Appeal to Reason

OPEN FOR BREAKFAST
DRIVE-THRU

Appeal to Reason

25 YEARS IN THESE TIMES

EDITED BY
CRAIG AARON

A SEVEN STORIES PRESS FIRST EDITION

SEVEN STORIES PRESS
140 Watts Street
New York, NY 10013
http://www.sevenstories.com

IN CANADA
Hushion House, 36 Northline Road, Toronto, Ontario M4B 3E2

IN THE U.K.
Turnaround Publisher Services Ltd., Unit 3, Olympia Trading Estate, Coburg Road, Wood Green, London N22 6TZ

IN AUSTRALIA
Tower Books, 2/17 Rodborough Road, Frenchs Forest NSW 2086

Library of Congress Cataloging-in-Publication Data

Appeal to reason : 25 years in these times /
edited by Craig Aaron.
p. cm.
ISBN 1-58322-275-8 (pbk.)
1. In these times—History. 2. Press, Socialist—United States—History. 3. United States—Social conditions—1980– 4. United States—Politics and government—1945–1989. 5. United States—Politics and government—1989– 6. Socialism—United States. I. Aaron, Craig.
HX3 .A67 2001
335'.00973—DC21
2001041092

9 8 7 6 5 4 3 2 1

College professors may order examination copies of Seven Stories Press titles for a free six-month trial period. To order, visit www.sevenstories.com/textbook, or fax on school letterhead to (212) 226-1411.

Book design by POLLEN

Printed in the U.S.A.

Contents

IN THESE TIMES
Politicians get foreign aid—from Korean CIA
Jamaica—another socialist island? 3
Left revival in Bay Area 6
China's new direction 11
50,000 tenants can't be wrong 12
Albert Maltz on a popular front 17

IN THESE TIMES
Anti-Nuclear War In New Hampshire
HONK FOR NO NUKES

IN THESE TIMES
HEAVEN AND HELL ARE THE SAME PLACE

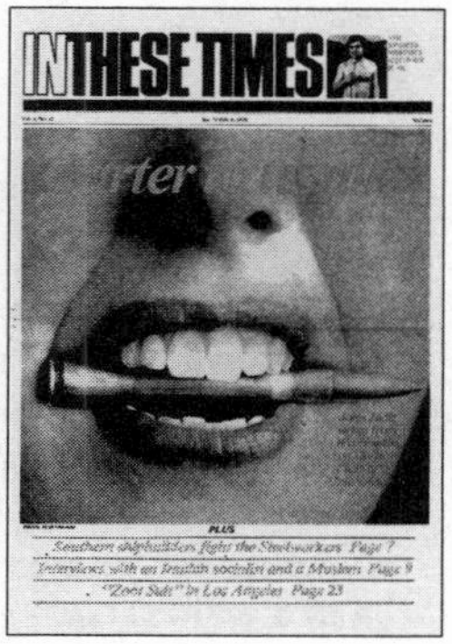

IN THESE TIMES

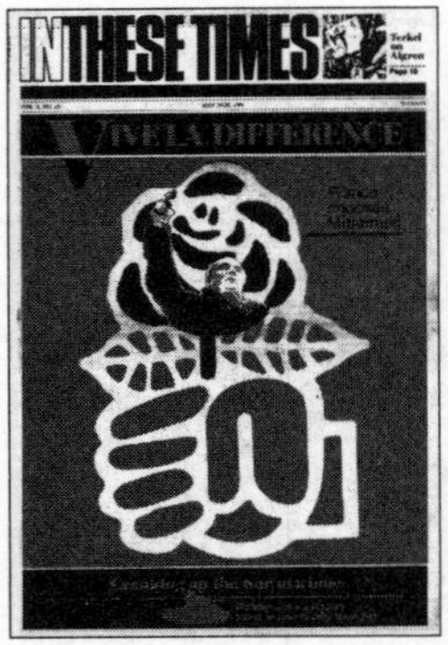
IN THESE TIMES
VIVE LA DIFFERENCE

IN THESE TIMES
Right
Makes
Might

IN THESE TIMES
Reagan's First Strike

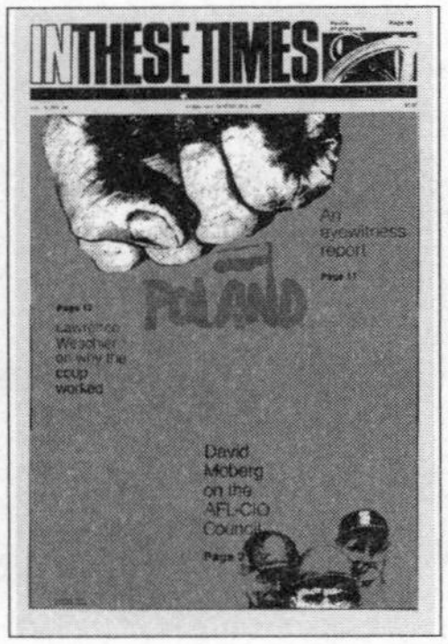
IN THESE TIMES
POLAND

IN THESE TIMES
BANG THE POTS
LOUDLY

IN THESE TIMES
The politics of
COMPARABLE WORTH

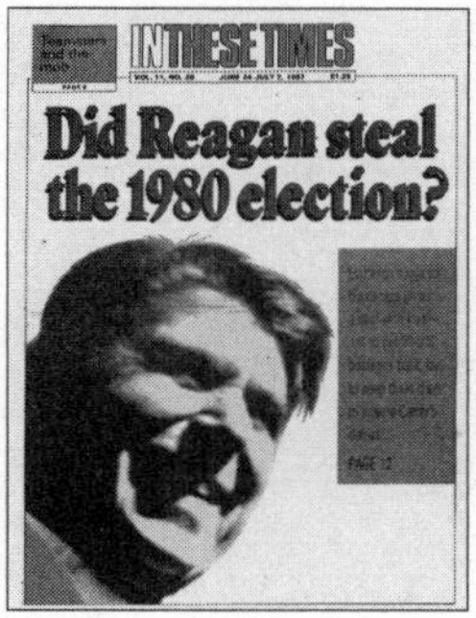
IN THESE TIMES
Did Reagan steal the 1980 election?

IN THESE TIMES
New abortion battles
LIVING
PERESTROIKA
Soviet democratic groups in the age of Gorbachov

Top Story: Hooked on self-help books
InTHESETIMES
the alternative newsmagazine
"Every lawbreaker can point to scars from the past and claim exculpation. And if all are excused, who is responsible?"
GANGING TOGETHER

NOAM CHOMSKY ON DEMOCRACY'S SLOW DEATH
InTHESETIMES
BRAVE NEWT WORLD

HAZARDS OF BIOENGINEERED FOOD
InTHESETIMES
STARBUCKED!
The predatory tactics of America's largest gourmet coffee chain.

LOS ANGELES R.I.P.?
InTHESETIMES
Slaves of NEW YORK
REPENT!
Rudolph Giuliani is replacing union labor with a new underclass of welfare recipients.

South Africa:
IN THESE TIMES
The TOWER OMISSION
The story they didn't tell
OFFICIAL

THE GREAT DIGITAL TV HEIST
IN THESE TIMES
In Maggie's Closet
New Labor's political cross-dressing
Hilary Wainwright reports

Interviews with Edwidge Danticat and John Hume
In These Times
Finding the Third Way
Directions for a "post-ideological" world

Dreaming of Eugene Debs • WTO Showdown
In These Times
Class Ceiling
Can Feminism Survive?
Barbara Ehrenreich
Julianne Malveaux
Annette Fuentes
Mimi Abramovitz

MUMIA'S LAST CHANCE • STUDENTS VS. SWEATSHOPS
In These Times
AFTER THE FALL
The stock market will crash. Then what?
By Dean Baker

TERROR IN EAST TIMOR • INFO-WAR IN KOSOVO
In These Times
Pride and Politics
Gay Rights 30 Years After Stonewall

SEX SLAVERY IN CHICAGO • BITTER LENNON
In These Times
INDEPENDENT NEWS & VIEWS
THE NEXT WAVE
FEMINISM FOR ALL

THE CHARLESTON FIVE • INSIDE BURMA • NUCLEAR TEST ANXIETY
In These Times
INDEPENDENT NEWS & VIEWS
WHATEVER HAPPENED TO GUN CONTROL?

James Weinstein: Let's Crash the Democratic Party
In These Times
BUSH II
The Return

Camp Ruckus • Fast Food Jungle • Taxes for Terrorists?
In These Times
GLOBAL WARNING
It's Now or Never
By Bill McKibben
The Myth of Living Safely in a Toxic World
By Sandra Steingraber
Plus:
10 Green Heroes
Bush's Hostile Environment

Fast Track Is Back • Our Foundering Fathers • McCensored
In These Times
The Pentagon's
TROJAN HORSE
Geov Parrish reports
Plus:
David Bacon investigates the dirty war against Colombian unions

Chechnya's Forgotten War • Battleground Alaska
In These Times
AMONG THE THUGS
GENOA AND THE NEW LANGUAGE OF PROTEST

New Columnist Naomi Klein: Bin Laden and the Damage Done
In These Times
Are You Ready for the Long War?
Doug Ireland
Slavoj Zizek
George Lakoff
Susan Douglas
David Moberg
and more...

War Profiteering • It's Not Over In Afghanistan
In These Times
THE STORIES WE TELL OURSELVES...
Special Books Issue
An Afterlife in Fiction
Istanbul in the Shadows
Rushdie Does New York
Naipaul's Comic Journey
Franzen's Therapy
The Lonely Tribune

Foreword

JAMES WEINSTEIN

WHEN CRAIG AARON INDUCED ME TO WRITE THIS FOREWORD, HE ASKED WHAT I HAD LEARNED IN MY 20-PLUS YEARS AT THE HELM OF *IN THESE Times*. My initial response was negative: Not to start a project like this so grossly undercapitalized. Not to misjudge the political situation so badly when launching a political magazine. Not much.

Then I remembered why I have been accused of being a pathological optimist, and I realized my initial responses were too pessimistic. So here's the flip side: I learned that if you are committed to doing what you have always wanted to do, you will succeed against the odds. And I learned that as small as *In These Times* is in the world of American media, it has played a vital role in keeping honest journalism alive and giving talented progressive journalists a place to do what they want to do most—to write about important things without ideological restrictions.

It's no secret that these past 25 years haven't been easy for *In These Times*, or for its staff. How could they have been for those putting out a socialist publication in the era of Reagan, Clinton and the Bushes? But unlike almost every other left journal that began publishing in the '70s—and many long-established ones on the left before that—*In These Times* has survived. It did so for two reasons: From the beginning, we have been resolute about our editorial mission. And from early on, our readers generously and consistently have supported us.

As a result, we have gained a reputation for integrity and excellence among journalists and leaders of progressive political and social movements. Unfortunately, our impact on the world has fallen far short of our initial hopes. This has been disappointing but not a total surprise. When I set out to create what was then to be weekly newspaper, I knew that our fate was not entirely in our own hands. In the prospectus I produced the year before we began publishing, I acknowledged that the prospects of a publication like ours ultimately depended not only on its quality, but also on the state of the left in the United States. If the left grew and prospered, I was confident that we would also grow rapidly. If, on the other hand, the left stagnated, I knew we would have to scratch and claw our way through bad times. The left didn't grow and prosper. In fact, it didn't even stagnate. It foundered and shriveled, leaving us to paddle furiously against the tide just to keep from being swept into oblivion.

But here we are in a new century, and we're publishing a book that recounts what we've done in our first 25 years and looks at future prospects—for ourselves and for the American left. Our mission and our vision remain unchanged, while the need for a viable New Left is greater than ever. Popular satisfaction with our present political leadership is at an all-time low, and yet vigorous voices on the left exist only on the outer margins of American political life. To this optimist, the opportunity for a well-informed left to engage the political mainstream seems substantially greater than it did when we began publishing in 1976.

Now, as then, we need a vigorous left to reach our full potential as a journal of news and opinion. But more importantly, a viable New Left cannot exist without principled, rigorous publications to inform it, and to help give it direction. That was what we intended to do in 1976 when we cobbled together *In These Times'* initial staff in Chicago. It remains our purpose today.

Editor's Note

CRAIG AARON

WHEN JAMES WEINSTEIN MOVED TO CHICAGO IN 1976, HE SET OUT TO CREATE A FIERCELY INDEPENDENT JOURNAL THAT WOULD INFORM, EDUCATE and critically analyze an emerging popular movement on the American left. A historian by trade, Weinstein modeled his newspaper on the *Appeal to Reason*, a socialist weekly that boasted more than 750,000 subscribers at its peak around 1912 and featured the writing of Upton Sinclair, Mother Jones and Eugene Victor Debs.

Weinstein's newspaper did resemble the *Appeal*—in its Midwestern sensibilities and populist tone, in its orientation toward the labor movement and electoral politics, in its commitment to avoid sectarianism and foster open debate. And like the *Appeal*—which challenged the robber barons of the Industrial Revolution—this newspaper was being launched, as Weinstein would recall a few years later, at a time when "Americans were beginning to lose faith, not just in a particular politician or administration, but in the existing system."

But 1976 was also a time of great optimism and promise on the left, with memories of the anti-war movement still fresh, a newly elected Democrat in the White House, and progressive institutions popping up everywhere. When the first issue of *In These Times* appeared on November 15, 1976—just 40 cents for a 24-page tabloid—the staff saw itself at the vanguard of a new majority. As a *new* New Left grew and prospered, they reasoned, so would the newspaper.

Instead of riding the wave to mass appeal, *In These Times* has struggled to keep its head above water. Yet against the odds—and the newspaper-cum-magazine has been published during some dark days for the American left—*In These Times* has survived, even thrived, for 25 years. With this book, named in honor of the *Appeal to Reason*, we commemorate and celebrate that achievement. How did we make it this far?

Though I didn't join the staff until 1997, I am uniquely qualified to answer that question. Working on this book, I combed through the *In These Times* archives, reading thousands of articles from each of the more than 900 issues we've published over the years. While searching for the best articles to excerpt here, I came to a better of understanding why—when so many other publications have come and gone—*In These Times* has persevered.

Above all, *In These Times* has never wavered from its fundamental mission, as Weinstein defined it succinctly in the very first editorial, "to speak to corporate capitalism as the great issue of our time." *In These Times* no longer hails itself as "the independent socialist weekly" on the masthead, but the magazine has maintained a remarkably consistent worldview and never relinquished its vision of nurturing a viable progressive movement with broad, popular appeal. (As J. A. Wayland, founder the *Appeal*, always insisted: "Socialism is merely more democracy.")

In These Times' dedication to a pluralistic, pragmatic left has been exemplified in the diversity of its contributors (and readers): socialists and Democrats, liberals and anarchists, journalists and academics, novelists and organizers, greens and union members, even the occasional conservative or Silicon Valley tycoon. *In These Times* has always committed its limited resources to honest (not objective) journalism, upholding the traditions of its muckraking predecessors (like the *Appeal*, which first serialized Sinclair's *The Jungle*), challenging the conventional wisdom, and refusing to follow the agenda dictated by political hacks or PR flacks. Our writers and editors have set high standards for what an *In These Times* story should be: provocative, clear, concise, exhaustively reported.

This book continues in that tradition. Rather than simply reprinting the magazine's "greatest hits" in an instantly antiquated anthology, I approached 20 or so *In These Times* contributors—some old friends of the magazine, others more recent additions to its pages—and asked them to reflect on the lessons of the past 25 years and to answer that ever important question: Where do we go from here?

Each of the following chapters features one of these essays, which cover an array of progressive concerns. These pieces offer a range of opinions and styles, in accordance with the broad, diverse left they represent. Interspersed within each chapter are previously published excerpts from *In These Times* that complement or elaborate on the themes and issues raised by the essayists. These selections showcase some of the most interesting ideas and intriguing stories that have appeared over the years. Each chapter ends with a "coda," an article that explores another dimension or adds a dose of humor to the essays raised by the essayists.

Not unlike the early days of the *Appeal*, or the summer of 1976 when James Weinstein headed for Chicago, progressives are again at a crossroads. The time seems ripe for a reawakening of the left. The dissatisfaction with our corrupt political system has only grown more widespread. Young people are more politically aware and—surveys tell us—progressively inclined than at any time in decades. The nation is more diverse than ever before. Globalization, for all its negative effects and connotations, has brought us closer to potential allies across the world.

Yes, many challenges lie ahead. The divide between the rich and the rest of us is widening. At this writing, George W. Bush is still in the White House, enjoying astronomical approval ratings. Our political opponents on the right, under the guise of patriotism, have exploited the tragedies and tensions of 2001 to avoid public scrutiny, stifle dissenting voices, and reward their corporate benefactors. Indeed, at no time during my tenure at *In These Times*—and perhaps in the magazine's history—has clear-headed, truly independent journalism been needed more.

It is my fervent hope that this book will help provide a political and intellectual foundation for the discussions and debates that will sustain and set forward the progressive movements of the next 25 years.

Clearly, I could not have done this book alone. I would like to acknowledge the following people:

Without James Weinstein, there wouldn't be an anniversary to commemorate; thanks to him for many nuggets of wisdom. Joel Bleifuss, who has given me so many opportunities at *In These Times*, pushed me to pursue this project and offered advice on early drafts. David Moberg (at the magazine since day one) and Salim Muwakkil, not only performed double-duty, each contributing two essays for this collection, but their writing and reporting have long been a hallmark of the magazine.

I'm grateful to all of the essayists for their fresh and insightful prose. It was a pleasure working with each of them to shape this collection. And this book would be incomplete were it not for the authors, publishers, photographers, illustrators and others who granted permission for their work to be reprinted here.

I am particularly indebted to all of the editors who came before me at *In These Times*. Without their careful editing and wise choices, this would have been a much more difficult project. Special thanks to Sheryl Larson (who held the managing editor position longer than anyone), Miles Harvey, Jim McNeill, Chris Lehmann, George Hodak, Dave Mulcahey and Deidre McFadyen (who first taught me how to *really* edit). I'm also blessed to have worked with and learned from colleagues like Jefferson Decker, Kristin Kolb-Angelbeck and Joe Knowles (who lent his critical eye to several chapters as well).

Jim Rinnert (who too has worked at the magazine in various capacities for more than two decades) deserves special mention for helping track down much of the art for this collection. The rest of the current (and recently departed) staff also helped out in numerous ways. Thanks to Steve Anderson, Luli Buxton, Julie Fain, Seamus Holman, Kristie Reilly, Joshua Rothkopf, Aaron Sarver, Beth Schulman and all of my hardworking interns.

Dan Simon and the staff of Seven Stories Press were enthusiastic about this project from the very beginning. Thanks for having confidence in this editor and giving plenty of sage advice (some of which I actually followed). Special thanks to the staff of Pollen for their splendid design and editorial work.

My friends and family all offered support and encouragement during my long nights and weekends lost in the archives. As for Sheryl Fred, my cherished companion, confidant and copy editor, well, I don't even know where to start.

Most importantly, this book and the magazine it celebrates would not have been possible without the generous and loyal support of *In These Times* readers, donors and sustainers. Here's to all of you. Happy anniversary.

Why We Need *In These Times*

Illustration by Peter Hannan

Introduction

ROBERT W. McCHESNEY

I REMEMBER SEEING THE VERY FIRST ISSUE OF *IN THESE TIMES* BACK IN NOVEMBER 1976. I WAS JUST A MONTH AWAY FROM GRADUATING COLLEGE, and a close friend pulled me aside when it arrived in the mail. As a couple of young radicals, we had all the excitement opening up *In These Times* that I used to get 10 years earlier opening up the latest Beatles LP. I had heard rumblings about some new weekly newspaper that the great historian James Weinstein was launching, and now here it was in my hands. I was taken by it immediately. Finally, a publication written in plain English that covered politics from a left perspective and did not assume a working command of left-wing theory or membership in a sect. It was a paper I could show a committed activist, my neighbor, or my uncle who worked in a factory his whole life. I immediately subscribed and have seen nearly every issue published.

My God, the world sure looked different then. It seemed like progressive politics were on the rise, not just in the United States but worldwide. To my friends and me, the '60s had been an epiphany for the human race, and there could be no turning back to the dark days of racism, sexism, militarism and the capitalist (or communist) status quo. We thought we were part of a movement that would radically change the world for the better, and do so in our lifetimes. In the mid-'70s, there remained a whole coterie of left-wing and alternative institutions founded in the preceding decade, from food co-ops to underground newspapers to community radio stations. Even Middle America dumped the Republicans in 1976. We thought the best was yet to come. The early *In These Times* confirmed our enthusiasm, with reports on the socialist government in Jamaica, left-wing victories across Europe, the rise of the Sandinistas in Nicaragua, and Dennis Kucinich, the boy-wonder mayor of Cleveland. The members of the best rock band in the world, the Clash, were committed socialists. The times, they were a-changing, and now we had a national weekly newspaper to link us all together.

And that was Jim Weinstein's plan. "We wanted to create a magazine that was independent but would serve as a source of information and education for the movement's popular constituency," he recalled a few years ago. "You cannot have a viable political movement of the left, right or center if it doesn't have its own press."

The premise for *In These Times* was that there was a resurgent left and the newspaper would ride the popular wave to a large circulation and considerable influence over political affairs. Instead of marking the dawn of a new progressive era, however, the mid-'70s proved to be exactly the opposite. Politics moved rightward with a vengeance. First under Carter, and then with no holds barred under Reagan, Bush and Clinton, the United States embraced neoliberalism, the ugly notion that business is the rightful and necessary ruler of society. Corporations were in the driver's seat, while labor, poor people and traditional left constituencies were getting run over. They had less influence than at any other time in memory.

But that doesn't mean *In These Times* has been a waste of time and money. To the contrary, *In These Times* has been invaluable over the past 25 years, shining the light of journalism on subjects generally left in the dark by the mainstream news media. The impact of *In These Times* has gone far beyond its subscriber base. *In These Times* has broken numerous stories that have been picked up by larger media, stories that otherwise would not have seen the light of day. *In These Times* also has provided a platform for some of the nation's finest political writers.

Moreover, progressive politics require progressive media just as much in moments of darkness as in moments of growth and triumph. Indeed, without such media, the darkness may become permanent. Over the past quarter-century, *In These Times* has provided a trenchant critique of U.S. politics, giving

A Job Whose Time Has Come

JAMES WEINSTEIN

November 15, 1976

The following editorial appeared in the first issue of In These Times.

The election returns are in, but the future of the United States remains in doubt. Almost everyone was dissatisfied with the available choices. Few are delighted with the result.

Yet this campaign was not significantly worse than most presidential contests of recent decades. The difference between this and past elections was not that most voters acted against rather than for a candidate or party. That has been common in this century. Nor were the two major parties less different from each other than before. Their differences were as real and explicit as at any time since the '30s.

The new element in this election is that more and more people find these differences inadequate to meet the problems facing our society. Voters and nonvoters alike know, or sense, that the limits to public discourse set by the major parties prevent shedding old alternatives and defining new ones.

To more and more people it is clear that the political system is at an impasse. It presents us all with little more than dilemmas: choices between equally obnoxious or no longer credible alternatives. That is why the more exposure President Ford and President-elect Carter got, the harder it was to choose between them.

Since World War II, Republicans have won the presidency by promising to end wars presided over by Democrats and to bring prosperity with peace. Democrats have captured the White House with promises to end recessions presided over by Republicans and to bring progress through growth. But it is difficult to believe in, no less remember, prosperity without war. And it is no longer believ-

citizens the information they need to organize and fight back. The world is a better place thanks to *In These Times.*

Accordingly, *In These Times* has joined an illustrious list of political media in U.S. history, going back to the revolutionary era. From abolitionists and feminists to populists, unionists and socialists, every progressive movement in U.S. history could almost be defined by its press. If there was no press, there was no movement. Consider, for example, the United States in the early 1900s. Members and supporters of the Socialist Party of Eugene V. Debs published some 325 English and foreign language daily, weekly and monthly newspapers and magazines. Most of these were privately owned or were the publications of one of the 5,000 Socialist Party locals. They reached a total of more than 2 million subscribers. *Appeal to Reason,* the socialist newspaper that inspired Jim Weinstein to launch *In These Times,* alone had a readership of more than 750,000.

All of that changed over the course of the 20th century. Most important, the nature of our media system changed dramatically. Rather than being a competitive industry where newcomers could enter on the margins and make a go of it, the media became dominated by large firms operating in oligopolistic markets. This reduced the ability of leftist media to survive, let alone prosper. It also caused a major shake-up in journalism. Publishers realized that to continue using their monopoly newspapers as partisan engines might discredit the legitimacy of their enterprise, so they instituted "professional" journalism as the new model for their newsrooms. In this new world, trained editors and reporters would run the newsroom while owners and advertisers would concern themselves with the business side of the operation. The news would be fair, accurate and reflect no political bias.

Of course, it is impossible to have such nonpartisan journalism, and the newly minted code for professional journalists had three distinct biases written into it that reflected the

able that simple material growth in the pursuit of private gain signifies progress.

The polls show that people want peace without unemployment, economic insecurity and lost opportunities. They want progressive development and a healthy economy without war. They want stable prices and full employment, not one at the expense of the other. They want good education and health care, adequate housing and livable communities, honorable work and dignified leisure without crushing taxes and bankrupt cities. They want a compassionate society without paternalism and dependence.

They don't want the moon, just modest attainments in what the politicians never tire of telling them is "the best country in the world"—and the richest beyond ancestral dreams. And increasingly they know, or sense, that the system of economics in this country is unable to deliver the standard of living and quality of life they want, and that the system of politics is unwilling to make it do so.

It is true that inflation and unemployment, crime and health care, education and housing, free enterprise and big government, liberty and equality, even Karl Marx and "socialism" are discussed in election campaigns. But never the underlying reality. Corporate capitalism, this society's system of property, investment, resource- and labor-allocation is a political taboo. And yet, without that discussion all the rest remains abstract, hollow and unconvincing.

Capitalism is the unspoken reality of American politics. That is the one thing the major parties agree upon: Praise capitalism (not too often and preferably by another name) but don't discuss it. Preclude serious discussion of the central reality of our times.

This is to be expected. The major parties are the protection agencies of corporate capitalism. They are committed in bipartisan consensus to accommodating government policy and public expectations to the capacities and limits of the system. It is their job to keep corporate capitalism out of, "above," politics, just as it was the job of the pre-Civil War Whig and Democratic parties to keep slavery out of politics. They failed then because determined people brought the reality of slave power into the electoral arena, giving birth to the Republican Party. It remains to be seen whether the Democratic and Republican parties will succeed in keeping corporate power out of electoral politics. If they do, they will only be doing their job, and socialists will not be doing theirs.

That job is to bring capitalism into politics as the great issue of our time. This newspaper is committed to beginning the job and to seeing it through. It is a job whose time has come.

commercial and political needs of the owners. First, to remove the controversy connected with the selection of stories, it regarded anything done by official sources—e.g., government officials and prominent public figures—as the basis for legitimate news. This gave those in political office (and, to a lesser extent, business) considerable power to set the news agenda by what they spoke about and what they didn't.

To cite a recent example, this bias explains the truly dreadful news coverage of the Republican theft of the 2000 presidential election. Journalists were reduced to volleying between the official opinion in the Republican and Democratic camps. Republican sources were unified in their insistence that the White House was theirs, regardless of the vote count. The Democratic high command was unwilling to fight for what we now know they clearly had won (and many spoke of how it would be best if Gore threw in the towel), as such a fight would have required mobilizing labor unions, feminists, environmentalists and African-Americans in massive demonstrations, something the party's big-money backers wanted to avoid like the plague. The press therefore accepted the debatable premise that Bush had won the election, and Gore was grasping at straws to save his flawed position. For journalists to stick their necks out to call for a full and accurate tally of the votes—without Gore or other leading Democrats assuming an aggressive posture—would have left them exposed as being "partisan." So they retreated inside the walls of elite debate, and democracy was the loser.

The second bias is that professional journalism tends to present news in a decontextualized and non-ideological manner. In theory, one could read every professional news story on a topic and they all would be pretty much the same. An irony of professional journalism is that those stories that generate the most coverage—the Middle East, President Clinton's health care plan—often produce a confused and uninformed readership. In professional code, this decontextualization is accomplished in part by positing that there must be a news "hook" or "peg" to justify a story. Hence crucial social issues like racism or environmental degradation fall through the cracks of journalism unless there was some event, like a demonstration or the release of an official report, to justify coverage. So journalism tends to downplay or eliminate the presentation of a range of informed positions on controversial issues. This produces a paradox: Journalism, which in theory should inspire political involvement, tends to strip politics of meaning and promote a broad depoliticization. That is very bad news for the left.

Both of these biases helped to stimulate the birth and rapid rise of the public relations industry. By providing slick press releases, paid for "experts," neutral-sounding but bogus citizens groups and canned news events, crafty PR agents have been able to shape the news to suit the interests of their mostly corporate clientele. Or as Alex Carey, the pioneering scholar of PR, put it, the role of PR is to muddle the public sphere so as to "take the risk out of democracy" for the wealthy and corporations. PR is welcomed by media owners, as it provides them with filler at no cost. Surveys show that PR accounts for anywhere from 40 to 70 percent of what appears as news.

The third bias of professional journalism is more subtle but most important: Far from being politically neutral, it smuggles in values conducive to the commercial aims of the owners and advertisers as well as the political aims of the owning class. Ben Bagdikian, author of *The Media Monopoly*, refers to this as the "dig here, not there" phenomenon. So it is that crime stories and stories about royal families and celebrities become legitimate news. (These are inexpensive to cover and they never antagonize people in power.) So it is that the affairs of government are subjected to much closer scrutiny than the affairs of big business. And so it is that those government activities serving the poor (like welfare) get much more critical attention than those serving the interests of the wealthy (the CIA, for instance). The genius of professionalism in journalism is that it tends to make journalists oblivious to the compromises with authority they routinely make.

Labor and the left are among the leading victims of this third bias. In professional journalism, business is assumed to be the natural steward of society, while labor is seen as a less benevolent force. Left politics are almost always suspect. As the concentrated commercial media system developed, progressives began a sustained critique of the limitations of mainstream news for democracy. Beginning with Edward Bellamy and Henry Adams at the end of the 19th century, the torch was carried by John Dewey and then Upton Sinclair in the first few decades of the 20th century. By the middle of the century, radio and television broadcasting had joined newspapers and magazines as the primary organs of journalism, and they, too, were the domain of a few large private firms. With professionalism by then pretty much the rule across the board, the news was decidedly hostile to the left. A cartoon from the late '40s in the *CIO News* captured progressive sentiment toward the news media: It showed the cigar-smoking fat boss caricature manipulating two levers that led directly to a skull cap fitted over the head of a person identified as the American public. One lever is for radio, the other for newspapers. The message being pumped into the head is "business is good, labor is bad."

A left and labor press remained alive on the margins throughout the past 50 years, but its survival increasingly required a subsidy. This is where an awful Catch-22 occurred. The dominant commercial news media made it more difficult for the left to organize its constituency; but as the left declined in strength, there were fewer resources to provide for progressive media, so outreach became all the more difficult. (It has not helped that the progressive philanthropic community has avoided subsidizing progressive media—quite unlike right-wing foundations, which devote a large percentage of their funds to the promotion of conservative media.) Some militants, especially in the labor movement, attempted to develop their own radio and TV stations, but these efforts met fierce resistance from business, and many in labor did not have the stomach for a fight.

Of course, professional journalism has not been explicitly or viciously anti-labor or anti-left in most instances. The process is more subtle. And in moments of resurgence for the left and social movements, professional journalism is malleable enough to improve the quantity and quality of coverage. In the '40s, for example, full-time labor editors and reporters abounded on U.S. daily newspapers. Even ferociously anti-labor newspapers, like the *Chicago Tribune*, covered the labor beat. The 1937 Flint sit-down strike that launched the United Auto Workers was a front-page story across the nation. By the '80s, however, labor had fallen off the map and there were no more than a dozen labor beat reporters remaining on U.S. dailies. (The number is less then five today.) Hence the 1989 strike at Pittston Coal—the largest since Flint—was virtually unreported in the mainstream national media. Of course, poverty among workers is growing and workplace conflicts are as important as ever, but this is no longer considered news. And that has made the prospect of rejuvenating the labor movement vastly more difficult.

The experience with the mainstream media has been the same for other progressive social movements over the past 50 years. From peace and the environment to civil rights and feminism, news coverage has tended to be bad and filtered through elite lenses. The initial response to these movements by the press was to ignore them, trivialize them or, at times, demonize them. All in all, evaluations of all major progressive social movements conclude that the lack of a viable media outreach to the general population, or even to the progressive constituencies they were seeking to organize, has been a major barrier to success. That, of course, is much of what *In These Times* has aspired to provide.

During the past 25 years, it has gotten even more difficult for progressives to receive satisfactory press coverage in the mainstream media. This is due primarily to the tightening corporate ownership over the news media that has resulted from government deregulation of broadcasting and lax enforcement of antitrust statutes. Over the past two decades, the U.S. media system has been consolidated in the hands of a small number of colossal conglomerates. To give some sense of proportion, in 2000 AOL purchased Time Warner in the biggest media deal ever, valued at around $160 billion. That was 470 times greater than the value of the largest media deal that had been recorded by 1979. The nine or 10 largest media conglomerates now almost all rank among the 300 largest firms in the world; in 1975 there were only a couple of media firms among the 500 largest companies in the world.

These media conglomerates often pay a premium price for TV networks or newspaper chains, so they have incentive to apply the same commercial logic to their newsrooms that they apply to their other divisions. Why should they grant editors *carte blanche* when their other managers are held to a strict accounting of all their moves? The logical result has been a reduction in resources for journalism, a decline in costly and controversial investigative reporting, and a softening up of journalistic standards to permit less expensive and more commercially attractive journalism. First in line for the corporate guillotine was international reporting, which costs a great deal of money and adds little to the bottom line. Stories about celebrities and glorified puff pieces have come to play a larger role in the news. Some media are worse than others: Local TV news has become a commercial sewer. Indeed, in this era of narrowly drawn demographic profiles, the one thing that seems to unite all Americans is the firmly held belief that their local TV news is the worst in the nation.

One measure of the attack on the autonomy of the newsroom can be found in the plummeting morale of working journalists. Well into the '80s, journalists were among the staunchest and most sensitive defenders of the media status quo. They enjoyed their privileges and were convinced that they used them for the betterment of society. Over the past decade, in what amounts to a sea change, journalists have grown despondent over the collapse of their autonomy. One Harvard study of working journalists observed that a significant percentage of contemporary editors and reporters could qualify as being "clinically depressed." The Pew Center surveys of journalists showed a marked increase in demoralization over the course of the '90s. The editor of the *Chicago Tribune*, James Squires, quit his job, arguing that he had witnessed the "death of journalism" due to the "corporate takeover" of the news.

This does not bode well for the left or for democracy. Mainstream news and "business news" have morphed over the past two decades as the news is increasingly pitched to the richest one-half or one-third of the population. The affairs of Wall Street, the pursuit of profitable investments, and the joys of capitalism are now presented as the interests of the general population.

The dismal effects of this became clear in 1999 and 2000 when there were enormous demonstrations in Seattle and Washington, D.C. to protest meetings of the World Trade Organization (WTO), the World Bank and the International Monetary Fund (IMF). Here, finally, was a news hook that would permit journalists to examine what may be the most pressing political issue of our time. The coverage was skimpy and paled by comparison to the round-the-clock treatment of the John F. Kennedy Jr. plane crash a few months earlier. News coverage of the demonstrations tended to emphasize property damage and violence and, even there, it downplayed the activities of the police. There were, to be fair, some outstanding pieces produced by the corporate media, but those were the exceptions.

Media firms are among the leading beneficiaries of these global capitalist trade deals, which helps explain why their coverage of them throughout the '90s was so enthusiastic. The sad truth is that the closer a story gets to corporate power and corporate domination of our society, the less reliable the corporate news media are. And, in the final analysis, the U.S. mainstream media covered the extraordinary demonstrations against the WTO and global capitalism in Seattle in a manner not all that different from how the Chinese Communist Party press covered Tiananmen Square in 1989.

Indeed, the WTO demonstrations launched a troubling degeneration of media coverage of large public demonstrations that grew worse in Washington in April 2000 and at the Republican and Democratic conventions that summer. By the time of the conventions, demonstrators were being ignored altogether in the press or treated with contempt. As police in Philadelphia and Los Angeles effectively terminated the right of free assembly, the corporate news media regurgitated the press releases of the police and the flacks inside the convention halls. Even compared to the deplorable news coverage of anti-war demonstrations in the '60s and '70s, there was a striking lack of concern for the termination of basic civil liberties. What this means is that the one surefire method for generating a news peg—the demonstration—may no longer be a viable option for protesters.

Over the past five years, there has been a rebirth of the left in the United States, but it has passed by almost entirely undetected by the same corporate news media that can tell you who Monica Lewinsky is dating or how many times Bill Gates picked his nose while at the World Economic Forum in Davos, Switzerland. This *new* New Left is dominated by young people and is organizing around human rights, labor rights, opposition to the death penalty and the criminal justice system, environmental issues and corporate power in general. It manifested itself in Seattle and then in Ralph Nader's 2000 presidential campaign. And there are numerous signs of openings for progressive politics among broader segments of the population. The soil for left politics is fertile, but nothing can happen without an organized left and a viable independent media.

One of the more exciting aspects of this burgeoning progressive movement has been the rise of the Independent Media Centers, which use inexpensive new communication devices and the Internet as a basis for providing alternative and independent coverage of politics. They provide a wonderful global bulletin board where citizen journalists can post their stories. But just like the underground press of the '60s and '70s was not a sufficient alternative to the corporate news media, the Indy Media Centers cannot and should not be expected to carry the entire load of democratic and progressive communication on their shoulders. The left also needs media with the resources to pay people, so it can have experienced and talented journalists working full time on stories. It needs managers who work full time promoting the medium and seeing that its ideas are widely disseminated. Indy Media Centers—or, more broadly, the notion of generating noncommercial fare via the Internet—and traditional progressive media are not competitive notions of an independent press, but complementary ones.

On September 11, 2001, the world was turned upside-down. Following the attacks on New York and Washington, the United States launched a worldwide war against terrorism—Operation Enduring Freedom—that could last for a generation and reach the far corners of the globe. In a democratic society, the decision to go to war must be made with the informed consent of the population. That requires a press system to provide the citizenry with the information and perspectives to make such a decision. In some respects, for the notion of a free press, this is the moment of truth.

Whereas Americans once tended to be misinformed about world politics, now they are uninformed. The U.S. citizenry is embarrassingly and appallingly ignorant of the most elementary political realities in other nations and regions. This is an unmitigated disaster for the development of a meaningful democratic debate over international policy and highlights a deep contradiction between the legitimate informational needs of a democratic society and the need for profit of the corporate media.

The historical record suggests we should expect an avalanche of lies and half-truths in the service of power—in the both World Wars, Korea, Vietnam and the Gulf War, the government employed sophisticated propaganda campaigns to whip the population into a suitable fury—and that is exactly what we have gotten. But the U.S. news media, which love nothing more than to congratulate themselves for their independence from government control, did not so much as blink before they became the explicit organs of militarist and imperialist propaganda.

The Manichean picture conveyed by the media was of a benevolent, democratic, peace-loving nation brutally attacked by insane, evil terrorists who hate the United States for its freedoms and affluent way of life. Thus the only option was for the United States to immediately increase its military and covert forces, locate the surviving culprits and exterminate them; then prepare for a long-term war to root out and destroy the global terrorist cancer. Those who do not aid the U.S. campaign for justice—domestically as well as internationally—are to be regarded as accomplices who may well suffer a similar fate.

No skepticism was showed toward U.S. military, political and economic interests that might benefit from militarism and war. No hard questioning demanded evidence that the proposed war might actually reduce terrorism or bring justice to the terrorists responsible for the September 11 attacks. Those concerns, which would be applied to any other government that proposed to direct a world war, were avoided by the mainstream press. The entire political establishment fell in line for the war effort, leaving little wiggle room for journalists to challenge the jingoist sentiment without being accused of acting unprofessional, partisan or unpatriotic.

Fundamental issues remain decidedly off-limits. The notion that the United States is a uniquely benevolent force in the world remains undisputed. The idea that the United States is the proper judge and jury to determine who is a terrorist is beyond question. The premise that the United States alone—unless it deputizes a nation like Israel—has a right to invade any country it wants at any time will remain undebatable. And any objections that U.S. military action may violate international law are not on principle, but only because it might harm U.S. interests to be perceived by other nations as a lawbreaker.

U.S. media corporations exist within an institutional context that makes support for U.S. military natural. Indeed, the U.S. government is the primary advocate for the global media firms when trade deals and intellectual property agreements are being negotiated. Coincidentally, at the very moment the corporate broadcasters were singing the praises of "America's New War," their lobbyists appeared before the Federal Communications Commission seeking radical relaxation of ownership regulations for broadcasting, newspaper and cable companies.

The current war may be the most serious global political crisis in decades. The need for viable democratic journalism has never been greater, and the performance of the mainstream news media has fallen far short of that goal. In this context, *In These Times* has been nothing short of heroic. Its issues in the fall of 2001 bristled with superb investigative journalism and trenchant political analysis reminiscent of Andrew Kopkind and I.F. Stone. The magazine published voices—from Doug Ireland and Joel Bleifuss to Naomi Klein and Arundhati Roy—urging caution and restraint, relentlessly questioning the conventional wisdom and never swallowing the official line. In this moment of darkness, our need for *In These Times* has never been greater.

After 25 years of feisty independent journalism, *In These Times* may finally be on the verge of the times for which it was intended. As the events of the next several years unfold, we are all going to be fortunate and thankful for the long and rich path *In These Times* has traveled, and all the hard lessons it has learned. It will serve us well in the coming struggle to radically transform this nation and the world. We should hope that someday *In These Times* will be regarded as having been 25 years ahead of its time.

Appeal to Reason

Photograph by Lionel Delevingne

A New Majority

AWAITING THE SECOND COMING OF LIBERALISM

Photograph from ITT Archives

One

JOHN B. JUDIS

IN THESE TIMES BEGAN IN A SPIRIT OF GREAT OPTIMISM. JIMMY CARTER HAD JUST BEEN ELECTED, AND THE DEMOCRATS HAD SECURED MAJORITIES IN the Senate and House. As Carter took office in January 1977, liberal Democrats prepared an ambitious agenda for moving America from New Deal liberalism to European-style social democracy. It included campaign finance reform, the creation of a consumer protection agenda, labor law reform, progressive tax reform, and the Humphrey-Hawkins full-employment bill. Two years later, the first three had been defeated outright; a tax bill had passed, but without a scintilla of reform (its centerpiece was a reduction of the capital-gains tax); and Humphrey-Hawkins had been modified to the point where it was, in the words of the president of the Chamber of Commerce, a "toothless alligator."

What we thought was a second coming for liberalism turned out to be "the emerging Republican majority" that Kevin Phillips had predicted in a 1969 book of the same name, only delayed by the Watergate scandal. It would dominate politics until 1986, when Democrats would regain control of both houses of Congress. Since then, America has witnessed a political stalemate—typified by the first Bush administration and Bill Clinton's second term. While Democrats have not been able to pass their most ambitious initiative—Clinton's national health care bill of 1993—Republicans were stymied in their attempt in 1995 to gut the Environmental Protection Agency and the Occupational Safety and Health Administration. As the century opens, the stalemate continues, but there are some indications that the country—and perhaps Washington itself—may be moving to the left.

Liberals blamed Jimmy Carter for their setbacks in the late '70s, and conservatives blamed George Bush two decades later for failing to carry forward Ronald Reagan's agenda. Carter and Bush, of course, were not the most adept politicians, but they were victims of broader historical trends and political movements. A major shift in power and political ideology took place in the Carter years and began to abate during Bush's presidency. To understand it, you have to go back to Richard Nixon's first term.

Nixon is remembered by blinkered historians as a conservative, but his six years were a high-water mark of American liberalism in the 20th century. They saw the creation of the EPA, OSHA and the Consumer Product Safety Commission. Social Security benefits were expanded. Nixon's proposal for national health insurance, which liberals opposed for being too timid, was far more generous to consumers than Clinton's 1993 plan. A moderate Republican, Nixon wasn't uncomfortable with these initiatives, but they passed because the environmental, labor, civil rights and consumer movements enjoyed great popular support. In a 1974 survey, *U.S. News and World Report* found Ralph Nader to be the fourth most-influential American.

At the same time these liberal movements were triumphing, however, a counter-reaction had set in. Business leaders, who had viewed Lyndon Johnson's Great Society with equanimity, suddenly became worried that a revolution was imminent. In a special December 1969 issue on the coming '70s, *Business Week* warned that through the power of "blacks, labor unions and the young . . . business will still be business in 1980, but the meaning of the word may have undergone some significant change." In response to this long-term threat, and to the new regulatory agencies, business began to get organized in Washington. In 1971, only 175 businesses had registered lobbyists in Washington; by 1982, 2,445 had. Fortune 500 CEOs formed the Business Roundtable in 1972; both the Chamber of Commerce and the National Association of Manufacturers, which had slumbered through the '60s, revived; and NAM moved its headquarters from New York to Washington.

IN THESE TIMES

BULK RATE U.S. POSTAGE PAID Chicago, IL Permit No. 4881

Vol. 1, No. 1 | Nov. 15-21, 1976 | The Independent Socialist Newspaper | 40 cents

Politicians get foreign aid—from Korean CIA

By Sarah James And Tim Frasca

Washington. Relations between the U.S. and South Korea have been thrown into question by recent revelations that South Korea operated a wide-ranging network of intelligence gathering and repression inside the U.S. and that South Korean agents have bribed U.S. congressmen.

There is speculation that the revelations, most of which originated in leaks from government sources, are not coincidental, but represent the beginnings of an American policy shift concerning the Park Chung Hee regime in South Korea. The revelations are seen as reflecting both the anger of American policymakers at "highly improper" interference in American affairs and their concern that the Park regime is not fundamentally stable and secure.

The U.S. currently maintains 40,000 troops in South Korea and there is widespread fear that if they were to be removed—as President-elect Carter has hinted—the Park regime has so little support that it would be unable to sustain itself.

According to this interpretation, the leaks are seen as warnings to Park to change his policies and to stop trying to influence American policy. As former ambassador to Japan Edwin O. Reischauer says, "What is going on in Korea right now is making Korea a harder place to defend against the North.... Conceivably President Park has it in him to change course.... If he can't do it, there probably are others that could."

The various leaks and revelations, however, have revealed a wide variety of questionable activities by South Korean officials and agents in the U.S. and, until now, the apparent unwillingness of the government to put a stop to them.

►A list of 90 congressmen. The current inquiry centers on a Washington-based Korean entrepreneur named Tongsun Park. Park, who came to the U.S. as a student in the late '50s and began working for the Korean CIA in 1965, reportedly has dispensed $500,000 to $1 million to legislators during the past few years.

Government sources, corroborated by Korean sources quoted in the *New York Times*, report that Park met in Dec. 1971 with Korean President Park Chung Hee Col. Pak Bo Hi of the Korean Cultural and Freedom Foundation—also chief adviser and translator for the Rev. Sun

Continued on page 14

In this issue

Ron Dellums: "I think democratic socialism will prevail in this country because it makes an enormous amount of sense." **Page 6.**

Chiang Ch'ing and Chairman Mao: She was the most hated and he was the most revered person in China. **Page 11.**

Ronald Reagan and Robert Taylor: They both hated Communists and Communist sympathizers in Hollywood (seen in earlier, unhappier days). **Page 17.**

The first cover of *In These Times*, November 15, 1976.

ITT Archives

Q&A: Ron Dellums

JOHN B. JUDIS

November 15, 1976

You are the closest thing to a socialist elected to Congress in 20 years. Your approach seems like the socialist ideal of uniting working people against corporate power to establish popular ownership and democratic control of society's basic wealth. Is that your view?

Business also broadened its strategy. Instead of simply strong-arming a few key legislators, businesses formed coalitions to put grassroots pressure on legislators within their own districts. They also organized political action committees. And they began to fund research organizations and think tanks. While older think tanks like the Brookings Institute had claimed to be objective and nonpartisan, the policy groups business funded were devoted to its lobbying agenda. In the '70s, business threw its support behind the doddering American Enterprise Institute, helped to found the Heritage Foundation (whose first president came from NAM) and started numerous ad-hoc policy groups like the American Council for Capital Formation. These groups initially commanded the prestige and status of the older research groups without adhering to their standards of objectivity. Reading an op-ed piece on capital gains taxes from an economist associated with the American Council for Capital Formation, for instance, the public thought it was getting a dispassionate expert opinion, when in fact it was getting a paid message.

In the face of this mobilization by business, liberal and left-wing movements faltered. Unable to defend itself against more aggressive anti-union attacks, the AFL-CIO began to lose members. The labor movement also suffered from the shift in the work force from manufacturing, where it was strongest, to services, where it was weakest. The labor movement's share of the private work force fell precipitously from 27 percent in 1973 to 22 percent in 1979. The civil rights movement split between a nationalist black power and an integrationist wing. The consumer movements suffered from a loss of political activity on campuses after the Vietnam War's end. Only the environmental and women's movements sustained themselves—and they, too, had to face more powerful adversaries.

The Democratic Party coalition that had reigned since 1932 also began to disintegrate. It split over the Vietnam War, of

I think democratic socialism will ultimately prevail in this country because it makes an enormous amount of sense. We have to ask if the problems in society can be solved while we are propping up the major corporations. Right now the politician's code word is the "tradeoff of unemployment for inflation," but that's simply a way to ask if one is committed to the 10 or 12 million unemployed, or to the top 50 corporations in the United States.

Obviously, the Ford administration, and perhaps President-elect Carter, are committed to fighting inflation, to propping up the corporations as opposed to dealing with the human misery of unemployment. But if democracy means anything, it should mean a government of all the people, by all the people, for all the people. . . .

The government ought to be in the business of delivering health, education, housing and basic services to people without a lot of game-playing. There ought to be comprehensive childcare, a comprehensive approach to housing, a sane, rational way to finance education. But I also strongly believe in the notion of fundamental individual freedom. The government should not do everything for everybody all the time, but it should provide basic services to everyone who needs them. Education ought not be contingent on income or where you live. Neither should health.

Over the past few years, a number of candidates who share your views have been elected to office in the East Bay. Do you see this as the beginning of a movement?

Yes, people in this community are trying to develop a continuity of critical ideas, so that a person who carries the banner of "new politics" into the electoral arena is no more than that—someone who carries a banner. It's not a machine; it's the beginning of a movement.

course, but the more lasting damage came from the defection of Southern whites and working-class Northern whites over the civil rights movement. Except in 1976, when Jimmy Carter ran as the candidate of the South, the Democratic Party would never recapture the Southern votes it lost in 1968 when George Wallace ran as an independent. Most of the Wallace voters eventually shifted to the Republicans. The Democrats also lost some votes in the South and among Northern Catholics in reaction to the party's identification with the counterculture. And in the late '70s, many voters held the Democrats' expansionary policies responsible for stagflation and recession. Voters started blaming big government—rather than the older target, big business—for the economy's woes.

As the Democrats were disintegrating, conservative Republicans were building a new majority coalition of their own. As Phillips had foreseen, they were able to unite traditional business Republicans with the Wallace voters of 1968. In addition, they were able to attract a "new right" of evangelical Protestants. This coalition first emerged in the 1978 Senate races. By 1980, it had swept the presidency and won the Senate, with a functional majority of Republicans and conservative Democrats in the House. And for the next six years, it dominated American politics. Regulatory agencies were not disbanded, but they were rendered dysfunctional by hostile appointees. The tax system was rewritten on behalf of corporations and the wealthy, and social programs for the poor and unemployed were gutted, while defense spending skyrocketed.

This new conservative majority reigned during the Reagan years, but it began to unravel in the late '80s. By then, the economy, which had picked up after a severe recession in 1982, had begun to slow down. With budget and trade deficits mounting, Democrats who had defected because of Carter-era stagflation began to return to the fold in Senate and House elections. The Democrats won back the Senate in 1986. The conservative majority also began to suffer its own internal divisions. To a great extent, it had been held together by the looming threat of Soviet Communism, but with Cold War's end, the different factions

Carter Kills Populist Hopes Early

ALAN WOLFE

January 12, 1977

"If, after the inauguration, you find Cy Vance as secretary of state and Zbigniew Brzezinski as head of national security, then I would say we failed," said Hamilton Jordan, Jimmy Carter's key aide, last summer.

Rarely has an administration failed, by its own standards, even before assuming office. Carter is not yet president and he has already broken just about every progressive promise he made during the campaign. Populism is out, and the Trilateral Commission is in. The appointments made by Carter reflect the greatest domination of the federal government by Wall Street since Herbert Hoover. . . .

By deciding to go all the way with the Trilateral Commission, Carter has told blacks and working-class people who made his election possible what he thinks of them. There is no question that it was these folks and not the bankers who elected Carter, and he has responded by rubbing power in their faces. He is not even making an attempt to mystify the power with kind words. After two decades of economic mismanagement, political scandal and increasing illegitimacy, Carter has cast his lot with the mismanagers, corrupters and illegitimizers. His gall is phenomenal, but in truth his only two options were to do what he did or be a real populist, and the latter was never a serious option.

began to quarrel among themselves. Business groups complained of the Reagan budget deficits; Northern suburban Republicans who had backed the party's economic agenda became increasingly uncomfortable with the role of the religious right within the party. But the religious right, led by the Rev. Pat Robertson and his Christian Coalition, became unwilling to subordinate its own goals to those of the party's secular leaders. In 1992, some small business and working-class Republicans, concerned about the trade deficit and the threat from Japan to American economic superiority, defected to Pat Buchanan and his economic nationalism. In all, a party that had once seemed greater than the sum of its parts now seemed less.

The Democrats probably should have won the presidency in 1988, but they ran a candidate who was too closely identified with the party's discredited liberal faith. Under the direction of Lee Atwater, the Bush campaign turned Reagan Democrats into Bush Democrats. But Bush had to govern with a Democratic majority in Congress, and when the economy faltered in 1991, he became vulnerable (although his weakness was temporarily shrouded by the routing of Saddam Hussein from Kuwait).

Chastened by their past defeats, the Democrats went looking for a candidate who could inoculate liberalism from its associations with the worst excesses of the '60s. In 1990, Bill Clinton became chairman of the Democratic Leadership Council, which had been formed by party moderates and conservatives in the wake of Walter Mondale's landslide defeat in 1984. Some DLC members, such as Georgia Sen. Sam Nunn, wanted the party to embrace moderate-to-conservative social *and* economic policies, including opposition to raising the minimum wage. But other DLCers, including Clinton, advocated distancing Democrats from left-wing social policies to win back support for liberal economic policies. They figured correctly that many voters had been so alienated by Democratic positions on crime and wel-

ITT Archives

In These Times **wrote of Jimmy Carter: "Rarely has an administration failed, by its own standards, even before assuming office."**

No to Liberalism by a Landslide

JOHN B. JUDIS

November 12, 1980

The 1980 Republican landslide was a vote of "no confidence" in an entire generation of Democratic politicians. The results would have been the same—if not worse—if Sen. Edward Kennedy or Secretary of State Edmund Muskie had been the democratic nominee. The message was unmistakable: Liberals of all kinds, from Sen. George McGovern to President Jimmy Carter, *get out*.

The liberalism voters repudiated had its roots in Harry Truman's 1948 Democratic synthesis, later to be updated by a succession of Democratic presidents and presidential candidates. In this broad form, it spanned both self-styled liberals and moderates, as well as many Republicans, including Richard Nixon.

This liberalism held that through limited state intervention, the federal government could smooth out the business cycle and eliminate the inequalities of modern capitalism. It held out to all Americans the promise of a rising standard of living. It conceived of the United States as the guardian of world democracy, as the leader of the battle against Communism. And it saw the world's non-Communist nations as a vast marketplace in which a superior American industry could ply its wares, harvest its capital and purchase raw materials at discount prices.

The viability of this liberalism depended on the United States being the most powerful nation militarily and economically. It depended upon a peculiar situation in which the United States could help a war-torn Europe and Japan rebuild and in which it could gain privileged access to Third World markets as the champion of anti-colonialism. Given these circumstances, the American private economy, with a hefty boost from arms spending, was able to expand with few interruptions from 1948 to 1969, and the American state was able to apply the benefits of this prosperity to finance highways, supermarkets, unemployment compensation and Medicare.

With the American defeat in Vietnam, the Soviet achievement of nuclear parity and the reconstruction of Europe and Japan, the United States lost its absolute military and economic superiority. Under these new conditions, which saw simultaneous inflation and unemployment, a declining dollar and continuing rebellions against American power overseas, liberal policies could no longer sustain liberal promises. It was time for a re-evaluation.

Liberals had two choices: They could either go beyond liberalism to substantial state intervention in the economy—wage-price controls, a federal energy corporation and investment planning—and

Lionel Delevigne

Ronald Reagan built his conservative majority by uniting traditional business Republicans with the Wallace voters of 1968 and the "new right" of evangelical Protestants.

fare, they overlooked their opposition to Republican economic positions and their support for Democratic ones.

In 1992, Clinton advocated "ending welfare as we know it," called for tougher crime measures and supported the death penalty. But he also put forward the most populist economic program ("Putting People First") since that of George McGovern in 1972. He won the votes of many of the Reagan and Bush Democrats who had feared the party was soft on work and crime. Even so, Clinton could not win a popular majority. He defeated Bush, but third-party candidate Ross Perot took almost a fifth of the voters—many of them opposed to Bush, but unwilling to embrace what they saw as the enduring "big government" agenda of the Democrats.

Clinton mistook his narrow victory for a mandate to revive the liberalism of the New Deal and the '60s (he even promised a Roosevelt-style "Hundred Days"). When he advanced a comprehensive national health insurance program, the Republicans and health industry lobbies exploited popular fears of big government. When he backed eliminating the prohibition on gays in the military, Republicans branded the Democrats as anti-family.

But when voters repudiated Clinton in the November 1994 midterm elections, the Republicans made the exact opposite mistake. Believing they were the harbingers of a new conservative revolution, they set about trying to expand upon what Reagan had done in the early '80s. By the time the Democrats were able to show that the Republicans were trying to take money out of Medicare to fund a tax cut for the wealthy, the Gingrich revolution was over. The Republicans found themselves repudiated at the polls in 1996, and the country was left with a government evenly divided between Republicans and Democrats, conservatives and liberals.

Liberals blamed Bill Clinton's turn toward the center in 1995 and 1996—epitomized in his statement that "the era of big government is over"—on the nefarious influence of campaign consultant Dick Morris. But Morris brought a needed realism to Clinton's presidency, bringing his liberal aspirations more in line with what was politically feasible with a Republican Congress, a Washington dominated by business lobbies, and a populace skeptical of large-scale government measures. To the extent that Clinton moved leftward during his second term, it was because many Americans became less wary of government action due to continuing prosperity. But prosperity's effect on liberal hopes was double-edged. While it made voters less fearful of Democratic initiatives, it also deprived them of their urgency.

Looking back on the Bush and Clinton years, one sees a changing mixture—a conservative president and liberal

to a more pluralistic, egalitarian view of American relations to the rest of the world, or they could try to maintain liberal promises of world economic and military superiority by reverting to a combination of pre-liberal conservatism—which attempts to encourage economic growth by redistributing income toward the wealthy—and Cold War militarism, which attempts to restore the American hold over the less developed countries.

During the late '70s, the majority of liberal Democrats—Jimmy Carter most prominent among them—refused to choose between the two paths. Instead, they vacillated. Carter tried to use fiscal policy to cut unemployment, beginning with his proposal for tax rebates, but finally had to use recession rather than wage-price controls to curb inflation. Carter came into office committed to a post-Vietnam pluralistic world, but in the face of Soviet challenges in Africa and then Asia, he was convinced to revert to more traditional Cold War policies. The results were the worst possible: He created new unemployment without curbing inflation; he increased America's military posture toward the world, without increasing the respect with which the United States was treated. . . .

Using his mix of liberal promises and conservative programs, Reagan reached around Carter's collapsing Democratic constituency and picked up half of the blue-collar, Catholic, Jewish and trade union votes. These votes, along with his expected Republican vote, provided the winning margin. When Carter lost the South and the Northern middle class, the election became a landslide.

Congress for some years, a liberal president and conservative Congress for others—but surprising continuity in what policies were actually adopted. It was a centrism that tilted toward business rather than labor on economics, and toward liberals rather than conservatives on social issues. Both the Bush and the Clinton administrations backed conservative fiscal policies and deferred to Federal Reserve Chairman Alan Greenspan on monetary policy. There was continuity between Bush's 1990 budget, Clinton's 1993 budget and the Clinton-Gingrich budget of 1997. Liberals won a slight increase in the minimum wage, but only by ceding a raft of subsidies to small businesses and multinational corporations. Republicans got some tax cuts for the wealthy in the 1997 budget agreement but gave the Democrats a clumsy yet well-mentioned health care program for children. Business got the North American Free Trade Agreement, the World Trade Organization, the Telecommunications Act of 1996 and China's entry into the WTO but failed to roll back environmental and workplace regulations. Unions were able to block conservative assaults, but unable to reform labor laws.

George W. Bush's split decision in the 2000 election and the almost evenly divided Senate represent a continuation of this stalemate, but there are some indications that the electorate, if not Washington itself, has been shifting toward the Democrats and, perhaps, toward a yet-to-be-defined new liberalism. Together, Democrat Al Gore and Green Party candidate Ralph Nader won 51 percent of the vote, and a more effective (though not more left-wing) Democrat campaigning without the handicap of the Clinton scandals probably would have done much better.

In the '70s, it looked as though Democrats were becoming the party of the older, decaying Rust Belt states, and the Republicans the party of the growing, prosperous Sun Belt states. But by 2000, the geographical advantage looked like it was shifting toward the Democrats. Republicans had estab-

ITT Archives

George Bush didn't express a powerful unifying myth—he simply imposed a pejorative label on his opponent.

The Scarlet Letter

DAVID MOBERG

November 9, 1988

Finally, near the end of his campaign, Michael Dukakis owned up to being a "liberal." But for a couple of months, George Bush, pronouncing the "L-word" with a derisory sneer, was able to define the term. Dukakis simply whined about being labeled, confirming a sense that there must be something wrong with the politics that dare not speak its name. It looked like the final collapse of a political tradition. Liberalism was taking a terrible drubbing with nobody to defend it. What had happened?

lished a stronghold in the most culturally backward parts of the South (that still resonated with the Wallace vote) and in states like West Virginia and Kentucky that depended on embattled industries (coal, tobacco) and were populated by hunters and fundamentalists. The Democrats did surprisingly well in many of those areas that have been most touched by computer technology.

The Milken Institute of California constructs a New Economy Index that grades states according to such factors as their proportion of doctorates, scientists and engineers, and how much they spend per capita on academic research and development. Eight of the top 10 states on the index are now solidly Democratic. Of the 20 states with the highest proportion of scientists and engineers, Gore won 15. Gore and Democratic candidates also won in new economy areas of the South, like North Carolina's Research Triangle.

The Democrats' success among these voters probably reflects the coming-of-age of the college-educated '60s generation that was raised on women's equality, environmental and consumer protection, and civil rights. To these voters, and to many upper-middle-class suburban voters, the Republicans are the party of religious intolerance and social bigotry. Women used to vote disproportionately Republican, but since 1980 they have swung sharply to the Democratic side. Some women—African-Americans, for instance—may have done so for reasons that have little to do with their gender. But for many, the overriding reason they vote Democratic is because it's the party of women's rights. Unmarried women backed Gore by 63 percent compared to 48 percent for single men. Sixty-three percent of women with advanced degrees backed Gore. And more than half of women making more than $75,000 backed Gore compared to only 34 percent of their male counterparts.

Since the '60s, African-Americans, Hispanics and, to some extent, Asians also have become loyal Democratic voters. Hispanic voters are largely responsible for California becoming a Democratic state, and they may yet make Texas

Ronald Reagan managed to knit together his coalition out of the fragmented electorate partly by elaborating a powerful myth that a return to a simple, carefree, omnipotent America could be reached through the magic of slashing big government. But the Democrats have lost any comparable ability to reassemble their fragmented constituency with a unifying, compelling sense of mission. Dukakis threw in the towel in his convention speech when he declared that competence, not ideology, was the issue.

Bush and his unwitting but persuasive ally, rapist Willie Horton, certainly proved that wrong. The Republican didn't express a powerful unifying myth in the Reagan manner; he simply imposed a pejorative label on Dukakis. Bush associated liberalism with a general softness, especially on crime and defense, alien values, threats to the family, rampant permissiveness, anti-Americanism and radicalism.

The continued perplexing irony for people on the left is that public opinion seems strongly . . . on the side of many "liberal" programs, except welfare. Majorities favor increased spending for most major domestic needs, such as education, health, childcare and the environment. But there are big worries about how effective government programs are and about who should pay for them. And without a strong alternative vision, conservative ideology triumphs. . . .

If there is any lesson in Dukakis' encounter with the "L-word," it is that liberals—even people who call themselves "progressives," "populists" or "leftists"—can't make much headway if they are not prepared to defend their views politically and to win the consent of the governed.

My Date with the Transition Team

PAT AUFDERHEIDE

January 11, 1993

I felt like a *Doonesbury* character. I finally got it. I got The Call.

Actually, I just got a call. A brisk, generic, very young person asked me if I could show up for a meeting with the presidential transition team, to discuss the immediate future of a federal agency.

Well, sure I could. I'd spent the Reagan-Bush years at ground zero, where public-interest advocates like me had been cheerfully treated as beneath contempt. I'd even gotten used to it. It had come to seem almost normal, or at least a sour personal fate, that our crowd should spend its adulthood on the sidelines in the biggest power game around, occasionally issuing a Bronx cheer but mostly being ignored. When the right-wing would get cranked up about the liberal threat, it was actually kind of touching—at least somebody noticed us.

So this was big news, the kind of occasion in which you wake up thinking about what to wear. There was, as it turned out, no need to bother about such niceties. The transition team works out of several floors of a downtown Washington office building, where it seems not a single person has had a moment to so much as tape a family photo to the wall. It's a rabbit warren of paper, desolate desks and impromptu equipment arrangements. Vending machines offer an eerie simulacrum of sustenance. Once ensconced, it's possible to believe you might never figure out how to get out.

But getting in is a scene. There's an airport ambiance. Security gates are up, with very unfunny people guarding them. They channel a steady, seemingly nonstop stream of visitors that spills out of the elevators. Files, documents and briefs in hand, they step out ready to give their best policy recommendations to the teams, clusters, liaisons of the transition.

Democratic again. In the 2000 election, minority voters, swelled by Hispanics and Asians, now constitute 19 percent of the electorate. If a candidate wins 76 percent of these voters, which Gore did in 2000, he needs to win only 44 percent of the white vote to capture a majority.

In addition, Democrats clearly have benefited from the party's identification with prosperity during the Clinton years. Voters now have little memory of Carter. And as the surplus has risen, many voters no longer conjure up craven images of government bureaucrats whenever they hear of a new social program. As the Bush administration has recognized, these voters are willing to contemplate government spending on education and health care, although they would still look askance at programs as ambitious as Clinton's 1993 plan.

In American two-party politics, majority coalitions are never homogeneous. They always include what seem at the time to be improbable political bedfellows. Franklin Roosevelt's New Deal coalition included, for instance, Texas oil men, Jewish investment bankers, white Southern racists, Northern blacks, Midwestern farmers, urban ethnics and newly organized industrial workers. Reagan's coalition included Eastern patricians and upscale suburbanites, Jewish neoconservatives, Southern Wallacites and fundamentalists, and Italian and Irish Catholics. Similarly, the Democratic coalition that began to emerge in the '90s joined wealthy suburbanites in Evanston, Illinois, or New Jersey's Bergen County with inner-city blacks and Hispanics, and labor union members in Michigan's Macomb County with entrepreneurs in Silicon Valley.

Whether this coalition will form the basis of a new majority will depend partly on the willingness of Democratic leaders to recognize the heterogeneity of their own coalition. In the wake of Gore's defeat, the different factions within the party were pointing fingers at each other. The DLC, in particular, was blaming Gore's problems on his "populism" and his unwillingness to stress its "quality of life" agenda. But all the factions in the party have to realize they won't have a majority unless they can uphold both these kinds of appeals—unless they can maintain the loyalty and enthusiasm of both working-class and upper-middle-class Democrats. Clinton understood this and managed to include both groups in his 1996 campaign, which stressed both "building a bridge" to a high-tech future and defending Democratic social programs against Republican attack, but Gore was far less deft in combining these parts of the Democratic coalition.

The success of the Democratic effort will depend, too, on the ability of the Republicans to adjust to the new America of the 21st century—an America that will probably more closely resemble California and New Jersey than Mississippi and Utah. Just as the Democrats had to create distance between themselves and their extreme left, the Republicans will have to find a way to jettison the religious right. If the party moves closer to the center, as Arizona Sen. John McCain and others have advocated, it could certainly hold off the emergence of a Democratic majority. In that case, we could be in for a long period of transition, such as occurred from 1876 to 1896. During that period, there was a split-decision between the electoral and the popular vote twice (and a third near-miss). But if the Republicans remain the party of House Majority Whip Tom DeLay and the most retrograde business lobbyists, they will probably cede majority status to the Democrats within the next three elections.

What would the emergence of a Democratic majority mean, finally, for the nation's politics? Not as much as liberals might hope. While majority coalitions are always heterogeneous, certain parts of these coalitions usually define most clearly the party's direction and that of its leading politicians. The New Deal coalition was the party of Franklin Roosevelt, not of his conservative vice president John Nance Garner (or the more liberal Henry Wallace, for that matter). Likewise, the new Democratic majority is likely to be defined by moderates—by

This is not the lockstep look of the passing era. The diversity of the crowd looks more like what you might encounter at a bus stop than at a Washington policy conference. The buzz is infectiously enthusiastic, uncool. It's policy input gone retail—the Kmart of political reform. We're all here with our blue-light specials, our little piece of the answer. Happy to serve.

Once we all get our badges and our escort, we wend our way up and down staircases, down corridors and finally into a conference room increasingly crammed with people with something to say. That's when the transition team guy explains what we're here for. After us, he says, the briefing-book team will meet with trade associations and industry groups. Our conversation will guide their next one. The team's big question for us: "We need to find out ways for this agency to get all kinds of input justly and fairly represented, not just from people with money."

Say what? People can't quite believe their ears. The honcho goes on to belabor the obvious: "Frankly, the corporate community has a lot more money than all the people in this room." Consensus comes easy on this point. The librarian and disabled spokesman and children's advocate and public-interest computer programmer and the rest of us accede without a peep.

Then the honcho explains that another top-down "directive" is to figure out how to get the agency's staff itself to reflect the demography of the American population. The equal-opportunity mandate is, according to him, one of the president-elect's priorities. The sincerity quotient appears to be pretty high. We listen, trying hard to separate rhetoric from reality. It has been a long time since anyone in power spoke our language.

Then we all go to work, resolutely trying to rein in impulses to tell horror stories. They leak out anyway. We can't quite believe we're talking to people who really care about the fact that for 12

Al Gore or Joe Lieberman rather than Jesse Jackson or Minnesota Sen. Paul Wellstone.

As the Democratic Party evolved under Clinton, it became socially liberal—supportive of women's and civil rights, but not necessarily of gay marriage—more protective of the environment and consumer safety, willing to contemplate new spending on education and health care and attentive to workers' insecurity in the new global capitalism. But the Democrats have been largely unwilling to challenge the prerogatives of American multinationals within this new order.

If you distinguish two kinds of liberalism—one that attempts primarily to use the power of government to reduce insecurity and increase opportunity and another that puts government squarely on the side of labor and consumers—then the new liberalism is much more of the former variety. That's because within the new global capitalism, multinational corporations still hold the upper hand. They can move their facilities around the world in the face of threats from labor and consumers. And in the United States, while the growth of the Internet is spurring new kinds of virtual political communities, the labor movement has not yet figured out—and may never figure out—how to organize these workers. Even under John Sweeney's more militant leadership, unions have continued to lose members.

Under a new Democratic majority, those liberals who still nourish dreams of a new participatory democracy that extends from the workplace to the White House are likely to find themselves frustrated. But the upshot is that their frustrations will not compare with those suffered by the liberals of 1976, who thought they were about to ascend Mt. Olympus only to find themselves, in Bob Dylan's immortal words, "stuck inside of Mobile with the Memphis blues again." Twenty-five years later, those of us who identify with the left's historic goals of liberty and equality are certainly better off than we were in that Indian summer of 1976.

ITT Archives

Democrats clearly benefited from the party's affiliation with prosperity during the Clinton years.

years this agency has sabotaged its mandate, buried basic data, hidden and charged for basic procedural documents, and cavalierly ignored or dismissed our properly filed and entered interventions. But we warm up to the task.

Then, suddenly, it's all over. The transition team is driving this afternoon like a bus, and we've arrived at our destination. No one offers to lead us out of temporary office hell. We bump into a few vending machines and leave.

Never Mind the Bollocks, Here's the Republican Party

BILL BOISVERT

September 4, 2000

PHILADELPHIA—It's a strange sight as the glitz and snap of MTV rudely shove the innate dorkiness of a Republican Convention to the side; stranger still is the Clintonian tone of seductive come-on. But this is the year the Republicans finally said, *we get it.* They remember the 1992 and 1996 conventions, the disastrous results of Pat Buchanan's truculence and Bob Dole's last hurrah on behalf of once-potent GIs. And they've concluded from the Monica Lewinsky fiasco that a way with women is Bill Clinton's strength, not his weakness. So they have determined that this year the convention *will not be a guy thing.*

Hence the focus on health care, childcare, tax relief for young families—what Republican operatives, giving up the euphemism of "compassionate conservatism," simply call "she issues." Tonight's session is about education, the ideal theme to appeal to suburban obsessions and to showcase the Republicans as the party of social workers of color. The usual Republican boilerplate about character and discipline is repackaged into a softly therapeutic rhetoric of self-esteem, as a parade of African-American and Latino educators extol their own successes at turning inner-city kids into neatly uniformed readers, using nothing more expensive than high

Joeff Davis

With the glitz and snap of MTV, the 2000 Republican National Convention tried to put a new face on the GOP.

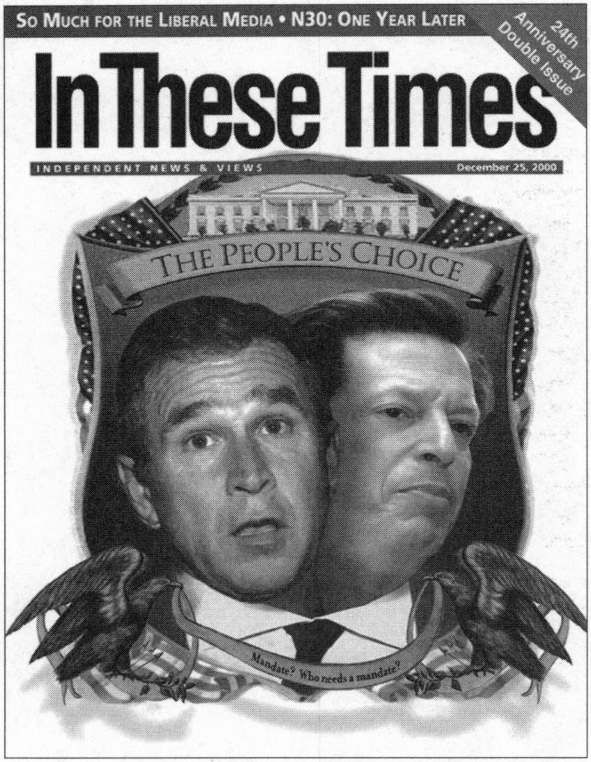

Jim Rimnert

Despite a split decision in 2000, there are indications that the electorate, if not Washington itself, is shifting to the left.

expectations. The evening ends with a speech by the famously reluctant Laura Bush, who tells of George's enthusiasm for parenting and literacy. Her message to other women is clear: *Like you, I thought a Bush presidency would ruin my family, but I was wrong. . . .*

Later in the week, I sat in as a group of Young Republicans listened to a Florida State Health Department official admonish them that Republicans could be a majority only when they claim the She Issues. But commitment seemed to waver, especially in the back of the room, where some of the more boisterous in the group loudly commented on the short skirt worn by the national co-chairwoman. She turned to them with a pained expression and brought her thumb and forefinger together in the universal symbol of tininess, a sort of genteel "fuck you" gesture I've seen a lot of Republican women use when Republican men are around.

At a College Republican luncheon with Newt Gingrich, everyone seemed to have been exhaustively briefed by the party leadership. None would admit to being McCain supporters, although they support campaign finance reform. When asked about Dick Cheney's embarrassing congressional voting record, they uniformly responded that legislative acts are vast and compendious, so we can't be sure exactly what he was voting against, as if the Clean Water Act had been some obscure rider on a pork-barrel appropriation. They don't seem to realize how lame that sounds. They're for sales taxes but against estate taxes; for sin taxes but against gas taxes.

They worship Gingrich, who ends his speech on his usual note of self-satisfied futurism about the unstoppable "rate of change." Then, inevitably, in walks ex-Sex Pistols frontman Johnny Rotten, an MTV camera crew in tow, his blazing yellow shirt festooned with drawings of the Bohr atom and the word "Web," symbols of unstoppable change. The original anarchist punk clasps hands with the original conservative globalist, the College Republicans gather round and send up a whoop of joy, and the circle is unbroken.

Fighting my way out of the dream logic of American political culture, I walk over to four waitresses standing in the corner. We talk about She Issues. Three of them have no health insurance. Should the government pay for health care? Yes, but not for the rich. How about a sliding scale? A sliding scale works for them. What about the estate tax? Not for ordinary people. How about for big estates, say over a million dollars? Yeah, rich people should have to pay the tax.

None of the four are Republicans. One is a Democrat. One likes Ralph Nader. I ask her why. "Because this," she says, sweeping her hand around the marble ballroom, toward the chandeliers far above, toward the red-white-and-blue streamer on the walls, toward Johnny Rotten sadly intoning "this space is for rent" as he poses for photos, "all this is bullshit."

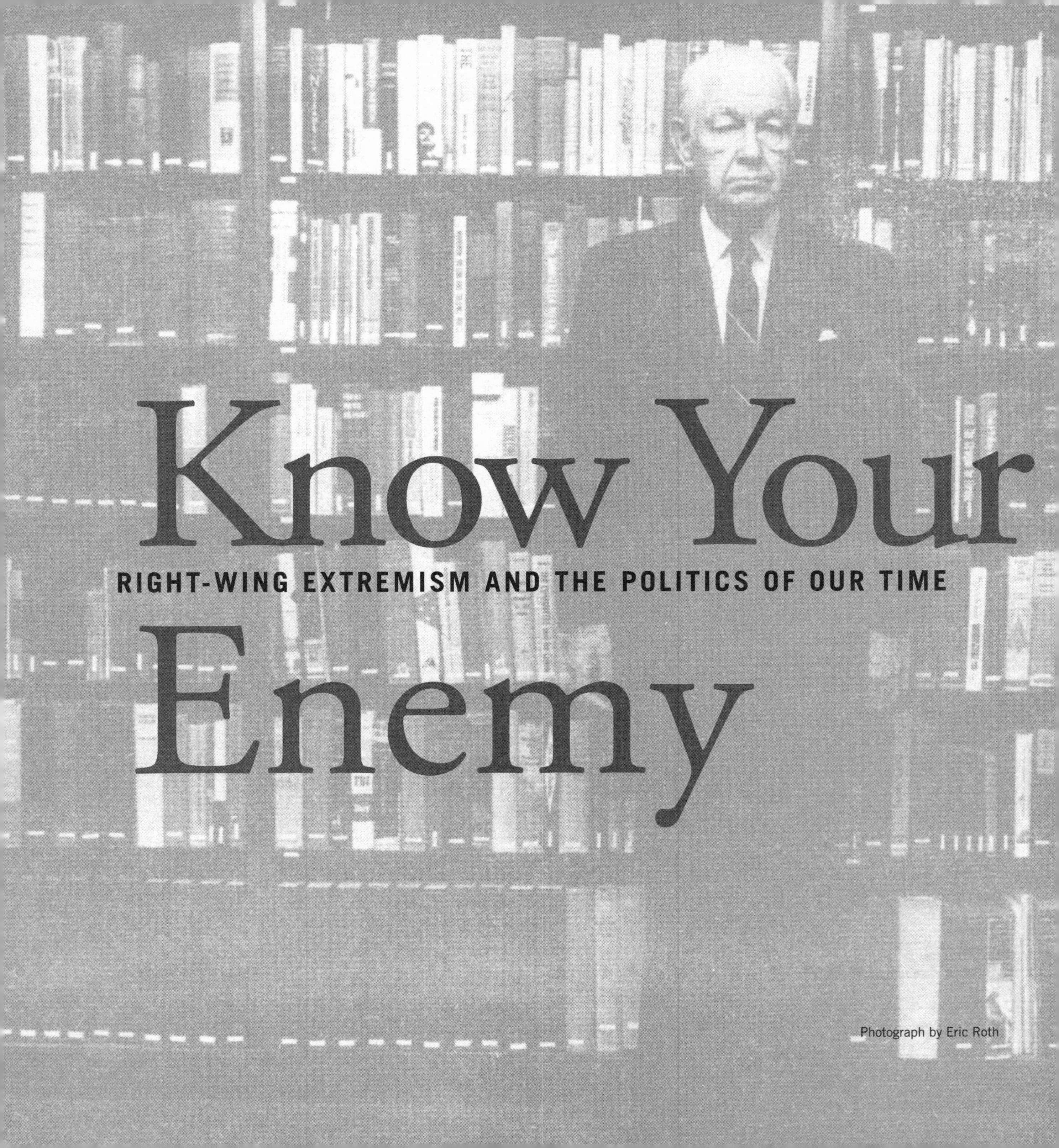

Know Your Enemy

RIGHT-WING EXTREMISM AND THE POLITICS OF OUR TIME

Photograph by Eric Roth

Two

RICK PERLSTEIN

BACK IN 1961, SOME OF THE 2,200 NEW YORK-AREA MEMBERS OF THE NEWLY MINTED CONSERVATIVE YOUTH ORGANIZATION YOUNG AMERICANS FOR Freedom used to leaven their crowded political schedules by repairing to the backroom of the White Horse Tavern on Hudson Street, celebrated hangout of longshoremen, folk singers and scribes. There, they were joined by members of the Young People's Socialist League. Revolutionary and counter-revolutionary gravitated to one another in the White Horse back room; the YAFers even joined in the YPSLers in rowdy choruses of old radical songs. Reliable witnesses attest to this.

This is not so strange. Recalled one of the White Horse lefties: "We had more common ground of conversation and interest with one another, than with all those people who didn't give a hoot about politics, the great yawning masses of the middle." It was a time when men like Dwight D. Eisenhower uttered epithets like, "Those who take extreme positions in American political and economic life are always wrong." John F. Kennedy proudly announced that whatever obstacles to well-being America faced were "technical problems."

Critic Karl Meyer called the political ideal-type of the day the "Smooth Dealer"—"too obsessed by the problems of his 'image' to explore the controversial issues of his time . . . too impressed by opinion polls and lacking in interior conviction . . . too prone to conceive of electoral survival as an end in itself; his nose is so implanted in the middle of the road that his eyes lose sight of the horizon."

Plus ça change. Nowadays we live in a less romantic age—backroom rendezvous between "far right" and "far left" are more likely to be tactical than recreational (say, Roger Milliken and Ralph Nader sharing intelligence on the latest outrageous international trade deal); that young Democratic and Republican congressional staffers occasionally lift a glass together at D.C. watering holes serves merely to show how debased the coin of ideology has become. And yet that certain strange bond remains. A common enemy—the half-conservative, half-liberal faith in the *is* that we might as well call "centrism"—renders those who occupy far ends of the political spectrum objects of mutual fascination.

That is why a wild-eyed reader of *The National Review* is more likely to follow the goings-on in a magazine like *In These Times* than your average sober-sided subscriber to *The New Republic.* It is why a magazine like *The New Republic*, in fact, has tended to react to right-wing advances with either a sniff, a laugh or a posture. And why publications like *In These Times* have consistently been the best sources for reporting about the right: Free from hang-ups about desecrating the sacred center, those souls to the left of liberal have better been able to see conservatives plain—as adversaries to fight, not cases to be studied; as givens in political life, not aberrations that wither away once that inevitable mantle of reason, procedure-driven pluralism and ideological equilibrium settles calmly over the earth once and for all.

But we get ahead of ourselves.

The practice of judging political temperaments as either "left" or "right" has been with us so long—"Every boy and every gal that's born into the world alive / Is either a little liberal or else a little conservative," japed Gilbert and Sullivan—as to seem almost primal. Certainly the elements of what we call conservatism in the United States—reverence for rugged individualism and contempt for government, aggression against the forces of international radicalism and selected resident others, the grandstanding embrace of personal piety—were well in place by the end of World War I, when anti-immigrant panic and postwar labor militancy, a public cult of patriotic godliness,

Sugar Daddy Welch

BARRY STAVRO

October 4, 1978

The home office of the John Birch Society is in Belmont, Massachusetts. The sedate, ivy-covered brick building flies an enormous Old Glory out front. On the ground floor is an American Opinion bookstore, one of 250 across the country. Most of the titles are published by Western Islands, their own firm, and have a Birchian flavor: *Naked Communist*, *Reds in America*, *I Was a Slave in Russia*, *The Red Web* and so forth. Also for sale are bumper stickers, flag kits, plus innumerable books and recordings by Society founder Robert Welch.

Welch occupies a regal-sized office on the second floor. At 78 he is a bit hard of hearing but has made few other concessions to old age, often putting in 20-hour days and sleeping over on the couch in his office. Welch fiddles with a cigar as he discourses on the Society's primary goal: "To get rid of Communists. To throw out the Communist forces and powers and influences in this country."

Each summer the Society publishes a "scoreboard issue" in their monthly magazine, *American Opinion*, listing the percentage of Communist influence among the nations of the world. Twenty years ago the United States was assessed at a 20 to 40 percent share; today it's pegged at 60 to 80 percent. A common criticism against Welch has been his tradition of crying wolf: the Reds are coming, coming.

"I'll bet you the people in Cambodia don't think so," Welch snorts. "Or Vietnam. Or Portugal. The point is the people who say we're crying wolf are the damn wolves. Most of my feelings about actual Communists is pity for them. They are a stupid bunch of cattle being used by a superior bunch of tyrants."

and a new assertiveness among urban African-Americans combined to produce the most ruthless wave of strike-breaking, race riots and Klan-building America had ever known. In its wake came a decade's interregnum of closed-lipped, straight-laced Republican presidential administrations; the air was conservative.

A truly self-conscious, institutionalized conservative movement, however, would have to await the coming of an American state large enough to be worthy of its contempt. In Franklin Roosevelt's '30s, with press barons like William Randolph Hearst and Col. Robert McCormick leading the way (McCormick blared from his editorial bully pulpit that FDR was creating "a centralized, despotic government different in no essential detail from Hitler's despotism"), conservative troops began massing, especially in the Midwest. But there was a problem. An organizing principle of Midwestern conservatism was isolationism. And whatever that position's honorable historical pedigree, after Pearl Harbor conservative forward motion found itself arrested by one of history's true juggernauts: American globalism.

The Party of Lincoln had always been a fair-weather home for conservatives; however, after FDR won his second term with a record 61 percent of the vote and the slogan, "If you want to live like a Republican, vote Democratic"—then a third and a fourth—liberal and internationalist party elites in the East won the day once and for all with the argument that since registered Democrats outnumbered Republicans as much as 3-to-2, the only way to win was to field candidates who appealed to this majority.

The postwar Red scare proved an unsteady rock upon which to rebuild the conservative church. Whatever Sen. Joe McCarthy's extravagant success in winning, according to polls, over half of Americans to his conviction that the true enemies of the nation burrowed secretly within its own innards—politically, McCarthyism lost when it won. If you actually removed the fear of subversion by catching subversives, you ended the fear that brought you to power in the first

Terry LaBan

Those who fled the Birchers for saner outlets always left better informed about how to effect political change.

The Conservative Movement

SIDNEY BLUMENTHAL

July 18, 1979

"It's a sign of our strength that there is no candidate in the Republican Party who is going to run a left-of-center campaign for president," Viguerie says. "This will be the first time in our lifetimes that no serious candidate for president will appeal to that liberal perspective. Slowly but surely we're moving the political balance much more to the center. Not to the right. But things are definitely moving our way."

Viguerie is relaxed in his corner office, surrounded by paintings of famous golf courses. His head is a gleaming sculpted dome with a few strands of hair brushed across it. He bubbles with optimism. "There isn't a Communist leader in the world worth his salt who doesn't feel that Communism isn't the wave of the future. That's place—though, of course, you could never catch all the subversives, for the conspiracy was a bottomless murk, a menace greater the more it was flushed out. Such a politics was too frightening, too *un-American*, to acquire much more than a fleeting popular hegemony.

A new generation of conservative intellectuals was beginning to realize there were better enemies to target—more dangerous, in their subtle way, but also far more efficient as a catalyst to populist resentment. McCarthyism was, Brent Bozell and William F. Buckley Jr. assured readers of their 1954 book *McCarthy and His Enemies*, something around which "men of good will and stern morality may close ranks." But in retrospect, what made this particular book a signal document of a more mature conservatism struggling to be born was the number of critical references to McCarthy it included. Unmasking subversives? Buckley and Bozell were more interested in fighting liberals. "We are interested in talking, not about 'who is loyal?' " they wrote, "but about 'who favors those politicians that are not in the national interest as we see it?' "

The national interest as conservatives saw it came rather dramatically under threat from three separate directions around 1956. Eisenhower's re-election that year ended all hopes that he would lead a charge to turn back New Deal reforms. Ike declared that "gradually expanding federal government" was "the price of rapidly expanding national growth." And among opinion-makers, the notion of moderate liberalism as a national consensus calcified. This stoked conservative fears and hardened their resolve to take back their party once and for all.

New formations were arising, new alliances set in motion—not least the beginnings of outreach efforts to the nation's other significant body of conservatives: Southern Democrats, for whom Midwestern isolationism once made them anathema. The Supreme Court's *Brown II* decision also came in 1956, mandating school integration go forward with

ITT Archives

The Reagan revolution sought to make "less government and more responsibility" the national creed.

what we have going now: The conservatives believe that they will govern America. They are totally convinced that they have the ability to govern and that they *will* govern in the foreseeable future. There's an electricity, an excitement that wasn't here six years ago."

Viguerie is fundamentalist in his political beliefs. What sets him off from mossbacks of previous generations is his sophistication. He has been willing to learn from sources other than fellow rightists. He is an apt pupil of George McGovern, the New Left and the AFL-CIO. "We've taken close to 100 percent of the left's tactics," he confesses unashamedly. "What we're doing is what they did. We have been 30 years late in realizing how the left did it. We're into making a list of all the things they do and doing the same things."

On Viguerie's desk when I paid him a visit was a thick book containing copies of the direct-mail solicitations from the 1972 McGovern for President campaign, which Viguerie holds in high professional esteem. "I'm studying it," he says. "I'm trying to build a movement. I don't know if you've heard that word much. Among us conservatives that's a word that's used constantly. The movement."

"all deliberate speed." Across Dixie, a new political culture of "massive resistance" blossomed almost overnight. And lo and behold, its sympathizers were not only Southern: In a Gallup poll, Arkansas Gov. Orval Faubus was listed as one of the 10 most admired men in America. Federal overreach, it appeared, was an issue to organize around.

And though the third catalyst in the rise of modern conservatism was more localized—newly aggressive attacks by smaller manufacturers against the growing bargaining and political power of the AFL-CIO, personified in the figure of hated Autoworkers chief Walter Reuther—this development was perhaps the most politically portentous of all. Once upon a time, union power was broken at the point of National Guard bayonets. But after the Wagner Act of 1935, and the routine corporate acceptance of collective bargaining that slowly followed, the weapon devised by smaller manufacturers was political: a "right to work" movement.

The argument was extravagantly made: By "forcing" workers to join, union shops violated the most sacred principle in the American civil religion: liberty. The "right to work" clamor that followed in the 1958 off-year elections happened to fail as a practical matter—the ballot initiatives and the candidates who supported them were trounced, bringing down much of the House and Senate Republican caucuses with them. But for the long-term project of movement building, it was a quantum leap. It set the stage for decades of masterful repackaging of plutocratic interests into populist language.

After conservatism was crushed in the 1958 elections, mainstream opinion read the right wing its last rites, and not for the last time. But, also not for the last time, the dead horse was stirring. Arizona Sen. Barry Goldwater, having resoundingly won re-election in 1958, became the new conservative hero. His manifesto *Conscience of a Conservative* somehow became a national sensation. Populist conservatism had arrived, and the tribunes of respected opinion were startled. *Time* noted how it "thoroughly belies the U.S. Liberals' caricature-belief that an Old Guardist is a deep-

Right-Wing Confidential

JOEL BLEIFUSS

August 8, 1994

On a spring night in May 1981, under a tent in the backyard of political strategist Richard Viguerie's suburban Virginia home, 160 New Right political leaders celebrated the change in their political fortunes. President Reagan had been elected that previous November. And though a taste of power was the main entrée, the New Right's best and brightest also dined on cold lobster, Peking duck, sushi and a strawberry-festooned elephant.

As members of the press looked on, Interior Secretary James Watt, Office of Management and Budget Director David Stockman, Phyllis Schlafly, Joseph Coors, Sen. John East (R-North Carolina), Sen. Orrin Hatch (R-Utah) and New Right *wunderkind* Paul Weyrich, among others, quenched their thirst with drinks served in coconut shells by kimono-dressed waitresses. And with coconuts raised on high, this collection of administration officials, congressmen, industrialists and conservative Christians inaugurated a political federation that was to coordinate their political agenda, the Council for National Policy (CNP).

After this public kickoff, the CNP went underground. Consequently, we do not know much about the CNP's actions or agenda. What we do know is that the radical right is clearly ascendant within the Republican Party. It has taken over state GOP organizations in Texas, California, Minnesota, Hawaii, Iowa, Nevada, Arizona, Idaho and Virginia. These coups give credence to Weyrich's contention that "we are no longer working to preserve the status quo. We are radicals, working to overturn the present power structure in this country." . . .

The CNP meets quarterly behind tightly closed doors. The group is so secretive, in fact, that its Washington office will neither confirm nor deny where, or even if, the group meets. It is known, however, that the council has quietly gathered in such far-flung places as Sinaia, Romania. The roster of the 500 people who are members of this organization is also confidential. . . .

[But] members of the CNP are known to include Jerry Falwell; Oliver North (a longtime member who sits on the CNP executive committee); Sen. Don Nickles (R-Oklahoma); Sen. Trent Lott (R-Mississippi); Sen. Jesse Helms (R-North Carolina); Rep. Bob Dornan (R-California); Brent Bozell III of the Media Research Center; Iran-Contra figure Gen. John Singlaub; Richard Shoff, former leader of the Ku Klux Klan in Indiana; Republican pollster Richard Wirthlin; Robert Weiner, head of Marantha, a Christian cult; Howard Phillips of the Conservative Caucus; Linda Bean Folkers of the L.L. Bean Co.; televangelist John Ankerberg; and Bob Jones III, president of Bob Jones University. . . .

It would be easy to dismiss the CNP as a collection of right-wing nuts. But that would be a mistake. "These groups move with unswerving determination," investigative journalist Russ Bellant told *In These Times*. "Virtually all the people I see in the leadership of the CNP are committed to either an anti-democratic or theocratic social system. Once they really gain the upper hand, they do not intend to ever let their enemies come back again." . . .

Bellant puts some of the blame on liberals. "The liberals are genuinely ignorant of who the right is and how they operate," he says. "They keep acting as if all that matters is the bottom line on voting day, and they ignore all the base-building that goes on in the preceding years. Remember, it was the far right that used so-called social issues—abortion, guns, taxes—to split the coalition of the Democratic Party. But the leadership of the constituency groups of the Democratic Party and of the party itself largely ignores the right wing. It beats me why people can't see where it is all coming from and go right to the heart of it. The Republican establishment is married

dyed isolationist endowed with nothing but penny-pinching inhumanity and slavish devotion to Big Business."

The impression that *Conscience of a Conservative* was a humanitarian manifesto, not a reactionary tract, was achieved through lines like: "Every man, for his individual good and for the good of his society, is responsible for his own development. The choices that govern his life are choices that he must make; they cannot be made by any other human being. . . . The conscience of the conservative is pricked by anyone who would debase the dignity of the individual human being." Words like "dignity," "autonomy" and "authenticity"—words that answered to the spirit of an age of post-scarcity, of a generation that could afford to forget the culture of limits wrought by the Depression—gave birth under the establishment's nose to a newly ideological politics both on the left and on the right.

And on the conservative side, certain old reliable appeals never went away. When the manager of the tiny Hudson Valley town of Newburgh, New York scapegoated black welfare recipients for the town's fiscal decline and instituted draconian, nationally publicized relief strictures (uncannily similar to those imposed by the 1996 welfare reform bill) the guardians of civic reason were disgusted ("Cruelty anywhere is the concern of mankind everywhere," declaimed the *New York Times*) but relatively unconcerned. "A substitute of police methods for welfare methods" (Hubert Humphrey's words) could never catch on, editorialized Henry Luce in *Life*: "It is simply not in the American character to let anyone starve."

But what happened next was that it caught on. The modest town manager was soon fielding thousands of letters in praise. Beyond the old game of scapegoating the poor, it was the new, high-flown conservative appeal to humanist values of autonomy that truly had traction. During this little-remembered affair, millions of ordinary Americans simply tuned out the voices of the experts who pointed to the evidence that should have made them know better, moralists who demanded they care more, and intellectuals who compared them to Nazis. Nothing quite like it had happened before: The experts and intellectuals were resentfully styled as tribunes of conformity, bureaucracy and the violation of common sense. "I willingly join those you defame as 'know nothings,' " ran a typical angry letter to the *Times.*

It was 1961. A new, right-wing vibe pulsated through American life; it was grassroots, it was growing, it was stubbornly political, it was approaching the ordinary. And *The New Republic* types hardly noticed. But as it happened, the forces of conservative normalcy arose amid spectacular examples of right-wing lunacy. Astonishing passages from an underground book published by a man named Robert Welch were read into the Congressional Record accusing President Eisenhower of being a Moscow-directed agent. For a time, Welch's John Birch Society and its cognates became one of the most talked about subjects in cocktail-party America.

But the talk was not of a right-leaning political mood bubbling up from below. Centrist liberals believed they had a handle on the right-wing upsurge: It was one of those periodic outbreaks of what Richard Hofstadter called America's "paranoid style" of politics. The idea, both theoretically and empirically dubious, was that a certain proportion of our fellow citizens, unable to cope with the confusions that face them in a modern, complex world, react by acting nutty and irrational. This was worrisome to the degree it reflected the innate baseness in the heart of man, but dismissable—even laughable—to the degree that, after all, the future would soon roll over these pathetic anomalies. Hofstadter himself joked that he welcomed the Goldwater-for-president movement when it sprung up because it was providing conservatives "a kind of vocational therapy, without which they might have to be committed."

In fact, the history of modern American conservatism from here on is inseparable from the story of mainstream liberalism's condescension toward it. Even in 2001 *The New*

Peter Hannan

If new right *wunderkind* Paul Weyrich were a Democrat, he would advise the party to "go for the jugular."

to the Christian right; it can't win an election without them. But the Democrats refuse to address the essential role of the Christian right in the Republican Party, so the coalition is allowed to thrive and defeat them."

If Paul Weyrich were a Democrat, he would advise the party to follow his lead and, as he has said, "go for the jugular." The Democrats could learn other things from Weyrich, such as the value of building a national political infrastructure to support grassroots actions, the importance of forging political coalitions and the need to communicate ideas forcefully and effectively.

But in order to communicate ideas, the Democrats would first need to have some.

The New Old Right vs. The Old New Right

DANIEL LAZARE

March 25, 1992

Has Pat Buchanan really gone soft? Has the White House pit bull who once talked (metaphorically, of course) of "firing from the upper floors" on the Iran-Contra committee turned into just another sensitive guy given to Donahue-esque emanations over the plight of the downtrodden and oppressed?

Not quite. Pat, for better or worse, is still Pat. What is different, though, is that the politician whom William Safire calls an "anti-intellectual intellectual" has been on a mission lately, an ideological quest of sorts, scouting out new territory on the radical right. It's not a terrain that policy wonks and spinmeisters in Washington are terribly familiar with, which explains their surprise at what he has brought back.

And indeed, the new right (more properly, the new *old* right) is radically different from the neoconservatism that dominated the Reagan White House. The old new right—led by William Bennett, Irving Kristol, Norman Podhoretz, Midge Decter and Elliott Abrams—was corporate, internationalist and largely secularist. Many of the top figures (most notably Kristol) were lapsed Marxists who still believed in the capacity of human beings to remake the world in their own image. The new old right, by contrast, is often religious, always nationalist, hostile to big cities and big business, culturally traditionalist and profoundly suspicious of any notion of social engineering.

Unlike neocons, who regard themselves as proselytizers for democracy (provided said democracy does nothing to challenge corporate prerogatives), paleoconservatives regard "democratism" as a species of totalitarianism hardly less intrusive than Stalinism or fascism. Rather than championing majority rule, they want to restrict it by limiting

Republic featured a story chalking up the election mess to the right's paranoid style, complete with an old phrenology chart—as if paranoia could never, ever dwell in the center, that precinct of eternal wisdom, as if every centrist political reform from welfare reform to the progressive income tax had not first issued from outside the blob.

There was always a gaping flaw in the paranoia theory. For many of those who flirted with the Birchers, the appeal wasn't, say, Welch's lunatic insistence that the United States was "already 50 to 70 percent communist." They often joined as political orphans at a time when conservatism's profile in American political culture was at an all-time low. Often the local Birch organizer, armed with the slogan "less government and more responsibility," was the only conservative game in town. Members of this and other fringe groups regularly defected as they found other, saner, outlets for their conservative instincts. They always, however, left better informed about how to effect political change.

The failed Goldwater campaign; Nixon's election on the back of "silent majority" rhetoric; heightened moral clamor over matters like sex-ed and troublesome youth; anti-busing crusades; stronger and more entrenched conservative organizing all through the '70s—ever bubbled the dialectic. But the churning at the grassroots faced establishment indifference and condescension. (Reagan may win the Republican nomination, perhaps even the presidency, *The New Republic* reported in December 1979, but only because he is cutting himself adrift from "the kooky fringe of the GOP, on the likes of Jesse Helms [and] Phil Crane." Phil Crane. Wasn't he the one who introduced the welfare reform bill that President Clinton signed?)

Of course, kooky-fringe-cutting was part of the process all along. The act of identifying, isolating and purging the Birch taint from institutions like *The National Review*, the Goldwater presidential and Reagan gubernatorial campaigns, and various sundry local crusades for moral reclamation was one of the key trials-by-fire that tempered the conservative movement to fight for actual political power. Those on the fringe were the foil. Without them, the plane might never have gotten off the ground at all. They were the ones who left liberals to be utterly blindsided when the right was ready to seize the day.

Enters our hero. *In These Times* was born at a time of exhausted energy on the New Left but extraordinary momentum on the part of a self-identified "New Right"—new not for its ideology, but for its hunger for conservative governing power. It was also a time when the right-wing economic agenda was becoming a bona fide Washington interest-group hustle, with outfits like the Business Roundtable bidding adieu to older corporate notions of responsible citizenship and light-touch Keynesianism in favor of a politics that equated the national good with what they called "capital formation." And those to the left of liberal were often the new climate's most discerning observers.

"Like the tortoise, the John Birch Society has a tough shell and has endured a long and hard drubbing, only to steadily plod on," ran a 1978 *In These Times* article. It went on to observe how the Society had managed to beef up its membership and influence in the late '60s with its grassroots campaign to "Support Your Local Police"—coining a new item for the conservative agenda, one that is still with us today. The Birchers' campaign for 1978, *In These Times* noted, was "Tax Reform Immediately." This is significant because 1978 was the year of California's Proposition 13 and of a remarkable tax revolt across the country—astonishing to those in the establishment, but not to conservative activists or those who were reading the right left-wing magazines.

"One of the remarkable things about American politics is a substantial growth of right-wing opinion that is not necessarily represented in voting trends," *In These Times* observed then. "The causes of anti-government feeling should not be underestimated." This at a time when the journalistic standard for reporting on the far right, when there was any, was to recall

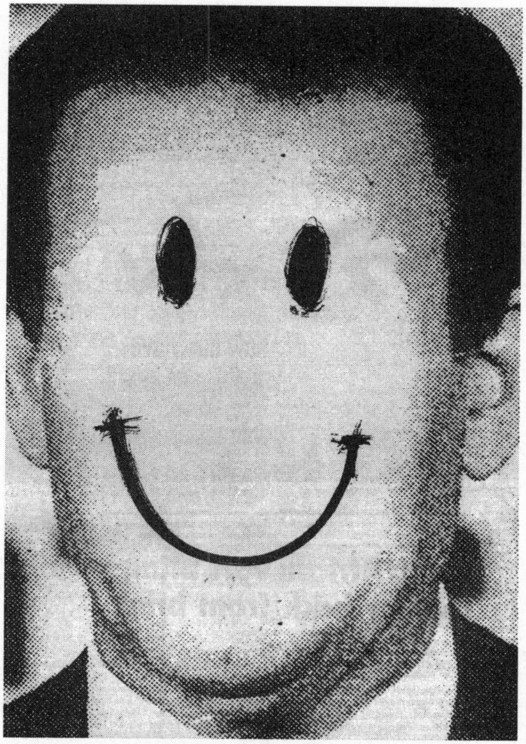

ITT Archives

Pat Buchanan offered a different vision of "compassionate conservatism."

areas of human activity subject to government purview. In wanting government out of the lives of individuals, they are no less hostile to government by majority than to autocracy.

The paleoconservatives also have a different take on the compassion issue. Liberals, we all know, like compassion. Neoconservatives, we're equally aware, don't, believing that compassion is a condition imposed by sob sister social workers that prevents unemployed workers, among others, from adjusting to the fast-changing demands of the global economy. Instead of sympathy, they think the jobless need a kick in the pants to encourage them to learn skills.

Paleoconservatives, on the other hand, disagree with both. Unlike neocons, they believe in compassion (as Buchanan asserted over and over again in New Hampshire), but in the context of a nationalist ideological framework, as opposed to a liberal-humanitarian one. If their hearts bleed for hard-pressed New Hampshire residents tossed out of their homes, it's not because they're human beings, but because they're Americans and are therefore entitled to a helping hand. All others—starving Ethiopians, typhoon-stricken Bangladeshis, European Jews on the run from Hitler, etc.—must go to the end of the line.

readers to Robert Welch's statements about Communist adulteration of the water supply and the disloyalty of General Eisenhower, perhaps going on to dismiss the right's great presidential aspirant, Ronald Reagan, on account of the Birch-linked past of some of his associates, and leave it at that.

What *In These Times* watched happen over the next 20-some years is a familiar story. The Reagan revolution sought to make "less government and more responsibility"—and less cultural freedom and more defense spending—the national creed. Success was stuttering at the time: Despite Reagan's lip service, government spending and government programs grew during his tenure, and his promise to melt the federal deficit in a warm bath of trickle-down fiscal policy was undone by the brazen doctrine that there could be "no price ceiling on American security." (Reagan had no problem with price ceilings on American health care, American economic security and American education, however.)

But over time, much of his program found redemption. Reagan's politically bountiful Third World- and U.N.-baiting came back in the form of "structural adjustment" programs that regovern the Third World under the guise of trading with it; his fear-mongering on crime and sub-rosa racism reached their apotheosis in Clinton's civil-liberties-shredding anti-terrorism and immigration laws (which themselves set the stage for George W. Bush's further gutting of constitutional protections after September 11).

But the real damage has been quieter. It resides at the level of what your ordinary, everyday well-dressed man—the guy who graduated from college, follows politics loosely, wants to make a decent living in an honest way—thinks as a matter of habit. In the early '60s when "Smooth Dealers" were being accused by a few scattered critics of ignoring certain forces for social justice roiling just beneath the surface, at least the somnolent consensus they were trying to wake people out of included, among its tenets, decent respect for the power of government to countervail that of corporations, a mild form of civil rights, and the fair distribution of income as a moral *and* economic good. Winning a landslide victory in 1964, Lyndon Johnson had proclaimed: "The government is not an enemy of the people. It is the people."

Three decades later, half of Americans agreed, according to pollsters, that "the federal government has become so large and powerful that it poses a threat to the rights and freedoms of ordinary citizens." And when "experts" remark on today's sweeping embrace of market thinking, the retreat of the regulatory state, America's military role as the "indispensable nation," a shorthand rolls off their tongue: "There is no alternative."

When experts said that same thing in 1964, it was one of the most dramatic failures of collective discernment in American intellectual history. Can an "extreme" seize the center? It has happened before.

Conservatism is our enemy and our obsession, a repository for our seething rage and our middle-of-the-night anguishes. Each of us has our own theories about its provenance, its perversities, the secret of its success. We trade tidbits about its latest outrages and get gauzily reverent about its fiendish organizational brilliance (forgetting that, long ago, they stole the playbook from us). We know its story because we have to. We know it too well because, against all of our dreams and most of our expectations, it has become all too nearly the sum total of politics in our time.

But in writing about a neglected component of the intellectual genealogy of the left—the astringency with which the socialistically inclined have been able to understand the geography of the other shore, and with it, that of the deceptively lulling terrain of the Great Boring Central Plains in between—I am reaching here, on the occasion of *In These Times*' 25th anniversary, for something broader: a subject yet beyond the grasp of journalists, historians and activists, but that somehow seems the skeleton key to all of our hopes.

That is the matter of the paradox of a nation riven to the core with conflict and division and resentment and contempt, that remains ever unable—by nature? by design? by the malign cunning of an unbreachable status quo? by the timorousness or blindness of our attempts to outfox it?—to acknowledge its own nature as a society of conflict and division and resentment and contempt. This is a society that *changes*—and, perhaps, a society we can change.

The first step is to make it so those who appreciate a true ideological catfight don't have to hide in the backrooms of bars, while Smooth Dealers too obsessed by the problems of image to explore the controversial issues of their time, too impressed by opinion polls and lacking in interior conviction, too prone to conceive of electoral survival as an end in itself, noses so implanted in the middle of the road their eyes lose sight of the horizon, unaccountably hog all of the conventional wisdom. The next step is to engage the opposition—and win.

By Our Mark Shall Ye Know Us!

TERRY SOUTHERN

October 18, 1993

The persons most responsible for the deterioration of the quality of life in this country are not, as is generally assumed, the drug lords or the crazed addicts looking for their next fix. No, it is a group of citizens less conspicuous than they; it is a loose coalition of rabid xenophobes whose minds perceive government as an abstraction, which is either "intrusive," "incompetent" or simply "too big."

Their regard for government suggests nothing so much as the reaction of Pleistocene Man when confronted with that first stone scoop of *fire*: scuttling crabwise away from it, grimacing crazily, eyes agog, arms akimbo, fending it off in grotesque squeals and grunts of animal panic.

It's vividly analogous to the behavior of the Sam Nunns, the Bob Doles, the Bob Grahams and the Newt Gingriches when regarding such simple notions as "group planning" and "group endeavor." They have managed to poison and corrupt these ideas and to cloak them in bugaboo superstitions of "bureaucratic socialism" so that we are deprived of much of what other civilized nations take for granted, especially in the realm of the nation's health. Apparently they have never grasped the principles upon which our society was founded: Whatever body of laws might *govern* it, those laws would be *of* and *by* the people—an *extension* of our society, not something distinct from it.

Compared to the more common and perhaps more "natural" follow-the-leader (and devil-take-the-hindmost) forms of social structure, ours is fairly complex, relying less on instinct, cunning and strength than on resorting to such acquired

ITT Archives

The Proud-as-Punch Nitwits, or "Pee-Pees" for short.

notions as planning and cooperation. It is understandable how the "Leader of the Pack" types might not be comfortable in a society pledged to utilize its resources for the benefit of all its members, weak and strong. Indeed, it can be argued that the Doles, the Nunns, the Gingriches, the Grahams—those people whose behavior flagrantly defies the most basic principles of our social contract—have no morally justifiable place in the culture. It is outrageous when they express, as they frequently do, a concern for "law and order," since their own conduct frequently resembles that of "anarchists."

But even anarchists need organization, and an organization of sorts has evolved, an organization whose principal founders are Sens. Strom Thurmond and Jesse Helms. This group, first calling itself the PPNs (the Proud-as-Punch Nitwits), was born following the appearance of a spunky article by *New York Times* columnist Anthony Lewis wherein he described the two senators as a "pair of nitwits." To this, Helms testily responded: "Nitwits and proud of it!" while Big Strom, added, with characteristic bravura: "Yes, as proud as punch, you little Commie wop!"

Both men are known to be avid history buffs and to have expressed great admiration for the old Know Nothing movement of the 1850s. It is understandable why they welcomed the Proud-as-Punch Nitwit sobriquet with hearty fervor. Their "PPN" designation, used with great frequency by the media, soon became shortened to the "PPs" and then was vulgarized by the tabloids and the general public into "Pee-Pees."

It is an indication of the temper of Helms and Thurmond, and of their followers, that they did not shy away from this new moniker. To the contrary, they embraced it with defiant relish and almost immediately adopted the gesture of public urination as part of their collective persona. "By our mark shall ye know us!" they proclaimed at a press conference on the lawn of the U.S. Senate and promptly demonstrated their meaning to the gaggle of gawking reporters. These are persons, bear in mind, whose public paranoia regarding "socialism" or anything that might somehow remind them of it, has denied us not merely the common-sense single-payer solution to health care, but also the very keystone of industrial/economic infrastructure of every other non-Third World country on the planet: a nationalized or subsidized high-speed rail transportation system.

In keeping with their typical ("Give 'em Hell, Jesse!") exuberance, the group's device of public urinations eventually spilled over into the smart salons of their fundraising patrons (usually against velour drapes), a practice which remains a matter of sharp controversy among even their most devoted followers.

Be on alert, then, Mr. and Mrs. Joe Six-pack, for the following known and dedicated members of the PPN:

Lloyd Bentsen, David Boren, Orrin G. Hatch, Arlen Specter, Bob Packwood, Alan Simpson, Alfonse D'Amato, Bob Dole, Robert Dornan, Newt Gingrich, Charles Grassley, Howell Heflin, Henry Hyde, Richard Lugar, John McCain, Sam Nunn, John Danforth, Donald Riegle, Pete Domenici, etc. etc., etc., etc., etc., etc., etc., etc., etc. etc., etc.

Stick and Win

FORGING A REAL PROGRESSIVE ALTERNATIVE

Photograph by Steve Kagan

Three

JOHN NICHOLS

IN THAT BLEAK WINTER OF 1983, I WAS A KID IN RECESSION-RAVAGED RURAL WISCONSIN, AND RONALD REAGAN WAS THE PRESIDENT OF THE UNITED States. By just about any measure I could figure, mine was the losing end of that equation—I was so outgunned, in fact, that rather than bang my head against the wall of politics, I poured my post-adolescent energy into weighing with similarly disengaged friends the relative merits of Grandmaster Flash versus the Cure. Some perverse motivation—perhaps it was patriotism—kept me reading the left press, particularly *In These Times*.

The publication had grabbed me a few years earlier when the editors displayed what appeared to be appropriate enthusiasm at the election of François Mitterrand as president of France. On the outside prospect that a wellspring of democratic socialism might explode in the United States sometime soon, I figured these folks were best prepared to recognize the signs. In January 1983, it seemed my faith in the radical dowsers at *In These Times* might be rewarded.

Harold Washington, an African-American congressman with a reassuring penchant for pointing out the parallels between Reagan and the Central American dictators the United States was propping up in those days, was running for mayor of Chicago. Washington was rough and radical. He despised social and economic injustice, and he was talking about busting up Chicago's corrupt machine politics to make way for a government that—if not quite the Paris Commune—sounded better than anything I could see taking shape inside the Beltway.

Chicago's daily newspapers, which found their way to the farm town where I lived, were unimpressed with Washington's candidacy. To them, he was a footnote in the dismal Democratic primary battle that year between Mayor Jane Byrne and the guy they called "Richie" Daley—the son of "The Boss." Washington

Low Vote and the Left

JAMES WEINSTEIN

November 22, 1976

The inability of Republicans or conservatives to attract the millions of people who either have never voted or have been dropping out speaks to the left's opportunities. The continuing disenchantment not simply with major-party leadership, but also with politics as such, speaks to the left's failures.

Politics in the United States, as in the rest of the West, has meant and continues to mean, among other things, participation in electoral activity. This is true because representative government is the most democratic form of government yet put into practice, despite limitations imposed on it within capitalist society. But socialists in this country have made only token use of our electoral system and then either to pursue narrow factional ends or as invisible partners in liberal campaigns.

One other thing seems clear: It is in the left's interest to bring the 70 million nonvoters into the electoral arena, because to do so would be to change the face of American politics by vastly increasing the number of labor, low-income, women and ethnic

ITT Archives

Republicans and conservative Democrats have a vested interest in keeping the number of voters low.

was not viable, editors and Democratic insiders explained, because he was, uh, black. That didn't seem like a very sophisticated analysis, considering the fact that most Democrats in Chicago were, uh, people of color. Nor did the dismissal of Washington seem particularly sporting, as he was smart and cool and right on the issues, while Byrne and Daley were, uh, not, not and not.

I learned some powerful lessons about the necessity of a left press during those first months of 1983. As the *Chicago Tribune* and *Chicago Sun-Times* meticulously missed the story of the most historic campaign in the city's history, *In These Times* got it. Its writers recognized in this remarkable campaign a potential for the multicultural "Rainbow Coalition" of African-Americans, Asian-Americans, Latinos, lakefront liberals, rank-and-file trade unionists, gays and lesbians, old-school Democrats and lifelong lefties who had never before bothered to back a party that listed Sam Nunn and George Wallace among its "elder statesmen."

After Washington dispatched Byrne and Daley in the primary, I took the train to Chicago and volunteered on the campaign that *In These Times* said was breaking all the rules of Chicago (and American) politics. I even developed an undeserved reputation as a political pundit—upon which I capitalize to this day—because I parroted the theory advanced by *In These Times* that a reasonably radical black man could, with maximized minority turnout and just enough support from white progressives, claim the chair once occupied by "The Boss."

Washington's win that spring was everything a Reagan-era youth suffering from rapidly diminishing faith in electoral politics could ask for. Harold beat the racists, booted the machine, built a rainbow administration, and inspired dozens of other African-American mayoral candidates who turned 1983 into a critical breakthrough year in urban progressive politics. Inspired by Washington's win, one of the mayor's Chicago supporters announced that he would seek the presidency; the Rainbow Coalition went national with the Jesse Jackson campaign of 1984.

Mistakes were made, opportunities were squandered, Washington died too young. Jackson did not win the elections of 1984 or 1988, and he did not prevail in the even more important post-elections—when the Rainbow Coalition needed to be turned into a permanent force. But Jackson's campaigns and the coalition-driven, unapologetically progressive, necessarily grassroots politics they represented did change the playing field within the Democratic Party—so much so that the corporatists had to form the right-wing Democratic Leadership Council and pour tens of millions of dollars into a project they euphemistically referred to as "getting our party back." The fight over the soul of the Democratic Party continues to this day, but no one should question that the left's opening salvo came in Chicago—where the Washington campaign broke down the barriers of class, race, gender and sexuality to initiate a new model for electoral coalition-building.

Something like an eternity has passed since those heady days, when the results of a single election in a single city sent shockwaves through the politics of the nation. We are less innocent now about the prospects for electoral politics, less hopeful about the coalitions that can be built, and woefully less prepared for the presidency of another deceptively doltish Republican president. Yet we are no less in need of a politics as inspired as the revolutionary campaign that Harold Washington mounted almost two decades ago. And we will have it as soon as those of us who experienced the exhilaration of that victory night in 1983—and those who cannot imagine yet still hope for such a moment—begin to worry a little less about Washington, D.C., and a little more about Chicago and Cleveland, Los Angeles and Laredo, Seattle and Sheboygan.

This is not to suggest that we should be any less enraged over the sorry state of political affairs that has put a Confederate crank like John Ashcroft in charge of civil rights enforcement, that has seen Congress cripple the Bill of Rights with a misguided anti-terrorism bill, and that has seen minority representatives in Congress and in state legislatures.

Republicans and conservative Democrats have a vested interest in keeping the number of voters low. We do not. The answer is not a campaign to get out the vote, however. People abstain from voting for good reason. The answer is to take the task of providing a good reason to vote as central to this time.

Marc Pokempner

"Are you a serious candidate," a TV reporter asked Barry Commoner, "or are you just running on the issues?"

On the Road with Barry Commoner

DAVID MOBERG

October 22, 1980

With a TV crew following him through the shopping center, the Citizens Party's Barry Commoner suddenly seemed plausible as a presidential candidate. It was a sign of how the campaign, lacking money for TV, is essentially shut out of what is presidential politics for most Americans—the tube. Since he does not have a shot at winning, his ideas—however interesting—are little more newsworthy than if he were still just a professor. The TV reporter from CBS even suggested that he risked losing influence by running, since he might now appear kooky rather than continue to be the respected Dr. Commoner. Politics is still basically a horse race for the mass media—and for most people, even if they wish it were a different horse race. One of Commoner's favorite stories from the campaign concerns an Albuquerque TV reporter who started the interview, "Mr. Commoner, are you a serious candidate, or are you just running on the issues?"

Mayor Bernie Sanders Speaks

BERNIE SANDERS
AS TOLD TO DAVID MOBERG
March 23, 1983

BURLINGTON, VERMONT—Politics is not dissimilar to art. What is it that makes a great novel or film different from a fair novel or film? In a sense you've got to inspire the people, and you've got to talk to them where they're at today. Two years ago a lot of people in the progressive community in Burlington didn't think that I should run. I was too individualistic. You're always right after you succeed. Right now, I'm the smartest person in the world, but two and a half years ago a lot of people didn't think I was very smart.

People have got to develop confidence in themselves. They've got to get inspired. They've got to believe they can do it. Sometimes you have groups of people sitting around in endless discussions, and they go absolutely nowhere. I'm elected because I probably knocked on more doors than anybody in the history of Burlington. In [three campaigns] I've probably knocked on half the

America launch another war without the debate that past wars should have taught us is necessary. The point is that the only way out of the mess we find ourselves in is to stop thinking that the Democratic National Committee or dumb luck—which are pretty much the same thing these days—will deliver us from the valley of the Bush. The answer will come, as it always has, from a Chicago of our own making.

What is it that we're making? A new politics?

Let's hope not.

The next time some "visionary" shows up with a line about how the left has to find a new way of talking to America, run away as fast as you can. Stop only when you reach a good, independent video store and grab a copy of *Northern Lights*, Rob Nilsson's timeless film about the farmers who in the early years of the 20th century birthed the most successful left-wing electoral experiment in American history, the North Dakota Non-Partisan League. Toward the end of that film, there is a scene where Ray Sorenson, the NPL's reluctant organizer in one of the most barren corners of what could be the most barren state in America, is trying to convince a circle of skeptical Norwegian homesteaders that their only hope for survival lies in banding together in a political movement that sees the Democratic and Republican parties as mere shells—to be occupied and discarded, as the need be, by a freewheeling band of activist voters whose only loyalty is to one another and to their movement for economic democracy.

The Non-Partisan Leaguers had a slogan, "We Stick, We Win." The message was simple: Get the great mass of voters into a coalition of the disempowered, set some basic goals for achieving economic fairness and common decency, pursue them with a vengeance and without respect for political labels or partisan dogmas, gut out the hard times, grab the good, and win. The Leaguers did exactly that—to such an extent that their ideology still guides the shell they eventually crawled into, which even now is officially known as the Democratic-

Non-Partisan-League Party of North Dakota. And for 85 years, North Dakota has sent one of the most consistently anti-corporate delegations to Congress of any state.

For half that time, its members raged as Republicans; for a time, some of them raged as political independents; now they rage as Democrats. (Check out Sen. Byron Dorgan's proposed legislation to break up agribusiness monopolies if you find yourself in need of a dose of the NPL's lingering prairie populism.) When I was covering the anti-WTO protests in Seattle, I heard D-NPL state Rep. April Fairfield from rural Eldridge chanting, "This is what democracy looks like!"—and I knew that the "D" was not nearly so dominant as the "NPL" in her political bloodstream.

The great lesson of left electoral politicking—from the abolitionists of the Liberty and Republican parties, to the Non-Partisan Leaguers and the Progressives of the '20s and '30s, to the Rainbow Coalition, to the radical foes of gentrification who took over San Francisco's Board of Supervisors in December 2000—is simple. It is always about sticking and winning, about building broad coalitions and keeping them together beyond Election Day. Whether we call our cause democratic socialism, progressive populism or liberalism is, for the most part, inconsequential. Whether we come together around an open fire in rural North Dakota, at a church in Chicago or in an Internet chatroom is entirely meaningless.

What matters is that we move beyond the tiny circle of the committed core and create a movement that incorporates the vast majority of Americans, who polls tell us want, in the words of sociologist Joel Rogers, "a living wage for the work we do, a great education for our kids, a guarantee of health care if we get sick, economic security when we grow old, and an end to the false divisions along lines of race, gender, sexuality and physical ability that prevent our true voices from being heard."

How can we fail to recognize that, in the aftermath of the September 11 terrorist attacks, America turned not to the private sector for a response, but to government—at the local, state and national levels? Now more than at any time in

doors in the city. You can't be afraid of the people—and you've got people who sit around talking continually about the people, the people, the people, but God forbid they'll ever go out and knock on a door.

The word 'socialism' has value, because what it says is that we believe in a different vision of society rather than a handful of banks and corporations. But what can I do as mayor of Burlington to bring that about? There are limitations. I work with banks for economic development. We are not going to nationalize the banks. We couldn't if we wanted to.

But talking about what must happen in this nation and getting the support of people here is a very frightening thing to the people who own the city and the state. They are outraged that working people are supporting us and our vision even if we freely admit that we can't bring that vision about—that poverty is unnecessary, that we could eliminate it in a few years with sane economic development.

Can I do that in Burlington? I can't. But even saying those things and pointing the way toward public ownership of the major means of production, for example, and involvement of workers in day-to-day decision-making infuriates those people. What infuriates them even more than 3 cents tax on a bottle of beer is that we're talking about a vision of society where the ruling class isn't going to be in the driver's seat anymore.

People are supposed to repudiate that. You're supposed to get 2 to 3 percent of the vote, if you're lucky. That's what all the textbooks and shows on radio and TV are all about, that these ideas are foolish and not worthy of being discussed in the United States. Well, I discuss them, and I just beat my Democratic opponent by 20 percent and the Republican candidate by 30 percent.

The issue of socialism is not of tremendous importance in the day-to-day running of city government. It is of tremendous importance in raising the consciousness of people who are now saying,

"Gee, this can be a different world." Do you think it makes the ruling class happy that the turnout in this election was so heavy? They much preferred it the old way when the more conservative elements would come out, and working and poor people wouldn't vote because they'd given up, and that's just what the system wants.

If I get criticized for not being radical enough for some people, that's fine. But I'm not a Democrat, and I'm not a Republican. We've stood up, taken them on and beaten them. We're talking about a vision that will not be brought about tomorrow, maybe not in a hundred years, but it's a vision, and maintaining a vision of an alternative society is probably the most important thing we can do.

ITT Archives

"You've got people who sit around talking about the people, the people, the people," Bernie Sanders says. "But God forbid they'll ever go out and knock on a door."

recent American history, polls show that the American people recognize the wisdom of progressive appeals for a greater government commitment to stimulate a slowing economy, to protect public health, to regulate everything from airport security to the safety of our food.

It's no secret, of course, that our majority status when it comes to issues is not a guarantee of victory. As any savvy electoral organizer will tell you: Winning is easy, it's the sticking together part that's difficult. The problem is that sticking necessarily precedes winning. And right now there are way too many people on the left, people of goodwill, who are so disinclined to stick that winning has become unimaginable to them. It is not that people on the left disagree over issues; in fact, there is more coherence now than at any point in recent history (even the AFL-CIO is now in favor of immigrant rights, while the Humane Society has emerged as one of the most cogent critics of globalization). What divides people on the left is a combination of strategic disagreement—remember that whole Nader vs. Gore thing?—and self-loathing.

Let's deal with the self-loathing first, since it is easier to dispense with. Anyone who has spent five minutes at a symposium of progressive politics knows that the left has come to believe a media message that essentially says: "We really have reached the end of history. From here on out, it's all free-market capitalism and pseudo-democracy. Everybody on board because the train is leaving the station." For the better part of two decades, unbiased "reporters" have told us that "liberal" is the dirtiest word in politics, while right-wing pundits label Bill Clinton "a Marxist" because he favors ergonomics regulations.

If there was even the slightest hint of truth in the militant mischaracterization of the left and its potential appeal to the great mass of Americans, I too would embrace our footnote status. But at a point in history when people are more questioning of corporations, more wary of deregulation, more certain that politicians are bought by big business, more inclined to hold favorable views toward unions, more doubtful about the drug war and the death penalty, and more supportive of gay rights and gender equity, the footnote consignment is a crock. I don't expect the media to get it right, but I do expect the left to get over it. The time has come to end the lie that left-wing ideas are unpopular and that progressives must settle for the likes of Bill Clinton and Al Gore to protect against total right-wing hegemony. Recognizing that Clinton and Gore were not even moderates is an important first step on the way to the left reasserting itself as a political force. It is not, however, an easy one for many of us to take—as Campaign 2000 and its dismal aftermath illustrate.

The beginning of a Republican administration is always a time for hand-wringing on the left. Rarely, however, does this behavior so exhaust left hands that they are incapable of finger-pointing. In the aftermath of the Gore-Nader race (which was the only real contest on the left in 2000), the progressive blame game is being played with so much energy that wise speculators might want to invest in champagne cork futures in anticipation of Dubya's re-election party. You can just hear Republican strategists chuckling over the news that Democrats on Capitol Hill are reportedly refusing to work in coalition with Ralph Nader and his "collaborators." "Please, please, please, Lord God of Texas football and political gaming," Bush *consigliere* Karl Rove must surely be pleading. "Let Barney Frank and Jim Hightower keep fighting with one another for the next four years."

The absurdity of the bitterness is that our petty differences mask startling ideological unity and agonizing necessity. There should be little doubt that, in a no-Nader context, the overwhelming majority of progressives would have cast grudging ballots for Gore. But what would there have been to say about those ballots except perhaps that, once more, in the contest between voting and not voting, the lessons of fourth-grade civics teachers won out?

Washington Victory Ushers in New Era

JAMES WEINSTEIN

April 20, 1983

"We were slow to move from the protest movement into politics," Harold Washington said just after he won the Chicago Democratic mayoral primary in February. "We were lulled to sleep thinking that passing a few laws was enough. But we've got to be involved in the mainstream political activity. That's what's happening here in Chicago, and that's the lesson that's going out across the country."

This "coming into political maturity" of minority groups that, as Washington says, once thought simple street protests were enough, took a giant leap forward on April 12 when a sizable majority of Hispanic voters and enough left and liberal whites joined the overwhelming majority of blacks to give Chicago its first black mayor.

This was a victory for the left, both in the sense that the natural left constituencies—blacks, Hispanics and the labor movement—were its basis, and in the sense that organizational support for Washington outside the black community came from left groups ranging from unions like AFSCME to the National Organization for Women to the Democratic Socialists of America. And it was a victory over racism in the most highly segregated of American cities, even though the election also demonstrated how deeply divided Chicago's working people are by race. . . .

The left—especially the socialist left—has long talked about coalitions of labor, blacks, women and others. But while such coalitions frequently have been assembled on paper, and occasionally around demonstrations and protests, they rarely, if ever, have been effective in electing our own people, either black or white, to office. . . . Prudently, Washington is promising no miracles. But he is promising, within the limitations imposed upon him by forces over which he has no control, to provide all groups in the community their fair share of the city's resources. That promise alone, if carried out, would be a giant step forward.

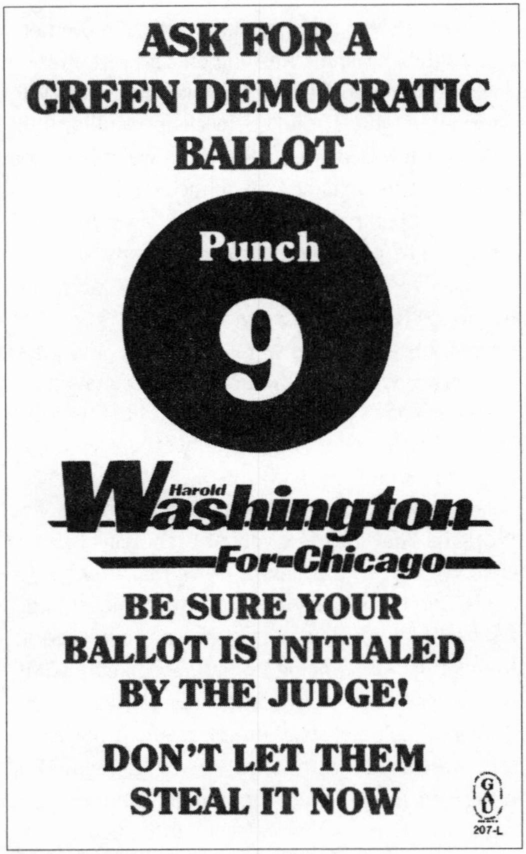
ASK FOR A
GREEN DEMOCRATIC
BALLOT
Punch
9
Harold
Washington
For Chicago
BE SURE YOUR
BALLOT IS INITIALED
BY THE JUDGE!
DON'T LET THEM
STEAL IT NOW
207-L

ITT Archives

Harold Washington used to refer to his election not as a personal victory, but as a "mandate for a movement."

Face Reality

JOEL BLEIFUSS

June 12, 2000

If Ralph Nader were serious about influencing the national discourse, he would have run in the Democratic primary, where progressive candidates

I spent the long 2000 campaign season traveling on the left borderlines of the American political landscape—with Sen. Paul Wellstone on the back roads of Iowa and New Hampshire; with Jesse Jackson Jr. on the streets of Chicago; with Ralph Nader on May Day in Madison; with the wizened pacifist-gay-Socialist David McReynolds in New York; with the Greens in Denver; with the Democrats in Los Angeles as they cheered the suddenly but not quite credibly populist Al Gore; with the rabble in the streets outside George W. Bush's Republican Convention in Philadelphia; with Frank as he bashed Nader; with Hightower as he bashed Gore.

Amid the great disappointment that was Campaign 2000, I most fondly recall the remarkable scenes at the Shadow Conventions in Philadelphia and Los Angeles, where Democrats and Greens, U.S. senators and Ruckus Society members, teen-age girls in "Smash the State" T-shirts and retired businessmen in bow ties found themselves in complete agreement about the need for a radical response to growing income inequality, a failed drug war and a corrupt political system. The single most electric moment of the entire 2000 campaign season came in a sweaty Los Angeles basement on the second night of the Democratic National Convention, when Wisconsin Democratic Sen. Russ Feingold, fresh from condemning his own party convention for its organizers' embrace of corrupt soft-money fundraising practices, entered a room filled with young people clad in Nader T-shirts to thunderous applause.

From a tiny stage where a band had been rocking out just moments before, Feingold spoke with a rare mix of passion and eloquence about the collapse of the Democratic and Republican parties into the abyss of corporate free-market dogma, about an arms race that steals from our schools and our hospitals to pay for weapons that at their best fail to function (and at their worst might actually work), about the fundamental injustice of the death penalty, about the ability of America with simple debt reduction strategies to dramatically reduce the suffering of Africa. "I refuse to believe that the American people want my party to ignore these issues," Feingold declared. "I believe they are ignored because so many of our leaders are listening more to campaign contributions than to citizens."

There was no light between the Nader campaigners and the Democratic senator that night. And while there is no need to downplay the legitimate doctrinal and tactical differences that divide the most rigid of my comrades, there is a need to put it in perspective. And perspective tells us that, even if Gloria Steinem and Barbara Ehrenreich may have voted for different candidates for president, they agree on 99.9 percent of the issues facing the world.

Sadly, however, Washington is packed with turf-protecting interest groups and party hacks who thrive on the bitterness that divided the left throughout the critical early stages of the Bush presidency. There will be no rapprochement in the short term at the national level. Indeed, squabbles over how to mount an effective opposition during a time of war and economic instability have divided Democrats themselves and put an even greater distance between the Democratic and Green parties. The blame game will go on. This could do actual damage by maintaining the absurd fantasy that, to paraphrase the sheriffs in grainy old westerns, "This left ain't big enough for the both of us."

But the fact of the matter is that there can and must be a left within the Democratic Party and outside of it. And this left—yes, "this left," not "these lefts"—can and must be united at critical moments, not on the basis of partisan agreements that are necessarily difficult to come by, but on the grounds of electoral prospects that are tantalizingly real. There are critical local and state elections to be won this year and in the years to come. A left that gets serious about politics can win them—just as the Non-Partisan League and Harold Washington did—and in so doing we can again transform the politics of the nation. Is the left ready to get serious? The one good lesson of the 2000 campaign tells us the answer to that question is "Yes."

have an opportunity to present ideas that normally don't get a public hearing. By debating Al Gore and Bill Bradley, Nader could have reached an audience of millions. This year, more than any other, we needed a challenge to the somnambulant corporate centrism of Gore and Bradley. Absent a third party that is well organized from the grassroots up, progressives must stay focused on putting pressure on those Democrats who claim to represent them, something a Nader run for the Democratic nomination would have done admirably.

Since Nader and the progressives who support him have neither built a third party nor challenged the Democratic establishment, one must conclude that candidate Nader fulfills another role—that of civil confessor. Citizens disgusted with the status quo can leave a voting booth with their integrity reaffirmed.

Their message is clear: We are not serious about political change. For too many on the left, electoral politics has devolved from civic participation into a lifestyle choice. One eats organic food to stay healthy, exercises to stay fit, and votes for Nader to avoid tainting principles with the give-and-take of real politics. . . .

Those progressives disengaged from party politics are understandably alienated. The current campaign finance system functions as a form of legalized bribery that allows the rich and powerful to pick and choose who gets elected. The Democratic Party, increasingly in thrall to corporate interests, has seen its popular base whither.

There are exceptions: In states like Minnesota and Vermont and in congressional districts like those around the Bay Area, the progressive movement is part and parcel of the political establishment. Those are the models to emulate if we want to move beyond the current quadrennial exercise of hitching our wagon to the latest progressive star.

Love Ralph Nader or hate him, recall his candidacy as an inspired challenge to politics as usual or as a dangerous fool's mission, but, please, don't deny the tremendously positive impact of his campaign on progressives. In the thick of the debate, especially when Gore backers labeled Naderites naive cogs in a right-wing Republican machine, or when Greens countered by decrying Democrats as naive cogs in a right-wing Democratic machine, the whole endeavor may have seemed unsettling. And so it was—thankfully. The dialogue over how to approach the 2000 elections shook up the left, rousing it from a long neglected and frequently dysfunctional relationship with electoral politics. Finally progressives began asking the right question: How do I use my vote, my energy, my talent, my influence, my resources to achieve the most left-wing result possible?

The need for another Chicago is clear. The Democratic Party at its highest levels is incapable of mounting an effective progressive challenge to a conservative Republican president and Congress—a lesson learned too late during the Reagan years, and now being painfully retaught in the Bush era. The challenge will come from below, at the level of local and regional politics. As *In These Times* taught me back in 1983, this is where the action is. Besides, once you've lost the White House and the Capitol, you cannot afford to lose City Hall.

The beauty of a local strategy is that it allows—perhaps the right word here is "requires"—us to stop bickering and get down to the serious business of winning. Indeed, even as national Democrats were so busily laying blame on the Greens for the ideological and strategic failures of Al Gore's 2000 campaign, San Francisco Democrats and Greens were working together to win a smashing victory for what may well have been the most left-wing slate of local candidates in the nation. Faced with dot-com gentrification that is turning the city into a "millionaires-only" enclave, immigrants, artists, retirees, gays and lesbians, trade unionists and the

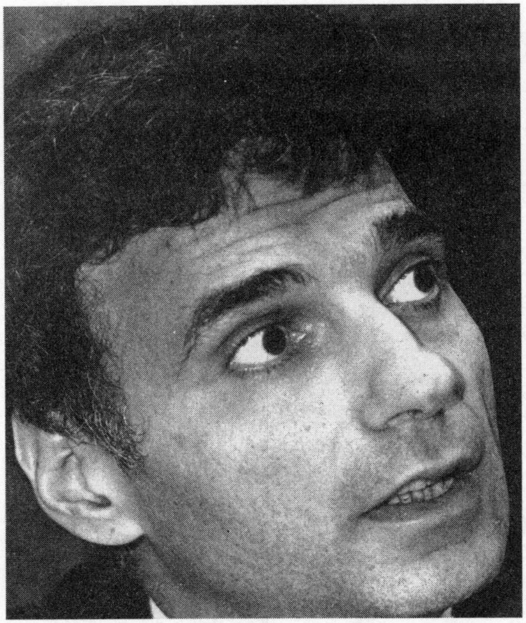

Lionel Delevingne

Back in 1978, *In These Times* first asked: "Will [this] be the year that Ralph Nader plunges into electoral politics full blast?"

Nader's Moment

ROBERT W. McCHESNEY

August 21, 2000

We have to think in broader terms than the immediate election. The Nader campaign is a necessary step in building a progressive political movement in this nation. There is no better time than now, and no better standard-bearer on the horizon than Nader. It will take time; we not only have to attract current voters, but we have to get the millions and millions of disaffected voters to come to the polls because they will finally see politics as addressing issues that mean something to their lives and their communities.

There are grounds for optimism. There may be more political vibrancy today—around issues like corporate-run globalization, the death penalty, sweatshop labor, the environment—than at any fearless *Bay Guardian* newspaper came together to back a slate of candidates committed to fight for affordable housing, sustainable development, locally owned small businesses, and an end to campaign corruption. When a key candidate on the slate switched his registration from "Democrat" to "Green," corporate interests sought to open Gore-Nader wounds on the local level, hoping they could stir up enough resentment to elect a developer-friendly Democrat. The scheme failed. No matter who they had supported at the national level, progressives stuck and won at home.

There will be plenty of new hurdles and plenty of opportunities to stick and win in the months and years to come. The grassroots victories in these battles will forge the real alternative to the conservative politics of George W. Bush and his minions. These are exciting times. And in them we will see history made by activists who choose to stick and win first in their hometowns, then in their states, and ultimately by taking their winning strategies national. The promise of 1983 was never fully realized. But that need not mean that the promise of 2003 will be thwarted. Indeed, if we learn not just from the right moves of 1983, but the wrong moves that followed, this can be our moment.

Sometime in the months and years ahead, a farm kid in Wisconsin, a suburban kid in California, or a city kid in New York will read an *In These Times* article about a grassroots campaign that has forged a broad coalition in support of the principles of economic and social justice that are shared by the whole of the left—and by the great majority of Americans. And when the campaign prevails in a local election that may or may not be noticed by the national media, that kid will rightly recognize that she has a part to play in building an opposition not merely to George W. Bush, but to the whole sordid right-wing compromise that cheats most Americans out of their share of the American dream.

Harold Washington used to refer to his election not as a personal victory, but as a "mandate for a movement." He was right. The movement is a constant. But the mandate must be

time since the '70s. The Nader campaign is part of this progressive resurgence. Indeed, if we try to stoke progressive non-electoral movements on the one hand, while adhering to a lesser-of-two-evils support for Gore on the other, the resulting confusion can be disastrous for any nascent left. It makes progressives look like a bunch of political nincompoops.

All told, a strong Nader showing in 2000 can be a platform for rejuvenating progressive politics in the United States for the coming generation. It is a risk that must be taken.

Terry LaBan

Nader's candidacy: An inspired challenge to politics as usual or a dangerous fool's mission?

regularly renewed. That renewal will never come from inside the Beltway, where big money and bigger egos cast shadows over the prospect of a reinvigorated democracy. It will come from Chicago and Cleveland, Corpus Christi and Casper, Centralia and Compton, and the dozens of other cities and towns where citizens form new coalitions on old models, where these coalitions learn to stick and win, and where their victories will signal—as Washington's did, lo those many years ago—that a change is gonna come.

Building a Citizen Politics

SEN. PAUL WELLSTONE

June 14, 1998

Everywhere I go, I hear people say, "We are concerned about how to earn a decent living and how to give our children the care we know they need and deserve." If you think about all of the issues that we talk about—from welfare reform and reducing poverty, to stabilizing the middle class and how we perform in an international economy, to how we can do well in the next century—over and over again, we come back to a focus on a good education, good health care and a good job. Those are issues that are important to the vast majority of people in this country.

I've said in Minnesota and around the country, that I would take citizen politics over money politics any day. We will build that citizen politics, and that is how we can win elections. It is one thing to focus on these economic issues, which are so important to people's lives, but they just don't hear, they just don't see the conviction behind it, they just don't know whether it's for real. People don't organize unless there's something to organize for. The question is not to be better at communicating, it's to have an agenda that's worth communicating.

There are a whole lot of people who know that we ought to have elections and not auctions. It's an interesting coalition that believes you have to get money out of politics. I've been in people's living rooms where you've got a woman who says, "I'm here because the big corporations dominate politics." And then in the same room, you've got a CEO who says, "I'm here because I'm tired of being shaken down and getting 14 calls a day." This interesting coalition forces progressives to

Richard Stromberg

If we learn not just from the right moves of 1983, but the wrong moves that followed, this can be our moment.

talk to a lot of people with whom we don't necessarily agree and to build coalitions. That's really important.

The policy work and the intellectual work and the ideas that people in Washington work on are important too, but we can't just make the fight in Washington. We have to galvanize people around the country. We have to get people organized, speaking for themselves and advocating for themselves. We have to build that grassroots politics again.

Pushing this economic agenda and this reform agenda forward is one thing. Beyond that, I'm saying to a lot of people in the country (not necessarily even middle-income people, just American citizens): You know what? You don't like special-interest politics? You think when it comes to concerns for yourself, your loved ones, your family, your community, that those concerns aren't of concern in Washington? Well, you shouldn't be surprised because the truth of the matter is the greatest ally of special-interest politics is not the parties and not Congress—it's when people don't register, don't vote, don't organize and when people don't get involved in public affairs.

You can't check out when it comes to your citizenship. You have to be part of this. You have to speak up. We're going to need you to move our country forward on an agenda of reform, opportunities, education, good jobs, decent wages, health care and building communities—making the United States of America all it can be going into the next century. That's our politics, and we can win on it.

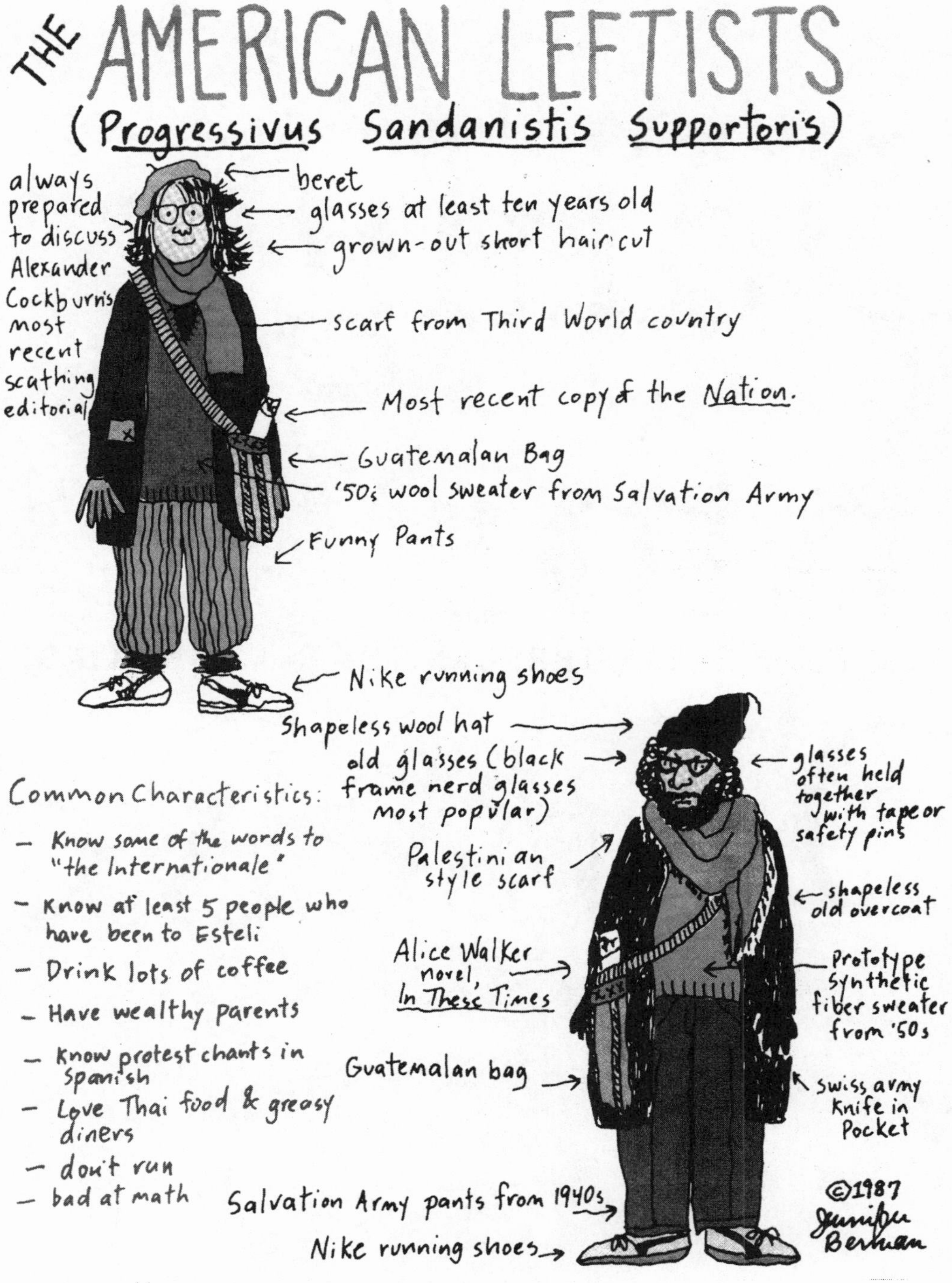

Jennifer Berman

Doing It for Ourselves

CAN FEMINISM BREAK THROUGH THE CLASS CEILING?

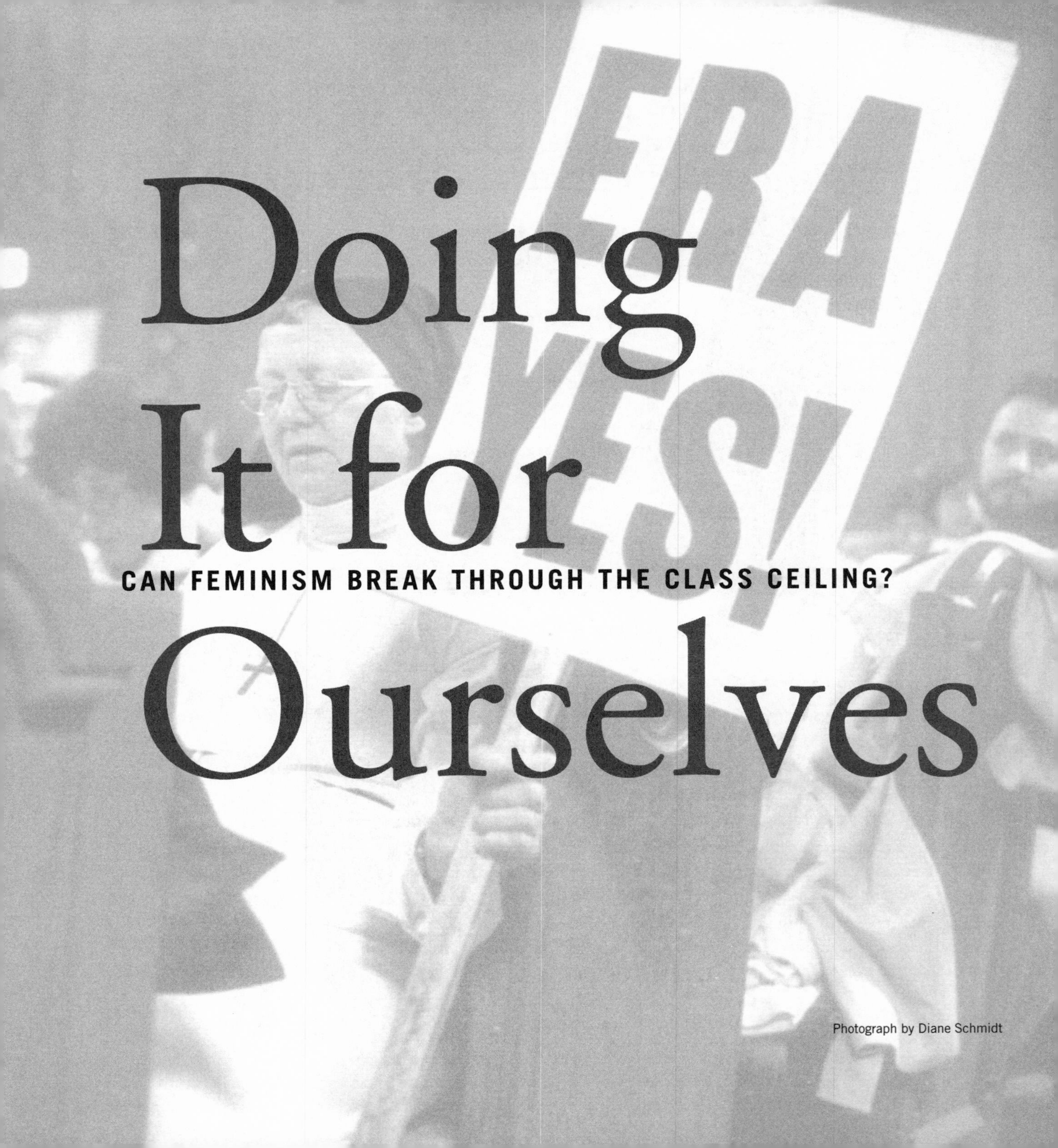

Photograph by Diane Schmidt

Four

BARBARA EHRENREICH

HERE'S A SCENE FROM FEMINIST ANCIENT HISTORY: IT'S 1972 AND ABOUT 20 OF US ARE GATHERED IN SOMEBODY'S LIVING ROOM FOR OUR WEEKLY "women's support group" meeting. We're all associated, in one way or another, with a small public college catering mostly to "nontraditional" students, meaning those who are older, poorer and more likely to be black or Latina than typical college students in this suburban area. Almost every level of the college hierarchy is represented—students of all ages, clerical workers, junior faculty members and even one or two full professors. There are acknowledged differences among us—race and sexual preference, for example—which we examine eagerly and a little anxiously. But we are comfortable together, and excited to have a chance to discuss everything from the administration's sexist policies to our personal struggles with husbands and lovers. Whatever may divide us, we are all women, and we understand this to be one of the great defining qualities of our lives and politics.

Could a group so diverse happily convene today? I tend to suspect the answer is "very seldom" or "not at all." Perhaps the biggest social and economic trend of the past three decades has been class polarization—the expanding inequality in income and wealth. As United for a Fair Economy's excellent book, *Shifting Fortunes: The Perils of the Growing American Wealth Gap*, points out, the most glaring polarization has occurred between those at the very top of the income distribution—the upper 1 to 5 percent—and those who occupy the bottom 30 to 40 percent. Less striking, but more ominous for the future of feminism, is the growing gap between those in the top 40 percent and those in the bottom 40 percent. One chart in *Shifting Fortunes* shows that the net worth of households in the bottom 40 percent declined by nearly 80 percent between 1983 and 1995. Except for the top 1 percent, the top 40 percent lost ground too—but much less. Today's college teacher, if she is not an adjunct, occupies that relatively lucky top 40 group, while today's clerical worker is in the rapidly sinking bottom 40. Could they still gather comfortably in each other's living rooms to discuss common issues? Do they still have common issues to discuss?

Numbers hardly begin to tell the story. The '80s brought sharp changes in lifestyle and consumption habits between the lower 40 percent—which is roughly what we call the "working class"—and the upper 20 to 30 percent, which is populated by professors, administrators, executives, doctors, lawyers and other "professionals." "Mass markets" became "segmented markets," with different consumer trends signaling differences in status. In 1972, a junior faculty member's living room looked much like that of a departmental secretary—only, in most cases, messier. Today, the secretary is likely to accessorize her home at Kmart; the professor at Pottery Barn. Three decades ago, we all enjoyed sugary, refined-flour treats at our meetings (not to mention Maxwell House coffee and cigarettes!). Today, the upper-middle class grinds its own beans, insists on whole-grain organic snacks, and vehemently eschews hot dogs and meatloaf. In the '70s, conspicuous, or even just overly enthusiastic, consumption was considered gauche—and not only by leftists and feminists. Today, professors, including quite liberal ones, are likely to have made a deep emotional investment in their houses, their furniture and their pewter ware. It shows how tasteful they are, meaning—when we cut through the garbage about aesthetics—how distinct they are from the "lower" classes.

In the case of women, there is an additional factor compounding the division wrought by class polarization: In the '60s, only about 30 percent of American women worked outside their homes; today, the proportion is reversed, with more than 70 percent of women in the work force. This represents a great advance, since women who earn their own way are of course more able to avoid male domination in their personal lives. But women's influx into the work force also means that

In Our Own Image

BARBARA EHRENREICH

November 16, 1977

The women's movement is beleaguered—in some regions, almost cornered. The ERA has been defeated in every state except Indiana where it has come up in the past two years. Abortion rights have gone through so much legislative surgery that it's questionable whether they'll survive at all. And perhaps the most bitter pill of all: The rank-and-file opposition to the ERA and abortion is not coming from bands of testosterone-crazed males, but from *women*. . . .

Aside from conscious right-wingers, there's a whole other constituency for anti-feminism. Most of them are housewives. Unlike anti-ERA leader Phyllis Schlafly, though, they don't have their own housekeepers, secretaries and private family bomb shelters. But they're scared, too. The sexual and cultural "revolution" of the past 10 years didn't liberate *them*. . . . Right-wing anti-feminism at least seems to offer some simple comforts: That motherhood will be respected. That families will hold together. That things will go back to being more or less like they were supposed to be when you first got engaged.

But, of course, the right-wing can't offer any real security because its *class* interests are opposed to those of the average working-class or lower-middle-class housewife. Right-wing anti-feminists rhapsodize about the glories of homemaking but oppose pensions for women who have put in a lifetime of it. They "honor motherhood" but oppose measures—like a guaranteed annual income—that could free mothers from total economic dependence on a man. They adore all fetuses until the moment they exit the birth canal and add to the welfare rolls, the school tax rate and the nation's Medicaid bill. And, of course, the right has nothing to offer the working mother try-

fewer and fewer women share the common occupational experience once defined by the word "housewife." I don't want to exaggerate this commonality as it existed in the '60s and '70s; obviously the stay-at-home wife of an executive led a very different life from that of the stay-at-home wife of a blue-collar man. But they did perform similar daily tasks—housecleaning, childcare, shopping, cooking. Today, in contrast, the majority of women fan out every morning to face vastly different work experiences, from manual labor to positions of power. Like men, women are now spread throughout the occupational hierarchy (though not at the very top), where they encounter each other daily as unequals—bosses vs. clerical workers, givers of orders vs. those who are ordered around, and so on.

Class was always an issue. Even before polarization set in, some of us lived on the statistical hilltops, others deep in the valleys. But today we are distributed on what looks less like a mountain range and more like a cliff face. Gender, race and sexual preference still define compelling commonalties, but the sense of a shared condition necessarily weakens as we separate into frequent-flying female executives on the one hand and airport cleaning women on the other. Can feminism or, for that matter, any cross-class social movement, survive as class polarization spreads Americans further and further apart?

For all the ardent egalitarianism of the early movement, feminism had the unforeseen consequence of heightening the class differences between women. It was educated, middle-class women who most successfully used feminist ideology and solidarity to advance themselves professionally. Feminism has played a role in working-class women's struggles too—for example, in the union organizing drives of university clerical workers—but probably its greatest single economic effect was to open up the formerly male-dominated professions to women. Between the '70s and the '90s, the percentage of female students in business, medical and law schools shot up from less than 10 percent to more than 40 percent.

ing to make ends meet on $3 an hour—except perhaps some literature on her "right" to work in an open shop.

I still think the women's movement has a fighting chance to become a *majority* movement. Phyllis Schlafly—plus the rest of the John Birch Ladies' Auxiliary types—is an enemy, no matter how many hormones we have in common. But the woman in curlers pushing a shopping cart with a few toddlers in tow and worrying about the price of ground chuck is, or should be, a sister.

If feminism is going to mean anything to her, the movement will have to rethink its image and revamp its program. Somewhere along the line the image of "feminism" got taken over by the gray-suited businesswomen with attaché cases and the purveyors of assertiveness training for managerial women—as if all we wanted was a chance to integrate, one by one, into a man's system. But the radical thrust of feminism always lay in its insistence on our connectedness as women: that we would support each other, stand together and remake the world for *all* women, for all people.

Is it too late to remake our public image in our *own* image?

ITT Archives

Back in the day: Gloria Steinem, Betty Friedan and Marlo Thomas.

There have been, however, no comparable gains for young women who cannot afford higher degrees, and most of these women remain in the same low-paid occupations that have been "women's work" for decades. All in all, feminism has had little impact on the status or pay of traditional female occupations like clerical, retail, health care and light assembly-line work. While middle-class women gained MBAs, working-class women won the right not to be called "honey"—and not a whole lot more.

Secondly, since people tend to marry within their own class, the gains made by women in the professions added to the growing economic gap between the working class and the professional-managerial class. Working-class families gained too, as wives went to work. But, as I argued in *Fear of Falling: The Inner Life of the Middle Class*, the most striking gains have accrued to couples consisting of two well-paid professionals or managers. The doctor/lawyer household zoomed well ahead of the truck driver/typist combination.

So how well has feminism managed to maintain its stance as the ground shifts beneath its feet? Following are some brief observations of the impact of class polarization on a few issues once central to the feminist project:

WELFARE

This has to be the most tragic case. In the '70s, feminists hewed to the slogan, "Every woman is just one man away from welfare." This was an exaggeration of course; even then, there were plenty of self-supporting and independently wealthy women. But it was true enough to resonate with the large numbers of women who worked outside their homes part-time or not at all. We recognized our commonality as homemakers and mothers, and we considered this kind of work to be important enough to be paid for—even when there was no husband on the scene. Welfare, in other words, was potentially every woman's concern.

Flash forward to 1996, when President Clinton signed the odious Republican welfare reform bill, and you find only the

Politics of Abortion

ELLEN WILLIS

June 15, 1983

The abortion rights movement is a paradigm of the women's movement as a whole. . . . In demanding unrestricted abortion, women's liberationists dramatically rejected the traditional definition of woman as womb, as passive extension of the fecund earth. We declared that like men we were human beings with an autonomous existence that transcended our reproductive freedom. We pointed out the blatant injustice of a system in which men made abortion laws while women got pregnant and assumed the full responsibility for child rearing. We attacked the sexual double standard, the open determination of abortion opponents to preserve the threat of unwanted pregnancy in order to deter and punish female sexual activity.

Finally, inherent in the demand for abortion rights was rejection of our supposedly innate feminine altruism: We recognized no special female obligation to be life-givers and nurturers at the expense of our own needs and desires. Of all the subversive implications of "free abortion on demand," this one was perhaps the most threatening. . . . The thought of "liberated" women pursuing sexual pleasure for its own sake was bad enough, but the specter of women denying that their purpose in life was to serve others haunted every institution from family and church to corporation. . . .

The right understands—as the left too often has not—that the rejection of biological determinism implicit in the act of abortion is the moral bedrock of women's liberation. Just as the threat of rape affects the feelings and behavior of all women, not just those who are raped, the right to abortion changes the condition of all women—gay as well as straight, those who abhor abortion as well as those who are thankful for it. To refuse to have an abortion now is an act of choice and will, weakest and most token protests from groups bearing the label "feminist." The core problem, as those of us who were pro-welfare advocates found, was that many middle- and upper-middle-class women could no longer see why a woman should be subsidized to raise her children. "Well, I work and raise my kids—why shouldn't they?" was a common response, as if poor women could command wages that would enable them to purchase reliable childcare. As for that other classic feminist slogan—"every mother is a working mother"—no one seems to remember it anymore.

HEALTH CARE

Our bodies, after all, are what we have most in common as women, and the women's health movement of the '70s and early '80s probably brought together as diverse a constituency—at least in terms of class—as any other component of feminism. We worked to legalize abortion and to stop the involuntary sterilization of poor women of color, to challenge the sexism of medical care faced by all women consumers and to expand low-income women's access to care.

In many ways, we were successful: Abortion is legal, if not always accessible; the kinds of health information once available only in underground publications like the original *Our Bodies, Ourselves* can now be found in *Glamour*; the medical profession is no longer an all-male bastion of patriarchy. We were not so

rather than acquiescence to the law and fate. Legal abortion is not just one reform, one new freedom among many: It is a basic precondition of freedom.

(m)Otherhood

SUSAN J. DOUGLAS

September 20, 1989

This past winter I had a baby.

That means my thighs look like semi-deflated Michelins, I've got eyebags like George Shultz, and all I'm supposed to be able to talk about is the consistency of infant excrement. It also means I've had to confront, in more personal and immediate ways than before, the soft-focus, honey-hued symbolism surrounding moms and babies. I've had to sit there in my husband's sweatpants (the only thing that fits) and watch the likes of *Good Morning America*'s Joan Lunden chirp on cheerfully at 7:15 A.M., insisting we can do it all. Nowhere is the gap between image and reality wider than the one separating the smiling, serene,

ITT Archives

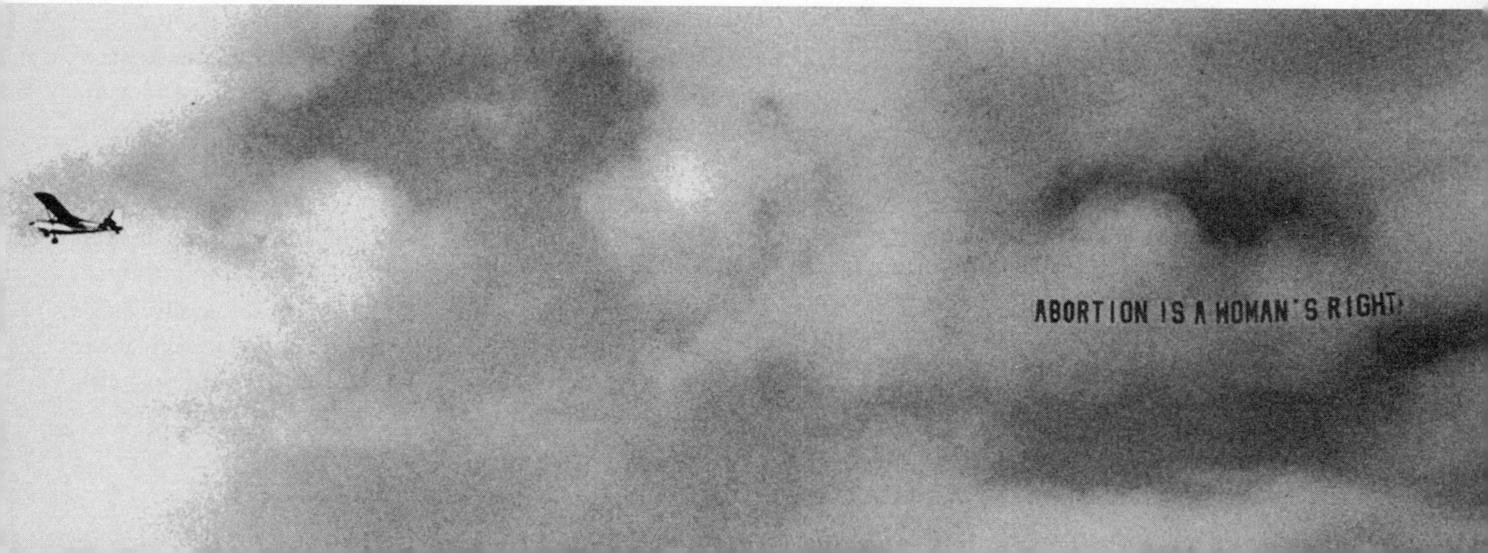
ABORTION IS A WOMAN'S RIGHT

financially comfortable and perfectly coiffed media mom from her frazzled, exhausted, spit-up-covered, real-life counterpart. . . .

One of the first things new parents learn is that it's considered gauche to talk too much about the baby. This is especially true for mothers. Baby-talk is supposed to be boring, unserious, not quite legitimate: It means you've lost your critical edge, your connection to the "real world."

Have people ever considered how deeply sexist this bias is? During the first few months of my daughter's life, I was in another dimension, in which clocks and schedules didn't matter and the ordered, the logical, the rational had no place. It was the realm of sensations and instincts and, of course, profound emotions—a realm completely at odds with the way our work, indeed, our entire society, is structured. . . .

ITT Archives

It is in and around the nursery that a new feminist politics must be born.

successful, however, in increasing low-income women's access to health care—in fact, the number of the uninsured is far larger than it used to be, and poor women still get second-class health care when they get any at all. Yet the only women's health issue that seems to generate any kind of broad, cross-class participation today is breast cancer, at least if wearing a pink ribbon counts as "participation."

Even the nature of medical care is increasingly different for women of different classes. While lower-income women worry about paying for abortions or their children's care, many in the upper-middle class are far more concerned with such medical luxuries as high-tech infertility treatments and cosmetic surgery. Young college women get bulimia; less affluent young women are more likely to suffer from toxemia of pregnancy, which is basically a consequence of malnutrition.

HOUSEWORK

In the '70s, housework was a hot feminist issue and a major theme of consciousness-raising groups. After all, whatever else women did, we did housework; it was the nearly universal female occupation. We debated Pat Mainardi's famous essay on "The Politics of Housework," which focused on the private struggles to get men to pick up their own socks. We argued bitterly about the "wages for housework" movement's proposal that women working at home should be paid by the state. We studied the Cuban legal code, with its intriguing provision that males do their share or face jail time.

Thirty years later, the feminist silence on the issue of housework is nearly absolute. Not, I think, because men are at last doing their share, but because so many women of the upper-middle class now pay other women to do their housework for them. Bring up the subject among affluent feminists today, and you get a guilty silence, followed by defensive patter about how well they pay and treat their cleaning women.

In fact, the $15 an hour commonly earned by freelance maids is not so generous at all, when you consider that it has to cover cleaning equipment, transportation to various cleaning sites throughout the day, as well as any benefits, like health insurance, the cleaning person might choose to purchase for herself. The fast-growing corporate cleaning services like Merry Maids and The Maids International are far worse, offering (at least in the northeastern urban area I looked into) their workers between $5 (yes, that's below the minimum wage) and $7 an hour.

In a particularly bitter irony, many of the women employed by corporate cleaning services are former welfare recipients bumped off the rolls by the welfare reform bill so feebly resisted by organized feminists. One could conclude, if one was in a very bad mood, that it is not in the interests of affluent feminists to see the wages of working-class women improve. As for the prospects of "sisterhood" between affluent women and the women who scrub their toilets—forget about it, even at a "generous" $15 an hour.

The issues that have most successfully weathered class polarization are sexual harassment and male violence against women. These may be the last concerns that potentially unite all women, and they are of course crucial. But there is a danger in letting these issues virtually define feminism, as seems to be the case in some campus women's centers today: Poor and working-class women (and men) face forms of harassment and violence on the job that are not sexual or even clearly gender-related. Being reamed out repeatedly by an obnoxious supervisor of either sex can lead to depression and stress-related disorders. Being forced to work long hours of overtime, or under ergonomically or chemically hazardous conditions, can make a person physically sick. Yet feminism has yet to recognize such routine workplace experiences as forms of "violence against women."

When posing the question "Can feminism survive class polarization?" to middle-class feminist acquaintances, I sometimes get the response: "Well, you're right, we have to confront our classism." But the problem is not classism, the problem is class itself: the existence of grave inequalities among women, as well as between women and men.

When you become a parent, a new abyss of consumerism opens. As with other areas of buying, this one provides great pleasure mixed with equal doses of horror. Stores like Toys-R-Us that you never dared enter before, or eyed with smug derision, now become part of your routine, as you seek to find some happy little playthings between the toy Uzis, let's-play-Contra outfits and Donald Trump's "The Game."

One thing you quickly notice is the way that sexism and violence are avidly reinforced for the children of the "lower classes," and determinedly eschewed for upper-middle-class kids. Upscale department stores specialize in unisex clothes made out of 100 percent cotton; trendy mail-order catalogs offer top-of-the-line, over-engineered car seats and kiddie backpacks, as well as educational and safe toys.

But a trip to Kmart exposes you to a distinctly different line of goods. The polyester clothes (which often produce rashes on babies) are highly gendered. The girls' outfits (in pink, of course) read "Future Miss America" and "Daddy's Little Girl." And you won't find the science, geography or conceptual playthings here: This is the land of Barbie and G.I. Joe. A child whose mother must shop at Kmart begins his or her life adorned in clothes laden with class and gender codes, reliant on inferior baby technology and surrounded by toys that train little girls to be sex objects and little boys to be cannon fodder. . . .

Time and again, my husband and I have been struck by the cushy privilege of our position: We are not rich, but we have health insurance, a pediatrician around the corner, childcare centers where we work and, for now anyway, two incomes. I'm constantly humbled by this good fortune. And I'm haunted by the class and racial divisions that undermine the women's movement.

How do middle-class mothers, without seeming patronizing, arrogant or invasive, help their less privileged sisters have the same decent circumstances within which to raise their kids? This is a crucial question that no one, parent or not, can afford to ignore much longer. The problem is that the media's soft-focus imagery of middle-class mom-dom encourages us to regard motherhood through solipsistic and narcissistic eyes and never to think that the nursery is the proper place for politics. But it is in and around the nursery that a new feminist politics must be born.

We should recall that the original radical—and, yes, utopian—feminist vision was of a society without hierarchies of any kind. This, of course, means equality among the races and the genders, but class is different: There can be no such thing as "equality among the classes." The abolition of hierarchy demands not only racial and gender equality, but the abolition of class. For a start, let's put that outrageous aim back into the long-range feminist agenda and mention it as loudly and as often as we can.

In the shorter term, there's plenty to do, and the burden necessarily falls on the more privileged among us: to support working-class women's workplace struggles, to advocate for expanded social services (like childcare and health care) for all women, to push for greater educational access for low-income women and so on and so forth. I'm not telling you anything new here, sisters—you know what to do.

But there's something else, too, in the spirit of another ancient slogan that is usually either forgotten or misinterpreted today: "The personal is the political." Those of us who are fortunate enough to have assets and income beyond our immediate needs need to take a hard look at how we're spending our money. New furniture—and, please, I don't want to hear about how tastefully funky it is—or a donation to a homeless shelter? A chic outfit or a check written to an organization fighting sweatshop conditions in the garment industry? A maid or a contribution to a clinic serving low-income women?

I know it sounds scary, but it will be a lot less so if we can make sharing stylish again and excess consumption look as ugly as it actually is. Better yet, give some of your time and your energy too. But if all you can do is write a check, that's fine: Since Congress will never redistribute the wealth (downward, anyway), we may just have to do it ourselves.

Operation Queen Esther

PAULA KAMEN

April 16, 2001

On the surface, at the dawn of the Bush administration's Old World Order, things look pretty gloomy for feminists. Right-wing fundamentalist men in their fifties and sixties, some cast directly from Margaret Atwood's *The Handmaid's Tale*, have taken over all three branches of the federal government. A disquieting percentage have affiliations to an obscure fringe Southern university with the name "Bob" in the title.

At the same time, generally unprepared to defend their sexual freedoms, young women lack a sense of women's history, even for events as recent as the '60s and '70s. They think *Roe v. Wade* is the newest midseason replacement character on *Walker, Texas Ranger*, and that *The Feminine Mystique* is the latest fragrance from Estee Lauder. Through the '90s, many have come to define political rebellion strictly in personal terms, by watching *Charlie's Angels*, reading *Cosmo*, defiantly wearing hotpants and stiletto heels, and writing memoirs about their affairs with their fathers—all acts with limited potential to get rid of John Ashcroft.

But thanks to my secret plan, there's hope.

Here is what we do: Send another voluptuous, crafty Jewish Generation Xer to seduce the president. Call it Operation Queen Esther, after the brave Jewess who saved her people in ancient times by getting cozy with the gentile king, a noble lesson I learned so many years ago as an impressionable tot in Hebrew school. It's just fighting fire with fire, Bush with bush.

Yes, what we feminists need is a juicy White House scandal—certainly one involving SEX. Not an anemic DUI

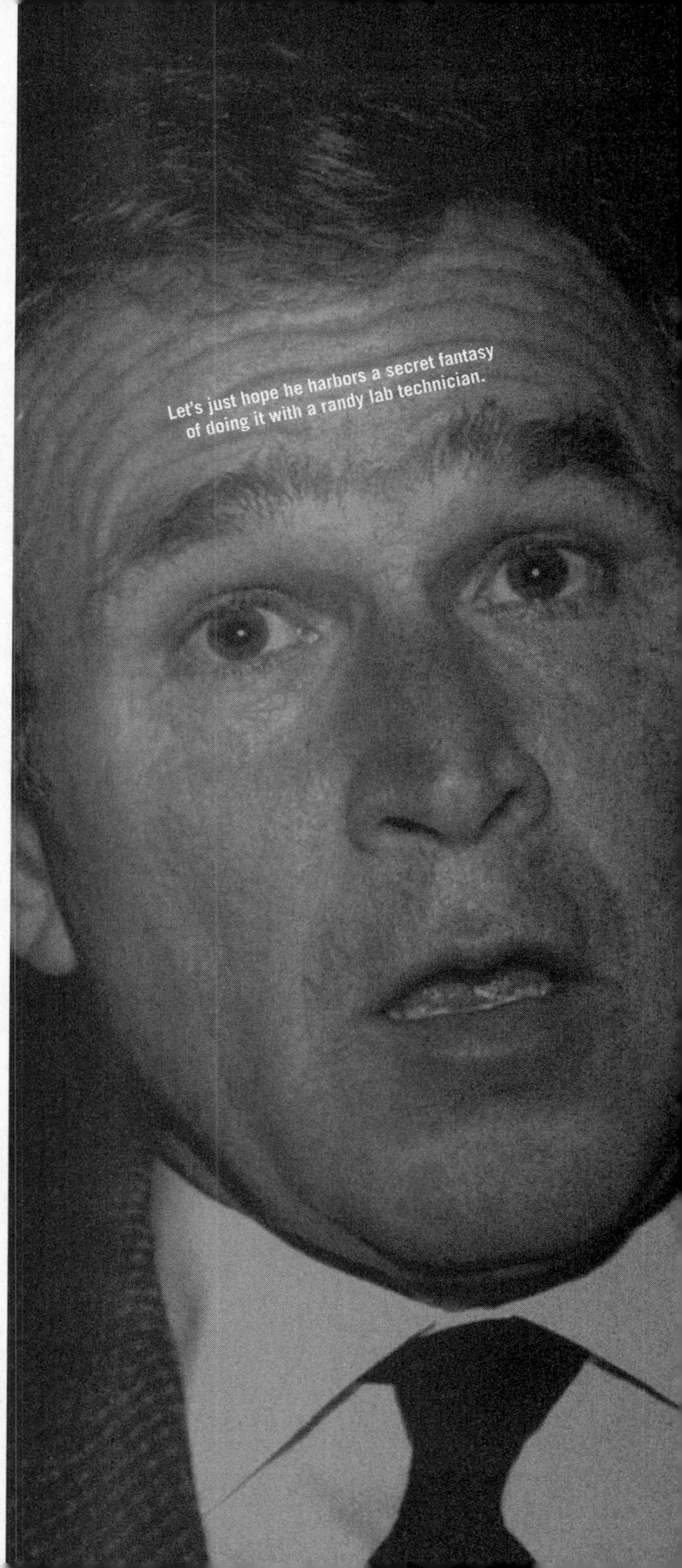

Let's just hope he harbors a secret fantasy of doing it with a randy lab technician.

Jeoff Davis

or drug-taking scandal or the bombing of a helpless Third World nation, which, as we've seen, no one really cares about. A scandal involving sex is the only guaranteed way to really make headlines and capture the fancy of the people with the real power: the twenty- and thirty-something male late-night comedy writers who fill the evening airwaves and determine the country's political agenda. After all, to them, nothing can guarantee more yuks and laffs than a Hoover—Jay Leno still makes hay out of the Lewinsky scandal to this day.

And, no matter what the gamble, think of the expense this will save already beleaguered feminist groups, who won't have to do all those dreary mailings, collate all those photocopies, conduct all that tedious lobbying and hire all those extra temps. Our only challenge is finding the proper Jewish Gen Xer with a strategically face-slimming haircut. My first impulse is to make a Nader supporter do it, as an appropriate and long-overdue act of penance for getting us into this quagmire to begin with. . . . But after much rumination and soul-searching, I have decided to personally step forward.

I can't approach Dubya as myself. I need a guise to be properly welcomed into the White House. So, here's the plan: I will pose as a fundamentalist Christian pro-abstinence activist, Tammy Faye Cherry. Bush will eagerly admit me to a private meeting because of my catchy new pilot campaign for chastity for unmarried women over 30.

Our affair, not to be rushed, will start slowly and tenderly, with the exchange of whimsical gifts. I'll get Dubya the director's cut of the original *Stepford Wives* movie. He'll share with me the secret three-part Skull and Bones handshake. Then, oh so gradually, my true fiery Semitic passion will eventually rise to the surface and win him over. I will lure him in for the kill by offering to do *all* of the things that Laura would find the most risqué and humiliating, such as talking dirty about the Dewey Decimal system. And of course, as a last resort, I'll reveal my secret erotic trick, the Kennebunkport.

But I have to be very careful. I can't bear to do this more than once. (I'm a hero, not a saint.) I have to make sure that, as I compromise his integrity, I don't also compromise the integrity of his key DNA sample. So, I'll take no chances, arriving at our long-anticipated meeting wearing a lab coat, hair net, eye goggles and rubber gloves, and carrying a full set of test tubes and Petri dishes. I'll just cross my fingers and hope that he harbors a secret fantasy of doing it with a randy lab technician.

And then, armed with only my own courage, sense of justice—and at least three full milligrams of Xanax—I will carry out my mission.

After we get the lab results back, I'll leak the news to the press and brave the political firestorm to follow—and, of course, the pressures of celebrity and dealing with the media. In the inevitable interview with Barbara Walters, I can see myself lying prostrate before millions of TV viewers, confessing my deep remorse, sense of shame, long-lived insecurities and lingering self-hatred. And: "Yes," I'll add, "the lipstick shade is 'glace.' That's g-l-a-c-e. Glace."

So, young male comedy writers, get ready. Your jobs are about to get a whole lot easier. And the laughs will get stronger and stronger, until they peak at the targeted day of impeachment. And then, to be sure, my personal sacrifice—both so honorous and onerous—will pay off in saving generations of women to come, or at least those in the next four years.

Color Bind

RADICALISM AND THE BLACK FREEDOM STRUGGLE

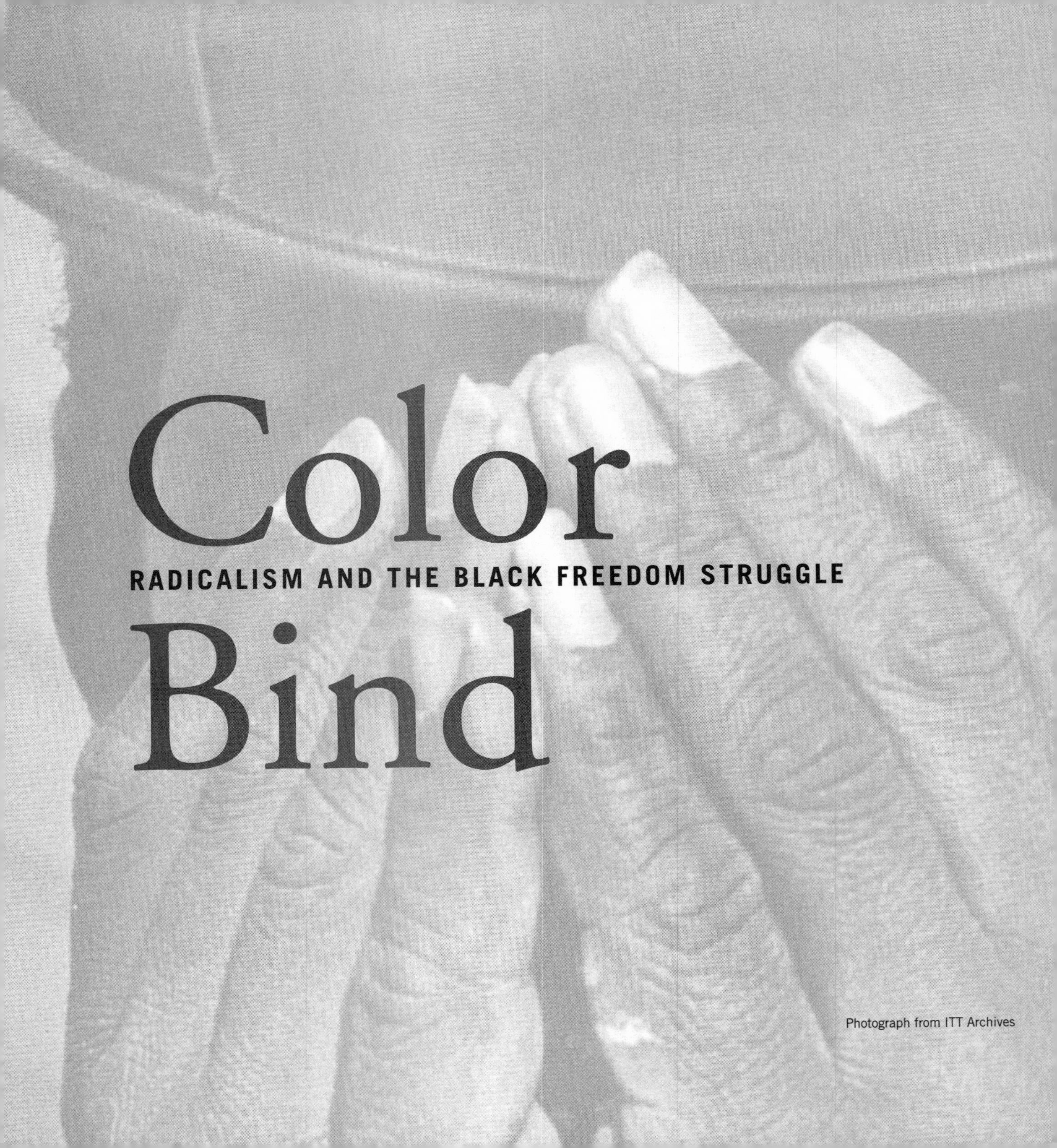

Photograph from ITT Archives

Five

SALIM MUWAKKIL

WE ARE ENTERING THE NEW CENTURY WITH THE SAME PROBLEM OF THE COLOR LINE THAT W. E. B. DU BOIS CORRECTLY PREDICTED WOULD PLAGUE the last one. The disparities between the bulk of America's black and white citizens remain wide and various. Yet there seems to be no sense of undue distress among the African-American masses. A veil of quietism has enveloped the black freedom movement.

The final years of the last century were booming days for the U.S. economy and relatively good for African-Americans, with record levels of employment, a surge in home ownership, the steady growth of the middle class and a strong push into higher education. Poverty reached record lows, and median income hit a record high. Crime and teen-age pregnancy rates also dropped precipitously during the last half of the '90s. The improving figures are relative, of course, but they're improving nonetheless. They fuel the argument that African-Americans are just another ethnic group struggling to make its incremental peace with the American system through absorption in employment, business and electoral politics. The Joint Center for Political and Economic Studies released a poll in October 2000 noting that 75 percent of African-Americans surveyed were optimistic about their future in the United States.

But all is not well in black America. Racial disparities are everywhere apparent, and the rush to privatize public resources (from schools to health care to housing) means the government is abandoning its role to provide redress for the disparate realities bequeathed by a unique racist history. A typical black worker with a college undergraduate degree still earns less than a white employee with a high school education. The unemployment rate for black Americans is still more than double that for whites. According to 2000 Census figures, white Americans' average net worth is $49,030; African-Americans' is just $7,073.

Meanwhile, as police shootings and racial profiling continue with frightening regularity, the criminal justice system now looms as the major impediment to the vitality and growth of the African-American community. At current levels of incarceration, newborn black males in this country have a greater than 1-in-4 chance of going to prison during their lifetimes, while white males have a 1-in-23 chance of serving time, according to the Justice Department. Black women make up the fastest growing prison population, and more than half of them are incarcerated for nonviolent offenses. The steady transfer of so much youthful energy into the criminal justice system cripples the black community's ability to defend itself against institutional assaults. Problems with re-integrating inmates who return from prison embittered and unskilled, add another level of irrationality to the insanity of the criminal-industrial complex.

These confounding problems don't come with easy answers for the leaders of black America. The protest and boycott strategies of the civil rights era, which remain the movement's primary tactics, seem antiquated. The rewards of electoral politics have been more symbolic than substantive. Congress and the Supreme Court have mounted a full-scale assault on the movement's small gains. The "unity" promised by events like the Million Man March has proven ephemeral. Black leadership, these days, requires a combination of qualities that can speak to a people wizened by a history of dashed hopes and repeated disappointments. It's a requirement with an indeterminate portfolio.

But for years, the Rev. Jesse Jackson has held the title of honorary president of black America. A summer 2000 poll on the issue of black leadership conducted by the Joint Center on Political and Economic Studies found that Jackson had an 83 percent favorable rating among African-Americans. No one else even comes close. (Louis Farrakhan was next in line with a favorable rating of 27 percent.) But early in 2001, news that the leader of the Rainbow/PUSH Coalition had fathered a child with a top aide, threatened to knock Jackson off his throne. (And eager successors like the Rev. Al Sharpton were waiting in the wings.)

Divided They Stand

DAVID MOBERG

June 28, 1978

"The freedom movement is not dead. It is merely over."

The Rev. Jesse Jackson stood before the several hundred committed and curious people at the weekly Saturday morning PUSH meeting on Chicago's South Side. . . . "Freedom means options," he intoned. "When we were on the back of the bus without the option of sitting in the front, we were unfree. Sometimes we don't vote, but we are free to vote. We have options. But too often we don't take advantage of our options. Freedom doesn't mean you catch up. It means we have to get in the race for equality. Whether you go to the hospital as a doctor or a patient is your decision. Whether you go to court as a criminal or a judge is your decision."

The PUSH choir launched into a forceful version of what approximates the current organizational hymn, "Save the Children," with its watchword chorus: "Ain't nobody gonna save us from us for us but us."

The slogan is a long way from "black power." But political and economic power is still what the black community needs and wants. The old clenched-fist salute scared conservative power-holders in this country, but many of them feel quite at home with the new PUSH slogan. It fits their view that blacks are their own worst enemies and that they could progress quickly toward the "Great American Dream" if they simply cleaned up their act.

Yet in many ways it also fits the mood of blacks today, who have lost faith in the likelihood that white goodwill or government action will soon redress poverty or unemployment and eradicate institutionalized racial inequities. This is a time of reflection and regrouping among those who are not completely disillusioned and frustrated. . . .

Some black activists fear that the movement is not merely "over." One Chicago organizer said

Among African-Americans, this possibility provoked much discussion of a successor, the nature of black leadership, and whither the black movement. This was not a new discussion, of course. Jackson has long been a bone of contention within the black community; he is as loathed in some quarters as he is loved in others. His incredible longevity in the national spotlight is surely a product of his singular talents, but it also highlights the stalemate of the black movement.

Might it be time for a radical alternative?

For most African-Americans, radicalism means black nationalism. It's no mystery why race remains the indelible feature of the African-American worldview. Their hybrid identity was fused together by slavery and crippled by cultural opprobrium. Being black in a white supremacist culture, their strength had to come from the source of their shame. Black nationalism, as an expressed demand for African autonomy and freedom, has been around since the first enslaved Africans arrived in the colonial territories, according to Sterling Stuckey, whose 1972 book, *The Ideological Origins of Black Nationalism*, is perhaps the most definitive study of the concept. Black nationalism crystallized into an ideology circa 1850, Stuckey notes, and has been the most consistent tradition in the African-American struggle for racial equality.

Since the mid 1930s, the Nation of Islam has been the most prominent champion of black nationalism. Malcolm X emerged in the early '50s as the NOI's chief spokesman, and he soon became one of the most influential of all African-American leaders. He was killed by NOI members in 1965 following a feud with the NOI's patriarch and "divinely" appointed leader, the Hon. Elijah Muhammad, but Malcolm's charismatic presence lit the fuse for the black power explosion that followed: The cultural nationalists, the Pan-Africanists, the black arts movement, the Black Panther Party and collegiate black studies all were ignited by Malcolm's black nationalist vision.

privately what many feel in moments of discouragement: "The movement is dead, ground to a halt. There's not even any reaction to racist outrages. If blacks are organizing, it's in the newspapers and not in the streets. Every time I think about the nuclear arms race and look at the cities decaying, I get sick.". . .

An even harsher judgment comes from Manning Marable, chairman of the political science department at the Tuskegee Institute: "Because of the self-destruction of the black movement in the '70s and the hostile political climate, the black movement is the most fractured and disoriented it has been since 1905. We have 'black leaders' who are not leaders. Blacks are accepted within the state as elected representatives, but the material condition of black people hasn't been worse."

ITT Archives

For years, Jesse Jackson has held the title of honorary president of black America.

Although many of those movements have withered, the NOI has survived and grown. When Elijah Muhammad died in 1975, his son Wallace D. Muhammad (now known as Imam Warithudin Mohamed) took over, transforming the organization into an American outpost of Islamic orthodoxy, changing its name and discouraging expressions of black nationalism. Louis Farrakhan, who once served as Malcolm's lieutenant but had become a caustic critic at the time of his death, initially pledged fealty to the son. But he broke away three years later to restore Elijah Muhammad's race-centered vision and re-establish the NOI.

Black nationalism gains adherents when white Americans swing to the right, and Farrakhan steadily increased his influence during the dark days of Ronald Reagan and George Bush. He gained unprecedented public visibility following his active participation in Jesse Jackson's 1984 presidential campaign. But that exposure also begot an ongoing feud with the Jewish community. Farrakhan was accused of praising Hitler and calling Judaism a "gutter religion." Both charges were overblown and taken out of context, but Farrakhan found he could exploit the controversy to provoke a "circle-the-wagons" response in the black community.

In the early '90s, when the shrill voice of the Republican right increasingly dominated public discourse, Farrakhan's stock in the black community continued rising. Just before the midterm elections of 1994, when Republicans took over the House and the Senate, a poll named Farrakhan black America's "most effective leader." For at least a decade before that, Farrakhan had been the only black leader capable of attracting thousands to his speeches. With his fiery oratory and "no sell out" persona, he attracted the hip-hop generation—who had been lulled to sleep by the conciliatory leadership of the '80s.

Yet even after pulling off the enormously successful Million Man March—the largest gathering of African-Americans in the country's history—Farrakhan was still dismissed as an unstable eccentric or dangerous demagogue by most mainstream pundits. Oddly enough, Farrakhan seemed to encourage that perception.

Farrakhan Nation

SALIM MUWAKKIL

October 23, 1985

NEW YORK—The huge crowd attracted by Minister Louis Farrakhan to Madison Square Garden was growing impatient with the slow process the security-conscious Nation of Islam was using to allow entrance into the arena. Portions of the crowd were threatening to get out of hand when an amplified voice boomed this message: "I'm sure Mayor Koch has planted some troublemakers in this crowd to create a disturbance so the press can have a field day with negative propaganda about Minister Farrakhan. If you brothers and sisters see someone making trouble, please inform them that Koch's plan won't work." The crowd calmed down immediately.

That shrewd manipulation of popular passions is emblematic of how the NOI, through the charismatic leadership of Farrakhan, has harnessed the spirit of the times to fuel the kind of mass popularity that has been absent in the black community since the days of Malcolm X. He also inspires the same kind of hatred. . . .

The crowd, though diverse, roared in unison when Farrakhan said such things as: "No matter what they've said against me, black people are still coming out to hear what I have to say. This means that their propaganda no longer has any effect on them. Black leaders, you are finished if you stand with the enemy of your people."

The "enemy" reference was in response to a news conference held a few days earlier in which a multiracial range of political and religious leaders denounced Farrakhan and repudiated his message. The collective denunciation was orchestrated by Koch, one of Farrakhan's harshest critics. Among the black leaders denouncing him was City Clerk David Dinkins, who is the city's most powerful black politician. Farrakhan singled out Dinkins for special ridicule, calling him a "silly Tom."

He had to tarnish his mainstream credibility to retain his legitimacy as a black nationalist. The NOI leader remains plagued by this dilemma. His success is based on his extremist image, but extremists are seldom successful in the mainstream. As prospects for power have improved, Farrakhan has de-emphasized the racial component of his message and has started hewing closer to the racial egalitarianism of Islamic orthodoxy.

Farrakhan's "marching millions" phenomenon seems partly to have been a reaction to a growing concern about spiritual torpor within the African-American community. Spiraling crime and illegitimacy rates, the scourge of crack cocaine, the incarceration epidemic, the terrifying specter of HIV/AIDS, all seemed to spell doom for African-Americans, especially for black men. Farrakhan's emphasis on morality and discipline pleased cultural conservatives as well as those in the wider black community who witnessed the NOI's rehabilitative powers, watching stone-cold sociopaths sternly rerouted into hard-working family men. In many ways, the Nation of Islam's racial rhetoric has disguised the theocratic cultural conservatism at the group's core. The Million Man, Million Woman and Million Family marches all focused more on personal responsibility and spiritual transformation than on challenging the institutional structures of power. The NOI's leitmotif of entrepreneurial capitalism also resonated strongly with the era's prevailing faith in market populism.

This encroaching conservatism was noticed by one of Farrakhan's most visible disciples, Khallid Muhammad. He gained fame in January 1994, when the Anti-Defamation League published a full-page ad in the *New York Times* featuring excerpts from a 1993 speech that Muhammad, then Farrakhan's "national spokesman," gave at Kean College in Union, New Jersey. In that infamous speech, he lauded Nazi Germany's treatment of Jews, issued vulgar insults about Catholics and the pope, and threatened black leaders who failed to toe the NOI's "white-man-is-the devil" line. The negative reaction to that speech provoked Farrakhan to excommunicate Muhammad in 1994.

He said the reason people of Dinkins' ilk did "the master's" bidding is because they don't properly fear black people. "They fear white people," Farrakhan told the adoring throng. "But they have to learn to fear the people they are supposed to represent."

He finished the subject with this question: "Do you feel we ought to let them live?"

The fired-up crowd answered: "No!"

ITT Archives

For most African Americans, radicalism means black nationalism and Louis Farrakhan.

Race and Candor

SALIM MUWAKKIL

May 22, 1991

A new candor about race is at large. Taboos are tumbling from the left to the right, and suddenly Americans are expressing long-forbidden thoughts about racial matters.

Not surprisingly, this new mood has provoked much anxiety among those who fear it is premature to relax cultural constraints against an evil not fully exorcised from the country's psyche. The embers of racism can too easily be inflamed by any skillful demagogue, they warn. Although they are clearly on the defensive, those people who urge the retention of selective social taboos—most of whom are on the left—have become demonized as promoters of political correctness. Yet the full-blown furor now raging around the notion of PC is actually a rear-guard action. The right has already won the high ground this time around in America's ongoing culture war.

The left richly deserves this defeat. Left-liberal orthodoxy—as diffuse as it was—stifled frank debate on racial issues. Whenever some wayward lefty dared to suggest that African-Americans actually bore some responsibility for the decay corroding their communities, he promptly would be chastised for failing to understand economic subtleties. By refusing to face certain realities of the time, the left missed the boat.

Reality for many African-Americans featured premature pregnancies, a soaring crime rate and a debilitating drug epidemic. But the left either ignored that reality or ceded it to the right. Those problems involved issues of "values" and thus were beyond the ken of the left-liberal axis. And since the right-wing seemed to be the only segment of society willing to openly discuss the hot issues of crime and other kinds of social dislocation that characterized too many black communities, its voice gained increased currency.

At first, it seemed that Muhammad's confrontational style, caustic rhetoric and fierce appearance had captured the interest (and perhaps the allegiance) of the hip-hop generation. As Farrakhan had before him, Muhammad made several cameo appearances on rap albums and attracted large crowds on college campuses. Outrageousness fueled his celebrity, and he used that notoriety to build a shadow organization, the New Black Panther Party. Muhammad sensed that young black people were growing increasingly uncomfortable with the Nation of Islam's conservatism, and he knew how to tap into that dissatisfaction.

But he had little but rhetoric to offer as an alternative. His New Black Panthers had a sartorial resemblance to the black-bereted Black Panther Party of old, but there was little ideological connection. When they created the Black Panther Party in 1966, Bobby Seale and Huey Newton crafted a jerry-built ideology, combining elements of Karl Marx's dialectics, Mao Tse-tung's cultural revolution, Frantz Fanon's theories of anti-colonial violence and Malcolm X's black nationalism. It was a messy concoction, but it was at least an attempt to bring some analytical rigor to black protest.

In attempting to create a new version of the Panthers, Muhammad substituted attitude for rigor. And while his attempt was exploitative and self-serving, it had an unintended effect. By taking the NOI's demonology to its most noxious, name-calling extremes, Muhammad revealed the fake militancy at its heart. By the time of his death in February 2000, Muhammad had become increasingly irrelevant. However, the group—carried on by his acolytes like Malik Zulu Shabazz—remains a popular draw on the college circuit. The allure of the New Black Panthers' militant pose reveals black youth's continuing hunger for a radical response to their condition.

Many seasoned black activists recognized that Farrakhan's NOI was striking a radical pose to sell reactionary messages of theocracy, patriarchy, homophobia and petty capitalism. So in June

1998, a group of black academics, intellectuals and activists (full disclosure: I was one of them) convened the first Black Radical Congress (BRC), seeking to attract that same youthful curiosity by presenting a radical critique of American society. "The realization of genuine democracy in the United States requires radical solutions," begins the group's manifesto, titled "A Black Freedom Agenda for the Twenty-first Century."

The BRC formulated 11 "principles of unity," which essentially reaffirmed conventional wisdom among longtime activists. There were two positions unique to the BRC document: a call for slavery reparations and a denunciation of "homophobia and discrimination against lesbians and gay men." Attempting to ensure that the black community keeps its eye on the real culprit, the group has made "education not incarceration" the theme of its first national campaign.

The BRC positions itself as an alternative to and critic of the kind of black nationalism that posits biological or "essentialist" differences between the races. "We reject racial and biological determinism, black patriarchy and black capitalism as solutions to problems facing black people," reads the fourth plank in the group's principles of unity. By making this explicit distinction, the BRC is marking a boundary similar to the one that separated the Black Panther Party from the black nationalist groups of the '60s like Imamu Amiri Baraka's Congress of African Peoples. While the BRC accepts and recognizes the "revolutionary nationalism" that the Panthers embraced, it decidedly rejects "cultural nationalism." This is a risky delineation. The BRC seems to recognize this with its sixth principle of unity: "We need to meet people where they are, taking seriously identity politics and single-issue reform groups, at the same time we push for a larger vision that links these struggles."

But the BRC has struggled for legitimacy. Internal divisions have hampered the group's attempt to establish a well-defined identity. (In New York City, for example, the BRC has already split into three separate chapters.) Although the group presumes to speak for the African-American masses, particularly those on the lower rungs of the economic ladder, the BRC's leaders (and

Instead of co-opting the conservative message—as adroit conservatives have done with liberal themes such as "colorblindness" and "empowerment"—the left dug in its ideological heels. . . . Because of the left's reluctance to engage in the debate and provide context, words such as "quota," "crime" and "welfare" in recent years became highly charged euphemisms for matters of race. And by leaving conservatives alone to frame those important issues, the left now finds itself isolated.

Ted Soqui

Leaders of the Los Angeles gang truce fashioned a treaty based on a copy of the 1978 Camp David accords between Israel and Egypt.

Ganging Together

SALIM MUWAKKIL

April 5, 1993

An unexpected spirit of *détente* is alive and kicking in America's black inner cities as street gangs in urban communities across the country seem suddenly smitten with the idea of peace.

In Los Angeles, a deadly 20-year feud between the Crips and Bloods has been officially terminated.

In Chicago, a similarly bloody rivalry between gangs connected to the Black Disciples and those aligned with the Gangster Disciples also has been called to a halt.

Organizers of the truce give a simple reason for the action. "This started because we got tired of seeing so many innocent black children getting killed for so much dumb shit," explains Kevin "T-Roc" of the Nickerson Gardens (Watts) Bloods.

"We started out in Watts before the riots, just trying to get three major projects together: Nickerson Gardens, Jordan Downs and Imperial Courts," he says. The group fashioned a treaty based on a copy of the 1978 Camp David accords between Israel and Egypt. "After the riots the truce just caught on everywhere across L.A., and it's still holding." . . .

Wallace "Gator" Bradley is a major architect of the "United in Peace" effort among Chicago's estimated 50,000 gang members. A former enforcer of the Gangster Disciples—one of Chicago's largest gangs—the 40-ish Bradley remains a well-respected figure in Chicago's gang subculture. . . . Although Bradley's gang-banging days are far behind him—he has even run for political office—he retains the trust of many imprisoned gang leaders, including GD legend Larry Hoover. According to prison officials, Hoover is among the most powerful gang leaders in the city's history.

"The brothers in the penitentiary as well as many of the younger brothers on the street have all come to realize that we as a people have become part of a genocidal plan to annihilate black males," Bradley says, explaining the larger reasoning behind the peace. "We understood that we could no longer be a part of that plan." . . .

Organizers of the peace effort face skepticism on all fronts. Traditional black nationalists are suspicious of gang members' lack of ideology; the civil rights fraternity is put off by their proletarian sensibilities; law enforcement agencies see nothing

much of its membership) are secular academics or high-ranking labor bureaucrats. This is not an indictment of the organization; academics have been invaluable to the black freedom struggle. But it's important to recognize the BRC's academic character to better understand the group's context and its limitations.

Launching a new organization is always a daunting task. These problems were compounded because the organization offered radical solutions to the economic and social problems of African-Americans during a period of record-high employment, low poverty and falling crime rates. The BRC recognized the temporal incongruity of the word "radical" in the boom times of the late '90s. "Radicalism means to get at the root of real problems, seeking effective solutions," reads part of the "Freedom Agenda." But African-Americans don't seem to be in a very radical mood these days.

Despite this sense of complacency, there are some rumblings of discontent and glimmers of hope for a resurgence of activism. Jesse Jackson's temporary tumble was a signal to African-American activists and organizers that it was time to regroup. New challenges overlay unfinished business and, despite their torpor (or perhaps because of it), black Americans seem more receptive to new approaches than in the past. One example of this new attitude is the unlikely popularity of a traveling seminar, organized under the heading "New Paradigms for Progress," which has been making the rounds in the black community and attracting big crowds as it dissects the state of black America. Tavis Smiley, an author and popular media personality (who was fired in 2001 by Black Entertainment Television, some say, for his activist inclinations), was the primary organizer of this road show. Smiley was bucking tradition: The notion that large audiences of African-Americans would gather, much less pay, to hear assorted black intellectuals, preachers, entrepreneurs and activists pontificate was an odd one. But his show is a hit wherever it appears.

One reason may be that in recent years, a cadre of media-genic black intellectuals (like Cornel West, Michael Eric Dyson, bell hooks, Henry Louis Gates Jr. and others) have caught the public's attention with their entertaining mixture of showmanship and scholarship. Moreover, the mass marketing of political protest—as per the Million Man March—has introduced the idea of activism to unprecedented numbers of black people. Combine that rising level of interest with the 2000 presidential election fiasco, and you have the ingredients for a popular road show on the state of the black union. Whether anything of importance is uttered during these gatherings is another question altogether. The one certain thing revealed is the diversity of opinion among black leadership. Those who criticize monolithic portrayals of the black community certainly were vindicated by the variety of views on display at these mobile seminars.

Crowd-pleasing intellectuals like West and Dyson invariably are near the top of the list of invitees, as are the requisite sprinkling of old-school preachers like Bishop T. D. Jakes and militant firebrands like the Rev. Al Sharpton. Leaders of the iconic civil rights groups—the NAACP, the National Urban League and the Southern Christian Leadership Conference—also are sure to get an invite, as are crusty contrarians like Stanley Crouch. The need for ideological balance often requires including black conservatives like Armstrong Williams, the opportunistic lightweight who is ever ready to blurt out his banal aphorisms. Active elders, like Randall Robinson, founder of the black foreign policy lobby TransAfrica, and poet Nikki Giovanni invariably are paired with youthful figures like journalist Farai Chideya and Aaron McGruder, creator of the comic strip *Boondocks*. Smiley is also sure to include a sampling of Afro-eccentrics like Professors Na'im Akbar, a psychology professor from Florida A&M, or Sonia Sanchez, an English professor from Temple University. His goal is to project an image of inclusiveness by covering most ideological bases. (Though the absence of any representative from the NOI or the BRC was a glaring omission.)

Watching these gatherings, it's not hard to think of Adolph Reed Jr., who scathingly criticized the "public intellectual" phenomenon that presaged this current popularity. Reed concluded that this media fad was fueled by a class of black but scam; and community organizers question their commitment. I share some of that skepticism. Nonetheless, these vibrant but confused African-American youth are our future. And we all have a stake in how that turns out.

Face the Nation

SALIM MUWAKKIL

October 30, 1995

WASHINGTON—Early on August 28, 1963, I joined a few friends from northern New Jersey for a trip down the turnpike to Washington, where, rumor had it, thousands of women would be assembled. Those rumors were correct, and when Dr. Martin Luther King Jr. made his historic "I Have a Dream" speech, I was busy with other concerns; I missed the moment. But despite my lack of attention, the 1963 March on Washington had an indelible effect on my political consciousness. The spirit of camaraderie and common purpose I felt that day still tempers my occasional bouts of pessimism.

I went to Washington again this month for the Million Man March, and the event's purpose was underlined by a sad realization: I'm the last one left alive of the five friends who made the 1963 trip. All of them fell victim to one of black America's contemporary plagues, afflictions so dire that even moderate voices are shouting about our "endangered" status.

Concerns about that status and its implications propelled hundreds of thousands of black men to gather in the nation's capital on a chilly Monday in mid-October. The huge gathering shocked many Americans into recognizing that an enormous racial rift still divides the country. . . .

No other black leader in the country could have supplied both the organizational discipline and emotional inspiration provided by the NOI's head man. For several years, Minister Louis Farrakhan has been addressing male-only rallies in packed venues across the country. With his uncompromising message of moral rectitude and self-discipline—some would say, despite this message—the fiery 62-year-old is alone among contemporaries in attracting the attention of black youth. Farrakhan's voice is among the most sampled sounds in hip-hop music, and members of America's most notorious black street gangs speak of him in reverential tones. Farrakhan speaks like no other leader to the rage of a generation of black men that feels abandoned by the inadequate integrationist agenda of the civil rights movement.

But Farrakhan's appeal extends far beyond alienated black youths. Some of the men on the mall fit that profile, but most did not. The crowd was vast and diverse, buoyant but orderly. The odd assortment of fringe groups often found at Farrakhan's events was there: Ardent acolytes of the late black nationalist Marcus Garvey were well-represented, as were members of the Five Percent Nation—a mushrooming New York-based offshoot of the NOI. Allah's Black Army, donning black uniforms sprinkled with silver studs, set up shop just east of the reflecting pool. And a few feet in front of them a contingent of Rastafarians unfurled a banner proclaiming the late Haile Selassie's divinity. A group of austere men in Islamic skullcaps and African dashikis held up a sign announcing "Orthodox Muslims in Praise of Farrakhan." . . .

Farrakhan's appeal for self-sufficiency, his insistence that black male agency can make a difference in reversing the decay of the African-American community, brought them together. Fraternity was the reigning spirit, and warm embraces were the preferred greeting. Many men wept openly. The gathering spanned every conceivable spectrum—class, color, religion, political ideology, gang affiliation, even gender. A large number of black women

intellectuals bereft both of academic discipline and ideological rigor. He dismissed their style as "don't worry, be happy politics" and derided their pop-culture-peppered scholarship as a "Pigmeat Markham-meets-Baudrillard coon show." But Reed's analysis has not aged well. Rather than degrading the notion of intellectual activism, these public intellectuals have energized and mobilized a generation of black youth newly interested in intellectual pursuits. One reason for the popularity of Smiley's gatherings is the black community's growing appreciation of intellectual analysis. Whatever the reason, that's a good thing.

This intellectual revival of sorts is bringing different issues to the forefront of the black agenda. Most notable has been the emergence of a movement calling for reparations. This is not a new phenomenon. But historically reparations advocates were ridiculed as starry-eyed idealists pushing implausible schemes. Marcus Garvey's Universal Negro Improvement Association, Omari Obadeli's Republic of New Africa, and the NOI have been the primary pro-reparations voices in the black freedom movement, and typically they were seen as antagonists of the left. There is also a class aspect to this reparations story. The black nationalist groups that pushed the concept all had mostly lower- and working-class constituents. Thus, the issue typically was given short shrift by the class-conscious, "talented tenth" who dominated the leadership of major civil rights organizations.

But in a very short time, the issue of reparations has left the fringe and become an important aspect of the national discourse on race. The emergence of the issue can be largely credited to a group of activists who came together in 1987 to form the National Coalition of Blacks for Reparations in America (N'COBRA) after Congress voted to award $1.2 billion in reparations to Japanese-Americans interned in concentration camps during World War II. N'COBRA helped change the image of reparations advocates; no longer were they automatically dismissed as hapless eccentrics as they were during the civil rights years.

Now several groups of high-powered attorneys are preparing a class-action suit for reparations against the U.S. government on behalf of the progeny of enslaved Africans. Other lawyers are investigating possible litigation against a number of U.S. corporations whose fortunes were built on slave labor. In 2000, city councils in Chicago, Cleveland, Dallas, Detroit, Nashville and Washington passed ordinances supporting a bill that has been languishing in Congress for many years. Introduced annually since 1989 by Michigan Democratic Rep. John Conyers, that bill seeks to "establish a commission to examine the institution of slavery . . . and economic discrimination against African-Americans . . . to make recommendations to the Congress on appropriate remedies."

One reason for the re-emergence of reparations as an issue has been the failure of affirmative action. Although the logic of compensation helped justify the "Great Society" programs of President Johnson, few uttered the word reparations. In fact, Johnson provided a lyrical rationale for the concept in a 1965 speech in which he said, "You do not take a person who for years has been hobbled by chains and liberate him, bring him up to the starting line, and then say, 'you are free to compete with all the others.' "

In effect, affirmative action is just a euphemism for reparations. Although the policy was originally designed as a means to help compensate African-Americans for slavery and its lengthening legacy, the racial aspects of the program were eventually toned down. By de-emphasizing race, liberals succeeded in making the program more palatable but less effective. Consequently, white women have been the major beneficiaries.

A program of reparations, as framed by its more sensible proponents, would be a national investment in human capital, providing resources for education, training, housing and business creation over two to three generations. Many analysts now argue that reparations would have been a logical remedy for African-Americans' social disadvantages if the problem had been correctly defined as one of unjust enrichment and structural

decided to join the march, and there were occasional white faces as well. . . .

Black feminists have long criticized the NOI's cultural conservatism and its veneration of a patriarchal order. Julianne Malveaux, economist, author and Pacifica Radio talk show host, questioned the "macho assumptions" implicit in the demonstration. "Farrakhan's doctrine is just a dark-skinned version of the Christian Coalition's dogma, with some racism thrown in," Malveaux argued. . . .

Writer bell hooks echoed Malveaux's point. "How can we teach and model for our children that patriarchy is a bad thing, when we adopt its very patriarchy and warlike sensibilities for our own models?" hooks asked. "Stevie Wonder was the only speaker to mention the word 'love.' Everyone else was on a warlike and militaristic footing."

For me, it was no contest. The march was an enormously satisfying event, part therapy, part mobilization. The sense of fraternity and common purpose was overwhelming, and I embraced everyone as if they were Edward Patterson, William Foster, "Duck" Givens and Richard Hudson—all of whom probably would have attended, had they survived urban America.

Talking About Race

SALIM MUWAKKIL

February 8, 1998

When President Clinton announced a year-long initiative on race relations, he said that he hoped a candid discussion on this vexing American problem would help "perfect the promise of America" and "build our more perfect union." Media commentators were deeply cynical, portraying the initiative as the vain preoccupation of a legacy-hungry lame duck. It is that. But it is also a serious effort by a president who is genuinely concerned about racial divisions. Clinton deserves credit for tackling a problem that many deem intractable, and that other contemporary presidents have either ignored or exploited.

Still, it appears that Clinton's well-intended foray into the maze of race relations may fare no better than the malign neglect of his predecessors. In its first six months, the effort has mostly provoked sharp arguments between increasingly fractious antagonists. That is exactly what Clinton hoped to minimize. By proposing a seemingly innocuous idea of a national discussion on the subject of race, "when we are not driven to it by some emergency or social cataclysm," Clinton thought he could keep the panel from being hijacked for partisan advantage. "Now is the time we should learn together, talk together and act together to build one America," he said. . . .

Clinton, however, has never been one to put inequality—racial or economic—on his agenda. His moral appeals to topple the barriers of racial exclusion are actually motivated by economic incentives. "With just a twentieth of the world's population, but a fifth of the world's income, we in America simply have to sell to the other 95 percent of the world's consumers just to maintain our standard of living," Clinton explained recently in a burst of candor. "Because we are drawn from every culture on earth, we are uniquely positioned to do it."

That's his fundamental argument: We can be more effective salespeople in the international marketplace if we look like our potential customers.

Unfortunately, the real race problem in this country is not commerce, but anti-black bias. The advisory board set up by Clinton to oversee a national dialogue on race issues could accomplish some good if it were to tunnel to the core of our racial miasma, analyzing the social cost and long legacy of 250 years of slavery and a century of Jim distribution of resources, rather than one of social hostility amenable to moral suasion.

As right-wing judicial rulings are forcing policy-makers to turn away from affirmative action and other compensatory programs, the need for reparations becomes clearer. In his enormously influential book *The Debt: What America Owes to Blacks*, Randall Robinson shows the connection between contemporary racial disparities and the legacy of race-based chattel slavery, arguing eloquently for social investment in communities crippled by that legacy. "At long last, let America contemplate the scope of its enduring human-rights wrong against the whole of a people," Robinson writes in the introduction. "Let the vision of blacks not become so blighted from a sunless eternity that we fail to see the staggering breadth of America's crime against us."

The inequities set in motion by the history of slavery and the Jim Crow apartheid that followed have been reinforced by a society that presumes black inferiority and still has a problem providing African-Americans equal access to goods and services. Reparations advocates argue that if Americans remain ignorant of slavery's social and economic legacy, they are unlikely to ever get to the root of those inequities. Furthermore, Robinson contends that the struggle for reparations will work wonders for African-Americans whether it's successful or not. "The issue is not whether or not we can, or will, win reparations," Robinson writes. "The issue rather is whether we will fight for reparations because we have decided for ourselves that they are our due."

For African-Americans to "get their due" they must first confront the "internalized oppression" (or more prosaically, self-hatred) that has been one of the most debilitating consequences of socialization in a white supremacist culture. Generations of black people were taught to believe that "the white man's ice is always colder," and that reinforced self-abnegation takes a cultural toll. People convinced of their own impotence lack the sense of agency necessary for any struggle. Thus, the appeal of black nationalism—which deals with issues of identity, culture and agency—is likely to persist. These approaches surely have their place in the arsenal of the freedom movement—whether from the NOI or from Christians like Boston's Rev. Eugene Rivers—but such inner-directed strategies do little to alter the disparate distribution of goods and services that cripples the life chances of too many African-Americans. Black leadership must learn how to attend to those issues of identity while cultivating coalitions and building wider alliances. Getting to the root of these problems is a radical enterprise. But will African-Americans, grown relatively fat on the entrails of the booming '90s, enlist in this enterprise?

There are few signs of a new youth movement on the horizon, but such movements usually arrive unexpectedly. The radical voice that had expressed itself historically from the slave revolts to the Black Panther Party seemed especially mute in recent years, but it was in full throat in the cultural realm. Because there was such a lack of relevant movement voices in the late '80s and early '90s, hip-hop artists often stepped into the breach. Never before in African-American history had musicians made such bold claims for social authority. Hip-hop music and the subculture it spawned also became a focal point for the widening class divide within the African-American community—a divide growing faster among blacks than in the rest of the population.

But neither nationalist nor cultural solutions will be adequate to deal with the crisis I see quickly closing in on many African-American communities. The spirit of the times should provide the needed elements for a renewed sense of black activism and new prominence for radical critique. The requirements for the necessary kind of leadership are daunting, perhaps impossible. This is a good thing. The unwieldy portfolio necessary for traditional, "big-man-style" leadership may force black Americans finally to embrace the kind of collective leadership needed to move them to the next chapter in their national narrative. There is no one person who can liberate black people, and the widespread recognition of that reality is a measure of the freedom movement's growing maturity.

Crow apartheid, determining how best to intervene to prevent American institutions from reproducing race-based inequality, or studying the corrosive effect of the U.S. media on race relations.

Clinton has chosen an anti-racist theme for his legacy. In doing so, he has offered the country an opportunity to pick the scab that covers the festering wound of racism. It's a chance that comes around infrequently, and it can hurt. But if we're to move beyond the tired choreography of blame and denial, the wound must be examined fearlessly. Clinton has demonstrated some political courage by raising the contentious issue of race. Now if he were only courageous enough to do something significant with this opportunity.

Terry LaBan

In a very short time, the issue of reparations has left the fringe and become an important aspect of the national discourse on race.

They change their attitudes, or they change the subject. But who so far has changed their address?

Bill Stamets

Don't Go There

WILLIAM UPSKI WIMSATT

October 30, 1995

At a book reading in San Francisco, I was challenged "not to go" to Hunter's Point (the largest black neighborhood in the city). A tough white guy named Mike (former graffiti writer in training to be a cop) offered to give me a tour of San Francisco, then drop me off in Hunter's Point. "Just don't go to Sunnydale," he added.

"Don't go there!" emphasized a black woman. "It's really not worth it. You won't be able to do anybody any good if you get killed. The ghetto in San Francisco is not like on the East Coast. Black people here are so isolated. So in a way, they're even angrier."

Everyone has a *reason* why *their* black people are the *scariest.*

It was Saturday night. A bunch of people standing around. No one said anything.

"I'll come," said a small, well-dressed young woman. She hadn't spoken all night. Everyone glanced at her nonchalantly then quickly looked away. Even her friends didn't say anything to her.

Her name was Lisa—from Newton, Massachusetts, a student at Pomona College. She had never been to a ghetto before. Mike drove us to the far end of Sunnydale. It was midnight. He tried to convince us not to get out of the car.

Lisa and I walked in circles until 4 A.M. through Sunnydale, Hunter's Point and a couple of projects, all the way back to the Mission District.

"Get the fuck out of here!" someone shouted from a slow-moving van. We were on a dark side street. Lisa didn't flinch.

Lisa went the furthest I've seen anyone go in curbing the Ghetto Avoidance Pattern, among the least talked about gaps in American life. Our literature suffers from an analogous gap. We need a literature about being spoiled. Enough of this literature about struggle! Most people who read in this country are spoiled and boring, yet all they want to read about is struggle and adventure.

The only white people I know who realize it's safe to live in the ghetto are the ones who've actually lived there. A few other whites tell me that I'm wrong, naive, lucky, lying, crazy. At least they're up-front about it.

Most whites I meet are neither experienced nor up-front. They tell me that they agree with me, or they admire me, or they change their attitudes, or they change the subject. But who so far has changed their address?

Why should they? Every place I've lived or person I know well brings out a different side of me. My mother brings out one side. My father brings out another. The more kinds of people I know on their own terms, the more sides of my personality get developed. Any people I don't know, not only do I not know them; I don't even know that part of myself. Most people are walking around with less than half a personality.

People with underdeveloped personalities aren't really in a position to make informed choices in their personal lives, let alone figure out how to organize against racism or struggle for social justice. I don't care how long you've been reading *In These Times.* Or how astute you are when talking to like-minded buddies. Without friendship among disenfranchised groups, leftist organizing is impossible and leftist principles are empty. Social justice grows out of your social circle.

The Return of Juan Seguín

LATINOS AND THE REMAKING OF AMERICAN POLITICS

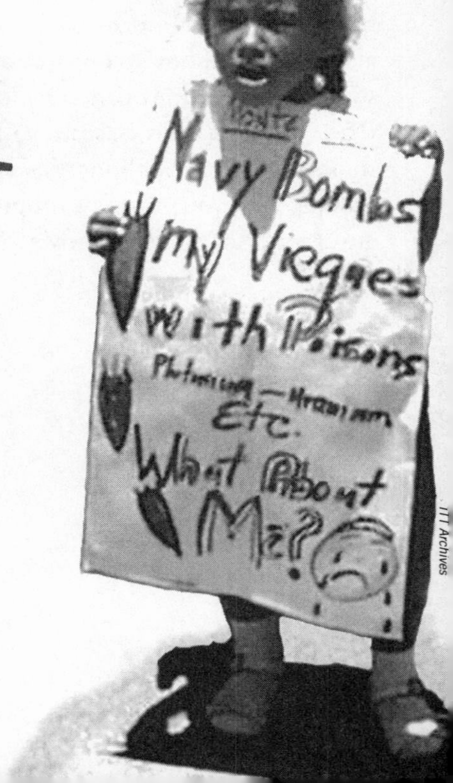

ITT Archives

Six

JUAN GONZALEZ

EVERY AMERICAN RECOGNIZES THE NAME DAVY CROCKETT, THE FRONTIER LEGEND WHO DIED DEFENDING THE ALAMO, BUT JUAN SEGUÍN, WHO FOUGHT with Crockett and survived, is virtually unknown.

Seguín's ancestors settled present-day San Antonio 50 years before the American Revolution. A rich landowner and federalist opposed to Mexican President Santa Anna, Seguín was part of the small group of Mexicans who joined the Texas rebels at the Alamo, but he was dispatched from the fort with a message to Sam Houston before the shooting began and thus escaped the massacre. Seguín went on to fight with Houston's army at the Battle of San Jacinto, was later elected a senator of the Texas Republic and served several terms as mayor of San Antonio. Then, in 1842, white newcomers chased him from office at gunpoint, seized his land and forced him to flee to Mexico, making him the last Hispanic mayor of San Antonio until Henry Cisneros took office 140 years later.

Seguín is the forgotten father of Latino politics in the United States. The story of his life and career has left Hispanics with a somewhat different political legacy than that which Washington, Jefferson and the founding fathers bequeathed to white Americans, or which Nat Turner, Sojourner Truth and W. E. B. Du Bois symbolize for black Americans. Yet how our nation comes to terms with that legacy will determine much of American politics during the 21st century.

The reason is simple. The political influence of Hispanic Americans is growing at breakneck speed. Between 1976 and 1996, Hispanic voter turnout in the United States grew by 135 percent, compared to only 21 percent among non-Hispanics. Fifty years ago, Latino registered voters could be counted in the thousands; today, they number more than 10 million. In 1950, there were a few hundred Latino elected

Crossing the Frontier

CARLOS MORTON

September 13, 1978

Elizondo left his native village in Michocán to study electronics in Mexico City but had to drop out after his father died. There were brothers and sisters to support. "I had trouble getting a job in Mexico City," says Elizondo, a tall, good-looking young man of 22. "I had been involved in some union organizing, and I fear that I was blacklisted. So I hitchhiked to Tijuana and joined a flock of *pollos*. I got caught two times by the *mosco* (one of two 500C hawk helicopters) and once by the *migra* jeep. On the fourth try, I finally caught a good ride all the way to Salinas."

Guillermo, 32, left his small city in Aguas Caliente in search of better pay and came by bus to Tijuana. "You can't live on 60 or 70 pesos per day anymore," he says, "and I had a family of five to support. So I hung around the bus station, and before long I was approached by a 'coyote' who offered to take me to Los Angeles for $200. I had a little money saved up, and so I struck a deal. Then he told me to wait in a nearby bar until late afternoon. I paid for my trip, and I was told to stay out of sight."

Once it starts to darken the *pollos* are roused from their hiding places in garages and bath houses to prepare for the rites of passage. Many wait to be sent into the United States from the *Colonia Libertad*, a *barrio* on the international border. Here there is no fence, and it is easy to cross freely into Spring Canyon, a rugged area notorious for being the scene of brutal attacks and robberies on the unsuspecting by gangs from both sides of the border. Here the Border Patrol has placed electronic sensors to detect movement.

Nothing can stop them. They hide in the bushes, smoking and talking in hushed whispers, waiting for the coyote's whistle to move out. Border

officials, almost none in major cities. Today, there are more than 5,000, and Latinos comprise the biggest ethnic voting blocks in Los Angeles, New York, San Antonio and Miami.

The release of figures from the 2000 Census finally awakened the nation to the astounding growth of the Hispanic population. The number of Hispanics in the country jumped to 35.3 million, a more than 50 percent increase from the 1990 Census (and that's not including the 3.8 million residents of Puerto Rico). Not only has the Hispanic population drawn virtually even with the nation's black population, but it has spread to every part of the country. In Nevada, for example, the fastest-growing of the 50 states for the past four decades, the Latino population tripled, with Hispanics now comprising nearly 20 percent of the state. In Oklahoma, Latinos are now 5 percent of residents, but they represent 38 percent of the state's population growth since 1980.

Unfortunately, the left in this country has failed to pay sufficient attention to this growing Hispanic population. Black-white relations and conflicts so dominate political discourse among American radicals and liberals that many still unconsciously resist coming to grips with the more racially and ethnically mixed nation we have become. While there are, for example, hundreds of studies done in recent decades analyzing the historical development of the fight for political equality among African-Americans, similar studies of Latino political history are nearly nonexistent. But even a cursory examination of that history reveals remarkable lessons for progressives and points to ways in which the new Latino political awakening has the potential to reinvigorate and reconfigure the American left.

The most decisive influence on Latino politics this century was World War II. Thousands of Mexican-Americans and Puerto Ricans who served their country in that war (and in the Korean War a few years later) returned from the battlefield with a new confidence regarding their rights as Americans.

The giant barrios of Los Angeles and San Antonio emerged as the centers of Hispanic ferment. In San Antonio, Henry B. Gonzalez, a war veteran and former juvenile probation officer, began organizing the *tejanos* of the West Side through his Pan-American Progressive Association; while in Los Angeles, social worker Edward Roybal, another veteran, rallied *mexicanos* to register to vote. They were the first Latino councilmen in their respective cities since the mid-19th century.

John F. Kennedy's nomination as the Democratic Party's presidential candidate in 1960 was a watershed moment for Latinos. "Viva Kennedy" clubs formed throughout the Southwest, and, nationwide, JFK amassed 85 percent of the Mexican vote. In turn, he threw his support to González in a victorious run for Congress in a special election the following year; he would be followed into Congress by Roybal in 1962 and Eligio "Kika" de la Garza and Joseph Montoya in 1964. To this day, you will find Mexican homes in the Southwest where a faded photo of Kennedy hangs prominently near one of the Virgin of Guadalupe.

During the '60s, the Johnson administration pushed a series of landmark bills through Congress. Those laws, the Civil Rights Act of 1964, the Voting Rights Act of 1965 and the Fair Housing Act of 1968, toppled the legal underpinnings of discrimination against both blacks and Hispanics. While new laws and federal court decisions during the Kennedy-Johnson era spurred Latino political involvement by eliminating legal discrimination, they did little to alter economic and social inequities.

But the pervasive new influence of television—whether in transmitting stories of dilapidated Harlem tenements, Bull Connor's dogs or the riots in Watts—suddenly made social inequity more glaring. The 1965 Watts riots, in fact, signaled the end of this incremental integration period. Hispanics, along with everyone else in America, entered a new psychological and political era—one of rebellion and social polarization.

For several years, riots became an annual reality for the inner cities, and many white Americans began to regard

Patrol jeeps jockey for position on the American side. The sun has set. One group suddenly bolts out into the open, and just as quickly dives into a ravine, out of sight. Was that just a tactic to divert the *migra*? *El Mosco* appears out of nowhere—its searchlights probing, loudspeaker blaring. The drama has begun. . . .

They constitute one of recent history's largest migrations and, like the Irish, Italians, Eastern European Jews and Africans before them, their children will be demanding a share of the American pie. U.S. Border Patrol spokesman Robert D. McCord is right: "The problem is bigger than all of us."

As for the men awaiting deportation behind bars, what do they think?

A stocky, broad-shouldered man of 35, says, "I am thinking about my family, my job, the time and money I lost. I am thinking about what a big game this life is, in one door and out the other. But most of all, *compadre*, I am thinking about how long it will take me to get back into the United States this time."

Diana Claitor

"Most of all, *compadre*, I am thinking about how long it will take me to get back into the Untited States this time."

Cesar Chavez of the United Farm Workers eventually became the most admired Hispanic leader in the country.

protests by blacks and Hispanics as a threat to the nation's stability. At the same time, African-American and Latino youth concluded that their parents' attempts at integration within the political system had failed. Only through massive protests, disruptive boycotts, strikes and even riots, the new generation decided, could qualitative (some called it revolutionary) change be accomplished.

Brash new groups—the Brown Berets, La Raza Unida, the Alianza, the United Farm Workers, the Young Lords, Los Siete de La Raza, Crusade for Justice, Movimiento Pro Independencia, MECHA, the August 29th Movement—were invariably more radical, their membership younger and usually from lower-class origins than the established civic organizations. They saw the older organizations as too tied to the status quo, too concerned with appearing respectable and reasonable to white society.

Inspired by the black power and anti-Vietnam War movements at home and by the anti-colonial revolutions in the Third World, especially the Cuban revolution, most offered a utopian, vaguely socialist vision of changing America. They also insisted that both Puerto Ricans and Mexicans were descendants of conquered peoples who had been forcibly subjugated when America annexed their territories during its expansion. They considered themselves more comparable to American Indians and African-Americans than to Scottish, German, Irish or Italian immigrants. This was also the period when the Latino community itself became more ethnically diverse. Dominican and Cuban refugees arrived in massive numbers to New York and Florida in the late '60s, followed by Colombians, Salvadorans, Guatemalans and Nicaraguans in succeeding decades. Meanwhile, Mexican immigrants—both legal and illegal—as well as Puerto Ricans spread beyond their original enclaves in the Southwest and Northeast.

While the Mexican-Americans and Puerto Ricans tended to form nationalist groups with left-wing orientations, the Cubans almost exclusively had right-wing outlooks. The overriding goal of Cuban immigrants was returning to a

Seeds of Justice

JOHN GARDNER

May 17, 1993

I remember vividly a July 1975 dawn in Oxnard, California. Helicopters suddenly appeared over the windbreak of trees, spraying pesticides on tomato fields still wet with dew.

Dozens of people were already working the wet rows. Most were Mexicans, but everyone got hit—African-Americans, Syrians, Filipinos and a solitary homeland free from Fidel Castro and communism. That obsession gave them the character of an exile group more than a traditional immigrant community. But it didn't take long for Cubans to make their presence felt in local politics, thanks to a law Congress passed in 1966 that made it easier for Cubans to secure U.S. visas and shortened the normal five-year waiting period for citizenship. A surge of Cuban naturalizations followed, and with it an explosion of Cuban voting power.

As the civil rights and anti-war movements deepened, however, division took root among Latino radicals, who refused to participate in the traditional electoral process and sought alliances instead with revolutionary groups outside the Latino community such as the Black Panthers, the Students for a Democratic Society and other New Left organizations. Eventually those coalitions splintered and evolved into scores of fringe Marxist factions. In the case of Puerto Ricans, those splinters included several clandestine urban groups that resorted to terrorist bombings, such the FALN (Fuerzas Armadas de Liberación Nacional) and Los Macheteros. In the Cuban community, the most extreme counter-revolutionaries began taking actions jointly with other anti-communist movements in the United States and Latin America, often with CIA sponsorship.

But these factions, whether from the left or from the right, became increasingly divorced from everyday reality. All failed to understand that despite the inequality and stubborn racism that Latinos faced in the United States, conditions here, even for the most destitute, were substantially better than in the Latin American nations they came from, a reality that to this day has doomed revolutionary Marxist movements in our country to tiny followings.

A second trend in Colorado and Texas was represented by Rodolfo "Corky" Gonzalez's Crusade for Justice, Reies Tijerina's Alianza de los Pueblos and La Raza Unida Party. While their rhetoric mirrored the militant nationalism of the Marxists, these groups opted for working within the U.S. electoral system. But they rejected both the Democratic and Republican parties as bankrupt, seeking instead to build

Chinese. One man's forearms erupted immediately in red blotches that kept expanding. "It lasts a few days," he told me resignedly. Mothers covered infants with blankets, then wet the blankets with drinking water, improvising cocoons to protect their babies' faces. Two old men coughed, examining their spit for blood. Nobody seemed surprised except me, the newly arrived United Farm Workers organizer from New York City.

I was there organizing because Cesar Chavez and the United Farm Workers of America (UFW) had suddenly and unexpectedly won the historic 1975 California Agricultural Labor Relations Act. . . . For the first time in this country, farmworkers could elect union representation, if they dared. . . .

Others had tried countless times since the '30s to organize agricultural workers: labor unions, compassionate liberals and earnest Christians, immigrant fraternal societies, Wobblies, Communists, Socialists—everyone in 20th-century America committed to labor justice. But it was Cesar Chavez who made real headway. . . .

"You can't organize on money," Chavez used to tell us. "There isn't enough money to organize now. There never was, and there never will be. Once you depend on money, you're dead." He lived on the UFW stipend of room, board and $5 a week. He challenged his constituencies—unions and religious communities—as hard as he challenged the growers he targeted.

I remember hosting a meeting for him at an Oxnard labor camp. Workers kept reciting fearful threats from labor contractors, growers and Teamsters henchmen. "You know something, *compañeros*?" he said. "There's nothing that can stand in the way of people committed to justice. When we have a vision of justice to share, nobody and nothing can possibly hold us back."

He contradicted everything they said, yet they believed him. Their belief gave them the courage to win the next week's election. He invented a type of organizing that synthesized the tactics of the civil rights and anti-war movements, cooperatives, labor unions, community organizing and religious ministries. Everyone in the union was uncomfortable with at least one aspect of this bizarre medley. But he got us all to live with each other because the union needed every one of these tactics and constituencies. Nowhere else then or since could you find nuns working beside immigrant laborers and college students, a routine combination in the UFW. He didn't care whether he had to march 1,000 miles or set up a shrine outside a vineyard—if it worked, we were going to do it.

Most of all, he had a will so strong that it frequently felt as if nothing could get in its way. "There's a moment," he would tell us about growers, politicians, corporations, sheriff's deputies, "when they believe we want it more, stronger and longer than they want to keep it from us. That's the moment we win."

ITT Archives

"There's a moment," Cesar Chavez would say, "when they believe we want it more, stronger and longer than they want to keep it from us. That's the moment we win."

independent Chicano organizations that would try to win elected office in what they called Aztlán, the original Aztec homeland that encompassed the territory ceded by the 1848 Treaty of Guadalupe Hidalgo. The party they formed, La Raza Unida, made some impressive showings in small towns in South Texas, but it proved unable to spark widespread *mexicano* desertions from the Democrats.

A third trend was represented by Cesar Chavez's United Farm Workers, the National Council of La Raza and Puerto Rican civic leaders like Gilberto Gerena Valentín. These groups concentrated on winning the basic rights that *mexicanos* and Puerto Ricans had as American citizens—the right to unionize, the right to vote, the right to basic government services like schools, public housing, sewers and drinking water. Chavez, the foremost representative of that trend, eventually became the most admired Hispanic leader in the country.

After 1975, Latino involvement with revolutionary organizations and nationalistic independent politics declined. The movement reverted to political equality as a primary goal, only now it was infused with the cultural and ethnic pride awakened by '60s radicalism. But in the face of a conservative backlash, the issues that minority leaders were raising—equal housing opportunity, school busing for desegregation, affirmative action, equal political representation, bilingual education—were blamed for subverting "American values."

In this new climate, the second generation of postwar Latino leaders discarded its illusion of overthrowing political power and instead sought a proportional share of it. But several new factors distinguished this period: Latino leaders filed an unprecedented number of federal civil rights lawsuits; they formed the first lasting national coalition across ethnic and racial lines; and they expanded their movement beyond just middle-class professionals into poor Latino communities by combining '60s-style mass protests with voter registration and election campaigns.

The climax of this period came in 1983, with the stunning mayoral victories of Harold Washington in Chicago and Wilson Goode in Philadelphia. Suddenly, the nation awoke to a new reality. Power in the Democratic Party's urban areas had slipped from organizations of white politicians and their ethnic constituencies to coalitions of African-Americans and Hispanics. In both cities, Hispanic voters, who until then had been ignored by political candidates, demonstrated a newfound ability to tip an election by voting in startling numbers.

In South Florida, meanwhile, a drastic change had begun. Between 1973 and 1979, according to one study, those who said they planned to return to Cuba if Castro were overthrown plummeted from 60 percent to 22 percent. By 1974, some 200,000 Cubans in South Florida had become citizens, and many were voting regularly. After several unsuccessful attempts, the first two Cubans—both Bay of Pigs veterans—were elected to office in 1973. In 1975, Cuban professionals launched a citizenship campaign, and 26,000 exiles were naturalized the following year. By 1980, 55 percent of the exiles had become citizens.

With Ronald Reagan's election that year, powerful Miami groups like the Cuban American National Foundation perfected a well-bankrolled, behind-the-scenes lobby in Washington for their special projects—Radio Martí, TV Martí and aid to the Nicaraguan Contras. At the same time, they adopted a new pragmatism in public, focusing less on controversial issues like bilingual education. By the mid-'80s, Cuban immigrants had turned South Florida into the center of Hispanic conservative power throughout the country.

When Jesse Jackson began his first campaign for the Democratic presidential nomination in 1984 by calling for a new "Rainbow Coalition," his attempt was dismissed as a meaningless protest. He promptly shocked all the experts by winning the majority of African-American votes and a substantial minority of Latino and white votes. Four years later, Jackson garnered 7 million votes against the eventual Democratic nominee, Michael Dukakis.

California Steaming

MARC COOPER

November 28, 1994

In the yawning political space left open by the enfeebled Democrats, a new social movement was inadvertently ushered into existence. Some 100,000 liberal and Latino opponents of Proposition 187 took their cause onto the sidewalks last month, organizing the largest demonstration in recent Los Angeles history. When they arrived at City Hall, there were no Democratic candidates on hand to encourage them. Instead, the first speech from the rally platform came from Ron Unz, the young millionaire Republican businessman who had challenged Pete Wilson in the June primary from the *right*, but who at least had the backbone to say what Kathleen Brown and Dianne Feinstein didn't: that Proposition 187 was morally repugnant.

Grassroots organizing against Proposition 187 grew quickly, and Brown and Co.—who had initially opposed the street mobilizations—now changed course and quickly tried to take advantage of the popular movement. But all this took place *after* the deadline for voter registration had passed, and the tens of thousands of new voters that the Democrats could have brought into the electoral process were already shut out.

Nonetheless, this other, alternative political campaign continued ahead. Given no expression in the electoral campaign, and inspired by the mammoth kick-off street demonstration, groups of high school students staged scores of walkouts, marches and protests in Los Angeles, San Francisco and outlying communities. While the Republicans and the media excoriated the kids for carrying Mexican flags, the Democrats cowered in fear of being associated with the young militants. The police readily skirmished with the angered students, but the protests continued right up through Election Day.

Now it is the Republicans and Governor Wilson who will have to deal with the stirrings of a new Latino civil rights movement. But at least for the moment, Wilson seems happy to ride the wave of xenophobia he helped unleash. No sooner than the day after the vote, with Proposition 187 already tied up in the courts, he signed a unilateral decree cutting off state-funded prenatal care for undocumented women. No matter that the affected children will be born as U.S. citizens—they are still aliens as long as they are in the womb.

Dennis Dunleavy

Anti-immigrant laws sparked a Latino political backlash; from 1994 to 1997, citizenship applications nearly tripled, the overwhelming majority from Hispanics.

The 1984 and 1988 Jackson campaigns brought millions of first-time voters to the polls in the South and the northern ghettos, and those same voters sent blacks and Hispanics to Congress in record numbers. In some states, blacks showed higher election turnouts than white voters for the first time, and candidates who identified themselves as part of Jackson's Rainbow Coalition started to win isolated local elections. In 1989, David Dinkins won the mayoralty of New York City—the first black to hold the post—by capturing 88 percent of the black vote, 64 percent of the Hispanic vote and less than 35 percent of the white vote. As blacks and Hispanics gained greater influence with Democrats, however, white middle-class and suburban voters kept deserting the party.

The Rainbow's revolutionary potential came from its appeal to those sectors of the nation's voting-age population that had remained alienated and disenfranchised throughout most of the 20th century—blacks, Hispanics, the young and the poor. For decades our country has had one of the lowest voter turnout rates of any industrial democracy, assuring that those elected to office represent only a minority of the voting-age adults. In 1972, for instance, 77 percent of middle-class property owners voted, compared to 52 percent of working-class Americans. And well-educated Americans usually vote at twice the rate of less-educated citizens.

Jackson's Rainbow movement, by contrast, placed prime importance not only on registering new voters, but on removing legal obstacles to simple and universal voter registration. Yet in both the 1988 and 1992 elections, Democratic presidential candidates chose to continue competing with the Republicans for the same small number of already registered voters who had fled their party—the so-called Reagan Democrats—in the hope of getting them to "swing" back. Little attention was paid to Jackson's strategy of getting millions of new voters from the lower classes—where blacks and Hispanics are disproportionately concentrated—onto the rolls, where they could become the basis of a new political majority.

After that initial breakthrough of the late '80s, the Rainbow Coalition stalled. In a country so long fixated on the contradictions between black and white, the Rainbow fell victim to similar divisions. Jackson and many of the veteran black officeholders around him started treating the white, Hispanic and Asian members of the Rainbow as permanent junior partners. While the leaders argued, their followers clashed over government contracts and patronage jobs.

Differences in attitudes toward race also tore at the Rainbow Coalition. Jackson portrayed the Rainbow as "common ground" for all Americans seeking economic justice; he urged an inclusive approach toward all minorities. Many African-Americans, however, believe Latinos aspire to be considered white, while many Hispanic regard blacks as obsessed with race. In fact, Latinos simply view race relations from a historically different perspective. This country's stark black-white dichotomy is alien to them. To varying degrees, ethnic identification or nationality remains at the core of Latino identity. Rather than air these different views and resolve them through debate and education, the Rainbow swept them under the rug, thus undermining its own unity.

By 1995, the mayoralty in four of the country's largest cities—New York, Los Angeles, Chicago and Philadelphia—had passed from a liberal or moderate black incumbent to a more conservative white leader. In each case, Hispanic voters shifted in significant percentages from the previous black mayor to the new white candidate, and, each time, those who switched sounded the same: "We weren't treated as equals by the black leaders." Even as the number of black and Hispanic leaders in Congress reached a record high, the cohesiveness of the alliance fractured, especially as black voters, along with whites, grew increasingly uneasy about the country's population of Hispanics and Asians. In November 1994, for instance, a majority of black Californians voted for Proposition 187 to cut off all benefits to illegal immigrants. Even though Jackson never officially declared its demise, the Rainbow Coalition was over.

¡Vieques Libre!

JUAN GONZALEZ

October 3, 1999

Empty bullet casings litter the sun-baked beach and the narrow dirt trails that disappear into the underbrush. From the top of a nearby hill, you can spot the pockmarks of bomb craters and the fins of unexploded missiles and shells, some four feet high, poking out from the mangled landscape like deadly pickup sticks.

This 20-mile-long island just off the east coast of Puerto Rico, a once-lush paradise, is now a denuded and contaminated indictment of American colonialism. Here on Vieques, an island most Americans have never heard of, a major political upheaval has erupted during the past few months, taking Washington by surprise and sparking unprecedented unity among Puerto Rico's 3.8 million inhabitants. The conflict is rapidly turning into a battleground over the meaning of democracy and human rights, one that has the Pentagon's top brass scurrying to ward off a major defeat.

Manuela Santiago was born and reared on Vieques and has been mayor of its 9,300 inhabitants for the past 16 years. Despite her post, Santiago had never seen the easternmost part of the island, called Cayo Yayi, until August 13, when she traveled there in a rickety fishing boat with an American delegation headed by the Rev. Jesse Jackson and Roberto Gonzalez, the archbishop of San Juan.

This section of Vieques has been off-limits to local residents since the '40s, when it came under control of the U.S. Navy, along with more than two-thirds of the rest of the island. During the following decades, the Navy has used the area as a live-ammunition practice range, which the Pentagon calls the Atlantic Fleet Weapons Training Facility. At the other end of the island, the Navy operates a huge munitions dump. The people of Vieques are squeezed in between the dump and the range.

Practice at the range goes on for as many as 200 days out of every year. Combat planes bomb and strafe the island. Destroyers bombard it from sea. The U.S. government even lends Vieques out to the navies of NATO and Latin American countries so they too can fire their shells at it. Maneuvers have included, on occasion, practice with depleted uranium shells, napalm and cluster bombs. That several thousand Puerto Ricans, all of them U.S. citizens, live next to a bombing range on an island only twice the size of Manhattan has never seemed to bother the Pentagon, which claims Vieques is essential to national defense. . . .

The people of Vieques always knew a disaster was bound to happen. It finally did this year on April 19. That's when two Navy pilots on a bombing run missed their target and hit an observation post with a couple of 500-pound bombs. David Sanes Rodriguez, a Puerto Rican security guard, was killed and four others were wounded.

Sanes' death was the final straw. A few days later, a group of fishermen led by several sons of Carlos Zenon—the fisherman who led protests against the Navy in the late '70s—moved their boats into the Navy zone and set up a protest camp on the hill where Sanes was killed. They rechristened it Mount David in honor of the dead man. They were followed by Ruben Berrios Martinez, longtime head of the Puerto Rican Independence Party, who led a group onto another part of the Navy land, Allende Beach, where they set up another protest camp. Then yet another group of fishermen headed by Carlos Ventura set up its camp at Cayo Yayi, followed by one of the Puerto Rican teachers unions, which established a fourth camp. Each of the groups has kept supporters living in the camps day and night since May. They are vowing to remain until the Navy leaves or they are arrested. So many protesters have moved into the area that the Pentagon has been forced to suspend all maneuvers. . . .

Following the disintegration of the Rainbow, Latinos entered a new stage, which I have dubbed the Third Force period. From 1994 to 1997, citizenship applications to the Immigration and Naturalization Service nearly tripled, the overwhelming majority from Hispanics. This stampede to citizenship was caused by several factors. Most important was the spate of restrictive immigration laws that began with Proposition 187 in California and spread across the country. Until then, Mexicans had the lowest naturalization rates of any immigrant group. One study showed that only 3 percent of Mexicans admitted into the country in 1970 had become citizens by 1979. Many Mexicans had lived and worked in this country for years, but they rarely sought citizenship since they invariably expected to return home someday. Likewise, the Central Americans who fled civil wars in the '80s expected to return once those wars ended.

But the new immigration laws sparked a Latino backlash. Of the 3 million illegal immigrants who became legal U.S. residents under the 1986 amnesty, for instance, 2.6 million were from Latin America; as soon as they were eligible for citizenship in 1992, most opted for it. In addition, the Republican-sponsored ban in 1996 on federal benefits for legal permanent residents (later partially repealed) prompted hundreds of thousands who were here legally to seek citizenship. As soon as they were sworn in, those new citizens registered to vote.

Another factor in the rush to citizenship was the peace accords in Nicaragua, El Salvador and Guatemala, which ended the fighting but not the economic chaos in those countries. Once the wars ended, the Central American refugees suddenly turned into the main source of economic aid to their beleaguered nations through the billions of dollars they sent home each year. Because of that, both the immigrants and their home governments resisted their repatriation. More recently, Latin American governments adopted dual citizenship laws that allow their nationals to retain home country rights even if they become U.S. citizens.

The combination of all these factors turned the dormant potential of Latino politics into reality starting in 1996, when the Hispanic vote shocked political experts with both its explosive growth and its unpredictability. More than 5 million Latinos went to the polls that year, an astounding 20 percent increase from 1992. Those who came to the polls voted overwhelmingly for Bill Clinton and the Democratic Party. Clinton garnered 72 percent of the Latino vote, compared to 61 percent in 1992. Even in Florida, where Cubans had always voted solidly Republican, he grabbed 44 percent to Bob Dole's 46 percent. The seismic shift was best exemplified in California, where relative unknown Loretta Sanchez narrowly defeated right-wing congressman Robert Dornan in Orange County, historically a conservative stronghold.

The following year, local elections in many cities repeated the same pattern of high Hispanic turnout but showed the Latino vote was becoming less predictable. In the New York and Los Angeles mayoral races, for instance, not only did the number of Latino votes exceed that of blacks for the first time, but Latinos gave substantial backing to victorious Republican incumbents—45 percent to New York's Rudy Giuliani and 48 percent to L.A.'s Richard Riordan—while blacks voted heavily against both.

Overall, the number of Latinos casting votes nationwide more than doubled between 1980 and 1996 (from 2.1 million to 5 million), then it shot up an astounding 30 percent in the 2000 presidential election—to 6.5 million. In other words, the size of the nation's Latino vote has more than tripled in just two decades, and it seems sure to continue this phenomenal rate of increase, even if current immigration restrictions remain in force. The demographics leave no alternative. Those 6.5 million votes amount to less than a third of the 21 million Latinos of voting age in the country today, since many Hispanic adults are still not citizens and a good portion of those who are have yet to register. Furthermore, with nearly half of all Latinos in the United States under 25 compared to just a third of non-Latinos,

Two Navy commanders went to Jesse Jackson's San Juan hotel room at 6 A.M. to plead their case. . . . The two spent half an hour explaining to the civil rights leader why the live-fire practice conditions on Vieques can't be replicated anywhere else in the world. "You guys don't get it," Jackson told them, shaking his head. "These people don't want you here."

In the Philippines and in Panama, the people reached a point where they said the Navy must leave, Jackson told them. "Now they are saying it in Puerto Rico. It is undemocratic of us not to listen. Colonialism is a sin anywhere."

Rainbow/PUSH Coalition

The Rainbow Coalition was over, but Jesse Jackson still went to Vieques. "Colonialism is a sin anywhere," he said.

and with Hispanic fertility rates higher than non-Hispanics, the pool of potential voters will mushroom irreversibly for decades.

As the nation headed into the 2000 presidential elections, the Republican Party began a major internal debate. One wing of the party, realizing that the backlash of new Hispanic voters against the party's anti-immigrant policies had cost them the White House in 1996, urged a rejection of those polarizing views. This group—exemplified by George W. Bush—argued that, given the nation's rapidly changing population, the party would doom itself if it continued to be seen as anti-immigrant.

But there was another new force working feverishly for the allegiance of the millions of new Latino immigrants. The AFL-CIO, which for decades had supported legislation against undocumented immigrants because they supposedly threatened the jobs of union members, suddenly reversed itself under President John Sweeney and backed amnesty proposals for the undocumented. More importantly, the labor federation directed millions of dollars into new organizing drives in California, North Carolina, Florida and other states that were aimed specifically at low-paid immigrant workers.

As a result, exit polls during the 2000 presidential elections reported that Latinos nationwide gave Gore 62 percent of their votes, Bush 35 percent and Ralph Nader 3 percent. Bush's numbers were especially buoyed by his showing in his home state of Texas, which has the second-biggest Latino population in the nation and where 43 percent of Hispanics backed him. If the 2000 presidential race was the first where the American people began to realize that Hispanics were a new major factor in national politics, the local elections of 2001 soon brought home just how this growing vote could directly affect major centers of power.

Antonio Villaraigosa, former speaker of the California Assembly, electrified the country's largest Latino population with his campaign for mayor of Los Angeles. While

Return to South Central

JUAN GONZALEZ

September 18, 2000

Around the time the Democrats opened their convention at the Staples Center downtown, Margarita Reyes and her husband, Carlos, were having an afternoon sandwich inside the tiny shoe and clothing store they own near the intersection of Florence and Normandie avenues. The corner sits at the center of a story most politicians—both New Democrats and New Republicans—would like America to forget.

It was at Florence and Normandie in April 1992 that a crowd of angry blacks gathered after hearing that a Simi Valley jury had acquitted the cops who were caught on videotape brutally beating Rodney King. What followed was the nation's worst riot of the 20th century. By the time it was over, the arson and looting had spread throughout this sprawling city, more than 50 people were dead and thousands had been arrested. . . .

Even before the rioting, this had been a neighborhood beset by drug trafficking and violence, long abandoned by the scores of factories that once provided its residents with jobs and some measure of hope. At the time, the rest of the country saw it as a black riot, even though the biggest group of people arrested during the disturbances was Hispanic, most of them immigrants picked up by police and National Guard troops for violating curfew or petty looting.

South Central, like the rest of this city and like so much of our nation, was a place undergoing a startling transformation. It was not only poor, but longtime black residents were moving out and being rapidly replaced by Mexican and Central American immigrants—newcomers fleeing a poverty and desperation in their homelands that could make the worst ghetto in this country seem like paradise.

Villaraigosa led the vote in the first round of balloting in a crowded field of the nonpartisan election, he eventually lost a hard-fought run-off to James K. Hahn, a white liberal. Latino voter turnout, however, skyrocketed. Hispanics, who comprise more than 40 percent of Los Angeles, had been 15 percent of the electorate in 1997, but jumped to 22 percent in 2001. Hahn's victory showed that the fault lines of Jesse Jackson's Rainbow Coalition had become a chasm. While Villaraigosa claimed more than 80 percent of the Latino vote, Hahn, whose father had been a longtime backer of civil rights, captured 80 percent of the black vote.

In San Antonio, however, a different scenario emerged. With the city's Latino population at a record 58 percent, Ed Garza, a 32-year-old urban planner, won a landslide vote. Garza racked up huge support among the city's Latinos, and he managed to win close to 40 percent of the white vote, a far better share than Villaraigosa in Los Angeles. But the overall turnout in the election was astoundingly low—barely 15 percent of registered voters went to the polls.

Finally, in New York, Public Advocate Mark Green, a white liberal who had long been considered the front-runner, found himself locked in a neck-and-neck race with Bronx Borough President Fernando Ferrer. Ferrer, who was born in Puerto Rico, fashioned a black-Latino coalition for the main part of his support, but that very success prompted the city's political establishment to attack his campaign as racially divisive. Ferrer surprised many observers by leading the first-round vote, which was delayed by the September 11 attack on the World Trade Center, but Green won the racially charged run-off two weeks later (yet would lose to Michael Bloomberg in the general election). Still, the emergence of Ferrer as a credible candidate alerted the city's ruling elite that Latinos are a force that can no longer be ignored.

Most experts argue that the new Latino electorate will never function in nearly the unified fashion that blacks have done

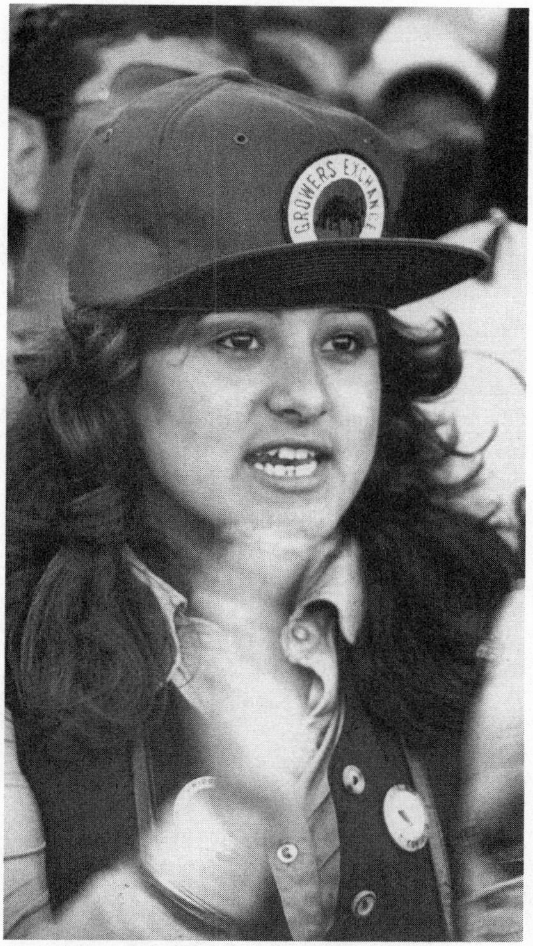

Nick Allen

A new Latino political awakening has the potential to reinvigorate and reconfigure the American left.

Only eight years later, that transformation is even more pronounced. You see it in the businesses around Florence and Normandie. Margarita Reyes, who is from El Salvador, and her husband, who is from Guatemala, opened their store only three months ago. Up the street is the Cuba/Mexico Night Club. There is Pancho's convenience store and Rosa's Party Supplies and Hilda's Hair

Salon and Club Las Hadas—all owned by Latinos. None existed there before the riot. And so it goes all over Los Angeles, where Hispanics now comprise 45 percent of all residents. The same scenario is being repeated throughout the country. The number of Hispanics turning out at the polls, joining labor unions and getting involved in American civic life in general has skyrocketed.

Paul Mauldin, a black man and longtime resident, was busy repairing an engine at the Baby I'm Back Auto Care Shop, just down the street from the Reyes' clothing store. Mauldin, 47, moved to Los Angeles from Tyler, Texas, in 1977. "All the blacks are moving to Riverside or San Bernardino," he says. "Nothing but Spanish moving in." . . .

After decades of broken promises, local blacks are deeply bitter. They seethe at a Clinton-era prosperity that whizzed past South Central like traffic on the freeway. I asked Maudlin about the Democrats and the convention downtown. "I don't pay them no mind," he says. "Never voted in my life. Never heard one of them say something that made me want to."

The Latino newcomers on the other hand, haven't had time to become disillusioned. Margarita Reyes became a citizen only this year; her husband is still a permanent resident. She concedes she hasn't followed Gore or Bush, and doesn't know what either of them stands for. "It's my first chance to vote in November," she says. "I'm looking forward to it."

Over at the Staples Center, the Democrats, allegedly the party of working people, spent the week raising more money from big corporate donors and putting on a glitzy performance for television that blissfully ignored the growing number of workers so turned off to politics that they refuse to vote; or those, like Reyes, who can't tell Bush and Gore apart. In South Central, and in the neighborhoods like it across America—those places where people make less than $20,000 a year—

historically. The terms "Hispanic" or "Latino," they note, are useless umbrella categories masking huge ethnic differences, and they predict Latinos will gradually adopt voting patterns closer to the old European immigrants. While the first conclusion is certainly true, the second fails to grasp the emergence during the past several decades of a rich new Latino identity. From what was at first a largely Mexican-American population in the Southwest and a Puerto Rican enclave in New York City, the different Hispanic groups have undergone cultural amalgamation among themselves—through intermarriage, through shared knowledge of one another's music, food and traditions, through language, through a common experience of combating prejudice and being shunted into the same de facto segregated neighborhoods. No longer do a handful of Mexican-American or Puerto Rican or Cuban groups dominate the national debate on Hispanics; rather, the leaders of once disparate groups are now speaking with a more unified voice.

Some studies claim the Latino electorate is conservative at heart. True, wherever Hispanic communities achieve relative prosperity—in places like Miami and Orlando, northern New Mexico and Contra Costa County, California—they inevitably become more conservative in their voting patterns. But Hispanics remain overwhelmingly concentrated among the country's working- and lower-middle-class sectors. Latinos are constantly influenced by news of how people in their homelands are struggling to survive in the new global economy. Those economic realities, together with the anti-Hispanic bias they confront each day in the United States, continually force Hispanics of all nationalities to bind together to defend their interests.

Furthermore, Latin American immigrants are more politically sophisticated than most of us realize. They come from countries where civil wars and political strife have forced them to pay attention to politics. Because the continuing economic crisis in Latin America means more immigrants will keep coming, and because of the maturing of interethnic Hispanic identity here, I have no doubt that the 21st century will lead to a full awakening of the voting power of Latinos. According to one recent study, by 2025 Latinos and African-Americans will constitute 52 percent of the population of Texas, 50 percent in California and New Mexico, 43 percent in New York, 41 percent in Florida, 36 percent in Arizona, 34 percent in Nevada, and 31 percent in Illinois; and in each of those states, Latinos will be the dominant group.

What does the rapid growth of Latino political power signify for the American left? Does it merely represent the emergence of a new Latino petty capitalist class that will use nationalistic appeals to grab a share of political power but end up only dividing American workers? That danger certainly exists, but just because a particular historical development contains pitfalls doesn't necessarily mean it must be avoided—even if it could be. The fact is that for many Latinos, especially for the Mexican-Americans and Puerto Ricans, the bourgeois democratic revolution was never completed.

Much like African-Americans did in the '70s and '80s, the Latino masses must pass through a period of fighting for equality of political representation, of completing their democratic revolution. Only then—after they have learned through their own experiences that whether a political leader is black, white, Asian or Hispanic has very little to do with his or her commitment to radical social change, will they thoroughly grasp the class nature of American society. Those who would seek to skip this stage of political development and just tell people to forget their racial and ethnic differences, or to forget the very real ways that those differences are used to target specific groups of national and racial minorities, do not understand the actual process by which political consciousness evolves among masses of people.

To the extent that the awakening Latino political movement in this country allies with organized labor and the environmental, women's and anti-globalization movements, and to the extent that it helps to limit the strategic options available to the capitalist class in the United States, it should be welcomed as an important new front in the fight for progressive social change.

barely two out of 10 adults vote these days. These are neighborhoods neither party has ever really cared about, except for those moments when they explode and spoil the show.

ITT Archives

"Raza Sí, Guerra No," a mural by Aurelio Diaz.

Mexico 2061

ILAN STAVANS

October 14, 1992

I had a dream in which I saw Mexico's future. It must have been short—a matter of seconds, not even a minute. Yet I get the feeling I spent months, perhaps years, talking to the nation's proud inhabitants, spending nights at the home of perfect strangers, gathering every kind of information with journalistic thirst. A perplexing vision. What follows is not a scene-by-scene recreation, but a summary, incomplete yet faithful to the overall message.

According to my calculations, the dream must have been set in the year 2061—surely the month of April, when heavy rains clean the nation's capital. The urban landscape of my childhood had vanished, replaced by ultra-modern architecture without the slightest hint of Baroque colonial style. The North American Free Trade Agreement, I was told by a polite Asian lady almost fluent in what sounded like Spanish, was signed in early 1993. While dissenting voices in Montreal and Washington criticized important parts of its content, a moratorium was introduced, and popular support grew overwhelmingly. Thus a new global culture emerged, one with Hispanic, French and Anglo elements intermingled. Mexico was not part of Latin America anymore.

In a matter of years, jobs multiplied and businesses big and small boomed across the hemisphere. Supermarkets in cities as distant as Anchorage, Quebec, Hermosillo and Atlanta were invaded with once-restricted goods and technology, like exotic fruits (mango, papaya, sapote, chirimoya) from Chiapas and Japanese cellular phones.

In a matter of decades, the geographic border between the United States and Mexico was abolished. A high-speed highway was built between Tenochtitlán (as Mexico City had been re-renamed) and Los Angeles, now the city with the highest population of Mexicans. According to a computer network, a few years before my visit the peso was replaced by a new kind of dollar as the hemisphere's currency. Patriotism acquired a different dimension. Interviewees told me the capital was the city of Texasville, yet many government offices, including the Defense Department, were located in downtown Tenochtitlán.

After NAFTA was signed, Mexicans quickly learned English. People thought it would become Mexico's new official language. But a strange phenomenon took place: Spanglish—what some referred to as *calo pachuco*, a hybrid half Shakespeare, half Cervantes—became an astonishing linguistic force. Television, radio and the print media soon modified their communication codes to accommodate the new dialect. By 2061, a vast quantity of unrecognizable words circulated, to such a degree that I had difficulty understanding passersby and waitresses.

Almost simultaneously, with the fall of communism in China, a monumental influx of laborious Asian immigrants settled in California and Tenochtitlán. Miscegenation began. Children of mixed marriages among Asians, Mexicans and Anglos increased in number. *Hunger de Poder*, and epoch-making book by Dr. Alejandro Morales III, a theoretician at the University of Ciudad Juarez, claimed a new race was born: *la arroza de plata*—the silver race of the rice people. The once-called Chicanos or Mexican-Americans, some 25 million in the early decades of the 21st century, became a collective symbol, the precursor to the current racial mix. Cesar Chavez, the agrarian union activist, was stamped on redesigned $100 bills.

Mexico, as I knew it, had vanished into oblivion. Yet the day-to-day reality of the United States and Canada was transfigured at least as drastically. The Rio Grande, once an artificial division, was just like the Mississippi River—a natural sight, a commercial avenue. Purity in culture was unretrievable.

I woke up uneasily at dawn with Nietzsche's dictum in my mind: Only the past, not the future, is a lie.

Pride and Politics

WHATEVER HAPPENED TO GAY LIBERATION?

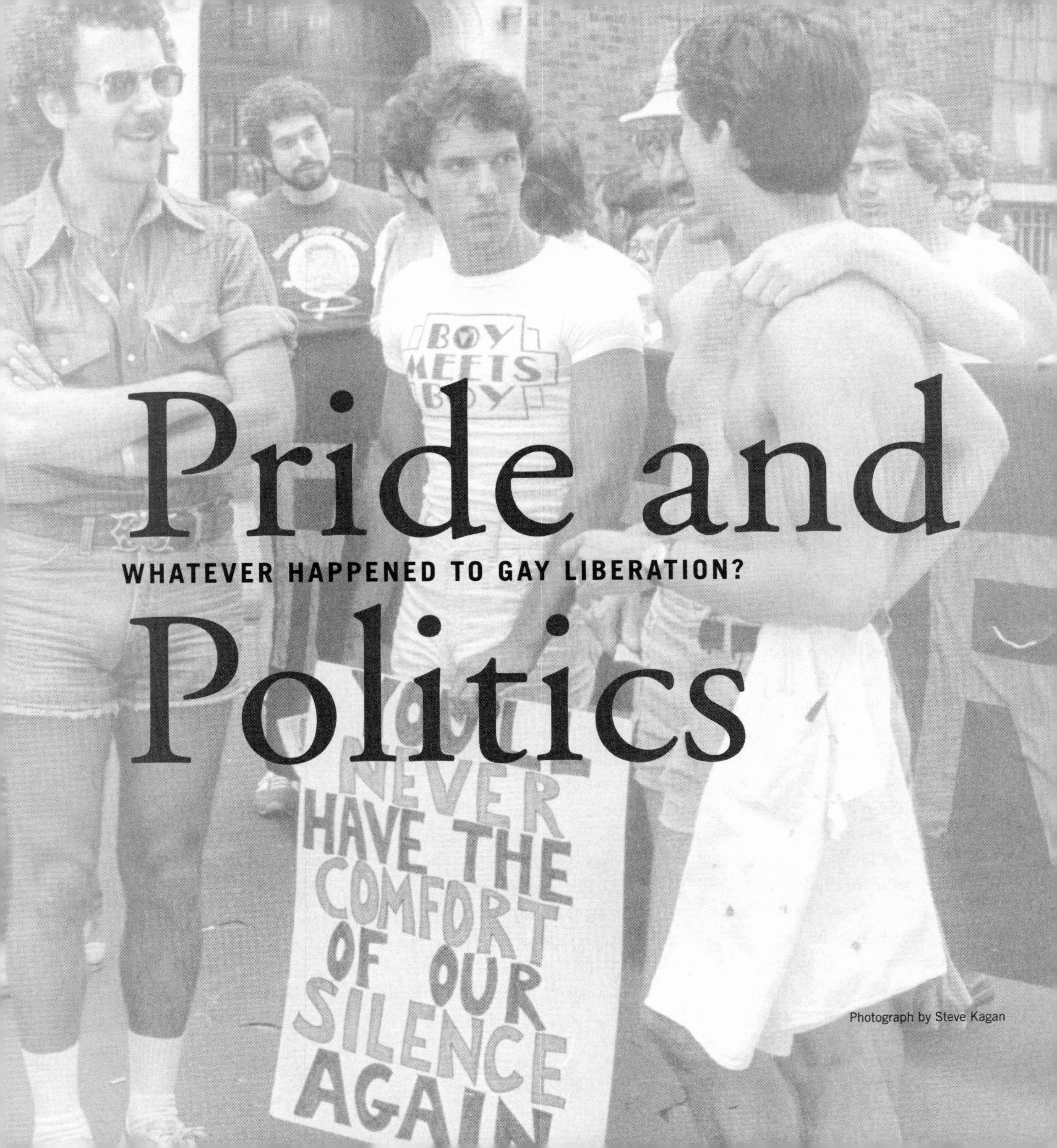
BOY
MEETS
BOY
NEVER
HAVE THE
COMFORT
OF OUR
SILENCE
AGAIN

Photograph by Steve Kagan

Seven

DOUG IRELAND

WHEN I MENTIONED TO A LESBIAN FRIEND OF MINE THAT I HAD BEEN ASKED TO CONTRIBUTE A REFLECTION TO THIS VOLUME ON GAY POLITICS OVER THE past 25 years—where we have been and whither we are tending—she laughed. "My poor dear," she said, "all you have to do is write two sentences: There is no movement. The guppies have won." (Guppies, for those who don't know, is a queer term for "gay yuppies.")

Those who are not gay, or younger queers who have come of age in an enlarged cultural space they now take for granted, may find my friend's half-joking comment incomprehensible. Are there not more same-sexers (Gore Vidal's useful term) out of the closet and open about whom they choose to love than ever before? Are there not more gay organizations, associations, lobbies and community centers than ever before? Aren't the annual gay pride marches larger than they've ever been—and more numerous?

But like me, my lesbian friend grew up politically in the social movements of the '60s and embraced gay activism in the first days of its flowering in the early '70s. In the early years after the 1969 Stonewall riot in Greenwich Village, and well into the '70s, the project of the gay movement was called "gay liberation." Let me suggest what that meant to us then.

In the first quarter-century after World War II, homosexual attraction was still "the love that dare not speak its name," to quote from the famous poem that helped send Oscar Wilde to prison. Love between two people of the same gender was defined by medicine and law as a "sickness" and a danger; it was illegal, a fact underscored by the witch hunts that purged homosexuals from the government during McCarthyism. Historian Allen Berube has documented how the war played an important role in fostering the growth of the homosexual subcultures that already existed in the large urban centers of the two coasts. But the mob-connected gay bars and public cruising areas that defined that subculture then were subjected to regular (often brutal) police raids. Same-sexers were forced by their families and the state to undergo institutionalization, electroshock and other torturous "cures." When homosexuals were portrayed in mass culture, they were presented as stereotypic figures of derision or tragedy. The dominant culture taught homosexuals to hate themselves.

Gay liberation was a radical rebellion against all this. It insisted—to borrow from the title of an early film by the German *cineaste* Rosa von Praunheim—that "it is not the homosexual who is perverse, but the society in which he lives." Drawing from feminist critiques of the tyrannies of patriarchy and the family, it rejected the white, middle-class male culture's patriarchal attitudes, hierarchies and rituals (homophobia and misogyny were seen as two sides of the same coin). It insisted on the right to plural desires and opposed "any prescription for how consenting adults may or must make love," as Martin Duberman put it. Gay liberation was, he said, "a rite of passage—not into manhood or womanhood as those states have been traditionally defined; not sanctioned by supernatural doctrine; not blueprinted by centuries of ritualized behavior; not greeted by kinship rejoicing and social acceptance; not marked by the extension of fellowship into the established adult community," but rather to placing "ourselves in the forefront of the newest and most far-reaching revolution: the recharacterization of sexuality."

Gay liberation saw itself as "a paradigm of resistance" to the stultifying political culture of the Nixon years and was infused with a sense of commitment to unleashing the collective energies of a hitherto invisible people as part of the much larger effort to maximize social justice and human liberation for all. Since official liberalism rejected gay liberation as a "pathetic" celebration of "perversion," we felt it was doubly subversive and were proud of it.

The accomplishments of the gay liberation movement were many. It shattered forever the silence that had imprisoned same-sexers in untenable solitude and alienation; its

Founder of a Movement

BRUCE MIRKEN

March 20, 1991

On a November afternoon in 1950, five men gathered at Harry Hay's house on Cove Avenue in Los Angeles. What they were there to do seemed so daring, so dangerous, that it had taken Hay years of persuading, prodding and cajoling to find even five who were willing to attempt it. That day Harry Hay, Chuck Rowland, Bob Hull, Dale Jennings and Rudi Gernreich founded the Mattachine Society, the first ongoing gay organization in the United States.

It is hard to remember how utterly different things were for gays in 1950. Gay sex was illegal in every state. Many localities, Los Angeles included, had laws forbidding gatherings of "deviants," and any bar or other establishment that served homosexuals was in constant danger of being shut down by the police. Gay meeting places were "totally underground," Hay recalls. "Were it open knowledge, the cops would be all over the place, and you'd be in the clink in nothing flat, because to make a pass at another person was a lewd act, and a lewd act opened you up to five years in jail. You'd have to register as a sex offender for the rest of your life."

In such a poisonous atmosphere, getting people to show up for a meeting of gays was impossible. As a fig leaf, Hay concocted the idea of establishing a discussion group on the subject of the recently published Kinsey Report, which had dealt extensively with the subject of male homosexual behavior. Even so, he says, his gay friends "wouldn't touch it with a 10-foot pole," because they were "absolutely terrified" at the thought that the police might be there. Only with two years of effort and the assistance of his lover, Gernreich, did he manage to bring off that first small, furtive meeting.

It wasn't the first time in his life Harry Hay had done something daring, and it wouldn't be the last. In the '30s and '40s, he had been an active member raucous, media-savvy confrontations changed the nature of public discourse on homosexuality (symbolized by the insistence on the word "gay"—a code word for same-sex love for over a century—instead of the clinical, one-dimensional term "homosexual"). The most significant victory was the successful fight to have the American Psychiatric Association drop same-sex attraction from its catalog of "disorders" in 1973. And, of course, it made coming out—the most radical act in a homophobic society—not only the basis of mental and emotional health for gay people, but the imperative for creating the political movement that could carry through the fight for civil rights.

As more and more people began to come out, thanks to the liberationists' clamorous visibility, the out gay community increasingly began to reflect the demographic, political and cultural makeup of the society as a whole. The gay liberation movement—the one my lesbian friend laments—became the gay rights movement. Gay liberation considered innate homosexuality as much of a challenge to a suffocating and unjust social order as the political radicalism that many of its proponents embraced. But it was transformed in a relatively short time into a quest for full citizenship. Or, as former *Socialist Review* editor Jeffrey Escoffier put it in his 1998 book *American Homo: Community and Perversity*, the liberation movement "celebrated the otherness, the differentness, and the marginality of the homosexual; whereas the gay politics of citizenship acknowledges the satisfaction of conforming, passing, belonging and being accepted."

The deradicalization of the gay movement was accelerated by a number of factors. For one thing, gay liberation was largely the work of people who had been participants in or influenced by the '60s movements for black civil rights and against the Vietnam War or by labor struggles. As the first generation of activists began to burn out, the movement was populated with younger people with little or no previous history of political protest. Simultaneously, the fulgurant rise of the commercial gay ghetto and the emergence of the gay mar-

of the Communist Party, deeply involved in party organizing. His dedication to leftist causes was one of the reasons he suppressed his homosexuality in a heterosexual marriage for 13 years. The party at that time had no room for deviants.

His Communist past eventually forced him out of his role in the Mattachine Society. In February 1953, at the height of the McCarthy era, Hay was named in a Los Angeles newspaper as a Marxist music teacher—the one thing more scandalous than being a homosexual. Mattachine, which by this point had grown into a network with roughly 2,000 members, put out a statement disassociating itself from any political, cultural or religious ideology, and its governing council agreed unanimously that Hay could not have any public association with the group. It turned out to be the first step in the decline of Mattachine as a politically active group; as the '50s progressed, the organization became quiet, respectable and assimilationist, bent on blending in with mainstream society.

This assimilationist tendency of many gay groups still rankles Hay today. "One of the big problems," he says, "is that we ourselves trigger the homophobia that we suffer from when we rush up to tell the heteros that we're exactly the same as they are except in a minor particular. They know fucking well we aren't."

ket contributed to the rapid growth of an out gay middle class, which saw itself as having more of a stake in the existing social order than the younger marginals and intellectuals who made up the movement's first wave. Finally, the backlash against visible homosexuality and against the demand for full gay citizenship drove the movement to seek political advances through a more traditional form of interest-group politics. The need to appeal to the non-gay electorate helped water down and eventually dim the radical liberationist discourse (in this, the gay movement did not escape the fate of other initially radical social protest movements).

Two symbolic events, which may be said to mark the end of gay liberation, contributed to putting the changing movement on the defensive and to adopting a less radical coloration: The crushing defeat of the Dade County, Florida gay civil rights ordinance by Anita Bryant's "Save Our Children" crusade in 1977, and the murder of openly gay San Francisco City Supervisor Harvey Milk the following year. The results of the Dade County referendum and the light prison sentence for murdering Milk and pro-gay mayor George Moscone given to Dan White, the homophobic fireman-turned-politician, underscored just how profoundly resistant society was to assuring even minimal rights or protections for its same-sexers. So did the defeat in 1978 of gay civil rights ordinances in St. Paul, Minnesota; Eugene, Oregon; and Wichita, Kansas.

And then came AIDS.

From 1981, when it was first identified as a "gay cancer," until well into the '90s, AIDS was used to stigmatize homosexuals, especially gay males, by the political homophobes of the right. Whatever shreds of liberationist thinking and attitudes that remained in the gay community were effectively snuffed out. First, the epidemic and the social opprobrium it brought with it forced the gay community to turn back in upon itself in a struggle to survive: Government was entirely absent from the fight against AIDS in the Reagan years, so the burden of prevention, education and even care for the sick fell

On Their Own

JOSHUA DRESSLER

June 22, 1977

There seems to be a backlash already visible from the Dade County vote. Anita Bryant has announced that she plans to carry her crusade to Minnesota and to California to organize a movement against "permissive" laws in those places. Indeed, one Minnesota state senator has announced that he and other anti-gays (can you imagine a state senator in 1977 saying he was leading an anti-black crusade?) would take advantage of Bryant's presence not only to urge repeal of the Minneapolis anti-discrimination statute, but to enact a state law that would require the imprisonment of convicted homosexuals.

Whether gays can combat this ignorance and fear is unclear. But one of their main obstacles comes not from the fundamentalist right, but from the so-called progressive left. Although many of us may agree that Anita Bryant is crazy, few of us seem willing to stand side-by-side with gays. We seem afraid of being thought of as gay, thus demonstrating our own prejudices.

Consequently, much of the support from the left, when it has come at all, has been narrow. Until the left gets its collective head as straight as some of its sexual leanings, and until the left—especially socialists—demonstrates the courage it has historically shown in support of other oppressed groups, gays will be on their own.

on homosexuals themselves. AIDS consumed an enormous amount of the gay community's money and energies, as we took day-to-day responsibility for our afflicted "extended families" of friends and lovers. This grimmest of reapers also took thousands of gay liberation's most original and tireless activists, a loss unparalleled in the history of any other American social movement.

Furthermore, any radicalism that still existed in the gay community—primarily from younger activists—was increasingly channeled into the fight against AIDS with the founding of ACT-UP. The struggle for simple survival took primacy over the larger issues of social and sexual transformation. (One positive element of the AIDS crisis: Many of the tensions between men and women that had bedeviled the gay movement from its inception were dramatically lessened. The outpouring of solidarity and compassion from lesbians in combating the epidemic was impressive and moving.)

By the end of the '90s, the institutionalization of the gay movement was complete. The largest and most visible national gay political organizations—like the Human Rights Campaign (HRC) and the National Gay and Lesbian Task Force (NGLTF)—have adopted a top-down, corporate structure that demands little more of their members than writing a check (or occasionally a letter to a public official). In their endless search for corporate sponsorships for gay events and activities, in their insistence on presenting a homogenized and false image of gay people, the gay institutions and their nest-feathering and access-obsessed gaycrats are committing serious strategic and tactical errors that play into the hands of our heavily funded and organizationally sophisticated enemies on the right.

The image of gay people these groups present is often an alarmingly false one. When the religious right coalesced to put on a national advertising campaign asserting that "homosexuals can be cured," the HRC, a Washington lobby

Gay Body Politics

RICHARD KAYE

October 19, 1983

Now that some of the dust has cleared from the subject of this mysterious and deadly ailment, it is worth examining just what the recent appearance of AIDS—as well as the scare it has caused—means for the homosexual community, the gay movement and those who consider themselves friends of—the phrase seems almost quaint these days—gay liberation.

However the gay community has been represented or misrepresented by the mainstream media,

ITT Archives

AIDS took thousands of gay liberation's most original and tireless activists.

nearly all gay leaders argue that the appearance of a deadly disease affecting gay men for which there is as yet no cure will have a radical effect on the gay community. "It has presented the most radical challenge to the homosexual community, since the legacy of the Stonewall Riots, which occurred more than 10 years ago," insists Dennis Altman, author of a number of books on the gay movement.

"Curiously enough, gay identity, once secured, is now endangered by two perils, one tragic, the other theoretical and possibly benign," wrote Edmund White recently. The theoretical danger he refers to is the right-wing backlash that has come with AIDS, from groups like Dallas Doctors Against AIDS—working for the criminalization of homosexuality for health reasons—and the Moral Majority, whose newsletter regularly warns that "America's families" are under attack by a hazardous gay lifestyle. But for White and other gay leaders, the issue that is at least as important as the reactionary response to AIDS is the question of how the gay community will respond to the medical threat to gay relations that AIDS presents.

For a large number of gay men, sexual promiscuity has been a key means for the expression of gay identity. "Sexual promiscuity," maintains White, "or at least the possibility of sexual adventure, has for a long time now been the essential glue holding the urban gay ghetto together. The bars, the baths, the discos are still sites for cruising. Whereas lesbians united over feminist issues—economic, legal and sociological—gay men have few ideological banners everyone is willing to march under other than the oriflamme of sexual freedom."

The oriflamme of sexual freedom, one of the more permanent holdovers from '60s activism, has not been a banner solely for the homosexual community (women, too, learned the value of shedding some of the more suffocating restraints on individual sexual freedom). But it has been gay men who in the past 10 years have sought sexual libertarianism

with a $14 million budget (growing every year), responded with an ad campaign that portrayed gays as white, middle-class and religious. That may be the profile of the HRC's fundraising base, but it's hardly an accurate picture of real life as lived by same-sexers. Antics like these contain a hidden danger. There have been any number of studies in recent years showing that homosexuals are far from being the privileged, affluent types of media clichés and HRC ads. The average gay man earns less than his heterosexual counterpart, and the earning gap for lesbians with straight women as well as men is even more striking. By ignoring the poor, the black and the brown, groups like the HRC are playing into the attempts by right-wing homophobes to portray gays as a powerful, privileged group with insidious influence that is demanding "special rights" denied to others.

Neither does this do much for gay civil rights at the ballot box. In the 2000 elections, supposedly tolerant Maine voters *repealed* an anti-discrimination law for gays passed by the state legislature; gay-bashing Defense of Marriage acts passed in Nebraska and Nevada; and a vicious anti-gay education referendum was only narrowly defeated in supposedly liberal Oregon. The professional homophobes of the religious right, meanwhile, have adopted a highly effective strategy in the past few years aimed at states and localities. Every year there are more referenda and anti-gay bills being introduced in state legislatures, aimed at everything from prohibiting gay couples from adopting kids (in a country where there are scads of orphaned and abandoned kids waiting to be adopted), to criminalizing AIDS transmission, to banning realistic sex education that could save the lives of kids both straight and gay.

Increasingly, money is dominating the gay political agenda. Gays gave at least $20 million to the Democratic Party in the 2000 election cycle, most of it from rich fat-cats. The Gill Foundation, launched a few years ago by Tim Gill, a computer mogul who founded Quark, gives away $25 million a year to gay groups, but nearly all of that money goes to "mainstream" gay institutions. Because the foundation has a policy against funding "urban concerns," it rarely gives to organizations representing or serving people of color or doing local organizing (of which there are at least 45 vibrant organizations in New York City alone). The Gill Foundation also hosts an annual summit retreat in Aspen, Colorado for gay funders. Where their money goes significantly influences what direction organized gay activities will take, yet the folks who don't conform to the preferred gay stereotype rarely get a hearing, let alone a check.

Nothing better illustrates the shortcomings of the institutionalized gay movement than its total co-optation by the Clinton administration. Some may find it comforting that an executive order now makes it possible to be openly gay and work for the CIA or FBI without fear of discrimination, but I choose to remember the long list of Clinton's betrayals. They include instituting the infamous "Don't Ask, Don't Tell" policy on gays in the military, which led to a huge upswing in verbal and physical assaults on gay people in uniform (who could not complain since that would be "telling") and an annual increase in the number of gays discharged; asking for so little money that Congress actually increased AIDS appropriations *every year* over what Clinton requested; overruling the entire medical community in refusing to support clean needles for drug users; hypocritically preaching the failed policy of "abstinence only" sex education for the young (among whom AIDS infections are soaring); signing the gay-bashing Defense of Marriage Act (and then boasting about it in ads played in Middle America but not on the more gay-friendly coasts) to secure re-election; and so much more.

But by a clever combination of symbolism, rhetorical prestidigitation and patronage jobs, the Clinton administration lulled the overwhelming majority of the out gay community—now a mass phenomenon, with the increasingly significant gay vote much sought after in a number of states—into a false sense that it had a sure ally in the White House (just as the administration that abolished welfare

as a means of dealing with a felt disenfranchisement from mainstream society.

It is worth remembering that, whatever the exceptional gains of the gay liberation movement—and this includes everything from gay rights legislative wins in cities such as Madison, Wisconsin, to the appearance of gay characters on prime-time television programs—the vast majority of homosexuals in this country feel compelled to hide their homosexuality from their families and employers. It is still a weighty task to come out as a homosexual today, no better summed up than in a recent AIDS joke making the rounds: "Question: What's the hardest part of telling your mother you have AIDS? Answer: Persuading her that you're Haitian." . . .

After years of political bickering within the gay activist community, which often prevented a full-fledged mobilization of forces, AIDS has politicized homosexuals in a way Jerry Falwell could never quite do. "The number of people AIDS has brought out into the politically active community—many of them out of the closet—is very exciting to me," insists Jeff Levi, the Washington representative for the National Gay Task Force. "When it's life-or-death, it's worth risking your job. I haven't experienced this kind of caring or activism since the very early days of gay liberation."

"My hope," adds Edmund White, "is that the current health crisis and the philosophical quandary about gay identity will somehow lead to a more profound vision of community."

Our Lips Are Sealed

DAVID FUTRELLE

June 14, 1993

I have a dream.

I have a dream that one day in the office of Sam Nunn, an office now cluttered with nervous men in suits, little gay soldiers and sailors will be able to join hands with little straight soldiers and sailors, without anyone really knowing which of them is which. And no one asking or telling. I have a dream today.

I have a dream that one day this nation will rise up and live out the true meaning of its creed: "Our lips are sealed." This is no time to engage in the luxury of cooling off, or to take the tranquilizing drug of gradualism: Now is the time not to speak. Now is the time not to ask, not to tell.

I have a dream that one day, in the showers of our great Army barracks, the water shall be neither too hot nor too cold, and the tile surfaces will be shiny and bright and not too covered with mildew, and gay men and straight men will share soap together, and not one of them will publicly admire the buttocks of another, except in the spirit of brotherhood. I have a dream today.

This is our hope. With this faith we will be able to work together, pray together, shower together, sleep together—uh, in separate bunks, I mean—without anyone the wiser.

This will be the day when all of God's children will be able to sing with new meaning: "It doesn't matter what they say / In the jealous games people play / Our lips are sealed." Our lips are sealed in the halls of Congress. Our lips are sealed in the mess halls of Fort Bragg. Our lips are sealed, especially, in the bunks and the showers of our great naval vessels on the high sea. In every barrack, our lips are sealed, our eyes are averted and our knees are locked together.

When our lips are sealed, as per official military protocol, we will be able to speed up that day

hornswoggled the black community to get re-elected). That the HRC traded access to the White House for its independence, and photo-ops for silence, is hardly surprising: The treasurer of the Democratic National Committee is a member of its board. But even the NGLTF, putatively the more progressive of the Washington gay lobbies, decided to celebrate the lame-duck Clinton administration by throwing a December 2000 party for all of its gay patronage appointees. Meanwhile, there wasn't a peep out of either group when Clinton never lifted a finger to help pass the Employment Non-Discrimination Act in the year it failed the Senate by only one vote.

The eclipse of gay radicalism meant that there were few voices raised in the Clinton years to say that the emperor had no clothes. There was one notable exception: the protests by AIDS radicals from ACT-UP, the Health Gap Coalition and campus groups over the Clinton administration's use of economic and political blackmail to prevent the nations of Africa and the Third World from making generic versions of AIDS drugs to fight the global pandemic. The point man in the administration's policy of carrying water for the pharmaceutical industry was Al Gore, and by targeting his presidential campaign, the younger AIDS radicals—using the confrontational tactics and civil disobedience that were employed in the first years of gay liberation to great effect—forced a partial retreat, at least on South Africa. (But once Gore lost, the lame-ducks launched a new assault on Brazil for making cheap copies of AIDS drugs for free distribution.) However, these AIDS radicals found their anti-Gore protests criticized by mainstream groups like the HRC and AIDS Action (the Washington lobby representing the 3,500 local AIDS service organizations, almost all initially founded by the gay community, that are now dependent on federal funding to maintain their bureaucracies).

Cutting-edge politics and radical critiques have found little echo in today's gay press, which, instead of serving as a watchdog, has become a homogenized creature of its advertisers. Gay people are more visible than ever before, especially on television. But despite the camp sensibility that is apparent in hit shows like *Will and Grace* and *Queer as Folk*, this is little more than gay minstrelsy. Most of the product being mass-marketed as gay culture, in fact, is just as insipid as its heterosexual counterparts. Yet the gay press celebrates them uncritically, as it does any cultural offering with a gay theme, no matter how trivializing it may be of real gay life.

A 2001 merger combined the largest gay media outlets—*Out* and *The Advocate* magazines, the Internet companies PlanetOut and Gay.com, the largest gay book publisher, Alyson, and more—into one giant media conglomerate. (*Out*, by the way, tried for two years to market a kind of designer apathy under the label "post-gay," while *The Advocate* long ago turned into an entertainment-oriented fanzine, a kind of gay *People*.) Even *New York* magazine, the chronicler of yuppie consumer chic, which consecrated the triumph of gay commercialism with a March 2001 special issue on "Gay Life Now," commented: "These media outlets, once valuable to the extent they served the community, are now redefined purely as assets and sold to the highest bidder."

Major investors in the merged company will include such mainstream players as Chase Capital Partners, Silicon Valley's Mayfield Fund, AOL Investments and the Creative Artists Agency. The purchase of the *Washington Blade* and its chain of gay weeklies by a gay PR company that has hired itself out to corporations (like United Airlines) targeted by boycotts for anti-gay discrimination is further evidence of the corporatization of the gay press.

◎

What remains of the movement my lesbian friend pronounced dead? About the only place one can still find shards of liberationist thinking is in the academy. But none of this ever reaches a mass gay audience or gets noticed in an understandable way by the gay media. Sex Panic, a liberationist agitprop group launched in 1997 by two gay intellectuals—

when all of God's children, gay men and straight men, butches and femmes, rubber fetishists and those who prefer leather, those who do it standing up and those who prefer the missionary position, will be able to join, um, hands—without anyone disclosing any of these various proclivities or mentioning the National Gay and Lesbian Task Force or RuPaul or Judy Garland or any of those other dead giveaways—and sing, in the words of that great Go-Go's song, "Our lips are sealed, our lips are sealed, our lips are sealed!"

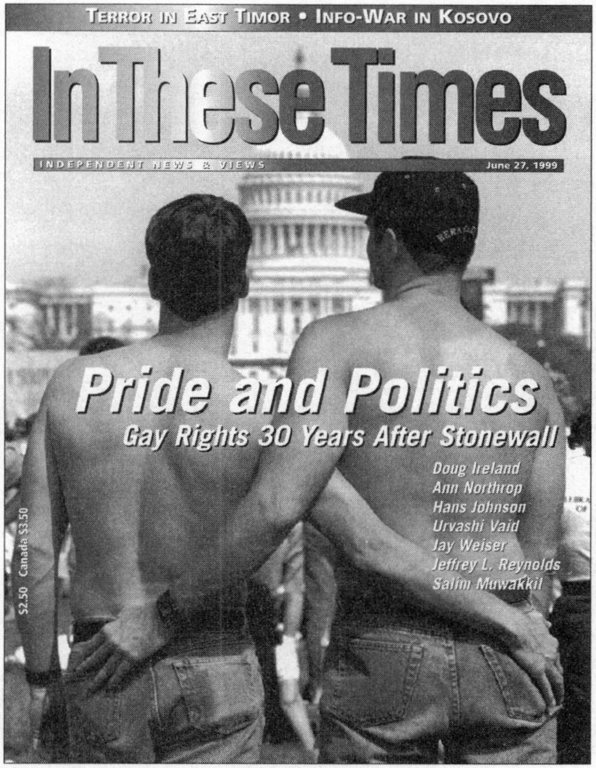

ITT Archives

The eclipse of gay radicalism meant there were few voices raised in the Clinton years to say that the emperor had no clothes.

Michael Warner, author of *The Trouble With Normal*, and Douglas Crimp, former editor of *October*—folded after only two years.

One of the few contemporary liberationist thinkers who writes well enough to be readable by a large audience is Michael Bronski, whose brilliant book *The Pleasure Principle: Sex, Backlash, and the Struggle for Gay Freedom* deserves a wider readership. As Bronski writes:

> The reality for gay people is two-fold. Most gay men and lesbians lead lives in which they worry about their jobs, paying the rent, and making ends meet; some gay people have children and all the responsibilities that come with them. They share, then, many of the same economic anxieties as heterosexuals, although these similarities are almost never discussed in the mainstream media. Yet as social outsiders, gay people have a unique vantage point from which to critique mainstream culture, explore new concepts of gender and sexual relationships, and create innovation and liberating social and cultural endeavors.

Unfortunately, most of what reaches a mass gay audience fails miserably at meeting this challenge (with a few exceptions, like the plays of Tony Kushner). In his attempt to revive our understanding of homosexuality as subversive, Bronski suggests:

> What is most threatening about homosexuals, however, is that their very existence demonstrates not only that there are other options besides heterosexuality, but also that pleasure—emblematically non-reproductive sexual pleasure—needs no justification and can be used to prioritize and evaluate human experience, moral decisions, and the living of life. This is such a daunting and frightening idea that it must be constantly attacked, obscured, disguised, or marketed as something else. This simple truth about homosexuality and gay and lesbian lives is so difficult to state in our society that even homosexuals—hiding behind the temporary and

Lesbian Chic

HEATHER ZWICKER

September 30, 1996

Near the end of my first year as an assistant professor at the University of Alberta, I was invited to bring my "spouse" to a faculty dinner party. With some trepidation (after all, Alberta is hardly the hotbed of Canadian radicalism, at least not of the left-wing variety), I brought my female partner along. Somewhat to my surprise, people were not merely friendly toward us, but actually vied for our attention all night long. Where did we meet? When did the penny drop for the two of us? Had we thought about having children together? What was San Francisco like, and did we miss it a lot? What did we think of the same-sex spousal benefits initiative on campus? After eight years as an out lesbian, I had grown accustomed to being treated with puzzled tolerance, so I found this sudden informed interest baffling. Don't get me wrong—my colleagues are wonderful people, but I had no reason to

Don Hammerman

When the media made lesbians chic, they also tried to define and control them.

ineffective relief of the "gay moment" or attempting to hide the reality of gay sexuality by insisting, "we are just like everyone else"—are reluctant to speak it.

Bronski is on to something. Homosexuality is, of course, natural—but it can never be "normal," nor even "virtually normal" (the title of a dreadful book, dripping with self-hatred, by the gay conservative writer Andrew Sullivan). The right seems to understand just how subversive the existence of same-sex love is to the established order better than the contemporary gay movement does: Did not Bill Kristol's *Weekly Standard* recently proclaim that "heterosexual monogamy within the context of marriage is the only relationship compatible with our republican form of government"?

The election of George W. Bush as president and the events of September 11 have, I think, ushered in a profoundly conservative period for at least a decade—and it may well last longer. This is something that the Democratic Party—which in the Clinton years stood for nothing except gaining and holding on to power—is too ethically, politically and intellectually bankrupt to challenge. In a country drowning in religion, I think the fragility of the small gains the gay citizenship movement has made will all too soon become apparent, especially in the land between the coasts.

The generation that will come of age in the new millennium shows signs of being ever more conservative than its predecessors—for example, a 1998 poll of nearly 5,000 students taken by *Who's Who in American High Schools* showed an alarming 20 percent increase (to 48 percent) of those who admit they are "prejudiced" against homosexuals. Surveys by the Gay, Lesbian and Straight Education Network (GLSEN) demonstrate that gay students hear anti-gay slurs 25 times a day on average. And violent gay-bashings, usually the work of young people (as in Matthew Shepard's murder) have been on the upswing for a decade, a trend that hate crimes legislation can punish but not halt.

believe they lived completely outside of the casual heterosexism that characterizes everyday life.

And then it struck me: As out lesbians at a dinner party in the early '90s, my girlfriend and I were chic. We were part of the social craze over lesbians. Everyone at the dinner party had seen the *Newsweek* cover story about lesbians, and some of them had no doubt read the *New York* magazine feature, too. Good Albertans, a few of them had undoubtedly lingered over the k.d. lang/Cindy Crawford spread in *Vanity Fair*, though they might not admit it. Between the tiramisu and the after-dinner grappa, I realized that lesbian chic was real, and it had cachet in my neighborhood.

All this visibility is good, to a degree. Even if the dykes I know don't exactly measure up to the image of the well-heeled, highly educated, multicultural, marriage-oriented, deficit-cutting, law- and capitalism-abiding suburban lesbian subject that *Newsweek* has in mind, at least a major mainstream news organ has admitted that lesbians exist. At the same time, lesbian chic makes me nervous, because media representations can function as a strategy of containment, just as medical, psychiatric and religious discourses do. Medical explanations of homosexuality, psychiatric theories of inversion and religious prohibitions against same-sex desire lay claim to a certain knowledge about lesbianism; they give it names, causes, prognoses and, usually, cures. In a similar way, the media render lesbianism visible, knowable and accessible to the world at large. In so doing, they attempt to make it controllable.

The downsizing of government social services and the subsidizing of programs run by organized religions (a goal of the Bush administration that gives a new meaning to the phrase "voodoo economics") means that economically disadvantaged Americans, especially young people, will be increasingly exposed to anti-gay prejudices and propaganda inherent in "faith-based" institutions. Remember that only 12 states have adopted any form of legislation outlawing discrimination against gay people (and that religious-affiliated institutions are broadly exempt from them, as they are in the proposed federal Employment Non-Discrimination Act as well).

Resisting what I fear will be the coming backlash against the new mass-marketed gay visibility will require a strategic reorientation of organized gay politics that embraces and acts on issues of race and class—thus expanding the potentially mobilizable gay electorate to reflect gay reality, and enabling gay organizations to build coalitions with other groups in society more solid than the temporary alliances of convenience we sometimes are able to arrange.

For example, the problems of working-class gay people are seldom addressed by the mainstream gay groups, with their middle-class orientations. A number of unions have sizable gay caucuses—the Service Employees, Hotel Employees and Restaurant Employees, AFSCME and others—yet the leading gay groups have yet to reach out to them. And while Pride at Work, the organization of gay trade unionists, now has been officially recognized and given a small subsidy by the AFL-CIO, it has received almost no help from the institutionalized gay community.

Another example: Even though Latinos are now the largest nonwhite group in the population, and even though they so desperately need help to combat the rampant homophobia and inculcated self-hate fostered by cultural machismo and religious primitivism, few gay dollars go toward organizing that community. Indeed, only pennies of the money raised by national gay groups goes to any local organizing—a fundamental strategic error. Reorientation for resistance requires

In Defense of Identity Politics

MARTIN DUBERMAN

July 9, 2001

We hold on to a group identity, despite its insufficiencies, because for most non-mainstream people it's the closest we have ever gotten to having a political home—and voice. Yes, identity politics reduces and simplifies. Yes, it is a kind of prison. But it is also, paradoxically, a haven. It is at once confining and empowering. And in the absence of alternative havens, group identity will for many of us continue to be the appropriate site of resistance and the main source of comfort.

The anti-multiculturalists' high-flown, hectoring rhetoric about the need to transcend these allegiances, to become "universal human beings with universal rights," rings hollow and hypocritical. It is difficult to march into the sunset as a "civic community" with a "common culture" when the legitimacy of our differentness as minorities has not yet been more than superficially acknowledged—let alone safeguarded. You cannot link arms under a universalist banner when you can't find your own name on it. A minority identity may be contingent or incomplete, but that does not make it fabricated or needless. And cultural unity cannot be purchased at the cost of cultural erasure.

a tactical shift of gay resources from building national bureaucracies to strengthening local organizing, community by community, city by city, and state by state. All this is in the short term.

But in the long term, developing new strategies of resistance and liberation will require the gay movement, which has become so *embourgeoisé*, to begin a serious and radical rethinking of homosexuality so as to understand at a deeper level why fear and loathing of same-sex love is so deeply ingrained in society and culture not only here in the United States, but around the world. This also means breaking the forms of social control implicit in the gay market ideology. As important as the demands of the gay citizenship movement are, one cannot change minds and hearts by legislation. Only a redefinition of human freedom that includes a recharacterization of human sexuality—the original project of gay liberation—can do that.

Terry LaBan

Identity politics are at once confining and empowering.

Resisting the coming backlash will require a strategic reorientation and a radical redefinition of gay politics.

Nick Allen

Back to the Future

JEFFREY L. REYNOLDS

June 27, 1999

Make no mistake about it, the AIDS crisis is over. It doesn't matter that tens of thousands of people are still infected with HIV every year. It doesn't matter that many of those on the much-ballyhooed AIDS "wonder drugs" are getting sicker, or even that our family, friends, neighbors and co-workers are still dying. The AIDS crisis ended in 1996, damn it, and it seems nothing can convince us otherwise.

America's AIDS landscape changed dramatically three years ago with the advent of protease inhibitors—a new class of powerful anti-HIV medications. Unlike earlier AIDS drugs, protease inhibitors block replication of the virus in a person's body, thereby limiting the damage to the immune system and potentially preserving their health for longer periods of time. How long? No one knows for sure. But protease inhibitors are an important step along the way to a cure, if only in keeping people alive long enough to find something better.

What'd we do next? We walked away. Most of America was happy to declare an end to an epidemic it never wanted to acknowledge in the first place. But after 15 years of gloom, doom and AZT, hope turned into complacency just as quickly among the battle-fatigued on the front lines. We didn't renew our commitment to a cure or plot new strategies to ensure everyone could reap the potential benefits of protease inhibitors. We didn't develop a back-up plan for those who fail on the medications. We didn't refocus our prevention efforts. Instead, we packed up and went home, precisely as AIDS was moving beyond the gay community and into other populations—women, people of color, drug users and the poor.

The widespread notion that living with HIV simply means popping a few pills each day has given a green light to unsafe sex. Contentious debates about "barebacking"—latex-free sex—have re-emerged throughout the gay community. Young people—who never embraced safer sex—continue to dismiss warnings and will account for half of all new infections in the next few years. The ad campaigns on MTV, the school-based educational programs and prevention efforts are gone.

That our sloth-like clinical advances outpace social advances is sad but not surprising. We seem to be repeating the same mistakes that gave HIV an unrecoverable advantage during the early days of the burgeoning epidemic. We still underestimate the power of HIV. We still demonize those with HIV, restrict access to clean syringes and deny health care to 43 million Americans. We refuse to talk openly about sex, unless, of course, it takes place in the Oval Office. But our president, who refuses to adequately fund prevention efforts, now fails to even mention AIDS in the State of the Union.

Coming full circle, we appear as unprepared and unwilling to deal with the third decade of the AIDS epidemic as we were the first. HIV, on the other hand, has grown quietly and steadily stronger, cutting an even wider path of destruction in communities already saddled—not coincidentally—with other problems we abandoned long ago. To expect that the next clinical advance will push us effortlessly into victory against AIDS is to ignore the fact that HIV is a distinctly different virus now than it was 10 years ago. If you thought the '80s were ugly, just wait.

Steve Kagan

The image of gay people presented by the Washington lobby groups is an alarmingly false one.

Stuck but Stirring

IS THERE STILL POWER IN A UNION?

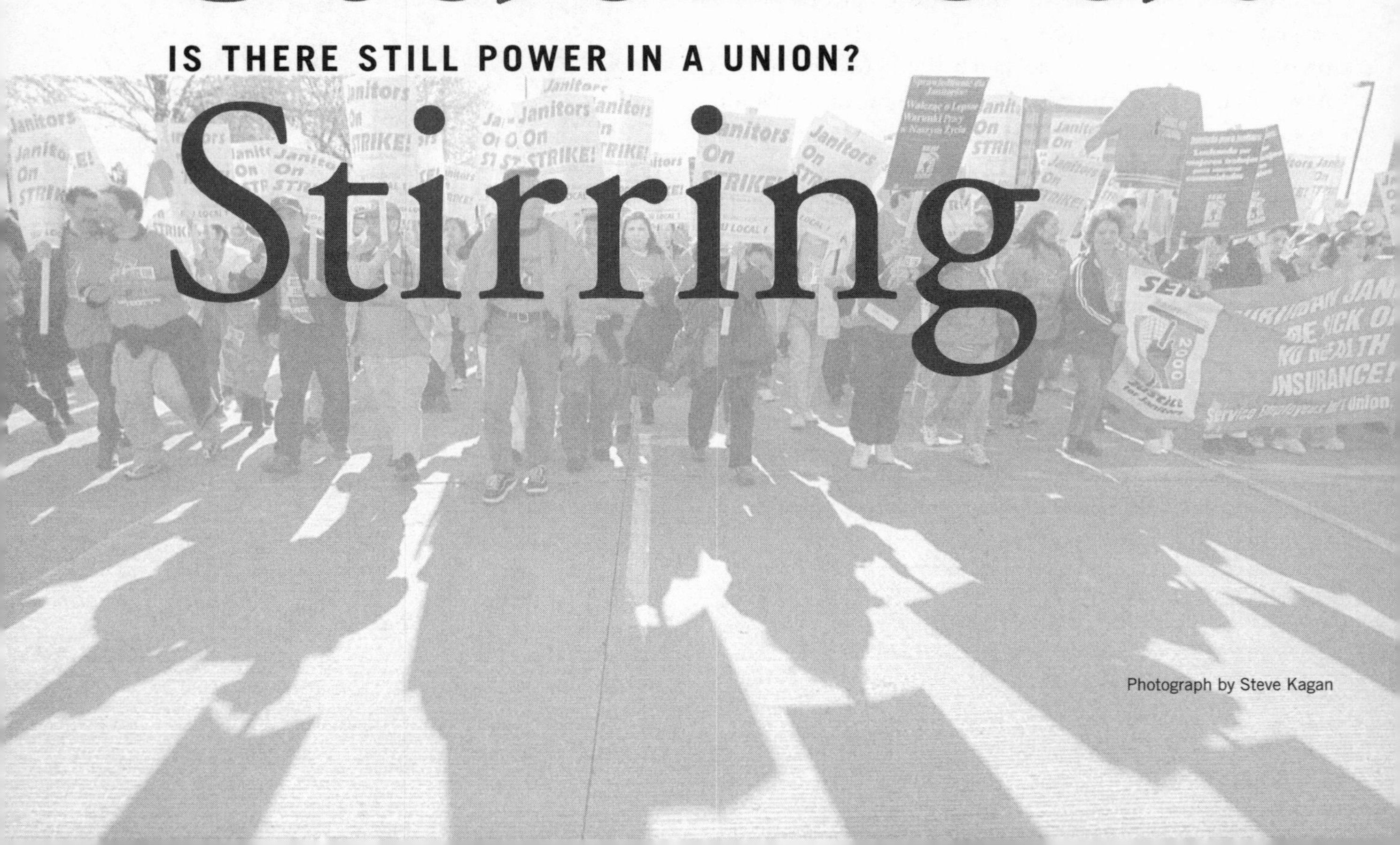

Photograph by Steve Kagan

Eight

DAVID MOBERG

THERE WAS SOME GOOD NEWS FOR THE BELEAGUERED AMERICAN LABOR MOVEMENT AT THE END OF THE 20TH CENTURY. DESPITE OVERALL DECLINE, unions showed they could organize on a grand scale: The Hotel Employees and Restaurant Employees kept pace with booming Las Vegas and built a local union of more than 50,000 members; the Service Employees conducted a 10-year battle to win union recognition for more than 60,000 low-paid home care workers in Los Angeles. After two decades of vicious union-busting strategies from employers, unions also proved they could win strikes: UPS workers prevailed against a tough employer in a nationwide battle that won strong public support; Boeing engineers established that high-tech workers could strike as effectively as their fellow machinists against a leading global corporation.

Unions learned to fight in new ways, attacking corporations on all fronts and drawing on global alliances, as the Steelworkers did in the early '90s against a lockout by Ravenswood Aluminum Corporation. Organized labor demonstrated a new ability to build alliances in local communities, with other social movements (especially student, religious and environmental groups) and on a global basis, playing a key role in the dramatic 1999 protests against the World Trade Organization in Seattle. And they displayed a new capacity to organize politically, turning out union households for elections in rising numbers.

But there was just as much bad news. The number of union representation elections plummeted in the '80s and remained low. The number of strikes also reached record lows, and some of the most militant battles—such as strikes by workers at Caterpillar and Bridgestone/Firestone and the lockout at Staley Corporation that occurred simultaneously in the small town of Decatur, Illinois, in the mid-'90s—

collapsed in defeat. Unions got little from supporting the Clinton administration (except some defense against Republican assaults), which passed plenty of legislation labor opposed, such as NAFTA. Despite the election of AFL-CIO President John Sweeney in the federation's first contested presidential vote in a century, only a few unions substantially reworked their own organizations, strategies and budgets. And one big transformation that was showing promise—the rank-and-file reform movement in the Teamsters—stumbled badly because of union campaign finance abuses, returning the union to some of its old ways.

By far the worst news was that the labor movement continued nearly a half-century of steady decline in the percentage of workers who are union members—from a high of nearly 33 percent in the early '50s to 13.5 percent in 2000, with only 9 percent of private sector workers in unions. The five-decade slide in the union share of the work force, the most prolonged and profound crisis of the trade union movement in American history, is both a cause and a symptom of the erosion of union power. This loss of strength had consequences far beyond the union movement itself, contributing significantly to the decline of the Democratic Party—both in its electoral success and its commitment to a progressive agenda—and to the evaporation of popular consciousness about social and economic class.

There is no single, simple explanation of why labor unions have slipped so dramatically since the '50s, and there is no equally simple road back to greater numbers and influence. Many external influences have weakened unions, but a variety of internal factors—in the structure, ideology and leadership of the labor movement—also contributed to their decline. For decades many union leaders denied that there was any problem. Most simply hunkered down, hoping that some day—maybe when Democrats regained power—the tide might turn on its own.

The labor movement needs to change itself, to make its organizations the center of a much broader movement of

As Patco Goes, So Goes the Union

DAVID MOBERG

August 26, 1981

DENVER—"Reagan is taking on unionism," says Carl Conant, vice president of the PATCO local at Stapleton Airport. "He has taken on PATCO No. 1. Then the rest are ducks in a row."

Controller Dave Rambeau figures that the direct and indirect costs of the strike to the economy run close to $100 million a day. Firing all the controllers will cost the government $200 million for retirement and vacation pay, plus millions more in legal fees and other efforts to break the strike. The initial training of each new controller (3,000 to start, but obviously more if PATCO members don't return) is $175,000 plus additional on-the-job training costs. "If you add all these things together," Rambeau says, "it's at least $3.5 billion or so. Our ideal contract would have cost $575 million. So it is simply blatant union-busting."

Most of the controllers thought of themselves as solid patriots and ordinary, scrupulously law-abiding folks. "I'm married, with one child, one dog and one cat," Rambeau says. "I'm just Joe American."

But their view of America is changing. "There's something wrong with America when a man on strike is taken to prison in shackles," Conant says. "There's something wrong when people with $30,000-a-year jobs risk those jobs to go on strike. I love America, but if they tear down the unions, you might as well move to Russia. Here's the same man who wants to get government out of our personal business destroying our union. It seems like a contradiction."

working Americans from farmworkers and janitors to college professors and nurses. Unions must rework their own culture, making it more participatory and democratic, but they also need to remake working-class culture and popular political dialogue to resurrect the values of solidarity—the real "counter-culture" to American acquisitive individualism, as Thomas Geoghegan argued in *Which Side Are You On?* If the labor movement hopes to expand its influence, it must promote a fairer social contract for all Americans as well as better contracts for members. The very survival—not simply the power—of the labor movement depends on it.

Labor's decline started at a point in the mid-'50s when the Cold War was flourishing at home and abroad, Republicans had regained political power nationally, and large American corporations were consolidating oligopolistic power domestically as they dominated a world economy from which they were protected by distance, culture and temporary technological superiority. While the New Deal had given workers rights and made collective bargaining a centerpiece of the new economy, the law did not amplify union influence as much as it did in parts of Europe, where, either by law or government action, negotiations between unions and major employers set a standard that was extended to an entire industry.

Business leaders in America, imbued with the spirit of laissez-faire capitalism and facing a weaker left-wing political challenge than in Europe, had long been extremely anti-union. Despite acceptance in some industries of unions, whose demands employers nevertheless strongly resisted, many major corporations and smaller businesses worked aggressively to avoid unionization, either through preventive management, flight or fight. As Richard Freeman and James Medoff concluded in *What Do Unions Do?* one of the main deterrents to union growth over the past 50 years has been adamantine resistance of employers, who have exploited, stretched and broken the law with impunity. Resistance to

ITT Archives

The smashing of PATCO legitimized union-busting and harmed the entire labor movement.

Austin City Limits

DAVID MOBERG

January 29, 1986

AUSTIN, MINNESOTA—Heavily bundled against the cold, five members of the Erickson clan, ranging in age from their early twenties to long past retirement, huddled across from the line of National Guard troops arrayed up and down Hormel Drive. Along with other relatives, they had put in a combined 250 years working for the Geo. A. Hormel Co., the prosperous meatpacking company that has long dominated—sometimes benevolently, sometimes oppressively—this normally placid town of 23,000 not far from the Iowa border.

Since August, the Ericksons have been among the 1,500 members of the United Food and Commercial Workers (UFCW) Local P-9 on strike to resist concessions demanded by Hormel. On January 13, the company reopened its new $100 million flagship Austin plant, told strikers to come back or be replaced, and began taking applications for new workers. Although about 70 workers crossed picket lines during the first week, the company claimed as many as 3,000 people had applied for jobs. Then on Monday, January 20—after workers and union supporters from Minneapolis-St.Paul blocked gates with slow-moving or parked vehicles and taunted strikebreakers from the curb opposite the entrances—Minnesota's Democratic governor, Rudy Perpich, sent in the National Guard.

Only a few minor incidents were the reported reasons for calling in the Guard—a few tire slashings, a scuffle reportedly provoked by a company photographer, an alleged gunshot far from the plant. At the very moment that local authorities later claimed the

David Moberg

P-9? "I wish I had a hundred local unions with leadership like that."

unionization intensified in the '70s, as profits were squeezed in an era of stagflation, then became even more aggressive as the political assault on unions grew during the Reagan era.

Beyond the political, legal and managerial assault, unions faced new challenges from structural changes in the economy. The service sector, where unions had little presence, grew rapidly along with a variety of white-collar, technical and professional occupations. In many cases, labor made little effort to enter fast-growing industries or occupations, while employment in traditional union strongholds declined. Manufacturing industries were dramatically affected by the new global economy. Cheaper or better imports displaced jobs, and U.S. companies—often incorrectly blaming their workers and wage costs for their inability to compete—shifted production out of the country and intensely fought unionization.

At the same time, corporations placed a growing emphasis on "shareholder value," pushing for short-term profit at the expense of long-term strategy. Deregulation, privatization, outsourcing, mergers, corporate restructuring and consolidation of national franchises led to an ever-changing fragmentation and rearrangement of work and authority. Increasingly, employers relied on contingent workers—contract, temporary, part-time, non-tenured or leased. All of these trends made it harder for unions to enforce contracts or even to preserve unionization of the work force.

As much as external attacks and changes in society undercut union power and membership, the labor movement itself bears much of the responsibility for failing to respond forcefully, imaginatively and quickly. The postwar period of prosperity, combined with a Cold War ethos shared by many labor leaders, created a conservative, complacent culture in the labor movement. Unions benefited from and identified with oligopolistic or regulated industries: Because they were often largely immune to foreign competition, wage and benefit increases could be passed along to consumers. But when business as usual collapsed in the '70s with greater foreign competition and deregulation, unions weren't ready to fight back.

The structure of American unions complicated their problems. The labor movement was fragmented, with many small national unions, industries or occupations divided among multiple unions, and with too much control in union locals. In theory, this could have given the labor movement greater flexibility and an opportunity for more democratic accountability. And innovative and democratic locals did carry on dramatic struggles (such as the Steelworkers local at Danly Manufacturing in the Chicago suburbs or the United Food and Commercial Workers Local P-9 at the Hormel meatpacking plant in Austin, Minnesota) and organize aggressively (such as the Local 1199 hospital workers union in New York). But in practice, decentralization was no guarantee of effectiveness or democracy.

The AFL-CIO itself has been a tenuous federation, which might make policy statements on national or international affairs but has had no power to command affiliated unions to do anything—not even to pay dues properly. During the tenure of presidents George Meany and Lane Kirkland, the federation offered only occasional strategic guidance, and unions undertook most efforts on their own. Kirkland brought unions together for the 1981 Solidarity Day March on Washington, for example, but when the air traffic controllers went on strike that same year, the squabbles and resentments among unions, especially in the airline industry, led to minimal solidarity, the smashing of PATCO by Reagan, and the legitimization of union-busting that harmed the whole labor movement.

The tendency of many unions to haphazardly add "dues units" wherever they could find them, rather than pursuing strategic organizing, compounded these problems. The result wasn't the "one big union" the Wobblies had envisioned, but a grab bag of many tiny unions. This contributed not only to less effective organizing, but to weaker bargaining positions. Union staff have more difficulty serving workers in many unrelated industries, and workers within an industry are weaker if they are divided among many unions.

crowd had turned into a "mob," local police were chatting amiably with picketers. The main problem had been the stalled traffic, usually not a problem requiring 500—later 800—soldiers with clubs, visored riot helmets and flack jackets.

At 7 A.M. on Tuesday, labor consultant Ray Rogers, who had crafted a wide-ranging, year-long assault on Hormel by Local P-9, arrived at the intersection, and, using a bullhorn, reminded strikers once again that "our whole struggle is opposed to violence." . . .

"Don't think one moment or one hour will win this struggle," he cautioned. "It's a process." . . .

The battle at Austin goes beyond the drama of a small town torn apart by a bitter labor conflict. In the eyes of many, it is a testing ground for a more militant union built on broad solidarity and tough-minded principles. It has become not only a bare-knuckle battle between workers and management, but also a conflict within labor ranks. . . .

Whatever the ultimate success of its bargaining goals, the P-9 campaign—of which the strike is only part—has been a great success in forging a determined, enthusiastic, democratic local union, whose members easily understand and casually discuss the links between their problems and the struggles of others, whether local farmers, PATCO strikers, Polish workers or blacks in South Africa. Night after night, crowds of 500 or more gather for open and democratic meetings. There is an enthusiasm and loyalty—which often erupts in spontaneous chants of "P-9, P-9, P-9!"—that outsiders, even from the international union, underestimate.

Even a former labor movement official who is very critical of what he sees as the local's commitment to "total victory or total defeat," said, "I wish I had a hundred local unions with leadership like that."

While greater cooperation and strategic cohesion would make a difference, centralization by itself isn't an adequate answer. Unions aren't armies to be commanded. They are voluntary organizations that work when leaders motivate members and provide opportunities for them to experience the power of solidarity in action. That requires a strong participatory democracy. Labor leaders are right in calling their movement the largest democratic organization in the United States, but it often hasn't been as democratic as it needed to be for unions to work at their best.

The old business or insurance unionism model—where union leaders promise to provide protection and services for members—created a culture of cynical detachment and individualism, which in the worst cases led to corruption. The soul of unionism is solidarity, a sense of camaraderie and cooperation that must be dominant even if a hierarchy of officeholders is necessary to run the organization. At a time when employers recognize they must give their employees at least the illusion of being "associates," it is imperative for labor to nurture the strong democratic voice that workers are denied in corporations, in corporate-dominated politics and—tragically—in too many unions as well.

And most unions simply haven't put much money into organizing. In the early '90s, few unions devoted more than 5 percent of their budgets to organizing. By the end of the decade, many had increased their commitment (sometimes through budgetary sleight-of-hand, sometimes through real changes) but only a handful came close to the AFL-CIO's target of deploying 30 percent of resources for organizing. There were many reasons for the foot-dragging. Organizing is hard work, with long and disruptive hours. It is costly and risky, especially in industries exposed to global competition. In most cases, however, existing union members simply want their dues money spent on services for themselves, and the internal politics of unions reward leaders who serve existing members rather than organizers. Many union leaders fear bringing in new members because they are unpredictable

Peter Hannan

Labor's biggest challenge isn't figuring out what to do, but systematically applying the lessons that a few successful unions have already learned.

Down in Coal Country

DAVID MOBERG

November 15, 1989

CARBO, VIRGINIA—Both Raymond and Shirley Harrison grew up poor. Now they feel Pittston Coal threatens the life the union won for them. "People don't understand how deep it goes," Shirley says. "They owned my grandfather and they owned my father, and I resented that. They harassed me while Raymond was lying on the hospital bed fighting for his life. I had to guard him to prevent them from coming in trying to get a statement to make the accident look like it was his fault. I was angry then; I'm even angrier now."

In the tight-knit coal communities, where nearly everyone has relatives working in the mines or relying on Mineworkers retirement funds, roots run deep and strong. The traditional culture remains lively, voters who might upset a comfortable tenure in office.

But for organized labor to gain numbers and power, those leaders must put forward a vision of unions as part of a social movement. They must educate and organize members to devote energy and resources to organizing. After all, except for their own co-workers, the most persuasive organizers are people who share life and work experiences and can personally explain what it means to be in a union.

The labor movement has the capacity to revive itself, if only it had the will. Labor's biggest challenge is not figuring out what to do, but systematically applying the lessons that at least a few unions have learned. That doesn't mean there are no problems left to solve. Even if all the best practices were employed, labor would still face difficulties in taming the forces of unregulated global corporate capitalism. Also, as long as the United States retains its current electoral rules (which make it next to impossible for alternative parties to emerge), labor will be hampered by its problematic dependence on the Democratic Party. But the future need not be as bleak as the current numbers suggest.

By the late '80s and early '90s, individual unions had started trying new, ambitious efforts on their own. For example, although much of the growth of the Service Employees under John Sweeney came from mergers with smaller unions, the SEIU did begin aggressively organizing with it is "Justice for Janitors" campaign. This noteworthy effort organized low-income immigrant workers (many of them undocumented) using militant tactics such as sit-ins or street blockades and applying pressure to the real economic powerhouses (the downtown building owners or big corporations like Apple Computer) to win contracts for janitors employed by smaller firms.

During the same period, AFSCME (the union of state and local government employees) took the initiative in pulling groups of unions together for political action.

melding heartfelt religion, uncompromising unionism and proud patriotism. The distinctive symbol of the strike—camouflage clothing, often emblazoned with a "stop Pittston" symbol and the slogan, "overcome evil with good"—grew out of this culture. It originated in an earlier long strike against A.T. Massey Coal, when workers were angered at being arrested on the basis of brief descriptions—like the wearing of a blue shirt or red hat. In a Spartacus-style gesture of solidarity, they all dressed alike, picking camouflage in part because everyone already had hunting clothes. . . .

Jack Kiser, a striking miner, estimates that 90 percent of local merchants back the union, most of them proudly displaying UMW support cards in their windows. "It's not union vs. company, but corporate greed out of Connecticut against local people like me who they've known for years and helped make them," he explains.

In the heart of the strike zone, gas station owner Wayne Rasnick displays a sign saying his Chevron station respectfully refuses to serve state police during the strike. Throughout the area, homes are decorated with hand-lettered signs of support such as "I may be poor, but I ain't no scab."

Cleaning House

ZACK NAUTH

May 1, 1995

WASHINGTON—Middle-aged men in suits and women in dresses looked around uneasily as the police carried off one demonstrator after another, many still brandishing signs and chanting slogans. Well-compensated bureaucrats and office workers from labor's conservative center, the AFL-CIO headquarters a few blocks away, stood shoulder-to-shoulder with their counterparts on labor's most militant wing: janitors from El Salvador and Pittsburgh, union organizers from Guatemala and Milwaukee.

What brought these unlikely comrades together in mid-March for a five-hour ordeal of handcuffs and jail time?

The march and the rush-hour sit-down action were the work of "Justice for Janitors," an innovative organizing campaign of the Service Employees International Union (SEIU). The missionary zeal of the Justice for Janitors organizers is understandable: Founded a decade ago, it is now the most successful organizing campaign among service industry workers in the private sector. And, remarkably, it has succeeded among a work force that other unions have failed to reach—part-time, low-income workers, predominantly African-Americans and Spanish-speaking immigrants, who hold jobs at the bottom of the U.S. economy. As organized labor continues its seemingly inexorable slide into irrelevance, the Justice for Janitors model—which has won new contracts and registered impressive membership gains—looks increasingly attractive. . . .

Justice for Janitors uses strategies—like the sit-down strike—made famous during labor's golden age in the '30s, and combines them with the nonviolent tactics of the civil rights movement. Justice for Janitors molds them into a simple formula: The disruption of business as usual, plus moral authority, equals change.

But this approach often runs into legal obstacles. For example, the time-honored tactic of warehouse workers refusing to handle the goods of a company whose employees were on strike—like many other successful union strategies—has been outlawed by Congress, the courts and the National Labor Relations Board (NLRB). So, Justice for Janitors has been forced to be creative.

The campaign rejects the standard organizing method most unions now use: site-by-site, NLRB-supervised elections. Justice for Janitors organizers

And thanks to a court-ordered consent decree and a strong rank-and-file opposition, Ron Carey took control of the Teamsters and began changing the image and practice of a union that had been labor's historic bad boy. Meanwhile, the unions that would form UNITE (garment and textile workers), the United Electrical Workers (a tiny union outside the AFL-CIO) and the United Mine Workers began to forge a new internationalism, criticizing President Reagan's policies in Central America, fighting for workers rights in countries where U.S. companies had shifted production and linking with foreign unions to combat multinational corporations.

But many unions that undertook such innovative efforts in organizing, politics or international affairs had to contend with a hostile AFL-CIO. By the time Newt Gingrich led the Republicans to their congressional triumph in 1994, the sense of crisis and internal dissatisfaction with the AFL-CIO among a key group of unions reached the breaking point. They launched an internal challenge to Lane Kirkland, who was seen as aloof and ineffective. Before Kirkland agreed to step down, the dissatisfaction had erupted into a full-blown campaign—the first in more than a century—for a changing of the guard.

The challenger was John Sweeney, a portly man with a fringe of white hair and a pleasing smile, who had a rare ability to work with stodgy, conservative union leaders, while giving wide latitude to an innovative, militant and politically leftish staff. He seemed guided more by his Catholic faith and classic trade union values of solidarity than by any more fully developed political ideology. But despite his personally conservative style and willingness to compromise, he usually articulated a progressive vision, even on issues like gay rights that labor usually had shunned. He was willing—too willing, many said—to sit down and talk with employers to find common ground, but he also sought allies among progressive causes and constituencies, from environmentalists to the clergy to academics. And no AFL-CIO leader within memory has been as willing as Sweeney is to join picket lines and demonstrations, moving easily beyond the Beltway to join in labor struggles.

Once in office, Sweeney beefed up the organizing department, established an organizing fund, and gave top priority in talks, meetings and publicity to organizing (though his decision to get rid of organizing director Richard Bensinger, a relentless gadfly on behalf of more aggressive and expansive organizing, tarnished his record). In the able hands of Steve Rosenthal, the AFL-CIO Political Affairs Department helped rebuild labor's grassroots political army, roughly doubling the share of union household turnout in national elections from 1994 to 2000. In 1998, the labor movement pulled off an upset rejection of California Proposition 226, the so-called "paycheck protection" initiative that would have crippled unions' ability to use dues money for political work. At least in theory, unions also began to emphasize issues over candidate endorsements. That not only made members more knowledgeable and more willing to trust their unions' advice, but also helped to shift Democratic political focus to bread-and-butter economic issues.

Increasingly, labor linked its organizing and political work, demanding that union-backed candidates provide real support for workers when they faced obdurate employers. With innovative new leaders providing guidance in places such as Atlanta, Milwaukee and Silicon Valley, the AFL-CIO launched a "Union Cities" program to revive central labor councils (and later a "New Alliance" program to do the same with state labor federations). The AFL-CIO Corporate Affairs Department has tried to expand union influence over workers' pension fund money and to use that leverage (through shareholder resolutions, for example) not only to pressure corporate miscreants, but to change how capital markets reward and punish corporations—hoping to increase support for companies that pursue long-term strategies based on a skilled work force rather than for slash-and-burn executives hunting for quick bumps in stock prices.

liken the NLRB to a black hole that sucks in the union's time, stalls momentum and eventually bores workers to death. Worse, they claim, many members feel that the often lengthy proceedings that accompany an NLRB election only underscore the union's weakness. Consequently, when Justice for Janitors organizes a workplace, it insists the company agrees to simultaneously recognize the union and negotiate a contract.

Other unions prefer the NLRB strategy because it's more predicable: set an election and win or lose on that date. But Justice for Janitors organizers dig in for the long haul, with a high-profile, multifaceted pressure campaign. . . .

Justice for Janitors has proven that, with the right issues at stake, workers will take risks. In Los Angeles, dozens of janitors marched into Century City—and faced a brutal beating by the LAPD that sent 60 of them to the hospital. But they emerged stronger, with a court settlement, a majority of the industry organized and a new contract. "We need to figure out how we use our remaining power to organize now," says organizer Stephen Lerner. "We need to relearn how to capture the imagination, generate excitement, and articulate a vision that can mobilize union and nonunion workers. . . . Only by targeting on a grand scale and by taking big risks can we succeed."

War Zone

DAVID MOBERG

July 24, 1995

DECATUR, ILLINOIS—Brian and Tyna McDuffie, a middle-aged couple, could easily serve as the poster family for the harshness of contemporary American blue-collar life.

While the AFL-CIO still fought to preserve good, American jobs, the strategic emphasis under Sweeney shifted to writing new rules for the global economy that protect workers rights and the environment everywhere. (Trade battles, especially since the NAFTA fight in 1993, fostered an alliance between labor unions and environmentalists, but the short-sighted, misguided view of a key group of unions on global warming has created a rift between the allies.) The AFL-CIO joined with critics of the International Monetary Fund and World Bank, advocated cancellation of the foreign debts of very poor countries, criticized the corporate rights and financial structures of the new global economy and forged tighter alliances with militant labor movements in countries like Brazil, South Africa and South Korea. Starting with the "Union Summer" program for college students and young workers, Sweeney's AFL-CIO helped strengthen a new student movement, which has been standing up for workers on college campuses and in overseas sweatshops.

Sweeney and the AFL-CIO were swept forward by a developing movement they had helped to inspire but could not control. In 1999, for instance, when the AFL-CIO called for hearings on its new immigration policy proposals (which jettisoned earlier support for sanctions against employers of illegal immigrants), the federation explicitly ordered meetings of no more than a couple hundred people. The Los Angeles Federation of Labor refused and instead joined with immigrant groups to turn out an estimated 20,000 Latino workers and their families, chanting for "union" and "amnesty."

In the late '90s, a tightening labor market strengthened the hand of unions, especially outside the manufacturing industries, but the external social pressures on the labor movement remained inhospitable. Unions started to confront the internal obstacles to restoring their numbers and power, but progress on some fronts was limited. For example, while mergers reduced the number of unions in the AFL-CIO

Jim West

Labor should have made Decatur a rallying point for a national political campaign.

Since last June, Brian, a stocky electrician partial to the red T-shirts that have become the emblem of labor militancy in this central Illinois city, has been on strike against Caterpillar over the construction equipment maker's hostile treatment of its UAW work force. Although Cat has been consistently profitable for years, the company has pressed the union for concessions in a series of increasingly bitter contract negotiations. In April 1992, after a 163-day walkout, Caterpillar threatened to permanently replace its striking workers, and the union called off the strike.

Once the workers returned to the plants, however, they began a "work-to-rule" campaign, with many UAW members doing only the minimal work required in their contract. Like other union members, Brian faced steady harassment from Cat management. Workers wearing union T-shirts and buttons were disciplined. Cat's opposition has been so extreme that the National Labor Relations Board (NLRB) has filed 167 complaints against Caterpillar—the most ever lodged against a single company in a labor dispute. With Caterpillar showing no signs of backing down, UAW members walked out again last June.

Five years ago, Tyna, then a divorced mother of four, abandoned three minimum-wage jobs to take a unionized $11.50-an-hour job at A.E. Staley, a from 81 in 1995 to 64 in 2001, the planned merger of the Steelworkers, Machinists and Autoworkers was abandoned. More significantly, most unions continued to pursue all available targets instead of developing a focused strategy, although there were a few exceptions like the Hotel Workers, Service Employees and UNITE. Also, while unions increasingly mobilized their members, there was much more halting progress in educating workers and organizing them to exercise greater decision-making power.

Sweeney still faces the same problems as past AFL-CIO presidents: For the labor movement to change dramatically, each affiliated union must change from the top on down through each local. Even in the best international unions, only a minority of local unions are actively organizing or doing political work. Many internationals continue to drag their heels, neither actively fighting nor seriously implementing the new strategies. Sweeney can only cajole, nudge, exhort, educate and inspire. The major barrier to progress remains the failure of much of the labor movement to widely implement the best strategies and practices.

Even without major changes in the law and other external obstacles, workers can successfully organize—either in elections under the National Labor Relations Board or by direct action with employers to win recognition. They more likely will succeed if they start with a comprehensive campaign to pressure businesses, strategically target employers to take advantage of existing bargaining power, build strong internal committees of workers, employ members as volunteer organizers (and hire trained organizers who reflect the work force, including women and people of color) and utilize political and community allies.

Unions can win politically if they build grassroots movements of workers who are educated about political issues on the job, if they make direct "labor to neighbor" connections in working-class neighborhoods, if they emphasize issues of economic well-being and family security, if they educate politicians and if they work closely with progressive allies. Unions can win fights in the global economy by extending the same organizing

leading maker of corn syrup and starch owned by British conglomerate Tate & Lyle. When Staley let its contract with the union expire in 1992, the local's leaders figured that management wanted workers to strike so the company could permanently replace them and break the union. Instead, the workers stayed on the job, mounted a work-to-rule campaign, and simultaneously launched an attack on Staley's corporate and financial allies. Production plummeted, and in June 1993 Staley locked out Tyna and her 760 fellow workers.

After a stint driving a school bus, Tyna got a job at the Bridgestone/Firestone tire plant last spring. Two months later, the plant's 1,250 workers—members of the United Rubber Workers—also went on strike. In January, the company informed Tyna and her co-workers that they had been permanently replaced. In May, the union called off the strike, but the company has offered jobs to only 185 strikers.

Brian and Tyna, whose early dates were on the Cat picket lines and who got married a few days after the Bridgestone/Firestone strike started, remain undaunted. They travel around the country as "road warriors" spreading the word about Decatur. Why do they do it? "Part of it is because I've read history—and understand why I have what I have," Tyna says. "Part of it is my kids: I want a good job for me, but mostly I'm fighting for my kids and the people who fought and died for what I have." . . .

One of the main reasons that workers do not join unions today—or even think about organized labor—is that they're skeptical that unions have the power to solve their problems. As long as unions fail to join together—forgetting that "an injury to one is an injury to all," as the old slogan goes—those skeptics will be right. Employers everywhere will be more emboldened to pursue "restructuring." And organizing will be more difficult for everyone. . . .

Labor could have made Decatur a rallying point for a national political campaign. Concerned about family values? Then it's time to rein in corporations that impose disruptive work schedules and slash wages—not because their survival is at stake, but simply because they can get away with it. Union leaders could have argued that what America really needed—instead of middle-class tax cuts—was an end to middle-class pay cuts. Want cooperation at work? Give workers the power to be equal partners and protect their interests. Unions could make the case to the vast unorganized majority that "empowerment" does not mean being tossed alone into the stormy seas of the market, but having the right to act together and have a voice at work.

If labor, or the Democrats, hope to revive themselves in the coming years, they must embrace and trumpet that clear alternative. That, at least, is one message from Decatur, the hottest front in a war being waged in quieter ways against workers everywhere—and political strategies—cooperating with unions in other countries, forming broader alliances with other constituencies, targeting renegade corporations and demanding new rules that restrain capital and raise standards for workers everywhere.

Even as unions are at their lowest point since the bleak '20s and are being written off as relics of a bygone age (if not being targeted for extinction by their business and conservative Republican opponents), there are signs of life stirring throughout what had seemed like an inert institution narrowly hanging on for survival. This sense of hope and openness to new ideas may be as important as any specific program or policy in creating the possibility—and it is still only a possibility—of a labor revival.

Even as unions are being written off as relics of a bygone age, there are signs of life stirring.

ITT Archives

Roll the Union On

NELSON LICHTENSTEIN

October 18, 1998

I recently visited my local Burger King to pick up an employment application for my 16-year-old son. Right at the top, under the heading "Equal Employment Opportunity Employer" was this bold assertion: "Employer does not discriminate in employment because of race, color, sex, religion, national origin, age, disability, martial status, or liability for service in the armed forces of the United States."

This statement is on the Burger King application for two reasons. First, it is the law of the land. Second, Americans consider discrimination on the basis of race and religion and creed "un-American." Of course, there is a debate as to the meaning of "non-discrimination" and the way in which society can make up for past discrimination. But the overwhelming majority of workers, employers and politicians believe that the government has a right to insist that active discrimination not take place against anyone covered by Title VII of the 1964 Civil Rights Act.

But when it comes to the rights of workers as mere employees, the spirit of the Burger King application is entirely different. On the back there's a bit of boilerplate language that asserts the right of the corporation "to terminate my employment at any time for any reason, or for no reason. . . . Employment handbooks, manuals, personnel policies and procedures are not employment contracts and do not modify my status as an at-will employee."

This ideological dichotomy—between civil rights and workers rights—represents an unprecedented opportunity for the labor movement. Just as the CIO made the generation-long quest for "industrial democracy" a powerful theme that legitimized its strikes and organizing campaigns, so too can the contemporary labor movement capitalize upon the nation's

ITT Archives

The ideological dichotomy between civil rights and workers rights represents an unprecedented opportunity for the labor movement.

AFL-CIO

Unlike any other AFL-CIO leader in recent memory, John Sweeney has moved easily beyond the Beltway to join the picket lines of local labor struggles.

well-established "rights" culture of the past 40 years. Indeed, the AFL-CIO is now in the midst of a concerted effort to make the right to organize a part of our broader civil rights culture. This is not an entirely new idea, but it needs to be pushed forward with vigor, intelligence and commitment.

To give this ideological campaign the kind of concrete political and organizational meaning that can generate a massive shift in the nation's political culture, I offer three propositions.

First, the union movement needs more militancy. But even more important, American labor as a whole needs to stand behind those exemplary instances of class combat when they occur. The '80s were a tragic decade for American labor, not because workers did not fight, but because when they did take a stand—at International Paper in Jay, Maine, at Hormel in Austin, Minnesota, at Continental and at Greyhound—their struggles were both physically isolated and ideologically devalued. We remember Pullman in 1894, Lawrence in 1912, Gastonia in 1929 and Memphis in 1968, not because the workers engaged in those strikes were any more militant or victorious than those of the '80s, but because the labor movement as a whole—and liberal and left-wing intellectuals in particular—defended these struggles and gave them a transcendent meaning.

The second key is internal union democracy. Unions need tens of thousands of new organizers; but the AFL-CIO cannot recruit, train and deploy such an army, and even if it could, organizers who parachute into a campaign are far less effective than those who are part of the community and the workplace. Such a homegrown group cannot be recruited in the absence of a democratic union culture. Unfortunately, thousands of local unions—and not a few national or international organizations—are job trusts that exist to protect the incomes of an entrenched stratum of officials. Democratization threatens their security, but without it the union movement will remain a shell.

Finally, the road to a revitalized union movement lies not just through a vigorous organizing drive, but through politics as well. Here, following the footsteps of John L. Lewis is more problematic. Early in the 20th century, Samuel Gompers first declared, "Reward your friends and punish your enemies." Three decades later, Lewis ordered UAW radicals to drop their support of a Farmer-Labor Party and endorse President Roosevelt if they wanted $100,000 from the CIO treasury to organize General Motors. Such hard-nosed, seemingly pragmatic calculation has long captured the essence of mainstream labor's political activism. AFL-CIO President John Sweeney's stepped-up political commitment to Clinton and the Democrats in the 1996 campaign season lay squarely within this venerable tradition.

But such a pragmatic calculus is not enough, for politics is not simply a question of rewarding friends and punishing enemies. Instead, a political party can be far more: An educational instrument that crystallizes an entire worldview and generates a compelling vision of social change. In the fall of 1936, when FDR ran for re-election on a radical platform that condemned the "money-changers and economic royalists," he brought millions of workers into the streets and set the stage for the dramatic sit-down strikes that followed two months later. The Democratic Party has never played such a role again.

Labor-based political parties have been almost universal in the industrial West because they arise out of compelling logic that urges unionized labor to reach beyond its own ranks and forge alliances with those natural allies who are either unorganized or immobilized. Today, no trade unionist would dare to hope that the Democrats might actually become the kind of party that spoke forthrightly on behalf of labor.

Labor, therefore, needs its own voice, as well as its own party. Because the obstacles to the latter remain formidable, the need for the unions to have an independent profile within our political culture becomes even more important. Such a task requires not simply money for TV ads, but a public posture that puts an abrasive edge between the labor movement and the ambiguous politics of even the most progressive Democrats. Such independence breeds not isolation, but respect, leverage and legitimacy in our increasingly atomized and ambiguous world.

Terry LaBan

It's not too late: The road to a revitalized union movement lies through vigorous organizing and independent politics.

Gang Green

THE CHANGING FACE OF ENVIRONMENTALISM

Photograph from ITT Archives

Nine

JEFFREY ST. CLAIR

ON MAY 3, 1969, AFTER HOURS OF BITTER DEBATE, THE SIERRA CLUB FIRED DAVID BROWER. THE ORGANIZATION'S FIRST PAID STAFFER, BROWER HAD transformed the club from an exclusive, white male hiking outfit of 2,000 members into the world's most recognizable environmental group with more than 70,000 members. But the old guard didn't like the direction that Brower, its executive director, was taking the staid organization: toward political confrontation, grassroots organizing and attacks on industrial pollution, nuclear power and the Pentagon.

This kind of aggressiveness in the face of entrenched power alienated funders and eventually the Internal Revenue Service, which, after Brower's successful international campaign to stop the construction of two dams in the Grand Canyon, moved to strip the group of its tax-deductible status. The IRS action proved to be the final straw, and Brower was booted out. Brower was 56 when he was sacked. He could have retired then to his home in the Berkeley hills to write books, hike in the Sierras with his wife, Anne (if anything, an even more radical environmentalist), and travel the world doing what he loved most: running wild rivers.

But it turned out that Brower's ouster was more of a beginning than an ending. In fact, many greens point to that moment as the start of what has become known as the "New Conservation Movement." Brower went on to form Friends of the Earth, the League of Conservation Voters, Earth Island Institute and the Alliance for Sustainable Jobs and the Environment. He was nominated three times for the Nobel Peace Prize.

When the militant Earth First! movement sprang from the rubble of the Reagan era, many mainstream environmental leaders were quick to denounce them and their tactics of tree-sits and road blockades. Not Brower. "I thank God for the arrival of Earth First!" Brower said. "They make me look moderate." It was

Lionel Delevingne

After the press left Three Mile Island, people living near the plant were left to deal with the aftermath.

Crimes Against Nature

HARVEY WASSERMAN

April 16, 1980

GOLDSBORO, PENNSYLVANIA—The catastrophe at Three Mile Island has barely begun. While nearly $2 billion in radioactive machinery simmers unused in the middle of the Susquehanna River, animals in the surrounding farm country are dying off. . . .

"In 1976, I began to notice strange goings-on," explains Jane Lee. "Nobody would listen to me, of course, but I began collecting sworn affidavits from as many of the farmers as would give them to me. The evidence is pretty damn frightening." . . .

this sense of optimism that defined Brower most: His delight in how the movement he helped found continued to grow in unpredictable directions.

The evolution of environmentalism over the past quarter of a century has been spurred by any number of competing internal tensions: between national and grassroots, apolitical and partisan, international and domestic, lobbying strategies and direct action tactics. But more than anything else, the character of the American environmental movement has been shaped by the unexpected threats it has had to confront: Three Mile Island, Love Canal, James Watt, Chernobyl, the *Exxon Valdez*, rainforest destruction, the ozone hole, the decline of the spotted owl, global warming, the World Trade Organization.

Yet the environmental movement has always been the most existential of social movements, willing to change tactics on the fly, use what works and discard what doesn't. "In our business, you've got to be fast on your feet," said Brower, who died in November 2000. "When industry wins, they win forever. The most we can hope for is a stay of execution. It means we've got to be eternally vigilant, be very creative and be willing to take risks."

The modern grassroots environmental movement probably got its start in the citizen uprisings against nuclear power, beginning in the '70s with the Clamshell Alliance, a decentralized coalition put together to fight the Seabrook reactor in New Hampshire and its rowdier counterpart on the West Coast, the Abalone Alliance, which targeted the Diablo Canyon plant in California. Indeed, in her book *Political Protest and Cultural Revolution*, Barbara Epstein says, aside from the civil rights movement, these groups were the "first effort in American history to base a mass movement on nonviolent direct action."

The debate over nuclear power also exposed one of the first great schisms inside the green movement. Many environmental groups, fixated on a looming energy shortage, seized on the dream of nuclear power as a safe, clean alternative to oil-burning and coal-fired power plants. Indeed,

Brower lost his job at the Sierra Club partly because of his lonely and persistent opposition to the Diablo Canyon reactor, which was built on a major fault line.

But public attitudes toward the use of "atoms for peace" changed permanently on March 28, 1979, when the No. 2 reactor at Three Mile Island experienced a partial meltdown, emitting radioactive gasses into the air near Harrisburg, Pennsylvania, and contaminated water into the Susquehanna River. Most Americans first learned of the meltdown from the unimpeachable voice of Walter Cronkite, who opened the nightly news by saying: "It was the first step in a nuclear nightmare. As far as we know at this hour, no worse than that. But a government official said that a breakdown in an atomic power plant in Pennsylvania today is probably the worst nuclear accident to date." After four days of trying to keep details of the extent of the accident under wraps, officials finally suggested that nearby schools should be closed and pregnant women should evacuate the area. Public confidence in this supposedly safe and cheap form of energy collapsed.

But after the press left, people living near the plant were left to deal with the aftermath. Within a few years, the inevitable respiratory illnesses, kidney ailments and cancers began to sprout up around the nuclear complex. Yet the media, wrapped up in the apocalyptic fervor of a meltdown scenario, seemed bored by these relatively minor tragedies and tended to side with the utilities and nuclear industry in dismissing the link between the disease clusters and the release of radiation as the ranting of paranoids. (In fact, studies have found that just living near a nuclear plant–where cancer clusters tend to occur and where there are higher rates of infant mortality, blood disorders and kidney problems–can be dangerous for your health.)

If the nuclear industry was hoping for a quick comeback in the United States once public anxiety calmed over Three Mile Island, those dreams were shattered on April 26, 1986, when Ukraine's Chernobyl reactor blew its containment vessel during a test, bringing about the most serious industrial accident in

Leafing through a pile of Xeroxed documents, she talks calmly about what has happened. "We have had a long run of duck eggs not hatching, with some of the ones that have made it being born deformed. We have had rabbits giving birth to stillborns, with a drop in fertility. Same with the cats. In 1978 we had a rabbit and a barn cat drop dead for no apparent reason. We thought they might have gotten poisoned, but the autopsy showed no sign of it. We've also had a decline in fertility of the goats. And, of course, you've heard about all the cows that have been lost." . . .

Charles Connolly is 74 years old and has lived on his farm, less than two miles from TMI, since 1913. Connolly explains that in the past year he has lost three out of four calves to a strange, inexplicable disease that waterlogged their bones and made them unable to walk or stand. "Right after the accident," he says, "that maple tree in the front yard just up and died. Bark peeled right off it. Birds disappeared too. Used to be you'd have 25 robins out there in the back yard. This year I've only seen one. I found a bunch of starlings that just flew into the hay mow and died, and my brother found a robin that just keeled over in a peach basket."

As I head toward Goldsboro, directly across from the plant, it occurs to me that there is no "definitive" evidence that anything these farm people have told me is true. There has been no government study of area animals—a fact that infuriates the locals. Many believe that the authorities are afraid of what they'll find, preferring to keep the damage to the level of folk myth rather than official reality.

But it's all pretty real to Clair Hoover, who lost 30 of the 105 milk cows off his Bainbridge farm within months after the accident, and his six neighbors, who suffered similar losses. Hoover has moved and is suing Met Ed for $50,000 in business losses, plus other damages. "The wind," he says, "must have been blowing right at us."

history. The radiation released was greater than that from both the Nagasaki and Hiroshima atomic bombs, contaminating farm and dairy land and forcing the evacuation of more than 135,000 people. Thirty people were killed in the initial blast, and within five years there was a tenfold increase in thyroid cancers in the most-contaminated provinces.

After the accident, the Soviets delayed releasing any information to the public, grudgingly acting only after Sweden had revealed the disaster to the world. "The accident at the Chernobyl nuclear plant . . . has painfully affected the Soviet people and shocked the international community," Soviet President Mikhail Gorbachev said in a televised address. "For the first time, we confront the real force of nuclear energy, out of control." (Gorbachev would later claim that Chernobyl was a key event in giving momentum to *glasnost.*)

In the United States, the '80s saw numerous nuclear plants shuttered due to a combination of relentless citizen-organizing and their own financial extravagances: Marble Hill in Indiana, the Clinch River Breeder Reactor in Tennessee, Shoreham in New York and the Trojan reactor in Oregon. In 1989, the Rancho Seco reactor in Herald, California, became the first nuke plant shut down by popular vote.

There hasn't been a new nuke plant built in the United States since the Three Mile Island disaster. But that doesn't mean the nuclear industry went into hibernation. Instead of focusing on the United States, Westinghouse, General Electric, ABB and Bechtel set their sites on the developing world: India, Indonesia and Brazil. Their forays were often gladly backed by the U.S. government with financing through the IMF and World Bank.

An even bigger problem in the United States has become how to deal with the accumulating mounds of spent fuel from the nation's 104 commercial nuclear reactors. The nuclear industry, backed by politicians with nuclear plants in their states, wants to truck the radioactive waste to the Nevada desert and entomb it inside vaults in Yucca Mountain, a site on traditional lands of the Western Shoshone. The Shoshone have

Under the Rainbow

DIANA JOHNSTONE

September 4, 1985

PARIS—The first hypothesis suggested by the French daily *Le Monde* after the July 10 bombing of the *Rainbow Warrior* in New Zealand was that Greenpeace had sunk its own flagship. "If one sticks to the adage 'who profits from the crime?' it is obvious that it's the movement itself," it wrote, before excluding the hypothesis as "too Machiavellian."

Four weeks later it came out that the couple of suspects arrested by New Zealand police were French agents, and all clues pointed to the DGSE (General Direction of External Security), the French version of the CIA. Suddenly the tune changed. Now everybody was not against Greenpeace, everybody was against France. . . .

The *Rainbow Warrior* was preparing to lead a protest campaign against French nuclear weapons

ITT Archives

Greenpeace's provocative protests earned the group some powerful enemies—including bomb-wielding French agents.

tirelessly fought the plan for more than a decade, joined by anti-nuke groups such as the Snake River Alliance and the Nuclear Information and Resource Service.

They've nicknamed the entire scheme the "Mobile Chernobyl" plan. It calls for more than 30 years of continuous shipping by train and truck of 60,000 casks filled with irradiated reactor fuel. A single rail cask harbors nearly 200 times as much cesium as was released by the Hiroshima bomb. One study predicts that more than 300 "accidents" can be expected involving the shipment of this high-level nuclear waste. And Yucca Mountain itself is far from safe. For one thing, geologists say the site leaks, posing the real threat of nuclear waste hemorrhaging into groundwater. For another, it's on unstable terrain. This area of Nevada has been rocked by more than 650 earthquakes in the past 20 years. Of course, the nuclear industry doesn't want the liability when something inevitably goes wrong, so they pushed a bill through Congress transferring the liability for spent reactor fuel to the U.S. government.

But where there's a risk, there's also opportunity. In 1997, a strange amalgam of former Pentagon officials, CIA officers, venture capitalists and a couple of neoliberal environmentalists hatched a scheme to ship commercial radioactive waste to Russia, for disposal at a site in the Ural Mountains. The plan was fiercely opposed by many American and Russian environmental groups. Indeed, Russian greens mounted the largest campaign in the nation's history, gathering 2 million signatures to place the issue on the ballot as a public referendum. But the Kremlin rejected the signatures and the powerful Russian nuclear agency Minatom, which stands to make as much as $20 billion on the deal, persuaded the Russian parliament to give the go ahead.

It's the old story: privatize the profits and socialize the costs.

Back in the spring of 1978, residents of the working-class community of Love Canal, New York discovered that a chemical dump site had been leaking toxins into their neighborhood,

tests in the South Pacific when it was sunk by two explosive charges attached to its hull by divers. The technique is known as a specialty of the French secret services. Portuguese photographer Fernando Pereira was killed by the second blast. The death toll could have been much higher. Seven international leaders of Greenpeace who had planned to spend the night aboard the *Rainbow Warrior* changed their minds and decided to go ashore shortly before the explosions.

Since the DGSE has been incriminated, the usual word used in France to describe the operation has been *bavure*, or "snafu."

Alaska Aftermath

TERRY CARR

May 3, 1989

ANCHORAGE, ALASKA—For 12 years, the 48-inch Trans-Alaska pipeline was a gun barrel leveled at Prince William Sound. Since 1977, when oil began pouring down from the North Slope, nearly 9,000 tankers departed the pipeline's Valdez terminal fat with crude. Each tanker, its load ranging to more than 50 million gallons, held the potential to kill the Sound.

Then on March 24, a tanker captain with too much to drink, an unqualified mate at the helm and pathetic oil cleanup preparations joined to pull the trigger. The tanker *Exxon Valdez*, for reasons still not thoroughly explained, went aground miles out of the normal tanker route. More than 10 million gallons of oil bled from its holds and spread unchecked in one of the world's most magnificent bodies of water. . . .

Walking the shorelines of Prince William Sound's islands—at a time when, normally, the colors and noise of spring would be breaking out all around—calls to mind a messy mechanic's oil-changing pit. The spill smeared rocks and gravel with dirty, black slime resembling used motor oil with 10,000 miles on it. The smell is something belonging deep underground, in the filth and fires of hell, not among the Sound's mountains, unblemished snow and green spruce.

In high tide, the oil crawls up the beaches, laying on a new coat of swill that is smothering kelp, eel grass, mussels and clams. When the tide departs, it leaves birds and sea otters. Death clenches most of the animals. The oil stiffened them into a black mass barely distinguishable from the rocks. It suffocated some, starved some by killing their food and poisoned some with its toxins. A few carcasses have been shredded by eagles attracted by an easy, though probably fatal, meal.

The worst ones to see are those found alive. For then the otters lie on their backs, rubbing their eyes or licking their stomachs, trying to groom themselves clean of the oil. The birds hunker down, too weak and too heavy with oil to stand. Their wings tremble in apparent effort at flight.

Under Attack

DAVID HELVARG

October 17, 1994

"You can't reason with eco-freaks but you can sure scare them," brags Rick Sieman, leader of the Sahara Club, a California-based anti-environmental group. . . .

The Sahara Club's newsletter and computer bulletin board list environmentalists' names, addresses, phone numbers and license plate num-

saturating their schools, playgrounds and homes with a poisonous stew of more than 200 chemicals. The prime culprit was Hooker Chemical Company, a subsidiary of Occidental Petroleum. One study showed that 56 percent of the children born in Love Canal between 1974 and 1978 had suffered birth defects. Another study showed that the rate of urinary-tract infections had increased by 300 percent over the same period. A similar spike in the rate of miscarriages also was reported.

The government was slow to act to protect the residents, probably because it was a working-class neighborhood with little perceived political clout. Then a group of mothers and housewives, led by Lois Gibbs and going by the name the Love Canal Homeowners Association, sprang into action, filing petitions to close contaminated schools, pressuring Gov. Hugh Carey to evacuate the area and even commanding the attention of President Carter, who signed a bill funding the permanent relocation of 660 families.

The Love Canal campaign became a model for a new kind of citizen action, a blue-collar environmentalism that was uncompromising, creative and community-based. "The words 'Love Canal' are now burned in our country's history and in the memory of the public as being synonymous with chemical exposures and their adverse human health effects," Gibbs says. "The events at Love Canal brought about a new understanding among the American people of the correlation between low-level chemical exposures and birth defects, miscarriages and incidences of cancer. The citizens of Love Canal provided an example of how a blue-collar community with few resources can win against great odds, using the power of the people in our democratic system."

Since Love Canal, Gibbs has been a leader of one of the most exciting and powerful strains of conservationism: the environmental justice movement. It springs from a simple truth: People who are poor, disenfranchised and dark-skinned are the most likely to be victimized by chemical plants, hazardous waste dumps and myriad other industrial effluvia.

Hazardous waste facilities continue to be constructed

with a chilling regularity in poor areas inhabited largely by minorities. This is not a statistical phenomenon, but a deliberate business and political strategy. A leaked 1984 memo from the California Waste Management Board spelled out the strategy in stunningly clinical language: "All socioeconomic groups tend to resent the nearby siting of major [hazardous waste] facilities, but middle and upper socioeconomic strata possess better resources to effectuate their opposition. These neighborhoods should not fall within the one-mile and five-mile radius of the proposed sites."

A 1992 investigation by the *National Law Journal* unearthed another ugly dimension of environmental discrimination. From 1985 through 1991, the fines handed out by the Environmental Protection Agency for violations of federal environmental laws were 500 to 1,000 percent higher if the crimes were committed in white communities as opposed to black and Hispanic areas.

These incidents aren't abstractions. They occur in real American communities: Navajo forcibly removed from their homelands on Big Mountain to make way for the expansion of Peabody Coal's strip mines, the largest on earth; Mexican-American families in the southern Texas town of Sierra Madre who are forced to live next to a 70,000-acre ranch where New York City dumps its sewage sludge; the black community of Convent, Louisiana, in the heart of cancer alley—surrounded by three oil refineries, 17 chemical plants and eight hazardous industrial facilities; the Appalachian hamlet of East Liverpool, Ohio, home to the world's largest hazardous waste incinerator; Gary, Indiana, dumping ground for U.S. Steel.

It's hard to escape the conclusion, as environmental justice organizer Richard Moore says, that "people of color don't have the complexion for protection."

By the summer of 1992, the attention of the world was focused on Rio de Janeiro, for the international confab

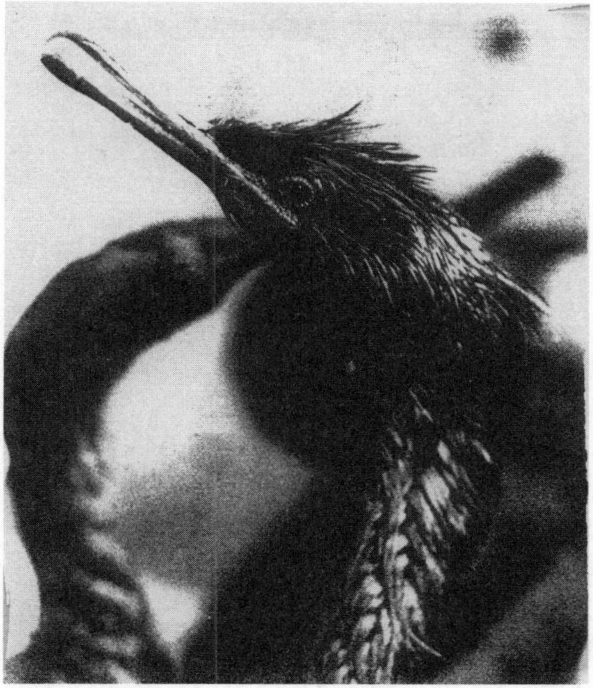

ITT Archives

The Trans-Alaska pipeline was a gun barrel leveled at Prince William Sound.

ITT Archives

bers. The lists are usually followed with this admonition: "Now you know who they are and where they are. Just do the right thing and let your conscience be your guide."

The Sahara Club is not alone. Across the country, the past six years have seen a startling increase in intimidation, vandalism and violence directed against grassroots environmental activists. Observers of this trend have documented hundreds of acts of violence, ranging from vandalism, assaults, arson and shootings to torture and rape, much of it occurring in rural and low-income communities.

ITT Archives

Recent years have seen an increase in intimidation, vandalism, and violence against environmentalists.

known as the Earth Summit. The Rio Summit was billed as the first major huddling of world leaders to grapple with some of the most intractable environmental crises: global warming, ozone depletion, species extinction, rainforest destruction. More than 170 nations attended—but the U.S. government almost didn't show up. Eventually, President Bush was embarrassed into sending a delegation, although it quickly left without signing the most important protocols, including the International Convention on Biodiversity.

Much of the attention in Rio and in the press was focused on the fate of the rainforest, the so-called lungs of the world. The forest was being plundered at an almost inconceivable rate: upward of 149 acres every minute, 214,000 acres per day. Much of the forest was simply going up in smoke, in a kind of modern slash-and-burn regime designed to rid the land of forest and indigenous tribes and clear the way for huge cattle ranches. The loss of forest cover has presaged a staggering loss of species. The extinction rate in tropical rainforests worldwide was compared by biologists to that which jolted the earth during the Cretaceous Age. Biologist E. O. Wilson estimates that 137 species are extirpated every day—50,000 each year. Indigenous cultures too have been torn asunder, victims of acculturation, government-sanctioned murder, enforced starvation and Western diseases. The population of indigenous people in the Amazon basin prior to Western contact has been estimated to have been as high as 9 million. In 2000, less than 200,000 indigenous people remained.

All this saw the proliferation of hundreds of new groups battling for the rainforests. Three stand out: Rainforest Action Network (RAN), Project Underground and the International Rivers Network (IRN). These groups share a number of features: they are international, aggressive, confront corporations directly, engage in direct action and work side-by-side with indigenous groups. RAN set the model, which ranged from boycotts of Mitsubishi (a prime destroyer of rainforests in Malaysia and Indonesia) to aiding the cause of indigenous groups such as the Penan of Borneo, the Kayapo of the

Amazon and the Pygmies of the Ituri forest in Africa. RAN has worked with many of these tribes and rainforest ecologists to advance sustainable uses of intact rainforests.

The loss of tropical forests has mostly been linked to the rapacity of timber companies. But throughout much of the tropics, the rainforests harbor other treasures the corporations are eager to exploit: namely oil and gold. Project Underground was started as a way of helping local communities in the tropics and elsewhere fight off the depredations of the transnationals. Much of Project Underground's early work focused on the Grasberg gold mine in Indonesia. One of largest mines in the world, with deposits of gold, silver and tin valued at more than $70 billion, Grasberg started as a joint partnership between the New Orleans-based mining giant Freeport McMoRan and the regime of former Indonesian dictator Suharto.

But the riches haven't found their way to the Amungme tribe, who live next to the mining site and consider the mountain it's carved into to be sacred. Instead, the Amungme have been forcibly evicted from their homes and killed by Indonesian troops acting as security forces for the mining company. As many as 2,000 people have been murdered by security forces near the mine. As horrifying as these acts are, the long-term environmental consequences from the mining operation may take an even greater toll. Throughout the '90s, Freeport dumped more than 150,000 tons of toxic mine waste into the Ajkwa River system, poisoning the Amungme's drinking water and toxifying or killing the fish that are a staple of their diet. In 1996, the Amungme filed a $6 billion class action suit in U.S. federal court against the company. "Freeport has killed us," says Tom Beanal, an Amungme tribal leader. "They've taken our land and our grandparents' land. They ruined the mountains. We can't drink our water anymore."

The Berkeley, California-based IRN was one of the first groups to confront the malign environmental role played by international finance institutions. Their focus is on dams, which have proliferated across the developing world in the name of economic aid, too often destroying ecosystems and

The threats and bloodshed have coincided with the rise of a self-styled "movement" whose members call themselves either "Wise Use" or "Property Rights" activists and support unrestricted timber cutting on public lands as well as offshore "energy development," mining and drilling in national parks and wilderness areas, abolition of the Endangered Species Act and rollbacks in other environmental-protection laws.

Most Americans have probably never encountered the Wise Use philosophy except in the rhetoric of Rush Limbaugh or Pat Buchanan. Nevertheless the movement has developed its own social base, idiomatic language and support network, which reaches from unemployed loggers, off-road motorcyclists and rural county commissioners to the top levels of industry and government.

To date, the strength of anti-environmentalism has been not in its membership rolls, but in its ability to mobilize a network of core activists to intervene in and politicize local conflicts, creating a perception of power that they hope can be used as a springboard for further expansion. But where politics have failed, elements of the Wise Use movement have shown a willingness to use violence. The movement's key players—many of them upscale conservatives—have often tried to distance themselves from the bullying tactics. "When I say we have to pick up a sword and shield and kill the bastards, I mean politically, not physically," explains Ron Arnold, a former Sierra Club member who went on to become a founder and leader of the anti-green movement. Nonetheless, if—as Arnold himself has put it—Wise Use is engaged in a "holy war against the new pagans who worship trees and sacrifice people," it's the pagans who have suffered most of the casualties.

indigenous communities for the sake of U.S. corporations. IRN made its mark tackling the biggest dam of them all: China's Three Gorges. This monstrosity would rise 575 feet above the Yangtze, the world's third-longest river, and would create a reservoir more than 350 miles long, compelling the forced resettlement of nearly 1.9 million Chinese. Construction on the $24 billion dam began in 1994, backed by financing from a myriad of Western institutions, including Morgan Stanley Dean Witter, First Boston, Goldman Sachs and the World Bank, the largest financier of dams worldwide.

But IRN led an international coalition of groups that targeted these funders and international construction firms. This was an entirely new kind of environmental campaign, which targeted and exposed the complex political economy of mega-construction projects. By 1996, they won a key opinion from the National Security Council, which determined that the U.S. government should withdraw financial support for the project. A few months later, the Export-Import Bank announced that it would not guarantee loans to U.S. companies seeking contracts at the dam. Then, in the biggest victory of all, the World Bank announced it would not underwrite Three Gorges.

Planet Care

DAVID BROWER

January 23, 1995

There is no mandate for *greedlock*. You won't find the term in *Webster's* yet. It was invented by my wife, Anne Brower, to describe what the earth was suffering from before the Earth Summit in Rio.

The senior Republicans elevated to leadership last November promise to make greedlock far worse—yet they have absolutely no mandate to wreak such havoc. Did anyone mandate that Congress stop protecting public lands, and instead put them up for a liquidation sale? Or vote for a budget-cutting race with hardly a thought about how much the cuts might cost if we keep postponing the overdue maintenance of our planet? Or insist that these cuts ignore the cost to those who have not yet reached voting age? . . .

We have taken too much from the earth and restored too little. We have spent too much of our children's hope on our own instant gratification. We have unwittingly substituted the poverty of materialism for prosperity.

The news isn't all bad. Polio is gone. Life expectancy is up in the North if not the South. There is instant replay on TV. We have Rush Limbaugh to assure us that everything that enviros fret about isn't really a problem. And we have the Far Righteous to see that we pray enough as long as we pray right.

But, as Thoreau asked so long ago, "What's the use of a house if you haven't got a tolerable planet to put it on?"

On a 1992 trip to NASA headquarters to examine the latest in geo-satellite technology, President George Bush was presented with two large satellite images. One depicted a million acres of forest in the Brazilian Amazon. Another showed the same amount of acreage on the Olympic Peninsula of Washington State. Bush shrugged his shoulders and wandered away. But the following day the photos landed on the front page of the *New York Times*. The contrast in the images was striking. The Brazilians, so often the target of American condemnation, had logged off and burned about 10 percent of the Amazon's primary forest. By contrast, the United States had logged off more than 95 percent of its original forest. The ensuing battle over the fate of the remaining 5 percent of old-growth forests in the United States would become one of the fiercest in the history of American environmentalism. The ecological symbol for this struggle became a diminutive and secretive bird that inhabited the temperate rainforests of the Pacific Northwest: the northern spotted owl.

Traditionally, green groups such as the Sierra Club and the Wilderness Society had tended to ignore forests for easier targets: alpine wildernesses or so-called "rocks and ice" terrain. So through the '60s and '70s, millions of acres of old-growth in Oregon, Washington, California and southeast Alaska were leveled with little organized opposition. All that began to change in the early '80s, when a new, more confrontational group of activists began blockading logging roads and hanging from trees slated for cutting.

Inspired by the writings of Edward Abbey and fed up with the timid and top-down nature of many big environmental groups, the Earth First!ers placed their bodies between big trees and chainsaws. The '80s saw repeated confrontations between the Earth First!ers, the Forest Service and the timber giants: in the Siskiyou and Klamath Mountains, at Millennium Grove (where the oldest trees in Oregon were logged illegally on Easter Sunday), at Opal Creek and along the Breitenbush River. These battlegrounds evoke the same resonance for environmentalists that Shiloh, Vicksburg and Bull Run do for the Civil War buff.

In the end, the fate of the spotted owl ended up in the hands of a Reagan-appointed federal judge named William Dwyer, who confounded his Republican allies by dealing the Bush administration a string of stinging setbacks, culminating in an injunction against any new timber sales in spotted owl habitat. In his landmark ruling in 1991, Dwyer denounced the Forest Service for "a remarkable series of violations of the environmental laws."

The spotted owl injunction became a contested issue in the 1992 presidential election, with Bush pledging to overturn the logging ban if re-elected. Bush lost, but Bill Clinton and Al Gore came to the timber industry's rescue anyway. The scheme was pure Clinton: convene a staged "town hall"

The Myth of Living Safely in a Toxic World

SANDRA STEINGRABER

April 30, 2001

I call it the myth of living safely in a toxic world. It works like this. Environmental education in this country tends to focus on individual actions. From Earth Day pamphlets to college environmental science textbooks, we are exhorted to recycle, compost our food scraps, turn off the tap while brushing our teeth, and insulate our attics. . . .

We pretend that we can all live safely in a toxic world if we as individual consumers just give up enough stuff: stop eating meat, stop eating fish, stop drinking tap water, stop swimming in chlorinated pools, stop microwaving in plastic, swear off dairy products, remove shoes at the door so as not to track lawn chemicals into the living room, handwash silk blouses rather than drop them off at the dry-cleaners. Or worse yet, we pretend we can shop our way out of the environmental crisis: buy air filters, buy water filters, buy bottled water, buy pesticide-removing soaps for our vegetables, buy vitamin pills loaded with anti-oxidants to undo whatever damage we can't avoid. . . .

Lionel Delevingne

Fed up with the timid nature of many big environmental groups, Earth First!ers placed their bodies between big trees and chainsaws.

meeting, put out a prefabricated plan and induce your liberal friends to swallow their principles and sign off on it. This shadow play was the April 1993 Forest Summit, a ridiculous display of consensus-mongering that saw some of the nation's leading environmentalists play footsy with executives from Weyerhaeuser.

Shortly after the Portland summit, the political arm-twisting began. "They told us that during the campaign they'd made commitments to the timber lobby that logging would be restarted before the end of 1993," recalls Larry Tuttle, then head of the Oregon Natural Resources Council, a plaintiff in the original suit. "They said we had to agree to lift the Dwyer injunction or they'd get Congress to come up with something worse."

Tuttle and many other grassroots greens objected, but the big national groups went along with the deal. By the fall of 1993, the ancient forests were once again being clearcut. The consequences for the spotted owl were dire. Under the Clinton plan, the spotted owl population plunged more in five years than the plan's environmental impact statement had predicted it would decline under a worst case scenario over 40 years. But the owl was always just a symbol for an entire ecosystem on the verge of collapse. Among the other species caught in a tailspin toward extinction: marbled murrelets, coho salmon, cutthroat trout, Pacific fisher, pine marten, red tree voles, bull trout, dozens of salamanders, mollusks and hundreds of deep forest wildflowers and plants.

Eight years of Bill Clinton and Al Gore yielded few rewards and many more bitter disappointments. During the early days of the administration, Clinton and Gore played it smart. They tapped more than 30 environmentalists for key positions in the administration, from Carol Browner as head of the EPA to Bruce Babbitt as interior secretary. That gave the environmentalists the kind of access they hadn't had in more than a decade. But it turned out that access was about all greens got out of Clinton and Gore. The 1993–1994

ITT Archives

The disparate strains of environmentalism converged in the streets of Seattle on November 30, 1999.

Fortunately—and I do think it is fortunate—few of these lifestyle sacrifices actually offer much real protection for public health. The reason I think this is good news is that the sooner we quit trying to turn our bodies and homes into fortresses against toxic invasions, the sooner we'll realize that we have no choice but to rise up and demand an end to the invasion. The hard fact is that we cannot opt out of the water cycle or the food chain.

Consider drinking water. You might think you can save yourself from exposures to carcinogens in tap water by purchasing bottled water. But the sense of safety offered by bottled water is a mirage. Because the industry is unregulated, there is no telling what's actually in the bottle. It frequently contains trace contaminants. In some cases, it even is tap water. Moreover, it turns out that congressional session, when Democrats controlled all branches of government for the first time in 12 years, was one of the least productive environmental legislatures in half a century. And the Republican takeover in 1994 put greens back on the defensive, having to battle both Congress and a reluctant administration.

The failures of the Clinton years are perhaps best illustrated by the issue that Gore made his own: global warming. By the mid-'90s, global warming had gone from a theory to a harshly experienced fact. A wave of searingly hot summers and droughts scorched the Midwest, accompanied by fierce storms and prolonged El Niño conditions in the Pacific. The '90s would be the hottest decade on record. The Kyoto convention in 1997, convened as a follow-up to the Rio summit, was supposed to put the brakes on this perilous warming trend, but the event itself would become emblematic of the shifting alliances and competing interests in global environmental policy. Kyoto was doomed from the start. The U.S. Senate voted 97-0 to reject anything that came out of the meeting before it began. And the U.S. negotiators, led by Gore, started backpedaling from previous commitments almost as soon as they arrived. In the end, the accord was a feeble one, requiring signatories to reduce their carbon emissions an average of 5 percent below 1990 levels by 2012.

But three years later, Congress still had not ratified the treaty, and, at a meeting in The Hague, the United States outraged the European community by attempting to back out of even these meager commitments by pushing for more flexibility in evaluating emissions reductions. U.S. representatives pushed for the use of credits for carbon "sinks"—forests and other lands that absorb carbon dioxide pollution—and emissions trading to help nations meet their goals. This was particularly appalling considering the fact that although the United States contains only 5 percent of the world's population, it is responsible for more than 23 percent of greenhouse gas emissions.

American environmentalists now find themselves in a paradoxical fix: popular support for their causes has never been

breathing, not drinking, constitutes our main route of exposure to volatile pollutants in tap water. This is because most of them—solvents, pesticides, by-products of water chlorination—easily evaporate. As soon as the toilet is flushed or the faucet turned on, these contaminants leave the water and enter the air. Drink a bottle of French water and then step into the shower for 10 minutes, and you've just received the exposure equivalent of a half-gallon of tap water. . . .

Or consider breast milk, that most perfect form of infant nutrition, with its unsurpassed powers to boost IQ, fend off infectious diseases, encourage the development of the immune system, and prevent diabetes, allergies and obesity. Because it exists at the top of the human food chain, mothers' milk has become the most chemically contaminated of all human foods. It carries concentrations of organochlorine pollutants that are 10 to 20 times higher than cows' milk. Indeed, prevailing levels of chemical contaminants in human milk often exceed legally allowable limits in commercial foodstuffs. Thus, on average, in industrialized countries, breast-fed infants ingest each day 50 times more PCBs per pound of body weight than do their parents. The same is true for dioxins.

We cannot ask newborns to become vegetarians. (Soy-based formula is far inferior to human milk. Even as chemically compromised as human breast milk is, breast-fed babies still end up smarter, healthier, less prone to leukemia and exhibiting superior motor skills when compared to their formula-fed counterparts.) We could encourage their mothers to make changes in their diets, but it turns out that the lifestyle approach to cleaning up breast milk is not very effective. Unless they are strict vegans, vegetarians have just as much dioxin in their fat tissues—from which breast milk is manufactured—as meat-eaters. . . .

On the other hand, political action works great to purify breast milk. I am pleased to report that average concentrations of certain key breast milk higher, but their political influence seems on the wane. The 2000 presidential election saw the movement divided, in conflict with itself. Pragmatists sided with Gore, despite his ineffectual record; idealists and radicals threw themselves into the Green Party run of Ralph Nader. Both sides would be disappointed.

George W. Bush, however, may turn out to be the unwilling savior of the environmental movement—even as he, and his slate of cabinet appointees from the corporate world, plot to plunder what's left of the natural world. That's because of a simple truism: Environmentalists are better on the defensive. "Bush is a mobilizing force," says Tim Hermach, director of the Eugene, Oregon-based Native Forest Council. "He's just like James Watt. He's got all the green fundraisers salivating. For those of us on the frontlines, Bush brings clarity—there's no chance of mistaking his intentions, the way so many did under Clinton."

In the past 25 years, U.S. environmentalism has become big business. Nine nonprofit organizations enjoy budgets of more than $20 million a year, while four have budgets of more than $50 million. This newfound wealth inevitably has made these groups more cautious. Thus the divisions between inside-the-Beltway greens, national groups and more radical groups seem likely to widen. Even Earth First! has been out-radicalized by the emergence of the Earth Liberation Front, which has torched ski resorts, luxury homes built in the wilderness and buildings housing biotech operations.

The future of environmentalism will also likely be far more internationalist. On matters such as global warming, ozone depletion and pesticides, the European Union has taken more protective stands than the U.S. government. Greens have come to political power in Germany, amassing seats in parliament and forming part of the cabinet. In France, José Bové and his group of peasant farmers have attracted international headlines for challenging corporations such as McDonald's and Monsanto. New environmental movements are also

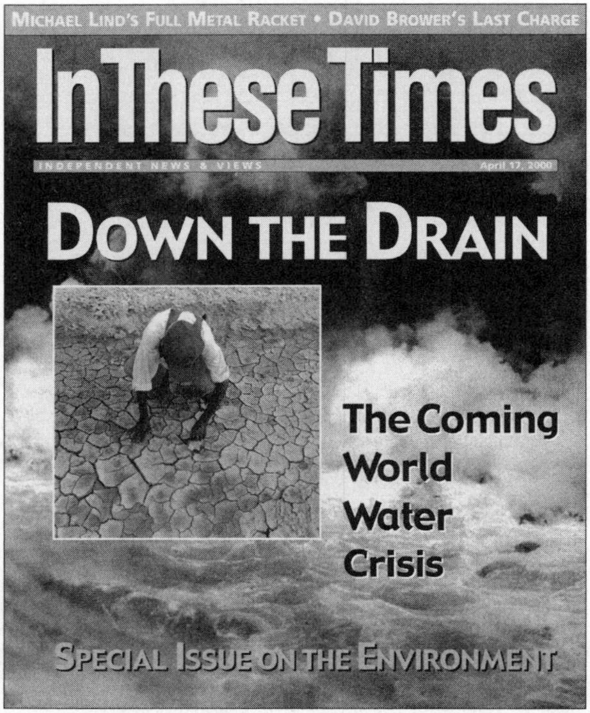
MICHAEL LIND'S FULL METAL RACKET • DAVID BROWER'S LAST CHARGE
In These Times
INDEPENDENT NEWS & VIEWS
April 17, 2000
DOWN THE DRAIN
The Coming World Water Crisis
SPECIAL ISSUE ON THE ENVIRONMENT
ITT Archives

The future of environmentalism will be far more internationalist.

contaminants—DDT, PCBs and dioxins—have declined dramatically since the '70s. This improvement is a direct consequence of bans, tighter regulations, incinerator closings, emission reductions, permit denials, right-to-know laws and tougher environmental enforcement. We nursing mothers owe a great debt to thousands of anonymous citizens from all around the world who worked to stop toxic pollution at its source.

The way we repay this debt—and continue the process of detoxification—is to stop distracting ourselves with individual sacrifices and get involved with the political struggle.

springing up in India, Russia and across Latin America. When Subcomandante Marcos led his Zapatista army of Mayan rebels into Mexico City in March 2001, the 150,000 people who packed Zocalo Plaza heard Marcos deliver a fiery speech that linked indigenous rights, economic justice and environmental protection.

All of these disparate strains of environmentalism converged on the streets of Seattle on November 30, 1999, protesting the World Trade Organization. Organic farmers stood shoulder to shoulder with Earth First!ers and human rights groups, trade unionists and animal rights activists—all united in their desire to shut down this coven of global finance ministers. The WTO was seen as the mouthpiece of a global economy that tramples indigenous peoples, exploits workers, circumvents laws and ravages nature. In a sense, the consolidation of the corporate world had served the function of consolidating the opposition to it. The movement assembled on the streets of Seattle was a snapshot of what environmentalism had become: internationalist in perspective, anti-corporate in tone, grassroots oriented and unified by a desire for social and ecological justice.

Terry LaBan

In Seattle, Brower said: "Our future is out on the streets. It's alive and well and fighting harder than ever."

David Brower was in Seattle that week and, though weakened by cancer, there was a fire in his eyes and it was clear that his 88-year-old heart was with the protesters. Brower's life as America's pre-eminent environmentalist was in many ways a testament to the arc of the movement itself, from elitist hiking clubs to militant opposition against the ravages of transnational corporations. What defined Brower most was his unremitting optimism. Brower always spoke for the possibility of radical change and the ability of popular movements to take on and defeat entrenched power.

On that rainy day in Seattle, Brower pointed toward the clouds of tear gas and said: "Our future is out on the streets. It's alive and well and fighting harder than ever."

The only way global warming will become a political issue is if it becomes a personal issue first.

ITT Archives

Now or Never

BILL McKIBBEN

April 30, 2001

In the face of global warming, what is an environmentalist to do? The normal answer, when you're mounting a campaign, is to look for self-interest, to scare people by saying what will happen to us if we don't do something: all the birds will die, the canyon will disappear beneath a reservoir, we will choke to death on smog.

But in the case of global warming, those kind of answers don't exactly do the trick, at least in the time frame we're discussing. At this latitude, climate change will creep up on us. Severe storms have already grown more frequent and more damaging. The seasons are less steady in their progression. Some agriculture is less reliable. But face it: Our economy is so enormous that it handles those kinds of changes in stride. Economists who work on this stuff talk about how it will shave a percentage or two off GNP over the next few decades—not enough to notice in the kind of generalized economic boom they describe.

And most of us live lives so divorced from the natural world that we hardly notice the changes anyway. Hotter? Turn up the air conditioning. Stormier? Well, an enormous percentage of Americans commute from remote-controlled garage to office parking garage—they may have gone the last year without getting good and wet in a rainstorm. By the time the magnitude of the change is truly in our faces, it will be too late to do much about it: There's such a lag time with carbon dioxide in the atmosphere that we need to be making the switch to solar and wind and hydrogen right about now. Yesterday, in fact.

So maybe we should think of global warming in a different way—as the great moral crisis of our moment, the equivalent in our time of the civil rights movement of the '60s.

Why a moral question? In the first place, because we've never figured out a more effective way to screw the marginalized and poor of this planet. Having taken their dignity, their resources and their freedom under a variety of other schemes, we now are taking the very physical stability on which they depend for the most bottom-line of existences.

Our economy can absorb these changes for a while, but for a moment consider Bangladesh. A river delta that houses 130 million souls in an area the size of Wisconsin, Bangladesh actually manages food self-sufficiency most years. But in 1998, the sea level in the Bay of Bengal was higher than normal, just the sort of thing we can expect to become more frequent and severe. The waters sweeping down the Ganges and the Brahmaputra from the Himalayas could not drain easily into the ocean—they backed up across the country, forcing most of its inhabitants to spend three months in thigh-deep water. The fall rice crop didn't get planted. We've seen this same kind of disaster in the past few years in Mozambique or Honduras or Venezuela or any of a dozen other wretched spots.

ITT Archives

This century seems poised to see extinctions at a rate not observed since the last big asteroid slammed into the planet. But this time the asteroid is us.

And a moral crisis, too, if you place any value on the rest of creation. Coral reef researchers indicate that these spectacularly intricate ecosystems are also spectacularly vulnerable—rising water temperatures will likely bleach them to extinction by mid-century. In the Arctic, polar bears are 20 percent scrawnier than they were a decade ago: As pack ice melts, so does the opportunity for hunting seals. All in all, this century seems poised to see extinctions at a rate not observed since the last big asteroid slammed into the planet. But this time the asteroid is us.

A moral question, finally, if you think we owe any debt to the future. No one ever has figured out a more thoroughgoing way to stripmine the present and degrade what comes after. Forget the seventh generation—we're talking 70th generation, and 700th. All the people that will ever be related to you. Ever. No generation yet to come will ever forget us—we are the ones present at the moment when the temperature starts to spike, and so far we have not reacted. If it had been done to us, we would loathe the generation that did it, precisely as we will one day be loathed.

But trying to make a moral campaign is no easy task. In most moral crises, there is a villain—some person or class or institution that must be overcome. Once they're identified, the battle can commence. But you can't really get angry at carbon dioxide, and the people responsible for its production are, well, us. So perhaps we need some symbols to get us started, some places to sharpen the debate and rally ourselves to action. There are plenty to choose from: our taste for ever bigger houses and the heating and cooling bills that come with them; our penchant for jumping on airplanes at the drop of a hat; and so on. But if you wanted one glaring example of our lack of balance, you could do worse than point the finger at sport utility vehicles.

SUVs are more than a mere symbol. They are a major part of the problem—one reason we emit so much more carbon dioxide now than we did a decade ago is because our fleet of cars and trucks actually has gotten steadily less fuel efficient for the past 10 years. If you switched today from the average American car to a big SUV, and drove it for just one year, the difference in carbon dioxide that you produced would be the equivalent of opening your refrigerator door and then forgetting to close it for six years. SUVs essentially are machines for burning fossil fuel that just happen to also move you and your stuff around. . . .

So that's why some pastors are starting to talk with their congregations about what car they're going to buy, and why some college seniors are passing around petitions pledging to stay away from the Ford Explorers and Excursions and Extraneouses, and why some auto dealers have begun to notice informational picketers outside on Saturday mornings, urging their customers to think about gas mileage when they go inside.

The point is not that by themselves such actions—any individual actions—will make any real dent in the production of carbon dioxide pouring into our atmosphere. Even if you got 10 percent of Americans really committed to changing energy use, their solar homes wouldn't make much of a dent in our national totals. But 10 percent would be enough to change the politics of the issue, to ensure the passage of the laws that would cause us all to shift our habits. And so we need to begin to take an issue that is now the province of technicians and turn it into a political issue—just as bus boycotts began to take the issue of race and make it public, forcing the system to respond. That response is likely to be ugly—there are huge companies with a lot to lose and many people so tied in to their current ways of life that advocating change smacks of subversion. But this has to become a political issue—and fast. The only way that may happen, short of a hideous drought or monster flood, is if it becomes a personal issue first.

Terry LaBan

SUVs essentially are machines for burning fossil fuel that just happen to also move you and your stuff around.

Color and Criminal Justice

AMERICA'S INCARCERATION EPIDEMIC

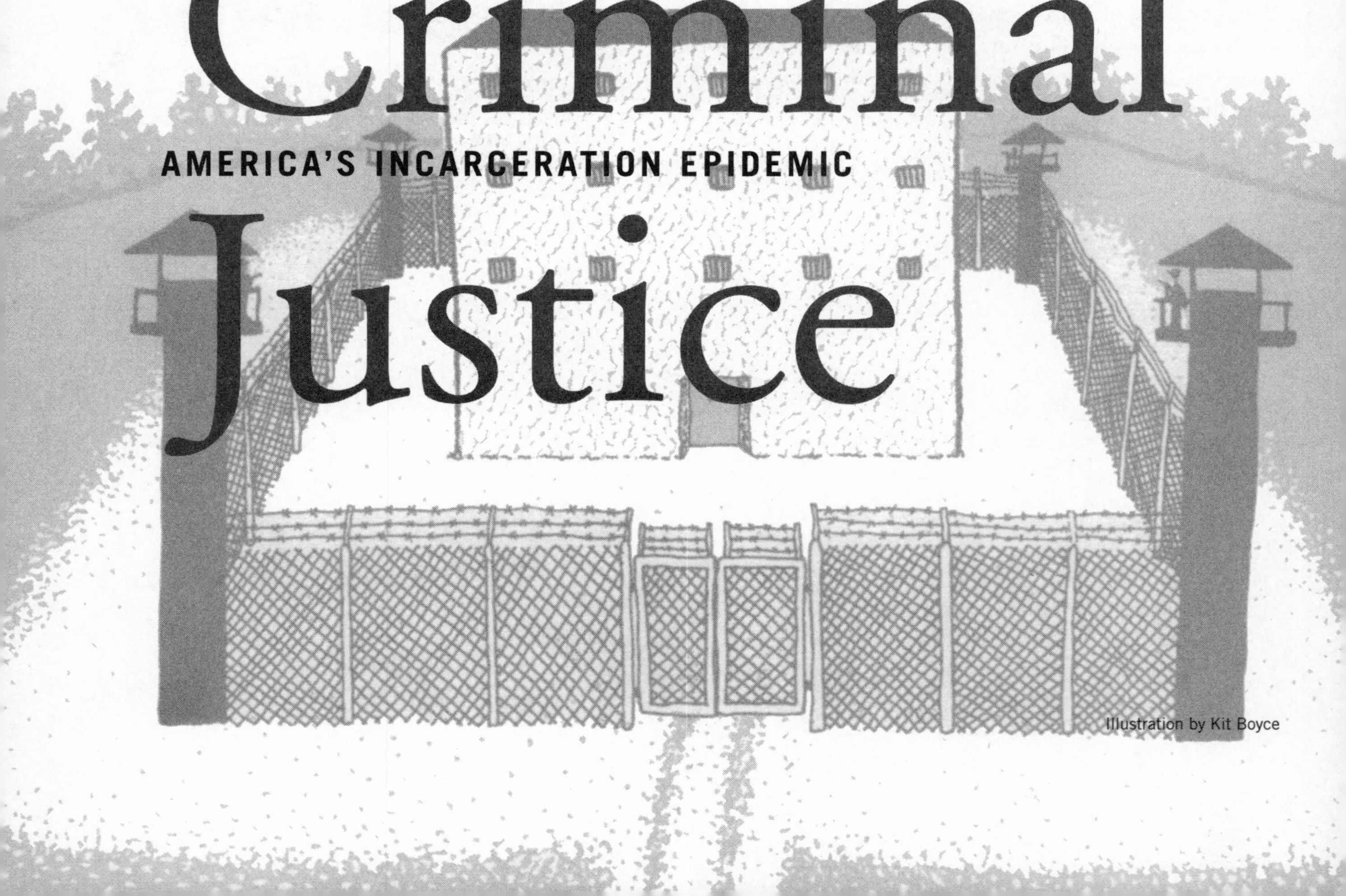

Illustration by Kit Boyce

Ten

SALIM MUWAKKIL

ABANDONED HOPES SHARE SPACE WITH DECAYING BUILDINGS IN THE ENGLEWOOD NEIGHBORHOOD ON CHICAGO'S SOUTH SIDE. OTHER THAN A thriving drug trade, there is little commercial activity among the vacant lots and squalor. This is Gangster Disciples territory, and the notorious street gang has cornered the market on cheap, high-grade marijuana. On just about every block at any hour, customers come from all over the city to purchase $10 bags of weed. Many of these drug merchants are just out of prison, men who have flocked to the area for gang camaraderie and employment in the only industry unconcerned with criminal records.

This is hardly the only Chicago community afflicted with this problem. "In some cases there are more people who have come home from prison living in the neighborhood than residents," says Rep. Danny K. Davis of some areas in his Chicago district. "Since prisons are no longer interested in rehabilitation, most of these ex-inmates are unskilled and unqualified for employment in good-paying jobs. Many are illiterate. How can we have a desirable quality of life in a community with so many jobless, ex-inmates concentrated in one neighborhood?"

Davis' rhetorical question focuses on just one aspect of an incarceration epidemic. According to the Sentencing Project, a Washington-based reform group that researches criminal justice issues, at least 2 million people are already incarcerated in the United States, and about half—or 1 million—are African-Americans, although they comprise only around 13 percent of the U.S. population. Three out of 10 black boys will spend time in prison, and about one-third of all black males in their twenties are currently under the control of the criminal justice system (including parole and probation). The Bureau of Justice Statistics reveals that, as of 1999, the incarceration rate for black men was 4,617 per 100,000; 1,802 for Hispanic men;

and 482 for white men. For black women the rate was 375 per 100,000; 142 for Hispanic women; and 53 for white women.

This disparity reflects a legacy of racial oppression and social exclusion, contemporarily reinforced by anti-drug police practices that target blacks disproportionately. The viability of black America is being undermined as youth are sucked into the maw of an insatiable U.S. criminal justice system. Yet the conditions that Davis bemoans will invariably worsen as increasing numbers of inmates return from prison to communities woefully unprepared. Their increasing menace will clearly demonstrate the insanity of a criminal justice system that serves more as an apartheid academy of criminality than a venue of rehabilitation that could reduce crime's social harm.

How did we get to this point?

The association of black men with criminality is as old as America itself. The fear of slave revolts prompted officials in early America to ban all gatherings of black men, as John Hope Franklin notes in his landmark volume *From Slavery to Freedom*. The "slave codes" forbade black men from congregating for purposes other than laboring for whites. Yale University scholar Robert Perkinson argues that the measures taken to control the black population in the South—particularly black males—are the true antecedents of modern criminal justice. The first organized American police force, for example, was the slave patrols.

After slavery was abolished, the "black codes" enforced similar prohibitions. Since America had an enormous economic stake in enforcing the racial hierarchy, it was essential to eliminate any threat to that color-coding through draconian legal restrictions, repressive social constraints and the criminal justice system. "By the 1880s and 1890s, Southern criminologists were talking about the 'innate criminality' of black people," explained Christian Parenti, author of *Lockdown America*, in a 2000 interview. "Those last 20 years

MOVE Massacre

ALICE WALKER

December 17, 1986

Was the bombing of black people, with a black person ostensibly (in any case) responsible, too much for the collective black psyche to bear? Were people stunned by the realization that such an atrocity—formerly confined to Libya or Vietnam—could happen to us? Did I simply miss the controversy? Were there town meetings and teach-ins and pickets around the clock in every city Wilson Goode and his police officers appeared? Or did the media (and Philadelphia officials, including the black mayor of which black Philadelphians were so proud) succeed in convincing the public that the victims were indeed the aggressors and deserved what they got? Ramona Africa, after all, was arrested for assault and sentenced to prison for "riot"—and it was her house that was bombed, her friends, colleagues and loved ones who were slaughtered.

Thumbing through the stacks of articles I've been sent on the MOVE massacre, I see that an earlier assault on their house occurred in 1978, when a white man, Frank Rizzo, was mayor. Under Rizzo, MOVE people were evicted, often imprisoned, their house eventually razed. Under Goode, a black mayor, their house was bombed, their neighborhood destroyed, and many of them killed. And why?

Through both administrations, the city officials and MOVE neighbors appeared to have one thing in common: a hatred of the way MOVE people chose to live. They didn't like the "stench" of people who refused, because they believe chemicals cause cancer, to use deodorant. Didn't like orange peels and watermelon rinds on the ground. Didn't like all those naked children running around with all that uncombed hair. They didn't appreciate the dogs and the rats. They thought children should be in school and that the adults and children should eat cooked food; everybody should eat of the 19th century saw a huge explosion of incarceration in the South. Black people, rather than being kept as slaves, were being put in prison camps. Traditionally, Southern prisons had been very small. The period after the Civil War brought the first great wave of imprisonment in American criminal justice."

The defeated Confederate states were essentially able to re-enslave many blacks by crafting laws that criminalized their behavior. In Alabama, for instance, loitering without proof of gainful employment was a crime. The 13th Amendment may have officially abolished slavery, but it didn't apply to forced labor by convicted felons. And the new convict-lease system (in which prisoners were "leased" to landowners and corporations) had great advantages; landowners didn't own the convicts and thus had no financial stake in their well-being. Many were simply worked to death. Similarly, when the 15th Amendment extended the vote to former slaves, southern states hastily enacted laws forbidding ex-felons from voting. (Although disenfranchisement laws have been on the books since the founding of the republic, all previously excluded groups except for convicted felons now have the right to vote.)

The media too did its part to demonize blacks. According to a 1954 study by historian Rayford Logan, blacks were regular targets of blatant bias in U.S. magazines and newspapers at the turn of the century. "The magazines repeated derogatory epithets, inconsistent dialect and stereotypes; they glorified the Plantation Tradition and condemned Reconstruction," Logan wrote in the study, which has been republished as *The Betrayal of the Negro: From Rutherford B. Hayes to Woodrow Wilson.* The newspapers weren't any better: They regularly used such terms as "nigger" and "darky."

Worse, by focusing relentlessly on the "stereotype of the Negro brute," Logan writes, the media "provided the principal basis for Southern justifications of lynching." The mob murders of black people even became a popular form of entertainment in some regions of the country. A 1999 book called *Without Sanctuary* featured extraordinary photographs of

meat. They probably thought it low-class that in order to make money MOVE people washed cars and shoveled snow. And appeared to enjoy it.

MOVE people were not middle class. Many of them were high school drop-outs. Many of them mothers without husbands. Or young men who refused any inducement to "fit in." Yet they had the nerve to critique the system. To reject it and to set up, in place of its rules, guidelines for living that reflected their own beliefs.

The people of MOVE are proof that poor people (not just upper- and middle-class whites and blacks who become hippies) are capable of intelligently perceiving and analyzing American life, politically and socially, and of devising and attempting to follow a different and, to them, better way. But because they are poor and black this is not acceptable behavior to middle-class whites and blacks who think all poor black people should be happy with Jheri Curls, mindless (and lying) TV shows and Kentucky Fried Chicken.

This is not to condone the yelping of 50 to 60 dogs in the middle of the night. Dogs MOVE people rescued from the streets (and probably subsequent torture in "scientific" laboratories), fed and permitted to sleep in their house. Nor the bullhorn aimed at airing their neighbors' backwardness and political transgressions, as apparently they had a bad habit of doing. From what I read, MOVE people were more philosophical than perfect; I probably would not have been able to live next door to them for a day.

The question is—did they deserve the harassment, abuse and, finally, the vicious death other people's intolerance of their lifestyle brought upon them? Every bomb ever made falls on us. And the answer is no.

white families obviously amused while viewing brutal murders. In retrospect, it's difficult to understand how mainstream Americans looked on as thousands of black people were summarily executed by white mobs from the 1880s to the 1920s. Yet civil rights activists struggled in vain to pass anti-lynching legislation. African-Americans had been so thoroughly dehumanized by the media that many whites knew them only as stereotypes and thus weren't unduly alarmed by the killing spree. Conventional wisdom at the time automatically assumed that murdered black men were guilty.

Yet how far have we really come?

The modern spurt in incarceration rates began in the late '60s in an atmosphere charged with political and social anxiety. By 1969, race-based riots had erupted in more than 300 cities, the Vietnam War had provoked vigorous, sometimes violent antagonisms, and American youth were engaged in a full-scale cultural rebellion. The social anxieties provoked by these varied challenges fertilized a public mood conducive to backlash politics. The right-wing politicians of that era—particularly Barry Goldwater, George Wallace and Richard Nixon—exploited those sentiments for public notoriety and some political success.

A powerful synergy of propaganda involving pandering politicians, law enforcement interests and the media—which presented lurid images of the most horrendous but rarest crimes—nourished the notion that criminal anarchy threatened our very civilization. The public mood darkened and became more receptive to the kind of politics that blamed liberalism for allowing crime to rage out of control. Crime rates were rising due to a number of factors, but the response to the uptick was distorted by candidates seeking political mileage by exaggerating the menace.

In 1968, the same year that Richard Nixon won the presidency running on a campaign theme of "law and order," Congress passed an anti-crime bill that allocated millions of

New Medium, Old Message

NELL IRVIN PAINTER

May 13, 1992

It is well past time that we read the past to realize that little in the Rodney King affair is new or mysterious. The very accessibility of the images seemed to set this case apart from instances of police brutality that went before. But the only part that is new is that this time a cameraman happened to catch it on video. Black people, other people of color and the poor of all races have been familiar with police brutality for generations.

Police brutality is as old as time, as old as slave patrols, as old as the Pinkertons. In recent decades and with uneven success, victims have taken their cases to court. This time the evidence perfectly suited the medium of television, and an old story reached a wide audience. This time the amazement—at the beating, at the verdict—spread beyond the people who were beaten and those who were on their side. Thanks to that cameraman, a lot of Americans discovered the crime of police brutality for the first time. . . .

The inevitable inquiries, findings, recommendations and remedies have a history as old as the riots. The immediate causes of the disturbances of the '60s were nearly always police brutality or rumors of police brutality. The underlying causes—explained in report after report—also began to sound familiar: discrimination, poverty, unemployment, lack of governmental services.

The most eloquent of the reports, the Kerner Report of 1968, is still read and still current. But its roots lie in the 1947 report of President Harry S. Truman's Committee on Civil Rights. The report, titled "To Secure These Rights," began by indicting lynching and police brutality—practices that proved how little America respected the value of black life.

An inclusive report that touches on most of the themes that reappeared in the civil rights move-dollars to local law enforcement agencies to modernize and militarize police forces. During this same period, state legislatures began passing laws that limited judicial discretion and instituted mandatory minimum sentences. New York Gov. Nelson Rockefeller set the stage in 1973 with harsh new laws that included mandatory 15-year terms for possessing small amounts of drugs.

In the '80s, President Reagan ratcheted this social hysteria up several notches. Politicians, particularly those on the right, could win praise for civic engagement and "moral courage" just by reciting a few well-chosen phrases of support for the "war on drugs." It was an easy ploy. But the militant rhetoric translated into a paramilitary approach to combating drug abuse. SWAT teams were bolstered and redeployed to conduct drug raids in the inner cities; a virtual army was stationed along the border with Mexico. Federal funding for the drug war increased from $1.5 billion in 1981 to $6.6 billion (in real terms) by 1989, when Reagan finally left office. Ten years later, the figure had reached $17 billion.

Police forces were suddenly flush with new revenue (often from property seized during drug "investigations") to help them carry out the absurd drug war. Many police departments have restructured their law enforcement techniques to better exploit those new incentives. This leads them to target the most vulnerable cogs in the machine of drug commerce. Their various "buy-and-bust" and drug-dealing "sting" campaigns focus law enforcement resources on small-scale street sales. Of course, most of this activity occurs in the poorest areas of the inner city, where open-air drug markets are more common and fewer resources are available for treatment.

Drug arrests doubled in the '80s, according to the Sentencing Project, and by 1999 had reached more than 1.5 million. Those arrested on drug charges faced a new punishment regimen that included more aggressive prosecutions and mandatory sentencing. The penalties enacted in the Anti-Drug Abuse acts of 1986 and 1988 imposed five-year mandatory prison terms for possession of as little as five

Ted Soqui

The immediate cause of the L.A. riots—as well as the riots of the '60s—was police brutality.

ment of the '50s and '60s, "To Secure These Rights" is well worth reading today, if only to remind us how long remedies have been recognized and agreed upon—and how long the political will has not been sufficient to sustain fundamental reform. . . .

One great lesson of the '60s that came out of the civil rights movement and the war on poverty was the importance of neighborhood-based organizations led by local people. The Student Nonviolent Coordinating Committee of the early '60s and the Model Cities Project of the late '60s have both been spoken of disparagingly since their time. But in different ways, each managed to bring poor and working-class people of color to an appreciation of their power as citizens. This, in turn, stretched prevailing notions of democracy—that officeholders are supposed to speak as though they are college educated and as though they share an identity of interests with the rich and middle-class.

Organization from the bottom up will be crucial in reform, and it will deliver an important lesson that we are perhaps ready to hear. South Central Los Angeles, like many other inner cities in the

United States, is no longer a study of monoliths coded in black and white.

For better or for worse, the '80s proved that black conservatives do, indeed, exist. Clarence Thomas, Anita Hill and their friends demolished completely easy equations of blackness with the liberal wing of the Democratic Party—with any wing of the Democratic Party. Working-class black people exhibit the same ideological heterogeneity.

The poor and working-class people who will need to organize toward the regeneration of their neighborhoods are also heterogeneous ethnically and racially. Effective organization, therefore, will need to reach out to people of many backgrounds. Allies from within and outside inner-city neighborhoods who want to be of help can't afford to remain racially or ethnically parochial. We are accustomed to using the language of race to talk about class, but recent experience shows that poverty and joblessness have more than a black face.

Rebuilding South Central Los Angeles in these recession-ridden, post-industrial times will prove challenging in the extreme, but the path may already be discerned. It leads from one beaten black body to a rainbow coalition organized from the grassroots.

The Other Side of Zero Tolerance

SALIM MUWAKKIL

October 5, 1997

I was 9 years old when I had my first direct contact with a police officer.

A beefy white cop knocked me down and busted my lip when I protested the way he manhandled an older cousin. "Stay the fuck out of this, you little fucking nigger," he snarled as the back

grams of crack cocaine. An offender in possession of powder cocaine—which has the same chemical composition—would have to possess 500 grams to receive the same sentence. These harsher penalties took a disproportionate toll on African-Americans. The U.S. Sentencing Commission reported that 86 percent of those charged with crack trafficking offenses in the federal system in 1995–1996 were African-American, while blacks represented 30 percent of persons charged with powder cocaine offenses.

While this disparity is among the most glaring, other features of criminal justice policy serve to focus the drug war's firepower on the black community. A 2000 Human Rights Watch study, titled "Punishment and Prejudice," found wide disparities in the way black and white drug offenders are treated within the system. Although the study found that there are five times more white drug users than black ones, black men are imprisoned for drugs at rates many times that of white men. The greatest disparity was in Illinois, where blacks are imprisoned for selling or using drugs at 57 times the rate of whites, and where African-Americans comprise 90 percent of the inmates imprisoned for drugs. Black women too are increasingly being sucked into the system, primarily as casualties of the drug war. According to a February 2000 study by the General Accounting Office, the number of women prisoners increased by more than 500 percent from 1980 to 1998.

Even as the black community is stripped of precious human resources, it is fueling a burgeoning corrections industry. For investors at big financial concerns like Goldman Sachs, Prudential Insurance, Smith Barney and Merrill Lynch, prison construction bonds have been lucrative sources of revenue. So many people have developed stakes in maintaining high incarceration rates that the system is offhandedly referred to as the "prison-industrial complex." A 1999 report by the Justice Policy Institute found that prison construction surpassed college construction by a 3-to-1 ratio over the past 20 years. In nearly every state, but especially in those states with the largest black populations, officials are diverting resources from schools to prisons. This is a textbook example of a scavenger enterprise, feasting on the entrails of social decay.

All of these disastrous policies have fueled a murderous underground economy, corroded the civil liberties of all U.S. citizens, and transformed the world's most boastful democracy into the world's leading jailer. Yet the drug war too has failed in its own goals of demonizing drugs and making them less available. According to the University of Michigan's "Monitoring the Future" survey, in 1999 nearly 90 percent of 12th graders rated marijuana "fairly easy" or "very easy" to obtain. Cocaine was rated "easily available" to 25 percent of 8th graders. And the U.N. Office for Drug Control and Crime Prevention found that over the past decade prices had fallen for cocaine by 50 percent and for heroin by 70 percent.

Despite all of these glaring disparities, there has been little public outcry beyond the usual suspects of civil rights activists and other rabble-rousers. Reaction to these studies tends to split along racial lines: Many African-Americans will applaud such reports for documenting clear racial biases in the brutal criminal justice system. But others seem reluctant to attribute racial disparities in imprisonment to bias. Racism is the cause, charge many blacks. Wrong, say many whites, it's criminal behavior.

◎

When W. E. B. Du Bois wrote *The Philadelphia Negro* in 1899, he noted and deplored the "criminal element" and "sexual looseness" within the city's black community. He criticized black parents for not emphasizing the value of formal education, and he upbraided the Negro church for failing to aggressively fight social corruption. But unlike his white contemporaries, Du Bois added historical context: "We have two great causes for the present conditions of the Negro: Slavery and emancipation with their attendant phenomena of ignorance, lack of discipline, and

ITT Archives

In most minority neighborhoods, the police are considered an alien, enemy force.

of his hand slammed into my face. The vitriol that dripped from his lips was more memorable than the pain from the slap. Like some perverse rite of combat, my encounter with that New York cop elevated my peer status in my Harlem neighborhood in 1956. The wound he inflicted was transformed into a mark of distinction, and I brandished it like a medal. I told my mother I fell out of a swing in a nearby park.

In the New York City of my youth, the police were considered alien and enemy forces—an occupying army from the land of white privilege sent to humiliate, vex and sometimes kill us. And the cops avidly fulfilled our expectations. They disrespected us routinely and gratuitously. Seldom did they miss an opportunity to humiliate us; routine searches usually included a demand that we drop our pants.

Those memories flooded back as I read about Abner Louima's horrifying tale of abuse at the hands of Brooklyn cops on August 9. After being arrested outside a Brooklyn nightclub, the 30-year-old Haitian immigrant was handcuffed, taken to Brooklyn's 70th Precinct Station and allegedly tortured by a gang of police officers. According to Louima, the cops pulled down his pants and dragged him handcuffed to the restroom where they rammed the handle of a toilet plunger deep into his rectum, ripping his colon and bladder, and then they shoved it down his throat, shattering his

moral weakness; immigration with its increased competition and moral influence."

In Du Bois' mind, environmental and historical factors were at the root of the higher black crime rate. This was as true for the 40,000 or so blacks living in Philadelphia during that period as it is for African-Americans today. As Du Bois concluded a century ago, the lack of opportunities for social and economic advancement, aggravated by the stresses of resource-poor living conditions increased the likelihood of criminal behavior. His analysis remains relevant.

During the mid '80s and early '90s, the period of most rapid growth in the inmate population, the rapid divestment

Joe Raedle

The number of women prisoners increased by more than 500 percent from 1980 to 1998.

of corporate and governmental resources from the inner city spawned a new level of joblessness that has been more damaging and far-reaching than anything urban blacks' had yet experienced in this century. As Harvard sociologist William Julius Wilson wrote in his 1996 book *When Work Disappears*, "For the first time in the twentieth century most adults in many inner-city ghetto neighborhoods are not working in a typical week."

Wilson argued that this chronic joblessness was the hidden hand in the community instability and burgeoning rates of violent crime that have plagued black America. The income that jobs provide is essential, of course, but Wilson held that the ancillary requirements of steady employment (regular hours, attention to hygiene, and so on) also serve to discipline community life. Wilson inundated critics with a torrent of data that persuasively made his point: The problems of the black community are rooted in the structural tangle of economic forces. To the drumbeat of market logic, capital marched away from the inner city and left behind a post-industrial wasteland.

But drug commerce thrived at the same time, and those plying the trade glittered in contrast to their grimy surroundings. The underground economy is often a less threatening, not to mention more lucrative, alternative for youth increasingly isolated in the nation's resource-poor inner cities. But when these youth make what, by all calculations, is a rational economic decision, they are marked as the enemies in the drug war. The ensuing incarceration epidemic has had devastating, intergenerational effects on the social dynamics within the communities from which these inmates are siphoned.

This focus on incarceration rather than treatment (although a number of studies clearly show that treatment would more effectively combat problems of drug abuse) has nurtured the spread of prison culture. Much of the imagery, metaphors and attitudes of hip-hop and gangsta rap are lifted from prison culture. Jail signifiers are ubiquitous in

teeth. While doing this, Louima said, they were spewing the same kind of racial epithets that were directed at me so many years past. . . .

Mayor Rudy Giuliani has consistently defended the questionable actions of the city's cops. He dismissed community concerns about excessive force after three police officers fired 24 bullets into an unarmed young black man named Aswon Watson last year in Brooklyn. When police shot a 16-year-old Dominican youth named Kevin Cedeño in the back earlier this year, Giuliani quickly offered the officers his official support. He charged that the Washington Heights residents protesting the shooting were being exploited by political opportunists like the Rev. Al Sharpton, a candidate for mayor.

Giuliani's enthusiastic support for a zero-tolerance crackdown on so-called "quality of life" offenses also contributed to the New York Police Department's lack of concern for the civil rights of people suspected—but not convicted—of crimes. City officials and police credit this new strategy, which is all the rage in police circles these days, with significantly reducing serious crime in the city.

Analysts trace this policing strategy to a 1982 *Atlantic Monthly* article by James Q. Wilson and George Kelling, titled "Broken Windows." The authors argued that neighborhoods with broken windows, graffiti, litter and other indications of "disorder" were crucibles for crime. If the laws against these symbols of disorder were enforced aggressively, they claimed, it would restore a sense of public safety and criminals would be less likely to make their move.

Not surprisingly, this zero-tolerance approach is practiced most conscientiously in poor, minority neighborhoods where "broken windows" predominate, serving, in essence, to give cops even more leeway in abusing the rights of community residents. Louima charged that the cops who assaulted him chanted, "it's Giuliani time now, not Dinkins time."

ITT Archives

The effects of high incarceration rates reverberate throughout African-American culture.

black culture these days. Most of the street gangs and other predatory street styles that hold such perverse allure for black youth are incubated in jails and prisons.

But the effects of high incarceration rates reverberate throughout African-American culture. The growing number of African-Americans who get ensnared in the criminal justice system are forever relegated to a kind of quasi-citizenship. An estimated 13 percent of black men currently are disenfranchised (permanently so in 10 states); experts predict that if current trends continue, 30 to 40 percent of the next generation of black men can be expected to lose their right to vote at some point in their lifetimes. In the states of Florida and Alabama, one in three black men is permanently disenfranchised, and in seven other states that ratio is near 25 percent, according to a 1998 report by Human Rights Watch and the Sentencing Project.

Men who have been imprisoned are not good marriage prospects because their records often prevent their successful reintegration into society, further undermining a fragile family structure disproportionately troubled by divorce and female-headed households. The federal Bureau of Justice Statistics estimates that 1.5 million children have a parent behind bars. Many of these children grow up in foster care, with relatives, or moving from place to place. Denise Johnston, head of the Center for Children of Incarcerated Parents, told *Mother Jones* that up to half of all male children of prisoners will go on to commit crimes themselves, perpetuating a cycle that will feed the prison boom for generations to come.

All along America's historical trajectory there have been social and economic disparities that were the result not of a failure of criminal justice, but a lack of economic justice. Instead of fighting crime, we should be fighting poverty. This is only possible through large-scale capital and cultural investments in black America. As a start, the failed war on drugs could easily and plausibly be replaced with programs of harm reduction comparable to strategies used by European countries that have successfully moved away from prohibition. Other policy changes should include support for community-based policing, on-demand drug treatment programs, expanded educational opportunities (with an aggressive focus on preschool and early education), job creation, greater support for small business and entrepreneurial efforts, and increased access to family services. Mandatory sentencing laws must be repealed.

Wishful thinking? For now, perhaps. But these changes will grow more appealing as the damning illogic of our current system begins to manifest in increased social disruptions. Even as the profit potential of the burgeoning corrections-industrial complex attracts more vested interests, society cannot survive this destructive spiral. Just as we now marvel at our past acceptance of lynching, one day we'll look back on this period of apartheid and injustice and shake our heads—if we've still got them, that is.

For every seven prisoners executed, one is set free.

ITT Archives

Innocence on Death Row

CRAIG AARON

December 27, 1998

By the time you are reading this, the United States has probably executed its 500th prisoner since 1976. If not, it's just a matter of days before Oklahoma, Texas, South Carolina or Arkansas straps Tuan Nguyen, Joseph Faulder, Joe Truesdale, Robert Robbins or another of the nation's more than 3,500 Death Row inmates onto the gurney or into the electric chair and kills them.

Number 500 easily could have been any one of the 29 former Death Row inmates who nervously lined up backstage at the National Conference on Wrongful Convictions and the Death Penalty on November 14. Each of these men and women were once sentenced to die; some came within hours of being executed—all were innocent. They each spent years, and sometimes decades, on Death Row for crimes they didn't commit. Only with a stroke of lottery-like luck, divine intervention and a few good lawyers were they freed. One by one, they marched onto the stage, stepped up to the microphone and told the crowd, "If the state had gotten its way, I'd be dead today."

Since the Supreme Court overturned *Furman v. Georgia* in 1976 and reinstated the death penalty, 75 Death Row inmates have been completely exonerated and released. That means for every seven prisoners executed, one was set free. . . .

The stories of the wrongfully convicted are overwhelming. Most involve some combination of incompetent defense lawyers, bloodthirsty or corrupt prosecutors, hanging judges, police beatings, hidden evidence or false testimony. Many are stories of simply being in the wrong place at the wrong time, poor or black: "We need someone for this," a police officer told

Clarence Brandley, who was wrongfully convicted for rape and murder in Texas in 1980. "Since you're the nigger, you're elected."

The wrongfully convicted tell of sitting in closet-sized cells for 23 hours a day, writing out legal briefs longhand with a dull pencil and fighting off the roaches and mice for table scraps; they speak of the endless waiting, always thinking about burning alive in the electric chair or being stuck with a lethal needle. "I just wanted to curl up in a ball, scream and holler and bang my head against the wall," says Carl Lawson, who spent six years on Illinois' Death Row. "I thought, I'd rather be dead than live here in this cell. I felt like the whole world hated me. I had to push so hard to keep from killing myself."

Even freedom comes with a price. After years in prison, most of the wrongfully convicted have struggled on the outside without any skills, job prospects or compensation from the state. Topping it off, they have been held up as examples of how the system works. Try telling that to James Richardson, who was on Death Row for 21 years. Or Sonia Jacobs: After spending 16 years in prison for the murder of two policemen, it was exposed that prosecution witnesses had lied at her trial. She was released in 1992. Her common-law husband, Jesse Tafero, wasn't so lucky. Convicted on much of the same evidence, he was executed in 1990 before the new information came to light. . . .

Of course, the only way to ensure that no innocent person is executed is to abolish capital punishment altogether. That remains a noble goal, but it's unachievable in the current political climate. However, issues of innocence, equality and fairness resonate with the public. Using the example of the wrongfully convicted as a springboard and focusing on the realities of the death penalty, opponents should push for specific, achievable systemic and legislative reforms. "We have to get back to putting fairness ahead of finality," says attorney Steven Bright, director of the Southern Center for Human Rights. "We need to get back to achieving equal justice under the law, or we should just sandblast those words right off the front of the Supreme Court building."

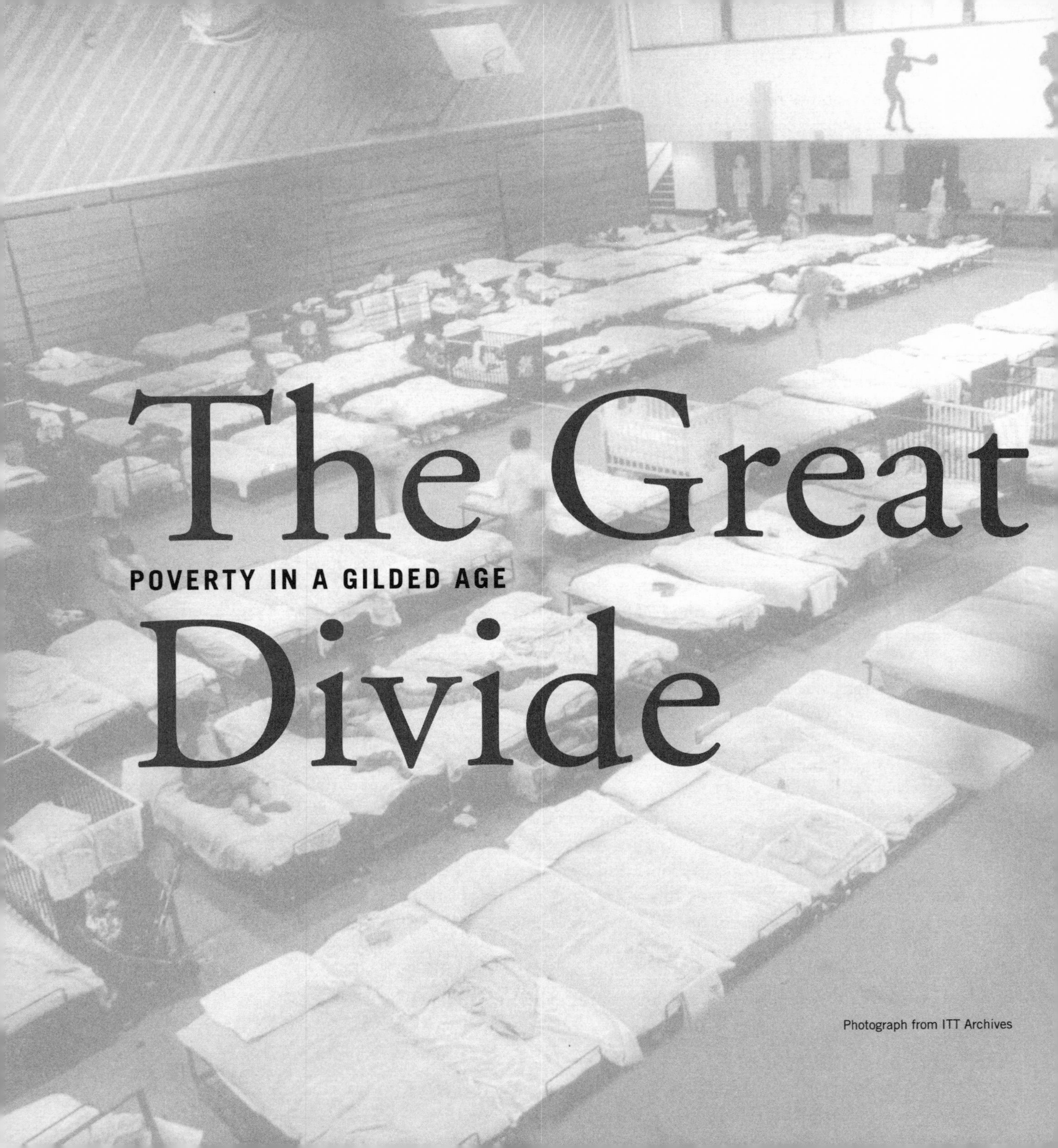

The Great Divide

POVERTY IN A GILDED AGE

Photograph from ITT Archives

Eleven

ANNETTE FUENTES

NO ONE EVER SAID, "THE RICH WILL ALWAYS BE AMONG US," EVEN IF IT IS JUST AS TRUE AS THAT BROMIDE ABOUT THE POOR. THE POOR AND THEIR poverty have been a defining social problem since before the turn of the last century, and they've hardly vanished as we hurtle headlong into the 21st.

But back in the late 1800s, as industrial capitalism hunkered down and dispatched the pesky naysayers with Pinkertons and police, the discourse on poverty was framed in frank terms of class and inequality. Marxism and socialism were debated by workers and the captains of industry alike. None other than steel magnate Andrew Carnegie wrote in 1908: "The unequal distribution of wealth lies at the root of the present Socialistic activity. This is no surprise to the writer. It was bound to force itself to the front, because, exhibiting extremes unknown before, it has become one of the crying evils of our day."

Chances are we won't read such sentiments flowing from the keyboard of Bill Gates, even if he has followed Carnegie's philanthropic tradition by creating a multimillion-dollar charity. Techno-barons like Gates, and Americans in general, don't talk about class anymore, much less the lopsided distribution of wealth and privilege. And not because it is no longer a "crying evil." More than a century after Carnegie blamed the concentration of wealth for fomenting revolutionary movements, the gap between rich and poor, the have-a-lots and the have-nots, is alive and well.

This is one of the most important stories of the past 25 years to be virtually ignored by the mainstream media, whose corporate owners no doubt consider the trend less than newsworthy. An occasional article appears in the *New York Times* or *Wall Street Journal*, reporting official data on the great wealth divide. But there are no banner headlines, no public outrage, no calls for congressional hearings, no task

Women's Common Ground
FRANCES FOX PIVEN
June 13, 1984

Imagine what might have happened. It is the summer of 1981. A new Republican administration, with the acquiescence or active support of most Democrats, enacts a program of massive cuts in social programs for the poor. Indignant feminist leaders, quickly realizing it is women and their children who will be the main victims, initiate protest marches in New York, Los Angeles, Chicago, Philadelphia and Boston. The TV networks feature Gloria Steinem, Betty Friedan and Bella Abzug holding aloft banners proclaiming the rights of mothers and children to food or health care or housing or heating fuel. The ranks of the marchers are not numerous, but outrage spreads, demonstrations continue, the ranks swell and the cameras turn to the increasing numbers of poor women of color hauling their infants and toddlers with them as they walk alongside the skirt-suited women from downtown offices.

Meanwhile, in state capitals, feminists who not so long before had chained themselves to statehouse columns in the battle for the ERA, chain themselves again, this time daring state politicians to pass along the federal cuts to poor women by slashing the AFDC or Medicaid programs. And here and there, sit-down strikes break out among women staff members in health and welfare agencies who refuse to implement new restrictions. . . .

The scenario is to me entirely credible. It could have happened. And it still could happen.

Many feminists share the prevalent American bias against the welfare state as such. They have come to associate emancipation with entry into the market and upward mobility within it. There is irony in these leadership attitudes (as there is in the similar attitudes expressed by some black leaders) given the increasingly impoverished circumstances

forces to study the causes of mushrooming wealth in the hands of fewer individuals and corporate entities and all the threats to democracy that represents. Instead, we are served up a regular diet of coverage of the poor and their pathologies, and an endless stream of political solutions to the problem of poverty, as if the gargantuan wealth of the few had no connection to the meager fortunes of the many.

Poverty grabbed the national spotlight in the early '60s, as one of many issues bubbling up from grassroots movements for social justice that would dominate the next decade. The civil rights movement, which so clearly articulated the racial divide in this nation, created the vocabulary and tools to identify and challenge class and income inequities. The postwar happy days of the '50s gave way to the emerging realities of urbanization, of the ghettoization of African-Americans, Puerto Ricans, Chicanos and other marginal groups for whom the American Dream was about as real as Goldilocks and the three bears.

Faced with mounting discontent and social unrest, President Johnson and Congress responded by enacting the Great Society reforms and the War on Poverty, establishing public assistance programs that would come to be known as welfare. Chief among them were the Medicaid and Medicare health insurance programs that assist the poor and elderly, respectively, and Aid to Families with Dependent Children (AFDC) and other income supports that were imperfect solutions to growing unemployment and income stratification in the post-industrial economy. The Great Society reforms did not address the structural inequalities and causes for shrinking opportunities or the loss of well-paying jobs. Neither did they redistribute power. Instead, their purpose and effect was "regulating the poor," as Frances Fox Piven and Richard Cloward describe the process in their classic study by the same name of public relief programs as social control.

Since the rise of the New Right during the Reagan years, however, those solutions have taken an increasingly punitive turn. The Great Society's redistributive programs have been attacked by revisionist historians, conservative economists and liberal politicians alike. Despite clear evidence that publicly funded social service programs reduce poverty—especially for the elderly—the new orthodoxy blames big government and its social largesse for breeding dependence and encouraging poor women to have children outside of marriage in order to collect ever-higher public assistance benefits.

In the '80s, neoconservative tracts like Charles Murray's *Losing Ground* and George Gilder's *Wealth and Poverty* became manifestos for a war on the War on Poverty and a mounting assault on the poor themselves. As Murray wrote: "We tried to provide more for the poor, and produced more poor instead. We tried to remove the barriers to escape from poverty, and inadvertently built a trap."

No group has been more vilified in this attack on the poor than people of color. Statistics showing that whites are the vast majority of welfare recipients are meaningless when stereotypes powered by racism have become so ingrained in the public consciousness. In fact, the right's success in engineering new antisocial policies that hurt the poor has depended upon nurturing and then exploiting the racism of working- and middle-class whites, who've scarcely gained ground themselves as the income divide widens.

Retrenchment of the welfare state and its income support programs began with a vengeance in Ronald Reagan's slash-and-burn budgets. In his first term, more than $70 billion was chopped from housing, food, health care and income-subsidy programs for the poor. George Bush maintained the trend in shrinking social programs for the poor with his "thousand points of light" privatization approach to public problems. (A decade later, his son George W. Bush calls his approach "compassionate conservatism," with its most compassionate policies saved for corporate America and the rich.)

of so many women and the unlikelihood of their escape from the low-wage, service-sector jobs to which the market consigns them. The irony is compounded because more middle-class constituents of feminist organizations work for welfare state agencies than banks or advertising companies or Silicon Valley entrepreneurs.

The bias among feminist leaders is not unmotivated. A good many women leaders, like black leaders, are trying to build their organizations by operating in political and business spheres where a spirited defense of the welfare state would not open doors or win points. So we have conflicting ideas, and we are deeply ambivalent; women object that women are being made the victims of program cuts, but we are not quite willing to defend the programs that are being cut.

Our ambivalence is thus producing narrow and short-sighted calculations of organizational interest, for it rules out the possibility of creating a new political force capable of opening doors and winning points on its own terms. It rules out the possibility of activating and leading a movement that includes poor and working women.

In the '30s, a union oligarch named John L. Lewis understood the enormous possibilities represented by the stirrings of industrial workers who were beginning to demand the right to organize. He sensed the potential power of a movement for industrial unionism, which the existing AFL craft unions were resisting, at least partly because of their dislike and distrust of industrial workers and their fear of mass strikes. Lewis broke with his longtime cronies among the leaders of the AFL and became the fiery spokesman for industrial unionism. He took a chance, risked his career and his organization, and helped create a movement that changed American history. Now women leaders have that same chance.

But it was Bill Clinton, a Democrat, who gave the coup de grace to "welfare as we know it," when he signed into law the Personal Responsibility and Work Opportunity Reconciliation Act of 1996, essentially icing a cake Reagan had started baking 16 years earlier. Gone was AFDC, which had been a necessary if flawed safety net for millions of women and children. In its place came Temporary Aid to Needy Families (TANF), with a five-year cap on benefits and work requirements, which have turned welfare recipients into an indentured labor force that undermines the bargaining power of organized labor.

The architects of welfare-to-work programs, like former Wisconsin Gov. Tommy Thompson (now Bush's secretary

Homeless on the Range

LOUIS DUBOSE

April 8, 1987

HOUSTON—In the chapel of downtown Houston's Star of Hope Mission sits a Saturday-night congregation that is a cross section of this city's hard-core homeless. Tired old men are here in mix-and-match clothing from the mission closet. While the physically disabled set their sites on lower bunks, the mentally disabled engage in long conversations with no one in particular.

Here, too, are groups of lean young men only a few days out of the Texas Department of Corrections

Mark Ludak

Statistics showing that whites are the vast majority of welfare recipients are meaningless when racist stereotypes have been ingrained in the public consciousness.

of health and human services) have bragged about the thousands of people moved off the dole. Yet it is not at all clear just where those people have gone, or if they've found jobs to support themselves and their families above poverty levels. Some studies of welfare-to-work in New York City, which has the nation's largest workfare program, indicate that without training and education, former welfare recipients are faring the same or worse financially than they did on public assistance. But data are hard to come by because the city is more interested in slashing the welfare rolls than in tracking what happens when people are cut loose.

Public agencies administering the new welfare programs have thrown up countless hurdles to discourage people from requesting and receiving even basic subsidies in time of need. A 2000 Department of Agriculture study, for example, revealed that 12 million people were eligible for food stamps but not getting them—chiefly because of the onerous application process and frequent, requisite visits to the welfare office. Other national studies indicate that millions of people were wrongly booted from Medicaid when they were moved off public assistance, even though the two programs have different eligibility levels.

Of course, we are told, the past decade has been a boom period of U.S. economic expansion, a heady time of dotcom millionaires and stock-option affluence. Anyone who is still poor is, well, just lazy and certainly not deserving of public sympathy or subsidy. In this giddy climate, discussion of poverty and the efficacy of welfare reform are dismissed as anachronistic or irrelevant. The sea of good fortune has swelled, raising the boats of all—the poor included—according to the supposed consensus. But is it really true? Using Census Bureau data, *Left Business Observer* editor Doug Henwood found that 1996 average incomes were no better than those in 1973—a 23-year period of stagnation despite the good times.

Poverty rates provide more contradictions of the national economic boom. Based on a measure developed in 1963,

maximum security facility at Huntsville, as well as a handful of Mexicans clustered together in the back corner. A few men in their thirties—new to the streets and ill at ease—talk to no one. All need a meal and a place to sleep.

Everyone stands when an old lay preacher asks, "Who loves the Lord?" But most are soup-kitchen Christians. A hard-driving rain and low temperatures forced them into the optional three-hour (Spanish then English) chapel service. After a closing hymn, those fortunate few with regular beds upstairs leave the chapel. Those remaining show their numbered bed-tickets and file out toward the 500-bed dorm. It's a place to sleep until breakfast call at 4:30 A.M. In the huge converted warehouse, the roof leaks and it's cold. Every man sleeps fully dressed.

All of this, three meals and a bunk—offered by what is arguably the most generous men's shelter in the state—is provided without the expenditure of a single tax dollar. In Texas, the homeless live off the kindness of strangers, not taxpayers. . . .

The homeless aren't at the top of the political agenda of anyone who might make a difference. And the little new money appropriated will probably go toward bringing the state prison system into compliance with a federal court order to provide more space.

Less regressive states may see something of their future in Texas—a state where social services are almost completely privatized. Yet help for the homeless might be one issue on which the public is way ahead of elected officials. A *Dallas Morning News* poll found that 52 percent of those sampled responded that they would pay more taxes to assist the homeless.

It's unlikely that Republican Gov. Bill Clements will be moved, however. In an earlier campaign, he said: "A lot of these people are going to have to realize that they've got to be mobile. They're going to have to realize that they've got to go where the jobs are. I started that kind of *modus operandi* when I was 17 years old and getting out of Highland Park High School. I didn't sit up in Dallas sucking my thumb. I got on a bus."

which used 1955 data on an average family's budget, the poverty level itself is a flawed standard that undercounts the true numbers of Americans living in need. Although in dollar terms the amount is adjusted for inflation, the formula fails to reflect the changed budgetary needs of families and the soaring costs of housing, childcare and other expenditures that didn't figure into that original formula. For 2000, the "poverty threshold," as it's officially known, was $8,959 for a single person under age 65 and $17,761 for a family of four.

Even using that flawed measure, the poverty rates among many groups are a discordant note in the good news gospel choir. The 1998 poverty rate was 12.7 percent, a drop from the previous year, but still higher than in the '70s. Child poverty is perhaps the most shameful indicator at 18.9 percent—representing 12.1 million children, and one in three African-American and Latino children. That's higher than the 1979 child poverty rate of roughly 16 percent and higher than the rate in most industrialized countries, including Canada and Western Europe. The poor are getting poorer, too, with their incomes falling below the official measure by ever greater dollar amounts. Even more jarring, given low unemployment, is the fact that the poverty rate among full-time workers grew from 2.5 percent in 1997 to 2.9 percent in 1998, representing half a million people—the largest such increase ever recorded.

◎

But enough about the poor and working poor. There is plenty of good news for some Americans. An analysis by the Center on Budget and Policy Priorities revealed that the after-tax income of the richest 1 percent of Americans rose 115 percent (adjusted for inflation) from 1977 to 1999. (Put in other terms, the richest 2.7 million people received as much after-tax income as the bottom 100 million, which is about a third of this country's population.) The top 20 percent didn't do too badly either: Their average after-tax income gain was 43 percent over the same period. This increased affluence probably helped shift the scrutiny away from the glaring advances of

Kit Boyce

The unstated and undeniable effect of "workfare" programs is to break the backs of labor unions.

Slaves of New York

ANNETTE FUENTES

December 23, 1996

NEW YORK—In 1995, Mayor Rudolph Giuliani launched the country's largest, most ambitious workfare program, designed to move thousands of adult welfare recipients into low-skilled jobs in exchange for their weekly checks. Called the Work Experience Program (WEP), it has injected a total of 100,000 workers into virtually every corner of the municipal labor force over the past two years. Riding the crest of anti-welfare sentiment, Giuliani has garnered accolades aplenty for WEP from the usual suspects. *Newsweek* put Giuliani on the cover of its November 11 issue, heralding him as "the most hated, successful mayor in America" because "crime has plummeted, workfare is working."

the super-rich. Meanwhile, that figure for those in the middle 20 percent of the income scale grew 8 percent—and the average income of the poorest fifth of Americans actually fell.

Talking about wealth, which includes more than income, the Center on Budget and Policy Priorities found that concentration at the top is greater than at any time since the Great Depression. The wealthiest 1 percent of households owns 40 percent of the nation's wealth, while the bottom 80 percent—the vast majority of Americans, mind you—owns 16 percent. As Henwood has framed this picture of rampant inequality, 95 percent of virtually all the benefits of economic boom in the past quarter of a century has been gobbled up by the richest 5 percent. Quite an achievement in a classless, democratic society.

This decades-long trend of stuffing more and more boodle into the bulging pockets of the wealthy is the real social welfare program, but it doesn't generate the ire public assistance to the poor does. Corporate welfare and subsidy of the rich through regressive business and personal income tax codes are just some of the ways federal and state governments have contributed to the great wealth gap. In the past 25 years, according to Congressional Budget Office data, revised tax policies bestowed an average of $40,000 in tax cuts to the richest 1 percent of households, which exceeds the average incomes of those Americans at the middle of the scale.

With Dubya now at the helm, we can expect an even further widening of the divide between the rich and the rest. Start with his $1.6 trillion tax cut proposal, the first major initiative announced with much hoopla just two months into his presidency. Dragging supposed average American families on stage with him at a White House press conference in February 2001, Bush declared that his income tax plan would offer working and middle-income families relief. A reality check, provided once again by those nit-pickers at the Center on Budget and Policy Priorities, finds that the bottom 40 percent of the population would get only 4 percent of the tax cuts. The wealthiest 1 percent would get 43 percent of the

But WEP is not just a New York story. National attention is fixed on the Big Apple and its workfare scheme as other cities and states begin to reshape their welfare systems in response to the new federal mandates. Yet despite glowing reviews, the real story of WEP is of hardship, exploitation and unfair labor practices that are roiling unions to their core. "There are other states monitoring us as a role model," says WEP worker Sandra White. "I want to let them know: It's bad. It's not working at all." . . .

While the ostensible purpose of WEP is to force people on welfare to "give back" something to the city, the unstated and undeniable effect of WEP is to break the back of labor unions. Viewed together with Giuliani's drive to privatize public services, the WEP program is a frontal assault on the most basic tenets of unionism: equal pay for equal work, a safe working environment and the right to organize.

WEP creates a pool of contingent workers, doing the same work as city employees and often working shoulder to shoulder with them, but for a fraction of their pay. With no sick leave, no vacations, no pensions or other benefits, WEP workers are a constant and not-so-subtle threat by management to workplace standards. "WEP workers are asked to work in conditions that unionized employees negotiated to avoid," says Ed Ott, political director of Communication Workers of America (CWA) Local 1180.

For example, WEP workers doing street cleaning get no gloves or uniforms or footwear, and have no locker facilities to change clothing, so they must go home wearing whatever filth the day brings. In the parks, WEP workers are forced to climb higher than union contracts allow in pruning trees.

How New York's unions approach the workfare issue could determine the face of organized labor for years to come. Is workfare an unmitigated threat that can only weaken unions, or a golden opportunity to bolster their diminishing ranks by organizing the most vulnerable and exploited members of society?

tax breaks, more than their 18.5 percent share of income taxes paid. A whopping third of all families wouldn't see any tax break under the plan because their incomes are so low that they have no federal income tax liability.

Wait, it gets better. Bush also proposed repealing the gift and estate taxes, as blatant a form of upward wealth distribution as you can imagine. Again using as props some farm families of modest means who simply want to pass on their property to their children, Bush called estate taxes an "unfair burden." What's unfair is that the repeal would mean the richest 2 percent of Americans could save $236 billion over 10 years. That money would be lost not only to the federal treasury, but to charities, which depend on the wealthy's bequests. Andrew Carnegie must be spinning in his grave. In that same 1908 essay called "Wealth," he declared, "A heavy progressive tax upon wealth at death of owner is not only desirable, it is strictly just."

The conservative campaign to delegitimize social spending requires that poor people—with limited exceptions—be discredited as unworthy of help. Their poverty must be cast as a

Move 'em Out

NEIL DEMAUSE

December 14, 1997

Alesha Nicholson is one of Bill Clinton's welfare reform success stories. Until last winter, the Milwaukee single mother was dependent on welfare benefits. She has since become one of the 1.4 million people who left the welfare rolls between August 1996 and last May, a statistic that led to Clinton's triumphant August announcement: "The debate is over. We know welfare reform works."

Nicholson accomplished this feat by opening her mail. "I was on welfare," she says. "I was told to do 15 job contacts a week, which I did. I complied with everything I was told to do." But the letter that arrived last December charged that Nicholson had failed to file a monthly report on her wage earnings (at the time, zero). She insists she filed the form; the state disagreed and cut off her benefits.

Paul Comstock

The conservative campaign to delegitimize social spending casts poverty as a matter of individual irresponsibility, not collective concern.

matter of individual irresponsibility, not collective concern. Piven and Cloward describe English laws passed during the reign of Henry VIII that penalized beggary with branding, enslavement and death. It was a time of economic dislocation and destitution for masses of peasants and landless poor. In 20th-century New York City, under the reign of Mayor Rudy Giuliani, panhandling on the subways is a crime punishable by a fine and imprisonment, and homeless people are swept up by police from the fashionable districts favored by tourists. If poverty is not quite a sin, it is apparently still indecent.

Devising new strategies to address poverty and protect existing government welfare programs is a never-ending challenge for advocates of the poor. Some activists are currently campaigning for a generous income tax credit for caregivers—parents caring for children, children caring for elderly parents and so on—that would acknowledge both the social and economic value of such labor.

This is a worthy and important crusade. But parallel efforts must also attack the income gap by reeling in corporate welfare and the government's collusion in the creation of wealth and all the power it puts in the hands of the few. The great wealth divide and the active government intervention that aids and abets it have coincided with government divestment of social programs. But the public has been so riveted by the image of Oz railing against welfare dependency, it has ignored the men behind the curtain doling out 10 times the benefits to corporate America and its minions.

Social welfare programs, as Piven and Cloward show, have always been the consequence of social activism and mobilizations. Yet in recent years, the poor and their advocates have had their backs to the wall as the nation's political atmosphere has veered sharply to the right. Faced with the institutionalization of workfare programs, the harsh sanctions of the new punitive welfare state, and a social climate devoid of compassion, the poor have not begun to mobilize

In the terminology shared by welfare bureaucrats and recipients, Nicholson had just been "sanctioned"—removed from the welfare rolls for violating the increasingly byzantine regulations. Finding a short-term factory job to pay the rent, but unable to afford childcare, she was forced to send her 3-year-old daughter to stay with out-of-town relatives, where the child was sexually abused.

Nicholson later retrieved her daughter and found part-time work at Welfare Warriors, a Milwaukee-based welfare mothers' activist group. There she discovered that the Opportunities Industrialization Center, the private agency that handled her welfare case, had been directed to reduce its caseload by 25 percent annually or face losing its lucrative state contract. Every public and private welfare agency in the state received the directive in February 1996. One way or another, all but one met the quota.

Even as Clinton, Mickey Kaus and other would-be welfare reformers insist that the 1996 Personal Responsibility and Work Opportunity Act—which freed states from the requirement to provide aid to all needy residents—has worked wonders in bringing the nation's welfare recipients into the working world, stories like Nicholson's indicate otherwise. States are just starting to implement programs designed under the new law. But in the months before signing the law, Clinton quietly granted waivers to 43 states, allowing them to experiment with such policies as rigid time limits and workfare for single mothers. It is these state programs that are credited with the startling 24 percent drop in the welfare rolls, a total of 3.4 million people, since the start of Clinton's first term. . . .

Exactly how this was accomplished is an official mystery. The White House doesn't even claim to know. Domestic policy adviser Bruce Reed could only speculate that "most have probably gone to work or gotten married so that their income no longer makes them eligible." The only national study to date, released by the federal Council of Economic Advisers in May, chalked up 44 percent of the caseload drop to an

Eileen Mullin

The only work skill valued by the new welfare regime is the ability to jump higher and higher hurdles on the road to a monthly check.

improved economy and 31 percent to the effects of workfare and other new restrictions. The other 25 percent were marked simply "other factors."

Welfare recipients and advocates for the poor agree that the economy has improved. But as for workfare and those "other factors," they paint a gloomier picture. Like Alesha Nicholson, many welfare recipients are discovering that the only work skill valued by the new welfare regime is the ability to jump higher and higher hurdles on the road to a monthly check.

on the scale and with the intensity that would force their needs back on the national agenda. Their natural allies among union ranks, for example, have largely failed to make the connections between workfare programs and the diluted strength of organized labor, acquiescing as workfare participants become a disposable army of low-cost labor.

What will it take to reignite the kind of social movements that can begin to address the wealth divide and redistribute the country's resources in a more equitable way? Perhaps things will have to get much worse before they can get better, and, at this writing, there are indications they certainly will. The uninterrupted economic boom has slowed, and working-poor and middle-class people are undeniably vulnerable to the economic rumblings. Their tolerance for conservative fiscal policies—for less government or government spending—won't hold when they start to feel the pain, no matter what the cheerleaders in Washington are selling.

The best hope for change that will address income and social inequalities lies in broad-based coalitions that target corporate wealth, elite privilege and the government policies that cater to their interests. The seeds of such a movement seem to be germinating in the burgeoning opposition to unfettered corporate reach into developing countries. The anti-sweatshop mobilizations among labor and student organizations and protest demonstrations against the World Trade Organization and the International Monetary Fund indicate the links activists have made between U.S. corporate policies that enrich the few and the mounting impoverishment of the many in all corners of the world.

The next stage is to bring home the message of corporate greed and popular disenfranchisement in all arenas of life—from the economic to the political. Let's reclaim the right to welfare for all and restore its meaning, as *Webster's* defines it: "the state of being or doing well, in respect to good fortune, happiness or prosperity." What could be more American than that?

Mother Courage

ARIEL GORE

January 9, 1995

A young woman with a sticky baby stroller stands ahead of me in line at the check-cashing place on Broadway. It is the ninth of the month, so the wait to pick up our food stamps is short. Her turn comes and she pushes the stroller to the counter. She slips her state ID card under the bullet-proof glass and watches the woman who picks it up.

"Sixty-four," the woman says, and passes a pink card to the young mother to sign.

"I'm supposed to get a hundred, not 64," she snaps.

"I don't know, I just give out the food stamps," the woman behind the glass says meekly.

I'm sure the flurry of profanities that escape from the young mother's mouth can be heard from the street. By the time she quiets, the woman behind the glass is holding the food stamps to her chest. "I'm not going to give them to you," she says matter-of-factly.

The mother suddenly assumes a diplomatic tone. "I'm sorry," she says. "I know it's not your fault. Can I please have my food stamps so my baby can eat?"

The woman behind the counter gives in to the plea, but as soon as the mother wraps her pale fingers around the small pile of bills and pulls them safely away from the glass, she starts in again.

I sign for my own food stamps quickly and rush out into the brisk morning. As the glass door shuts behind me, I can hear the mother screaming. "You think I'm going to kiss your ass." . . .

The mood in the food stamp line this month is more strained than usual. By now everyone has heard something of Washington's plans for "welfare reform," and we know the complaints aren't with the welfare system itself, but with us.

Peter Hannan

Welfare opponents have come together to declare open season on any woman who dares procreate without a husband and a stable income.

Even I, who have never made any secret about being on welfare and never apologized for procreating before my 20th birthday, have begun glancing over my shoulder when I am in line at the grocery store waiting to pay with brightly colored government coupons. At the bank, I now hesitate before taking my AFDC check out of the county envelope it arrived in and placing it on the counter in front of a manicured teller. And from long talks and brief encounters with other women on government aid, I know I am not alone.

At our most panicked, we envision a social worker hammering on the door and hauling our children off to an

Mark Ludak

One in three African-American and Latino children now live in poverty.

orphanage. On calmer days, we simply try to make ends meet, acutely aware that the climate has shifted, that our families have been judged and that the verdict is guilty.

Now the powers that be, from Newt Gingrich to Bill Clinton, are calling for an intensification of stigmas against teen-age pregnancy and out-of-wedlock births. Erstwhile political opponents have come together to declare open season on any mom who dares procreate without a husband and a stable income. Linking teen motherhood to gun violence "and other social pathologies" lends urgency to their arguments. As Jonathan Alter put it in *Newsweek*: "Every threat to the fabric of this country—from poverty to crime to homelessness—is connected to out-of-wedlock teen pregnancy."

I realize that I might be called a radical when I suggest that these stigmas should really be applied to lawmakers who cut welfare benefits without serious plans to end poverty. I might even be crossing the line when I suggest that they should be branded as batterers whose violence is responsible for displacing 50 percent of the homeless women and children in this country. The vast majority of young mothers I have come into contact with over the years are good mothers. But disrespect, shame and schemes to cut off the few available resources a woman has do not bolster good parenting. These assaults merely drain our spirits and shorten our fuses. And we all know that after food, clothing and shelter, what a mother needs most is patience and spirit.

It is possible that life had discouraged the red-haired woman at the check-cashing place long before she became a mother, or maybe her mood this morning had more to do with sleep deprivation than with Newt Gingrich. I don't know. But I am willing to bet my welfare check that what she needs isn't shame and stigma. The $36 worth of food stamps in question isn't likely to do the trick either. But they might feed her family through Christmas, and that would be something.

Kevin Weinstein

Out of sight, out of mind: Panhandling on the subway is a crime punishable by a fine or imprisonment, and the homeless are regularly swept up by police from the fashionable tourist districts.

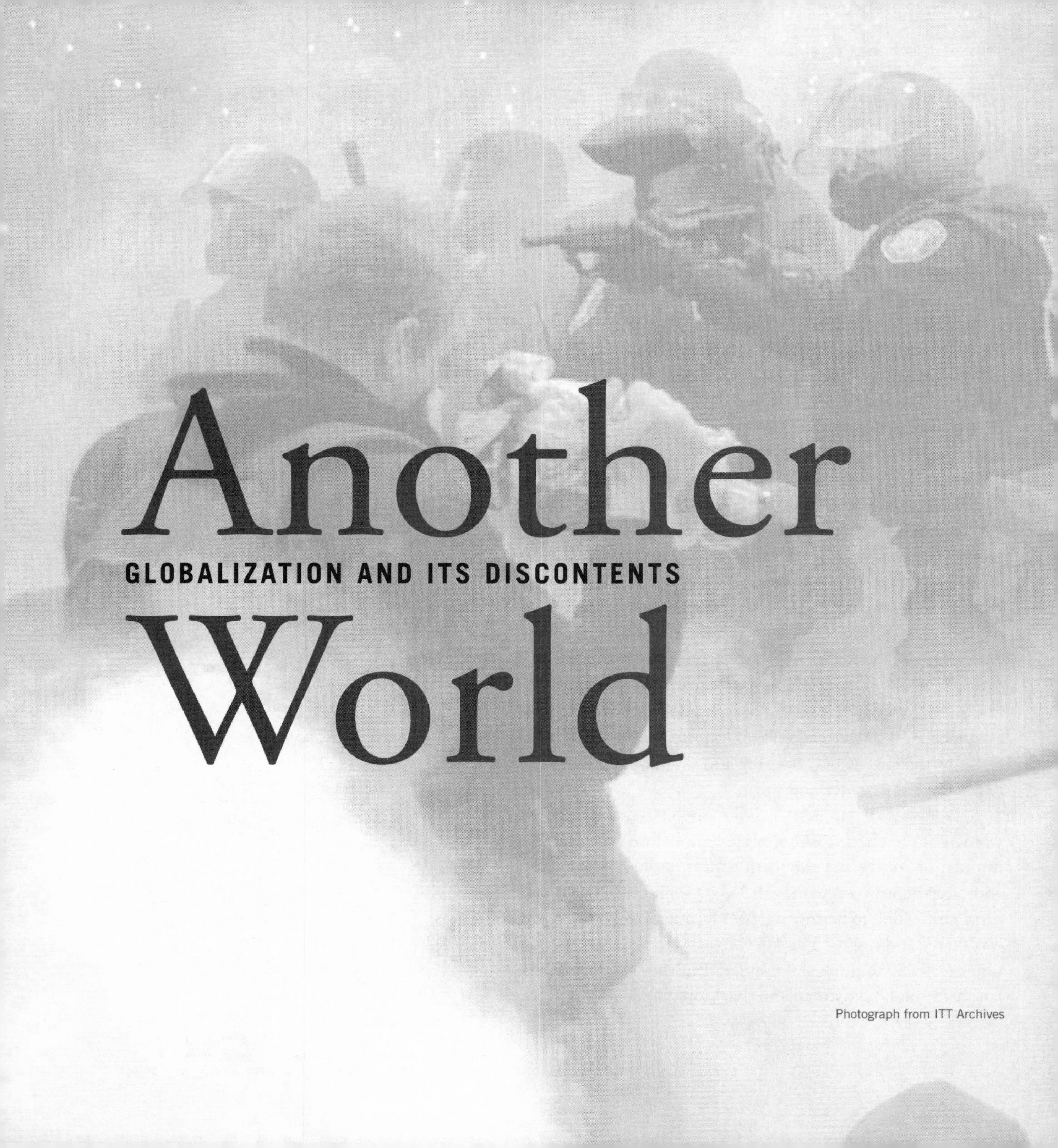

Another World

GLOBALIZATION AND ITS DISCONTENTS

Photograph from ITT Archives

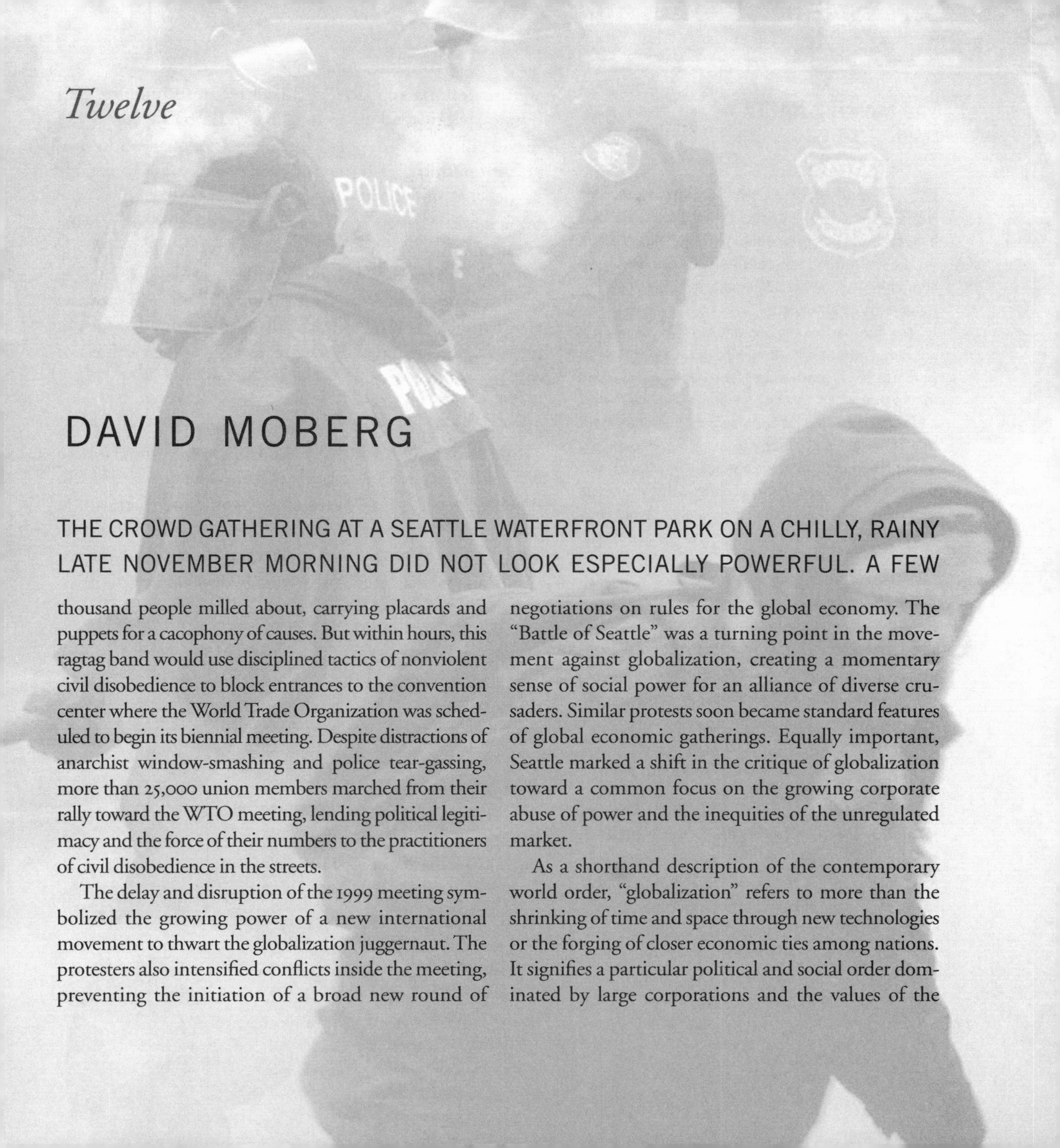

Twelve

DAVID MOBERG

THE CROWD GATHERING AT A SEATTLE WATERFRONT PARK ON A CHILLY, RAINY LATE NOVEMBER MORNING DID NOT LOOK ESPECIALLY POWERFUL. A FEW thousand people milled about, carrying placards and puppets for a cacophony of causes. But within hours, this ragtag band would use disciplined tactics of nonviolent civil disobedience to block entrances to the convention center where the World Trade Organization was scheduled to begin its biennial meeting. Despite distractions of anarchist window-smashing and police tear-gassing, more than 25,000 union members marched from their rally toward the WTO meeting, lending political legitimacy and the force of their numbers to the practitioners of civil disobedience in the streets.

The delay and disruption of the 1999 meeting symbolized the growing power of a new international movement to thwart the globalization juggernaut. The protesters also intensified conflicts inside the meeting, preventing the initiation of a broad new round of negotiations on rules for the global economy. The "Battle of Seattle" was a turning point in the movement against globalization, creating a momentary sense of social power for an alliance of diverse crusaders. Similar protests soon became standard features of global economic gatherings. Equally important, Seattle marked a shift in the critique of globalization toward a common focus on the growing corporate abuse of power and the inequities of the unregulated market.

As a shorthand description of the contemporary world order, "globalization" refers to more than the shrinking of time and space through new technologies or the forging of closer economic ties among nations. It signifies a particular political and social order dominated by large corporations and the values of the commercial marketplace. This package of technology, economics, politics and values is held together by an ideology of inevitability. According to its apologists, globalization provides not just the path to prosperity, but the only acceptable model for human society. This unified projection of the human future has emerged over the past three decades, rising triumphantly in the '90s but promptly facing a growing argument on many fronts that "another world is possible," in the ambiguous phrase of French critics. While this growing international movement has challenged the onward rush of globalization, it has only begun to sketch the outlines of other possible worlds.

World leaders were not always confronted with the claim, in Margaret Thatcher's words, that "there is no alternative." In the early '70s, the Cold War split the world into three camps: the capitalist "free world" (including industrialized countries with strong social democratic regimes), the Communist countries and the nonaligned, mainly developing countries. U.S. policy—military, political and economic—was focused on containing Communism.

After World War II, it did so partly through the framework of the Bretton Woods system of treaties and institutions such as the World Bank and International Monetary Fund. The United States encouraged freer trade, international stability and economic growth as a way of knitting together an alliance to contain Communism (and to suppress any movements that challenged capitalism). But in the interests of maintaining anti-Communist alliances and reducing popular discontent that might fuel radical political movements, postwar U.S. governments accepted a range of policies in other countries (even advocating programs such as land reform) that were far different from the American model of freewheeling capitalism. Among its Asian allies, for instance, the United States tolerated nationalist, export-oriented strategies that disadvantaged American workers.

The Morning NAFTA

DAVID MOBERG

December 13, 1993

The low road to President Clinton's victory on NAFTA was paved with political payoffs. But his high-road message appealed to nationalistic pride: Aren't we Americans confident of our ability to compete in the world, especially against a poor little country like Mexico?

The popular anxiety about NAFTA, however, was not about whether "we" can't compete, but about who "we" are. Increasingly, the average American thinks that when corporate leaders use "we," they are speaking only of themselves. Worries about NAFTA reflect a distrust, most pronounced among working people, that corporations will willingly jettison or threaten U.S. employees if they have an overseas opportunity to pay lower wages, avoid environmental and safety regulations, or escape public responsibilities.

This broadly based conviction is not just an expression of "insecurity" that can be pacified with promises of health security and job retraining, as the Clinton administration suggested. It reflects a deep, new fissure in the American sense of identity as a nation—as well as a growing sense of powerlessness over the economic forces that shape many people's lives.

Anger over NAFTA demonstrates the unraveling of a loosely formulated, psycho-social contract that most Americans have carried around in their heads for the past half-century. Those who, in President Clinton's oft-repeated phrase, "work hard and play by the rules" had believed that being part of the national economy offered them a solid hope of financial opportunity and individual material progress. Americans don't doubt their own abilities or willingness to work. They do worry increasingly that they have no control over whether they—or their children—will have a chance to use

By attempting to escalate the war in Vietnam in the mid-'60s without imposing higher taxes, the United States created an economic dilemma. Rising military expenditures contributed to an increase in the already troublesome U.S. balance of payments deficit (the difference between imports and exports, adjusted by flows of interest, profits and service income). But the basic underlying problem was the expanding trade deficit, as imports (especially from Japan) began to challenge auto, steel, consumer electronics and other industries that had been sheltered because of geographical distance or distinctive American cultural tastes (such as the consumer love affair with big cars, which was created by the Big Three auto companies and cheap U.S. oil policies). U.S. companies—often blaming high labor costs when the fundamental problems were poor management and lack of investment and innovation—increasingly tried to compete by moving overseas, further compounding the balance of payments problem.

Foreigners began to worry that inflation could erode the value of dollars in their possession. So they started buying gold, which led to fears that U.S. gold reserves could be exhausted. While the growing foreign holdings of U.S. dollars provided the world economy with an expanding means of conducting international business, it also created an international financial market largely beyond the regulation of central banks—the beginnings of "casino capitalism" in the global financial markets.

If any date qualifies as the debut of contemporary "globalization," it is August 15, 1971, when President Nixon ended the U.S. commitment to exchange dollars for gold, a linchpin of the Bretton Woods system. Nixon's action put the world economy on a "dollar standard," allowing the relative values of currencies to fluctuate freely in a global financial market. But the ripples from that policy splash spread much further. It marked the point of departure for several decades of systematic success in promoting the free market and attacking government in the creation of a new world economy in which corporations write the rules.

their abilities in a way that will provide a "middle class," moderately comfortable standard of living.

At the same time, the campaign against NAFTA opened up a new internationalism. It's striking how many Americans have come to realize that protection of their jobs and standard of living depends on expanding the political, labor and human rights of people in countries like Mexico—and in raising wages throughout the world. With some exceptions—especially in the Perot and Buchanan anti-NAFTA camps—American critics of NAFTA expressed genuine concern about poverty, exploitation, and health and environmental problems in Mexico.

Direct contact between U.S. labor groups and Mexican workers is one factor in this newfound solidarity. Moreover, the end of the Cold War has made it easier for American workers finally to identify with the aspirations of workers in poor countries. In the past, they had been blinded by an anti-communist obsession that led U.S. unions to help undermine democracy and effective labor and peasant organizations in less-developed countries. Now many U.S. unionists have come to see a mutual, shared interest in improving the lot of workers everywhere.

Unhappy Birthday

DAVID MOBERG

October 3, 1994

As the World Bank celebrates its 50th anniversary in Madrid this month, a growing chorus of critics from both rich and poor countries will be sending a sour birthday message: 50 years is enough. . . .

Established to help Europe rebuild after World War II, the World Bank actually played a tiny role there. Much of Europe's reconstruction was funded through Marshall Plan programs, which promoted

Peter Hannan

The World Bank's own internal review concluded that 35 percent of its projects were financial failures.

economic expansion and employment with grants and low-interest aid. Despite free-market rhetoric, the Marshall Plan gave European governments wide latitude in shaping national economic policies, often along social democratic lines.

By contrast, the World Bank and the IMF have—especially over the past two decades—pursued policies that have saddled poor countries with enormous amounts of foreign debt and deflated their economies in the name of free market discipline. At the same time that the bank has advocated austerity for the world's poor, it has supported a slew of development boondoggles that have enriched corrupt Third World elites while despoiling the environment.

The bank itself has always been an elite institution: its presidents have come mainly from the ranks of corporate America. Despite its talk about alleviating poverty, the bank has served primarily as an instrument of transnational financial interests. But it is important to remember—especially when contemplating possible reforms—that it has one other major constituency: the elites in many poorer countries.

Ostensibly a non-political technocracy, the World Bank has always been political. It was an important

While governments had encouraged more trade and reduced tariffs under the Bretton Woods system, they had also tried to stabilize it by regulating currencies and capital flows, giving countries leeway to adopt varied strategies to promote growth and reduce unemployment and providing development aid to poorer countries. The deregulation of the international money markets started the wave of corporate pressure to give markets—and the big players who dominate them—greater power. As the Bretton Woods system unwound, the floating exchange rate among world currencies created more financial turbulence. This financial instability and devaluation of the dollar contributed to OPEC's decision to force up the price of oil in 1973, leading to the first of two energy crises in that decade. The oil crisis spawned an economic crisis for many countries, especially poorer oil importers, but it also created a new pool of capital (so-called petrodollars).

With Bretton Woods dismantled, the IMF moved in during the '70s and '80s to create a new and expanded role for itself in providing loans to countries in financial crisis (followed by banks interested in enlarging their profits by recycling petrodollars). But when those countries couldn't repay their debts, the IMF set the terms for new loans. The IMF required governments to balance budgets, privatize government services, open markets to imports, eliminate subsidies (including those designed to help the poor), increase fees (including charges for education and health care), encourage foreign investment, maintain a stable currency and export, export, export. This set of policy prescriptions came to be known as the "Washington consensus."

The IMF and World Bank could enforce the Washington consensus in countries that were facing currency or debt crises not only because they were offering loans to sustain their national economies, but because private financial institutions typically would not lend to governments if they hadn't enacted IMF measures. Developed countries adopted the Washington consensus model under pressure to be globally "competitive." Corporations and the wealthy took advantage of the deregulated global market to pressure governments to reduce taxes or make rates less progressive in the competition for investment. That, in turn, made it harder to sustain the policies that had made earlier, moderate trade liberalization less disruptive or harmful.

After the stagflation and profit squeeze of the '70s, corporations had decided, as *Business Week* described the situation in 1974, to sell the American people on "the idea of doing with less so that big business can have more." A labor movement already in decline (partly because of its own internal weaknesses) was hammered by import competition, plant closings, capital flight and, by the late '70s and early '80s, deep recessions. The Reagan administration stuck the sword in deeper, with a public sanctioning of union-busting and economic policies that further devastated industrial union strongholds. Despite the emergence in the '70s of a vigorous environmental movement, labor's decline removed a major check on the radical anti-government, pro-market policies of the Reagan-Bush era. The Democratic Party increasingly adopted a tempered version of Reaganism, while still defending a few popular bastions such as Social Security and Medicare.

The demise of the Soviet Union and the Eastern Bloc made American-style cowboy capitalism, which itself was becoming wilder and less regulated, seem like the only option. Despite hopes in the '70s and '80s of a democratized Eurocommunism or of the emergence of democratic socialist alternatives in Communist countries, the political left—including the major European social democratic parties—largely failed to pose strong alternatives to the new neoliberal, free market global order.

Thirty years after Nixon's decision to abandon the gold standard, the Cold War has ended, and few people other than Fidel Castro still talk openly about American imperialism. Although America's defeat in Vietnam—the last major "imperialist" war of the Cold War era—set in motion the instrument of Cold War anti-communist policies. It has a sordid record of underwriting dictators—from Brazil, where the bank would not lend to the democratically elected leftist government of João Goulart but promptly aided the generals who ousted him in 1964, to Romania, where renegade communist Nicolae Ceausescu was one of the bank's biggest borrowers from 1974 to 1982.

The bank has also been extremely secretive, drawing up vast plans for countries without releasing any information to their citizens. In most decisions, the bank has been accountable to virtually no one—leaving bank projects notoriously susceptible to fraud and waste. Two years ago an internal review concluded that more than 35 percent of World Bank projects were financial failures.

After Seattle

DAVID MOBERG

January 10, 2000

After Seattle it will be difficult for any politician to talk about global economics without addressing links to labor rights, human rights, food supplies and the protection of both consumers and the environment. After Seattle it also will be critical that the protesters maintain their broad coalition, link up more with movements in developing countries, and define with greater clarity what they are for as well as what they are against.

It was easy for outsiders to be perplexed by the variety of issues raised by protesters. There were people costumed as sea turtles, dolphins and ears of genetically modified corn marching alongside Steelworkers, Teamsters and longshore workers. There were religious activists demanding cancellation of poor countries' debt and defenders of human rights in Burma and China. There were

FRANKENFOODS • NORTHERN IRELAND'S LASTING PEACE?
In These Times
INDEPENDENT NEWS & VIEWS
January 10, 2000
AFTER SEATTLE
WTO

ITT Archives

Since Seattle, the movement against globalization has become more international and more intent on building coalitions.

campus crusaders against sweatshops and child labor, eco-defenders of old forests and small farmers from around the world. There were calls for "vegan power" and flags invoking the American Revolution—"Don't trade on me." . . .

The new movement has become a more pointed international popular fight against corporate globalization and unregulated markets dominated solely by the needs of rootless transnational capital. At the turn of the last century, there was another movement of populists, progressives and socialists against laissez-faire capitalism and robber barons. "No one thought they had a chance," Minnesota Sen. Paul Wellstone reminded a labor audience in Seattle. "Their point was to civilize the national

emergence of the new globalization, it has been that new globalization that actually "won" the Cold War by making the whole world safe for capitalism. (American military power is still a bedrock of the new globalization, but it plays a more indirect role. Except for cases like the Gulf War, the United States increasingly has tried to act through proxy armies, from Angola and Central America in the '80s to the Colombian drug wars of today.)

As a combined political and economic phenomenon, globalization has gone further than even many of the most hard-nosed cold warriors ever imagined in constraining governments and undermining the most fundamental and popular public programs for health, education and income security. Indeed, the multinational corporation is now the dominant economic force in the world. In the late '60s, there were about 7,300 transnational corporations from a select group of 15 industrial countries, but by 1998 there were nearly 41,000 transnational corporations from those same countries and a total of 60,000 from all countries. Today, nearly half of world trade occurs within branches of transnational corporations, not as arm's-length transactions between independent businesses in different countries.

Through a vast number of multilateral and bilateral treaties, tariffs have been reduced and trade increased, growing much faster than overall production of goods and services. However, these agreements have gone beyond tariff reduction and trade liberalization to protect property, investor rights and the free flow of capital while indirectly—and sometimes directly—constraining protection of consumers, workers and the environment. In every case, corporate rights have gained new protections, and the powers of governments have been constricted in the name of free trade. These corporate priorities are enforced through the World Trade Organization—which was formed out of the Bretton Woods-era General Agreement on Tariffs and Trade (GATT)—trade agreements like NAFTA, as well as through the World Bank and IMF. Governments have been complicit in this giveaway of their powers to regulate the economy and, by extension, the democratic rights of citizens (in countries where those existed). At one level, the reason is simple: Countries wanted to attract foreign investment and increase exports so they could become wealthy. More particularly, political and economic elites saw an opportunity to become wealthy, even if most citizens enjoyed few benefits.

But what has the record been? The gleaming office towers and shopping malls of Singapore, Hong Kong and even Shanghai are testimony to a new wealth in formerly poor countries, and millions of people who would have been peasants now work in factories built by multinational companies. International trade has grown rapidly, accounting for a growing share of world economic output. Global financial markets have swollen: The daily foreign exchange turnover was $18 billion in 1977, but it had increased to $1.5 trillion by 1998. Although subject to erratic swings, foreign direct investment has increased over the years, growing most rapidly in developing countries but still mainly concentrated in the richer countries.

The countries first subjected to the IMF "structural adjustment" regime have a very poor record of economic growth. IMF conditions have been imposed mostly in Africa and Latin America, but a study by the Preamble Center, a Washington think tank, concluded that African countries following IMF mandates have experienced lower economic growth than other developing countries; they cut spending on health care and education but still suffered a rising debt burden. While the gross domestic product of Latin American countries has grown faster than in Africa, overall the growth rate has been slower for the past several decades than in Asia, especially since 1980.

Inequality has been rising, too: The global economy as a whole was strong during the '90s, yet by the end of the decade 80 countries—including many under IMF agreements—had per capita incomes lower than the previous decade. The ratio between incomes in the countries of the richest fifth of the world and those in the poorest fifth more than doubled from 1960 to 1997, from 30-to-1 to 74-to-1. The number of

economy. We are here—a broad coalition—to civilize the global economy." . . .

The dominant argument is that "there is no alternative" to the American model of cowboy capitalism and wide-open markets. But if that's true, key questions need to be asked: What is it about the way the world works that restricts the ability of communities or nations to create alternatives? What needs to be changed to give people more choices? Obviously, changing the WTO is only one part of that solution, and among critics there is an often fruitless debate about whether it can be reformed or whether new institutions must start from scratch.

What's needed instead is a debate about how to push simultaneously for what is achievable in the near term and what is needed in the long run, taking victories where they can be won without abandoning the more ambitious goals. The clearer the movement that coalesced in Seattle can become about those common, long-range goals, the better chance it will have to go beyond stopping the WTO and providing the much needed alternative to corporate globalization.

wretchedly poor people continues to increase: around 1.3 billion people live on less than a dollar a day. (Inequality has risen sharply within many countries as well. The United States leads the pack of industrial countries in the growth of inequality since 1973.)

The few countries that actually have moved from poverty to moderate wealth relied on a far different development strategy. Although Japan and the Asian tigers—Singapore, Hong Kong, Taiwan and South Korea—made dramatic leaps forward since the '50s, most (with the exception of Hong Kong) protected their domestic industries, invested in education, restrained the growth of inequality and developed national industrial strategies that relied heavily on exports.

A variety of studies have concluded that there actually is a strong correlation between lower inequality and higher growth rates. There also is a correlation between democracy and higher growth. As former World Bank chief economist Joseph Stiglitz has argued, empowering citizens and workers is important both to improve human rights and to foster economic development. But the policies imposed by the emerging global regime undermined equality and democracy. The instability of the global economy has also increased, and the more that countries are exposed to the global economy, the greater the risks.

Overall, the record of free market fundamentalism in the global economy has been unimpressive. Since the early '70s, economic growth has been slower worldwide than it was during the Bretton Woods era. Moreover, if economic progress is measured not simply in monetary output, but in quality of life, the escalating damage to the environment alone means there has been little or no gain under the regime of corporate globalization.

◎

Apart from opposition to American military adventures, early criticism of the new global order first came from industrial unions that faced surges of imports and job losses. American unions had long been supporters of free trade (and most also

The Insider

DAVID MOBERG

May 29, 2000

While pundits were quick to attack shortcomings in the international financial savvy of protesters at the April demonstrations against the International Monetary Fund and the World Bank, it is harder for them to dismiss the credentials of critic Joseph Stiglitz.

Stiglitz, who recently resigned as chief economist of the bank, is a distinguished academic and former chief of President Clinton's Council of Economic Advisers. He is pleased with the success of the protests in getting across a basic message. "What is at issue is a question of values," Stiglitz told *In These Times*, "of democratic processes, the environment, workers—and how partly because of the absence of democratic process, decisions were made that jeopardized the livelihoods, and even the lives, of many of the world's poor."

Stiglitz, chief economist from 1996 until last November, often got into trouble for his willingness to disrupt the "Washington consensus." Although Stiglitz worked to change World Bank practices from the inside, he was hampered by the power of the IMF to define the broad economic framework within which the World Bank functioned and by the enormous pressure to maintain a unified voice among global financial institutions. So last year he decided that he had to leave to express himself more freely.

Stiglitz is particularly unhappy with how the IMF and World Bank have responded to these calls for change. "There was certainly no engagement on the broad, fundamental question about democratic process—and whether there was a balance of representation in the decision-making process of financial interests versus workers," Stiglitz says. "What's remarkable, I see no indication of a grasp of that even as an issue." . . .

For many years, the IMF—with support from the World Bank—has insisted that the solution to global had supported Cold War militarism, including the Vietnam War). But by the late '60s—when the United States was no longer as economically dominant—unions began seeking import restrictions. They argued for protection against the "dumping" of goods below cost and advocated "fair trade," contending that exporters like Japan sold into the American market but restricted imports. They also insisted, as they had for many years, that countries given special access to the American market should respect internationally recognized labor rights.

Around the same time, environmentalists started strongly criticizing the World Bank for financing projects like big dams, which devastated natural regions and forced evacuation of indigenous populations. Other groups focused on the practices of individual corporations, as in the campaign to stop Nestle from promoting infant formula as an alternative to breast-feeding in poor countries. Although there were occasional expressions of "Buy American" sentiment, concern about the new global economy was largely restricted to people and communities who were directly hurt. Trade negotiators could rest assured that few people would ever know—let alone care—about their work.

NAFTA changed all that. During the '80s, there had been growing popular concern, first in labor unions and then among environmentalists, about the *maquiladora* assembly factories that were rapidly expanding along the U.S.-Mexican border. Deeply burdened by foreign debt, Mexican President Carlos Salinas had hoped to earn income from increased exports by luring foreign investment. The *maquiladoras* starkly illustrated crucial problems of globalization: corporations moving factories to seek low wages and avoid both unions and environmental regulations.

Building on the existing critique of *maquiladoras*, grassroots labor and citizen groups began agitating against NAFTA, which had first been proposed by Salinas in 1980, eventually getting the AFL-CIO and several national environmental groups involved in popular mobilization and Washington lobbying

Jim West

The guardians of global finance?

poverty is its draconian program of "structural adjustment." But "many developing countries need assistance because they're poor," Stiglitz says. "Structural adjustment suggests they're out of kilter, that they need a nose job. My point is they're poor and need more money to be less poor. If the IMF gets out of lending to developing countries, then the World Bank will be freer to move ahead in this direction."

But the fundamental reform needed to manage the global economy is more open and democratic debate, Stiglitz argues. "If there were more opportunity for discussion, there would be more scrutiny," he says. "We're getting more discussion today, but very little inside the institutions."

Stiglitz fears that IMF and World Bank responses to criticism will be superficial without some fundamental restructuring of who has a voice in their decisions. "The institutions themselves, in the process of fighting for their survival, will pay lip service to change while drawing up the bridge."

Enronomics 101

DAVID MOBERG

January 21, 2002

If there's any justice, the fall of Enron from miracle "new economy" corporation to bankrupt shell should land quite a few executives in jail. But Enron's demise is not only a tale of corporate hubris, greed and criminality. More important, it is a cautionary guide to many of the dominant trends in the American economy.

For the past quarter century, a growing ideological chorus has contended that markets are rational and efficient—therefore good—and any interference, especially by government, is bad. . . . The Enron story is a massive argument for government intervention. A gas pipeline company that transformed itself into a maker of markets in energy, water, metals and much more, Enron's executives bought political influence to push deregulation of energy and other markets. Like many U.S. companies, Enron shifted from providing real energy to selling a complex variety of financial "derivatives"—contracts abstracted from some real commodity.

against the deal. While earlier protests against foreign imports had sometimes taken an ugly, racist tone, by the early '90s, the anti-NAFTA campaign tried to link up with the few progressive Mexican groups opposed to the agreement. With their slogan "Not This NAFTA," unions implied that a regional agreement would be acceptable if it raised Mexican workers' standard of living and protected labor rights and the environment. But opposition to NAFTA also came from more nationalist and conservative quarters, led by Ross Perot and Pat Buchanan. Globalization and trade issues split both parties, but it caused the deepest rifts for the Democrats.

Although Bill Clinton promised in his 1992 campaign to take seriously the issues of labor and the environment, the side agreements his administration negotiated were weak and deeply flawed. The corporate globalizers won: NAFTA introduced an era of trade agreements with an equal emphasis on tariff reduction and protection of investor and corporate rights. NAFTA also broke new ground in granting foreign corporations, which have no responsibilities under the agreement, the right to sue governments for adopting policies that deprive them of potential profits.

NAFTA was sold as a winning proposition for all three countries. But seven years later, the Economic Policy Institute concluded that working people had lost ground as a result of the trade deal. More than 750,000 jobs, many of them moderately high-wage manufacturing jobs, were displaced from the United States, adding to the pressures that kept inequality growing throughout the '90s. Despite the growth of such jobs in the *maquiladora* sector, however, overall job growth was modest in Mexico (since many Mexican agriculture and small manufacturing jobs were eliminated as a result of new competition), and real wages in manufacturing declined by a fifth from 1993 (just before NAFTA took effect) to 1999. In Canada, growth and wages stagnated, and inequality rose.

Clinton was able to get NAFTA passed only by exerting more effort—and offering more favors—than he did on behalf of nearly any other initiative he put before Congress. But the fight against NAFTA elevated international economic issues to a new level in public consciousness, one that they hadn't occupied since the tariff fights of the late 19th century. Labor unions and environmentalists forged a new alliance with the potential (despite the divisive, pro-corporate views of some unions on global warming and energy policy) of creating a new, much more comprehensive progressive political movement.

After NAFTA passed, the WTO was approved in 1995 with only modest opposition and little public awareness of the arcane trade issues. But backlash was growing, spurred in part by new leadership of the American labor movement under AFL-CIO President John Sweeney, student anti-sweatshop efforts and the Jubilee 2000 movement for the cancellation of the debts of poor countries. The biggest U.S. legislative victory of the '90s was twice blocking the renewal of the president's "fast track" negotiating powers. More significantly, a global campaign helped to scuttle the negotiation of a Multilateral Agreement on Investment. There were defeats as well: Clinton pushed through a flawed free trade agreement for Africa, and China won admission to the WTO. Worse, George W. Bush resurrected fast track, pushing it through Congress in the wake of September 11.

Since Seattle, the movement has become more international and more intent on building coalitions, but there have been debates over strategy, tactics (from behavior at protests to the utility of electoral politics) and just who is the real enemy. (Big corporations? Globalization? Capitalism?) Although the U.S. critique of globalization has its roots in trade issues, a variegated movement against corporate power has emerged. Tackling issues from intellectual property to bioengineering, from rainforests to tax havens, the new movement is as concerned about loss of democracy as about loss of jobs.

Globalization may be a fuzzy and all-encompassing notion, but organizers have been able to make the problems and solutions concrete and comprehensible. The real work of

Terry LaBan

We have seen the end of Enron, but the problems the company exemplified live on.

These financial devices are the centerpiece of the new "risk management" game in which complex bets on the future of the economy are balanced against each other to eliminate risk. But real-life risk didn't disappear; it just sneaked up in a new way to bite Enron. . . .

Markets are always volatile, but big government spending and regulation stabilize them—helping both business and the general public. Free market fundamentalists argued that companies like Enron could provide better stability—and make big bucks. Enron quickly grew to No. 7 in the Fortune 500. It also went global, leading the crusade for privatization and deregulation worldwide through the World Trade Organization.

Like many of its brethren in the hot fields of Internet business and financial services, Enron greatly overstated its profits through a fiendishly complex scheme that included partnerships with privately held firms—many run profitably by Enron executives—that were used to shift debt off Enron's books. The result: a boosted stock price and inflated credit rating. The rah-rah stock "analysts" touted Enron even as it was collapsing.

Worse, Enron's auditor, Arthur Andersen, ignored the shenanigans, its vision apparently clouded by the $52 million Enron paid it last year in consulting and accounting fees. Meanwhile, top Enron executives made more than $1 billion over two years selling their overpriced stock while they lied to investors about the condition of the company and pressured lower-level employees to hold Enron stock in their 401(k) pension plans as the company fell apart.

The Enron debacle is an argument for stricter financial disclosure laws, new (and restored) restrictions on banks and auditors playing double roles (like consulting and auditing), tougher corporate law enforcement, rigorous regulation of financial derivatives and new rules to protect employee pension plans. (It's also an argument against privatization of Social Security.) Enron is a perfect example of American-style "crony capitalism," the misguided idiocy of energy deregulation and the social dangers posed by the risk-management craze.

Most of all, it is a reminder of how flawed markets can be—even in the holy sepulcher of deregulation—particularly when information is distorted by both outright fraud and the manic belief in market magic by a herd of willing investors and silent watchdogs. We have seen the end of Enron, but the problems that the company so boldly exemplified live on.

the anti-globalizers has focused on specific measures like implementing a "Tobin tax" on speculative currency transactions or targeting corporate bad guys like Nike and Citibank. There is widespread public sympathy with the critics of globalization, but there is also growing skepticism about the Washington consensus from such diverse figures as billionaire investor George Soros and Harvard trade economist Dani Rodrik. It is not just flat-earthers out there raising questions, despite the fulminations of such corporate toadies as Thomas Friedman of the *New York Times.*

Globalization critics have grave doubts that unrestricted trade is always a good thing, but their focus is now less on restraint of trade than developing new rules to make sure that trade yields more equitable, sustainable development. There is a growing recognition that simply tacking on a few new conditions doesn't get at the fundamental flaws in this model of global economics. The challenge for the critics of globalization is to devise new rules for the global economy that protect the environment, ensure the rights of workers to organize unions, defend human rights and strengthen democratic control. Corporations and markets should be subject to rules that give priority to values of individual rights and social solidarity, strengthening egalitarianism and democracy within individual countries.

This will require the movement against corporate globalization to continue its creation of an international grassroots coalition drawn from both rich and poor countries. This movement must also fight, through electoral politics and other strategies, to change policies and win political control over the national governments that will ultimately have the powers to assemble and write the new rules. It is a daunting task, but it is the prerequisite for the success of progressive politics on any issue in any country in the years to come.

After the Fall

DEAN BAKER

December 12, 1999

The roaring stock market is seen as a testament to the success of American-style, free-market capitalism. The stock market apostles want to get the government out of the way and let business run the show. This gospel is being applied in all areas of life, from schools and prisons to health care. It also has become a leading export item, as the administration tries to push the American model on Japan, Europe and the rest of world, with the strong arm of the IMF acting as a sales agent in the less-developed countries.

There is a major problem with this picture. By any reasonable measure, the stock market is hugely overvalued. Typically, the ratio of the price of a share of stock to the earnings per share has been about 14 to 1. Currently it is more than 30 to 1. Investors can bid up stock prices in the same way they can bid up prices of rare paintings. But ultimately people value shares based on the earnings they generate, not how pretty they are. This means that stock prices would have to fall 50 to 70 percent to allow stocks to offer a return that is competitive with other financial assets, such as bonds.

Furthermore, when the stock market crashes it is not going to bounce back like it did in 1987, when the market wasn't nearly as overvalued. After the fall, stock prices are likely to grow at about the same rate as the economy, around 2 percent annually after adjusting for inflation. This is an issue of logic and arithmetic, not ideology. To put it simply, stock prices must be based on profits and the expected growth of profits. Even the highest plausible assumptions about profit growth would still leave the current market overvalued by about 50 percent. There is no economist in the country who has been able to develop a scenario that would justify current stock prices.

Terry LaBan

What goes up, must come down.

In the wake of the coming crash, the whole relationship between the government and the market will have to be re-examined.

IT Archives

Stock prices will plunge—it's just a question of when. Prices are determined by the psychology of investors. Their enthusiasm for stocks, no matter how irrational, may keep prices at inflated levels for six months, two years, even a decade. Economics and logic can't predict exactly when reality will catch up with this enthusiasm: They only assure that at some point it will.

The crash of the stock market is the ideological equivalent of the fall of the Berlin Wall. The soaring market has allowed corporate ideology to dominate public debate as never before. In the wake of the crash, progressives should be prepared to propose clear alternatives to a failed worldview.

Some parts of the agenda are obvious. It will be time to clean up Wall Street. The simplest way to try to deter similar bouts of "irrational exuberance" in the future is to impose a small transactions tax on the exchange of stocks, options, currencies and other financial instruments used for speculation. A tax of 0.25 percent on each purchase or sale of a share of stock would have almost no impact on anyone who holds a stock for five or 10 years, but it could prove quite costly to someone who buys at two o'clock and sells an hour later. Similarly, a tax of 0.1 percent on currency trades, such as buying Japanese yen, won't affect the price of imported cars in any noticeable way, but it would make high-speed currency shuffling very expensive.

This sort of transaction tax would not necessarily prevent future bubbles, but it would at least treat this form of gambling like any other form, all of which are heavily taxed. There is no reason to prefer that gamblers place their bets in financial markets rather than casinos, horse tracks or state lotteries. In addition, the tax could raise more than $100 billion annually. This money could be used to finance social spending or a tax cut for low- and middle-income workers.

But the need for rethinking the nation's agenda goes much further. Over the past two decades, the nation's leading economists have told us (and the rest of the world, through institutions like the IMF and World Bank) that financial markets should be given full responsibility for allocating capital. They claim that governments are too incompetent and will inevitably get things wrong. But the current overvaluation of the stock market shows that the market can lead to misallocations that can outdo even the most inept government bureaucracies.

Consider the case of an Internet start-up, where the initial stock offering sells for hundreds of millions of dollars, but the company subsequently goes belly-up. It's a safe bet that many of today's high-fliers will end up in this category. The hundreds of millions of dollars that go into purchasing the company's stock constitute money that otherwise could have supported productive investment. Instead, the money ends up in the pockets of the company's founders, who will be able to enjoy a lavish lifestyle for many years to come. When this is repeated tens or hundreds of times, as it has been, it means that the stock market boom has diverted a vast pool of capital from productive uses to supporting the luxury consumption of Internet millionaires and billionaires. As a result of the stock market boom, the magnitude of this waste has been much greater than anything caused by crony capitalism in East Asia. The nation will pay an economic price for this diversion for some time.

In the wake of the crash, the whole relationship between the government and the market will have to be re-examined. New paths forward will be developed based on experimentation with new ideas and the implemention of old ones. But we should be sure that we never again trust the proselytizers of free-market capitalism at the Clinton Treasury, the Greenspan Federal Reserve Board and the IMF. These folks should be left in the dustbin of history, right alongside the central planners of the USSR.

Beyond Anti-Capitalism

NOTES FOR A FUTURE MANIFESTO

Photograph by Lionel Delevingne

Thirteen

G. PASCAL ZACHARY

I HEAR THE SAME CONVERSATION WHEREVER I GO. ONLY THE ACCENTS CHANGE, THE FACES, THE NAMES, THE PLACES.

In the former Soviet republic of Moldova, the god that failed is not socialism, but globalization. Ten years after the breakup of the Soviet Union, Moldova's material living standard is roughly one-third of what it was in Communist times. Many people have not had hot water for eight years, power outages are common, and even residents of the country's capital, Chisinau, suffer through weeks without any heat in the worst of winter. Educated people are leaving the country in droves to work as maids and drivers in middling-income countries like Greece. Despite the deepening poverty, Moldova is loaded with American advisers and receives the third-highest amount of aid per capita of any former Soviet republic. The foreigners preach self-reliance, but so far the one notable sign of entrepreneurship came from a shadowy peddler who convinced a Moldovan village to export their body parts for cash.

If globalization has failed absurdly in Moldova, it has produced more predictable setbacks in Africa. In Ghana, most people still live close to the land, and yet the country cannot feed itself. Ghana imports meat, juice, flour, even rice. Convinced a decade ago by the International Monetary Fund to open itself to imports and discover its own "comparative advantage," Ghana so far has found no edge and hence makes practically nothing. The small percentage of Ghanaians who attend university or have international businesses prosper from the country's conventional economic path, but the vast majority does not. Rents have skyrocketed, legions of people are trying to escape to rich nations, and many of those remaining are poorer today than they were in 1957, when Ghana became the first black African colony to win independence.

Snapshots of a World Coming Apart at the Seams

EDUARDO GALEANO

February 5, 1992

"We can be like them," proclaims the giant neon sign on the road to development. The Third World will become the First World. It will be rich and happy, as long as it behaves itself and does what it's told.

But "what cannot be, cannot be, and besides, is impossible," as the bullfighter Pedro el Gallo said so well. If the Third World produced and squandered as much as the rich countries, our planet would perish. Already acid rain kills our forests and lakes. Toxic waste poisons our rivers and seas. In the South, agro-industry rips both trees and humans from their roots. With delirious enthusiasm, mankind is sawing the branch on which it is seated.

The average American consumes as much as 50 Haitians. Of course, this statistic does not represent the likes of Baby Doc Duvalier or the average resident of Harlem, but we must ask ourselves anyway: What would happen if the 50 Haitians consumed as many cars, as many televisions, as many refrigerators or as many luxury goods as the one American? Nothing. Nothing would ever happen again. We would have to change planets. Ours, which is already close to catastrophe, couldn't take it.

The precarious equilibrium of the world depends on the perpetuation of injustice. So that some can consume more, people must continue to consume less. To keep people in their place, the system produced armaments. Incapable of fighting poverty, the system fights the poor. . . .

The West is euphoric in triumph. The collapse of Communism gives the West the perfect alibi: In the East it was worse. Were the two systems any different? The West sacrifices justice in the name of liberty on the altar of the goddess productivity.

Doubts even persist in places where globalization benefits many. Germans talk of the need to preserve social safeguards and standards under attack from a left-leaning government desperate to make Germany more business-friendly. China holds off from joining the World Trade Organization (WTO) while searching for a way to defend a myriad of laws and practices aimed at protecting domestic producers. South Koreans resist the layoffs and business restructuring that capitalists say are the best medicine for the country's economy, but which are certain to destroy jobs and lower wages. In the United States, AFL-CIO President John Sweeney calls for "a new internationalism" that would put "global fairness" on equal footing with the imperatives of capital.

The U.S. war on terrorism further underscores the widespread feeling that globalization has failed. President George W. Bush endorsed this interpretation in a speech a month after September 11 in Shanghai, accusing Osama bin Laden and the al-Qaeda network of seeking to "shatter confidence in the world economic system." Acknowledging that the unfettered nature of that system inspires hatred in some, Bush added that "terrorists want to turn the openness of the global economy against itself." The stark social and economic policies of Afghanistan's Taliban regime may not present an alternative path to globalization. But that country's dire state raises questions about the sustainability of a certain economic approach.

Whether in Berlin or Davos, San Francisco or Santiago, Moscow or Kabul, the conversation about globalization invariably ends on a down note. But seeing the failures of globalization isn't the same as seeing beyond globalization. So across the globe, a pattern is emerging: Backlash isn't enough. Decrying sweatshops and environmental degradation isn't enough. Bemoaning the volatility of financial capital and the rapaciousness of profiteers isn't enough. Loathing the growing divide between rich and poor nations isn't enough. Nor is trying to halt the spread of global trade and investment or undo the global concentration of corporate ownership. To be sure, resistance is admirable, but it is not enough. A positive vision is needed. Alternatives are needed. But alternatives to what?

The question might hardly seem worth asking, the answer is so obvious. Globalization is the cosmic force everyone loves to hate. Indeed, bashing globalization has become a popular sport: Not only anti-corporate activists do it, so do billionaire financier George Soros and World Bank President James Wolfensohn. The establishment's race to embrace critics of globalization makes a mockery of the painful re-evaluation of neoliberalism that remains to be done. Poverty pimping on a global scale is a beguiling sideshow. Calls for a new consensus around an "enlightened" or "humane" globalization collide with the reality that reforms are difficult to impose and often unpopular with the globalizers themselves.

Critics of globalization rarely do more than trash the great beast. Their failure obscures a fundamental issue. For all the hype about new technology and the speed of change, globalization is nothing more than a friendlier word for "capitalism." The C-word, I submit, does have its virtues. For all its emotional baggage, anachronistic connotations and negative associations, "capitalism" remains superior as a descriptive term, if for no other reason than it suggests the historical antecedents of today's global forces and underscores the need for fundamental thinking about radical alternatives to the status quo. Indeed, capitalism as an explanatory category is more relevant than ever because a single seamless world market seems closer to realization than ever.

The implications of bringing the whole world under capitalism have been appreciated for some time, however. More than 150 years ago, one observer wrote:

> The bourgeoisie has through its exploitation of the world market given a cosmopolitan character to production and consumption in every country. . . . In place of the old wants, satisfied by the productions of the country, we find new wants, requiring for their satisfaction the products of distant lands and climes.

The East used to sacrifice freedom in the name of justice on the altar of the goddess productivity.

In the South, let's ask ourselves if this goddess deserves our lives.

Kit Boyce

The precarious equilibrium of the world depends on the perpetuation of injustice.

The writer was Karl Marx. And though *The Communist Manifesto* was written in the 1840s, a time bereft of computers, wireless telephones and airliners, the hollow promise of the global village as well as capitalism's propensity toward speed and change were evident to Marx. He noted:

> The bourgeoisie, by the rapid improvement of all instruments of production, by the immensely facilitated means of communication, draws all, even the most barbarian nations, into civilization. . . . Constant revolutionizing of production, uninterrupted disturbance of all social conditions, everlasting uncertainty and agitation distinguish the bourgeois epoch from all earlier ones. All fixed, fast-frozen relations, with their train of ancient and venerable prejudices and opinions, are swept away, all new-formed ones become antiquated before they can ossify. All that is solid melts into air.

With the insight that it is not globalization but capitalism that holds the world in its thrall, the search for alternatives becomes more compelling. But questions immediately arise: Don't we live in a post-ideological age? Didn't the socialist and communist experiments of Europe and the Soviet Union crash and burn? Isn't "reform" the best we can do? There aren't really any alternatives to capitalism, are there?

The inevitability of the grin-and-bear-it embrace of capitalism is conventional wisdom among reformers the world over. Anthony Giddens, director of the London School of Economics and an adviser to Britain's ruling Labour Party, has submitted to the inevitability of capitalist hegemony. After all, socialism is dead, and local or national self-sufficiency is "equally unappealing." Protectionism is a dead end because it "produces lower (economic) growth" and unleashes national rivalries that yield wars. Voicing the confidence of legions of self-styled pragmatists, he concludes in his book *On the Edge: Living with Global Capitalism*:

Democracy's Slow Death

NOAM CHOMSKY

November 28, 1994

In the New World Order, the world is to be run by the rich and for the rich. The world system is nothing like a classical market; the term "corporate mercantilism" is a closer fit. Governance is increasingly in the hands of huge private institutions and their representatives. The institutions are totalitarian in character: in a corporation, power flows from the top down, with the outside public excluded. In the dictatorial system known as "free enterprise," power over investment decisions, production and commerce is centralized and sacrosanct, exempt from influence and control by workers and community as a matter of principle and law.

Systems of private governance have gained undreamed-of power. They have naturally used it to create the "de facto world government" described in the business press, with its own institutions, also insulated from public inspection or influence. National governments, which in varying ways involve some measure of public participation, are constrained by such factors to serve the interests of the rich and powerful even more than in the past.

But there is little that is new in neoliberal programs, trickle-down theories and the rest of the doctrinal baggage that serves the interests of privilege and power. The ideology of oppression may differ in form when applied to Third World service areas and domestic populations, but similarities are apparent, and current enthusiasms are hardly more than a recapitulation, often sordid, of earlier devices to justify the privilege of those who hold the reins. As in the early 19th century, we are now once more to understand that it is a violation of natural liberty and even science to deceive people into thinking that they have some rights beyond what they can gain by selling their labor power. Any effort to depart from such right thinking leads directly to the Gulag. . . .

> The task, surely, *in the absence of alternatives*, is to keep the current system going and improve it. It is all we have; it is both a source of creativity and global enrichment, but equally it faces risks from all sides that need to be confronted and managed.

But are the most serious ills of capitalism subject to the sort of piecemeal, gradual management that Giddens considers the best of all possible worlds?

Consider that the triumph of capitalist economies came about partly through default: The collapse of the Soviet Union, the conversion of China to freer markets and the failure of European social democrats to revitalize the welfare state all powered capitalism's re-emergence in the '90s as the one true way. But the economic system that took the name "globalization" after the Cold War also showed impressive strengths: the ability to marry technological innovation with human freedom; an astonishing expansion of productive capacity that nevertheless coincided with healthy job growth (especially in skilled fields); and the death of inflation, once the scourge of mature industrial societies.

Despite the heterodox sources of capitalist vitality, a simplified and distorted explanation of its power took hold. In this view, which came to be known as neoliberalism or the "Washington consensus," growth flowed inexorably from the removal of government controls on trade, labor and capital. At the same time, prosperity depended on two conditions: a legal system that protected private property and the "rights" of investors, and a sound currency that flowed from restraints on government spending. These twin pillars of neoliberalism, while actually a means to an end, became ends in themselves. What began in the '80s as a specific strain of capitalism ended the century as the only legitimate capitalist path. This was unfortunate. Neoliberal capitalism spawns two bad outcomes that threaten the viability of capitalism and, by extension, the whole cosmopolitan project of knitting together the globe through the fabric of commerce and culture.

Terry LaBan

There is little new in neoliberal programs, trickle-down theories and the rest of the doctrinal baggage that serves the interests of privilege and power.

Vast unemployment persists alongside of huge demands for labor. Wherever one looks, there is work to be done of great social and human value, and there are plenty of people eager to do that work. But the economic system cannot bring together needed work and the idle hands of suffering people. Its concept of "economic health" is geared to the demands of profit, not the needs of people. In brief, the economic system is a catastrophic failure. Of course, it is hailed as a grand success, as indeed it is for a narrow sector of privileged people, including those who declare its virtues and triumphs.

How far can this go? Will it really be possible to construct an international society on something like the Third World model, with islands of great privilege in a sea of misery—fairly large islands, in the richer countries—and with controls of a totalitarian nature within democratic forms that increasingly become a facade? Or will popular resistance, which must itself become internationalized to succeed, be able to dismantle these evolving structures of violence and domination, and carry forth the centuries-old process of expansion of freedom, justice and democracy that is now being aborted, even reversed? These are the large questions for the future.

Does Globalization Matter?

DOUG HENWOOD

March 31, 1997

My hope is that people will stop talking about globalization—and its sidekick, technology—in such analytical isolation. Focusing on them, and exaggerating their scope and novelty, leads to a sense of resignation and passivity, in part because it tends to erase human agency from the picture and transform foreign investment and technical change into forces of nature. People come to believe that you can no more resist globalization than you can resist the sunrise.

One reason so much attention is paid to these factors is that we're not allowed to speak critically of capitalism as a system anymore. Postmodernists chide beliefs in systems as either quaint or totalitarian, and most lefties these days despair of any more than marginal reforms around the edges of the almighty market. So we speak instead about aspects of the system in isolation from each other. But, incorrigible dinosaur that I am, I insist that the driving force behind social and economic policy today is the lust for profit. For a while, there were countervailing forces—notably unions and leftist political parties—but for various reasons these have either been crushed or neutralized.

Many of the forces that have been driving U.S. wage levels downward have nothing to do with "globalization." Take two notorious examples: airline and trucking deregulation. There was literally no foreign presence in either of these industries when deregulation was imposed in the late '70s, but it's hard to think of sectors where so many formerly high-wage jobs have been so massively transformed into low-wage ones. . . . These examples point to a larger issue: Most people work in service industries, and the service sector is largely insulated from foreign competition. Is it competition from Malaysia that keeps wages low at McDonald's?

The first bad outcome is inequality, or divergence in wealth, technology and living standards. In absolute terms, there are more poor people today than ever. Of the world's 6 billion people, 1.3 billion live on less than $1 a day, while 2.8 billion make do on $2 a day. This means that roughly half the world's people lack decent health care, education and jobs, and have little or no access to the information and communications technologies that are transforming life for the rest of the world.

To be sure, experts disagree over the remedy for deepening poverty. Demographers blame high birth rates in developing countries. Development economists, such as David Dollar of the World Bank in his oft-cited paper "Growth is Good for the Poor," insist that incomes of the poor rise in lockstep with overall growth. This is essentially the trickle-down theory writ large, and much evidence suggests it does not hold. But even if advocates of trickle-down are correct, inequality is still growing. This is for the straightforward reason that rich countries generally grew faster than poor ones in the '90s, and this pattern is likely to hold in the new decade.

There are exceptions, of course, notably China. But in the case of the poorest nations of the world, and some of the biggest (Nigeria, Russia), economic activity contracted over the past decade. And even when growth occurred (as in India), it failed to keep pace with the growth of the United States, Germany and some other advanced industrial economies. The ideal of convergence expected by global economic experts now lies in ruin. The world is split between haves and have-nots, and the consequences are more profound than the stubborn reality of widespread poverty.

Divergence is reshaping the landscape of capitalism, most significantly by sharply reducing the commitment of the professional and domestic business elites in developing nations to their own countries. On a personal level, the choices are stark. Ten years ago, a physician in Ghana might have believed his society was improving and growing more prosperous, and thus considered it worth investing his time and skills. Today, he can have no such illusions. His best bet is to leave, the sooner the better. Even in more dynamic India, investment of time and capital in the United States promises greater rewards.

Divergence also has created a crisis of capital in which every economic position is potentially threatened, every commercial advantage at risk. Consider how the growth of software services in India's Bangalore metropolis, an enviable achievement, is now challenged by backwaters that also wish to gain a foothold in technology industries. The competitiveness of hungrier rivals in the Philippines or Vietnam, who are supplying less-expensive software, has forced India to produce more sophisticated products. But when the Indian software star Wipro Technologies decides to build branded software programs that put it into direct contact with the Microsofts of the world, the company risks not only losing out to established leaders, but relinquishing its position as a supplier of simpler, generic code. This cycle of innovation, glut and overcompetition leads to oligarchy, as can be seen so clearly in the end-of-the-century mergers in every industry.

This crisis has been exacerbated by the inherent instability of capitalism. Management of instability has always been the chief preoccupation of political economy in Western Europe and the United States. Yet with the hegemony of neoliberal capitalism, instability has increased. This second bad outcome has been duly noted by such mainstream economists as Paul Krugman, whose analysis suggests that greater global economic integration has resulted in greater global volatility. This conclusion carries a certain common sense. If we are all in the same boat, economically speaking, then we all get seasick in rough waters.

For several years, there has been a concerted effort to raise safeguards against the chances that an economic crisis arising in one country will spread to other countries and spiral into a global capitalist meltdown. But efforts at creating such an

The wave of downsizings over the past five years and the war on welfare are yet other examples. Downsizings, though often blamed on the dynamic duo of globalization and technology, have in fact been mostly driven by demands from Wall Street for fatter profits and higher stock prices. And just what globalizing pressure made Clinton's promise to end welfare as we know it a centerpiece of his 1992 campaign? The entry of millions of desperate former welfare recipients into the labor market is almost certain to depress wages for the bottom third of wage earners—for almost entirely homegrown reasons. In all these cases, "globalization" diverts attention from the responsible parties.

Finally, there's a disturbing and largely unexamined xenophobia behind the critique of globalization. What, in principle, is wrong with commerce across borders? I'd like to see it practiced on terms different from what prevail now, of course—exchanges among equals, not between bosses and the bossed—but doesn't anyone have anything positive to say about cosmopolitanism anymore?

The reflexive "No!" to globalization is symptomatic, I'm afraid, of the fact that few people have any good idea of what to say yes to. We've said "No!" to NAFTA, to the abolition of welfare, to budget cuts and so on without any positive vision of what the alternative is. What should the economic world look like? The disappearance of socialism from the political agenda has left a terrible vacuum. So dire have things got that it's left to George Soros—a man who made his billions through socially useless forms of speculation—to critique capitalism.

On this lack of positive vision, I'm about as guilty as anyone. But we've got to recognize that a nostalgia for a past that never was is a losing proposition, intellectually and politically.

insurance policy have led nowhere. The International Monetary Fund—the subject of so much criticism for exacerbating the effects of the currency crises in Asia and Russia in the late '90s—remains unreformed. Bailouts of national governments continue, without lowering the risks of future crises (and perhaps increasing them by rewarding irresponsibility among financiers). And increasingly it seems as if countries in crisis are those—like Turkey and Argentina—that supposedly have "graduated" from a period of painful economic reform and are poised for what neoliberals call "takeoff." Instead, a surprising number of poor countries are crashing on the runway because of a failure to attract investment, retain domestic capital or stimulate local demand.

While some reformers call for the creation of a global central bank—a sort of Federal Reserve for the entire world—this is a political non-starter. Poor countries suspect that rich ones wish to impose global economic rules for their own advantage. After all, this was the lesson of the WTO, which oversees multilateral trading rules. Poorer countries say these rules are biased against them because they allow rich countries to protect against wholesale imports of food products and clothing—the very areas where poor countries are the most competitive (because of lower labor costs and lower skills). Efforts at reforming the world financial architecture run aground in this morass.

To be sure, some aspects of capitalist excess or imbalance are subject to reform. Controls on capital flows—whether in the form of fixed exchange rates or limits on the ability of foreign investors to move money in and out of countries—demonstrably cushion dramas associated with open markets at little cost. Malaysia's experience with such controls, following the Asian currency crisis of 1997, illustrates the benefits of taking firm, consistent action. Despite the shrill cries of neoliberals that controls would wreck Malaysia's economy, foreigners resumed their heavy investments in the country and adapted to restrictions on expatriating profits.

So, too, can the poor be helped with reform measures. In many developing countries, public spending disproportionately

Water War Zone

JIM SHULTZ

April 17, 2000

COCHABAMBA, BOLIVIA—A grassroots rebellion over the rules of economic globalization erupted in January in this city of half a million high in the Andes. This time the battle was over something very simple: the price of water.

Last year, under direct pressure from the World Bank, the Bolivian government sold off Cochabamba's public water system to a consortium of British-led investors. In January, the new owners, Aguas Del Tunari, handed local water users their monthly bills, emblazoned with a spanking new corporate logo and hikes in water rates that were more than double for many families. In a country where the minimum wage is less than $100 per month, many users were hit with water bills of $20 and higher.

In mid-January, Cochabamba residents shut down their city for four straight days with a general strike led by a new alliance of labor, human rights and community leaders. All transportation came to a halt, roads were blockaded, no buses were allowed in or out of town and the government was forced to the negotiating table, agreeing to a price rollback and a two-week deadline to work out the details.

However, it soon became clear that the government's promises were vanishing into thin air. Movement leaders announced plans for a massive but peaceful march to the city's Central Plaza on February 4. Bolivian President Hugo Banzer, who ruled the country as a dictator from 1971 to 1978, responded by bringing in more than 1,000 police and soldiers from outside the city and imposing a military takeover of Cochabamba's center. For two days, while popular leaders and government officials held tense negotiations, police showered tear gas and rubber bullets on rock-wielding protesters. . . .

benefits the well-off. In Ghana, for instance, primary school education is neither free nor universal, yet the government devotes a significant share of national education spending to a university system that mostly serves the children of the rich. Similarly, the country spends scarce tax revenues on advanced medical services in its capital city of Accra, when even rudimentary health care isn't available in many rural areas. By shifting priorities, many governments could direct far more resources to the most needy members of their societies. If they won't tax the better-off more heavily, they can at least reduce the public subsidies for services chiefly used by the wealthy.

The behavior of multinational corporations can also be reformed. Codes of conduct, voluntary or coercive, create a benchmark against which the behavior of the world's biggest corporations can be measured. In Cambodia, a non-governmental organization, London-based Global Witness, has been given power by donor countries supplying foreign aid to ensure the government's enforcement of logging regulations. Private corporations, from Nike to Levis, have empowered both internal and external auditors to monitor their environmental and labor practices in poor countries. Such monitors are hardly foolproof and sometimes provide a veneer of respectability. But "shaming and naming" can help curb corporate misbehavior.

But taking down a brand-name corporation is a far cry from reforming labor practices in an entire sector of the world economy, or even of a single country. No less than Naomi Klein, champion of consumer campaigns against scofflaw corporations, admits in her anti-globalization treatise *No Logo*:

> There is no doubt that anti-corporate activism walks a precarious line between self-satisfied consumer rights and engaged political action. Campaigners can exploit the profile that brand names bring to human rights and environmental issues, but they have to be careful that their campaigns don't degenerate into glorified ethical shopping guides: how-to's on

The privatization of water is just the latest in a decade-long series of sales of Bolivian public enterprises to international private investors—including the national airline, train system and electric utility—as government officials carefully toe the neoliberal line that "private is better." While the promises have been about an infusion of new investment, the more obvious results have been weakened labor standards, price increases and reductions in services (train service is gone altogether).

Privatizing Cochabamba's water was a major item in the World Bank's June 1999 report on Bolivia, which specifically called for "no public subsidies" to hold down water price hikes. Poor countries like Bolivia reject World Bank advice at the peril of being cut off from international assistance. In a process with just one bidder, local press reports calculated that investors put up less than $20,000 of up-front capital for a water system worth millions.

World Bank economists in Washington will now pay less for water per month than Tanya Paredes, a mother of five who supports her family as a clothes knitter. Her water bill went up in January from $5 per month to nearly $20, an increase equal to what it costs her to feed her family for a week and a half. "What we pay for water comes out of what we have to pay for food, clothes and the other things we need to buy for our children," she explains.

Price hikes like these led to widespread support for the protests. "Everyone took a role," says Oscar Olivera, the Cochabamba labor leader who has become the protests' most visible spokesman. "Youth were on the front lines, the elderly made roadblocks."

When protest leaders called on the radio for a citywide transportation stoppage in response to the police crackdown, little old women with bent spines were out in the streets within minutes, building blockades with branches and rocks. . . . "We're questioning that others, the World Bank, international business, should be deciding these basic issues for us," Olivera says. "For us, that is democracy."

saving the world through boycotts and personal lifestyle choices. Are your sneakers "No Sweat"? Your rugs "Rugmark"? Your soccer balls "Child Free"? Is your moisturizer "Cruelty-Free"? Your coffee "Fair Trade"? Some of these initiatives have genuine merit, but the challenges of a global labor market are too vast to be defined—or limited by our interests as consumers.

Tom Kruse

To protect corporate interests, Bolivia declared martial law.

The same can be said for many reform efforts: All too often the limits are reached too soon. Out of frustration, radicals and anarchists, mainly of European origin, have targeted the meetings of the global elite—a reminder that while the marginalized may lack answers, they possess plenty of anger and frustration. These protests are effective in their fashion, but they have succeeded mostly in convincing leaders of rich countries to gather discreetly in out-of-the-way (and out-of-sight) venues. The capitalist elite insists that improvements will come with or without the shrill attacks in the streets. Yet no reform agenda can promise to reverse deepening inequality and rising instability. The neoliberals only hope to hold these trends in check. This compels us to look for alternatives beyond the capitalist framework.

Rather than think in terms of a grand ideology, let's consider the benefits of a pragmatic approach that draws from various sources. The key to forging alternatives to capitalism is to adopt a principled heterodoxy, based on the understanding that radicalism will not yield a "one size fits all" model any more effectively than conservatism will. What, then, are the elements of a counterweight to capitalism? I see three. Each deserves an essay of its own, but here I'll quickly outline the basics.

SELF-RELIANCE

Economists have a sneering, technical term for self-reliance: autarky. Conventional wisdom equates self-reliance with inefficiency. Economists reason that in order to support local producers, barriers to imports must be erected. Having erected these barriers, local producers grow complacent and inefficient. Growth slows, living standards decline and the barriers ultimately collapse of their own weight. But critics miss the point: No country or region ought to attempt to become self-sufficient across the board. They should do so selectively.

In India, which sought to rid its economy of local impediments following independence in 1947, local industries did indeed grow stronger through protections against foreign competition. But rather than removing or easing protections in response, the government became a captive of domestic industries. In Ghana, state control of the export sales of cocoa, the country's most valuable cash crop, failed because farmers were paid too little for their crops in a misguided attempt by the government to unfairly profit from cocoa production (and to find the cash to pay the bribes that would perpetuate its political rule).

For the surest proof that self-reliance ought to be the cornerstone of an alternative, look no further than the behavior of the United States and European Union. Despite decades of proselytizing the benefits of free trade, both these economic actors vigorously protect their agricultural producers and communities at great cost to consumers (in excess of $300 billion annually). If self-reliance is good enough for the world's richest countries, it should be good enough for the poorest.

In early 2001, at the prestigious World Economic Forum in Davos, Switzerland, the presidents of Nigeria and South Africa called for a new approach to African development, based on local self-sufficiency and increased partnerships between African neighbors. The two countries say continued foreign aid remains essential (as does debt relief) for an African recovery—but more fundamental is the development of local industries. Self-reliance, of course, may not be anti-capitalist; it may serve to build or buttress the clout of a native bourgeoisie. But the same ethos can nurture producer

Trading on Terrorism

NAOMI KLEIN

November 12, 2001

There are many contenders for Biggest Political Opportunist since the September 11 atrocities. Politicians ramming through life-changing laws while voters are still mourning; corporations diving for public cash; pundits accusing their opponents of treason.

Yet amid the chorus of draconian proposals and McCarthyite threats, one voice of opportunism still stands out. That voice belongs to Robyn A. Mazer. Mazer is using September 11 to call for an international crackdown on counterfeit T-shirts.

Not surprisingly, Mazer is a trade lawyer in Washington. Even less surprising, she specializes in trade laws that protect the single largest U.S. export: copyright. That's music, movies, logos, seed patents, software and much more. Trade Related Intellectual Property rights (TRIPs) is one of the most controversial side-agreements in the run-up to November's World Trade Organization meeting in Qatar. . . . American multinationals are desperate to gain access to these large markets for their products—but they want protection. Many poor countries, meanwhile, say TRIPs cost millions to police, while strangleholds on intellectual property drive up costs for local industries and consumers.

What does any of this trade wrangling have to do with terrorism? Nothing, absolutely nothing. Unless, of course, you ask Mazer, who published an article September 30 in the *Washington Post* headlined, "From T-Shirts to Terrorism: That Fake Nike Swoosh May Be Helping Fund bin Laden's Network."

She writes: "Recent developments suggest that many of the governments suspected of supporting al-Qaeda are also promoting, being corrupted by, or at the very least ignoring highly lucrative trafficking in counterfeit and pirated products capable of generating huge money flows to terrorists." . . .

cooperatives, worker-owned factories and small entrepreneurs. In either case, the dependency on imported products can be lessened in a way consistent with growth and equity.

Self-reliance is nothing new, of course. Despite the cult-like authority of the belief in economic integration, powerful nations have always sought to protect their interests by keeping some significant part of their economy under national control. The events of September 11, 2001, may provide a stimulus for more nationalistic social and economic policies in the United States and among its economic rivals. Fears raised by terrorism on the scale executed by the al-Qaeda network invariably will roll back economic integration by raising costs of removing barriers to the flow of people, material and capital. But this may also stimulate fresh thinking about the forgotten benefits of self-reliance, one of which is strengthening community.

STATE OWNERSHIP

State ownership of key industries was subjected to relentless criticism in the '70s and '80s, but the failure of privatization in the former Soviet Union, as well as parts of Eastern Europe and Latin America, has triggered a re-evaluation. "In Eastern Europe the initial euphoria over the liberalization of the planned economies began to wane as the hard, grinding work of reconstruction continued," writes Italian economic historian Pier Angelo Toninelli in his book *The Rise and Fall of State-Owned Enterprise in the Western World.* "In Western Europe the recent success of center-left coalitions in France, Britain, Italy and Germany brought the social price of economic change back into consideration. . . . The challenge for the market economies of the 21st century will be to invent some new public-private mixture."

Individual governments must decide just what areas are most promising. In Israel, for instance, a state venture-capital fund stimulated the formation of high-tech companies in the '90s. In Malaysia, a government-owned auto company led to the transfer of jobs and know-how in this critical industry. In

Welcome to the brave new world of trade negotiations, where every arcane clause is infused with the self-righteousness of a holy war. . . .

What do new trade deals have to do with fighting terrorism? Well, the terrorists, we are told again and again, hate America precisely because they hate consumerism: McDonald's and Nike and capitalism—you know, freedom. To trade is therefore to defy their ascetic crusade, to spread the very products they loathe.

But wait a minute: What about all those fakes Mazer says are bankrolling terror? In Afghanistan, she claims, you can buy "T-shirts bearing counterfeit Nike logos and glorifying bin Laden as 'The great *mujahid* of Islam.'" It seems we are facing a much more complicated scenario than the facile dichotomy of a consumerist McWorld versus an anti-consumer *jihad*. In fact, if Mazer is correct, not only are the two worlds thoroughly enmeshed, the imagery of McWorld is being used to finance *jihad*.

Maybe a little complexity isn't so bad. Part of the disorientation many Americans now face has to

Terry LaBan

The crises of capitalism will spawn alternative forms of political economic organization.

Britain, poor performance by private railroad operators has raised the possibility of renationalizing the country's train companies. Here, too, the threat of terror highlights the need for state intervention, if only to improve the safety and security of financial transactions. An unintended consequence of the September 11 attacks may be to spawn a new optimism about the possibility of government, including direct participation in economic affairs.

But any resurrection of state ownership (through nationalization of companies or state-led entrepreneurship) must be accompanied by a greater role for independent watchdogs and monitors in the regulatory process. Independent regulators must promote healthy competition so that neither big business nor big government gains too much sway. At the same time, state ownership creates an opportunity for corruption and exploitation: Over the past three decades in Nigeria, for example, oil revenues of $280 billion have been stolen and squandered, leaving the country among the world's 20 poorest. Making state ownership a force for equity, rather than a foundation for corruption, stands as the greatest challenge to architects of alternatives to capitalism.

SUSTAINIBILITY

Any alternative to capitalism must have at its core an appreciation for the environmental and biological aspects of civilization. This often pits ecological concerns against growth. State socialism, the great modern challenger to capitalism, showed scant concern for the environment, trashing land and resources with a ferocity that perhaps even exceeded capitalism at its most outrageous. Because of this history of environmental negligence, anti-capitalists need to pay special attention to the question of sustainability.

As elsewhere, sustainable economics is heterodox at its core, relying on diverse strategies. In her perceptive critique of the "green revolution," Vandana Shiva highlights the way gains in food production came at the expense of water conservation. Water-intensive farming supplanted water-sensitive

Terry LaBan

What do new trade deals have to do with fighting terrorism?

do with the inflated and oversimplified role consumerism plays in the American narrative. To buy is to be. To buy is to love. To buy is to vote. People outside the United States who want Nikes—even counterfeit Nikes—must want to be American, must love America, must in some way be voting for everything America stands for.

This has been the fairy tale since 1989, when the same media companies now bringing us America's War on Terrorism proclaimed that their television satellites would topple dictatorships the world over. Consumers would lead, inevitably, to freedom. But all these easy narratives are breaking down: Authoritarianism co-exists with consumerism, desire for American products is mixed with rage at inequality.

Nothing exposes these contradictions more clearly than the trade wars raging over "fake" goods. Pirating thrives in the deep craters of global inequality, when demand for consumer goods is decades ahead of purchasing power. It thrives in China, where goods made in export-only sweatshops are sold for more than factory workers make in a month. It thrives in Africa, where the price of AIDS drugs is a cruel joke. It thrives in Brazil, where CD pirates are feted as musical Robin Hoods.

Complexity is lousy for opportunism. But it does help us get closer to the truth, even if it means sorting through a lot of fakes.

agriculture. While raising farm output, the shift also sowed the seeds of a water shortage crisis.

How best to ensure the sustainability of global and local resources remains elusive. But in an essay titled "Yoked to Death: Globalization and Corporate Control of Agriculture," Shiva links unsustainable farming techniques with the push to open agriculture to global competition. While theoretically offering small producers in poor countries access to a wider base of customers, the immediate effect of agricultural liberalization is to expose small farmers to the predations of global agribusiness. Traditional farming methods are swept away in the shift toward higher-yielding seeds and the latest fertilizers. In her native India, home to one-sixth of humanity, Shiva sees a rapid colonization of Indian food production by global corporations. The alternative, she argues, is to pursue the goal of "food security"—where success is defined not only by sufficient food supplies, but by sustainability and ecological farming practices.

A parallel challenge to capitalist exploitation of the natural world arises from resistance to the commercialization of the gene pool. Under the logic of capitalism, without the promise of profit useful innovations will not occur. The patenting of various life forms sets the stage, as Jeremy Rifkin has noted, "of claiming an actual animal as an invention." This absurd possibility suggests the need for a "biosocialism," whereby some portion of the planet's genetic heritage is declared off-limits to commercial exploitation. Just how the world establishes what Rifkin calls "a genetic commons" isn't clear. The mechanisms might include state ownership of genetic engineering firms or a revamped patent system that forces innovators who receive public support (essentially all of them) to place their inventions in the public domain. But the realm of bio-engineering and genetics has the potential to spur a re-examination of capitalist ends and the emergence of alternative means of achieving the fruits of the biological revolution: not greater profits, but better lives and a healthier planet.

Something along these lines already is happening in Brazil, which in 1999 enacted a law that gives the state the right to license patents in a national emergency. This Brazilian law has already been used to help lower the prices of AIDS medicines. The measure has provoked the wrath of capitalists. Prodded by the United States, the WTO wants to end this practice before 2006. But the rebels against pharmaceutical tyranny have scored monumental victories, forcing drug makers to drop a lawsuit against South Africa for following the Brazilian path and selling essential drugs at cost. Indeed, the anti-capitalist backlash to global pharmaceutical companies has been so successful that no major player in the worldwide industry claims any longer to have an unabridged and unassailable right to protect their products from copying. They insist only on controlling the mechanism for giving away or deeply discounting the drugs.

The idea that everything is for sale, even human life, is spawning a counter-philosophy based on a belief that some aspects of society and nature are not tradable and that market forces must not trump human values in these realms. Out of this contest may arise a full-blown alternative to capitalism. However, the capacity for multinationals to absorb and respond to even fundamental attacks remains a formidable barrier to those who wish to turn a radical critique of capitalism into concrete actions.

These alternatives aren't a revelation. Taken together, they are not capable of sweeping aside neoliberal capitalism. And they are hardly new. Indeed, each carries a whiff of the past. The 20th century provided a stage for ideological combat of the sort unlikely to be seen again. But history is not at its end. The crises of capitalism continue, and while they are unlikely to lead to its demise, these crises will certainly spawn alternative forms of political economic organization.

Whether this emerging alternative to entrenched capitalism ultimately constitutes a counter-ideology is unimportant.

By drawing on diverse roots, different parts of the world may create different alternatives to the one-size-fits-all capitalism that holds sway among the global elite. We may feel some nostalgia for the bygone era when contradictory ideologies squared off in a titanic fight for world supremacy. But this time around, the counter-capitalisms that arise may provide more human satisfaction because they will be based on a belief in diversity—and a realization that embracing one way of social organization as true and best carries too many costs.

However protean and robust, however quick to seize social, cultural and economic innovations, capitalism remains vulnerable from its failure to embrace heterodoxy and its overdependence on a canonical faith in markets and openness. From these vulnerabilities the alternatives to capitalism will arise. This ground is not fertile for grand theories, so tomorrow's radicals are unlikely to build sweeping ideologies. There may be no Marx toiling obscurely in a library somewhere, a manifesto waiting to be born. But there is room for more experimentation, out of necessity and opportunity.

Take It to the Streets

NAOMI KLEIN

March 19, 2001

PORTO ALEGRE, BRAZIL—It looks a little like one of those press conferences announcing a merger between corporate giants: a couple of middle-aged guys shaking hands and smiling into a bank of cameras. Just like on CNN, they assure the world their new affiliation will make them stronger, better equipped to meet the challenges of the global economy.

Only something is askew. More facial hair for one thing: The man on the left has a scruffy beard, and the one on the right has a rather distinctive handlebar mustache. And come to think of it, their alliance is not a merger of corporate interests—designed to send stock prices soaring and workers wondering about their "redundancy." In fact, the men say, this merger will be good for workers and lousy for stock prices.

Another clue we're not watching CNN: Someone passes a message to the man on the right. It seems the police are threatening him with arrest. That definitely doesn't happen during your average corporate-merger announcement—no matter how flagrantly the consolidation violates antitrust laws.

The man on the left is João Pedro Stedile, co-founder of Brazil's Landless Peasants Movement. The man on the right is José Bové, the French cheese farmer who came to world attention after he "strategically dismantled" a McDonald's restaurant to protest a U.S. attack on France's ban on hormone-treated beef. And this isn't Wall Street; it's the World Social Forum in Porto Alegre, Brazil.

To read the papers, these men should not be sharing a platform, let alone embracing for the cameras. Third World farmers are supposed to be at war with their European counterparts

Mauricio Lima

"Olé, Olé, Bové, Bové, Bové."

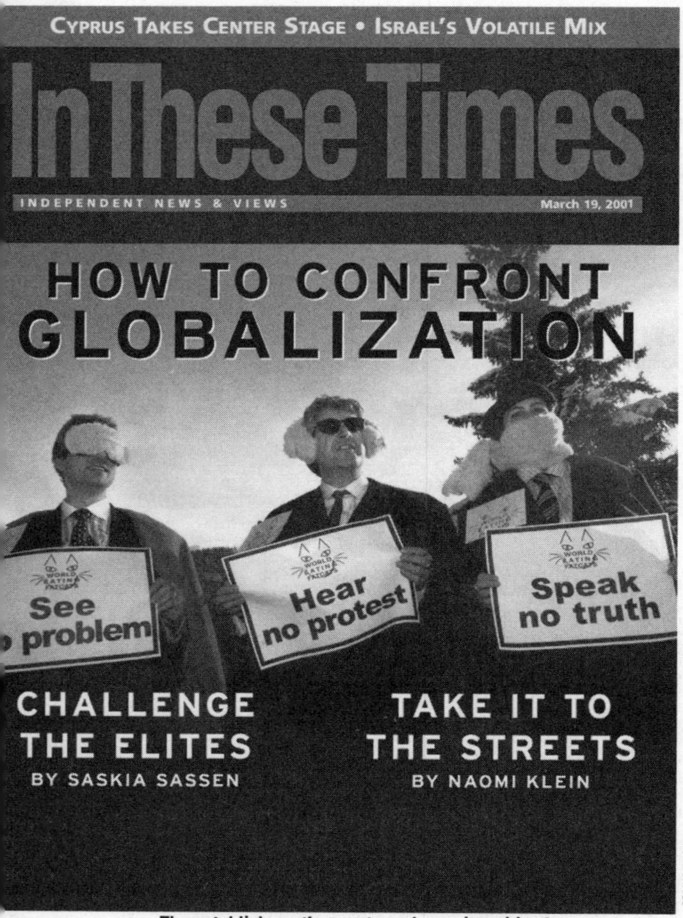

Cyprus Takes Center Stage • Israel's Volatile Mix
In These Times
INDEPENDENT NEWS & VIEWS
March 19, 2001
HOW TO CONFRONT GLOBALIZATION
See no problem
Hear no protest
Speak no truth
CHALLENGE THE ELITES
BY SASKIA SASSEN
TAKE IT TO THE STREETS
BY NAOMI KLEIN

ITT Archives

The establishment's race to embrace its critics has sidestepped the painful re-evaluation of neoliberalism that needs to be done.

over unequal subsidies. But here in Porto Alegre, they have joined forces in a battle much broader than any intergovernmental trade skirmish. The small farmers both men represent are attempting to fight the consolidation of agriculture into the hands of a few multinationals, through genetic engineering of crops, patenting of seeds and industrial-scale, export-led agricultural policies. They say that their enemy is not farmers in other countries, but a system of trade that is facilitating this concentration, and taking the power to regulate food production away from national governments.

"Today the battle is not in one country but in every country," Bové tells a crowd of several thousand. They break into chants of "Ole, Ole, Bové, Bové, Bové" and, in a matter of hours, hundreds are wearing badges declaring, "Somos Todos José Bové" ("We are all José Bové").

The World Social Forum was a chance to share ideas about social and economic alternatives. It is a new kind of intellectual free trade: a Tobin tax swapped for a "participatory budget"; national referenda on all trade agreements in exchange for local lending alternatives to the International Monetary Fund; farming co-operative models traded for community policing.

But there is one idea with more currency than any other, expressed from podiums and on flyers handed out in hallways, "Less talk, more action." It's as if talk itself has been devalued by overproduction—and little wonder. At the same time in Davos, Switzerland, the richest CEOs in the world sound remarkably like their critics: We need to make globalization work for everyone, they say, to close the income gap, end global warming.

Oddly, at the Brazil forum, designed to help talk our way into a new future, it seems as if talking has become part of the problem. How many times can the same story of inequality be told, the same outrage expressed, before that expression becomes a paralyzing, rather than catalyzing, force?

Which brings us back to the two men shaking hands. The reason the police are after José Bové (and why he is being treated like a cheese-making Che Guevara) is that he took a break from all the talk. While in Brazil, Bové traveled with local landless activists to a nearby Monsanto test site, where three hectares of genetically modified soybeans were destroyed. Unlike in Europe, where similar direct action has occurred, the protest did not end there. The Landless Peasants Movement has occupied the land and members are planting their own crops, pledging to turn the farm into a model of sustainable agriculture.

Why didn't they just talk about their problems? In Brazil, 1 percent of the population owns 45 percent of the land. In the past six years alone, 85,000 families have joined the ranks of the landless.

At the first World Social Forum, the most talked-about alternative turns out to be an alternative to talking: acting. It may just be the most powerful alternative of all.

New World Disorder

GLOBALIZATION VERSUS GLOBAL CONSCIOUSNESS

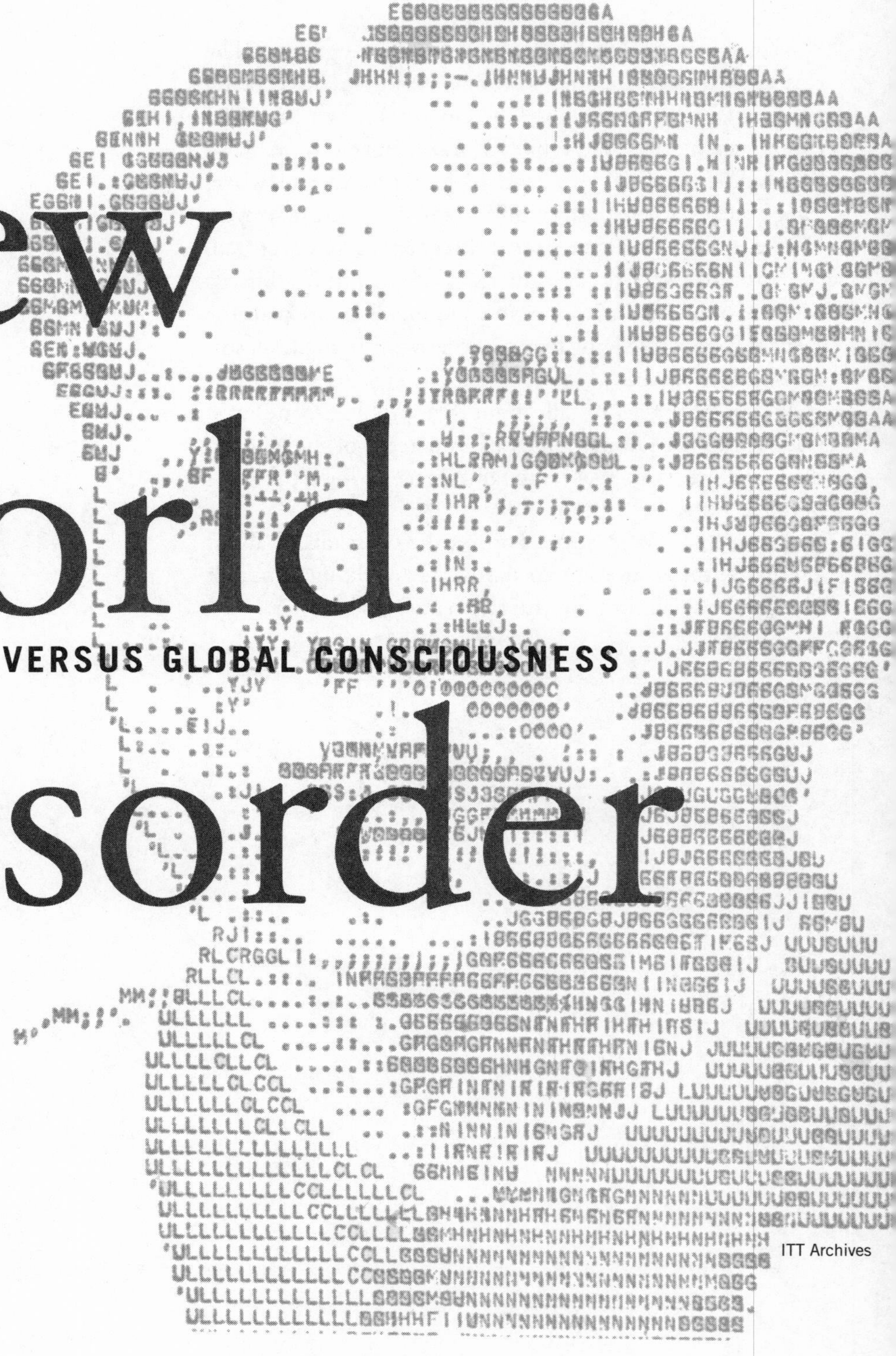

ITT Archives

Fourteen

JAMES NORTH

AT FIRST GLANCE, THE THIRD WORLD LOOKS MUCH BETTER TODAY THAN IT DID BACK WHEN *IN THESE TIMES* STARTED APPEARING IN THE FALL OF 1976.

Vicious dictatorships were everywhere. Of Latin America's 20-odd nations, only Colombia, Venezuela and Costa Rica enjoyed multi-party democracies; elsewhere, Augusto Pinochet of Chile was only the most notorious of the generals who had seized power and unleashed death squads across the continent.

In East Asia, it was much the same story. General Park Chung Hee in South Korea and Ferdinand Marcos in the Philippines had crushed all opposition. General Suharto had completed his first 10 years ruling Indonesia; in Taiwan, Chiang Kaishek's son, Chiang Chingkuo, continued the family dictatorship. Down in South Asia, Indira Gandhi had declared martial law in India, and generals dominated both Pakistan and Bangladesh.

In Africa, the biggest news in 1976 was the apartheid regime. The Soweto uprising had broken out that June, but unarmed black schoolchildren seemed to have no chance against a modernized police state. Nelson Mandela was in his 14th year in prison, nearly unknown to the outside world. Elsewhere in Africa, corrupt one-party states predominated, typified by Mobutu Sese Seko in Zaire, the murderous buffoon Idi Amin in Uganda, and the generals in Nigeria, who were already squandering that country's oil wealth. In the Middle East, there was stalemate between Israel and its neighbors, and even more instances of authoritarian rule: Anwar Sadat in Egypt, the Saudi Arabian princes, the Shah of Iran.

In the West, governments, banks and multinational corporations were not terribly worked up about this globe full of dictatorships. Back then it was business as usual with one dictator after another. After the

The Biko Tapes

December 6, 1977

This interview with Steve Biko was one of the few firsthand recordings of his thoughts in the last years of his life. The tape of this interview circulated underground in apartheid South Africa. Because of its clandestine origin, the interviewer was not identified.

Do you believe that by means of disturbances like the one in Soweto you will bring about a real change of this society?

I see this as only one form of discontent. I'm of the view that the change process is going to be protracted. It depends entirely on the degree to which the Nationalist government is prepared to hold onto power. My own analysis is that they want to hold on to power and fight with their backs to the wall. Now, conflict could be avoidable only if they would be prepared to avoid it. Those who are at the seeking end, that is those who want justice, who want an egalitarian society, can only pursue their aspirations according to the resistance offered by the opposition.

When you speak of an egalitarian society, do you mean a socialist one?

Yes. I think there is no running away from the fact that in South Africa there is such an ill distribution of wealth that any form of political freedom which does not touch on the distribution, the *proper* distribution of wealth, will be meaningless. The whites have locked up within a small minority of themselves the greater proportion of the country's wealth.

If we have a mere change of face of those in governing positions, what is likely to happen is that black people will continue to be poor, and you will get a few blacks filtering through into the so-called bourgeoisie. Our society would be run almost as of

Chilean people elected President Salvador Allende, a socialist, Henry Kissinger memorably commented, "I don't see why we need to stand idly by and watch a country go Communist because of the irresponsibility of its own people." The United States acted on his words with considerable covert support for Pinochet's brutal 1973 coup.

Citibank and Chase Manhattan loaned billions to the dictators in Brazil, Indonesia and Zaire without a nanosecond's hesitation. Ford, IBM and some 350 other U.S. corporations invested and traded with South Africa shamelessly. After the Argentine military nearly tortured to death the courageous (and politically moderate) newspaper editor Jacobo Timerman, neoconservative ideologues in America tried to discredit not the junta but Timerman himself, alleging that he had indirect financial links to the guerrillas who were fighting the regime.

Back in 1976 there were two things that did get the Western establishment worked up: the specter of Communism, and Third World talk of a new international economic order. The Soviet Union and its bloc in Eastern Europe still appeared strong and continued to aid certain leftist regimes around the world in places like Cuba, Ethiopia, Angola and Mozambique. In Asia, the Soviets continued to support Vietnam, which had finally won its 30-year war against the French and then the Americans. In China, Mao Zedong had died in September 1976, but the world's largest country still posed a significant challenge to Western hegemony.

Besides warning darkly about Soviet expansionism, the West was frightened by the vigorous new talk of a global redistribution of income. In 1973, the Organization of Petroleum Exporting Countries (OPEC) had quintupled the price of oil, and, in the mid-'70s, prices also rose for Third World commodities like coffee, copper and cocoa. Third World statesmen like President Julius Nyerere of Tanzania had been arguing for years that what economists call "the terms of trade" discriminated against poorer countries. Nyerere contended that over time primary commodities stagnated or even fell in price, but the cost of Western manufactured goods continued to increase. He pointed out that every year Tanzania had to export more bags of sisal, the fibrous plant used to make rope, to earn enough to import the same tractor.

But with OPEC leading the way, it looked like producer cartels might form in other commodities, and energetic debates started at the United Nations and in other international forums. The West whined about being "held hostage" by the Third World, making the unseemly suggestion that tin miners in Bolivia and coffee pickers in Brazil, who were lucky to earn a dollar a day, were greedy extortionists for wanting a better life for their families.

No one would have predicted the Third World that has emerged. Nearly all the dictatorships disappeared across Latin America, Asia and much of Africa. One ruler after another has fallen or been pushed aside. You can say and write things in Santiago and Seoul that you once would have hesitated to whisper. The Cold War ended and with it the vicious proxy wars between the superpowers, one of which, in the Horn of Africa, killed hundreds of thousands of people. Nelson Mandela did not die in prison, but emerged as the most widely respected political leader on the planet.

One of the most promising changes is that genuinely independent grassroots movements have started to flourish across the Third World. In 1976, no one had heard the expression "non-governmental organization." Environmental movements in India and Taiwan challenge dam-building and pollution; microcredit groups try to free the rural poor from the grip of moneylenders; independent newspapers wage war against national television monopolies and government corruption. Women have taken vocal roles in many of these groups, slowly reversing gender discrimination.

A Rip Van Winkle who woke up in 2001 in Rio de Janeiro or Bangkok would be astounded at these political and social changes, which exceed anything comparable in the West.

yesterday. So that for meaningful change to occur, there needs to be an attempt at reorganizing the whole economic pattern and economic policies within this country.

Clearly you see a country in which black and white can live amicably on equal terms together?

That is correct. We see a completely non-racial society. We don't believe, for instance, in the so-called "guarantee for minority rights," because guaranteeing minority rights implies an evolution of portions of the community on a race basis. We believe that in our country there shall be no minority, there shall be no majority—there shall just be people. Those people will have the same status before the law, and they will have the same political rights before the law. So, in a sense, it will be a completely non-racial, egalitarian society.

ITT Archives

Steve Biko's funeral procession.

No One Knows How Many

WILFRED BURCHETT

May 30, 1979

PHNOM PENH, CAMBODIA—In 16 different spacious rooms, the torturer-executioners were at work for seven days a week. Each seems to have disposed on the average of eight victims a day. A long list of guidelines personally drawn up by Pol Pot in his own handwriting stipulated that victims once in the torture chamber, "must know they are going to die so might as well make a full confession and get it over with quickly, but they must not be killed until a full confession has been extracted."

The period between arrest and being led into the torture-execution chamber was only a few days, during which the victims were confined two at a time in cells three feet wide by six feet long, chained by the legs. The torture chambers were simple enough: a bare iron bedstead with padlocked leg chains, a table with two chairs, one for the interrogator, another with a typewriter in front of it for the note-taker. A favorite type of torture was plucking out head hair with pincers; tufts of it lie at the head of each bedstead and copious blood stains the floor underneath. Executions were carried out with axes, hammers, short-handed spades and jungle knives.

In the neatly handwritten lists of each day's proceedings is noted the age and profession or education of each victim and the date of arrest and death. In some cases a notation in red ink is made of any exceptional form of execution. The small staff available for processing the great volume of data (which included separate files on their "confessions") had started classification under headings such as "students invited to return from France" (the number of those listed as killed, together with the nature of their studies or competencies, was 147), "former diplomats invited to return" and "members of original Sihanouk-led resistance government." In a haphazard selection of the daily lists of killed were 100 on

But much would be depressingly familiar. First, inequality between the First and Third worlds has not narrowed and in most places has actually gotten worse. Across Latin America, Africa and parts of Asia, the debt crisis hit in the early '80s, and the fledgling democracies spent a disproportionate amount of their export earnings repaying money (with usurious interest) that Western banks had loaned to the dictators. Latin Americans call the '80s "the Lost Decade," a Great Depression more biting for them than the worldwide slump of the '30s.

Some parts of East Asia did flourish economically. But on closer inspection, even here the grandiose claims of the market fundamentalists are exaggerated. Only four places had genuine, broad-based growth: two country-sized entities (South Korea, Taiwan) and two city-states (Hong Kong, Singapore)—all four total only 80 million people. Once the financial crisis of 1997–1998 swept through the region (nearly derailing the entire global economy in the process), the Asian economic miracle appeared much more fragile in nations like Indonesia (224 million), Thailand (61 million) and the Philippines (81 million). China was a special case: In the '80s, Deng Xiaoping's reforms did promote genuine economic growth across the entire country. But by the '90s, foreign investment was concentrated in certain coastal cities and enclaves, in a tawdry, soulless atmosphere of boom and corruption that left most of the Chinese people behind, with worsening health and deteriorating education.

Our Rip Van Winkle would also notice that the end of the Cold War didn't bring an end to violence. Ethnic killing blighted various places, including Indonesia, Sri Lanka and India; conflict also tore at Africa, the worst instance being the 1994 genocide in Rwanda, in which at least half a million people were slaughtered in 100 days. (If there wasn't a better Western response, at least there was greater awareness; in neighboring Burundi, massacres in 1972 had killed more than 100,000 people, but only one Western reporter, Stanley Meisler, wrote about it.) And violent ethnicity remained a terrible threat, especially in South Asia, where both India and Pakistan had developed nuclear weapons.

Yet the dire predictions of global chaos have not come true, and some countries, like Uganda and Mozambique, have largely restored peace and order. Despite a depression and a slow, halting recovery in Latin America, that continent has remained generally quiet; a similar economic catastrophe in Europe in the '30s gave rise to Adolf Hitler. In ways we do not fully understand but still demand our respect, Third World peoples have mostly not allowed massive dislocation and economic crisis to turn into mass violence and murder.

Even the horrible September 11, 2001, attacks on the World Trade Center and the Pentagon did not, at least at first, represent a mass movement for violence. Militant Islamism was visible in a number of Middle Eastern and South Asian countries, but it remained a minority view in all of them. People in nations like Egypt and Pakistan disagreed with U.S. policy in the region, particularly support of Israel. But despite suffering through frightening social and economic stagnation, very few actually endorsed the mass killing of American civilians.

Meanwhile, the solidarity among Third World peoples that seemed to be growing back in the '70s turned into a cruel joke. Instead of forming producer cartels, nations frantically competed with each other to export to the West and to attract multinational investment. One after another, even once independent-minded Third World nations like Mozambique, Angola, Vietnam and post-apartheid South Africa saw no choice but to open their economies to lure the global flow of investment. Though in most places outside East Asia the early results were not promising (and in the former Soviet Union, the free marketeers caused a historically unprecedented economic disaster), even the most honest and well-meaning Third World leaders saw no alternative.

How did the left respond to these dizzying changes? In the late '70s, leftists demonstrated against Pinochet and other

August 6, 1976; 191 on August 21; 92 on August 31; 120 on November 11; and 256 on June 20, 1977.

On the day that troops of the new Vietnamese-backed government of Kampuchea burst into the extermination center, they found 14 of the 61 bedsteads occupied by corpses in various states of mutilation. They also found four children—ages 4 to 11—the only survivors to pass through the gates of the former Tuol Sleng high school. Their parents had been killed a week or so earlier, and the children had been shown the corpses with the warning: "This will happen to you unless you support the Pol Pot revolution."

ITT Archives

A Khmer Rouge torture chamber.

Letter from Zimbabwe

JAMES NORTH

April 2, 1980

CHISANGANO, ZIMBABWE—The people gathered together under a grove of trees and waited expectantly. A young ZANU aide stepped forward, raised a clenched fist, and said calmly, "*Pamberi ne ZANU*—Forward with ZANU."

Three thousand people—women with infants strapped to their backs, barefoot old men—raised their fists and answered in a roar, "*Pamberi.*"

A young woman wearing a red kerchief then rose hesitantly and in a haunting voice sang the first line of a revolutionary song. The crowd joined in, and several hundred women began to dance. An old man stood on his head with excitement.

Ernest Kadungure, 42, who left in exile 16 years ago, stepped forward. "Thank you for giving us your sons and daughters to fight for our freedom. Let us pray for those who have died." Some people knelt, others, following the African custom, clapped rhythmically while the women wailed.

Then Kadungure began to speak, starting with the most crucial issue—the land. "They took half our country," he said. "They made large farms there. They left us with bad land, covered with anthills, sandy. We will divide up the big white farms, and everyone can have land. Then those who want to remain in the sand, can."

The crowd clapped and laughed. . . .

Then Joe Jokonya, a young lecturer in history at the university in Salisbury, rose from one of the benches the local committee had managed to borrow. Jokonya escaped from one of Ian Smith's prisons in the mid-'60s and lived in exile until last year. "Our struggle is not between blacks and whites," he began quietly. "Muzorewa is black—yet since he became prime minister he has commanded Rhodesian soldiers to kill our children. . . . Muzorewa says we are Communists. Britain and America have free education for all. That is what we want. Are they Communists in Britain and America? Muzorewa says if we win there will be no more marriage—all wives will be taken away and shared. Comrade President Mugabe told me if that happens, they can take his wife first."

The men chuckled with glee. The women did not find the joke as funny.

The rally closed with more songs, including a new one called "Vote for the Rooster." The British governor, Lord Soames, had banned ZANU's original symbol, the AK-47 assault rifle, as inflammatory, so the party, in a masterstroke, replaced it with a symbol that has great appeal to rural

dictators as well as against apartheid, pointing out that Western governments supported these regimes with loans, aid and investment. The global left did not topple the dictators, but leftists did help prevent even more murder and torture—at a time when Western governments said next to nothing publicly and privately offered no more than a nod and a wink. Apartheid fell mainly because of the resistance inside South Africa itself, but the new democratic government was quick to thank the worldwide movement for the economic and political pressure that helped bring about the miraculous change.

But honest leftists should also remember that 25 years ago some of us were inclined to explain away one-party Third World governments, in places like Cuba, Vietnam, Maoist China and Mozambique. We excused such regimes, sometimes uncomfortably, sometimes with embarrassing vigor, on several grounds: They represented the poor majority and were committed to better health, education and welfare; they were (we hoped) transitional and repressive partly due to vicious, often armed, hostility from the West; and right-wing regimes were worse, far more numerous and supported directly by our own governments, corporations and banks.

There was some truth to these arguments. (Indeed, Western hypocrisy continues to show today in the official attitude toward China, whose one-party state is overlooked now that the country has emerged from Maoist isolation to produce cheap goods for Western consumers and to provide investment opportunities for multinational corporations.) Even so, Western hypocrisy did not justify this attitude. Freedom of speech, freedom of assembly, freedom to publish a newspaper or form a political party are rights and absolute ends in themselves. To suggest otherwise is to fall into the same kind of immoral utilitarianism that imperialists used to justify their master plan—the arrogant assertion that some groups of people (never the speaker) must suffer today (regrettably, but we must be realistic) to reach a prosperous future.

But even cold utilitarian calculations show that individual freedoms are an indispensable part of genuine, broad-based economic and social development. The great South Asian economist Amartya Sen points out that famines do not happen in countries that have a free press. In his own home region, there have been no famines since Indian independence in 1947 because a vigorous press acts as an early warning system, pressuring the government into action. By contrast, more than 20 million Chinese died of hunger between 1958 and 1962 because no one could tell Mao that his Great Leap Forward was a disaster. Press freedom turns out to be not a luxury of rich countries, but a necessity in poor ones.

Today, leftists are a core element of the growing movement against an entirely new enemy: global financial institutions like the International Monetary Fund, World Bank and the World Trade Organization. Right away, the anti-globalization movement pushed its way onto the international agenda, changing the terms of the debate—and forcing the fearful global bodies to start holding their big meetings in out-of-the-way places like the Pacific island of Okinawa, and Doha, Qatar, to escape the creative and enthusiastic demonstrators.

In some sense, the free market fundamentalists have become the No. 1 enemy of the left. The traditional right in the West is no less committed to the welfare of the big banks and corporations, but it tends to be more cautious. One-time liberal allies are becoming more of a problem; the crusading zeal to remake the world was more pronounced in the Clinton administration and remains prominent at leading liberal organs like the *New York Times*. Plan Colombia, the (doomed to fail) billion-dollar effort to stop drug production by intervening in a Latin American civil war, may look like a characteristically right-wing militarized adventure, but we should not forget that Bill Clinton started it, endorsed by the *Washington Post* editorial page.

The free market fundamentalists think they can predict the future. They guarantee that opening markets and totally freeing trade and capital flows inevitably will lead to greater

Zimbabweans. Hundreds of dancing people, flapping their arms and crowing, escorted the ZANU cars out of Chisangano.

Kevin Danaher

Robert Mugabe's 1980 election was celebrated by the left—but 20 years later, he was despised as a dictator.

Twist of Fate

ALISA JOYCE

June 21, 1989

The most astounding consequence of the assault on Beijing is that, according to the people of Beijing and their government, the event never happened. History is being brazenly rewritten in China, with the compliance of the once-rebellious masses, through the formidable terror of the police state.

Some Beijing residents laugh if you try to question them about the events of 10 days ago and wave you away. Others, pressed further, say they know in their hearts what happened, but will never speak the truth with their mouths.

In Fuxingmen—where the troops plowed through the people to reach Tiananmen Square—they say things like, "I heard nothing on Saturday night, I was watching TV." A man with a bullet wound in his shoulder chases you away if you try to question him. Another man, whose 26-year-old wife died, says it was her own fault for breaking martial law.

ITT Archives

According to the people of Beijing and their government, the assault on Tiananmen Square never happened.

The culprits of Saturday night, indeed of the entire democratic movement, were "hooligans," "ruffians" and "counter-revolutionary elements," the government informed the people. After a few days of prudent silence, Chinese hard-line leaders Deng Xiaoping, Li Peng and Qiao Shi stepped forward to take credit for putting down the "counter-revolutionary turmoil" and to congratulate the People's Liberation Army for a job well done. . . .

The Great Wall has symbolized Chinese insularity for centuries. The current leadership, like their imperial predecessors, still lock arms and look only inward for means, methods and justifications for complete political authority. They are the traditionalists, the old guard, the guardians of Chinese harmony. They have never cared much for the concerns of the outside world and, while giving lip service to the platitudes of international accord, their first concern is to pacify their own Middle Kingdom. The barbarians—those living outside of the Wall—will be dealt with later.

prosperity everywhere. They contend that increasing flows of investment and trade will bind the globe ever more closely together and mutually dependent prosperity will promote democracy and deter war. They are not entirely wrong. Economic interconnectedness did make the apartheid regime in South Africa more vulnerable to global pressure. But potential leverage in a global economy does not automatically mean positive change. Their mechanical theory, as vulgar as the most primitive Marxism of the past, has already caused tragedy in Russia and elsewhere.

Yet free market fundamentalists push forward with their own end-justifies-the-means doctrine. They insist that Asian sweatshops will eventually disappear, but then they ridicule the principled Western students who actually carry out (increasingly effective) boycott campaigns. The fundamentalists say economic growth will bring democracy, but then they completely ignore China's leading democratic dissident, Wei Jingsheng, who after 18 years in Chinese prison camps lives right up the street from some of them in Washington, ignored by a mainstream press that once made Alexander Solzhenitsyn a household name.

In the early '90s, a Ugandan army major named Rubaramira Ruranga traveled to the Netherlands for an international convention on AIDS. The major had known he was HIV-positive since 1989 but had only told his family and his superior officer. He was ashamed of his medical condition and had just about given up hope. "I had decided that I was going to wait for death," he said.

In Holland, Major Ruranga met members of ACT-UP, the outspoken, predominantly gay organization of people with AIDS. He was deeply impressed with their courage and positive outlook. "I saw them dancing, singing, laughing—very energetic people," he remembered. "My heart changed. If people talk of being born again, I was born again. I said to myself, 'Ahhh, I am not going to die.' "

The major returned to Uganda a different man. He went public with his health status, started an activist organization, and gives talks in his own country and elsewhere in Africa. Ten years after his encounter with ACT-UP, Uganda has one of the most successful anti-AIDS programs in Africa, as openness by the major and others has reduced shame and increased awareness.

AIDS sadly illustrates the unjust economic order: If the disease—which by 2001 had already killed 22 million people, most of them in Africa—had hit the West with similar impact, the amount of money invested in research and vaccine development would have been many times higher. But Ruranga's story shows a positive side of globalization. You don't have to accept the feverish dreams of the techno-utopians to recognize that the Internet, fax machines, cheap jet travel and other advances have made the growth of global consciousness and solidarity more possible. The international campaign against land mines and the growing anti-sweatshop movement probably could not have happened without the new technology.

But caution is called for. In the 1800s, a campaign in the West against the slave trade and slavery did help contribute to abolition (its members communicated globally quite successfully using handwritten letters and sailing ships). But the capitalists of that epoch found other ways to exploit the developing world, and—just as significant—new ideological justifications for their actions. So, by the turn of the last century, "globalization" continued to grow enormously, measured by trade and investment, but the humanitarian sensibility of the early Victorian period had not expanded with it. Instead, the ruling idea in 1900 had become a more brutal, social Darwinist, scientifically racist rationalization for colonizing Africans and Asians and using the new machine guns against them when they resisted.

Anyone who tries to predict what *In These Times* will cover in the Third World over the next 25 years is asking for trouble. Despite globalization, international press scrutiny is

The Chinese language holds an infinite number of clues about the nation's state of mind. As a student of Chinese long ago, I was confused about their terms for time. The word for "the day before yesterday," for instance, can be literally translated to mean "front day," while the word for "the day after tomorrow" can be translated as "back day."

I asked a Chinese friend, a poet, to explain this seeming reversal of meanings. "That's easy to understand," he answered, laughing. "The Chinese are facing the past and walking backward into the future."

Up From Ground Zero

MATTHEW JARDINE

October 16, 2000

DILI, EAST TIMOR—Do you have any photos of my husband?" Senhora Quintas asks me upon learning that I had met her husband, pro-independence leader Verissimo Quintas, during a 1992 visit to East Timor. Unfortunately, I did not have any photos, nor did she.

On August 28, 1999, less than a day and a half before the start of a U.N.-run referendum, in which East Timor's citizens voted overwhelmingly in favor of independence, armed Indonesian soldiers surrounded her home in the town of Lospalos and opened fire. Then, before burning down the house, members of the local militia rushed inside and hacked Verissimo to death with machetes.

Countless East Timorese have similar stories. Indonesia's 1975 invasion and occupation of the former Portuguese colony was horrific, killing more than 200,000 East Timorese, about one-third of the pre-invasion population. As a parting act following last year's vote for independence, the Indonesian military and allied militias launched a wave of terror, destroying more than 80 percent of the territory's buildings and infrastructure, forcibly deporting about 250,000 people to Indonesia, raping untold numbers of women and killing an estimated 1,500 people—to create what they called "ground zero." . . .

It's easy to become depressed about the future prospects of East Timor. But it's also important to recognize the dynamism and creativity of the country's myriad activist groups and political movements as well as the strong international solidarity movement that supports them. Most importantly, we must remember how far East Timor has come in such a short time. Within the last year, the country has emerged from one of the most oppressive and brutal occupations in recent history. As many East Timorese told me, they may not have a house or a job, but at least they can talk freely and walk down the street without fear.

The importance of this new reality was evident when I visited Ana Lopes at the ruins of her family home in the most devastated neighborhood of Dili. Unlike a year ago, when militia regularly terrorized her family, she did not cry when she spoke to me. She now talks in a voice louder than a faint whisper, and no longer nervously rocks back and forth in her chair during an interview.

When I left, she walked me out of the house onto the street—something she never did during my many visits last year due to the fear of enraging the militia types who stalked the neighborhood. Perhaps most moving was when Ana proudly showed me the corn she is growing in a garden across the street from her house, amidst the ruins of the militia post—a beautiful symbol of the new order growing from the rubble of a very ugly past.

so lopsidedly biased toward the richer part of the planet that mass movements, whether cultural, religious or political, could emerge in India or Brazil, unnoticed at first elsewhere. Developments unimaginable today could suddenly alter our thinking in fundamental ways.

One thing does seem certain. Over the next 25 years, the battle of ideas will continue. World inequality is rising; the threat to the global environment is growing; and new communications technology does make increasing understanding of all this more likely, at least in theory. Yet the growing consolidation of the global mass media may mean more channels, but fewer points of view. International corporations and banks are increasingly adept at "green-washing" and other public relations manipulations. A different danger is compassion fatigue; the global media do intermittently flash pictures of Africans and others in the Third World, but only as victims—nameless, hopeless people who make you just want to turn the page or change the channel.

This is what makes independent media like *In These Times* so indispensable. The mainstream press stays in five-star hotels, interviews business leaders and politicians, and relies on "Western diplomats" for analysis. You could follow the established media for years and almost never stumble across an account of a collective effort in the Third World, whether a grassroots environmental group or a labor union. As a result, sophisticated Americans can name the dishes in a Thai restaurant, but they have never heard of Dr. Prawasi Wasi, a gentle physician who is that country's beloved social conscience. All the latest satellite technology is no substitute for curious, independent reporters who are determined to go out among ordinary people and listen to them.

Free at Last?

JAMES NORTH

September 5, 1999

DURBAN, SOUTH AFRICA—I had just arrived in South Africa, returning after 16 years, and I was motoring north along the steamy coastal road near the Indian Ocean port of Durban, the country's third-largest city. Right away, I saw mud, wood and tin shantytowns clinging to the sides of some of the green hills; these were the homes of poorer black people, the local equivalent of the *favelas* of Rio de Janeiro or the *kampungs* of Jakarta.

A first-time visitor might have reacted with some shock, contrasting the shacks with the big homes in the still largely white neighborhoods like Kloof and Morningside. A newcomer could have recoiled at the tremendous inequality that persists, even as Nelson Mandela's five-year term as president ended in early June and Thabo Mbeki succeeded him after the African National Congress won another election in a landslide. This disappointed reaction would have been understandable. . . .

But I was delighted to see those shacks on hills that were uninhabited when I left in 1983. Such shantytowns around Durban, Johannesburg and other South African cities actually represent tremendous progress since the alliance between the resistance movement inside the country and the solidarity movement around the world freed Mandela and ended the formal apartheid system.

Apartheid's central axiom was that 87 percent of South Africa, including all urban areas, gold mines and the best farmland, "belonged" to white people; blacks were allowed in those areas only on sufferance, as "temporary sojourners." Black people had the legal right to remain permanently only in the notorious Bantustans, desperately poor, overcrowded rural districts where infant mortality surpassed levels in the rest of Africa.

ITT Archives

Apartheid's central axiom was that 87 percent of South Africa, including all urban areas, gold mines and best farmland, "belonged" to white people.

Apartheid created a terrible oscillating migratory labor system. Millions of black men left their families behind in the Bantustans, staying in ugly single-sex hostels in the towns or near the mines for most of the year, returning home only at Christmas. Back in 1981, I befriended a woman in the Transkei Bantustan named Bandi Mpetha whose husband had recently died of overwork; over two decades of marriage, she and her five children had actually seen him for a total of less than three years. Today, people like Mpetha are free to move their families into what used to be "white" South Africa and live in the same shacks with

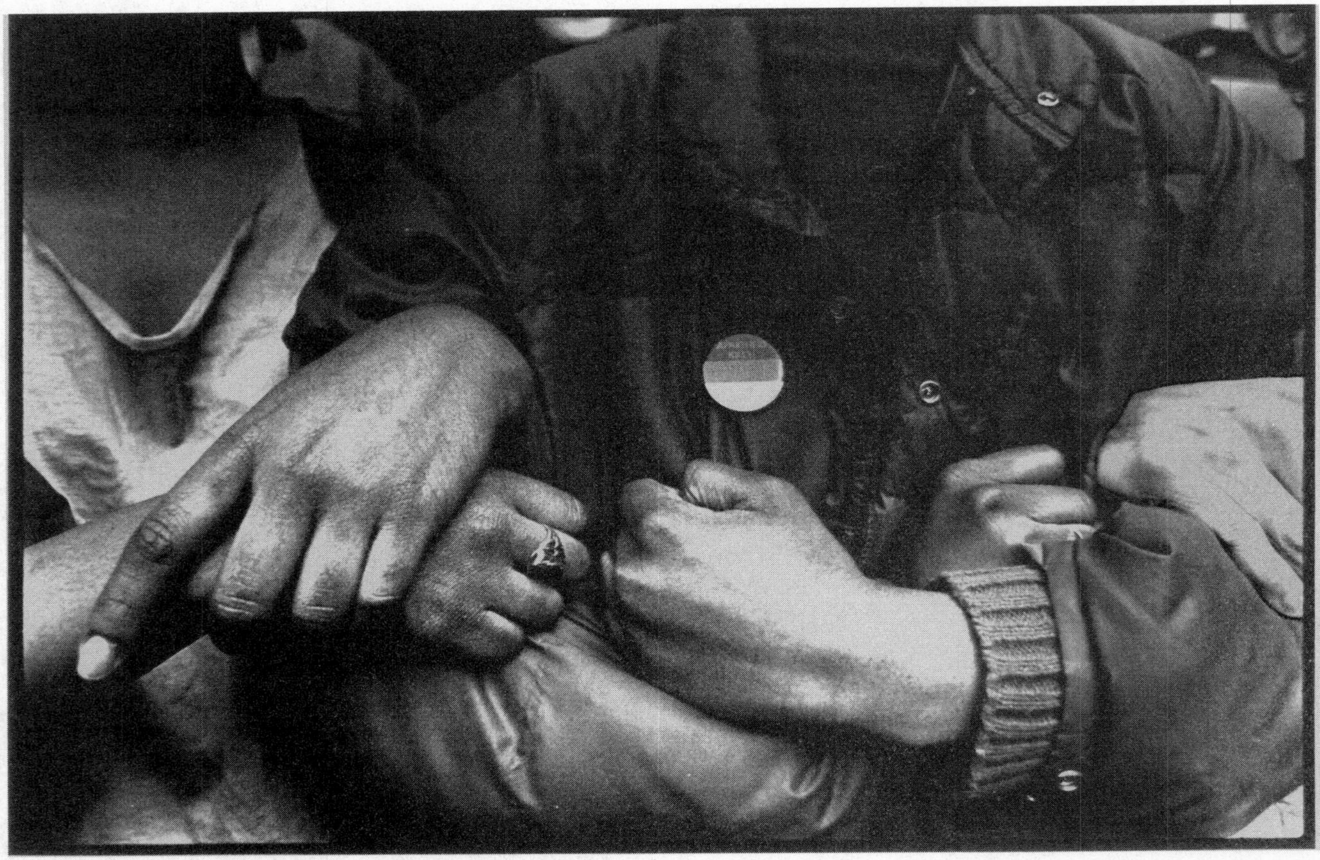

A global movement helped bring an end to South African apartheid.

their husbands. The new government is even starting to furnish the shantytowns with piped water, health clinics and other improvements. . . .

A week or so after my return, I stopped off for lunch in the interior town of Piet Retief. It is a conservative place that evokes in the South African consciousness something like what the words "Lubbock, Texas" do for an American. I was astonished to see black people calmly sitting and eating in the fast food restaurant on Voortrekker Street and to observe black women selling fruits and vegetables along the curb. I knew the segregation of amenities known as petty apartheid had been abolished, but I still felt that somehow out here in the conservative platteland, the old customs, protected by the threat of white violence, might persist. I waited uneasily for a white police constable to pass by and angrily drive the black people away. But nothing happened.

Then, an older black man approached me, bowed slightly, and offered to wash my car. He addressed me as *numzaan*, a Zulu word of respect, which literally means "householder." A first-time visitor would have noticed the man's tattered condition and imploring manner, contrasted it with the prosperous white farmers who strolled confidently up and down the street, and noted that social and cultural inequality persisted along with the economic variety. But I was again delighted at the change for the better. Twenty years ago, when I first came to South Africa, this man would have called me *baas*, Afrikaans for "boss." *Numzaan* is applied to both black and white people; I use it myself. But no white person in the history of South Africa has ever called a black person *baas*.

Revolution from Above

RUSSIA FROM *PERESTROIKA* TO PUTIN

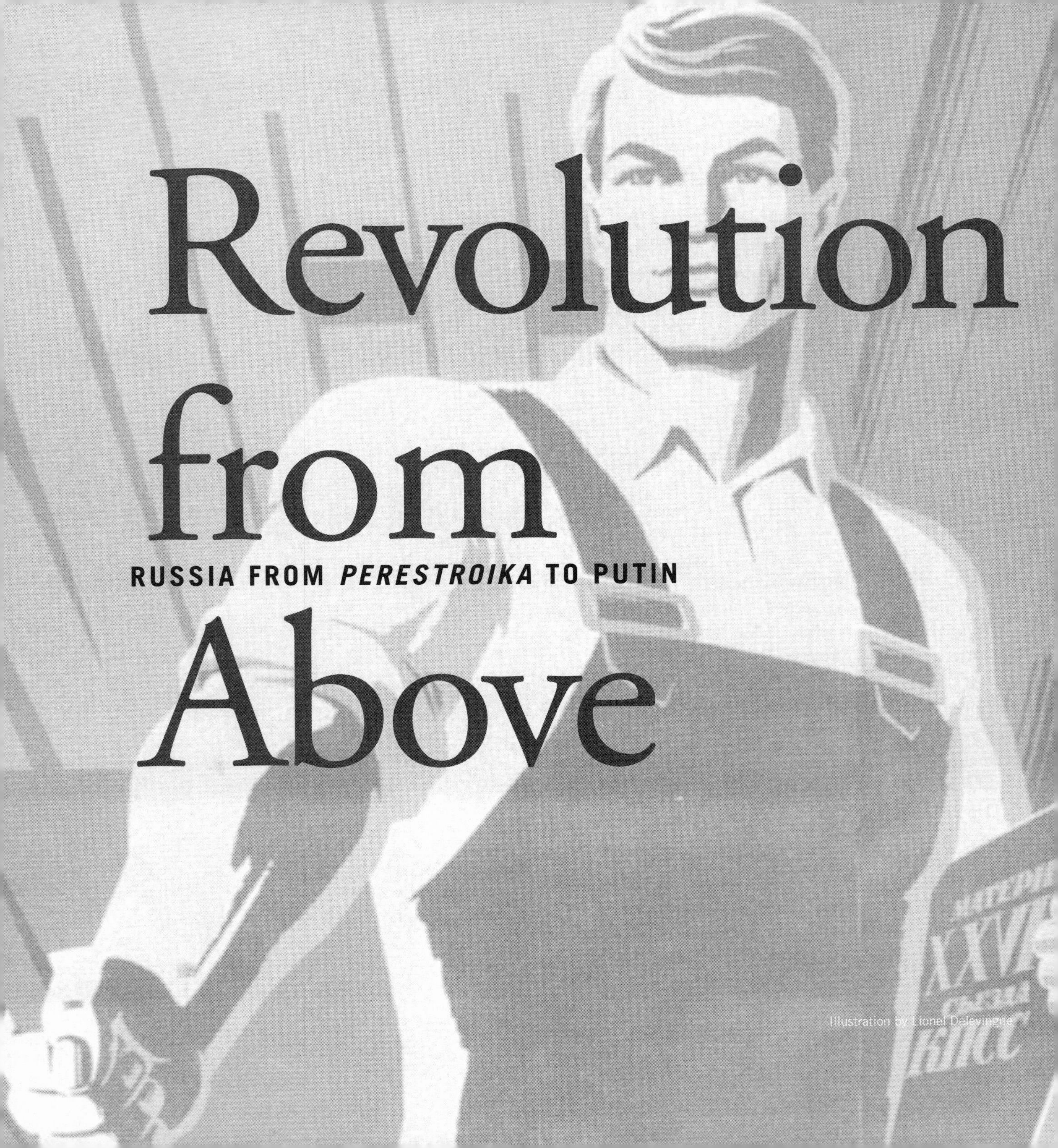

Illustration by Lionel Delevingne

Fifteen

FRED WEIR

ONE OF THE BEST JOKES TO EMERGE FROM THE FORMER USSR WAS AN EXTREMELY ACUTE SUMMARY OF THE COUNTRY'S POLITICAL HISTORY. Faithfully updated by each generation, it revolved around the solution each Soviet leader would suggest to the following problem: A train comes to the end of the tracks, the journey incomplete. What orders to give to the crew?

Vladimir Lenin, according to the joke, would tell his people to "go out and organize the peasants into work brigades, and teach them to build tracks so we can gradually move forward." Joseph Stalin would command his men to round up the peasants, shoot half of them, and lay their bodies down to serve as tracks. Nikita Khrushchev would say, "Go out, tear up the rails from behind the train and put them in front, and we'll carry on that way." Leonid Brezhnev would order his crew to "close all the curtains in the carriage, rock back and forth and make clicking sounds. The people will never know the difference." Finally, Mikhail Gorbachev would say, "We have *glasnost* now. Everybody run outside and shout at the top of your lungs: 'There are no tracks!' "

This running joke has not been continued into the post-Communist era. Soviet political humor has been in sharp decline since Gorbachev came to power, perhaps itself a victim of *glasnost.* It is tempting to imagine a red-nosed Boris Yeltsin sitting amid the train's ruins mumbling something while the crew steals the fixtures and floorboards. No image at all comes readily to mind for Vladimir Putin.

The West's central narrative on post-Soviet Russia, and certainly the stuff of most Moscow-based journalism over the past decade, has been of a country struggling to make a transition from Communism to free markets and democracy with the help of well-meaning Western governments and financial institutions. In most reporting, the stress has been on stock markets rising or crashing, privatization goals met, tough political medicine swallowed. The heroes have been a succession of liberal officials, emerging business tycoons and pro-market intellectuals, who are depicted as heralds of the future.

The old, dying part of society has been covered as well, sometimes even with sympathy. The impoverished majority has been personified by pro-Communist pensioners who subsist on a diet of bread and tea; angry coal miners who blockade railroads; women forced back into housewife status by the closure of cheap Soviet-era day-care centers. But until recently, Western coverage has always exuded the certainty that Russia is going to make it into the charmed circle of Western-style capitalist states. After all, where else can it go?

Few Russians share confidence in that inevitability. Although the Soviet Union is dead and gone, and no one really wants it back, the central perception for most Russians is that they live amid the crumbling urban and industrial wreckage of a vast, failed attempt to modernize their country—and the biggest catastrophes are yet to come. The market economy may be inevitable, but it's not particularly desirable. The usual crowd will benefit. One of the few decent political jokes of the past decade goes this way: "You know, everything our old Soviet leaders told us about communism was false," says one Russian to another. "But everything they told us about capitalism was true."

Americans were (and still are) accustomed to viewing the USSR in monochrome shades, as an economic failure, a brutal police state, an ideological mutant with unspeakable nightmares where a history should be. This view was not strictly false: If ever a system deserved to die, it was Soviet Communism. Yet to understand why Russia keeps collapsing a decade after its Soviet shackles were removed, it is necessary to consider the elements that were functional, even progressive and hopeful, about the USSR. It was an entire universe

Living *Perestroika*

JAMES WEINSTEIN

December 21, 1988

MOSCOW—Since April 1985, when *perestroika* began at Mikhail Gorbachev's initiative, a profusion of Soviet discussion clubs, informal independent press clubs, ecology clubs and social action groups have sprung up like mushrooms after a spring rain.

The first group in this renewal of the movement to democratize the Soviet Union—the Club for Social Initiatives—began a mere two years ago. But now there are hundreds of such groups in Moscow and an estimated 30,000 throughout the country, all of them dedicated to ending the stifling conformity imposed from above.

For now, the existence of these groups, if not always their activity, is tolerated. No one knows for how long, however. As a result, like mushrooms, all are vulnerable and some are ephemeral—springing up, spreading their spores and disintegrating. But resonating with each other under the surface of official society, these associations of citizens have a palpable vitality. As a social movement, they embody the best hope for the realization of the lofty democratic ideals proclaimed by the revolutionaries of 1917 but denied in practice. . . .

Virtually every group we met with expressed ambivalence about their situation. In our meeting with a group called Civic Dignity . . . one member talked about the enormous steps forward under *glasnost*. But she put the situation in perspective by saying, allegorically, that "now executions are only in the Central Square, not on every street corner."

This sense of the possibility of impending doom is based on historical experience. A member of Democratic Union, the most militantly confrontational of the groups we met with, made a point of telling us that every period of liberalism—the New unto itself, autarkic not only in economy, but also in political culture and social dynamics.

The history of post-Soviet Russia actually begins in 1985, when Mikhail Gorbachev was elected general secretary of the Communist Party. He was bent on a course of reform and, at least at first, had the backing of most of the country's power centers, including the Central Committee apparatus, the military and, crucially, the KGB. Gorbachev himself believed deeply in the socialist system and seemed convinced that once the USSR's historical horrors were exposed and renounced, and the population was freed from the daily coercion of party and state, a wave of popular creative energy would bring about the needed transformation of the country's economy.

He had some powerful arguments: In less than a century, Russia had risen from backwardness and collapse in World War I to become one of the world's two superpowers. The social transformation of Soviet times was profound: In 1920, some 80 percent of the population lived as peasants and worked the land; 60 years later, 80 percent lived in towns and cities and held recognizably modern jobs. The range and distribution of occupations was similar to that of a developed Western country, if somewhat behind the curve (the USSR had more workers in industry, fewer in services). Soviets were well educated as a population and heavily professionalized. Indeed, Soviet propagandists were fond of pointing out that the USSR had more doctors, scientists and engineers per capita than any other country. It was also way ahead of the rest of the world in integrating women into the work force. By 1985, more than 90 percent of Soviet women had full-time jobs outside the home and, even more impressive, 55 percent of graduates from higher educational institutions were female.

Another positive factor driving Gorbachev's vision was that the USSR appeared to have a highly developed civil society. This was not, as in the West, an intricate, self-organized community that had grown up over centuries. Rather, the Communist Party established a constellation of social organ-

Economic Policy of the '20s and the liberalization under Nikita Khrushchev—has ended in reaction. The same can be expected now, he said, although the changes now are deeper and will "probably not end as badly."

Such ambivalence accurately reflects the profound contradictions inherent in *perestroika* and *glasnost*—democratic reforms initiated by a party leadership with a monopoly on power that it intends to maintain. Gorbachev, and presumably the party leadership in general, understands that a modern society cannot continue to develop rapidly with an unmotivated work force and the absence of individual initiative.

But at the same time, the Soviet state, which Oleg Rumyantsev of Democratic Perestroika describes as "neo-feudal," does not allow for the possibility of citizens' associations intervening in the formation of social policy. Because decisions are "taken in a strictly hierarchical direction from top to bottom," the party sees no need for the development of an active citizenry—what Rumyantsev calls "civil society." And the result has been a debilitating lack of flexibility and a scarcity of the human resources needed to solve society's problems, he explained. . . .

If the democratic groups want to be free citizens and live in a free country, Rumyantsev insisted, they must learn to act under legal conditions. This requires compromise, but not surrender. "We cooperate with the power," he said, "but the power has to cooperate with us because we support *perestroika*."

This approach, however, irritates officials. According to Rumyantsev, they do not like the idea that "what we do is always half a step or a step ahead of them." To Rumyantsev and his colleagues, *perestroika* means rejection of the official idea that "the 'good' enlightened political leader tells us how to act and we must accept it without any objections."

izations according to its own ideological criteria, ensured that most people in each category would join, and set them into orbit around the party-state sun. Nonetheless, any visit to the Central Trade Union, the *Komsomol* (youth movement) or the Soviet Women's Committee during the '80s would bring one face-to-face with highly intelligent, ideologically capable, energetic and apparently well-motivated leaders who seemed the embodiment of Gorbachev's hopes. The political awareness of average Soviets, wherever one encountered them, seemed much higher than that of their Western counterparts. It was Gorbachev's oft-repeated belief that once freed from party control, all these organizations would automatically "right themselves," becoming bottom-up rather than top-down structures. They would naturally grow into true, self-organizing elements of a modern socialist society.

Most of Russia's key democratic reforms were enacted and reached their peak during the Gorbachev era. It has been commonplace, particularly among the U.S. press corps, to attribute these accomplishments to Boris Yeltsin, on the ideological grounds that no genuine freedoms possibly could have existed in the USSR. Yet it was in Gorbachev's time that the veil of fear lifted, and Russians began to breathe and speak freely. It was his policy of *glasnost* that turned the Soviet media, briefly, into a rich and unfettered garden of social debate. Gorbachev spun off power from the Communist Party to elected legislatures at every level. The parliamentary elections of 1989 and 1990 were far more open, competitive and scrupulously honest than any of the post-Soviet polls that followed. Above all, it was the political style of Gorbachev that enabled the USSR to break up in relative peace.

Yet under Gorbachev the economy and state unraveled, and his grand vision ended in personal disaster and national collapse. When the USSR imploded, it left an entire population stranded in an utterly strange world, amid the useless ruins of their former state, economy and society. Western governments had no idea what to do at the collapse of the USSR other than cheer. In subsequent years, financial aid

The Occidental Tourist

DIANA JOHNSTONE

September 20, 1989

LENINGRAD—The tourist longing to make contact with real people has an identity problem. She is no longer herself, but a "tourist." This means a bearer of hard currency. For the host country, the purpose of the tour is to bring in some of that hard currency, and the only reason for local people to approach tourists is to buy hard currency in order to shop in the *berioshka* stores, where rubles are not accepted. This very fact causes proud citizens to resent tourists and sometimes even to show it.

Still, speaking several languages and a smidgen of Russian it is possible from time to time to engage in snatches of simple conversation. There is a wedding party in our third-class hotel, and we are invited to drink to the happy couple. What do the members of the Leningrad wedding party think of Gorbachev? They shake their heads and say, "No good." Why? ask the Gorbiphile Westerners, disappointed. Shortages of soap, sugar, everything. Speculation and corruption are flourishing. Sure, Gorbachev is smart; he's fine for London or Frankfurt. But "the bad people obeyed Brezhnev. They don't follow Gorbachev." The Gorbiphile Westerners protest defensively that one man can't do everything, that it's up to all the citizens to reform the country. "Czar Peter the Great changed Russia all by himself," comes the answer. . . .

Even a tourist can see things to admire in the Soviet Union. The urban transport systems are cheap and excellent. The famous Moscow metro is not too grandiose—why shouldn't marble and statues be put where millions of people pass every day? The big cities are well equipped with schools, parks, playgrounds and theaters. There are cars on the streets, but not so many as to cause constant traffic jams and poison the air. There are no homeless people living in the street. Medicine is dirt-cheap. . . .

and political backing, particularly from Washington, aided and abetted the Yeltsin regime as it blasted away the elected parliament in 1993, made a mockery of electoral democracy in 1996, nurtured an economic oligarchy and exterminated tens of thousands of Russian citizens in the republic of Chechnya. But Russia's own Soviet-era elite—schooled, ironically, in Communist ideology—are the chief authors of the past decade's catastrophe.

The death of the USSR was earth-shaking news just about everywhere except in Russia, where people greeted the lowering of the hammer-and-sickle flag from the Kremlin on the last day of 1991 with a collective shrug. The moment of true euphoria had actually come and gone with the defeat of a putsch four months earlier, and Yeltsin's emergence as the real power in the country. Confronting the putschists had engaged only a relatively small number of politicized intellectuals in Moscow. But the handwriting was on the wall, and everyone began making their own personal adjustments. Most of the country's vast bureaucratic and security apparatus quickly jumped onto the Yeltsin bandwagon.

That watershed is still regarded with deep ambivalence, even by those Russians who benefited most. Current Kremlin leader Vladimir Putin gives a cryptic account of his own reaction to the coup's failure in his memoirs: He says he took his Communist Party membership card, placed it in a drawer and "made the sign of the cross over it." Whatever that means, it sounds fairly typical. My own mother-in-law, a very independent woman, had stopped carrying her party card months earlier, and only thought about it on the first day of the putsch when she spied a number of her academic colleagues lining up at a long-disused window to urgently pay their party dues. A few days later, they were all making sheepish anti-Communist declarations. Thus, the USSR went with a whimper, not a bang.

But whirlwind changes followed swiftly on the Soviet demise, and for many they altered life in fundamental ways.

There are mineral water dispensing machines all over. The customer rinses the glass provided (which users do not steal) and then for a kopeck (next to nothing) can have a glass of mineral water, or for two kopecks, a glass of mineral water with fruit flavoring. A soft drink, in short, with no bottle, can or plastic cup to throw into the growing heap of trash. This refreshing, environmentally harmless drink costs a fraction of the price of a Pepsi Cola.

What may look to Western green eyes like absence of waste is undoubtedly more widely viewed as a sign of backwardness. In Moscow, we asked Professor V., the Moscow reformist intellectual, what thought was being given to using Western technology without reproducing the harmful aspects of Western society. Reaching the Western level is one thing, we said, but following the Western model is another. The professor acknowledged that the current changes were indeed following the Western model. Eventually, he said, Communists in the Soviet Union would have to face this problem of a different model at the Western level.

Will they have the choice?

ITT Archives

It was in Gorbachev's time that the veil of fear lifted.

ITT Archives

This poster of Leonid Brezhnev reads: "Down with Stagnation."

The Second Russian Revolution

JAMES WEINSTEIN

September 4, 1991

On August 18, in an act of desperation, leaders of the dying and discredited Soviet Communist Party arrested President Mikhail Gorbachev and moved to stop the transformation of their country into a

The new Russian government, headed by neoliberal ideologist Yegor Gaidar, liberated prices for most consumer goods in the depths of the winter of 1992, triggering a wave of hyperinflation. The lifetime savings of millions were wiped out. I recall having 1,000 rubles in a bank account which, in the summer of 1991, would have purchased a complete two-week vacation at Yalta. A year later, the same amount would barely pay for lunch in an inexpensive cafeteria.

The hyper-inflation destroyed any optimism the public may have felt, but it did not bring on the much-predicted social explosion or mass starvation. That was because then—and to the present day—most Russians lived with one foot still in the Soviet economy. The Gaidar government, wisely, did not lift subsidies on heating, transportation, housing, energy or bread. Just about everyone inherited an apartment and a country *dacha*, or at least a rural kitchen garden, from the departing USSR. According to some experts, more than 40 percent of food consumed in Russia is still grown in those kitchen gardens. So the mass of Russians have survived in ways that are a testimony to their resilience, but no thanks to either Soviet state socialism or the new market economy.

For a small number, instant riches were on the menu. Russia is the world's largest country, and its vast wilderness contains a cornucopia of natural wealth. Even a few Soviet-era industries were economically viable, or at least had profitable sections. The Communist *nomenklatura* elite, freed from the strictures of the Soviet system and party oversight, moved en masse to transform their administrative power into private property, or at least into liquid wealth. I had an acquaintance, from a high Soviet official family, who briefly gained control over supplies of snake venom from the Central Asian republic of Turkmenistan. Purchasing the stuff at the old (very low) state prices from Turkmeni collective farms, he sold it on to international pharmaceutical companies at an astounding profit. He quickly became a multimillionaire and left the country.

In factories all over Russia, managers created private companies within their dying old state industries and began siphoning off whatever was of value. Much of this happened spontaneously, but it was aided and abetted by the Gaidar government. There were few sections of the old elite who were not involved, either in the form of direct plundering or its corollary, official corruption. The surest path to riches was to open a "bank." The early post-Soviet years saw thousands of these mushroom across the landscape, usually with grandiose names such as Bank Imperial and ProfitBank. Some banks were established by former Soviet economic ministries or big industrial conglomerates to move their own money, often in nefarious ways. But many were started by Kremlin insiders with few assets other than a government charter authorizing them to start a bank and begin receiving interest-free loans from the Russian Central Bank. The Gaidar regime publicly reasoned that capitalist bankers would naturally start greasing the wheels of commerce and investing in business, creating a new market economy even before the old state economy was dismantled. In fact, all that followed was an orgy of speculation that bankrupted what was left of the official economy.

Somewhere on the cusp of these events, I recall joking to my wife about how wonderful it could have been had I possessed the right connections and managed to secure a bank charter in 1992. With a (very modest) Central Bank interest-free loan of $1 million in rubles, I would have needed to perform just one operation: change it into dollars and hide the sum in my mattress. A year later, as inflation raged and the ruble nose-dived, I might have pulled $50,000 from the mattress, changed it back into rubles, paid off the loan and walked away with the rest. "We'd be rich now," I said. My wife, always swifter than me, remarked: "Yes, but you'd also be dead."

The life expectancy of Russian men has fallen precipitously over the past decade, but no categories plunged faster or further than bankers and *biznesmyen.* The Soviet KGB and security forces broke open in the early '90s, spilling thousands of highly trained killers, explosives experts and surveillance professionals into the job market. Many went to

democracy. Three days later, in a stunning defeat of the party, the coup collapsed and the Soviet people emerged victorious.

The defeat of the coup completed the first stage of a revolution that Gorbachev initiated in 1985 and that swept through all of Eastern Europe, only to return home for its climax. Unprecedented in history both in its scope and in the lack of violent opposition by the old regime, this second Russian Revolution has transformed the Soviet nation just as profoundly as the second American Revolution, initiated by Abraham Lincoln in 1860, transformed the United States. Like Lincoln, Gorbachev took the lead in emancipating the Soviet people. And like the United States when the Civil War ended, the Soviet Union now faces a dangerous and uncertain time of reconstruction. . . .

In the end, Gorbachev made two mistakes. He moved too slowly, thereby losing popular credibility as an advocate of fundamental change. And he remained convinced that a substantial core of party leaders shared his commitment to genuine democratization—in other words, that the party was a viable political vehicle for the realization of his goal.

As it turned out, both Gorbachev's faith in the party and the reformers' fears about the danger from hard-liners proved mistaken. Fortunately, the reforms had taken root not only among the people, but also in important sections of the army—especially on the secondary leadership level—and even in parts of the KGB. And fortunately also, although the leaders of the coup were willing to violate Soviet laws and the constitution, they hesitated at engaging in a bloody conflict that might secure their power but that would leave the country in chaos. . . .

Now, almost magically, the Soviet Union is free of the Communist Party. Not only has the party lost its property and its privileges but it is also thoroughly discredited, even among believers like Gorbachev. This is a situation at once exhilarating in the possibilities it presents and terrifying in the dangers it confronts. The party is gone, but nothing exists to take its place. Gorbachev remains in office, but at this point he has little power to stop the unraveling of the union, much less to lead the nation in a coherent direction. In the Russian republic, Boris Yeltsin reigns supreme at the moment, but his commitment to democracy and the preservation of a federal union may be weaker than his desire for power.

ITT Archives

What did Yeltsin accomplish in a few years that the Communists couldn't do in 70? He made Communism look good.

The Kitchen Counter-Revolution

FRED WEIR

March 22, 1993

MOSCOW—Seventy-five years after the Revolution decreed equality between the sexes, Russian women find themselves being ruthlessly prodded toward a giant leap backward.

Women, who until recently comprised 51 percent of the work force—and 60 percent of all Soviet workers with higher education—are today being urged, brainwashed and soon, very probably, work in the private armies of the new tycoons; others joined burgeoning organized crime gangs. In the first post-Soviet years, they slaughtered each other. But over time they have learned to work together. In today's Russia it is often difficult to discern the practical line between "criminal," "businessman" and "government official."

The post-Soviet period has seen mass impoverishment, authoritarian restoration, the rise of economic oligarchy, financial chaos and savage ethnic war. Some of this may have been inevitable, but a good deal must be laid at the doorstep of the arrogant, anti-social, former-Communist elite that came to power with Yeltsin at its head. Another rare joke from that era put that point eloquently enough: "Question: What has Boris Yeltsin accomplished in a few years that the Communists couldn't manage to do in 70? Answer: He's made Communism look good."

As a leader, Yeltsin was lackadaisical and fundamentally disinterested in the nuts and bolts of governance. That he spent the first half of his presidency glued to a vodka bottle and the second half flat on his back in a hospital bed is not an explanation for this. This political style is a time-tested way for clever mediocrities to govern Russia. Unlike his predecessor, Yeltsin had few ideas of what to do, so he permitted local elites to do pretty much whatever they wanted—provided they paid proper homage to the Kremlin.

On Yeltsin's watch, Russia splintered into dozens of semi-feudal regions where local governors ruled like satraps, decreeing their own economic, social and sometimes even foreign policies. The crown jewels of the former Soviet state economy, including most of the country's natural resources, were handed over to a group of Kremlin cronies, who milked them for quick profits. At one point in the late '90s, it was said that just seven "oligarchs" controlled 50 percent of Russia's GDP. During these years, official corruption ran amok, reaching deep into the Kremlin—even into the presidential family—to such an extent that it nearly sank the Yeltsin regime in the end.

On the positive side, the Yeltsin years will be remembered as a time of unprecedented personal freedom for the average Russian. These freedoms were not rights in the Western sense, based on the accountability of the state to the people. But those who could afford it built homes, traveled abroad and even started small businesses. No one paid taxes, it was easy to evade military service, and just about any problem could be fixed with a bribe to the right official. Although the Russian media fell under the sway of its new owners and became organs of commercial warfare and misinformation, the state made few claims on journalists during these years. With the exception of the 1996 presidential election, when all the stops were pulled to put Yeltsin back in office, political criticism flourished. Some of Yeltsin's biographers insist this is proof that despite all his mistakes the old man ruled by his core "democratic instincts." But there is a simpler explanation: He just didn't care.

On the other hand, Yeltsin reacted ferociously against any threat to his own position. As a result of power struggles in the early '90s, he moved to curtail Gorbachev's democratization and recentralize power in the Kremlin. In 1993, he shut down Russia's oppositionist parliament, and then stormed it with tanks and troops when lawmakers resisted. The Western press presented this showdown as a rebellion by a "Communist-dominated, Soviet-era parliament" against a beleaguered "reformist" president. In fact, the Russian parliament—in contrast to its USSR counterpart—was completely composed of deputies who were elected in multi-candidate constituency races. It was the same parliament that had elected Boris Yeltsin as its first chairman in 1990, and then passed the necessary constitutional amendments to enable him to run for Russian president the next year.

The parliament and president subsequently fell out over economic policy and the social costs of market reform. But the main issue was power: A parliamentary constitutional

legislated back to their premodern status as homemakers and mothers.

The rationale is familiar. In a declining labor market, available jobs are needed by men. The state can no longer afford the massive outlays it once invested in a universal network of day-care centers, generous maternity leaves, child nutrition programs and other measures designed to support a population of working mothers. In any other country, cabinet ministers might wring their hands, decry the circumstances and propose palliatives. But this is Russia.

Asked recently about the alarming growth of joblessness among women, Russian Labor Minister Gennady Melikyan achieved the rare feat of shocking a room full of hard-boiled Western journalists into stunned silence. "Why should we employ women when men are unemployed?" he demanded. "It's better that men work and women take care of children and do the housework. I don't want women to be offended, but I seriously don't think women should work while men are doing nothing. Russia is the only country that has so many working women." . . .

The Yeltsin government's message to women is stark and brutal: get back to the kitchen—and quick. "There is no event in modern history to compare with what is happening, except perhaps how North American women were forced to return to the home after running industry during World War II," says feminist scholar and author Elvira Novikova. "But that occurred in the context of an expanding economy, when it was at least conceivable that one male breadwinner could adequately support a family.

"Our economy is collapsing," she continues. "Poverty has engulfed the majority of our people, and it's impossible for most families to live even on two salaries. In this context, women are being commanded to sacrifice themselves, to give up all their rights, hopes and claims and willingly accept permanent serfdom as their lot."

The Kremlin War Machine

FRED WEIR

December 12, 1999

NARZAN, RUSSIA—If your only tool is a hammer, every problem looks like a nail. Russian President Boris Yeltsin has once again rolled out the one instrument in the unraveling Russian federation that still unquestioningly and efficiently obeys his edicts: the army.

With its professional officer corps and Soviet-era munitions stockpiles fit for World War III, Russia's military has been unleashed against the rebel republic of Chechnya to crack the Kremlin's two toughest problems with one blow. By crushing Chechnya's eight-year-old independence drive, it is hoping to end to Russia's post-Soviet orgy of regionalism and restore federal power and prestige. On the wings of that victory, the war's prime author and Yeltsin's heir apparent, Prime Minister Vladimir Putin, will—so the plan goes—be vaulted into the Kremlin in next year's presidential elections.

The army, bitter and angry after a decade of neglect and humiliation, seems almost eager to comply. Down along Chechnya's rugged, forested border with neighboring Ingushetia, where the high, snow-capped Caucasus Mountains seem to hang on the horizon, a huge war machine has been mobilized. Artillery batteries dug into hillsides pound the Chechen border towns of Bamut, Ochkoi Martan, and Sernovodsk around the clock. Helicopter gunships and fighter jets sweep in over the relative safety of Ingush territory to slam nearby rebel positions with rockets and bombs.

The roads are jammed with armored personnel carriers, tanks and truck convoys headed for the front. The young Russian recruits manning this war machine look miserable and scared. Their uniforms are ill-fitting and filthy, their high, cavalry-style boots are completely unsuited to the onrushing mountain winter, and they are often seen in the roads begging food

commission had recommended a draft post-Soviet charter that would make the legislature supreme, similar to the British system. Yeltsin broke with the parliament over that in March 1993, and published his own draft, defining a "presidential" state on the model of France. Yeltsin argued that parliaments were too fractious, that Russia needed a single strong hand. His opponents said that giving Russia one powerful leader was like handing a recovering alcoholic a stiff shot of vodka. In any case, the matter was settled by a two-day pitched battle that raged through downtown Moscow in early October, in which hundreds died. By the end of the year, Yeltsin's constitution, concentrating the lion's share of authority in the Kremlin and reducing parliament to little more than an ornament, was in force.

Few things better illustrate Yeltsin's style of running the Kremlin than his manner of leaving it. Nearing the end of his term, seriously ill, assailed by charges of corruption and facing political revolt from a big section of the regional elite, Yeltsin agreed to step down six months early in exchange for a rich retirement package and full immunity from prosecution for himself and his family. The Kremlin team selected Vladimir Putin, a former KGB agent, as its standard-bearer, and Yeltsin dutifully appointed him prime minister in August 1999. Putin utilized the public hysteria generated by a wave of still-unexplained terrorist bombings in Russian cities to launch a full-scale military invasion of the secessionist republic of Chechnya. In this atmosphere, a Kremlin-created party swept to victory in December parliamentary elections. On New Year's Eve, Yeltsin resigned, and Putin became acting president.

Unlike Yeltsin, Putin has clear ideas about how to use power, which he summarizes as "statism." This is not a new concept in Russia. Putin proposes to restore strong vertical authority to bring about economic modernization. Since coming to power, he has appointed former KGB colleagues to positions throughout the state apparatus. Though he has mobilized popular nostalgia for Soviet socialism—by reviving the Stalin-era national anthem, for example—the project at hand is not to restore Communism, but to build state-guided capitalism, perhaps on the model of Pinochet's Chile.

The Kremlin has already forced most of the Russian media to come to heel, launched a wave of treason trials against environmentalists, academics and others accused of interacting too freely with foreigners, and may be preparing to make sweeping constitutional changes to further consolidate central authority. The relative personal freedom that Russians have enjoyed since Gorbachev appears to be coming to an end, while the promised mass benefits of "market reform" are still nowhere to be seen.

Putin's election in March 2000—more a coronation, really—did produce at least one decent joke. In a variation on the familiar Aesop fable, a crow is sitting on a tree limb with a piece of cheese in its mouth. A fox, pacing below, looks up sharply and says, "Crow, are you planning to vote for Putin?" The crow remains silent. Adopting a more menacing tone, the fox asks again, "Are you going to vote for Putin or not?" The crow keeps his beak shut. "For the last time, will you vote for Putin?" demands the fox. The crow says, "Yes." The cheese falls to the ground, and the fox snaps it up. Looking down mournfully, the crow says to itself, "And would it have made any difference if I'd said no?"

and cigarettes. But the officers seem calm and confident, even cocky.

On October 27, a band of Chechen rebel fighters crossed the border and ambushed a Russian patrol in broad daylight near Verkhni Alkum, a hill post in southeastern Ingushetia. According to the Moscow media, dozens of Russian soldiers were killed. A Russian major, standing on the camp's perimeter a few days later, admitted the attack occurred but shrugged away questions about the price of war. "We're fighting here so that these boys won't have to fight one day in their own hometowns," he said, gesturing toward a nearby group of conscripts. "If we don't take strong measures now, all this instability will spread." He had kind words for Putin: "He knows what he's doing. It's time someone in this country faced problems head on."

Then he offered an analogy that speaks volumes about the mindset of the Russian military. After World War II, the Soviets fought a little-known war against CIA-backed, anti-Soviet insurgents in the Carpathian Mountains of Western Ukraine. "Those Ukrainians were the same kind of bandits, fighting us in similar terrain," the major said. "It took 10 years, but we ground them down and eventually wiped them out. We'll do the same here."

The irony of that comparison apparently escaped him. Ukraine today is an independent country, and those long-buried guerrillas are being rehabilitated and transformed into national folk heroes. The USSR may have won the war, but it failed in the long run to create a society to which any of its diverse peoples cared to belong. Post-Soviet Russia now appears irrevocably headed down the same path.

Heidi Hollinger

Instant riches were on the menu for just a small number of Russians.

What's the Big Idea?

FRED WEIR

November 2, 1997

MOSCOW—It's official: Russia is a country in quest of a fresh idea to guide it into the post-Soviet epoch and replace Communism, its former big idea, now deceased. Suitable suggestions should be sent to: National Idea Search Commission, c/o Mr. Georgy Satarov, the Kremlin, Moscow, Russia.

This is not a joke. The commission, which comprises a gaggle of Russian intellectuals, was formed by decree of President Boris Yeltsin last year, shortly after he narrowly defeated a tough Communist electoral challenge for his job. Apparently dismayed that 42 percent of Russians would vote pro-Communist half a decade after the death of the USSR, Yeltsin gave the committee of historians, philosophers, journalists and linguists one year to come up with a "New Russian Idea." The winning entry, Yeltsin said, would be a concept that is "above politics" but nevertheless capable of "consolidating society" and overcoming the contradictions that still confuse and divide Russians in the wake of the Soviet collapse.

In August, the Kremlin commission released its long-awaited preliminary report. The verdict: There are many ideas, but so far no "Idea." "World and historical experience has shown us that it is not just the national idea that is important, but the process of finding it, too," Satarov, a close adviser to Yeltsin, told journalists.

The committee's work has attracted ridicule from some quarters, but Yeltsin's flacks—and a surprising number of other Russians—take it with dead seriousness. "Russian society craves the elaboration of a central purpose, an idea that animates and directs us in this new epoch," says Nugzar Betaneli, director of the independent Institute for the Sociology of Parliamentarism. "Without a clear sense of identity, Russians always feel lost and despondent."

Russia's new political and economic elite are most in need of such an idea, given that their rapid rise to fabulous wealth and power has not been underpinned by any national tradition or much in the way of legal niceties. "Basically this is a problem of legitimacy, and how to manufacture it," says Vladimir Petukhov, an analyst at the Institute of Social and National Policy. "Having an official ideology is a great weapon for bashing enemies and settling arguments in your favor. Our present leaders feel they need this."

The commission's report fell within days of the sixth anniversary of the abortive August 1991 hard-line coup, in which Communist Party rule was destroyed and Yeltsin won effective control over Russia's government. As if to underscore the precariousness of that achievement, a recent public opinion survey found that if the same putsch occurred today, more Russians would support the coup plotters than Yeltsin. "Power may seem mighty, but it is very weakly grounded in Russia," Petukhov says. "The government does not control things, and when you come right down to it, cannot even explain to Russians why it is in power."

One rumor that keeps resurfacing in Moscow is that Satarov's commission was created to build a rationale for bringing back the czar. Some form of constitutional monarchy, with a corps of rich aristocrats to support it, is said to be in the wind. "This is not as crazy as it sounds," says Yevgeny Pashentsev, a political science instructor at the Moscow Mechanical Institute. "Russia is already an oligarchy, with a single all-powerful central leader. In other words, the social structure already resembles the czarist one, but lacks any semblance of stability or tradition."

But can any idea, even a good one, arrest the economic collapse and social deterioration that have beset Russians since the demise of the USSR? "The bottom line here is that 5 percent of Russians enjoy immense wealth while 55 percent live in dire poverty," Petukhov says. "If we want to consolidate society and bridge our social contradictions, we should start by addressing them with policies, not abstract ideas."

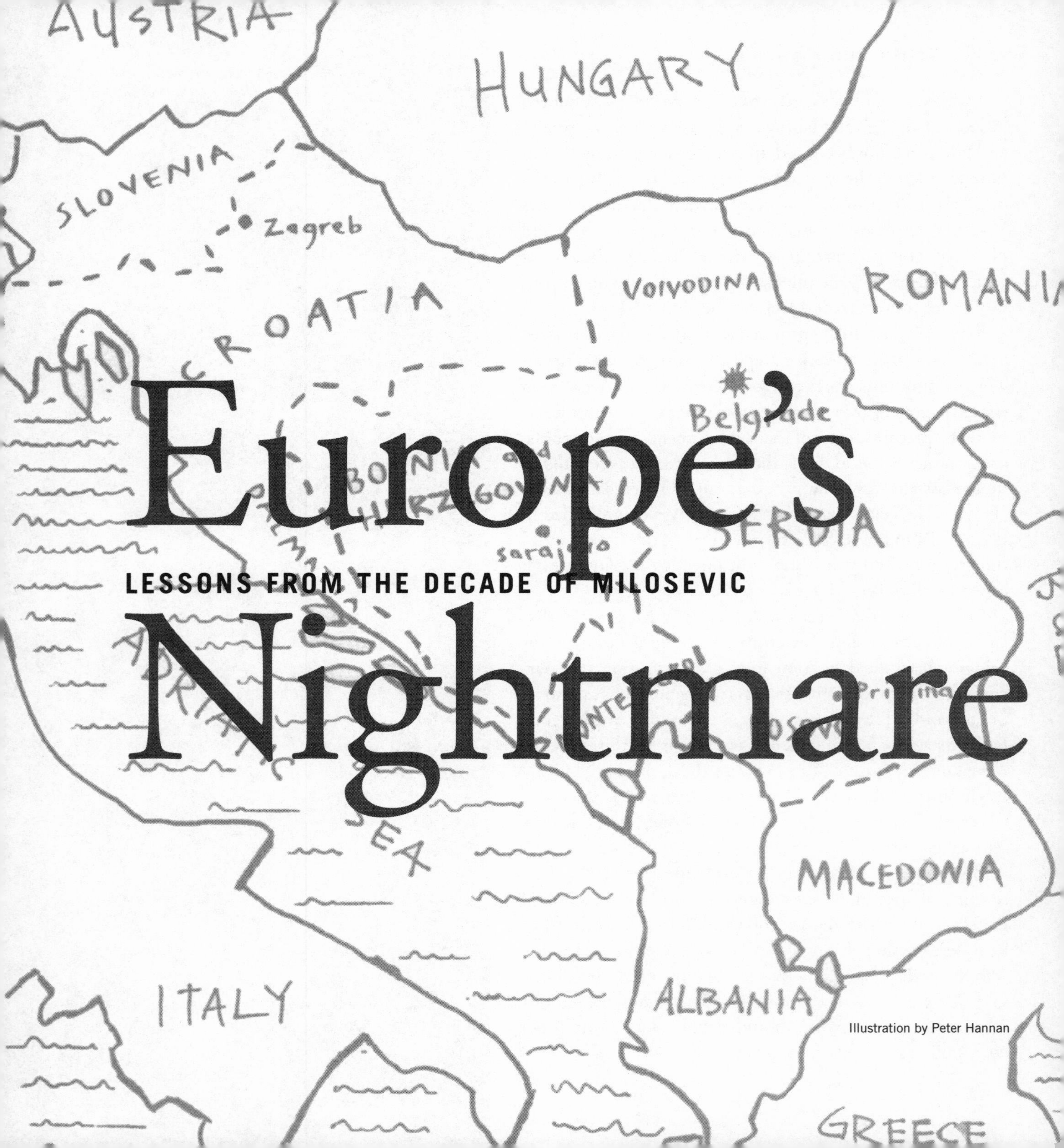

Europe's Nightmare

LESSONS FROM THE DECADE OF MILOSEVIC

Illustration by Peter Hannan

Sixteen

PAUL HOCKENOS

THE '90S WAS THE DECADE OF SLOBODAN MILOSEVIC. THE SERB LEADER WAS THE PRIME MOVER IN UNLEASHING THE FORCES THAT OVER THE COURSE OF four wars took 300,000 lives, displaced millions and destabilized all of Southeastern Europe. Yet to blame Milosevic personally, or to demonize him as single-handedly responsible for Europe's bloodiest conflicts since World War II, misses the point. The nightmare that befell Yugoslavia, the wars that must rank among the most absurd of the 20th century, could never have transpired had not all the major actors involved—rival politicians, ordinary citizens, Western diplomats—agreed to play by Milosevic's rules.

Milosevic alone never could have mobilized the kind of fervent nationalism he did without indispensable allies like Croatian President Franjo Tudjman and both leaders' gangster proxies in Bosnia, Herzegovina, the Dalmatian hinterland and Kosovo. But other players bear their share of blame as well. Bosnian leader Alija Izetbegovic's inconsistent political vision and slow-motion reflexes cost his country dearly. The Slovenian leadership's selfish dash to save its own skin only complicated the possibility of heading off Yugoslavia's pending catastrophe through some kind of negotiated compromise. The stubborn refusal of the Kosovar Albanian and Montenegrin leaders (at different points) to throw in their lot with the Serbian opposition simply prolonged Milosevic's political demise, and after his fall left Yugoslavia in an impossible legal conundrum. The list of accomplices goes on and on, and surely includes the United Nations, the European Union and the United States.

But perhaps most disheartening was the reaction of ordinary people. When I visited Belgrade and Zagreb in 1990, my friends there smirked a little at the democratic revolutions in Central Europe. The nerdy East Germans and Czechs in their polyester jeans surely had some catching up to do before they'd boast a punk rock scene like Belgrade's or summer vacations spent sipping Heinekens on the Adriatic coast. Northern Yugoslavia then had an economy that was a decade ahead of Poland's. The southern republics boasted periods of industrial growth and modernization during which living standards soared. Despite its obvious democratic deficits, by the late '80s, Yugoslavia possessed precedents for a functional civil society.

Yet the majority of people in multi-ethnic Yugoslavia would fall in line like zombies to surreal propaganda and hate speech, as if the previous 20 or 30 years of their lives had never happened. The radical convictions of peripheral slivers of the population were transformed into mainstream opinion and paraded as the nation's "natural" *staatsraison*, finally liberated after decades, if not centuries, of steely repression. Exceptions like the people of Tuzla in northeastern Bosnia were few. That places such as Tuzla and Sarajevo could maintain multi-ethnic communities during years under siege exposes the myth of the Balkan wars' historical inevitability—and speaks poorly of the others who succumbed so meekly to the jingoism.

Yet for all the ignominious *dramatis personae* involved, it was Milosevic's hollow, cynically manipulated nationalism and the repressive criminal regime he presided over that most accurately embodied the spirit that permeated the Balkan body politic for 10 long years. This nationalism resurrected old prejudices and historical fears with discourses of suffering and revenge, genocidal arch-enemies, and historically sanctioned greater states. The ensuing tensions upended the delicate ethnic relations of regions where different peoples had managed to co-exist for decades.

The personal identification with nation—and nation with state—became accepted as God-given truths, implicitly undermining the basic tenets of democratic pluralism. If you weren't part of the *volksgemeinschaft*, you were implicitly a second-class citizen or, worse, an enemy of the state. This essentially racist ethic of national exclusivity naturally concludes that people of different ethnic (or religious) backgrounds are

The Night of Jubilation When East Met West

GORDON LEWIS

November 22, 1989

The crowd in the restricted area had now grown into the thousands. People began to chant, "We want in." Everyone joined in. The border guards appeared nervous at this point; apparently they had not received any orders. The crowd sensed this and pushed forward toward the first of the red-and-white-striped barriers blocking the way, then we all climbed over.

My wife and I were both nervous, but there was no way we or anyone at the front could stop the surge. The next barrier came and went, the border guards retreating, until we reached a steel-barred fence on the eastern side.

Ahead of us, under the dim yellow lights of East Berlin, a line of cars extended as far as the eye could see, and pedestrians stood in line by the thousands. Everyone began chanting, "We want in! We want in!" Behind us the crowd continued to push.

And then the impossible happened. The East German border guards opened the gates. With a roar we ran into East Berlin. The East Germans cheered and laughed, not believing their eyes. A film of us storming the gate made the world news, with reporters claiming the pictures were of East Germans going to the West. But it was the other way around. The citizens of the GDR were orderly and extremely patient. As one man, Holger, a student from Zwittau, a town on the Polish border, told me later, "That was one line we were happy to stand in." . . .

In the East—without a passport, without a visa, without exchanging an obligatory 25 marks. It was remarkable. We moved toward the city center. The East Germans heading for the border weren't sure if this armada was an East German protest or what. We ran to the car windows, overflowing with ebullience. "They opened the border. No controls. It's free."

incapable of living together. "Puppies and kittens just don't get along," Bosnian Serb leader Radovan Karadzic liked to say.

Of course, Serbs, Croats and Bosnian Muslims are ethnically identical: They're all Slavs. Only religious identification separates them from one another, and most don't even go to church or the mosque. But never mind the obvious; reason doesn't help with this kind of brainwashing. Once the groundwork had been laid, including the emptying of jails to build militias, the massacres and rapes and concentration camps followed as if from a script. The logic of ethnic nationalism carried out to its radical conclusion ended in war and the fascist project of ethnic cleansing.

The Balkan leaders took great pains to promote the darkest caricatures of the region, a calculated strategy to legitimize their enterprises both in the eyes of their own people, who would have to act in kind, and abroad. The myths of age-old antagonisms and intractable blood feuds weren't propagated first by Western historians or bad foreign correspondents—but by the people of the Balkans themselves. The region's politicians were the most articulate salesmen of the pejorative stereotypes of "the Balkan," which Maria Todorova in *Imagining the Balkans* argues has become "a synonym for a reversion to the tribal, the backward, the primitive, the barbarian." Indeed, the image of the gangster-cum-freedom-fighter was elevated to the status of folk hero, while wars between nations were deemed natural and inevitable, just as was the ultimate victory of the superior *volk*. The irrationality that coursed through Balkan political rhetoric gave credence to a popular discourse of howling conspiracy theories and paranoid suspicions, which may take decades to exorcise.

These were the premises that everyone, including the West, would respect in one form or another across 10 years of conflict. The refigured maps of ex-Yugoslavia, the population exchanges, the international peacekeeping missions and the simmering conflicts of today all bear the imprint of Milosevic's logic. Neither the European Union, Russia, the United Nations

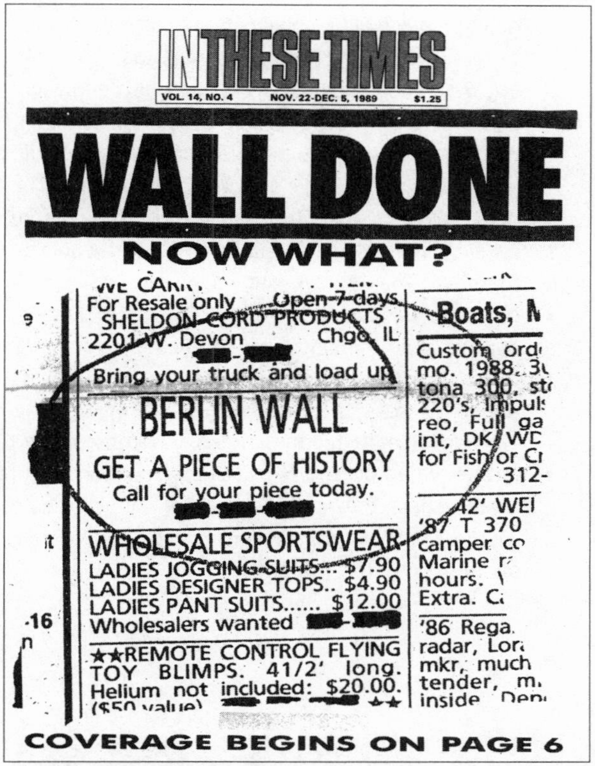

IN THESE TIMES

VOL. 14, NO. 4 NOV. 22-DEC. 5, 1989 $1.25

WALL DONE

NOW WHAT?

For Resale only Open 7 days
SHELDON CORD PRODUCTS
2201 W. Devon Chgo, IL
[redacted]
Bring your truck and load up

BERLIN WALL
GET A PIECE OF HISTORY
Call for your piece today.
[redacted]

WHOLESALE SPORTSWEAR
LADIES JOGGING SUITS... $7.90
LADIES DESIGNER TOPS.. $4.90
LADIES PANT SUITS...... $12.00
Wholesalers wanted [redacted]

★★REMOTE CONTROL FLYING TOY BLIMPS. 41/2' long. Helium not included: $20.00. ($50 value) [redacted] ★★

Boats,

COVERAGE BEGINS ON PAGE 6

ITT Archives

"We are about to enter the Twilight Zone."

The traditionally reserved Berliners were as fiery as Brazilians during Carnival. Every few yards we stopped and talked, shaking hands and even getting the occasional high-five. The cars on the streets honked their horns and flashed their lights as we made our way down Friedrichstrasse and turned back toward the wall on Unter den Linden, East Berlin's main street, at the end of which stood, bathed in light, the Brandenburg Gate.

At the end of Unter den Linden barriers blocked the path to the gate that stands in the middle of the restricted area. People began climbing over, and no border guards intervened. In front of the gate, however, a line of 50 soldiers stood before us, armed with machine guns. For a moment it was a standoff, but then somebody simply walked between them and they didn't respond. Everybody followed suit, running to the gate. On the wall to the West we could see hundreds of people screaming and yelling. The border police made a futile attempt to stop us from passing under the gate to link up with the people on the wall. They sprayed at us with hoses, which elicited more laughter than fear. The crowd charged, and the guards stood aside. For the first time in 28 years, somebody other than a soldier stood among the heavy columns of the gate.

In those early-morning hours, governments and authority had ceased to exist. It was a moment of timelessness between two eras. As my wife said when we ran toward the Brandenburg Gate, "We are about to enter the Twilight Zone."

ITT Archives

Tito salutes the troops in 1975.

nor the United States had coherent policies to address Yugoslavia's collapse. The muddled courses they took were marked by a lack of political will, ineptitude, cynicism and moral equivocation—all of which played straight into the hands of Milosevic and the rest of the Balkan autocrats.

Ironically, Milosevic was one of the few actors involved who didn't actually believe a fraction of his own bravado. In contrast to a die-hard nationalist like Tudjman or so-called pragmatists like Henry Kissinger, the old-Communist Milosevic never took seriously the crusty nationalist discourse of kings and lost kingdoms, medieval battles and blood vengeance. He ruthlessly abandoned his minions, amputated his state and sold out his people whenever it suited him. Milosevic's one priority above all others was to maintain his grip on power through the creation of a state, regardless of its size, that would perpetuate his rule until the next crisis. He succeeded for 14 years, as long as everyone played his game. It ended when the Croatians at long last rejected their ultra-nationalists, when the West finally drew the line in Kosovo, and when thousands of bell-bottomed Serbian teen-agers just said no to everything Milosevic stood for. Once exposed, a discredited Milosevic slunk from the stage like the king without his clothes.

Milosevic may now be gone, but international perseverance and vision are essential to keep the region from sliding backward. The hodgepodge of peacekeeping forces, observer groups and other assorted missions scattered across the former Yugoslavia today does not instill much confidence or respect. This dog's breakfast of mandates and missions has sprung up ad hoc mostly in reaction to the conflicts, or *ex post facto* to reverse their consequences. They certainly were not preceded by an informed debate over the universality of human rights, criteria for humanitarian intervention, or the *raison d'être* of post-Cold War peacekeeping missions. However, they have sparked such a discussion, albeit belatedly.

The question of intervention in the Balkan wars bitterly split the left in the United States and Europe. Leftist opponents of intervention point to the hypocritical legacy of Western military intervention in past decades, conjuring up images from Vietnam to Central America to the Persian Gulf. As thoroughly critical and intensely skeptical as the left must be toward interventionist policies, which are largely driven by blinkered national interests, a contemporary analysis should also reach beyond classic '70s imperialism theory and blunt reflexes that tend to brand all forms of Western international engagement as *a priori* sinister. Too much of the Western left remains mired in the logic of the Cold War. It reflexively rejects intervention when the *New York Times* or Bill Clinton supports it. The left has grown so accustomed to saying "no" that it appears incapable of demanding positive action when it could save lives and open space for democratic alternatives.

Today there is an ever broader consensus around the universality of human rights, which can be employed to deter repressive regimes and promote democratic forces. Even though in practice these principles are applied selectively, intervention in the name of human rights—political, diplomatic, economic and even military engagement—is not *ipso facto* a ruse to expand markets and establish spheres of influence. The issues for the United States in the Balkans were not primarily economic or strategic—but moral. There are progressive causes and movements that the left must identify and back in different ways, not least by promoting the constructive engagement of their own governments when possible.

Unlike in the United States, the European debate starts from the assumption that supranational bodies (for example, the United Nations, the Organization for Security and Cooperation in Europe [OSCE] and so on), conflict-prevention measures and peacekeeping missions are necessary for the kinds of conflicts likely to be faced in the next decade. In Europe, the question is more how to make these organizations work effectively than whether they serve any purpose at all. Europe sees human

Coming Apart at the Seams

DIANA JOHNSTONE

October 3, 1984

"There is no national power base in Yugoslavia today," says Praxis philosopher Svetozar Stojanovic. "The power bases today are in the six republics and the two autonomous regions."

The result is that there are no coherent policies or economic decisions on a national level. Instead, incoherent compromises are based on horse trading between local powers. . . . For years the Praxis philosophers have insisted that for the Yugoslavian system to work, self-management must be extended upward from the workplace to where real economic decisions are made. Tito and the party leadership balked at this extension of democracy that would threaten the party's leading role.

Instead, in the '70s, after purging Croatian nationalists, Tito proceeded to an extreme decentralization that saved the Communist Party role by dispersing it and attaching it to local economic interests. This was an ironic reversal for Tito, who had unified Yugoslavia through the Partisan resistance to the Nazis and later the defiance of Stalin. Four years after Tito's death, the danger menacing Yugoslavia is a sort of creeping re-Balkanization.

Local ethnic interests are reasserting themselves, but that is not all that is meant by "Balkanization." The danger is that these rival local interests may become involved in the rivalries of outside powers. That is how the Balkans in the past were a powder keg of world war.

Western multinationals have penetrated Yugoslavia and today may be better coordinated in the country than anything else. As in other indebted countries, the International Monetary Fund (IMF) has moved in and started giving orders. Today the only visible coherent economic policy is the severe austerity program being pushed by the IMF. Taking orders from the IMF is offensive to Yugoslavs' strong sense of national independence and self-respect. Moreover, the country already has one of the highest unemployment rates in Europe, and following IMF dictates could mean social disaster.

ITT Archives

Milosevic succeeded as long as everyone played his game.

The Case for Intervention in the Balkans

PAUL HOCKENOS

October 28, 1992

A full-scale, international military intervention in the former Yugoslavia, I am convinced, is the only alternative that remains to halt the barbarism enveloping the entire Balkans. A quick, decisive invasion of Bosnia-Herzegovina—on the scale of Operation Desert Storm—is an option the left should rally around as forcefully as any issue since opposition to the Vietnam War.

The six-month-old war has already claimed more than 50,000 lives and turned 2.5 million Bosnians into refugees. Each new report about the savagery loose in the former republic seems more inconceivable than the last. No longer can foreign observers feign ignorance about the war's carnage and the bestial crimes of its combatants, about the

rights and all that goes with them—respect for the rule of law, free media and minority guarantees—not only as a moral imperative, but as the key to regional stability and economic prosperity. The instruments of non-military engagement available are wide-ranging. But as a recourse of last resort, military forms of coercion must be considered. The United Nations or the planned 60,000-man E.U. rapid reaction force are the proper instruments for the military component to conflict resolution strategies, not NATO. But, as in the case of Kosovo, the United States and NATO will call the shots unless these security instruments are adequately funded and trained by the member countries. (Russia also must be included as an equal partner in European security structures, even if the self-serving role it played in the recent Balkan conflicts benefited no one.)

Still, the criteria for "humanitarian engagements," their goals and permissible costs remain largely undefined. What quantity (or quality) of human rights violations justifies—or compels—military intervention? Where do humanitarian priorities overlap, or, as the case may be, give way to economic and security interests? How can Western governments employ moral arguments to justify intervention in Kosovo, and then not in Chechnya or Rwanda? And what lessons have been learned from a decade of misguided policy in the Balkans?

In the Balkans, the international community took the path of least resistance at almost every turn. There were dozens of opportunities between the 1989 disintegration of the Yugoslavian Communist Party and Milosevic's fall in October 2000 when decisive international action could have made an enormous difference. The West's greatest failure in the Balkans, however, was its unwillingness to engage resolutely in the name of the same political values and moral imperatives that justified the Allied response to Nazi Germany in World War II.

Starting in 1990, the Bush administration's "hands-off" approach to Yugoslavia assumed that the United States had no legitimate interest in Yugoslavia's democratic transition, or the stability of Southeastern Europe in general, a patently absurd proposition that points to a complete absence of political vision. Furthermore, U.S. policy was that Yugoslavia should be held together in more or less its then present form, in some kind of superficially reworked federal structure that nationalists like Milosevic and Tudjman would negotiate among themselves.

It should have been clear then that neither a superficially democratic version of Tito's Yugoslavia nor a simple devolution of the six republics into nation-states was feasible. Neither were the antagonists capable of hammering out a compromise solution among themselves. Had there been the political will and a genuine spirit of cooperation between the European Union, the Soviet Union and the United States, an all-Yugoslavia conference to reconstitute the multinational state along confederal lines and according to democratic norms could have stood a chance. At the time, even in Croatia and Slovenia, there was serious talk of a loose confederal solution, an option vigorously pursued by Macedonian and Bosnian leaders. Even if such an arrangement eventually had fallen apart, it might have laid the groundwork for constructive working relations between neighboring entities and between minority and majority ethnic groups.

It's difficult to pinpoint the moment that recourse to military force of some kind became imperative. But by the early autumn of 1991, the eastern Croatian city of Vukovar was under siege, and the Yugoslavian Navy was shelling coastal Dubrovnik. A show of gunboat diplomacy would have sent Milosevic an early signal that the West meant business. Had U.S. or British battleships appeared on the horizon, or even fired warning shots in the direction of the Yugoslavian forces, they probably would have abandoned their pointless bombardment on the spot. A cease-fire could have created space for last-minute diplomacy. But the opposite message was conveyed: The West was willing to stand by in the face of naked aggression.

concentration camps and the massacres, about the mass rapes and the torture. If the Serbian siege of Bosnian cities and the "ethnic cleansing" of non-Serb communities continues into the winter—which it will—the body count is expected to soar into the hundreds of thousands. That suffering, however, is only a hint of what's to come should international inaction give in to the designs of Serbia's nationalist henchmen. . . .

It is a well-propagated myth that the peoples of the former Yugoslavia cannot live together. Every day in the bunkers of Sarajevo, Serb, Croat and Muslim citizens lock arms with their neighbors. They sing and share their last bits of food together as they had for the past 40 years. The war in the former Yugoslavia is not a popular ethnic conflict, but a territorial war manipulated from the halls of power and waged by extremists.

Either as a loose confederation or as independent states, the peoples of the Balkans could co-exist peacefully again. These states, however, must be civic states, based upon equality under citizenship, and not upon superiority according to nationality. They must constitutionally guarantee minority rights, the rights of regional and ethnic autonomy and the integrity of borders. . . .

A decisive international response six months ago could have prevented Bosnia from turning into the House of Usher. Once the conflict spills into neighboring states, Europe will find itself drawn into the Balkan melee anyway. The longer large-scale intervention is postponed, the more costly and complex it will become in the future.

Town Without Pity

PAUL HOCKENOS

June 12, 1995

BANJA LUKA—All trips within the Bosnian Serb state begin in Pale, whether or not the former mountain resort outside of Sarajevo is near one's destination—which, in the case of Banja Luka, it's not. There, after securing a press card, one is sat down for an informal little chat with Branko, a gruff, barrel-chested Serb in his mid-thirties. Branko explains "the Serb side" of ethnic cleansing (Muslims and Croats want to leave, we just help them), the siege of Sarajevo (they broke the

ITT Archives

In Serb-held northern Bosnia, the Muslim and Croat population dropped from half a million before the war to less than 70,000.

The different U.N. missions in Croatia and Bosnia from 1992 to 1995 followed a similar course of appeasement. In Croatia, a U.N. force protected Serbian territorial gains rather than minorities inside or outside the protected areas. And by implicitly promising to protect the Serbian rebels, the United Nations impeded the negotiation of a peace deal that could have given the Serbs substantial autonomy within a Croatian state. In the end, Croatia received U.S. and European support to settle the issue with force. In 1995, the Croatian army blitzed the Serb-held strongholds, sending 150,000 refugees eastward in the largest single forcible displacement of people during the war. Croatia thus became the ethnically pure state its ultra-nationalists had long dreamed of; the Croatian Serbs, who gambled all or nothing, ended up with nothing.

In Bosnia, the biggest and most expensive U.N. mission ever collapsed as a result of a mandate that, again, accepted the legitimacy of territorial aggression. The U.N. peacekeeping force, according to an excessively cautious reading of its Security Council mandate, maintained a strict neutrality between the three "warring parties." Thus it refused to distinguish between victims and perpetrators, or to employ force against one side. In effect, the United Nations watched over and even abetted ethnic cleansing. But the blame for this lies mostly with the Security Council. The United States refused to contribute troops to the ground force. And the ill-equipped, poorly directed mission was practically designed to flop, a debacle that both damaged U.N. credibility and prolonged the suffering in Bosnia.

Over the course of the three-plus years of war in Bosnia, every Western peace plan from Lisbon to Dayton entailed some form of ethnic apartheid. Implicit in all of these partitions was the assumption that the lion's share of territory captured and ethnically cleansed would remain in the hands of the aggressors. In 1994, the six-member Contact Group—a negotiating council comprised of the United States, Russia, and the Europeans—proposed maintaining a single sovereign Bosnian state divided into spheres of influence: one for the Bosnian Serbs on 49 percent of territory (though Serbs comprised only 31 percent of the population of Bosnia-Herzegovina in a prewar census), another for the Bosnian Muslims and Bosnian Croats on 51 percent of the territory.

Ultimately, the Bosnian Serbs rejected this plan, as it would have meant handing over territory its forces had occupied. Also, the stubborn Bosnian Muslim-held enclaves like Srebrenica, Zepa and Gorazde deep in Serb-controlled eastern Bosnia stuck out like irritated sores on a map that defied neat ethnic partition. "It is very hard to believe that the Muslim enclaves are viable in the long run," said Sir Michael Rose, the U.N. commander whose pro-Serb leanings typified U.N. moral ambivalence. There was talk of a land and population swap between the Bosnian government and the Bosnian Serbs that would address the problem of the maps. Perhaps, it was rumored, Sarajevo would trade its three Drina enclaves in so-called Republika Srpska for Serb-occupied territory around Sarajevo.

But in the summer of 1995, the thorny problem of the maps would be solved once and for all. In July, the world looked the other way while Bosnian Serb forces blitzed Zepa and Srebrenica, carrying out the bloodiest massacre in Europe since World War II. Neither the U.N. forces in Srebrenica nor the Bosnian army raised a hand to stop it. Weeks later, Croatia's Operation Storm (planned in conjunction with U.S. military experts) wiped out the rebel Serbs on Croatian territory. This time, it was Belgrade that averted its eyes.

The Croatian, Bosnian Croatian, and majority-Muslim Bosnian armies went on to take large swathes of Bosnian Serb-occupied land in Western Bosnia. The armies were advancing eastward through Serb territory to Banja Luka when they stopped in their tracks. The Bosnian Muslims and Bosnian Croats together now controlled 51 percent of Bosnia's territory, the prerequisite for a Western-backed

latest cease-fire), and the Contact Group peace plan, which the Serbs refuse to sign (this is a war we didn't even start, why should we give up land we won?). All journalists must travel with an official interpreter in order to avoid "false interpretations," he says—the kind that have unfairly turned the world against the Serbs. . . .

In all of Serb-held northern Bosnia, the Muslim and Croat population has dropped off from half a million before the war to less than 70,000 today. Driving through eastern and northern Bosnia, one finds former Muslim villages that today are ransacked ghost towns, the houses picked clean of doors, windows, anything looters could carry with them. Unlike the destruction in Sarajevo or Mostar, where bullets or grenades have done most of the damage, the buildings here have been plundered by human hands.

In Banja Luka, most of the former houses of Croats and Muslims are identifiable by small blue-white-and-red flags that their new Serb occupants have pinned or painted on their doors. "That means a Serb lives there now," sighs Ljubica, a French teacher and child of a mixed Serb-Muslim marriage. "They *want* you to know."

The most striking physical reminders of ethnic cleansing in Banja Luka are the empty, rock-strewn lots that stand out like scars along shady shrub-lined streets. In those lots, some of the oldest and most elegant mosques in the Balkans stood before Serbian extremists dynamited them. Before the war, there were 16 mosques in Banja Luka; today not a single one is standing. In fact, there is not a minaret to be found anywhere in Serb-controlled Bosnia.

On the corner where the stately Ferhadija Pasha mosque stood for 400 years, stray dogs lounge in the hot midday sun. The homeless animals belonged to Croats and Muslims who have fled the city. The first wave of ethnic cleansing, which began with the outbreak of the war in April 1992, relied on bombings, murders, rapes, mass arrests and arson to force Muslims and Croats from their homes. . . .

Ethnic cleansing is now in an "end phase"—the term foreign observers have assigned to the more subtle forms of intimidation that are forcing the remaining Croats and Muslims out of Bosnian Serb territory. Muslim and Croat men, for example, must perform compulsory labor service, often on the front lines. As the authorities surely anticipate, most would rather leave the country than risk their lives digging trenches.

It is now also cheaper to be ethnically cleansed. In the past, people paid 500 to 600 German marks ($350 to $450) to acquire the papers necessary to go to Western Europe. Today, the city's Civil Migration Authorities charge only 250 marks. At an informal flea market along a crumbling wall of the old city fortress, Muslims, Croats and Gypsies gather to sell their last possessions to get the money to leave. On old blankets, they display record collections, tool sets, door knobs, televisions—anything they can't take with them.

Six Gypsy women with colorful patchwork dresses and head scarves squat in a circle, hand-rolled cigarettes bobbing from their cracked lips. "One day some toughs came and said to us, 'What are you doing here anyway? Get lost or you'll be sorry,' " one woman recalls. She and her husband already have their papers to leave, but with the Croatian military offensive in western Slavonia the borders have been closed to everyone.

"Now you leave," she says, motioning to me with her head, "or I may never get out of here."

peace deal. The message came from Washington that they were to go no further.

The ethnic proportions were now right for a peace deal, which would be signed in Dayton, Ohio three months later. The General Framework Agreement for Peace in Bosnia and Herzegovina, commonly known as the Dayton Accord, enshrined the principle of ethnicity in Bosnia's future by splitting the country into two entities, one for the Bosnian Muslims and Bosnian Croats and another called Republika Srpska (the name of the wartime para-state) for the Bosnian Serbs. Although the Bosnian Serbs wouldn't achieve their wartime goal of breaking from Bosnia altogether, they received half the country, including Srebrenica, as the spoils of their battlefield victories. The wartime leadership and shrill propaganda machine remained in place, with its sights still set on eventually joining Serbia proper.

The architects of Dayton handed the country over to an inexperienced, underfunded peacekeeping mission with instructions to sew the country back together again, return refugees to their homes and then leave in a year's time. The peacekeepers in effect were expected to undo what Dayton had implicitly sanctioned, but without the tools or mandate to do it.

Six years down the road, the international mission's mandate is significantly stronger, and there has been progress to be sure, but much time and money has been wasted. The weak Bosnian state would crumble without the international community there to prop it up. Bosnia's most notorious war criminals, Karadzic and Gen. Ratko Mladic, remain at large. Only a fraction of minority refugees have returned to territory under control of another ethnic group. There are three ethnic armies, three ethnic police forces and three ethnic educational systems. The people of Bosnia are not surprisingly divided along the same ethnic lines laid down in the peace accord. Special blame lies with the NATO-led military force in Bosnia, which shamefully failed to assist the civilian implementation agencies in breaking down wartime power structures. (It is interesting to note that refugee return is markedly advanced in the regions, like Prijedor in Western Republika Srpska, where the indicted war criminals have been apprehended, and lowest where they are still free.)

Even after a decade of ethnic madness, there are still those in policy-making circles who advocate the division of Bosnia, as if this were a reluctant answer to, alas, an intractable problem. To the contrary, carving up Bosnia would satisfy no one and certainly could sow the seeds for renewed conflict in the near future. The region requires civic states with strong institutions that protect the rule of law in order to guarantee the equal rights of all the peoples within its borders. In the end, whether or not certain neighbors "want" or "don't want" to live next one another is completely beside the point. The rule of law must prevail.

The NATO military action against Yugoslavia in 1999 was the culmination of a decade of missed opportunities and inept decision-making. In Kosovo, ethnic tensions had long simmered closer to the surface than in Bosnia, Croatia or elsewhere. Even in a region with advanced traditions of democracy and tolerance, a problem of Kosovo's nature and magnitude would have been very tricky to resolve. But in Kosovo, there was no tradition of democracy at all. Still, some kind of political compromise probably could have been reached, leaving the region in better shape than it is now.

In 1990, the moderate Kosovar Albanian leadership was still ready to talk about autonomy within an overhauled Yugoslavian framework. Milosevic, however, responded to the Kosovar ambitions with ham-fisted repression, driving them in the other direction. The West refused to insist that Kosovo be included in an all-Balkan summit that would work out a comprehensive peace plan for the entire region. Instead, an uncoordinated patchwork of peacekeeping missions, alliances and piecemeal accords emerged—and Kosovo was ignored.

ITT Archives

The question of intervention in the Balkan wars bitterly split the left in the United States and Europe.

The New Military Humanism?

NOAM CHOMSKY

September 19, 1999

The crisis in Kosovo has excited passion and visionary exaltation of a kind rarely witnessed. The events have been portrayed as "a landmark in international relations," opening the gates to a stage of world history with no precedent, a new epoch of moral rectitude under the guiding hand of an "idealistic New World bent on ending inhumanity." This New Humanism, timed fortuitously with a new millennium, will displace the crass and narrow interest politics of a mean-spirited past. Novel conceptions of world order are being forged, interlaced with inspirational lessons about human affairs and global society.

If the picture is true, if it has even a particle of truth, then remarkable prospects lie before us. Material and intellectual resources surely are at hand to overcome terrible tragedies at little cost, with only a modicum of goodwill. It takes little imagination or knowledge to compile a wish list of tasks to be undertaken that should confer enormous benefits on suffering people. In particular, crimes of the nature and scale of Kosovo are all too easily found, and many could be overcome, at least significantly alleviated, with a fraction of the effort and zeal expended in the cause that has consumed the Western powers and their intellectual cultures in early 1999.

If the high-minded spirit of the liberation of Kosovo has even shreds of authenticity, if at last leaders are acting "in the name of principles and values" that are truly humane, as Vaclav Havel confidently proclaimed, then there will be exciting opportunities to place critically important issues on the agenda of practical and immediate action. And even if reality turns out to fall short of the flattering self-portrait, the effort still has the merit of directing attention to what should be undertaken by those who regard the fine words as something more than cynical opportunism. . . .

On June 3, NATO and Serbia reached a peace accord. The United States triumphantly declared victory, though not yet peace: The iron fist remains poised until the victors determine that their interpretation of the peace accord has been imposed. A broad consensus was articulated by *New York Times* global analyst Thomas Friedman: "From the start the Kosovo problem has been about how we should react when bad things happen in unimportant places." . . .

Even nine years later, after political tempers in the province had boiled over, some kind of political solution, though with an international military component, was still possible. At the Rambouillet conferences outside of Paris in February and March 1999, international mediators attempted to broker a last-minute deal between the Kosovar Albanians and Serbia that would offer Kosovo substantial autonomy inside Yugoslavia, with a plan to be overseen by international civilian and NATO-led military forces.

Historical hindsight will one day determine whether the Western mediators did everything in their power to reach a compromise between the two parties. Certain Western stipulations were unconstructive, to say the least. Nevertheless, it is no secret that the Serb negotiating team refused to take the summit seriously. At no point did it offer a viable alternative, like a U.N. force, to the proposed NATO presence. Milosevic had no intention of reaching an accommodation of any kind with the Kosovar Albanians. According to the British journalist Tim Judah, who attended the Rambouillet negotiations, Milosevic's strategy was based on two factors: "The first was his gamble that the Albanians would refuse to sign, and the second was skepticism that NATO countries really intended to carry out their threat to bomb."

Milosevic's miscalculation would cost Serbia dearly, probably losing Kosovo forever. After Rambouillet's collapse, the situation on the ground in Kosovo deteriorated further. The Yugoslavian army, local paramilitaries and criminal killer gangs—the same constellation that ethnically cleansed Bosnia—were at work in Kosovo. The very same forces responsible for the massacre at Srebrenica were expelling Kosovar Albanians by the tens of thousands and perpetrating atrocities with impunity.

Regrettably, the decision to launch air strikes lacked Security Council approval (Russia and China opposed it), violating international law. It further crippled the Serbian economy, exacerbated anti-Western feeling, and saturated the fields of Serbia and Kosovo with depleted uranium. The NATO occupation and U.N. police forces watched over a reverse ethnic cleansing as Kosovar Albanians vented their pent up rage and exacted revenge on Serbs and Gypsies. The ambiguous status of the Kosovo protectorate, neither independent nor a working unit of Yugoslavia, is a recipe for further instability. But at the time, there was simply no other choice.

Nowadays, international authorities in Kosovo and Bosnia too often act like colonial overlords, dictating policies and circumventing able local politicians. Yet as flawed as the post-conflict missions in Bosnia and Kosovo have been, they need to be rethought, not abandoned. The concept of protectorates runs the risk of creating dependent subjects in artificially stable conditions that will collapse once the international administrators leave. The international community must concentrate on creating self-sustaining structures, like independent judiciaries and professional police forces, that will continue to stand on their own once the scaffolding is stripped away. In Bosnia, there are constructive models of successful institution-building, like the Bosnian Central Bank and the Independent Media Commission.

Ultimately, the process of Southeastern Europe's integration into the established European structures, including the European Union, is the key to the region's transformation. Through the "Stability Pact for South Eastern Europe," the leaders of the European Union have committed themselves to a serious, long-term effort to help create the preconditions (functioning democracies and market economies, resolution of regional conflicts) to integrate all of the Balkan region into the Euro-Atlantic structures. The European Union pledged to grant membership to all countries of the region once they meet the membership criteria and to provide large-scale assistance to help meet those conditions. The Stability Pact is a process that supports the hard work of strengthening individual states according to European norms and thus sets the countries of Southeastern Europe on the same path that

While Friedman's own (and the conventional) answer to his rhetorical question is untenable, a credible answer appears in the same journal on the same day, though only obliquely. Reporting from Ankara, correspondent Stephen Kinzer writes that "Turkey's best-known human rights advocate [Akin Birdal] entered prison" to serve his sentence for having "urged the state to reach a peaceful settlement with Kurdish rebels."

Looking beyond the sporadic and generally uninformative or misleading news reports and commentary, we discover that the sentencing of the courageous president of the Human Rights Association of Turkey is only one episode of a campaign of intimidation and harassment of human rights advocates who are investigating and reporting horrendous atrocities and calling for peaceful resolution of a conflict that has been marked by one of the most savage campaigns of ethnic cleansing and state terror of the '90s. The campaign has proceeded with mounting fury thanks to the active participation of the United States. . . .

These events, continuing right now and taking place within NATO and under European jurisdiction, provide a rather striking illustration—far from the only one—of the answer given by the enlightened states to the question of "how we should react when bad things happen in unimportant places": We should react by helping to *escalate* the atrocities, a mission accomplished in Kosovo as well. Such elements of the real world of today raise some rather serious questions about the New Humanism.

In the Balkan war of 1999, these questions remain out of sight—within the "enlightened states," at least. Elsewhere, they are readily perceived, over a broad spectrum. To select several remote points for illustration, Amos Gilboa, a prominent Israeli commentator on military and strategic affairs, sees the enlightened states as "a danger to the world." He describes their new rules of the game as a reversion to the colonial era, with brought stability and prosperity to postwar Western Europe. Its far-sighted vision underscores that there is just one Europe, and the Balkans are part of it.

ITT Archives

Sightseeing in Novi Sad.

the resort to force "cloaked in moralistic righteousness" as the rich and powerful do "what seems to them to be justified." At a very different point on the spectrum, Alexander Solzhenitsyn, a Western idol when he is saying the right things, offers a succinct definition of the New Humanism: "The aggressors have kicked aside the U.N., opening a new era where might is right."

They and many others like them throughout the world might agree with an observation by the prominent and influential—though little celebrated—radical pacifist A. J. Muste: "The problem after a war is with the victor. He thinks he has just proved that war and violence pay. Who will now teach him a lesson?"

States of Denial

PAUL HOCKENOS

April 8, 1992

Milan Kundera opens *The Book of Laughter and Forgetting* with a parable about the treatment of history under Communism. On a snowy winter's day in 1948, Czech Communist leader Klement Gottwald posed for a photo with his inner circle. Next to him stood comrade Clementis, who took off his fur cap and set it on Gottwald's bare head. After the purges four years later, however, Clementis was air-brushed out of the photo. All that remained of him was his cap on Gottwald's head.

When the revolutions of 1989 brought down the Eastern bloc dictatorships, they swept away the facade of historical half-truths, distortions and lies upon which the ruling elites grounded their legitimacy. If the struggle of people against power is the struggle of memory against forgetting, as Kundera puts it, then in 1989 memory was victorious.

The close of a discredited historical epoch, however, poses new questions about remembrance and forgetting, about the new relationship between people and power. In a region so steeped in historical tragedy as Eastern and Central Europe, the form of democracy that evolves is implicitly informed by the post-communist systems' relation to their pasts.

In word, at least, all of Europe's new member-states concur that the dissolution of single-party rule constitutes a clean break with the Communist era. But like the will to erase a bad dream, the Eastern Europeans have tried to put the last four decades behind them as if they had never existed. To the detriment of their societies, the people of the former Eastern bloc have concentrated their collective energy on forgetting.

Of the many aspects of political transition, the Central and Eastern Europeans have taken little pain to confront Stalinism's legacy in their countries. Previously suppressed knowledge about

ITT Archives

The people of the former Eastern bloc have concentrated their collective energy on forgetting.

the political gulags and the secret police's Gestapo tactics have underlined the totalitarian essences of even the "soft" communist regimes. Yet that examination has stopped drastically short of a searching investigation into the past. As quickly as Romanian revolutionaries changed Lenin Strada to Strada Demokratiei, the complex questions of responsibility and guilt have been brushed aside to clear the way for the new era. The necessity of a penetrating *Aufarbeitung der Geschichte*—a coming to terms with the past—is nowhere on the young democracies' agendas.

Immediately after the East bloc regimes tumbled, even the top *nomenklatura* professed that they had been closet democrats all along, pushing relentlessly for change from within the power structures. For the discontented populations, the fact that the state outlawed political opposition and ruthlessly crushed popular uprisings served as a handy and not altogether unconvincing alibi for their political conformism. Unless one was prepared to sacrifice a normal life, Communism pressed the citizen into active compliance with the system. As party member, low-level bureaucrat or obedient fellow-traveler, the average person struck his or her compromise with power. In the former East Germany today, weekly revelations about the cooperation of even leading figures in the pre-1989 underground opposition with the secret police has exposed the shocking totality of society's complicity. In hindsight, the Vaclav Havels and the Adam Michniks stand out as the precious few.

Broad collaboration with the powers that were explains the readiness to skip over a full coming to accounts with the past. With the single exception of the former East Germany, the calls of yesterday's dissidents to open the secret police files have run into brick walls—and not to most people's displeasure. Neither is it simply a matter of politics that most of the democratic, dissident-led parties fared poorly at the polls. The majority of people not only identify better with the careerist-turned-nationalist, but also find their conscience better protected there.

The illusion of an automatic *tabula rasa* also undermines the need for society to reflect upon the consciousness that evolved under the conditions of the past 40 years. Since communism and "socialism" have been forever assigned to history's dustbin, there appears no pressing need for society to come to terms with just what that system was or how it continues to manifest itself in the present. In depoliticized societies, the totalitarian thought of the old fuels today's chauvinisms. A familiar authoritarianism, intolerance and provincialism persist in the reigning power structures—although now under the name of nationalism, "communism's opposite." And, by definitively closing the book on the past, the language of socialism also remains trapped in Stalinism's wreckage. Thus, the possibility of social democracy is also neatly nipped in the bud.

The denial of the Communist era has led political forces in Central and Eastern Europe in two general directions. In liberal-democratic circles, those most strongly identified with the dissident tradition, the 1989 revolutions are seen as the chance to embark upon a qualitatively new political future. Their model is contemporary Western democracy, something that most of them admit has never existed in Eastern Europe. The second and stronger tendency is a conservative nationalism that views the communist era as a Soviet-imposed interruption of a national democratic tradition that had flourished prior to World War II. The nationalists tout "a return to the past," a reversion to the interwar period when Hungarians ruled Hungary and Poles ruled Poland.

Fairy tales revisited: Unfortunately, today's elected rulers have sought recourse in historical myths no less perilous than those of their Communist predecessors. The nationalist revivals throughout the region have prompted sweeping historical revisions that uncritically glorify the nation's past from the Middle Ages to the present. Amid a new vacuum of power and ideology, the embellished histories remain one of the few legitimations of the post-Communist governments. With economic collapse and political instability looming, many liberals, too, have stooped to tap that national sentiment. The deficit of alternative political ideas has presented conservatives with an open field to define the nascent political culture.

Shifting Sands

THE MYTH OF ISLAM VS. THE WEST

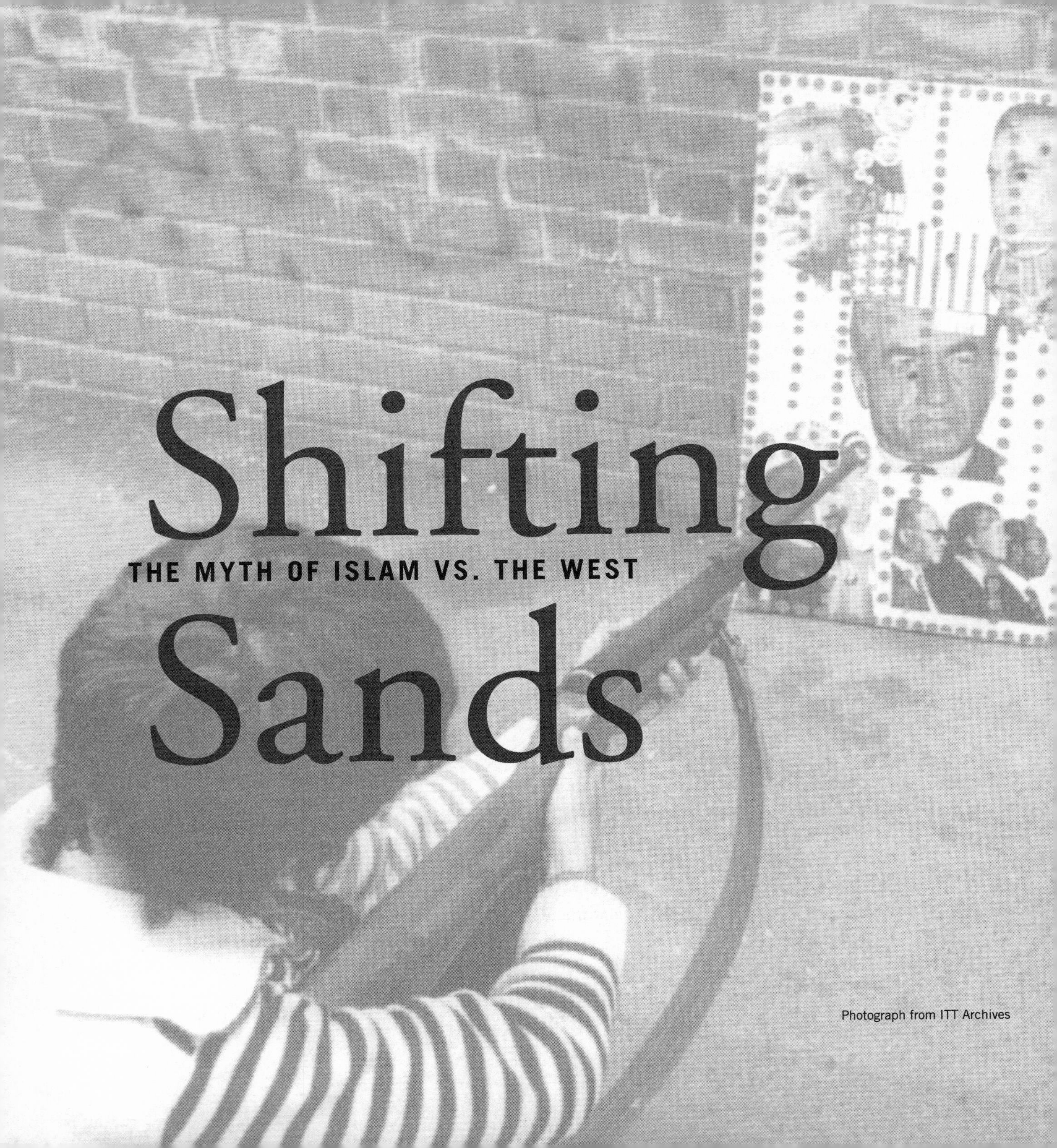

Photograph from ITT Archives

Seventeen

FRED HALLIDAY

ANALYSIS OF WORLD POLITICS SINCE THE END OF THE COLD WAR HAS BEEN MARKED BY A CARNIVAL OF GRAND GENERALIZATIONS, FROM "THE NEW world order" and "the end of history" to "the new middle ages" and "the clash of civilizations." Much of this speculation has centered on the prevalence of "cultural" conflict. While such conflicts have included that of "Asian" versus "Western" and "Christian" versus "Slavic," pride of place among the claims made in this category must go to the argument that the world is riven by an overriding conflict between "Islam" and "the West." If there is a grand narrative about conflict in the post-Cold War world, this is it.

Some political analysts argue the clash between Islam and the West has replaced the Cold War as the dominant fissure of international relations. Others make a somewhat stronger case that in a strategic vacuum left by the end of the Cold War, this conflict has been promoted by the West to fill the gap left by the disappearance of the Communist threat. Samuel Huntington's *A Clash of Civilizations* starts from a premise of international conflict, precluding international cooperation. "The clash of civilizations will dominate global politics," he writes. "The fault lines between civilizations will be the battle lines of the future." The events of September 11, 2001, have been offered as proof of his thesis.

Huntington asks: "If not culture, then what?" And this argument about cultural conflict goes well beyond Islam and the West. There have been recurrent claims about the place of cultural conflict in the contemporary international epoch as a whole: in Huntington's broader contention about the general primacy of culture and civilizational clash in international relations, in discussion of the cultural backlash to globalization, in invocation by academic cultural studies of deep structures of identity and antagonism within Western and non-Western politics. All of this, of course, has played into the "cultural turn" in contemporary social theory, according to which identity, symbol and discourse are more important than class or political power in determining the contemporary world.

There is limited validity in such theoretical approaches, and in the generalizations they lead to, beyond the fact that they are widely repeated. They are both comprehensive and elusive, resting on shifting sands of historical, cultural and political claims. When evidence fails, psychoanalytic speculation is invoked. Examination of this conflict may indeed tell us something about the world, but not what proponents of the myth themselves would argue.

The claim that the conflict with Islam has replaced the Cold War is often substantiated by reference to the rise of radical Islamist movements as a consequence of the collapse of the Cold War. This too might seem to confirm the post-Cold War "vacuum" theory. But the emergence of militant Islamic fundamentalism is not a substitute for the Cold War, but a product of that very conflict. It is as some ghastly relic of the Cold War, not some new strategic confrontation, that the deeper signifigance of these events should be seen.

In the Cold War, both the United States and the Soviet Union sought to use Islam for their own purposes. For its part, the United States played this card against secular nationalist and communist forces in a range of Muslim countries. Thus in the '60s, Saudi Arabia, Iran and Pakistan were encouraged to promote conservative Islamic forces against Soviet influence in the Middle East. This reached its apogee in the '80s when, following the Soviet invasion of Afghanistan, the CIA engaged in its largest-ever covert operation (costing more than $3 billion) in support of the Afghan opposition. These zealots and killers trained to fight the Communist forces have continued to spread violence. Whatever else, this history indicates that the politicization of Islamic movements predated 1989 and cannot be attributed to the end of the Cold War.

Defending Israel *and* Palestine

JAMES WEINSTEIN

May 17, 1978

From its inception, *In These Times* has been guided by basic principles respecting the Israeli-Palestinian conflict. We believe that:

- Palestine is the homeland of both Israelis and Palestinian Arabs.
- The right of each to self-determination in the form of recognized statehood is beyond question.
- Peaceful coexistence and friendly cooperation between the state of Israel and a Palestinian Arab state (in the areas of the West Bank and Gaza) are desirable and possible. The long-term security and progress of both peoples require coexistence and cooperation.
- The Israeli government should recognize the PLO as the legitimate representative of the Palestinian Arab people and their national aspirations; the PLO should recognize Israel as a legitimate state in Palestine and in the family of nations. On the basis of such mutual recognition, Israel and the PLO should engage in direct negotiations as part of the process leading to the establishment of a Palestinian Arab state.
- Both states should have secure and recognized boundaries, assured, if necessary, by international guarantees.
- The state of Israel and the Palestinian Arab state should cooperate in seeking the establishment of a refugee relief and resettlement fund under international auspices (preferably the United Nations) to facilitate the early development of the Palestinian Arab state, resettle Palestinian refugees, and aid Israel and Arab states to meet the just reparations claims of displaced Palestinian Arabs and displaced Jews.
- American socialists should not take the side of one nation against the other, but should support recognition of both Israeli and Palestinian Arab

Pro-Western secular regimes in the Middle East also played their own role in encouraging Islamism. In retrospect, it is striking how many of the Islamist forces that came into prominence in the '90s were promoted, for tactical considerations, by the states themselves during the Cold War. This was done to counter the secular opposition, whether it was from communists or nationalists. In Pakistan, successive military and civilian regimes sought to use Islamist parties against their opponents. In Turkey in the '70s, the military, faced with strong secular opposition, sanctioned increased activity by the Islamist forces. Israel too fostered Islamist opposition as a counter to the secular politics of the PLO. The rise of Islamism cannot be reduced to such state sponsoring, but it is a widespread and significant part of the story.

At the same time, the character of the opposition shifted, from secular to religious politics, because of the defeat of the former by internationally backed regimes. This was the revenge of the 1953 events in Iran: The CIA and the British MI6 backed the coup that restored the Shah and crushed the National Front and the Tudeh, laying the ground for the advance of Ayatollah Khomeini's Islamist politics a decade later. And the Islamists themselves in many ways were shaped by the Cold War: They took much in ideology, program and organizational form from their secular counterparts. While they deployed elements of the Muslim tradition for political ends, they also incorporated ideas—of imperialism, nationalism, economic change, political organization—from communism and secular nationalism. Khomeini even celebrated May 1 as the "Day of the Islamic Worker."

The one place where the Cold War did not produce Islamism, paradoxically, was the USSR, the most authoritarian, secular context of all. Neither under the Soviet system itself, nor (with the exceptions of Tajikistan and Chechnya) in the first decade of the post-Soviet period, did significant Islamist forces emerge in the Muslim republics or among the 50 million or so Muslims of Russia. Here, where the West and anti-Communist states in the Middle East had predicted an

nationhood and promote understanding and cooperation between the two states sharing Palestine. We should support or oppose acts and policies of other nations (including the United States) accordingly.

To be a true friend of Israel is to be a friend of Palestinian statehood. It is not possible to be a friend of one and an enemy of the other.

ITT Archives

Palestinian schoolchildren raise the "victory" sign during the first *intifada*.

The Idea of Palestine

EDWARD SAID

September 8, 1982

The idea of Palestine living in all Palestinians is not just a matter of land, water and a flag. They are important, but not the only thing. What matters about Palestine is what has always prevented Israel from converting its military superiority into lasting political gains: that invincible Palestinian desire to keep hold of what is right and to reject what is wrong. By most standards, the Palestinians are a

"Islamic" revival, politics took another form: corrupt clientelism at the top and consumer and democratic discontent below. Interestingly, there are very few remnants of the pro-Soviet communist movement roaming the world and creating havoc, but plenty of former clients of the West.

Turning to the post-1989 world, there seemingly was much to support those who believe in a growing clash between Islam and the West. The conflict between the United States and Iraq that began with the latter's invasion of Kuwait in 1990 seemed to reinforce this view, as did the unresolved Palestinian-Israeli conflict. Before September 11, this rift was exemplified by the U.S. missile attacks against Sudan and Afghanistan in August 1998, following bombings of U.S. embassies in Africa allegedly masterminded by Osama bin Laden.

While President Clinton, in his statement justifying the strikes, insisted that this was not the start of a war with the Islamic world, Secretary of State Madeleine Albright spoke in starker terms. "This is going to be a long-term battle against terrorists who have declared war on the United States," she said. Yet claims about the Western hostility toward the Muslim world—in press, radio, political speeches and mosque preachings—are at least as common in Muslim countries. Many Muslims saw themselves, not terrorist sites about which the evidence was uncertain, as the target of U.S. aggression.

One does not have to believe in a common Islamic politics or "threat" to identify a shared political feeling in which Muslims in different countries identify the West as their enemy. But this is a product of Islam only in a limited sense. This perspective combines attacks on Western imperialism in its historic form with a critique of contemporary politics and globalization. With local variations, there are distinct themes: the past and present of Western domination and intervention (Iran, for example, was invaded twice in the 20th century, by Britain and Russia); partition of Muslim states (Palestine being the classic case, southern Sudan and the safe haven in

modestly endowed people, although a people possessed by what is in the strict sense a secular ideal. They want justice, but not abstract justice. Rather, they want something that can be lived by them collectively in forms that can still be called just. In support of this, they have offered no metaphysical rationale, no divinely ordained transhistorical scheme. For them the idea of Palestine is adequate to their real memory, their actual present and their minimal requirements for the future.

Q&A: Ayatollah Khomeini

DIANA JOHNSTONE

January 24, 1979

In the Islamic republic you advocate, would all political parties, including those which are non- or anti-religious such as the Communist Party, be free to take part in elections and express their views?

Everyone under an Islamic government would be free to express his own ideas and to decide his own destiny. Yet principally, it is not acceptable, in a nation that has given that much blood of its youth and their children to establish an Islamic government, for some people then to come and build the nation according to their wishes, that is, destroying the results of what the people have been doing. Everyone is free to express his own ideas, but as for treason, the answer is no.

How could the Shiite clergy supervise the exercise of power in an Islamic republic without being corrupted by it?

First of all, the theory that one person should have power, whether it be a religious leader or any other person, and run the affairs of a nation without referring to the public opinion of the people, is

Iraq being recent examples); indifference to the sufferings of Muslims (Palestine, Bosnia, Eritrea, Kashmir); cultural corruption; support for Israel; support for dictatorial regimes; double standards in the application of human rights policies, sanctions and U.N. Security Council condemnations; and diffusion of anti-Muslim stereotypes in the Western press and media.

It sounds like an impressive list of denunciations, and it is. Yet it is only part of the picture. Once the supposedly unique conflict between Islam and the West is set in a comparative perspective, its supposedly religious or cultural character seems less dominant. First of all, not everything that is put forward as Muslim should be taken at face value: Saddam Hussein called for *jihad* and issued postage stamps with his own head next to that of Saladin, the defender of Muslim Jerusalem from the Crusaders. But despite these Islamic invocations, his is a thoroughly secular regime, which crushed the religious establishment and opposition in his own country.

On closer examination, it becomes evident that we are not dealing here with some clash or incompatibility of cultures, but with a clash of interests in a divided world. Many of the issues about which Muslims denounced the West in the '90s, though they may have been expressed in Islamic terminology, were not specifically Muslim at all. The sense of anger at Western colonial and post-colonial domination was also strong in China, India, Africa and Latin America. Much was made of the Islamic tendency toward conspiracy theory, but examination of the political culture of Serbia, China or even the United States would yield comparable perspectives. The attack on Western human rights policies for being hypocritical was heard as much in China as it was in the Middle East. Even terrorism is an instrument used worldwide by secular and religious groups. It is no prerogative of the Muslim or Middle Eastern world—as the Irish, the Armenians, Russian populists, Serbian nationalists and many factions in India, not to mention U.S. right-wing militias, would be the first to point out.

against Islam. And it's not accepted. But, in an Islamic republic, the supervision of affairs, to protect against any deviation from Islamic criteria and principles, rests with a group of Islamic scholars who know Islam very well and are righteous and pious and acceptable to the majority of the people.

Everywhere in the world, industrialization has entailed grave social upheavals and injustices. Do you think that even a government faithful to the moral principles of Islam could avoid the social evils brought about by economic changes in the world?

The answer is yes. If a nation is determined to be dependent only on the results of its own struggles and efforts, and avoids pursuing only its appetites and wasting its material and spiritual resources, and follows the instructions and principles of Islam, which are in fact congruent with the nature of the human being, this nation will overcome its difficulties.

ITT Archives

Ayatollah Khomeini and his associates made an issue of *The Satanic Verses* to reassert control over their own people.

By the same token, how much did culture—or more specifically, hostility to Islam as a religion—play a part in determining the foreign policies of Western states after the Cold War? (Or the policies of multinational corporations, for that matter?) How much was Islam, as a belief system, seen as a threat to Western interests in the making of foreign policy? At the strategic and economic levels, the answer is an overwhelming negative. The threat posed by individual states—Iran or Iraq, Sudan or Afghanistan—was a result of specific military policies they pursued, be they of territorial acquisition or procurement of weapons of mass destruction. All these states were also in conflict with other Muslim states. As such, the Western response was no different to that seen in regard to non-Muslim states, say Russia during the Cold War or North Korea in the '90s. Indeed, Western military policy showed at times considerable support for Muslim states: NATO carried out, in effect, three wars in the '90s—Kuwait, Bosnia and Kosovo—all in defense of Muslim peoples.

In clarifying the Islam-West relationship, it is equally important to get away from the image of a single united, or even coordinated, Muslim world. The impression of a growing conflict between Western states and the Muslim world misses the fact that despite the existence of common sentiments and political links, the Muslim world is composed of different states, 57 at last count. They may share a common stance on Palestine or Bosnia, but that's about it.

Iran, for example, has long put nationalist interests above Muslim solidarity. After the revolution of 1979 , Iran talked of Islamic solidarity and supported militant groups in other states. Yet in each case where it did so—Lebanon, Iraq, Afghanistan—it encountered local, state and national opposition. Its own foreign policy showed a flexibility that defies any religious community: Thus in the conflict between Shiite Muslim Azerbaijan and Orthodox Christian Armenia, Iran provided financial, diplomatic and security aid to the

Afghan Tragedy

DIANA JOHNSTONE

February 27, 1980

Afghanistan illustrates once again that the great powers' defense of their security is the biggest threat to the security of everybody else.

Leonid Brezhnev explained to *Pravda* that Soviet forces went into Afghanistan to save it from a "plot" to turn it into "an imperialist military bridgehead at the southern frontier of our country." The USSR could not just "sit back passively and watch the formation on our southern border of a serious threat to the Soviet state."

Now, it so happens there's a narrow mountain pass on the northeastern tip of Afghanistan that borders the far west of China. So of course China feels its security threatened. And the United States, although on the other side of the world, is so alarmed about *its* security that it is getting ready to grind its ploughshares into MX missiles and its grain into gasohol.

The giants see everything that goes wrong in the world as part of a plot by another giant. Or so they pretend. Leaving aside the propaganda and hyperbole, a fairly clear picture of events leading up to the Soviet invasion of Afghanistan emerges. . . . The heart of the tragedy is the failure of the country's Westernized elites in their efforts to pull the Afghan people out of age-old poverty and ignorance. It's the planetary problem of "underdevelopment," compounded by great power paranoia and meddling.

ITT Archives

A teen-age soldier killed by Soviet troops in Afghanistan.

Armenians. During its long smoldering conflict with Pakistan, Iran always maintained cordial relations with India. Its relationship with Beijing always overrode support for any secessionist movements in the Muslim province of Xinjiang. And, of course, Iran and Iraq fought a war from 1980 to 1988 in which hundreds of thousands were killed.

In the '90s, alongside the clamor about an Islamic-Western conflict, there were alarming confrontations between Muslim countries. Iran and Afghanistan nearly came to war in 1998 after the Taliban government killed Iranian diplomats and journalists. Here the issues included a long-running rivalry within Afghanistan between the militantly Sunni Taliban and the 15 to 20 percent of the population who are Shiites, and a growing sense in Iran that the Taliban were instruments of a Pakistani and Saudi expansion into Central Asia. Iran reacted as a nationalist state, marshaling troops along the frontier. Its spiritual leader Ayatollah Khamenei spoke of the need to defend the interests of what Ayatollah Khomeini had termed "the great nation of Iran." Khamenei classified the Afghans as *jahul*, a Koranic term literally meaning "ignorant," but with the implication of being un-Islamic. (Sunni-Shia tension also is evident in communal killings in Pakistan, in the growth of tribal and sectarian politics inside Iraq, and in social tensions inside Saudi Arabia and Bahrain.)

Nowhere is this variety of "Islams" more central than in regard to the issue of fundamentalism. Fundamentalists in the Islamic world, like their counterparts in the Hindu, Judaic and Christian worlds, denounce foreigners and alien corruption. But their prime targets are the secular forces in their midst. The main cause of the growth of fundamentalism is dissatisfaction with the post-independence, modernizing, secular state. This is as true of the revolt against the National Liberation Front in Algeria as it was of the Islamic revolution in Iran. Khomeini's "cultural revolution" of 1980 was, like that of Mao in China, supposedly directed against foreign influence, but was mainly directed against literary and ideological currents within Iran that he did not like.

Past Imperfect

FRED HALLIDAY

October 4, 1993

Israelis and Palestinians have behaved, and will continue to behave, in much the same way as other peoples in the world. And this is in part because of something neither side will admit—namely that, far from being the features of an ancient and determining history, they are the creatures of contingency, products of an arbitrary and quite recent history, which has created two nations, in the sense of distinct political communities, in a matter of a few decades. The real reconciliation will rest not on arbitrating the historical or ancestral claims, but rather on denying the relevance of history at all.

The Jews invoke their biblical claims; the Palestinians see themselves as the heirs of centuries of residence and descendants of the Canaanites before them. But here, as in so many other parts of the world, this invocation of history is spurious. The division of the world's people into nations, each claiming a separate state on the basis of distinct identities, is a recent phenomenon. The Palestinian nation is part of this process, with the added fact that it has been forged in the conflict with the Zionist project itself since the '20s.

Similar elisions occur on the Jewish side. A Jewish people has existed for millennia, but there is no Jewish "nation" in the modern political sense. Most Jews did not before 1948 live in Palestine; most do not now live in Israel. Out of a part of the Jewish people, an Israeli nation, Hebrew-speaking and resident in the Middle East, has been created. Its opponents deny it legitimacy on the grounds that it was created through immigration and settlement—but this argument would, if generalized, be true for many other nations the world over, including the United States.

Nationalists themselves, and those who invest nations with deep historical roots, deny the modernity of the nationalist project and try to divine the roots of today's claims in a long history. We can, if we try, locate those peoples and traditions that are the ancestors of today's nations. But the reasons why particular nationalisms arise and flourish today have much more to do with contemporary grievances and aspirations than with the distant past.

In the chaos of the post-communist world, all sorts of nationalisms have arisen. What is striking about so many of them is how, in their feverish invocation of the past, they ignore the lessons of other conflicts and reproduce the myths of other nationalisms. It is one of the paradoxes of nationalism that while each nation claims to be unique, they are, in their essentials, all the same.

ITT Archives

To be a friend of Israel is to be a friend of Palestinian statehood.

Collateral Damage

JOHN PILGER

May 15, 2000

Beside the road to Baghdad from Jordan lay two bodies: old men in suits, their arms stiffly beside them. A taxi rested upside-down beside them. The men had been walking along the road, each with his meager belongings, which were now scattered among the thornbushes. The taxi's brakes had

The best way to silence internal critics is always to brand them as agents of a foreign power. Here, too, rather than in some global cultural divide, lies the logic of the Salman Rushdie affair. Khomeini and his associates made an issue of *The Satanic Verses* in 1989 to reassert control over their own people. The charges of blasphemy and corrupting the young have long been used as a means of crushing political dissent: Indeed, this has been the charge on which many of the greatest dissidents have been condemned—Socrates, Christ and Spinoza among them.

Likewise, Osama bin Laden's main target is not the United States, but the ruling family in Saudi Arabia. He uses fictitious arguments, such as the claim that American troops are despoiling the holy places of Islam to mobilize domestic support. (Yet bin Laden and his associates were happy to take the money voted to them each year by the U.S. Congress in the '80s to support their war against the secular, pro-Soviet regime in Kabul and its Red Army allies.) The horrendous attacks on New York and Washington are only a latest chapter in what has been a long series of violent attacks by groups aspiring to power in Afghanistan, the Arab world and elsewhere. The aim is, in this sense, political and directed at discrediting and undermining the states of the region.

The events of September 11 mark the most dramatic example ever seen of what, in the anarchist tradition, is known as "propaganda of the deed." The purpose of such an action is not, in any substantial sense, to weaken the power of the state so attacked. The U.S. bombings may precipitate problems in the world financial system, global security and transportation arrangements. But they do not lessen the military power of the United States, the overall strength of its economy, or the tenacity of its political system and people. In some ways, by rallying the U.S. public to George W. Bush and by mobilizing a gamut of international support, they may even strengthen U.S. power.

What the actions do achieve is two other goals that the anarchists of a century ago, active in New York among other places, would have well understood. One is to inflict a symbolic humiliation and punishment on the United States and to publicize that humiliation. This was achieved in spectacular, unprecedented form. The other aim is to mobilize support for the movement against U.S. domination in the region and, of even greater importance, against those in the region who are associated with the United States. If the destruction of the Bamyan Buddhist statues by the Taliban in Afghanistan rallied Sunni fundamentalists in many countries, surely the attack on the World Trade Center will do so a thousand times more.

On closer analysis, the "long war" between Islam and the West is a sideshow to a much deeper conflict going on within Muslim societies themselves. We must look at the political and social interests being served by these internal calls to order—it is not the culture that explains what is happening.

What about the "vacuum" or "necessary threat" argument? According to this view, the West lost an enemy in Communism after 1989 and had to reinvent one in the form of Islam. This claim is not convincing for several reasons. First of all, the Western world did not *invent* the Communist threat: It existed, as Lenin, Stalin, Khrushchev or even Brezhnev would have been the first to acknowledge. The USSR participated in an arms race and a competition for influence in the Third World, which was sometimes exaggerated but not illusory.

Moreover, the underlying assumption of this "necessary threat" argument is that somehow the Western world *needs* a threat, an external enemy. Of course, external challenge can galvanize states and societies: War and economic competition formed the modern state. But what the West really wants is a world as much like itself as possible, with which it can trade, enjoy peaceful relations and so on. It was Voltaire who said that in the marketplace, "the Jew, the Mohammedan and the Christian treat each other as if they were the same religion, and

apparently failed, and it had cut them down. Local people came out of the swirling dust and stood beside the bodies: For them, on this, the only road in and out of Iraq, it was a common event.

The road on the Jordan side of the border is one of the most dangerous on earth. It was never meant as an artery, yet it now carries most of Iraq's permissible trade and traffic to the outside world. Two narrow single lanes are dominated by oil tankers, moving in an endless convoy; cars and overladen buses and vans dart in and out in a kind of *danse macabre*. The inevitable carnage provides a gruesome roadside tableau of burnt-out tankers, a bus crushed like a tin can, an official U.N. Mercedes on its side, its once-privileged occupants dead.

Of course, brakes fail on rickety taxis everywhere, but the odds against survival here are shortened to zero. Parts for the older models are now nonexistent, and drivers go through the night and day with little sleep. With the Iraqi dinar worth virtually nothing, they must go back and forth, from Baghdad to Amman, Amman to Baghdad, as frequently and as quickly as possible, just to make enough to live. And when they and their passengers are killed or maimed, they, too, become victims of the most ruthless economic embargo of our time.

The inhumanity and criminal vindictiveness of the sanctions struck me one afternoon in Baghdad, in the studio of the great Iraqi sculptor Mohamed Ghani. His latest work is a three-meter figure of a woman, her breasts dry of milk, a child pleading with her for food, the small, frail body merged into her legs. Her face is dark and ill-defined, "a nightmare of sadness and confusion," as he describes it. She is waiting in a line at a closed door. The line is recognizable from every hospital I visited; it is always the same, stretching from the dispensary into the heat outside as people wait for the life-giving drugs that are allowed into Iraq only when the U.N. sanctions committee feels like it—rather, when the Clinton administration and its sidekick, the Blair government, feel like it. . . .

While I was in Iraq, the list of "holds" on humanitarian supplies included 18 on medical equipment, such as heart-and-lung machines. Along with water pumps, agricultural supplies, safety and fire-fighting equipment, these were "suspected dual use": Saddam Hussein might also make weapons of mass destruction from wheelbarrows, which were on the list. So was detergent. In hospitals and hotels, there is the inescapable, sickly stench of gasoline, which is used to clean the floors, because detergent is "on hold." . . .

While I was in Iraq, Kofi Annan, normally the most compliant of U.N. secretary-generals, complained to the Security Council about "holds" amounting to $700 million. These included food, supplies and equipment that might restore the power grid, the water-treatment plants and the telephones.

The deliberate bombing of the civilian infrastructure in 1991 returned Iraq, a modern state, to "a pre-industrial age." The strategy was: bomb now, die later. It is the new style of "humanitarian war." The statistics of those who have since died are breathtaking; for this reason, no doubt, they have been consigned to media oblivion. In May 1996, U.S. Secretary of State Madeleine Albright was asked on the CBS program *60 Minutes* if the death of more than half a million children was a price worth paying. "We think the price is worth it," she replied.

they give the name of infidel only to those who are bankrupt."

This is the truth of what Marx and Engels wrote in *The Communist Manifesto*, that capitalism transforms the world in its own image. If there is a threat to the West today, it comes from the industrialization of East Asia and the shift of power to the Pacific. On this scale, the Middle East is marginal—it is, with Africa, largely outside the economic transformations of recent times—except insofar as it provides large quantities of oil and reinvests its rent in the West, to the tune of around $1 trillion. This is what makes talk of an Islamic threat so false. The most economically powerful Islamic states, those of the Arab Gulf, are cooperative partners in global energy and financial markets.

The Muslim world certainly has particular problems—of economic, social and political development—but they are not problems specific to the Muslim world. These include unemployment, income inequality, agricultural stagnation and corruption. Here, there are three common explanations: an inescapable history ("The Arabs were always like that"), imperialism ("We can blame the West for everything") and cultural reductionism ("It's all the result of Islam").

What should be examined are not the timeless cultures and religions, but the specific forms of state and class structures that have been established in the Arab world in the 20th century. We can then ask why democracy has not been achieved, what has happened to the money, why public administration may not be honest, why populations are dissatisfied. Beneath the appearance of international or domestic relations determined or shaped by cultural identity, we find the more familiar world of state interest in strategic calculation or opposition to that interest. We must look at what people do, not what they say or believe they are doing.

Culture certainly has a role in international relations. All political conflict, whether within states or between them, involves the invocation of history, and of religious texts derived from history, for selective purposes. "Getting its history wrong is part of being a nation," Renan said. While the past does not give the answer to present problems, it can be used to justify whatever position you want to take up today.

But culture rarely has been the basis for conflict in the international system—and is not so now. Indeed, conflict more often has been between states of similar cultural orientation: look at China and Japan, Germany and France, Iran and Iraq. Moreover, cultures are not static or given. They are defined and redefined by each generation, in response to current concerns and by some people at the expense of others. In the Islamic world, the same processes apply as elsewhere: Those in power resort to religion to justify their hold on power or, when people are out of power, to justify their claim to it. In Teheran and Mecca as much as in Washington and Paris, culture is flexible and instrumental. We should be looking at the structures of power and wealth to see in whose interests all this invocation of culture and tradition is working.

Which brings us to the general issue of myth, of what one may term "transnational paranoia." Here again we enter a world both transhistorical and particular: Each country or political culture sees its own tendency in this regard as unique. One can, for example, contrast literature on Islamic political myths with the literature on the paranoid in American politics. The cultures of paranoia have a historical component and historical causes, but their resurgence in the modern world reflects contemporary and transnational factors.

The myth of a deep clash between Islam and the West, on the one hand, confuses what are real and widely felt resentments in the Islamic world with culturally determined confrontation. On the other, it serves to reinforce a broader shift within Western academic and intellectual debate on the character of politics today. A more careful approach—looking at such criteria as state power, coercion and even class—may provide a different explanation, and in doing so, lessen the grip of cultural myths on debate about the contemporary world. Over the past decade, political philosophers have made a mess of analyzing the world. Our duty now may be to bring them down to earth.

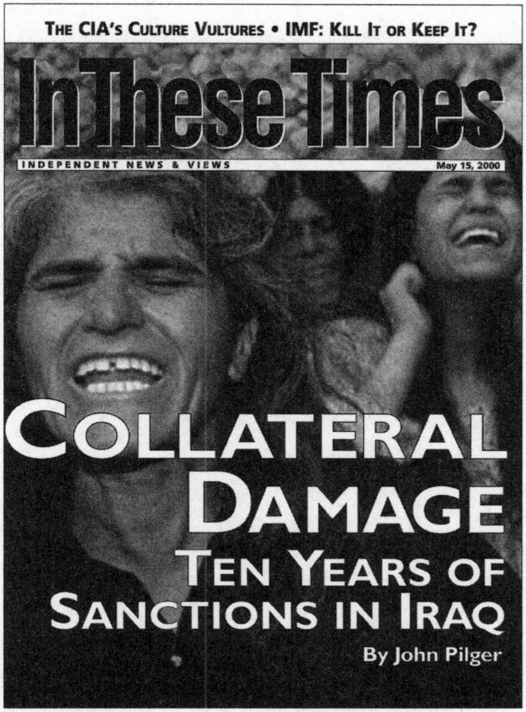

THE CIA'S CULTURE VULTURES • IMF: KILL IT OR KEEP IT?
In These Times
INDEPENDENT NEWS & VIEWS
May 15, 2000
COLLATERAL DAMAGE
TEN YEARS OF SANCTIONS IN IRAQ
By John Pilger

ITT Archives

"We think the price is worth it," said Madeleine Albright.

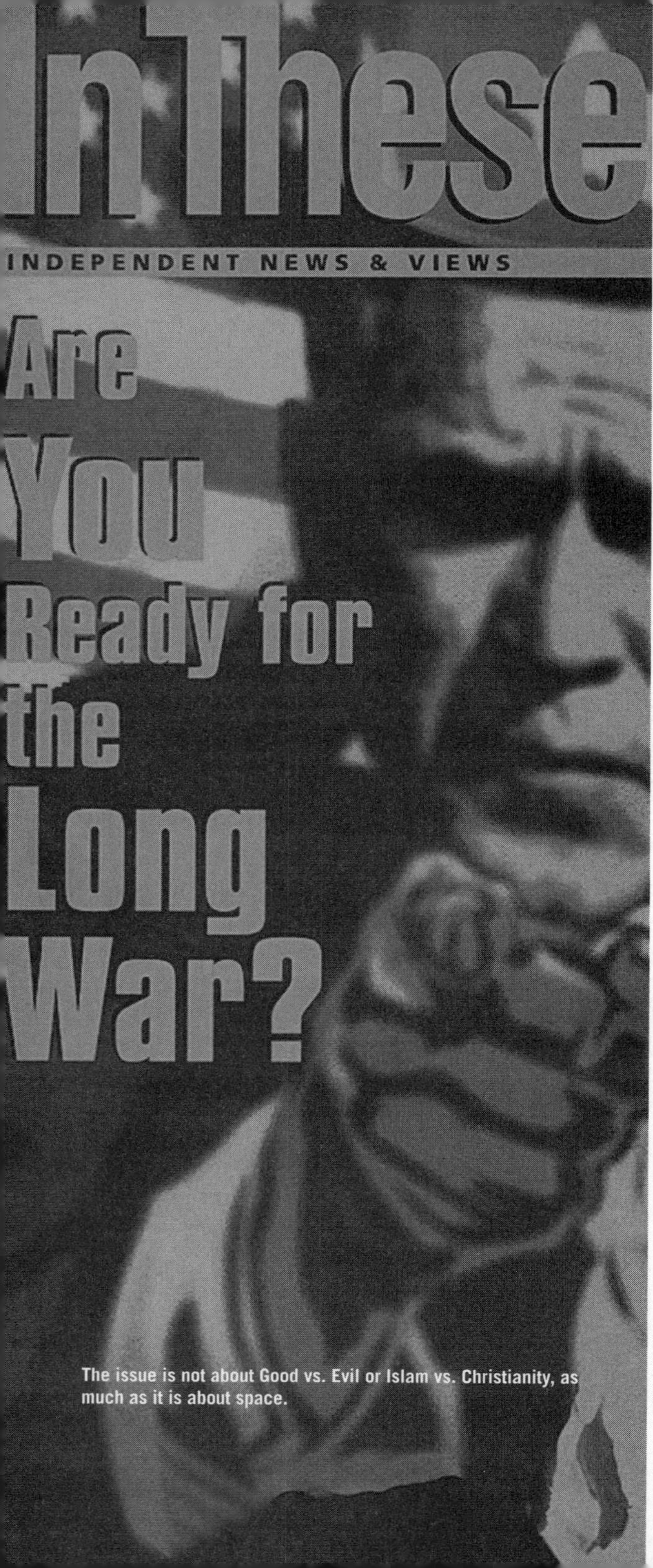
In These
INDEPENDENT NEWS & VIEWS
Are You Ready for the Long War?
The issue is not about Good vs. Evil or Islam vs. Christianity, as much as it is about space.

ITT Archives

False Choices

ARUNDHATI ROY

November 26, 2001

With all due respect to President Bush, the people of the world do not have to choose between the Taliban and the U.S. government. All the beauty of human civilization—our art, our music, our literature—lies beyond these two fundamentalist, ideological poles.

There is as little chance that the people of the world can all become middle-class consumers as there is that they will all embrace any one particular religion. The issue is not about Good vs. Evil or Islam vs. Christianity as much as it is about space. About how to accommodate diversity, how to contain the impulse toward hegemony—economic, military, linguistic, religious and cultural. Any ecologist will tell you how dangerous and fragile a monoculture is. A hegemonic world is like having a government without a healthy opposition. It becomes a kind of dictatorship. It's like putting a plastic bag over the world to prevent it from breathing. Eventually, it will be torn open. . . .

It is important for governments and politicians to understand that manipulating these huge, raging human feelings for their own narrow purposes may yield instant results, but eventually and inexorably will have disastrous consequences. Igniting and exploiting religious sentiments for reasons of political expediency is the most dangerous legacy that governments or politicians can bequeath to any people—including their own. People who live in societies ravaged by religious or communal bigotry know that every religious text—from the Bible to the Bhagavad Gita—can be mined and misinterpreted to justify anything, from nuclear war to genocide to corporate globalization.

This is not to suggest that the terrorists who perpetrated the outrage on September 11 should not be hunted down and brought to book. They must be. But is war the best way to track them down? Will burning the haystack find you the needle? Or will it escalate the anger and make the world a living hell for all of us?

At the end of the day, how many people can you spy on, how many bank accounts can you freeze, how many conversations can you eavesdrop on, how many e-mails can you intercept, how many letters can you open, how many phones can you tap? Even before September 11, the CIA had accumulated more information than is humanly possible to process. (Sometimes, too much data can actually hinder intelligence—small wonder the U.S. spy satellites completely missed the preparation that preceded India's nuclear tests in 1998.) The sheer scale of the surveillance will become a logistical, ethical and civil rights nightmare. And freedom—that precious, precious thing—will be the first casualty. It's already hurt and hemorrhaging dangerously. . . .

In America, the arms industry, the oil industry and the major media networks—indeed, U.S. foreign policy—are all controlled by the same business combines. It would be foolish to expect this talk of guns and oil and defense deals to get any real play in the media. In any case, to a distraught, confused people whose pride has just been wounded, whose loved ones have been tragically killed, whose anger is fresh and sharp, the inanities about the "Clash of Civilizations" and the "Good vs. Evil" discourse home in unerringly. They are cynically doled out by government spokesmen like a daily dose of vitamins or anti-depressants. Regular medication ensures that mainland America continues to remain the enigma it has always been—a curiously insular people administered by a pathologically meddlesome, promiscuous government.

And what of the rest of us, the numb recipients of this onslaught of what we know to be preposterous propaganda? The daily consumers of the lies and brutality smeared in peanut butter and strawberry jam being air-dropped into our minds just like those yellow food packets. Shall we look away and eat because we're hungry, or shall we stare unblinking at the grim theater unfolding in Afghanistan until we retch collectively and say, in one voice, that we have had enough?

As the first year of the new millennium rushes to a close, one wonders—have we forfeited our right to dream? Will we ever be able to reimagine beauty without thinking of the World Trade Center and Afghanistan?

ITT Archives

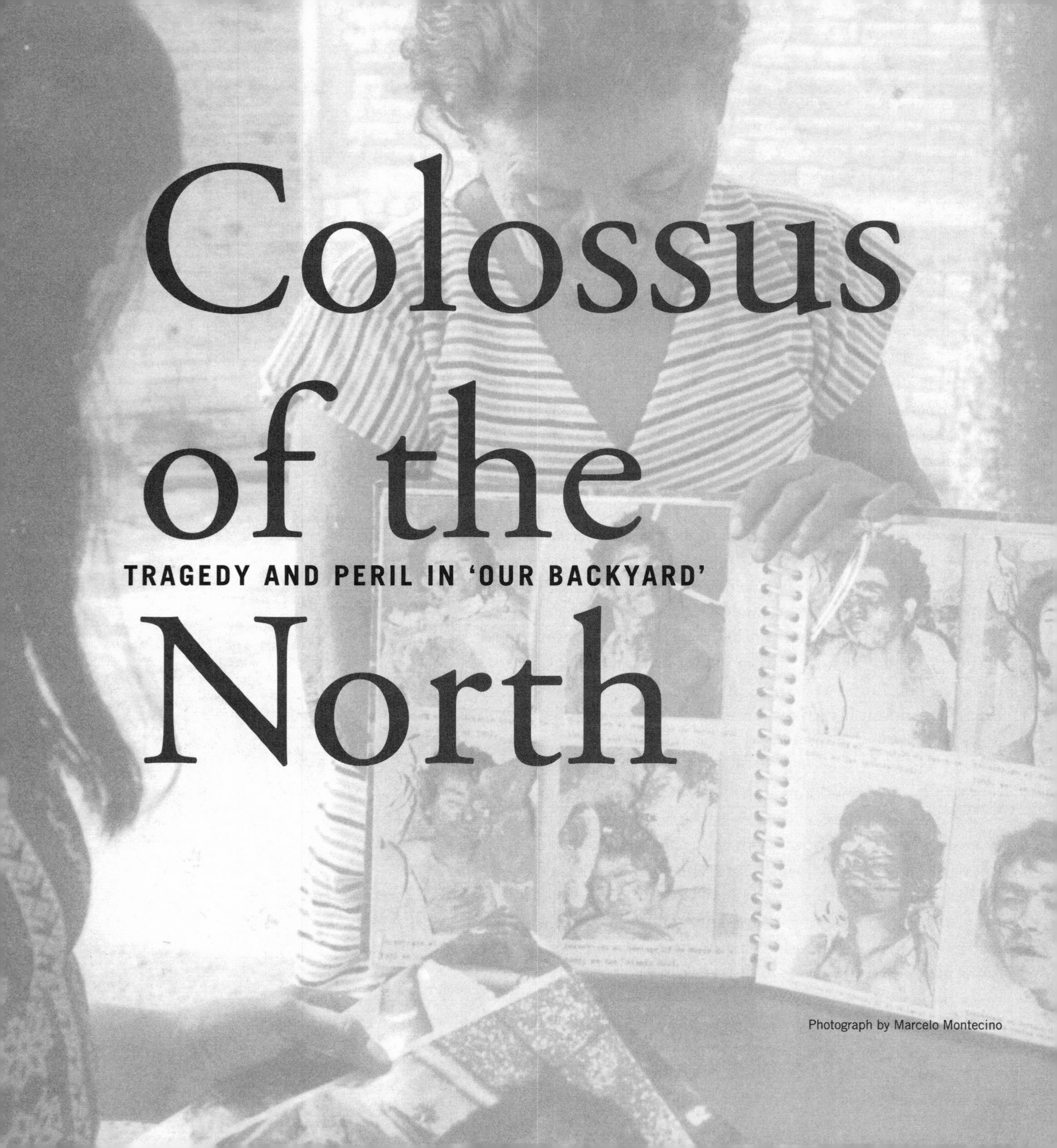

Colossus of the North

TRAGEDY AND PERIL IN 'OUR BACKYARD'

Photograph by Marcelo Montecino

Eighteen

ANA CARRIGAN

FOR MOST OF THE PAST 35 YEARS, I HAVE LIVED ON THAT NARROW ISLAND CALLED MANHATTAN, FROM WHICH PRIVILEGED LOCATION I CLOSELY FOLlowed the aspirations, dreams and nightmares of Latin America. I have traveled and reported in El Salvador, Nicaragua and Panama in the '80s, in Mexico in the '90s, and in my own maternal country, Colombia, since childhood. I have tried, in documentary films and books and articles, to be a translator-interpreter of sorts between two worlds, the northern and the southern, and three cultures, the Anglo, the Latin and the indigenous. What follows is a personal reflection on the complex role of U.S. policy in Latin America, seen from the perspective of someone who has been charting Washington's influence on its closest neighbors for many years, at a moment when it appears the relationship is disintegrating in ways that threaten to be perilous, even tragic, for both parties.

Where do I stand? Neither Che nor Fidel are my icons. Yet I am old enough to remember how it felt, on New Year's Day 1959, dancing in the streets of Bogota, swept up in the joyous fever of excitement and solidarity that raced across the Latin continent like an electric current to greet Castro's arrival in Havana. Castro, then, was the liberator of ideas and concepts far larger in Latin American terms than his own small island nation. When he and his youthful *barbudos* came down from the Sierra Maestra, they unlocked a door in the Latin psyche that released the spirit of "*¡Dignidad!*"—the Latin ideal so intimately wedded to concepts of sovereignty and independence from the overpowering "Colossus of the North."

My Latin American education was intense and radicalizing. Seven years after the Cuban revolution, I discovered in the Andean villages of Peru and Ecuador, the human face of poverty, neglect, racism and isolation. Then I understood who Che had gone to fight for in the

Bolivian mountains and why. In those wretched, filthy mountain villages, where the Indian carriers, chewing coca leaves to deaden their hunger, trudged barefoot through the broken streets, bent double under the weight of their loads, I learned that extreme poverty is a crime against the weakest, most vulnerable members of our common humanity, in the commission of which we are all complicit. I was young and very ignorant. I had gone to work for an Alliance for Progress program run by USAID because I believed in President Kennedy, and I thought his flagship policy for Latin America meant what the words said: an alliance between the rich and powerful North and the poverty-stricken South that would address the single most corrupting feature of their relationship—the vast disparity in political and economic power.

This program was billed as an effort to establish production and marketing cooperatives for Indians who had no access to a market for their beautiful traditional wares, which they sold for cents to a middleman out of a sack on the side of a muddy village street on market day. If any of my bosses had been serious about organizing craft cooperatives, they would have had to confront local business, land and political interests, all opposed to any change that might have dented a closed social system that kept the Indians in serfdom. But the Alliance for Progress was not interested in tackling social change. Thirty years before President Clinton replaced aid with the illusory promise of trade, JFK's program became another middleman, trading Indian crafts from some miserable street in the Andes via elaborate catalogs and commercial showrooms in New York. Everyone, right down to Sears Roebuck and the smallest gift shop in Key West was making money—everyone except the Indians—and I thought then that if I had the guts, I should be going to look for Che. I went north instead. The Indians remained, mired in poverty and despair. When the guns arrived in those sad and angry villages a decade later, they were brought by the monstrous "Shining Path."

Never Surrender

DAVID HELVARG

July 30, 1979

MANAGUA—We found an empty room in the Hotel Intercontinental and tried to go to sleep. Periodically, throughout the night, nervous guardsmen in the bunker next door would open up with their .30- and .50-caliber machine guns. Swarms of bullets sounding like angry wasps flew by the windows, occasionally snapping into the concrete walls and sending cement dust and fragments into the room.

Around 5 a.m., a young, blond German, one of the several mercenaries staying on the second floor, went up to the seventh floor and started robbing people at gunpoint while his drunken Guardia friend waved a bowie knife. Another soldier in civilian dress woke a newsman as he started piling M-16s along one wall of the newsman's room. "Don't worry," he said, "we'll never surrender." . . .

Around first light, we could begin to see men dressed in civilian clothes running away from the bunker. They were soon followed by army truckloads of soldiers in civilian dress, some armed, some not. In the lobby of the hotel and on the front lawn were piles of backpacks, web gear, rifles and grenades. Two men in civvies with M-16s asked me to help push-start their Chevy. In the backseat were the bodies of two dead Guardia and a case of scotch.

As the firing slackened, a group of us ran across the street to the main bunker complex. The gate was deserted. The door to Somoza's office complex was open. We went in. The interior was plush with wood-paneled walls and ceilings hiding a concrete wall. His bed was unmade. Next to it on the nightstand was a book titled *Hombre y Mujer*, a sex manual. His safe was left empty, its door open. A uniform hung on the wall.

In the war room, the phone was ringing, but there was no one there to answer it. In his private

Ten years ago, it seemed that relations between Latin America and the United States were on the threshold of change. The Berlin Wall had fallen. The Reagan administration's proxy interventions in the wars that had ravaged El Salvador and Nicaragua during the '80s had been discredited. Perceived as the final act of the Cold War on the American continent, those wars finally had ended in negotiations. New Latin American democracies had replaced old dictatorships. A Democrat in the White House had proposed a foreign policy agenda centered around economic engagement, and Europe was challenging the United States as the region's dominant economic partner. It appeared that a new era had begun.

Some things did change. One acid test of democracy is independent justice, and the arrest of General Pinochet by a Chilean court is only one of a number of steps—in Argentina, Guatemala, most recently Peru—by judges and prosecutors to apply the rule of law and end political impunity. But in other fundamental ways, obstacles to democracy, peace and economic prosperity are increasing, and the promised change in the relationship between Washington and Latin America is proving illusory. Washington's war on drugs and the deepening American military involvement in Colombia are destabilizing the entire Andean region. Clinton's superficial mantra, "trade not aid," heralded a new approach to economic development that has proved incapable of addressing the crushing, rural poverty that spawns all of Latin Americans' monsters: drugs, guerrillas, paramilitaries, mass rural displacement, soaring urban crime.

Much of Latin America has no goods to trade, and globalization has deepened existing poverty, heightened financial and political instability, and intensified social inequality and corruption. In the region with the highest level of income inequality in the world, the economic reforms of the past decade have benefited a traditional elite, failing to address the deep, structural problems at the core of the shocking

office, the military radio was still operating. Someone was calling his commander but getting no response: "The driver's been hit, over . . . over. . . . He's dying, over . . . over." . . .

The first Sandinista unit, under the command of Comandante Marcos from Leon, arrived at the bunker about 10 A.M. By 11 A.M. an ammunition warehouse had accidentally been set afire and exploding ammunition was shooting off all around the area. Kids who'd never fired a gun before were stripping Guardia positions of guns and ammo and celebrating with wild firing. Red-and-black flags sprouted throughout the city.

Three blocks from the bunker, I ran into my friend Marcio from Leon. "It's good to see you boys alive," he said, hugging me and my photographer, John Hoagland. He told us that our friend Ariel had been killed in combat. "A lot of people have died," he said. "But now with peace, we have a chance to rebuild, you know. That butcher Somoza—you look what he did to his own country, his own people, for what? For greed, for power. But it wasn't enough. We're free now. You know what it means? Free after 47 years. I'm 41, and I've never lived in a free country to call my own. This is the happiest day of my life, not only mine I think, but the whole Nicaraguan people."

Marcelo Montecino

A Sandinista militia on patrol.

imbalance between the haves and the have-nots. Fueled by hunger and a despairing perception that democracy has not delivered on its promises, social unrest and surging lawlessness now threaten the survival of several of the still weak democratic governments. In Washington, meanwhile, the re-emergence in the Bush administration of those responsible for U.S. policies in Central America during the '80s presages a retreading in the footsteps of the past.

Nothing about these developments should be surprising. Whenever Washington policy-makers are asked to define their goals in Latin America, they invariably respond that the United States wants to help "deepen democracy," "bolster respect for the rule of law" and "promote economic growth and stability." But Washington has yet to produce a coherent vision of what policies designed to accomplish these objectives might look like. In its absence, Latin Americans get something quite different: policies that sustain facade democracies in client states and that protect and advance the interests of American corporations—be they United Fruit in the Caribbean, American oil companies in Colombia, or Lockheed-Martin and McDonnell-Douglas in Chile. Sometimes, as in Guatemala in the '50s, Chile in the '70s, Central America in the '80s and Colombia today, Washington has intervened openly to frustrate Latin American efforts to determine their own model for development and take control of their own destinies.

From time to time, prominent American statesmen have defined America's attitude toward Latin America with candor and clarity. Franklin D. Roosevelt's famous statement about Anastasio Somoza, the dictator of Nicaragua—"he may be a son-of-a-bitch, but he's our son-of-a-bitch"—ripped away the mask from the president's own "good neighbor policy." The advice to the American foreign policy establishment of the '50s from eminent American scholar and diplomat

Back in Guatemala Again

ALLAN NAIRN

November 17, 1982

GUATEMALA CITY—Jesse Garcia, a 32-year-old captain in the Green Berets, is an expert in demolitions, combat arms, ambushes and helicopter assault tactics. For two years he commanded an airborne unconventional warfare unit at Fort Bragg, North Carolina.

Since July, Garcia has been posted in Guatemala, a country to which the United States officially sends no military aid. The Pentagon says Garcia is there "as an English teacher." But in a recent four-hour interview and on an armed patrol with 40 Guatemalan officers-in-training, Garcia described himself as a military trainer whose job is "not much different" from that of U.S. advisers in neighboring El Salvador. . . .

Garcia believes that he has come to the frontier of the next major war for the United States. During the interview he predicted that U.S. Green Berets would be fighting in Guatemala within one or two years. He estimated that two combat battalions—about a thousand men committed for a two-year stay—would be needed to do the job.

"Basically," he said. "they would train the government they wanted in power to stay in power and wipe out the opposition." He added that the American troops would serve as a "force multiplier," organizing the Guatemalans into Green Beret-style units and helping lead them into combat.

Garcia predicted a Guatemalan death toll of 50,000, most of them civilians. "It's going to be a big war. Korea in 1950, Vietnam in 1960, Central America in the '80s. And it's all because of Communism."

"The sting of Vietnam is still lingering," Garcia went on, "and it'll never go away. But it's just a matter of what's going to be more important—living with a memory that we can't get away from

George Kennan on how to deal with troublesome Latins is even more revealing. The United States, Kennan said, must never forget, and must constantly ensure that the people of Latin America never forget either, "that we are a great power, and that we need them far less than they need us; that we are prepared to abandon to their fate those [countries] that do not accept the form of collaboration that we propose; that the danger of causing damage to the relationship between us is far greater for them . . . and that it is more important to us that they should respect us, than they should like us, or understand us." Predictably, Kennan's recipe for achieving respect failed. As the Soviet Union discovered in Eastern Europe, the populations of satellite states develop many feelings about the great and powerful who dominate their destiny—fear, envy, anger, contempt—but respect is not one of them.

In Latin America, this dynamic between unequal partners depends on the collaboration of a permanent colonial caste: the rich, American-educated, English-speaking governing elites. Alienated from the majority of their own countrymen and women by reason of their wealth and foreign avocation, Latin America's ruling caste has far more in common with the global community in the developed world than with their own struggling populations. Endowed with a business degree from Harvard or Yale, standard equipment for Latin leaders, they feel far more comfortable in Paris or New York, on Wall Street or Fifth Avenue, than in some small, tropical, regional municipality in their own country, where most of the citizens, whose interests they claim to represent, strive to purchase a precarious toe-hold on modernity without losing what they value most: their connection to a shared, communal history and a multifaceted, complex culture, rooted in geography, climate and ethnicity.

Holding the exclusive on interpretation of their societies for Washington, Latin rulers have perfected the skills required to "accept"—and perpetuate—what Kennan deftly referred to as "the form of collaboration that we

or stopping something that's like a train coming down toward us . . . the Communist Express. How can we afford to lose Central America? We couldn't afford to lose South Vietnam."

ITT Archives

Guillermo, a Salvadoran refugee, found "sanctuary" at an Iowa church.

Sanctuary in the Heartland

BETH MASCHINOT

April 24, 1985

CEDAR RAPIDS, IOWA—The world goes by as Cedar Rapids watches unperturbed: that is how the people at Faith United Methodist Church portray their city. In fact, on April 14, the day that Faith United was publicly greeting Guillermo, a Salvadoran refugee who had come to the church for sanctuary, the Cedar Rapids press, and most of the city, ignored the event.

But Faith United's 77 members turned out in full force, along with another 80 people from neighboring churches in Mt. Vernon, Iowa City and Clinton. The stark church was packed as 20-year-old Guillermo told why he fled El Salvador. "In 1979, they killed my dad," he said. "He was coming home from work five minutes after curfew. The National Guard stopped him and beat him savagely. Finally, they ripped him up with a machine gun. . . . Two years later, they killed my mom. She was coming from the country to sell vegetables in the city. The

National Guard ransacked the vegetables, throwing them everywhere. Then they beat her and laughed, saying, 'Communist, tell me where the camp of your guerrilla friends is.' Finally, they poured gasoline on her and set her on fire." . . .

Faith United's members—mostly blue-collar and service workers with a sprinkling of professionals, including a few engineers at defense contractor Rockwell International—seem well aware of Guillermo's and their own risks. They've discussed sanctuary for more than a year. And before that, two years of Pastor Gil Dawes' preaching and two years of Bible study—an open forum for debate on current issues with a reflection on a biblical passage—had politicized the congregation.

Now there's a sense of common purpose that didn't exist before. But the calm has not precluded lively and often conflictive debate. Scores of Catholic missionaries who've worked in Central America have trooped through Faith United's doors, and often they contradict the mainstream media's version of the conflicts there. Church member Norma LeMaster says she still does not consider herself a "political person." But now she believes that there are two sides to every Central American question. And increasingly she thinks that "Gil and all the others we've heard who've seen it first-hand can't be all wrong."

Prisoner #01579-017

FATHER ROY BOURGEOIS

April 29, 1992

TALLAHASSEE, FLORIDA—Hundreds of Salvadoran soldiers, along with troops from Guatemala, Honduras, Bolivia, Colombia and seven other Latin American countries are now being trained

propose." When faced with the chaotic legacy of their corrupt and incompetent administrations, they have always turned to the Colossus for help to maintain control over their excluded, restless populations.

The most depressing feature of U.S. diplomacy in Latin America is that neither its imperial nature, nor its reliance on military solutions to complicated social and political problems, ever changes. For 100 years, U.S. policy has been driven by a bipartisan consensus that considers the countries of the Southern Hemisphere a potential threat to America's national security interests. At the height of the Cold War, Washington's fears of regional communist infiltration were well founded, as demonstrated by the 1962 Cuban Missile Crisis. Times have changed, but the notion that the United States is preordained to maintain a Latin American "Pax Americana," subservient to the priorities of Washington's political agenda, long predates Castro and has been unaffected by the end of the Cold War. From Theodore Roosevelt to George W. Bush, Washington's fear and distrust of Latin sovereignty and determination to maintain the Southern Hemisphere within America's exclusive sphere of influence and control, has provided justification for grievous distortions and betrayals of dearly held American principles. The American ideal, intended to balance moral purpose with U.S. interests, has not traveled well south of the Rio Grande.

To recover the pattern that recurs in Washington's relations with the Latin world, it helps to return to the feverish political debates that swept America in the last decade of the 19th century when, from the contest between the imperialists and the anti-imperialists, the concept of "Manifest Destiny" provided justification for a new spirit of American expansionism and militarism. In 1823, when President James Monroe drafted the doctrine that defined the Southern Hemisphere as an exclusive sphere of American interest, he introduced the metaphor that still encapsulates U.S. perceptions of its southern neighbors: "our backyard."

The Monroe Doctrine lay dormant until 1895, when President Cleveland pressured England to abandon its interests in Venezuela. With Britain out of the way, in 1898 the United States went to war with Spain over Cuba. There followed, in quick succession: the duplicitous annexation of Hawaii; the decision to transfer the sovereignty of the Philippines from Spain to the United States (which led to America's first counter-insurgency war against the rebel forces of a small nation struggling for independence); the annexation of Puerto Rico; and the establishment of a virtual American protectorate in Cuba. By the summer of 1898, America's imperial conduct, which still distorts the North-South relationship, had been established.

Though not without opposition. In 1898, on the eve of the Senate vote on the treaty with Spain, former President Cleveland and a group of 23 prominent Americans addressed a last-minute petition to the Senate seeking to halt the annexation of the Philippines and Puerto Rico. "In accordance with the principles upon which our Republic was founded" the petition read, "we are in duty bound to recognize the rights of the inhabitants . . . to independence and self-government." The Senate ratified the treaty, unaltered, by a single vote.

But as the debate over the treaty's fateful consequences escalated, half a million people joined the ranks of the Anti-Imperialist League, founded by an eminent group of intellectuals centered around Harvard University. Writing in the *Boston Evening Transcript*, William James proclaimed that America was now "openly engaged in crushing out the sacredest thing in this great human world, the attempt of a people long enslaved" to win their freedom and establish their own destiny. Harvard Professor Charles Eliot Norton, who had led the anti-imperialist forces from the start, wrote, "America has lost her unique position as leader in the progress of civilization, and has taken up her place simply as one of the grasping

ITT Archives

Salvadoran Bishop Oscar Romero.

at Fort Benning's School of the Americas (SOA). Established in Panama in 1946, the SOA has taught more than 54,000 officers and enlisted men to serve right-wing governments throughout Latin America.

Distinguished graduates of the SOA include: Manuel Noriega, former president of Panama; Gen. Hugo Banzer, former Bolivian dictator; Gen. Hector Gramajo, retired Guatemalan defense minister; and Maj. Joseph-Michel Francois, the Haitian chief of police who played a key role in the recent coup that ousted Jean-Bertrand Aristide. In 1984, when the school was forced out of Panama and relocated to Georgia, Panamanian President Jorge Illueca described the SOA as "the biggest base of destabilization in Latin America."

The foundation of the course work at the SOA is low-intensity conflict, which by military analyst Michael Klare's definition is "that amount of murder, mutilation, torture, rape and savagery that is sustainable without triggering widespread public disapproval at home." U.S. military instructors teach their soldier students that the enemy is not just an opposing force. Rather, the enemy can include anyone, armed or unarmed, who threatens political stability. Upon graduation, the soldiers return home and put their lessons into practice. Priests, nuns, teachers, union leaders and human rights advocates are among the victims of an SOA-inspired education. . . .

On September 3, 1990, 10 of us—Vietnam veterans, Salvadorans, a teacher and members of the clergy—began a water-only fast at the entrance of Fort Benning to protest the training of Salvadoran soldiers. When our fast ended after 35 days, our bodies were weak, but our spirits remained strong. On November 16, when we had recovered from the fast, three of us—Charles Liteky, a former Army chaplain who had received the Medal of Honor for heroism in Vietnam; his brother Patrick, who had trained at Fort Benning; and I—returned to Fort Benning to observe the first anniversary of the brutal murder of six Jesuit priests and two women at the Central American University in San Salvador by soldiers trained at the SOA.

We entered the post, placed a white cross with photos of the eight martyrs at the entrance of the School of Americas, and poured blood in one of the school's main halls. We wanted to impress on our country that we cannot wash our hands of the blood of innocent people killed in El Salvador by soldiers trained by the United States. . . .

Here at the federal prison in Tallahassee, we have 1,300 inmates living together in close quarters. Everyone has his own story to tell. "Was it worth it?" I am often asked by my fellow

and selfish nations of the present day." And Moorfield Storey, a former president of the American Bar Association, lamented: "We are false to all we have believed in. This great free land which for more than a century has offered a refuge to the oppressed of every land, has now turned to oppression."

Conquest and domination were never supposed to be the American way. The schism that split the United States at the turn of the last century revealed the tension between two Americas—the imperial country of global, hegemonic ambitions, and the country that harks back to the principles that gave birth to the original American dream. In the elections of 1900, American voters chose expansion, conquest and Theodore Roosevelt. As the American Century began, the forces of anti-imperialism were consigned to the past. Yet their legacy, and the schism in the American public psyche generated by their dedication to the original, democratic principles of the founding fathers, has survived. Among the populations of the client states of the victorious imperialist tradition, awareness of the enduring vitality of that schism offers a solitary space for hope that, at some future day, the Colossus will release its choke hold on their destiny.

Once, in the early days of the war in El Salvador, I believed that America's policy of recurring intervention would cease. In December 1980, four American churchwomen, three Catholic nuns and a young lay missionary, went missing in El Salvador. Two days after their disappearance, their bodies were recovered in an unmarked grave with evidence of their execution-style murders by a Salvadoran death squad.

At the time of their death, the women were working in the diocese of El Salvador's Oscar Romero, helping refugees flee the war in the rural north, where the Salvadoran army was carrying out a scorched-earth policy. As the military intensified the repression of its own people, the women's humanitarian work, and their intimate knowledge of the local situation, caused them to be perceived by the Salvadoran generals as a threat to continued U.S. military aid. Each journey the women made into the countryside to help frightened, hungry families trapped in the eye of a gathering storm, drew them deeper into Salvador's heart of darkness.

The fields and roadsides of El Salvador at that time were littered with the corpses of anonymous death squad killings. The "anonymous" was a lie, a mask to shield an American policy that supported the killers. But these were the first American citizens to be killed by America's allies. And they were women. And nuns. When the women's bodies were found, I was convinced Washington would be forced to cut off military aid to the government whose security forces had killed them.

It took 10 years and 50,000 more deaths before U.S. military assistance finally stopped. The Salvadoran FMLN guerrillas fought on to rid their country of a feudal elite that could not have survived for six months without America's military support. The United States spent $6 billion propping up the murderous Salvadoran security forces. The infamous Atlacatl Brigade, responsible for the most savage massacres of the war, was created from zero at the U.S. Army's School of the Americas and equipped with the latest American weaponry. Only when men of the Atlacatl dragged five Jesuit priests from their beds in the dawn hours of November 16, 1989, and blew out their brains on the campus grounds of the Jesuit University of Central America, did Congress finally pull the plug, and the war came to an inglorious end.

Today, the Pentagon has a different version of that dreadful history. According to the Pentagon, American military assistance transformed the Salvadoran army into a professional fighting force, respectful of human rights and the rule of law. By forcing the guerrillas to lay down their arms and negotiate from a position of weakness, the army hastened peace and restored Salvadoran democracy. The war in El Salvador has now emerged as the Pentagon's new model for all future "counter-insurgency" conflicts.

inmates and friends on the outside. Let me say that prison is hard, lonely and humbling—even with the support of family and friends, who also suffer. My Dad cried when I called home to tell him of my sentencing.

Yet I did what my faith and the poor demanded of me in the face of such violence, death and suffering. Like the Salvadoran people, I reached a point where I had to say, "*Basta!*"

Eyes on the Prize

DAN LA BOTZ

September 5, 1994

CHIAPAS, MEXICO—As the sun set, Subcomandante Marcos, the now famous mestizo spokesman for the Zapatistas' indigenous army, appeared on the amphitheater stage. Along with an indigenous leader of the EZLN, Comandante Tacho, he welcomed the delegates. Reverting to the poetic speech that has filled his widely published communiqués from Chiapas, Marcos explained that the meeting site had a been "a fort, a bunker, an armament factory, a military training center, an arms depot." But now it was transformed into "Noah's Ark, a Tower of Babel, the woodland ship of Fitzcarraldo, the raving neo-Zapatismo, the pirate ship."

The EZLN had literally carved Aguascalientes out of the jungle. The soldiers had cut down trees on a hillside to create the amphitheater. And the fallen trees served as benches, while dozens of tarps were sewn together to cover an area the size of a football field. After greeting the delegates, Marcos told the convention to do its duty, to come up with a strategy for achieving a democratic Mexico, so that the EZLN would not have to return to the armed struggle. . . .

A Zapatista mural in Chiapas.

A contingent of EZLN soldiers marched before the delegates. The crowd sat in awed silence, watching the soldiers pass by, shaking their heads at the little .22 rifles and ancient shotguns carried by the EZLN troops. What was impressive was certainly not the military might of this outfit, but the audacity and imagination of these soldiers who had seized the political initiative from the perfect dictatorship.

If there had been some feeling that Marcos and the EZLN were perhaps a throwback to the Communist guerrilla movements of the '70s, that idea was dismissed when Marcos displayed the Mexican flag. . . . The entire convention then sang the Mexican national anthem.

Historical fictions can be dangerous. This one now justifies Washington's agenda in Colombia, where the Pentagon is conducting a crash program to train and equip the Colombian army to pursue the identical goals the Reagan administration carried our in El Salvador. What's now at stake in Colombia is a "Pax Americana" designed to keep the local establishment in power and to permit the expansion of American interests. In Colombia, however, such a solution will be unattainable at any acceptable price, and its pursuit threatens to ignite a regional war across the Andes.

Thirty-five years after the Alliance for Progress abandoned the Peruvian villages, there are still no schools, no clinics, no roads, no doctors, no teachers, no weaving or knitting cooperatives, no communal pottery kilns, bakeries or chicken hatcheries, and no access to markets. There is no shortage of guns, however. Guns and guerrillas, guns and drugs, guns and paramilitaries, guns and American-trained Special Forces, guns and army battalions, helicopter gunships even.

Now, in these desolate Andean villages, American policies, ostensibly focused on the eradication of drug crops, are setting the fuse on a time bomb. This time bomb is the Andean Regional Initiative—the Bush administration's expanded version of President Clinton's $1.3 billion package for combating drugs and guerrillas in Colombia. Eighty percent of "Plan Colombia" funding went to the Colombian army. It included helicopter gunships and U.S. Special Forces training for three new "counter-narcotics" battalions to accompany American-flown crop dusters, fumigating coca fields in guerrilla held territory. Twenty percent of the funding was supposed to help the affected coca farmers switch to alternative crops, but this money has yet to reach its intended beneficiaries.

In response to demands from Colombia's neighbors for protection against the anticipated fallout from Washington's Colombia policy, the Bush administration has increased funding for a further two years and extended military aid around the region. But as dollars for training and equipment start flowing to Ecuador, Bolivia, Peru, Venezuela, Panama and Brazil, they too risk being drawn into a quagmire. In Bolivia and Ecuador, hungry Indian farmers are joining new guerrilla divisions to fight a patriotic war alongside the Colombian FARC rebels against American intervention. In Peru, where years of U.S. support for the sleazy duo of President Alberto Fujimori and his henchman Vladimiro Montesinos confirmed Latin suspicions of American complicity in dirty war repression and corruption, rural poverty has again opened a space for the "Shining Path" guerrillas; drug crops are once more flourishing in Peruvian fields.

If we want to avoid a reprise of the El Salvador war in Colombia, it is crucial that today's anti-imperialists mobilize to radically alter Washington's priorities. The policies of the last decade are in disarray. The Pentagon's millions have neither professionalized Latin American security forces, nor promoted more democratic and stable societies. The drug war is a catastrophe. To tackle the hemisphere-wide crises of drugs, disease, crime and instability, the United States must initiate a massive effort to eradicate the underlying cause—horrendous poverty. Three concrete steps could start a process that would transform the U.S.-Latin American relationship.

First, the Bush administration must increase American aid. With the exception of Chile, average economic growth across the hemisphere in the past decade has been insufficient to help 78 million Latin Americans living in poverty. America's aid budget, over the same period, has fallen to a scandalous 0.1 percent of GDP. This represents the lowest share of any country in the 22-member Organization for Economic Cooperation and Development and is derisory when compared to the 0.8 percent of GDP the United States gave in the '60s. Bolstering American aid should be the priority of any

The U.S. Embargo and the Wrath of God

JUAN GONZALEZ

March 8, 1998

HAVANA—Gilberto Durán Torres couldn't devote much attention to Pope John Paul II's historic visit here in January. While Cuban television and thousands of foreign journalists recorded the pope's every move, Durán and the other doctors at Calixto García Hospital, Cuba's largest and most prestigious medical center, spent another hair-raising week quietly concocting their own miracles—a string of patchwork procedures to keep their patients alive.

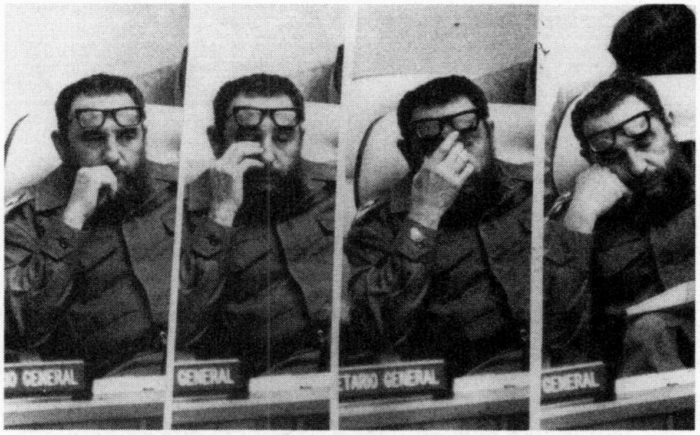

ITT Archives

Fidel Castro's influence spread far beyond his small island nation.

Durán is chief of the intermediate care unit. He has worked at the hospital for 25 years, but nowadays he watches helplessly as the country's awesome cradle-to-grave, free medical system slowly disintegrates. Durán's department, for instance, is making do with artificial respirators that are more than 20 years old. "We should have at least 12 for my unit," he says. "We have far fewer, and they are always breaking down. When one goes, we don't have the parts to fix it, so we have to search around

ITT Archives

Can the U.S. embargo survive much longer?

the city, find a hospital that's not using theirs, and transport it here."

So much of the world's advanced medical equipment and drugs are manufactured by U.S. firms that the three-decade-old American embargo is now literally killing Cubans. . . .

Nothing has drawn the Catholic Church and the Cuban government closer together than their mutual opposition to the U.S. blockade of medicine and food supplies to Cuba's people. "Even in warfare, you don't bomb hospitals and schools," says Patrick Sullivan, the pastor of a church in Santa Clara and the only American priest permanently stationed in the country.

A Cuban official in charge of finding and paying for food from abroad recounted her frustration with the embargo. "To ship a thousand tons of powdered milk from New Zealand, I must pay $150,000, when bringing the same amount from Miami would only cost me $25,000," she says.

While the U.S. government forces Cuba to pay six times more than necessary for children to drink

American administration interested in preserving democratic governments, for unless living standards are significantly increased and shocking levels of inequality reduced, a number of regional democracies will not survive the next decade.

Second, the dollars for Plan Colombia and the Andean Regional Initiative should be redirected to put American muscle and money behind land-reform programs and infrastructure for sustainable rural development. Suppose, for a moment, that a broad coalition—similar to the American human rights and religious groups who opposed the Reagan administration's Central American policies in the '80s—were to mobilize behind an imaginative blueprint to convert America's drug war into a war on poverty. Think what such a transformation would mean: tractors and road-building equipment would replace the helicopter gunships; doctors, agronomists, anthropologists and school teachers would take over from the counter-narcotics battalions; instead of American-trained "Rambos" spreading death and destruction, Andean villagers would get the experts they need to identify sustainable, small-enterprise projects and gain access to micro-credit lending programs.

This is an ambitious but attainable scenario. The World Bank, the U.N. Development Program and the Inter-American Bank have the expertise to carry it out. Only the leadership, the political will and the vision are lacking. Such a program would require an immediate halt to the aerial fumigation of drug crops, and the substitution of manual eradication programs with the collaboration and manpower of peasant growers. Aerial fumigation has not reduced the flow of cocaine and heroin to American cities, but it has fomented rebellion, deepened poverty and increased rural violence and displacement. Fumigation of drug crops in Colombia has strengthened the guerrillas and paramilitaries, and it has spread the Colombian drug plague to previously unaffected regions of Ecuador, Brazil and the Amazon rain forest. It is wreaking environmental havoc in the Amazon basin and undermining democracy in countries with fragile civilian institutions and long histories of military intervention in the political order.

An explosion is brewing in the Andes, which, once detonated, will not be containable. Dreadful and destructive though the conflicts in Central America were, Colombia is *sui generis*. War in Colombia has the potential to engulf the entire northern tier of the southern continent, and risks unleashing a humanitarian disaster on a scale never seen on this continent. There is no time to lose.

Since September 11, in Latin America as elsewhere in the poor southern countries, hopes for a change in Washington's policies have been all but extinguished. Henry Kissinger was the first Washington insider to identify the full scope and purpose of the new war on terrorism. Writing in the *Los Angeles Times*, Kissinger defined the newest challenge to American foreign policy: "The war on terrorism is not just about hunting down terrorists. It is, above all, to protect the extraordinary opportunity that has come about to recast the international system."

It is only a matter of time before a new front in this war opens in the Southern Hemisphere. The Southern Command has spent a decade training Latin American militaries and preparing for a regional anti-terrorist campaign. From Puerto Rico to the Amazon and beyond, the Pentagon's most sophisticated high-tech intelligence and weaponry, the battalions of Latin Rambos trained by U.S. Special Forces, and the strategically located bases are all in place. So is the enemy. "The most dangerous terrorist group in the hemisphere" is how Francis Taylor, the State Department's senior anti-terrorism official, characterized the FARC before Congress after September 11. FARC, the ELN and their bitterest enemies, the right-wing paramilitaries, all feature on the State Department's terrorist list. Since September 11, the Colombian government and the FARC have gone back to war, and the government has been lobbying for increased military aid.

milk and shuts off the supply for medical screening tests, it scurries to sell more Boeing planes to China, to open new Nike factories in Vietnam and even finds ways to ship food to North Korea. The last time anybody looked, these were socialist countries too, at least in name.

After all his homilies criticizing the lack of individual freedom and the evils of communism, the 77-year-old pope, no less a dictator within his church than the 71-year-old Castro is within his party, still managed in his parting words to condemn the U.S. embargo for striking "the population indiscriminately, making it ever more difficult for the weakest to enjoy the bare essentials of decent living."

Washington's embargo has now incurred the wrath of God. Can it hope to survive much longer?

Peter Hannan

An explosion is brewing in the Andes.

Until now, no matter how bad things were abroad, the domestic protections of American democracy and freedoms were sacred. So long as that other America existed, it offered a model, an ideal, that held out hope for a better future. But George W. Bush and John Ashcroft have discarded that bright, shining model. They have responded to American fears of terrorism with measures characteristic of a police state. The erosion of American laws and civil liberties sends a terrible message, one that governments around the hemisphere have been quick to understand as they scramble to draft their own draconian anti-terror legislation. Local human rights defenders are deeply alarmed, for they too understand the message. Constructed around the bedrock principles of the Bill of Rights, the civil liberties so adroitly ambushed by Bush and Ashcroft are the original principles of American democracy—that schism in the American psyche which gives others hope. What is to become of American society—and that hope—if these protections disappear?

In September 1939, on the brink of another worldwide conflagration, W. H. Auden wrote:

> Defenseless under the night
> Our world in stupor lies;
> Yet dotted everywhere
> Ironic points of light
> Flash out wherever the just
> Exchange their messages

As Auden took solace from those exchanges between "the just," we too must begin the search for our own points of light. We must create a space where, in a thoughtful context, we can address the serious questions about poverty and global injustice; about corrupt governments that masquerade as "democracies" with American support; of Washington's complicity in the state terrorism employed by its allies; the questions, in short, that will help us understand the underlying causes of terrorism.

Finally, we need to listen to those voices who are trying to reach out and open a dialogue with us across the gulf of our ignorance and indifference. The Egyptian novelist Adhaf Soeif could be speaking for Latin Americans when he writes, "The nation that once said, 'give me your poor, your weak, your hungry,' needs to look at itself through the eyes of the world's dispossessed."

It would be a good starting point.

In Colombia, the Pentagon is now pursuing the identical goals the Reagan administration carried out in El Salvador during the '80s.

ITT Archives

Big Stick Shtick

MICHAEL MOORE

September 2, 1987

INDIANAPOLIS—The United States overran Nicaragua this month, totally obliterating the tiny Central American nation. Within a matter of hours, the Nicaraguans were entirely stripped of any defense. It was annihilation of the likes of which have never been seen in this hemisphere.

Fortunately, it was just a baseball game.

The Sandinistas were clobbered by the United States, 18-0, in a game that was called after the seventh inning when the officials invoked the seldom-used "mercy rule," the sports equivalent of "enough already!" after one team is so far ahead it looks like a football score.

The unlikely setting for this meeting between the United States and Nicaragua was not the back forty of a recently firebombed Esteli medical clinic, but Bush Stadium in Indianapolis, site of the 10th Pan-American Games. . . .

The game of baseball is as American as Marines in Nicaragua. So it made sense that during a series of U.S. invasions and occupations of Nicaragua in the first two decades of this century, the Marines taught the Nicaraguans how to play baseball. Soon it became their national pastime, and the dictator Somoza fielded an all-star team that played local teams throughout the country. It was at these games that the peasants had their only chance to vent hostility toward Somoza by cheering on the home team. With the Sandinista victory in 1979, the repression ended, but the enthusiasm for baseball remained.

The Nicaraguan team was being housed and fed at the local U.S. Army base, Fort Benjamin Harrison, which gave the visiting press corps much to chortle about. Being surrounded by the U.S. military was nothing out of the ordinary for these players, though, and most remarked that they felt "right at home." . . .

The United States, unfortunately, didn't send the Contras to play ball for them in Indianapolis and opened up the first inning with a barrage of runs. When the Nicaraguans, who were ironically designated as the "home team," came to bat in the bottom of the first, they were unable to score off the American pitcher (and Flint, Michigan, native) Jim Abbott, who was born with only one hand.

That's the way the rest of the game went, with the U.S. coach ordering double steals even after his team was ahead 12-0. When the slaughter was finally called to an early end by the umpire in the seventh inning, Roberto Vargas of the Nicaraguan Olympic Committee commented that "the game was like sitting through the last three months of the Iran-Contra hearings."

All was not lost, though, as the Nicaraguans were winning, at considerable cost, the real-life competition for survival at home. The U.S. mercenary force still did not hold one inch of ground after five years of war, and the American public still opposed aid to the Contras. As one fan in the stands remarked after the game, "One thing's for sure: The peace process in Central America has a better chance of succeeding than the Nicaraguans had here today."

Armageddon It

NUCLEAR DANGERS PAST AND PRESENT

Photograph from ITT Archives

Nineteen

JASON VEST

THE YEAR 2001 WILL INDEED BE REMEMBERED AS THE YEAR A SPACE ODYSSEY COMMENCED, BUT UNLESS THE STARCHILD LOOKS TO EARTH'S orbit in search of lethal playthings, there won't be much overlap with Arthur C. Clarke's novel or Stanley Kubrick's film. Or will there? Fuse the delusionally murderous HAL 9000 with an apocalyptic player from *Dr. Strangelove,* and there are at least vague parallels between the stuff of fantasy (General Jack D. Ripper) and reality (Defense Secretary Donald Rumsfeld). Doubtless there are some who would characterize this view as both hyperbolic and hysterical. But there's the rub: The people George W. Bush has restored to the defense and disarmament establishment hail from a milieu where gross exaggeration and jingoistic fear-mongering are perpetually plied in the service of a philosophy that borders on the insane.

Twenty-five years ago, the denizens of this province held that defense policy should revolve around a massive nuclear buildup and active opposition to arms-control agreements, as the United States supposedly had let itself be outgunned by the Soviet colossus. Indeed, to hear these Armageddonists talk, nuclear conflict was inevitable; as Eugene Rostow—the man Reagan appointed to head the Arms Control and Disarmament Agency—wrote in a letter during Reagan's ascension, "We are living in a pre-war, and not a post-war, world."

Not to worry, another official of the same agency reassured us. Despite a close encounter with massive atomic megatonnage, it was possible for "any society" to survive nuclear war. (Semaphore signal: The Soviets could weather a nuclear holocaust, too—more money to the defense budget!) Indeed, Thomas K. Jones, then a senior Pentagon official, held that survival was simple: All you needed to do was "dig a hole, cover it with a couple of doors and then throw

Underground testing at Los Alamos.

Nuclear Backlash

MARK HERTSGAARD

December 19, 1979

Atop the posh St. Francis Hotel, the General Electric executive searched the lights of San Francisco for some way to describe the new mood that had come over the nuclear industry since this spring's Three Mile Island accident. "I think these guys," he gestured to a roomful of industry honchos crowded into GE's Hospitality Suite, "are tired of being kicked around. After Three Mile Island, they're ready to stand up and fight."

It was the first evening of the annual Atomic Industrial Forum (AIF), and the mood was festive, feisty and determined. . . .

The room grew quiet when Westinghouse boss Robert Kirby stood up to deliver the most important speech of the conference. It was significant that he spoke himself rather than sending one of his lieutenants. The senators and, later, the scientists could rally the troops. Kirby would provide them with a battle plan.

With the help of a slide projector, Kirby quickly linked nuclear power with America's national security. He called the '70s "the age of imminent oil catastrophe." Onto the screen flashed a global map. A thin white line stretching from the United

three feet of dirt on top. If there are enough shovels around, everybody's going to make it."

But then nuclear war was never really about the potential of total annihilation, our executive leadership insisted, but about playing the great game of nations. "I've always worried less about what would happen in an actual nuclear exchange than the effect that the nuclear balance has on our willingness to take risks in local situations," Cold War ideologue Richard Perle told the *Los Angeles Times'* Robert Scheer in 1981, summing up the dominant Reagan administration philosophy. "It is not that I'm worried about the Soviets attacking the United States with nuclear weapons, confident that they will win the that nuclear war. It is that I worry about an American president feeling he cannot afford to take action in a crisis because Soviet nuclear forces are such that, if escalation took place, they are better poised than we are to move up the escalation ladder."

More than a decade after the end of the Cold War, Perle and his compatriots should have been dispatched to the dustbin of history. But thanks to the graces of George W. Bush, this gang—Perle, Donald Rumsfeld, Paul Wolfowitz, Douglas Feith, J.D. Crouch, Paula Dobriansky, Dov Zakheim and Robert Joseph, to name but a few—has been restored to national security officialdom. Uncritically accepted by the Washington press corps, the strange history of this milieu has been largely neglected. This is all the more troubling given that the Pentagon seems obsessed with pouring billions of taxpayer dollars down the National Missile Defense drain and abandoning a variety of arms control treaties—at a moment, after the September 11 terrorist attacks on New York and Washington, that has exposed the utter folly of this insatiable boondoggle.

Ironically enough, the current defense junta truly began to come into its own just about the time *In These Times* started publishing. Like the self-declared pious elite of old, these arch-conservative, anti-communist crusaders established their own aristocratic league of ideological activism, an Order of Malta for the "pre-war" world: The Committee on the Present Danger.

The original Committee on the Present Danger, founded in 1950, redefined the nascent U.S. approach to the Soviet Union by subverting the containment policy originally advocated by diplomat George Kennan. Famous for his ruminative and gloomy diplomatic dispatches about the future of the USSR, Kennan called for containment of the Soviet bloc through diplomacy, not militarism. But after the explosion of the Soviet bomb in 1949, President Truman ordered a review of Soviet policy. The men of the first CPD produced a document known as NSC-68, which scrapped Kennan's more circumspect approach in favor of a policy promoting profligate military expansion, fused with the same fanaticism ascribed to the Soviets. Principally authored by Paul Nitze, NSC-68 argued that the United States must use "the same Soviet Cold War technique against the Soviet Union."

Once we had seen the enemy and realized he was us, the first CPD disbanded. But its spirit was carried forward by the emerging military-industrial complex, whose ideology emanated from Santa Monica, California—home of the RAND Corporation. Originally a shop in the Hughes Aircraft empire, RAND—shorthand for research and development—became a cerebral playground for defense intellectuals, whose research was (and still is) underwritten by the Defense Department. An institution devoted to "thinking about the unthinkable," it's hard to underestimate the influence RAND had on the scientific and policy development of the Cold War, nurturing the intellects of men such as future defense secretaries Harold Brown and James Schlesinger, Pentagon advisers Daniel Ellsberg and Andrew Marshall, and influential theorists Herman Kahn and Albert Wohlstetter, among others.

States to the Middle East illustrated the fragility of America's energy supplies.

"Russian bases and Russian ships are located strategically so that they can cut the bulk of our overseas oil supplies in hours," Kirby warned. The second that Kirby uttered the word "Russian," a gigantic, blood-red hammer and sickle exploded onto the screen, blotting out America's oil lifeline. Under today's conditions, Kirby continued, "imposing any moratorium on nuclear power, a source of oil independence, is absolutely ludicrous."

The Cold War theatrics hint at just how angry and threatened the nuclear industry feels, and how forcefully it plans to strike back. As the plenary session continued, it was clear that the corporations perceive the nuclear fight as being about more than just individual corporate profits. Consciously or not, they feel

Peter Hannan

Team B's efforts laid the foundation for the explosion of the defense budget in the Reagan years.

nuclear opponents are really attacking economic growth and, by extension, the private enterprise economy that it sustained.

The point was eloquently made in H-bomb creator Edward Teller's statement that, "We are in a desperate struggle against whatever you wish to call them—no growthers, environmentalists, elitists. They may well win the battle and, if they do, America is doomed and freedom is doomed."

No Fail-Safe

LAWRENCE WESCHLER

March 12, 1986

If there ever is a nuclear war, chances are it will go remarkably like the shuttle disaster. That's one reason the imagery of that disaster continues to hold such fascination for us, why we studied the video images every night on the evening news—new images, seemingly, each night from some fresh perspective, revealing some new angle. We realize, if only subliminally, that we are being afforded a premonition.

Mankind as a whole today sits perilously strapped to a doomsday machine of our own devising: The globe itself has become like a giant booster hurtling through space, enormous explosive potential held barely in check, atop which we sit huddled, secured to our fragile life-support systems. Like the seven shuttle astronauts, we've been assured that the machine contains safeguards two and three deep, checks and counterchecks and checks of counterchecks, that nothing can possibly go wrong. ("The space shuttle *Challenger*'s solid fuel booster rockets were not equipped with sensors," the *New York Times* reported within days of the catastrophe, "because designers thought the boosters 'were not susceptible to failure.' "). And

Ellsberg would become an apostate, but the others, as anti-nuclear activist Dr. Helen Caldicott wrote in 1984, had "no moral scruples in their writings or discussions about their systematic plan to murder hundreds of millions." There's a certain banality in Caldicott's description of the RAND scientists as boys who "spent all their time fascinated with the plans they had devised, drawing graphs, calculating models based on economic principles and playing never-ending war games," but it's not far off. Not only did RAND determine the first Soviet targets for U.S. nukes, but, as the Cold War went on, it became the death star by which the U.S. government steered.

No part of the star shone more brightly than Herman Kahn. Best known as the basis for the character Dr. Strangelove (of the "Bland Corporation"), Edward S. Herman once described Kahn as a man whose mission it was to "normalize the unthinkable" for the American public, specifically by "making nuclear war palatable." Author of 1960's 652-page opus *On Thermonuclear War*, Kahn wrote as if his brain had already been blasted into the stratosphere: "War is terrible thing, but so is peace. The difference seems, in some respect, to be a quantitative one of degree and standards." *Scientific American* called the book "a moral tract on mass murder: how to plan it, how to commit it, how to get away with it, how to justify it," and, as author Fred Kaplan later wrote, Kahn's most lasting contribution to the philosophy of nuclear war was clever use of the linguistic device "only" in conjunction with mass casualties, like "*only* 2 million killed."

Kahn's colleague Albert Wohlstetter wasn't quite as over the top, but he proved to be one of the longest-lasting hard-line influences on the Cold War. In some respects, his applied theories of defense embodied the schizoid nature of right-wing Cold War thinking: more faith in the abilities of the Soviet military machine to dominate than in the institutions of Western democracy to sustain. To some, this made perfect sense, as the godless, coercive Soviets surely could overwhelm the enlightened United States in terms of nuclear forces (a notion that—despite repeatedly being proved wrong—still endures in some corners). Thus rather than place bombers close to the Soviet Union, Kahn reasoned, the United States should keep them distant so they'd be more effective in a massive retaliatory counterattack.

To other Western scientists within the political-military establishment, the ideas propagated by Kahn and Wohlstetter sounded like the result of atomic overexposure. Sir Solly Zuckerman, the brilliant polymath and longtime scientific adviser to the British government, pointed out that relatively small nuclear arsenals on both sides were capable of inflicting devastating damage. Past a certain minimal inventory, stockpiling became not only superfluous, but demented. Writing in 1983 about the RANDy atomic policy zeitgeist of the late '50s, Zuckerman recalled, "Paranoia started to take over, masked by figures of numbers of warheads, and delivery systems which, for most people, completely obscured the facts of the destruction that could be wreaked by just a few nuclear bombs."

Horrified by a high-ranking Pentagon official who told him in 1961 that "we want waves of aircraft to drop enough bombs to tear up [Russia] down to a depth of 40 feet to prevent the Martians from recolonizing the country, and to hell with the fallout," Zuckerman and a few of his colleagues redoubled their efforts to inject at least an atom of rationality into nuclear defense policy. "A few of us were arguing for what we regarded as a more reasonable strategic nuclear policy: the concept of 'minimal deterrence.' It seemed to us inconceivable that in a rational world any country would try to further some aggressive aim if the risk were the total destruction of its own capital city, let alone that of its 10 largest cities."

But such a view was anathema to the RAND types, who had the ear of the only NATO power that really mattered.

But strategies about how to use the standard toys—planes, missiles, submarines—weren't the only provocative notions

indeed, things have been going right for so long that we've become inured; we've grown to take success—or at any rate, the impossibility of failure—for granted.

And then something happens. It begins with a pinprick leak over the side—along the rocket's South African rim, say, or over by its Iran-Iraq seal, its Israeli joint, its Polish latch. In retrospect we can now see the leak may have developed owing to a fluky set of extraneous climactic conditions—it was too cold the night before, the price of oil or gold was dropping, or rising debt pressures were straining established orders, a particular minority was refusing any longer to countenance its continued oppression. The leak rapidly grew in intensity: The hiss became a spout became a geyser, an assassination or a food price increase provoked a riot that provoked a mobilization, a pre-emptive raid, a counter-raid.

The entire structure began to shudder violently—as the crisis burgeoned, leaders and computers strained mightily to cope with a situation increasingly out of control, one that had never before been encountered in any of the exhaustive predictive models. The vibrations were becoming too extreme, a latch perhaps shook loose, one booster veered toward the casing of another—the superpowers went on red alert, they removed the safety latches from the weapons in their respective arsenals, just in case.

And then . . . it's already over. The climactic spasm, when it happens, it happens so suddenly and annihilates so completely that we can't even see it happening. We slow down the videotape, slow it down some more, and there's not a single moment, a single frame, when the explosion is just beginning. There are sparks, little flashes racing up and down the belly of the booster, but one moment the rocket is still there, entire, and the next it's utterly vaporized: There's *no* in-between. Just as it was *never* supposed to happen.

The analogy breaks down. The shuttle disaster *did* happen, the nuclear holocaust hasn't yet. Consciousness survives the horror of the shuttle disaster, tries to make sense of it, to assign it meaning, to fashion analogies, to derive lessons. There would be no consciousness on the far side of a nuclear holocaust; or if there were any, it would be so damaged as to be incapable of making sense of anything—there would be no meaning, no analogies, no lessons.

Catch F-22

DAVID EVANS

July 11, 1994

Welcome to the strange new world of the Blue/Gray Threat—a world in which the United States is competing in an arms race with its allies, its friends and, ultimately, itself.

Back in the Cold War days, of course, the Red Threat was always used to justify massive American military spending and large-scale exports of U.S. weapons. But with the Soviet Union's collapse, the Pentagon and the arms industry have had to find new potential adversaries. Thus, the Blue/Gray Threat was born. Now arms manufacturers are warning of the dangers posed by governments that are today either U.S. allies ("blue") or friends ("gray")—but that might one day take the superb military hardware that the United States has been selling them and use it against U.S. forces.

The first prominent use of the Blue/Gray Threat to justify a big arms project comes in a slick, full-color marketing brochure produced by the Lockheed Corp. in association with the Boeing Co. and engine maker Pratt & Whitney. The three contractors are distributing the brochure to key staff

being bandied about. After fathering the thermonuclear bomb, Edward Teller—one of the original Manhattan Project scientists—found himself at home with the hawks when many of his colleagues broke with the defense establishment. Teller burned for ever-expanding weapons research and development, and chief among his obsessions was an elaborate defense system that would destroy an incoming fusillade of Soviet nuclear warheads.

Such an idea had been kicked around in the '50s, but cooler heads and sound logic prevailed. Echoing a 1957 British study that concluded there were no effective means of protection against nuclear war, Zuckerman and others had at least managed to keep this debate in check, pointedly noting that the penetration of even one warhead or bomb would make a shield an airborne Maginot Line. Detractors also observed that development of an anti-ballistic missile shield would only inspire the Soviets to build and deploy more nuclear missiles to overwhelm it. Nonetheless, both the Americans and Soviets poured billions into ABM research during the '60s.

While the bombastic Nikita Khruschev postured that Russia would be able to "hit a fly in space," American engineers tinkered and experimented to no avail. In 1967, Lyndon Johnson convened an august assembly that included the Joint Chiefs of Staff, his own science adviser and the current and former directors of research and engineering at the Pentagon. LBJ wanted two simple questions answered: Could a system be devised that would effectively stop all incoming missiles? If so, should it be deployed? The answer to both questions was "No."

As the Nixon administration began to craft the ABM Treaty, it revisited the idea: If the possibility of using directed-energy weapons like lasers and particle beams—as well as the more conventional knock-down-a-missile-with-a-missile approach—was real, should the United States move forward? This time, the Joint Chiefs were less skeptical, but the State Department, CIA and Arms Control and Disarmament

Agency lobbied for a ban on the class of ABM weapons known as "exotics." In the end, compromise carried the day: Building a mobile ABM system was forbidden, but exploration of land-based measures would still be allowed. The Soviets agreed, and the first Strategic Arms Limitation Treaty (SALT) was signed in 1972.

Even before the Nixon administration began its policy of *détente*, hawks like Wohlstetter had started mobilizing against any curb on ABM research. In 1969, Paul Nitze incorporated the Committee to Maintain a Prudent Defense Policy, and, with the help of young Wohlstetter protégé Richard Perle, he mounted a campaign of ABM boosterism. Destined to become one of the most formidable and influential hawks in Washington, Perle made his bones with Nitze and proved that Zuckerman was not entirely right when he concluded in *Nuclear Illusions and Reality* that "it is the man in laboratory, not the commander in the field, who is at the heart of the arms race."

When the man in laboratory has groomed a stable of acolytes and placed them in powerful Washington policy jobs, the heart that pumps up the arms race beats with even more resilience. After Nixon and Secretary of State Henry Kissinger successfully negotiated the ABM Treaty (aka SALT I), the stage seemed set for SALT II, which would establish equal ceilings on offensive weapons such as missiles and bombers. But to Wohlstetter, Nitze and Perle, SALT II epitomized a soft-headed sellout of the American empire.

Taking up their standard was Ford administration Defense Secretary Donald Rumsfeld, who used hardball and subterfuge to kill the treaty and undermine Kissinger. Already fearful of Ronald Reagan's right-wing assault on his presidency, Ford thought he could satisfy the defense establishment hawks in both parties by nixing SALT II, a move that probably cost him the 1976 election. In a 1988 interview, the former president wasn't shy about explaining why SALT II

members and legislators on Capitol Hill as their F-22 supersonic fighter project comes up for its next booster shot of bucks, some $3 billion in the Pentagon's requested defense budget. The program is now in the final stages of development.

The F-22, which could cost U.S. taxpayers upward of $70 billion, is a strangely anachronistic airplane: It is arguably both ahead of its time and out of date. On the one hand, this new generation of fighter offers what Lockheed describes as a "quantum leap in technology," including stealth (which allows the plane to fly undetected past enemy radar) and supercruise (which enables the aircraft to fly efficiently at supersonic speeds for long periods of time). On the other hand, the F-22 is being developed for a battle situation that no longer exists. "The F-22 was developed for a highly specialized mission: offensive counter-air. It was designed to penetrate into Russia and break up their mass fighter formations before they got rolling to overwhelm NATO," explains Everest Riccioni, a retired Air Force colonel who was part of the now-famous "fighter-mafia" that designed the F-15 and F-16 fighters.

That mission died with the Cold War—and so should the plane, argue critics such as Riccioni. But with billions of dollars at stake, Lockheed and the F-22's other contractors aren't giving up so easily. They haven't totally abandoned the notion of a future threat from Russia or from Russian-built aircraft. But

ITT Archives

The F-22 is both ahead of its time and out of date.

they are also stressing the looming danger posed by foreign-owned, American-made fighter planes such as the F-16.

Indeed, according to Lockheed's booklet, the United States has exported top-line fighters like the F-16 to more countries (26) than the former Soviet Union exported its hottest combat jets (15). In the Lockheed view, the Cold War standoff has given way to an increasingly uncertain world, where the potential for conflict is greater, not less. Countries like, say, Egypt, are part of a new so-called "gray" category of nations armed with advanced fighters such as the American-built F-16 that could become potential foes. As one Lockheed official says, "We've sold the F-16 fighter all over the world; what if one of those blue/gray countries turns against us?"

Nuking It Out

KALPANA SHARMA

June 28, 1998

NEW DELHI—Following India's five nuclear tests on May 11 and May 13, thousands of euphoric supporters of the ruling Hindu-nationalist Bharatiya Janata Party (BJP) planned to spread radioactive sand from the Rajasthan Desert all over the country. Fortunately, they were dissuaded.

But the absurdity of this gesture says it all. The BJP, which came to power by appealing to regressive religious sentiments, is now using the quintessential statement of these "modern times" to assert its power. The nuclear tests by India, followed by at least one test by Pakistan on May 28, have altered security in the region permanently. For years, the world—and the Western powers in particular—assumed that even if India and Pakistan had

died. "The attitude in the Defense Department," he said, "made it impossible to proceed."

But killing SALT II wasn't enough for the hawks. With *détente* on the ropes, a group of like-minded gentlemen—including Nitze, Perle, Eugene Rostow and William Casey—continued to meet at Washington's exclusive Metropolitan Club for a series of discussions that spawned the second incarnation of the Committee on the Present Danger. Though originally seen as an extremist organization, the new CPD convinced the Ford administration to let its members have access to CIA data in the service of providing an "alternative" assessment of the Soviet threat. The CPD experts, who became known as "Team B," crafted a report that rampantly overestimated Soviet military capability and offered dire predictions.

The findings were submitted to the White House too late to be of any use to the floundering Gerald Ford, but the CPD mounted an incredibly effective media campaign of leaking and spinning to foment public hysteria. Despite Kissinger's condemnation of Team B's analysis, Rumsfeld was effusive in promoting it as a credible study. Two days before Jimmy Carter's inauguration, Rumsfeld fired parting shots at Kissinger and other disarmament advocates, saying that "no doubt exists about the capabilities of the Soviet armed forces" and that those capabilities "indicate a tendency toward war fighting . . . rather than the more modish Western models of deterrence through mutual vulnerability."

Team B's efforts laid the foundation for the explosion of the defense budget in the Reagan years. More than 50 CPD members entered the Reagan administration, manipulating data to argue that the Soviets were no longer subscribing to the deterrent principles of Mutually Assured Destruction (MAD) and were laying in wait to pounce on the West as soon as a "missile gap" was exploitable. As a result, Reagan took to the airwaves on March 23, 1983, explaining that the machinations of Sovieticus now required developing a system of earth- and space-borne weapons to deter against nuclear attack.

Dubbed "Star Wars" and owing much to the input of Teller, it did not take long for a few enterprising reporters to note that the president was drawing as much on celluloid science fiction as he was science. In 1940, movie screens had been graced with the serial *Murder in the Air*, a sparkling cinematic gem starring Reagan as secret agent Brass Bancroft. The plot revolved around the necessity of our hero protecting America's new super-weapon, the "death ray inertia projector," a device able to neutralize any mechanical airborne menace to U.S. national security.

Critics of "Star Wars" weren't the only ones who found the proposal loopy. Some of Reagan's defense *consiglieres*, Perle among them, considered it dubious at best. But to Perle, whether or not it ever worked was irrelevant; Star Wars' worth lay in its value as a propaganda tool, a device that could be used to scare the Soviets into submission at the negotiating table. Even the utopian-sounding proposals put forth by Reagan's people were done for propaganda purposes. Perle, for example, championed a "zero option" proposal that called for both sides cutting nuclear forces to nothing—not because he believed in it, but on the theory that the Soviets would never accept it.

But in 1986, Soviet Premier Mikhail Gorbachev announced he would do just that—dramatically calling for the abolition of *all* nuclear weapons. At a surreal summit meeting in Reykjavik, Iceland that October, Reagan and Gorbachev came close to an agreement on eliminating most or all of their nuclear arsenals. Star Wars was the sticking point: Gorbachev insisted on a ban on space-weapons research, which Reagan refused to consider. "In return for a small and probably meaningless concession on Star Wars, Reagan could at one time have had a strategic arms agreement of a scale that no predecessor would have ever tried for," wrote the *New Yorker*'s John Newhouse, a former assistant director of the Arms Control and Disarmament Agency, in his 1989 book *War and Peace in the Nuclear Age.* "But he must have sensed that a dream like Star Wars, once interrupted, cannot be resumed.

nuclear capability, they would not build weapons. . . .

Within days of assuming office, Prime Minister Atal Behari Vajpayee gave the green light to Indian scientists. With most of the preparations already in place, it only required the prime ministerial nod—which two previous prime ministers had refused—to set the tests in motion. Why did the BJP choose this moment to do it? As he flew over the test site on March 20, Vajpayee told the press that the tests were the only way for India "to silence its enemies and to show its strength." . . .

But rather than silencing its external enemies, China and Pakistan, which BJP portrays as collaborators in a conspiracy to encircle India, the government has given Pakistan the reason it needed to go public with its nuclear capability. As a result, South Asia has been plunged into a nuclear arms race that could prove disastrous for both countries. . . .

Domestically, the magic of the moment is already wearing off, and voices of dissent are being heard. The political opposition has been galvanized, peace activists are demonstrating their

Terry LaBan

National Missile Defense gives a bracing new meaning to getting more bang for the buck.

opposition and leading scientists have issued a statement opposing the tests. Even the urban middle class, which initially supported the decision to test, is now having second thoughts in the face of economic sanctions.

Within a week of the tests, people in New Delhi erected roadblocks to protest the lack of electricity. "You are making bombs," women shouted, "but not giving us water or electricity."

Neither Vajpayee, nor his colleagues, were listening.

Star Wars: Episode Two

JEFFREY ST. CLAIR

June 12, 2000

It's wrong to say that Star Wars is back. The harebrained scheme hatched on the fly by Ronald Reagan in 1983 has never gone away. Quietly but relentlessly a Star Wars industry, under the rubric of Ballistic Missile Defense, has mushroomed.

The corporate press, which rightly heckled the plan in its early days, soon got bored with the story and left it for dead. Then in 1992, the missile shield's putative critics took over the White House and became its new masters. In the intervening years, billions of dollars poured into the Pentagon's Space and Missile Defense Command Center in Huntsville, Alabama, to production plants spread across key congressional districts, and into the plump accounts of a portfolio of defense contractors and high-tech firms.

In a 1995 review of the program in *Defense Issues*, an internal Pentagon newsletter, Lt. Gen. Malcolm O'Neill, then head of the Ballistic Missile Defense Organization, rhapsodized about a "synergized" network of high-powered, space-based lasers, satellites, radar and sea-, air- and ground-launched "exoatmos-

To the end, he ignored the substance of progress in order to keep faith with its shadow."

"Communism will probably disappear altogether when the Russian experiment comes to a climax, and Bolshevism either converts itself into a sickly imitation of capitalism or blows up with bang," H.L. Mencken presciently sniffed in 1930. "The former issue seems more likely—for some of the chief Bolsheviks remain politicians all the same, and when the time of genuine stress comes they will think first of all of their jobs. To keep their jobs, they will be quite willing to make terms with capitalism."

Despite obvious signs Mencken's prophecy was coming to pass, as George Herbert Walker Bush took over the White House in 1989, the mandarins of the defense and intelligence establishments held that Sovieticus was likely to menace the world for at least another decade or two. But after the Berlin Wall came down and the USSR imploded, the phrase "peace dividend" was heard with increasing frequency.

In 1992, the American electorate sent a politician to the White House who seemed antithetical to the old prescriptions for global security. Yet Bill Clinton continued his predecessor's policy on Iraq, kept the nuclear arsenal well-funded and on a hair-trigger alert, and made frequent but inconsistent use of military force. And whatever animus some in the Pentagon might have had toward a draft-dodging president, the military-industrial complex got much of what it wanted during the Clinton years. The defense budget stayed high; dubious programs like the F-22 fighter jet retained their budget lines; the government worked with the defense industry to make sure its big-ticket arms were sold overseas.

But perhaps most remarkable was the continued funding for Star Wars. Clinton's first secretary of defense, Les Aspin, started reorienting the Pentagon away from a far-flung National Missile Defense (NMD) system, shifting emphasis to the limited combat applications of ballistic missile defense. While the Star Warriors were distressed that the program had been scaled back, they bided their time.

Thanks to the input of Rumsfeld acolyte Frank Gaffney, a more expansive missile defense system became a staple of Newt Gingrich's "Contract with America." While Clinton would veto a 1995 Gingrich-led effort requiring a full-blown NMD system deployment by 2003, he did grant the Pentagon a whopping $745 million—more than half of what the Pentagon asked for—to expand work on NMD. While Gaffney's defense contractor-funded think tank, the Center for Security Policy (a haven for former CPD members), bayed about the frightening vulnerability of the United States from incoming missiles, the public remained quizzical, if not unmoved. Advised by Gaffney, Perle, Rumsfeld and others, 1996 Republican presidential candidate Bob Dole flacked for NMD as well; again, the issue failed to take hold with the voters.

But the Star Warriors are a persistent bunch. After both the CIA and an independent commission concluded a ballistic missile attack on the United States from a rogue nation was highly unlikely, the graying acolytes of the CPD revived the "Team B" concept, creating yet another commission—this time headed by Rumsfeld himself. Predictably, the conclusions were dire, the analytical technique dubious; but it had the effect of pushing the Democrats—ever fearful of appearing "soft" on defense—to put forth a more expansive program of their own.

Three years and millions of dollars would be spent aggressively experimenting with a limited system designed to knock down one of the few missiles a "rogue state" might launch or a small number of missiles that might be launched accidentally from the aging Russian arsenal. As his days in office waned, Clinton—ever the politician—deferred the decision to deploy the system to his successor.

pheric kill vehicles" that would save U.S. cities from "theater-class ballistic missiles, advanced cruise missiles and other air-breathing threats as well." Feel safer?

Of course, there are problems. Namely, with the collapse of the Soviet Union and corporate America's coddling of China, why in the world would the United States need to deploy such a system? Such questions prompt the most absurd frenzy of threat-inflation since the notion that the Marxist government of Grenada posed a grave danger to the Western Hemisphere. A coven of atomic warriors has been rolled out to fulminate about "rogue nations" and "global terrorists" who threaten what the Pentagon brass calls the "early post-Cold War paradigm." . . .

What's driving the bipartisan push for an increasingly unpopular new missile defense system that is extravagant, inept, unnecessary and destabilizing? You don't have to dig very deep to find an answer: Raytheon, TRW, Lockheed Martin and Boeing. Each of these firms has secured a lucrative sector of the Star Wars program.

Of course, the companies do have to make some political offerings. And they haven't been miserly. Together these four companies have flushed more than $2.6 million to the two political parties in soft money alone since 1996. On top of that, the defense giants' PACs have sluiced $3.7 million to federal candidates in the past three years, making the Star Wars coalition one of the prime sponsors of our political system. What money can't buy, direct persuasion often can. These four companies spent more than $18 million lobbying Congress in 1998, sending out a legion of former senators, congressmen and retired Pentagon chieftains as their hired guns on the Hill.

This all gives a bracing new meaning to getting more bang for the buck.

Terry LaBan

The wizards of Armageddon are pursuing a more robust and offensive role for the U.S. nuclear stockpile.

Whereas Clinton dithered over missile defense, George W. Bush has brazenly championed it, reinstalling Rumsfeld and his minions at the Pentagon and irking our allies with unilateral pronouncements. Dismissive of the idea of a world community and the evolving problems it faces, Rumsfeld and his ilk are most comfortable with a global power dynamic in which the guy who controls the balance of terror with the biggest nuclear arsenal wins. As such they have set about tearing up international treaties and undermining the very edifice that arms control is built on. At his confirmation hearings, Rumsfeld dismissed the ABM treaty as "ancient history."

One of the Rummy's first acts as Defense Secretary was to commission a far-reaching blueprint on the Pentagon's future from Andrew Marshall—the RAND veteran who has been ensconced at the Pentagon since 1973 as head of the Office of Net Assessment. Marshall spent the Cold War years systematically inflating the Soviet menace. Since then, to the delight of defense-contracting executives and their advocates on Capitol Hill, Marshall has offered dire prognostications about an inevitably bellicose and hegemonic China and pushed for a "Revolution in Military Affairs"—a doctrine that serves as an intellectual cover for spending largess on Buck Rogers-type weaponry. In his book *Private Warriors*, journalist Ken Silverstein describes Marshall as "one of the most effective pork-seeking missiles ever deployed by the military brass."

But unlike the actual brass, who love to spend money on planes, tanks and ships, Marshall swoons over high-tech networked sensor systems and "brilliant" weapons—expensive procurements that are notorious for, well, not working. The most notorious of all is NMD, which has a record, in the words of John Pike of the Federation of American Scientists, "unblemished by success." Yet Marshall played a key role in convincing the Rumsfeld Commission that ballistic missiles from "rogue states" posed an imminent threat to the United States. (Among the commission's questionable conclusions: North Korea could strike America if China gave them a missile and the Aleutian Islands were the target.)

But while the Pentagon brass were busy searching for a new enemy, one came crashing down on them. The tragedy of September 11 would seem to suggest the need for new tactics and strategy. Indeed, as the United States began bombing Afghanistan in the weeks following the terrorist attacks, Paul Wolfowitz, Rumsfeld's top deputy (and yet another Wohlstetter protégé) said the United States is being forced to play a "different kind of ball game" on the "21st-century battlefield."

But in fact, Wolfowitz maintains his unilateralist, maximum-force mindset. Wolfowitz and others have argued that the new war on terrorism should be taken beyond Afghanistan to Iraq, Syria and Lebanon. Meanwhile, the wizards of Armageddon are pursuing of a more robust and offensive role for the U.S. nuclear stockpile. Rumsfeld has refused to rule out the use of nukes, and Wolfowitz has warned the Taliban that the United States is prepared to use a "very large hammer."

The Committee on the Present Danger itself may be a thing of the past, but its principles are already taking the United States back to the future.

"Light" weapons are now recognized as a major factor in the global outbreak of ethnic and communal warfare.

ITT Archives

Armed and Dangerous

MICHAEL T. KLARE

June 13, 1994

For most of the past 40 years, international arms control efforts have generally focused on the largest and most potent weapons systems: intercontinental ballistic missiles, nuclear missile submarines, nuclear bombers and so on. But now, in one of the most striking developments of the post-Cold War era, arms control experts are beginning to worry about the smallest and least sophisticated weapons, such as guns, grenades, mortars and landmines. Once considered irrelevant to the strategic calculus that defined international politics, such weapons are now seen as a major factor in the global outbreak of ethnic and communal warfare.

At the height of the Cold War, it was widely assumed that any major war would be decided by which side made more and better tanks, artillery pieces, warplanes and other "heavy" weapons. Today, however, many conflicts are being decided by sniper guns, assault rifles, mortars and other "light" weapons. Such weapons do not have the capacity to destroy a large and modern army, as the United States did in Operation Desert Storm, but are capable of depopulating rural areas, leveling villages and inflicting huge numbers of civilian casualties.

The current fighting in Rwanda provides a tragic case in point. Although the major factions are reported to possess a handful of heavy artillery pieces, almost all of the killing has been conducted with machine guns, assault rifles, mortars and landmines. According to researchers from Human Rights Watch, both the Rwandan army and the rebel forces have acquired large numbers of such weapons from foreign suppliers in the past few years.

A similar pattern can be seen in Kashmir and Sri Lanka, where brutal conflicts involving many thousands of soldiers on each side have been sustained for years by foreign deliveries of light weapons. In Bosnia, the heavy fighting around Sarajevo and Gorazde has entailed the use of tanks and heavy artillery, but most of the smaller battles and "ethnic cleansing" campaigns—not to mention the daily sniping—have been conducted with small arms.

The situation is all the more disturbing because there are no international controls on the spread of guns and other light weapons. Many millions of such weapons are sold through legitimate commercial channels every year, and millions more are transferred through black-market channels that reach into every corner of the globe. Surplus Cold War weapons, of both Eastern and Western manufacture, are available on a worldwide basis from black-market dealers at a fraction of their original purchase price. Yet the major arms-producing nations—including the United States—are continuing to pour new weapons into international markets, thus increasing the global glut in military firearms. . . .

All of these channels of trade add up to a massive and hugely destructive international market for light weapons Each day in conflicts across the globe, thousands of people die—most of them noncombatants. And many survivors are left with wounds—missing limbs, paralysis, blindness, despair—that make them unable to assist their families and villages, thus placing added burdens on the world's over-stretched humanitarian aid infrastructure.

But the cost to the international community extends far beyond this. At a time when the world is finding it increasingly difficult to control the spread of ethnic and communal warfare, the world's arms suppliers are making it easier and easier for potential belligerents to conduct wars of increasing scope, duration and intensity. This, perhaps more than anything else, is the lesson of Bosnia, Kashmir and Sri Lanka: So long as belligerents can obtain the guns and ammunition with which to carry on their crusades, the ability of outsiders to stem the bloodshed will be limited.

October Surprises

A TALE OF TREASON, PROPAGANDA AND THE PRESS

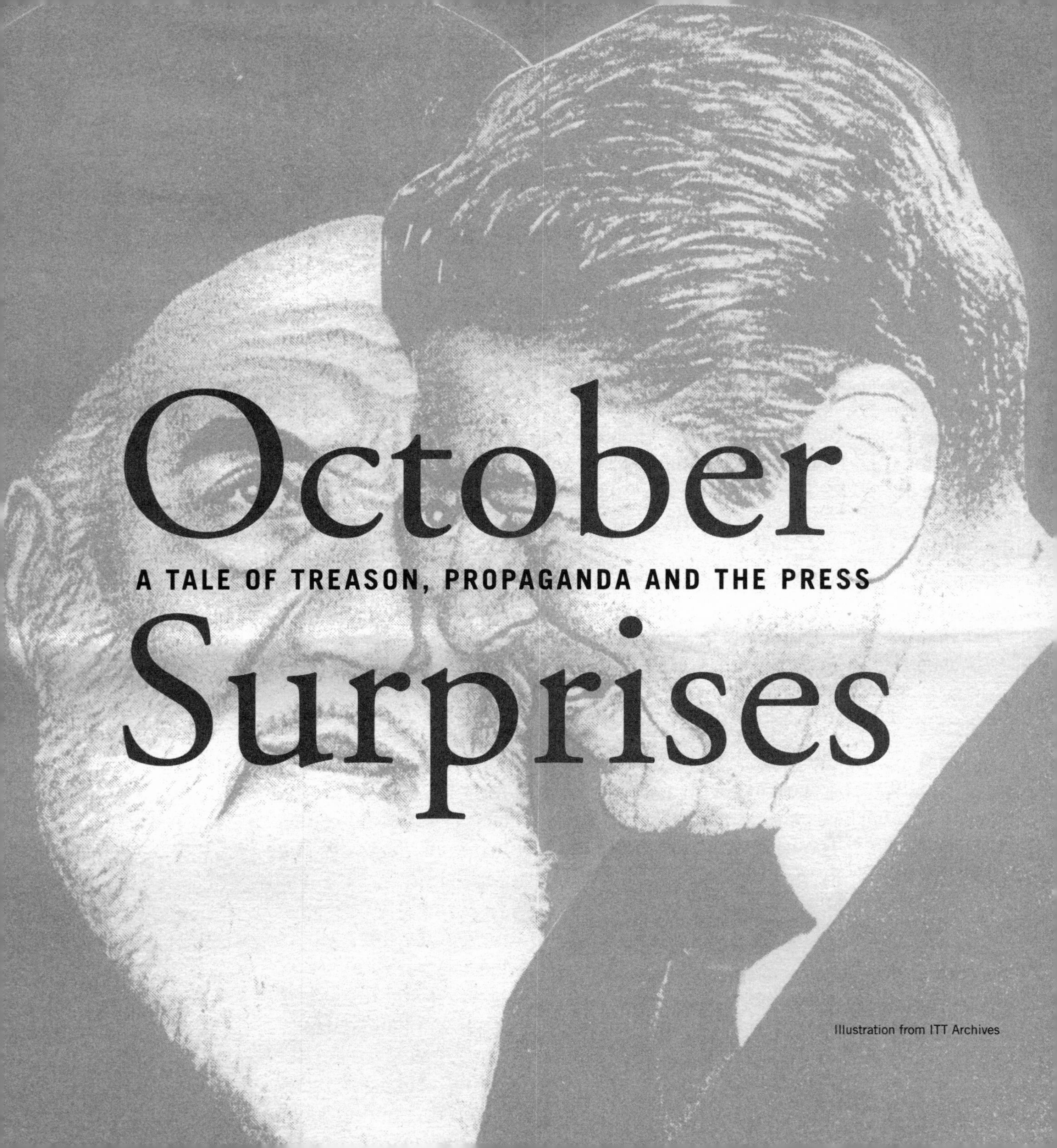

Illustration from ITT Archives

Twenty

JOEL BLEIFUSS

IN HIS INAUGURAL SPEECH ON JANUARY 20, 1981, PRESIDENT RONALD REAGAN BRAGGED, "IN THE EYES OF MANY IN THE WORLD, THIS EVERY-FOUR-year ceremony we accept as normal is nothing less than a miracle." If so, it was a day of miracles: Just minutes after Reagan was sworn in, 52 American hostages were freed after being held captive for 444 days by Iranian militants.

But in the cynical and calculated world of international diplomacy, real miracles are rare. As a large body of circumstantial evidence suggests, Reagan's eventful inauguration day had less to do with Providence than his campaign's illegal, covert efforts to persuade Iran to delay release of the hostages until after Election Day to ensure Jimmy Carter's defeat.

In my 15 years at *In These Times*, no story has so engrossed me as what came to be known as the "October Surprise." The scandal involved high crimes—the treasonous activity and subversion of constitutional government by a cabal of private individuals who would control the subsequent three presidential administrations. That skullduggery aside, in some ways the more chilling (and from a journalist's perspective, fascinating) part of the story is the conspirators' attempts to cover up their crimes through the manipulation and complicity of friendly journalists, media institutions and congressional investigators. This domestic covert operation employed Madison Avenue advertising techniques, the skills of psy-ops (psychological operations) military personnel and old-fashioned arm-twisting to discredit the allegations. Their success is undeniable: For the general public, at least those who ever heard the allegations, the October Surprise became nothing more than a fanciful conspiracy theory.

The October Surprise inaugurated an era of Republican dirty tricks and cover-ups—from Iran-

Contra to the CIA-cocaine connection to Whitewater—that continues to this day. As a casebook study of how Republican Party strategists have honed their ability to covertly influence foreign policy, domestic politics and media coverage, the October Surprise demonstrates that what matters is not the material evidence, but the ability to manage the public's perception of that evidence.

Key elements of the October Surprise story are not in dispute. Iranian student militants overran the U.S. Embassy compound in Teheran on November 29, 1979, taking 52 Americans hostage. For more than a year, the American public was consumed with the "hostage crisis." Xenophobia blossomed. Blow-by-blow crisis coverage was provided by ABC's *Nightline*, which was launched as a nightly update on the hostages.

The crisis stood as a symbol of Carter's impending downfall, its successful resolution his potential salvation. During the 1980 election, the Reagan campaign's top pollster, Richard Wirthlin, predicted a Carter victory if the White House could pull off an "October Surprise" and gain the hostages' release before the election. Journalists Jack Germond and Jules Witcover wrote that the Reagan-Bush campaign anticipated such a surprise with a "trepidation bordering on paranoia." To meet this threat, the Reagan campaign established an "October Surprise Group," headed by chief foreign policy adviser Richard Allen, to monitor the Carter administration's hostage negotiations and formulate countermoves.

That much is clear. But the crux of the entire October Surprise scandal hinges on whether Reagan campaign director William Casey, a World War II spymaster who would become CIA director, met with Iranian representatives prior to the election. If he did not, there was no secret deal. But an ever-growing body of evidence indicates that Casey did attend such meetings. Casey was never questioned about his alleged involvement in the October Surprise, having died in 1987 of brain cancer.

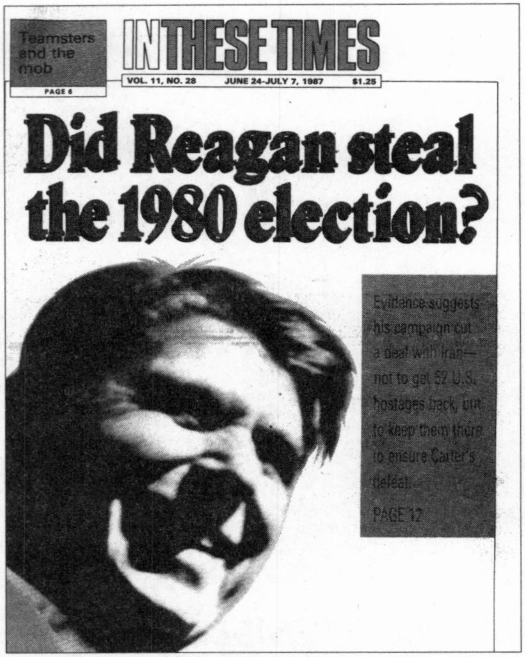

ITT Archives

"We don't have to worry," another Reagan campaign staffer told Barbara Honegger. "Dick cut a deal."

Did Reagan Steal the 1980 Election?

BARBARA HONEGGER AND JIM NAURECKAS

June 24, 1987

In October 1980, nothing worried the Reagan campaign so much as the possibility that the 52 hostages held by Iran might come home. The Reagan camp feared that the public perception of President Carter's weakness would evaporate if he could win the captives' release before the election—what Reagan staffers called an "October surprise."

According to the available evidence, here is what went down: In the summer of 1980, Casey went to Madrid, where he met with a pair of Iranian-born arms dealers, brothers Jashmid and Cyrus Hashemi, and an Iranian government representative named Mehdi Karrubi (who would later become speaker of the Iranian parliament). Over two meetings, held on July 27 and July 28, the four men first discussed the hostages being held in Iran and the possibility they would not be released until after the election.

Then a couple weeks prior to the election, Casey attended a second set of meetings, this time in Paris. At these meetings on October 18, attended by representatives of Iran, Israel and the Reagan campaign, the details of the deal were finalized. The incoming Reagan-Bush administration would supply Iran with American weapons and spare parts that it badly needed for its war against Iraq, which had started that September. In return, Iran would hold the American hostages until after the election.

Both Richard Allen and Robert MacFarlane, each of whom would later serve as Reagan's national security adviser, have admitted discussing an arms-for-hostages deal at an early October 1980 meeting in Washington with a man who claimed to represent Iran. Both men insist they dismissed the offer. But just such a deal would explain why Iran suddenly and inexplicably shifted its bargaining position in the ongoing negotiations with the Carter administration. Gary Sick, the Carter administration's expert on Iran, reports in his 1985 book *All Fall Down* that in early October the Iranians had demanded American weapons and spare parts in exchange for the hostages. But on October 22, Iran specifically limited its demands to frozen cash assets, a move that would only make sense if Iran knew it could expect those weapons and spare parts from Reagan.

After Reagan's victory on November 4, the Carter administration negotiated the release of the hostages in return for the release of Iranian assets. The hostages were released the moment Reagan was sworn into office. At the time, some wondered

But in the campaign's closing weeks, the mood of high anxiety suddenly changed. In late October, Barbara Honegger was working as a researcher for the campaign's Arlington, Virginia national headquarters. "We don't have to worry about an October surprise," a jubilant staffer at the campaign's operations center told her. "Dick cut a deal."

"Dick" was Richard Allen, Reagan's chief foreign policy adviser. And the "deal," research by *In These Times* suggests, was an agreement that Reagan would guarantee post-election arms shipments to Iran in exchange for delaying the hostages' release until after the November 4 election. Why would the Reagan campaign seek such a seemingly incredible arrangement? Because it saw an October surprise as the campaign's No. 1 threat.

In late fall, surveys still found the election too close to call. Reagan's top pollster, Richard Wirthlin, predicted that a pre-election hostage release would boost Carter at least 5 to 6 percent in the polls, and as much as 10 percent—giving him a sure victory—if the release came before the campaign's final week. The Reagan revolution would be over before it had begun.

Is the North Network Cocaine Connected?

DENNIS BERNSTEIN AND VINCE BIELSKI

December 10, 1986

In These Times has pieced together the outlines of what might yet become another major scandal for the Reagan administration. The picture that emerges is of two separate operations—one allegedly set up by Oliver North in 1984 to supply arms to the Contras, the other a Colombian-based cocaine trafficking operation that had been smuggling the drug into the United States for several years—that merged together for their mutual benefit.

Dan Sheehan of the Christic Institute, a Washington-based law firm, said two of Colombia's largest dealers of cocaine, Jorge Ochoa and Pablo Escobar, had been involved in smuggling cocaine into the United States in 1983. At this time, the North network was interested in creating a "southern front" of Contra forces in Costa Rica, he said. Operatives in the network, including anti-Castro Cubans Rene Corbo and Francisco Chanes and American John Hull, struck a deal with the Colombians, who agreed to provide them with hundreds of pounds of cocaine on a regular basis, Sheehan said.

A Nicaraguan Contra, who was known to reporters as David before his death last year, and other mercenaries have provided information that Hull's land in Costa Rica is used for training Contras and staging military attacks against Nicaragua. Massachusetts Sen. John Kerry's office also has information linking Hull to the CIA or National Security Council. According to a Kerry report: "Hull . . . has been identified by a wide range of sources, including . . . mercenaries, Costa Rican officials and Contra supporters, as a CIA or NSC liaison to the Contras on the southern front."

The cocaine is flown from Colombia to airstrips in northern Costa Rica located on land owned or managed

about the peculiar timing. More than six years later, it would be learned that Iran began receiving U.S. weapons and spare parts via Israel within weeks of the inauguration.

In November 1986, the Iran-Contra scandal shocked the nation with the revelation that the Reagan administration had been secretly negotiating an arms-for-hostages deal in an attempt to secure the release of Americans being held in Beirut by Hezbollah. What's more, the administration was diverting some of the profits from this secret arms sale to help fund its covert war in Nicaragua. This money supplemented the millions the administration had raised from private sources in its illegal attempt to circumvent Congress and defeat the Sandinistas.

It was in this atmosphere, as the Iran-Contra hearings were just about to get underway, that the October Surprise story first broke in a June 24, 1987, *In These Times* cover story titled, "Did Reagan Steal the 1980 Election?" In that article, reporter Jim Naureckas and former Reagan administration official Barbara Honegger first laid out the skeleton of the scandal, building on an April 1987 report by the *Miami Herald*'s Alfonso Chardy that an Iranian had met with Reagan campaign officials in October 1980 to discuss the hostages.

Honegger had worked in the national headquarters of the Reagan-Bush campaign, and after the election she was rewarded with a post as a policy analyst in the White House, where she served until 1982. She recalled that in the closing weeks of the campaign, the Reagan-Bush camp feared the effect if Carter could win the hostages' release. But as *In These Times* reported: "The mood of high anxiety suddenly changed. . . . 'We don't have to worry about an October Surprise,' a jubilant staffer at the campaign's operations center told her. 'Dick cut a deal.' " ("Dick" was Richard Allen.)

More evidence was added to the record in an article by Abbie Hoffman and journalist Jonathan Silver in the October 1988 issue of *Playboy*. Most notable was a letter to

Hoffman and Silver from Jimmy Carter, in which he wrote: "We have had reports since late summer 1980 about Reagan campaign officials dealing with Iranians concerning delayed release of the American hostages. . . . [I] have trusted that investigations and historical records would someday let the truth be known."

Carter's Iranian counterpart during the hostage crisis, President Abolhassan Bani-Sadr, told *Playboy* that he too had heard rumors of the alleged deal. Bani-Sadr said he received intelligence reports of two October meetings between Reagan-Bush campaign officials and an envoy for Ali Albar Hashemi Rafsanjani, the speaker of the Iranian parliament (who would later negotiate the Iran-Contra deal with Robert MacFarlane). One of the meetings was allegedly held in Washington, the other in Paris two weeks before the election.

These articles led to talk of a congressional investigation from Democrats in the House; that talk generated the first attack on the October Surprise and the reporters who dared to look into the story. Leading the backlash was freelance writer Mark Hosenball, who wrote in October 1988 in the *Washington Post* about the "conspiracy theorists" and "aficionados of intrigue" who were spreading a "rumor that just won't die." Hosenball was the first in a line of the October Surprise debunkers—journalists with unstated agendas who creatively interpreted the factual record to discredit the allegations. Congress decided not to investigate.

The October Surprise again broke into the mainstream media in 1991. Carter administration official Gary Sick, who in 1988 had publicly cast doubt on the allegations, undertook his own investigation and became convinced the evidence pointed to just such a deal. On April 18, he published an op-ed piece in the *New York Times*, making his case. Then PBS's *Frontline* aired interviews with Iranian arms dealer Jashmid Hashemi, in which he laid out his account of the two meetings in Madrid he attended in the summer of 1980. Records from Madrid's Ritz Hotel indicated that Hashemi was a guest there from July 25 to 29 and from August 8 to 13.

by Hull, Sheehan claimed. For the Colombians, Hull's land provides an ideal refueling point. In return, the Contra supporters receive $10,000 to $25,000 for each plane that refuels, Sheehan alleged.

The Christic Institute learned of this arrangement from intelligence officials in the Costa Rican Rural Guard, workers on Hull's land who claim to have unloaded the illegal substance from small planes and the pilots who transported the cocaine. Sheehan said he also obtained records of Corbo buying huge gasoline tanks in Costa Rica that are used for refueling planes.

Evidence of the Colombia-Costa Rica connection was provided indirectly by the Nicaraguan Contra named David. He revealed what he knew of the drug-trafficking activities to a Costa Rican named Carlos Rejos Chinchilla. According to Rejos' notes, obtained by *In These Times*, David said: "Drugs come from Miami and go to Colombia in small planes. Sometimes they are dropped by parachute to locations inside Costa Rica. Costa Rica is the perfect place for drug trafficking. There's no control here."

Sheehan said the drug is transported by two methods into the United States. It is flown to Memphis or Denver, or it is packed into container ships in Costa Rica belonging to seafood companies with which Chanes is associated, and is then transported to Miami, New Orleans and San Francisco. . . .

Jesus Garcia, a former Dade County, Florida deputy sheriff claims to have been an operative in the arms supply network. In a telephone interview from prison, where Garcia is now serving a three-year term for possession of a firearm, he told *In These Times*: "It is common knowledge here in Miami that this whole Contra operation in Costa Rica was paid for with cocaine. Everyone involved knows it. I actually saw the cocaine and weapons together under one roof, weapons that I helped ship to Costa Rica."

Casey, for his part, disappeared from public view between the afternoon of July 26 and the afternoon of July 28. (Casey's whereabouts on August 9 are also unaccounted for.) In an interview with *Frontline*, Mehdi Karrubi denied meeting Casey, calling the allegations "pure lies."

Days later, Hosenball again weighed in on the pages of the *Washington Post*. "The allegations have knocked around in fashionable publications and among the chattering classes in New York, Washington and Hollywood for years, but last week they hit the big time," he wrote. Sick's article and the *Frontline* exposé "gave a new lease on life . . . to a story which has obsessed a small brigade of conspiracy theorists and journalistic gadflies for years . . . a mischievous interpretation of highly circumstantial evidence."

Robert Parry was the chief reporter for the *Frontline* documentary. Parry had made a name for himself in Washington as one of the reporters who broke the Iran-Contra scandal. At the time, Parry told me this about Hosenball:

> It's become sort of a pattern. Any journalist who would quote or investigate these charges is attacked by Hosenball. . . . When reporters feel they are going to be ridiculed in Washington in this snotty, sophomoric way, they pull away from following the leads. As the psy-ops people always tell you, the best way to neutralize your opponent is to make them an object of ridicule. The effect of such ridicule has kept this story from being seriously treated for years, and right now Hosenball is working overtime being sure it goes back to the fringes.

◎

In the fall of 1991, both *Newsweek* and *The New Republic* featured cover stories that purported to debunk the October Surprise, arguing loudly—while quietly ignoring crucial evidence—that the Casey meetings never could have taken place. Both magazines claimed that Casey could not have attended such meetings because on the evening of July 27 he was

ITT Archives

In 1986, *In These Times* first reported allegations of collaboration between the CIA and cocaine traffickers.

Media Mindset

JOEL BLEIFUSS

August 5, 1987

At a recent Investigative Reporters and Editors conference in Phoenix, *New York Times* Iran-Contra editor Joel Brinkley posed this question: "Why did the press, the public and Congress have all this information and just sort of let it slip through their fingers?"

He then offered this example of his own slippage: On August 8, 1985, as one of the *Times* reporters responsible for covering the Contras, Brinkley came out with a story that began: "Rebels fighting to overthrow the Nicaraguan government have been receiving direct military advice from in London to attend a historical conference the next morning.

As for the October meeting in Paris, both magazines questioned the bona fides of former Israeli officer Ari Ben-Menashe, whose claims about such a meeting had been reported by *Frontline* and *In These Times*. "So far much of what Ben-Menashe says does not seem to check out," wrote *Newsweek*'s John Berry. For proof, he quoted David Kimche, a Mossad veteran and former director of the Israeli Foreign Ministry, who said Ben-Menashe was "apparently a minor clerk in some military branch."

How reliable a source was Kimche? Well, in July 1985, he met at the White House with Robert MacFarlane and discussed arms shipments to Iran. This conversation was the first step in the Iran-Contra deal. And this wasn't the first time the two men had met. A "former high-level State Department official" told Sick that Kimche had held three secret meetings with MacFarlane in December 1980 "to secure prior approval for arms sales to Iran."

Writing in *The New Republic*, Steven Emerson also accepted that Ben-Menashe was a low-level employee who lacked access. But that was directly contradicted by Moshe Hebroni, chief of staff for Israeli military intelligence, who told *The Village Voice*: "Ben-Menashe served directly under me. He worked for the foreign flow desk in external relations; he had access to very, very sensitive material."

Emerson further portrayed Ben-Menashe as an opportunist, whose "recall of the October Surprise came about belatedly" after he was arrested by the U.S. government in 1989 for trying to sell U.S. military equipment to Iran. But in 1986, Raji Samghabadi, an Iranian-born *Time* magazine correspondent, used Ben-Menashe as a source in compiling articles about the October Surprise and Iran-Contra that *Time* never published. In Ben-Menashe's 1989 trial, Samghabadi testified that Ben-Menashe had told him "there was a huge conspiracy between the United States government and Israel to supply Iran with billions of dollars in weapons off the books, without legal channels

White House officials on the National Security Council. . . . The operation has been run by a Marine officer who is a member of the NSC."

That story, Brinkley said, gave "the bare outlines of everything we have been hearing in these first six weeks of congressional hearings."

"I am not writing stories to cause parades in the streets," he continued "but when you write stories and nobody gives a hoot . . . you just lose the momentum to keep going with it. And that is not an excuse, but that . . . is an illustration of the mindset in a lot of Washington newspaper offices." . . .

"Every time we wrote one of the stories," he said later, "the White House would simply offer bald-faced lies and accuse us of being pro-communist. Maybe I shouldn't care about that, and I don't really, but after a year of Contra reporting . . . when you begin to challenge the White House and get in response accusations and direct lies of the facts, it simply wears you down. . . . And there begins to grow a seed of doubt in the minds of some editors: 'Is Brinkley really right? What's this all about?' That's not a good explanation. But I am human, and I did not follow it up."

And when asked if the ideology of the *New York Times* influenced decisions on what news is covered and what is not, Brinkley invoked journalistic objectivity. "That's just nonsense," he responded. "I know of no ideological strictures except my own that dictate how I direct our staff on Iran-Contra, and I try to ignore mine, just as we all do in journalism, not always successfully."

Objectivity is itself an ideology in the world of journalism. And it's this ideology that, on the basis of presenting the two sides of every question, obliges the press to rely on unidentified administration sources to give that other side. For the press to continue granting credence to these sources during the current scandal, when most White House officials are now on the record as public liars, seems risky, if not stupid.

WHAT'S THE DIFFERENCE BETWEEN A DIPLOMAT IN IRAN AND A STUDENT IN GRENADA?
1980: American hostage in the custody of Iranian terrorists.
1983: Student kisses American soil after being rescued by U.S. Army Rangers in Grenada.
PRESIDENT RONALD REAGAN.
Published by the College Republican National Committee, 310 First St., SE, Washington, D.C. 20003

ITT Archives

A poster designed for the 1984 elections by the College Republicans.

knowing anything about them, and it was still continuing at the time he talked to me."

That's not to say there weren't questions about the veracity of claims made by Ben-Menashe, who insisted that Casey was joined at the Paris meetings by vice presidential candidate George Bush and Carter national security staffer Robert Gates (who would become CIA director under Bush). Though Bush disappeared from public view for 20 hours between 10 P.M. on October 18 and 6 P.M. on October 19—enough time for a quick trip to Paris by private jet—the only other evidence to support this claim was the recollection of a *Chicago Tribune* correspondent who heard that Bush had gone to France that weekend.

Both *Newsweek* and *The New Republic* went to press a week before the publication of Gary Sick's *October Surprise*, preempting the large body of evidence Sick had accumulated. In *October Surprise*, Sick confirms the Paris meetings from two sources whom he describes as holding "high-level positions in their respective governments." One is an Israeli who had "first-hand knowledge of the 1980 deal," the other an Arab diplomat who was in Paris at the time.

Sick also demolishes the London alibi Emerson and Berry build for Casey. This was substantiated by Robert Parry, who concluded in a second October Surprise documentary for *Frontline* in April 1992 that while Casey was at the London historical conference by 4 P.M. on July 28, it is impossible to say where he was from the evening of

July 26 through the morning of July 28. Casey could have been in Madrid. UCLA history professor Robert Dallek told *Frontline*: "I have a very strong memory of not seeing Mr. Casey at the conference that morning [of July 28], because I was giving my talk at 11:30 in the morning, and I looked for him in the room. I knew he was a prominent figure. And I was interested to know whether he was going to be there or not."

For his perseverance, Parry was again subjected to public ridicule. Prior to the airing of the second *Frontline* documentary, Emerson wrote in *The New Republic*: "We're mystified by PBS's decision to air a second *Frontline* documentary (at a cost of $300,000) further hyping the October Surprise conspiracy. We haven't seen the program yet—but it's produced by Robert Parry, who is more accurately described as an active proponent of the theory than an objective reporter."

Following Emerson's slam, Senate Minority Leader Bob Dole held up federal funding of the Corporation for Public Broadcasting. "I have never been more turned off and more fed up with the increasing lack of balance, and the unrelenting liberal cheerleading that I see and hear on the public airwaves," Dole said. In the House, Reps. Robert Livingston (R-Louisiana) and Dick Armey (R-Texas) cosponsored a bill to end all federal subsidies to NPR, PBS, the Corporation for Public Broadcasting and *Frontline*.

These attacks set the mood for the ongoing House investigation, which had started in February 1992. The October Surprise Task Force, which released its report in January 1993, concluded that there was "no credible evidence" that the Reagan-Bush campaign had attempted to delay the release of the American hostages. As to the question of whether Reagan campaign officials met with Iranian representatives, the task force called the evidence "wholly insufficient"—a phrase that better describes the

Q&A: Gary Sick

JOEL BLEIFUSS

November 27, 1991

When asked about allegations of the October Surprise in 1988, you said you doubted whether any such deal took place. What first led you to reconsider your skepticism?

It has been a slowly growing process, a slow accumulation of information and evidence. There is no point like Saul on the road to Damascus where suddenly the light flashed on, and I said, "That's it." As opposed to the smoking-gun theory, where you come up with a piece of evidence that absolutely proves that this happened, I see this as putting pieces of a mosaic together. You stand back and look at it, and the pieces fit together. You have a lot of blank spaces, but nevertheless there is a picture there. Eventually, enough pieces were filled in, and I looked at and said, "It is very difficult for me to believe that this is really a picture of something else."

What does the coverage by Newsweek *and* The New Republic*—both of which support the administration's claims of innocence—say about the motives of these two news organs?*

I'm not going to speculate about what their motives may be. All I will say is that I was interviewed by both organizations before they printed their stories. They were working on that story one week before my book came out. I talked to both reporters. . . . I talked to them in considerable detail about what I had done in tracing the stories to particular sources. Unfortunately, they went ahead with their stories and were not willing to wait for the book to come out and to look at it. And the information that I gave them about my own procedures, and the way I worked, and the way I did my research, was simply never mentioned in the course of the stories. I've been very disappointed about that.

Flack Attack

JOEL BLEIFUSS

September 6, 1993

The Founding Fathers didn't have public relations firms to package their revolution. They wrote their own sound bites: "Give me liberty, or give me death." Media events like the Boston Tea Party were carried off without the help of corporate sponsors such as Celestial Seasonings.

These days something as momentous as a revolution could not happen without an army of corporate PR mercenaries churning out the information and putting forward hired experts to shoot down opposing ideas.

The PR industry's influence—often overlooked as a force in U.S. politics—is as pervasive as it is pernicious. PR professionals, when in their groove as apologists for the corporate ideal, define the subject of public debates and then frame the limits of that debate. As media critic Morris Wolfe has observed, "It is easier and less costly to change the way people think about reality than it is to change reality."

Manipulating the public's perceptions of reality takes special skills. Younger professionals in the field of "communications" earn PR degrees from journalism schools. Others get their start in government service and then, contacts in hand, cash in their experience with a high-paying job in the PR industry. But what the best in the business have in common is that they have rotated through a revolving door of government, journalism and PR, until their identities and allegiances have been blurred beyond recognition. . . .

One of the most successful broad-based PR efforts of the '80s accompanied the Reagan administration's budget-busting military build up. The growth in the Pentagon's coffers went hand in hand with a blossoming Defense Department PR staff. By the time Reagan left office, 3,000 public

House investigation itself, particularly regarding its answer to the crucial question of Casey's whereabouts in July 1980.

The congressional investigators couldn't ignore the evidence demolishing the London alibi for Casey. Instead, the task force decided that Casey could not have been in Madrid on July 26 and July 27 because he was at the Bohemian Grove, an exclusive male-only retreat north of San Francisco. Casey's desk calendar, which was in his personal files, was no help because the pages for that weekend were strangely missing. The investigators provided him with the Bohemian Grove alibi based on the recollection of Darrell Trent, who worked with the Reagan-Bush campaign in California. According to the task force report, Trent "was uncertain whether Casey was his guest" at the Bohemian Grove during the weekend of July 26 or the weekend of August 2, "but his best recollection" was that they attended the retreat during the first weekend.

But judging from evidence the task force itself uncovered, and then disregarded, Casey was clearly at the Bohemian Grove on August 2 and August 3:

- Trent told the task force that he remembered meeting Casey in Los Angeles and traveling with him to the Bohemian Grove.
- The August 1 page of Casey's desk calendar reads "L.A."
- Richard Allen provided the task force with meeting notes that indicate both Casey and Trent attended an August 1 meeting at 10 A.M. with Reagan and his campaign staff in Los Angeles.
- According to Bohemian Grove records, on August 1 both Trent and Casey incurred a $9 charge on their Bohemian Grove accounts for a "Playbook."
- On August 3, camp participant Matthew McGowan wrote in his diary: "1980 Bohemian Grove encampment closed this date. A very good encampment for me. We had Bill Casey Gov. Reagan's campaign mgr., as our guest this last weekend."

In the same way it fiddled with Casey's schedule in July to provide him an alibi, the task force manipulated his whereabouts on the weekend of October 18 and October 19, when he allegedly attended meetings in Paris. Nobody knows where campaign manager Casey was on October 19—just 16 days before the election—but according to the congressional investigators, Casey's nephew Larry remembered his father calling his uncle that day. (This same nephew previously had claimed on camera to *Frontline* that Casey had dinner in Washington with his parents on October 19—a dinner that actually occurred on October 15.)

The task force gave the nephew's uncertain recollection more weight than that of French intelligence official Alexandre de Marenches, who told a reporter he had provided "cover" for a meeting between representatives of the 1980 Reagan-Bush campaign and the Iranian government to discuss the hostages in Paris on October 18 to 19. When interviewed by a task force investigator, de Marenches denied knowledge of the Paris meeting. But his official biographer, former *New York Times* correspondent David Andelman, told the task force that De Marenches had "acknowledged setting up a meeting in Paris between Casey and some Iranians in late October 1980." Andelman said de Marenches told him this off the record.

Further corroboration of the Paris meetings came from a six-page Soviet intelligence report obtained by the task force, which read in part: "William Casey, in 1980, met three times with representatives of the Iranian leadership. . . . The meetings took place in Madrid and Paris. . . . [Robert] Gates, at that time a staffer of the National Security Council in the administration of Jimmy Carter and former CIA director George Bush also took part [in the October Paris meetings]. . . . In Madrid and Paris, the representatives of Ronald Reagan and the Iranian leadership discussed the question of possibly delaying the release of 52 hostages from the staff of the U.S. Embassy in Teheran."

Had it not been for Robert Parry, this explosive Russian report would never have seen the light of day. He found it in

relations officers were busy spending $100 million annually to manipulate the public's perception of the military-industrial complex.

The high-hog living at the Pentagon has been replaced by leaner times, at least relatively. The 1993 Defense Department budget of $278 billion is a little less bloated than the inflation-adjusted 1983 expenditure of $291 billion. Consequently, military PR is more important than ever. As industry trade journal *O'Dwyer's Public Relations Services Report* notes: "A key weapon the military has in its arsenal is an intern program in which top military PR people learn the tricks of the trade at leading PR firms."

In other words, the Pentagon PR flacks need some up-to-date techniques for congressional apple-polishing and public-propagandizing. Which raises the question: Who are these public servants really serving?

Mike Doble, an Army major who is chief spokesman for the Ballistic Missile Defense program—better known as "Star Wars"—is currently taking a 10-month sabbatical to work as an intern at Fleishman-Hillard, a leading PR firm. The major told *O'Dwyer's* that his goal is "to learn how pros at that firm get their message across to clients."

No doubt, when Doble returns to the Pentagon, he will have learned to better serve his Star Wars clients like a real professional.

Muddy Waters

ROBERT PARRY

August 22, 1994

From the start, the Whitewater inquiry has lacked both proportionality and fairness. Republicans, who ignored grave violations of law and ethics under presidents Reagan and Bush, have feigned horror over some real, some trivial and some imagined offenses by Bill and Hillary Clinton. While the unadorned truth about the Clintons in Arkansas is unflattering, Whitewater has always been less a scandal than a political strategy to enable the Republicans to regain control of the government. . . .

Terry LaBan

During the Clinton administration, the Republican propaganda apparatus went on the offensive.

a cardboard box containing many other documents collected by the congressional investigators. The box had been stored in a women's restroom being used a storeroom in a parking garage of the Rayburn House Office Building. Parry writes on his Web site:

> I contacted one well-placed official in Europe who checked with the Russian government. "This was real information based on their own sources and methods," the official told me. As for the possibility that the report was blowback from the U.S. media, the official insisted that the Russians "would not send something like this to the U.S. Congress at that time, if it was bullshit." Instead, the Russians considered their report "a bomb" and "couldn't believe it was ignored."

The suspiciously selective treatment of the evidence was capped by the carefully orchestrated manner in which the task force released its report. The morning before the document was released, the *New York Times*, The Associated Press and the *Washington Times* reported—based on a leaked copy of the "Executive Summary"—that investigators had concluded there was nothing to the October Surprise allegations. The 968-page report was finally released at the end of its press conference, preventing reporters from asking informed questions. But the national press corps was content to let the matter rest.

To do otherwise could jeopardize one's career. Just ask Parry, who writes in his 1993 book *Trick or Treason*:

> I had gotten a reputation around Washington as a "conspiracy theorist." Doors for possible jobs slammed in my face. My mood would darken with the personal attacks accelerated. . . . In this poisonous environment, I often found myself depressed for no other reason than that my faith in the profession of journalism had been shaken. Nearly all my Washington colleagues stayed away from the October Surprise story as if it were a new strain of the plague.

To fully understand why members of the national press corps shied away from controversial stories like the October Surprise, one has to go back to 1983, when, under the guidance of none other than William Casey, the Reagan administration set up an elaborate domestic propaganda apparatus with the help of corporate America. "A group of public relations specialists met with Bill Casey a few days ago," reads a 1983 National Security Council memo. "The group included Bill Greener, the public affairs head at Phillip Morris, and two or three others. They stated what needed to be done to generate a nationwide campaign . . . an effective communications system inside the government. The overall purpose would be to sell a 'new product'—Central America."

That "inside system" became the Office of Public Diplomacy for Latin America and the Caribbean, which was headed by Otto Reich (who has been named assistant secretary of state for Latin America by George W. Bush). Operating out of the State Department, though reporting directly to the National Security Council, Reich commanded a unit of psy-ops agents on loan from the Army. The mission of this covert operation was to sell Congress, the media and the American people on the administration's war against leftists in Central America. The overall theme of the propaganda campaign: "The Nicaraguan Freedom Fighters are fighters for freedom in the American tradition, FSLN [Sandinistas] are evil."

When it came to dealing with the national media, Reich was hands-on. In a memo to President Reagan, Secretary of State George Shultz praised Reich for helping "improve the quality of information the American people are receiving." As an example, Shultz mentioned a spring 1984 *CBS Evening News* report from El Salvador that "conveyed a deceptive image favorable to the guerrillas and distorting of U.S. and Salvadoran government goals." Reich paid a visit to CBS and spent hours with the CBS correspondent and CBS news executives "not in an effort to

The GOP accusers seem a strange lot for throwing stones. Alfonse D'Amato knows the inside of the Senate Ethics Committee like a delinquent student knows the principal's office. Still, he took the lead in lecturing Clinton aides on the fine points of honesty and ethics. When D'Amato's time expired, Phil Gramm stepped up to hurl more rocks, despite his own glass-house relationship with an S&L in Texas. Two other Republicans—Sen. Orrin Hatch of Utah and Rep. Bill McCollum of Florida—expressed outrage over Whitewater. But neither heard nor saw any evil while investigating the Iran-Contra scandal in 1987. Both signed the GOP's minority report that spotted no crimes and no "administration-wide dishonesty or cover-up" in that case.

The GOP's hypocrisy, of course, does not absolve the Clintons from criticism. But in the Whitewater affair, Republicans have shown a dedication to destroying a sitting president—both politically and personally—that has few equals in American history. With the selection of conservative partisan Kenneth Starr as special prosecutor, that GOP campaign has entered a dangerous new phase.

Media Snow Job

JOEL BLEIFUSS

October 28, 1996

On August 18, *San Jose Mercury News* investigative reporter Gary Webb began a three-part series describing how Contra-connected Nicaraguan drug dealers sold tons of cocaine to street gangs in South Central Los Angeles and then turned the profits over to the CIA's Contra army. The Nicaraguans, Webb wrote, supplied much of this cheap cocaine to dope dealer Ricky "Freeway Rick"

Ross, who "turned the cocaine powder into crack and wholesaled it to gangs across the country."

One profoundly troubling aspect of this burgeoning scandal is how the mainstream news media have chosen to cover—or not cover—this story. That the Contras were smuggling drugs is outrageous, but that has been reported in the alternative press, including *In These Times*, for years. That the Reagan and Bush administrations tried to cover up their knowledge of these operations is also old news. Nonetheless, the nation's newspapers of record, particularly the *Washington Post*, have failed to give the story broader exposure. Over the past decade, the *Post* has covered the Contra-cocaine connection only when it could not be ignored.

Kit Boyce

The official investigation into Gary Webb's allegations was an orchestrated PR stunt.

Perhaps there is a method to the madness. "In the '80s, to say 'Contras' and 'drugs' together marked you as a radical conspiracy theorist," says Jim Naureckas, who covered Iran-Contra for *In These Times*. "The story has gone from 'that's ridiculous,' to 'everybody knows about it,' without ever being news in between."

On April 14, 1989, the *Post* devoted one brief story to the final report of the Foreign

embarrass anyone, but simply to try to point out flaws in the information the American people are receiving." Reich conducted dozens of such visits, including one to National Public Radio, where he raged about coverage of the war in Nicaragua. Reich warned news editors that he had "a special consultant service listening to all NPR programs."

When the Iran-Contra scandal was exposed, the Office of Public Diplomacy closed shop, but its public relations functions, strategically integrated into the Republican Party, lived on. These same propaganda skills were very much in evidence during the unfolding of the October Surprise. Bush administration officials even called WBEZ, Chicago's NPR affiliate, after I appeared on a local news talk show to discuss the October Surprise. And in 1988, Abbie Hoffman said that Richard Allen had told him: "If we wanted to, we could have blown *In These Times* right out of history. But why make them famous?"

This public diplomacy *modus operandi* is a common thread that runs through the political events of the past 20 years, from Iran-Contra to Monica Lewinsky. A few examples:

• During his 1992 Christmas Eve pardons of six former administration officials for Iran-Contra related crimes, President George Bush portrayed his friends as the victims of a "profoundly troubling development in the political and legal climate of our country: the criminalization of policy differences." Of course, the six men Bush pardoned were not charged with committing bad policy. Four had been convicted on a total of 10 counts of lying to Congress, and two, former Defense Secretary Caspar Weinberger and Bush's CIA colleague Duane Clarridge, had been charged but not tried on 13 counts of lying to Congress. Among other things, as a result of the pardon, Colin Powell's role in Iran-Contra was never examined. The national media, while acknowledging that Bush pardoned those below him to protect himself, failed to treat the grants of clemency as a national scandal. Ditto for the Democrats. How different the situation was eight years later when President Clinton granted a scandalous pardon to fugitive financier Marc Rich.

• A 1986 *In These Times* story by Dennis Bernstein and Vince Bielski first reported allegations of collaboration between the CIA and cocaine traffickers. Stories about Sen. John Kerry's 1989 congressional investigation into the CIA-Contra-cocaine connection were buried. But the story resurfaced with new evidence in 1996 after an investigation by *San Jose Mercury News* reporter Gary Webb. At first, the national press ignored his "Dark Alliance" series. But as the story circulated widely via the Internet and public outrage began to build, particularly in the African-American community, the *Washington Post* took the lead in trying to discredit Webb.

In October 1996, Robert Suro and Walter Pincus, the *Post*'s national security expert, wrote a scathing critique that acknowledged the basic facts of the story but dismissed Webb's thesis that Contra cocaine-dealing fueled the crack epidemic. Explaining that "the CIA knew about some of these activities and did little or nothing to stop them," the *Post* reporters (and other critics who followed) ignored evidence that the CIA actively interfered with local efforts to curtail the Contra drug operations. And like the October Surprise Task Force, the official investigation into Webb's allegations was an orchestrated PR stunt, even though evidence further corroborating his story is buried in those reports.

• During the Clinton administration, this Republican propaganda apparatus went on the offensive, demonstrating that the same tactics—manipulating willing journalists, concocting official investigations, using the power of elected office (in this case control of the House of Representatives)—could be successfully deployed to attack a sitting Democratic president.

The national press ignored the manipulation of the federal judiciary by right-wing Republicans—which led to the appointment of Ken Starr—and painted a darker

Relations Subcommittee on Terrorism, Narcotics and International Operations, headed by Sen. John Kerry (D-Massachusetts), which found that Contras were involved in drug trafficking and that government agencies were aware of that involvement. After trivializing the report's findings, *Post* reporter Michael Isikoff concluded that claims of drug trafficking by high-level Contras "could not be substantiated."

The *Post* had nothing more to say on the subject until the fall of 1991, when Panamanian Gen. Manuel Noriega went to trial on drug-trafficking charges in Miami. Isikoff then wrote: "Allegations that the federal government worked with known drug dealers to arm the Contras have been raised for years, but congressional investigations in the late 1980s found little evidence to back charges that it was an organized activity approved by high-level U.S. officials."

That assertion was soon contradicted by the U.S. government's own witnesses against Noriega. In October, Floyd Carlton Caceres testified that his smuggling operation flew U.S. guns to the Contras in Nicaragua and brought cocaine into the United States on the return flight. However, federal Judge William Hoeveler, sustaining all objections from U.S. prosecutors, refused to allow Noriega's defense lawyer to press Caceres further on the subject. At one point, Hoeveler snapped, "Just stay away from it."

And in November, convicted Colombian drug lord and government witness Carlos Lehder told the court that an unnamed U.S. official offered to allow him to smuggle cocaine into the United States in exchange for use of a Bahamian island that he owned as part of the Contra supply route. Lehder went on to testify that the Colombian cartel had donated about $10 million to the Contras.

At this point, the *Post* finally took notice. "The Kerry hearings didn't get the attention they deserved at the time," its editorial concluded. "The

Noriega trial brings this sordid aspect of the Nicaraguan engagement to fresh public attention."

How does one square this editorial with Isikoff's dismissive coverage of Kerry's findings two years earlier? If, as the *Post* says, "the Kerry hearings didn't get the attention they deserved," why did the paper's editors at the time bury their one little story about Kerry's report on page 20?

portrait of the Whitewater scandals than examination of the evidence would bear out. *Washington Post* stories in late 1993 and early 1994 authored or co-authored by Michael Isikoff offered ominous-sounding revelations about bureaucratic maneuvers ("Justice Department officials are moving forward with two separate inquiries that have been expanded") and unsubstantiated speculation ("Bill and Hillary Clinton 'could possibly have benefited from the alleged scheme' "). The rest of the press followed suit.

David Brock, who first stoked the rumors of Clinton misdeeds in the pages of *The American Spectator* in 1993, admitted in 1998 that he had been duped. Appearing on CNN's *Crossfire*, Brock acknowledged that Hillary Clinton's charge about a "vast right-wing conspiracy" wasn't far off the mark. "There is a right-wing [apparatus], and I know what it is," he said. "I've been there, I was part of it and yes, they were trying to bring down Bill Clinton by damaging him personally . . . by any means necessary."

Despite evidence to the contrary, talk of a right-wing conspiracy has become a punchline on late-night television. The Clinton scandals, like the best lies, contain a kernel of truth: Clinton's behavior wasn't impeccable, and he lied under oath about an extramarital affair. But the scandal was just the latest example of what has been decades of Republican dirty tricks to subvert democratic government and further a right-wing political agenda. Abhorrent, yes, but not in itself all that surprising.

What's more disturbing is that the national media had incontrovertible evidence this was happening but chose to ignore it. Were it not for *In These Times* and other independent media institutions many of these misdeeds would have never seen the light of day. Yet numerous questions remain unanswered, including what is in the 4 million Iran-Contra documents that remain sealed?

The independent press will continue to investigate. Of course, doing so would be easier if it had the resources (the money and lawyers of the mainstream media) and the power (the congressional ability to subpoena) to get the full story. Lacking both, we make do with what we do have: integrity and faith in the fact that history will eventually show that the truth was on our side.

Oliver North is part of that large, confused group on the right that thinks the lesson of the Bay of Pigs is more air cover next time.

ITT Archives

Home Is Where the Enemy Is

CHRISTOPHER HITCHENS

March 25, 1987

German socialist Karl Liebknecht had a slogan with which he rallied people against imperialist war and Prussian chauvinism. "The main enemy," he would cry, "is at home!" After leading Germany to massacre and defeat in World War I, the German right adopted a paranoid distortion of this internationalist credo and began to preach menacingly about "the enemy within" and the "stab in the back."

Over the past months, we have had many revelations about the world of Oliver North. Yet these have been chiefly journalistic revelations about a world of dummy banks, cut-outs, bag men and secret government. Now it's time to consider what we have learned about the world of right-wing pathology and the powerful images and impulses that sustain it.

Recently I interviewed David Turkheimer, a former member of the Pentagon's Institute for National Strategic Studies and program analyst for the War Game Simulation Center. Last July, he attended a Defense Department "retreat" at Wintergreen, Virginia. A keynote speaker was Oliver North. According to Turkheimer:

> As [North] warmed to the task and realized that, surrounded by political allies, he was preaching to the choir, his talk became more freewheeling. His hostility to the freedom of the press became more open, and he came very near to calling the *Washington Post* traitorous. He added other dubious linkages as well, at one point dragging in a critic's opposition to nuclear power as being proof of the latter's inability to have a legitimate position on foreign policy. Such statements, combined with his continual interrupting of his talk to say to the ceiling, "Got that,

> Ivan?" did nothing to allay my growing suspicion that North was exhibiting symptoms of a paranoid personality.

What have we here? A nut, to be sure. But a certain *kind* of nut, with his own logic and his own theory—and his own mandate from the leader of the Free World. North is a leading member of that large, confused group on the right that is dedicated to wiping out that stain of defeat in Vietnam, that knows the defeat was inflicted by American liberals, and that thinks the lesson of the Bay of Pigs is the necessity of air cover the next time.

The Reagan doctrine was not an unsuccessful search for moderates in Iran. It was a successful search for extremists in the United States. It all reminds me of a warning that Robert Lowell gave to the anti-war movement nearly 20 years ago. "If we fail," he said, "I fear a reign of piety and iron."

While the liberals were making a concerted effort to forget Vietnam, the right was refighting the war in its head and swearing strange oaths. From the assumption that it was enfeebled democracy that had sapped the national will in Indochina, men like North made the deduction that a successful comeback had to be consciously anti-democratic. How astounded they must have been to find a president who so warmly shared their views, and so promiscuously gave them a free hand.

The "secrecy" of this operation, so decried by establishment critics, was its essence. Secret from whom? The Israeli right was told, and the State Department was not. The Iranians were told, and the cabinet was not. Carl Channell and Richard Secord knew, and Sens. Barry Goldwater and Daniel Patrick Moynihan of the Intelligence Committee did not. The Sultan of Brunei was taken into confidence, and the *New York Times* was kept in the dark.

Most of all, the voters and workers and citizens and taxpayers were systematically cheated and deceived. After all, they were at home—where the enemy is.

Get the Picture

WHY CULTURAL JOURNALISM IS MORE IMPORTANT THAN EVER

Terry LaBan

Twenty-one

PAT AUFDERHEIDE

WHEN I FIRST STARTED OUT AS CULTURE EDITOR OF *IN THESE TIMES,* THE NEWSPAPER WAS ONLY FOUR YEARS OLD, AND EVERYBODY HAD AN OPINION on what it should be. One board member told me he thought the culture section should offer an easy-reading entrée to the tough stuff of politics; why he thought this tactic would fool our clever readers into reading anything so boring was something I didn't try to figure out. Other editors were always sure the culture pages were available space if a "hard-news" story of theirs looked like it was running over. Academic readers told me I needed to get more poststructuralist theory into the paper and community organizers lamented the way the section didn't spend more space on locally produced activist theater. It was like flying through an asteroid belt of opinions while trying to navigate the section through a production week. And it was also excellent training in defining what good cultural journalism should be.

I always hope that as critics we engage readers with good writing, amaze them with insights and even make them laugh—but I also think that cultural articles form part of a journalistic mission, one that is growing in importance. The centrality of cultural production to the American economy at the launch of the 21st century—our No. 1 export by some calculations is information/entertainment—has shifted the space and place of cultural reporting. Cultural journalism at its critical best shows us that culture is a dynamic process, shaped not only by the strangling hand of the status quo, but by the wildly unpredictable effects of even small shifts in power. It helps us not only to understand the state of media today, but also gives us a way to imagine tomorrow's communications media—with ourselves in the picture.

That's not, of course, what most cultural journalism does. Most of it shamelessly sycophantic to media moguls and their darlings. It encourages us to think of culture as entertainment, of ourselves as consumers, and of production as something that happens within a branded space. This setup is so disempowering that couch-potato-hood never needs to be explained. Much more interesting is that even with billions of dollars poured annually into the infotainment industry, the setup regularly fails to disempower. In fact, sometimes it even fails to entertain. Certainly consumers value their own expression more than manufactured products: Consider that for every $1 Americans spend on a prepared entertainment product, they spend $10 on homemade, self-created communication using their telephones and computers. In fact, Americans refused to buy computers en masse until they could e-mail and instant-message with them.

Cultural production on a commercial basis is driven by the unforgiving logic of profit and executed with the endlessly repeated process of commodification. But the process of making that commercial culture is full of improbable and unpredictable turns. The people who create the most commercially successful forms of mass media, however jaded and cynical they may justifiably become, exhibit remarkable idealism and creativity along the way. They are acutely aware of their free will. On the front lines of the unending war for control of the sets of symbolic meanings that add up to "reality," every day offers a new battle. Anyone who saw *American Beauty* or *Men in Black* or *Three Kings* can testify to the ability of even the cineplexable product to surprise with its critical perspective on the culture that made it possible.

In an opinion magazine, cultural coverage once was simple. Book reviews held pride of place, as fora for the intelligentsia to disagree among themselves. Other art forms could also be reviewed. An occasional poem could be published (although only at the risk of editors being deluged with breathtakingly bad poetry from places where we didn't even know we had readers). The proliferation of forms of popular expression has widened the circle of relevant products vastly, to include

Q&A: Pauline Kael

PAT AUFDERHEIDE

May 7, 1980

Do you believe that newspaper and magazine film critics play an important role?

Yes, although it depends on the critic. In general, I think people are hostile to critics because they hear the stars and directors on TV jumping on them. But it's so silly, because without criticism you're completely at the mercy of advertisers. The influence of the critic is so small compared with the power of the advertiser. . . .

Not that journalism is in good shape in this country. News writing is awful. Everyone imitates the *New York Times*, and when it adopted all those sections—which was a kind of imitation of *People*—everyone else did. Now there's less space for other kinds of news and for criticism of the arts, and instead they want personality coverage.

The proliferation of gossip and unchecked rumors in journalism is startling. A lot of things are going wrong, and some of it is the result, I think, of Woodward and Bernstein. People are on the tail personally of people in office, but they don't investigate issues. They worry about whether the president stumbles or uses the wrong word, or they jeer at his family. . . .

I don't think the national magazine critics are doing the job they could, mostly because most of them don't stay in it for very long. They don't get involved in their art form enough to take the space to write. They have it if they want it. It has been years since anyone has complained that my *New Yorker* articles are too long.

The only chance for new work, innovative work, work that's disturbing in any way, to reach the public is if a few critics get behind it. Movie studios would be perfectly happy making the same kind of big, star-ridden, boring movies year after year. There would be no chance of new life in the industry.

movies, comic books, performance art, animation, fads, zines and Web sites. This proliferation has been fueled in part by more sophisticated, faster and sometimes cheaper forms of electronic communications.

These whizbang innovations have allowed more people than ever before to produce their own media. At the same time, they have increased the ability of powerful media brokers and producers to spy on customers, outbid rivals and stir up entire dustbowls worth of useless information. This expansion of media provides the visible evidence of an "information economy," in which marketing, media and communication are all both product and process. Ever-larger media companies—the mergers of ABC and Disney; CBS and Viacom; AT&T, TCI and Media One; AOL and Time Warner—relentlessly seek out new markets, cross-marketing opportunities and new products. Increasingly they sell, along with their products, a sense of personal meaning, a social location, a communal connection. AOL is your neighborhood on the Internet; instant-messaging is your buddy system for an untrustworthy world; Disney is your family's friend; and with *Barbie* and *Doom* video games (depending on your gender), you can play with your friends across time and space.

In the process, people of all classes and subcultures have become increasingly self-conscious about media production. But their curiosity and appetite for participation are often poorly served, especially on television. The "making of" documentaries on cable TV, the plugs for the entertainment industry on network TV, and the celebrity profiles of *Entertainment Tonight* neatly excise the "why" and "so what" from their coverage. They play on our understandable desire to make sense of the world through character and storytelling by turning gossip into news and cruelly distilling history into a few familiar story lines. If you watch VH-1's *Behind the Music,* you've seen one of the most tried-and-true formulas: "pride-fall-rehab."

Meanwhile, industry business decisions are cosseted in specialized trade publications or tucked away on the financial

The Empire's New Games

ARIEL DORFMAN

February 29, 1984

As the video game craze spread across the United States, parents complained of coins vanishing and doctors diagnosed new ailments like "joystick hand" and "asteroids finger." Some towns prohibited the coin-op games; others issued ordinances regarding age-limits and the times that arcades should close; and certain countries even forbade the entertainment as pernicious. . . .

But with billions in profits to be had, it is not strange that many justifications have appeared for video games. Educational consultants find them a means of acquiring computer literacy; behavioral scientists speak of "interacting with the technology of the future" and "confidence-building"; psychologists point out that kids are working out their aggressions on the games rather than spending their money on drugs, and that unathletic youths can use the games to acquire status with their peers.

Many of these explanations are probably true, but they do not account, by themselves, for the games' popularity. There may be another explanation. Video games in their present form would be inconceivable if the world did not have the means to blow itself to pieces—because the same technology that spawned real missiles with warheads also spawned those mock missiles with psychedelic flares on the screen. . . .

These computerized games of death are a way both of fulfilling a fear of nuclear death and of comforting the player at the same time; they are ways of "feeling" and "handling" the unthinkable. While they removed from nuclear warfare the distance and remoteness it has assumed in our society, they also allow the fake warrior to witness, and therefore survive, the end of the world. . . .

Computerized games, therefore, give back what the player has lost in society: some degree of participation—twisted, vicarious and tangled as it may be—in the preservation of the player's own existence. The game warns players that they are doomed and insecure and, at the same time, it tells them that, they must hustle, be suspicious, breed quick reflexes and go it alone. Like all mass entertainment, the video game helps its clients to play out their anxieties and identify them without having to acknowledge the loneliness, the hostility, the grinding terror inside.

The game, however, is not that innocent. The U.S. children of the '50s who were harrowed by subterranean visions of extinction and who had to live through the air-raid drills of the Cold War, are the ones who have invented the buttons on today's games. Many of the youngsters frantically playing video games may be in charge of tomorrow's real buttons. In fact, people who live life as a video game may, heaven and Pac-Man help us, be in charge of those weapons right now.

Publish and Perish

PAT AUFDERHEIDE

March 14, 1990

As barriers to freedom of expression fall around the world, here at home a major voice for human rights and diversity of expression was silenced when Pantheon Books was gutted by corporate managers on February 26.

The savaging of Pantheon shows why, under the current system, censorship is not necessary to suppress unfashionable or dissident opinion. Elimination of the vehicles of expression will come, indirectly, to the same thing. And the "invisible hand" never gets dirty.

Pantheon was one of the last enclaves of serious publishing of history and culture for a general

pages, and policy battles—those titanic struggles among industry stakeholders held at the taxpayer's expense—fall right off the news docket. It's easy to sneer at stinky media coverage, but it's harder to come up with good alternatives. Left-wing media and cultural reporting is also hobbled by other intermeshed problems—with the perennial lack of money cruelly conditioning them all. Many leftist writers on culture lack curiosity about popular media—particularly anything on television. They also lack access to the resources that let seasoned media reporters stay current on the terms of media business and of government policy-making. There is also a constant puzzlement of editors of any opinion magazine about whether a media story belongs in the "soft-news" cultural section or the "hard-news" section.

And there is the very real attitude problem—what constitutes a left perspective?—that goes hand-in-hand with the problem that the left these days is a community which shares discontent more than it shares a program or vision. People who can agree on the outrageousness of corporate executives' golden parachutes, or the dreadfullness of child labor overseas, or the ugliness of conditions in meat-packing plants can disagree about almost everything else, including how to fix any of it. This same problem leaves well-intentioned leftists united in their distaste for commercial culture—and little else.

The comfortable fallback position, in leftist cultural reporting and criticism, as elsewhere, is to rant. The old, Marxist-style criticism of political economy reliably yields outrage at the fact that media companies produce profits, benefit the rich, squander opportunities and squash competition when they merge. Unfortunately, all these insights usually end up with some version of the postmodern truism, "whatever is, is wrong." Such an approach doesn't do anything to explain what's different about these arrangements from the past, or how they reflect changes in capitalist production, or why so many people seem to find something they like within commercial mass culture. It can never reveal what the trade papers reveal every day: the enormous uncertainty and confusion among capitalists about how to navigate the transition to a digital era and an information society, whether it's in the form of giddy stock market bubbles that briefly buoyed up clueless upstarts or elephantine jockeying by old-economy titans.

Cultural journalists these days all find themselves deluged by products, overwhelmed by the range of marketing strategies that have created mini-audiences and niche markets in all directions, and often in the position of having their noses pressed to the window of this display of abundance. This has created new challenges for left critics. If they cater to a small demographic or niche product—say, Sundance movies or haute jazz—they hunker into a marginalized position. If they simply get in line at the feeding trough for mass media launches, they become part of the herd. Problems of access, by the way, are getting worse with new technologies. Publicity has become a fine-tuned business, incorporating everything learned from target marketing, and it has become a more vigilant and informed profession now that everybody's an Internet publisher looking for a press pass. Small publications get no respect, no matter their political orientation.

Still, readers have more places to go for cultural journalism than they have time. With so much to read, see and hear—and so little time and money—what is the cultural mandate for a small left publication? I think it's in focusing specifically on power. We should tell our readers about how media and political and social power intersect. We should offer critical readings of influential texts, and show them how to do it themselves. We should describe and evaluate, with all the skills of investigative reporters, attempts to expand media and communications opportunities for the disenfranchised. We should look hard at received wisdom but also crusade for sincerity—that is, for the good faith efforts of talented people to communicate new possibilities.

Peter Hannan

Creating public policy that can rein in the most destructive aspects of media conglomeration is a tricky business.

audience. It stood, over its 47 years, in the shrinking arena between cat calendars and the increasingly vanity-press world of academic publishing. . . .

In the absence of any public policy that recognizes the special role of the media in democracy, it will be difficult to do more than mourn the loss of such institutions. In the current brass-knuckles world of book publishing, any obligation to preserve and nurture cultural resources goes unrecognized either in law or corporate culture.

Creating public policy that can rein in the most destructive aspects of corporate capitalism in media industries is a tricky business. Preserving freedom of speech and the right to publish freely has been safeguarded in this country by keeping government out of press business, and there is little precedent for balancing corporate clout with regulation in the print media.

Part of the problem is rescuing legitimacy—in the deregulated, freewheeling economic environment fostered by the Reagan years—for the public's right to freedom of expression superseding corporate freedoms. That would mean acknowledging that, at times, the interests of media corporations are not wholly consonant with the crucial freedoms of speech and published expression upon which a democracy rests. And that would anger the powerful corporate interests that now cross-feed the biggest entertainment sellers through their publishing, broadcasting, cable and movie pipelines.

Info Bandits

JIM NAURECKAS

March 4, 1996

There's a Latin phrase—*cui bono*—which translates as "for whose good?" It means that you can figure out who is responsible for a situation by looking at who benefits from it. Sometimes, though, it's easier to figure out who benefits by looking at who is responsible.

This rule greatly simplifies the task of comprehending the sweeping Telecommunications Act recently passed by Congress and signed into law by President Clinton. Supporters widely praised the bill as beneficial to the public at large. It would lower prices and improve service, they claimed, by allowing the giant conglomerates of the telecommunications industry to compete with one another. Vice President Al Gore went so far as to call it "an early Christmas present to the consumer."

But the law was not created with consumers in mind. In effect, the bill was bought and paid for by the very telecommunications conglomerates it is supposed to bring under the discipline of the market. Far from mandating competition among telecommunications companies, the act encourages already mammoth corporations to pursue further mergers and allows businesses to form alliances with their supposed rivals in other sectors, greatly reducing the chance that

And what a wonderful, crazy-making time it is to be a media reporter and critic. The digital revolution has created whole new areas of interest. The Internet has been a showcase for bad behavior of all kinds, and for some spectacularly misguided legislation like the censorship-happy Communications Decency Act (since declared unconstitutional, although lookalikes keep popping up everywhere). But the Web, under the guidance of people who are committed to expansion of freedom of expression and democratic dialogue, also has sheltered creative new projects.

At Web Lab (www.weblab.org), for instance, you can visit extraordinary sites where people conduct open, honest and productive conversations on topics ranging from race to suicide to telemarketing. Web Lab is an ongoing experiment, a place to find out what works and what doesn't to make interactivity about more than shopping. (The people at Web Lab turn out to be children of the '60s; founder Marc Weiss was a longtime advocate of independent documentary film-making.) Meanwhile, human rights activists at www.witness.org have used the Web to host a site where you can watch a video, read about human rights abuses, and then act. Violence against women in war, the plight of widows in Nigeria, Colombian Indians threatened by oil producers—the stories told here bespeak not only grave problems, but the healthy effect of making those problems public with vividly produced media.

Public television, once a punching bag for leftists disillusioned with its milquetoast programming, has become a loose federation of entrepreneurial outfits, all of them agitated about what do with digital spectrum and how to pay for it. Since public TV types are acutely aware that the service can't survive without a distinctive identity, we are at a rare moment when notions of public service are actually front and center. PBS's proposal for a weekly show on civic culture as well as *Public Square*, a nightly national news program that would be like a television version of National Public

Radio's *All Things Considered*, has created new excitement among producers who thought they'd never again take public TV seriously.

Public Square is part of a much larger set of questions about the role of media in democracy and public life. The problem of how noncommercial values—the values of citizenship, family, community and civil society—are cultivated in a time of hypercommercial media and political instability is a burning international issue. This problem undergirds arguments, confrontations and even skullduggery in Eastern Europe, where people may have dozens of television and radio channels that mostly just recycle syndicated junk or pump out the propaganda of regional political thugs. The cultivating of civic space in communications media is of grave concern in Russia, where media magnates look warily at gangster-politicians, and in India, where the film industry is an incubator of populist leadership. Canadian indigenous people have won a cable channel of their own and are now puzzling out what to do with it, and whether it's worth the effort.

At a time when screens have proliferated right into ubiquity—they're on your Palm Pilot, in the airport, at the museum and the gas station—it's time to look at how people use those screens when they're trying to rechannel the flow of power. At the Chicago Video Project, for instance, short, punchy videos frame an issue—raising the minimum wage, worker safety, public housing—and are used in Alinsky-style organizing. Black churches nationwide are using a short version of the HBO documentary *Legacy* in community work with people leaving the welfare system.

The industries that propel this fantastic transition in communications need much more attention. There may be nowhere better to do that than at trade conventions where they congregate to hawk wares, float ideas and worry together. One of the key documents of the AOL-Time Warner merger surfaced when a public interest media advocate, Jeff Chester of the Center for Media Education, scooped up a sales pitch from Internet hardware company

new technologies will provide consumers with meaningful choice.

"This was conceived as: How do you get all the industries on board? You give everyone what they want legislatively," says Anthony Wright of the Center for Media Education. "You just give as many carrots as you can. Unfortunately, the consumers weren't invited to that feast.". . .

If the public-interest point of view was lost in the debate over the Telecommunications Act, it was because the bill's primary beneficiaries included media corporations—the same institutions that, in theory, are supposed to inform the public about what its elected representatives are up to.

"The broadcasters made no effort whatsoever to cover the huge giveaways they were getting under the legislation," notes Andy Schwartzman of the Media Access Project, which advocates for public-interest communications reform. According to the *Tyndall Report*, a newsletter that tracks the amount of time nightly newscasts devote to various issues, neither the passage nor the signing of the most sweeping telecommunications legislation in 60

Peter Hannan

The job of a progressive cultural critic should be to tell readers about how media and political and social power intersect.

years made the top 10 stories in their respective weeks.

What coverage there was focused on the probably unconstitutional restrictions on Internet indecency and on the V-chip. Rhetorical attacks on "immoral" speech, a routine many Republicans can probably now perform in their sleep, served to distract attention from the bill's pro-corporate economic agenda.

Print media covered the story little better—in large part because nearly every major newspaper group owns a stake in broadcast media, cable or both. When the *New York Times* editorialized that "after four years of legislative struggle, there was one clear winner—the consumer," it overlooked another clear winner: the New York Times Co., whose five TV stations and two radio stations will vastly appreciate as a result of this deregulation.

Cisco. The brochure spelled out in clear language how cable operators could spy on their customers and slow down their competitors' transmissions. That document helped convince the feds to require the merged company to behave fairly toward competitors.

We need to show up at the open-to-the-public events that establish government policy—the committee hearings in Congress, the regulatory agency workshops, the court proceedings, the international treaty discussions—decoding them and spelling out their implications for public life and democratic opportunity. When the experts argue in front of government officials about how to guarantee consumer privacy online—or how to make Microsoft take its foot off competitors' necks, or how to shape intellectual property laws so that fair use and public domain are protected—they are arguing about the basic terms of culture. Freedom of expression, creative resources, investment in cultural diversity—these are powerfully reshaped by policies that adjust for new digital realities. We also need to build memory, to remind people of the histories of struggle over what now appears to be ordinary fact. And we need to make our Top 10 lists not just from the latest flurry of products, but from work available on bookshelves, video stores and off the Internet, speaking to the concerns our readers have about their present and future.

It has been a privilege to be associated with this kind of project over the years. As these new challenges face us as engaged journalists, cultural reporters and critics of an endlessly inventive commercial culture, the questions we ask will inform and shape our readers' expectations as much as any answers we find. I can't wait.

The Toys Are Us

MATT ROTH

November 11, 1996

We can't be more than a couple of decades away from a time when Disney Inc.—already engulfing rival conglomerates and entangling us in an ever wider web of media events, product tie-ins, retail outlets, planned communities and theme parks—has completed its conquest of the world. We can scarcely imagine our exact place in the new order (will we be among the elite enjoying the servility of courtiers in animal costumes, or janitors interned in a super-efficient "underpark," or maybe workers assembling *Pocahontas* pajamas in a sweatshop?) or all the details of the global Disneyarchy (will Uncle Walt be awakened from his cryogenic slumber to be our leader?). But we do have one reliable oracle of the future: Disney's own propaganda. Thinly veiled in its animated full-length features are Disney's own ambitions, reactionary views of the world and blueprints for social change.

The Lion King, for example, constructs a nightmare from the paranoia of white, middle-class suburbanites. A ghetto full of street-talking, handout-seeking hyenas invade a sunny, well-manicured grassland with the aid of a scheming effeminate traitor who kills the legitimate ruler and converts his unholy alliance with the hyena underclass into a welfare state. The grassland degenerates into a wasteland until the king's rightful heir, Simba—who, thinking he caused his father's death, has retreated into the rainforest counterculture—can give up his decadent, alternative lifestyle; overcome his guilt; vanquish the false king, who rules by inciting class conflict rather than by natural right; and abolish the welfare state, restoring free competition among the species. Only then do prosperity and big-ticket consumer goods (such as antelope) return.

ITT Archives

Work hard. Play hard. . . .

In *Pocahontas*, Disney puts on its friendly face, shifting from grim enforcement of Americanism to the joyous embrace of the Global Village. Ostensibly a plea for tolerance (and an atonement for the Indians of *Peter Pan*), *Pocahontas* is at pains to show that the key to global harmony is communication. In its *West Side Story* take on the conquest of the New World, the clash between Native Americans and Europeans is wholly due to misunderstandings (and to the greed of an effete aristocrat who mistakenly believes there is gold in Virginia). John Smith and Pocahontas, able to understand each other by "listening to their hearts," avert the conflict. The story ends with the English leaving and Pocahontas longing for their return, as if to say that if only people had been able to *talk* to each other, hundreds of years of bloodshed might have been avoided. By implication, the coming communications revolution will bring nothing but benefits to Third World peoples awaiting "discovery" by multinational corporations.

Lest we get carried away with the visions of the upcoming global party, however, we can read the small print in *Toy Story*. This manifesto of the Disney Century amounts to a highly condensed version of the past 10 years' worth of management literature. It consists of two interwoven parables, exploring the riddles that will encompass our lives: The story of the children Andy and Sid teaches us to be proper consumers; the story of the toys Woody and Buzz, proper workers (or, to use Disney-speak, "cast members").

The movie begins in the room of Andy, by all appearances an isolated little boy. He's unable to muster up human friends unless he's having a birthday party, his faceless mother is too busy to do much besides shower him with toys and ferry him to theme restaurants, and his father seems to be nonexistent. Andy spends *a lot* of time with his toys.

For their part, the toys constitute Andy's harem, catering to his every need without troubling him with their lives: They flop into lifeless silence whenever he appears, to be used unprotestingly as he pleases. Even though they're inanimate objects to Andy, the toys actively manage the toy room, organizing themselves according to "team" principles. Woody the Cowboy, highest-ranked according to "play time" and therefore manager, leads not by giving direct orders, but by addressing the other toys' desperate need to provide quality service.

It's the Disney world writ small: Consumers so isolated from other humans they're willing to pay for ersatz social lives, and workers so selfless they willingly reduce themselves to objects for others' consumption. This happy arrangement is threatened, however, by the coming Third Wave. The plot of *Toy Story* begins with the two archetypal events of the new global economy: relocation (as Andy's family prepares to move to a new house) and the threat of human obsolescence.

Woody, having instructed the lower toys to be stoical about their "replacement" by more competitive toys, suddenly finds that he is outdated himself. Buzz Lightyear, Andy's new birthday gift, is a Space Ranger arrayed with gadgetry, including a push-button voice that outdazzles Woody's simplistic pullstring; his unscrewable arm reveals a robotic nature that contrasts with Woody's cloth-and-stuffing flesh. Woody, a cowboy, is the archetypal human nakedly confronting nature; Buzz the astronaut is encased in technology. Soon Andy starts paying more attention to Buzz, leaving Woody in the toy chest. In a fit of Luddism, Woody pushes the Space Ranger out the window, leaving both stranded "outside."

So there's a downside to the revolution; even managers can lose their jobs (and dirty tricks that sidestep honest competition will only backfire). But Disney shows the way out: Woody has to learn not to fight Buzz, but to work with him. Their joint journey of punishment and redemption, as they try to make it back to the toy room through the wastelands of suburbia, ends in a partnership of management and technology. In the final crisis, in which the two race to overtake the vehicles taking Andy's family to a new house, the subordinate toys are no help at all. But when Woody applies raw ingenuity (and a bottle rocket) to Buzz's technology, the two of them literally soar above the clouds. It's only the lower ranks who are obsolete after all.

The other climax of the movie resolves the Sid and Andy parable. Sid, the kid next door, is the embodiment of evil. In the Disney lexicon, he is the bad consumer, too much the content-provider of his own imagination. (Andy, on the other hand, rarely puts words into Woody's or Buzz's mouth that aren't part of their pre-recorded repertoire.) Sid's cardinal sin is disrespect for intellectual property: He breaks trademarked toys apart and rearranges them into personal creations (or simply uses them as fodder for explosives). Moreover, he finds or steals toys rather than acquiring them through authorized channels.

Sid's punishment is the revelation that the toys are alive—they *hate* him, and are policing his every move. Toys, who speak directly to the camera, command Sid to "play nice" and tell him "we are watching you." The threatening message to youngsters is as strong as the wish-fulfillment fantasy: The technology that suckles also surveils.

Sid, in any case, is left miles behind by the end of the movie. Paradise is regained in a presumably more upscale suburb. All of the toys have made it to the new toy room; the specter of replacement has vanished. How? Apparently by both the consumer and the cast working harder: Andy has increased his play-effort to accommodate both Woody and Buzz.

So, if we want to enjoy the global party of the next century, our roles are clear. We have to be good workers, self-negating and open to continuous change; and we have to be good consumers, properly paying for the content of our lives. If we obey these simple precepts, come what may, we will thrive.

Or will we? If the medium of *Toy Story* is the message, we're in trouble. The animation was subcontracted to Pixar Studios, whose computer techniques caused, in the words of the president of the animators' union, "a little bit of nervousness that happens with every revolution." The revolution was mainly a labor-cutting one. According to *Entertainment Weekly*, "*The Lion King* ran to $45 million and employed 810 animators, compared with *Toy Story*'s $30 million budget and a staff of 100." To save 30 percent in costs, human labor was cut by almost 80 percent. Disney obviously expects a windfall when the costs of the technology plummet; it's hard to say how much solace out-of-work animators will find in Disney's swelling profit margins.

Decrying the mode of *Toy Story*'s production, though, may get you kicked our of Dis-Topia. Instead, we must attend closely to the movie's instructions: Work hard. Play hard. And leave the rest to Mickey Mouse.

Red vs. Blue

HOW THE CULTURE WARS KILLED POPULISM

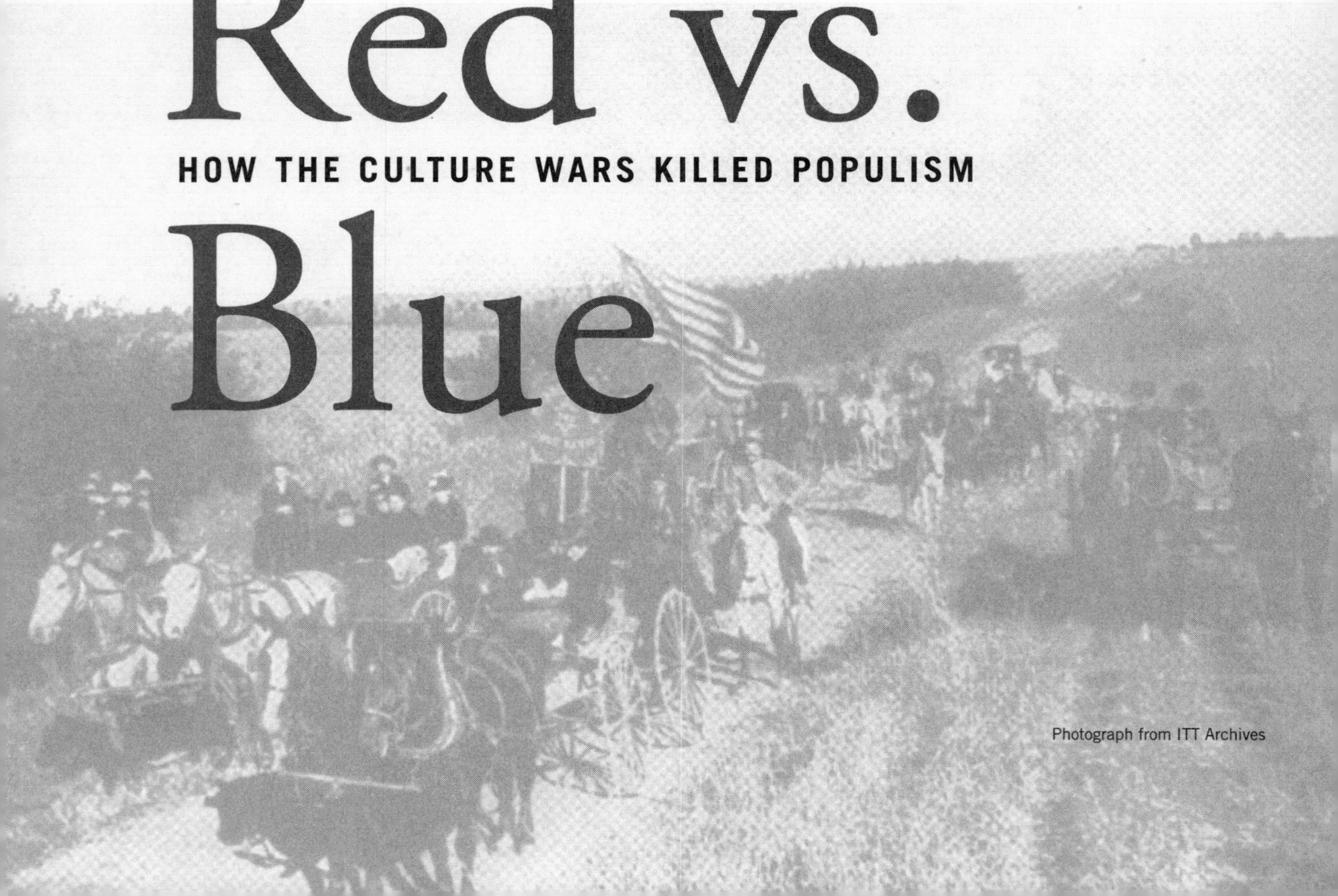

Photograph from ITT Archives

Twenty-two

CHRIS LEHMANN

EVEN AS A BLAND MANAGERIAL CENTRISM STEALS OVER MORE AND MORE OF THE NATION'S POLITICAL LANDSCAPE, AMERICA REMAINS INCONGRUOUSLY convulsed by culture wars. Every conceivable subject of debate—from Eminem's Grammy nomination to President Clinton's impeachment—now gets baptized, scripted and punditized in the image of a bipolar contest between caricatured fifth columns struggling to establish permanent control of our culture. The routine, overheated rhetorical depiction of these forces (barbarism vs. theocracy, decadence vs. censorship, narrow-minded bigots vs. "politically correct" puritans) guarantees they command no allegiance in the real world. And yet there they are, choreographing the course of American politics in ways that would have been unthinkable a mere three decades ago.

To take just the most obvious case study, consider the immediate fallout of the 2000 presidential contest. The actual questions of most urgent political moment—whether the ballots of the Florida electorate were tabulated fairly, whether the 14th Amendment has any meaning in our formal democracy—were consigned instantly to the courts (where they were laid to rest in just about the most unsatisfactory manner imaginable). The rest of us were tediously urged to mull over the breakdown of states that fell into the column for either major-party candidate as a Rorschach Test of our national psyche—and as evidence that America is bitterly divided, indeed "Two Americas." This notion was so simple-minded that it was quite literally color-coded: The coastal, heavily urban states carried by Al Gore were mapped out in blue; the heartland states that went for Bush were presented in red.

This image sent every pundit swooning. The very contours of the land were showing us the profile of our

"Two Americas": the red one being tradition-bound, moralistic, Bible-believing and (perhaps not coincidentally) sparsely populated; the blue one being urban, secular, relativist and liberal. In Redland, everyone supported school prayer, questioned evolution and reviled Bill Clinton. In Blueland, everyone supported late-term abortions, gleefully hurled government dollars at transgressive art and recognized Clinton as their sybaritic brother-in-arms, a virtual poster boy of Boomer rebellion. Red states all fell silent on Sunday mornings as the hard-working citizens sought forgiveness and comfort in Protestant houses of worship; Blue states shook every weekend with performance art shows and drug-saturated raves. The landlocked masses in the Red states consumed our most abject mass entertainment; the tanned Caligulas along the coasts cynically produced it. And so on.

There's no great need to dwell on the obvious here—that even in times of comparatively high turnout, an electoral map only charts the sadly limited preferences of less than a plurality of registered voters, let alone an "America." What's instructive about such official shibboleths is not so much their content as their form. The Red states, while actually harboring fewer citizens within their borders, are taken to be the home of the sensibilities of The People, plain and true, undistorted by the sophistries of the symbolic analysts and tax collectors. The Blue states, though more populous, are paradoxically taken to be the base of our powerful national elites, terrified of gun owners and church ladies, but determined to control all of our major cultural institutions with grimly earnest Leninist discipline.

Buried within this, and countless other set-pieces of culture warfare, is the political language of populism. And to account for the proliferation of the populist mythology of cultural warfare, we must briefly take stock of the historical fate of American populism. The People's Party of the late 19th century grew out of

Political Correctness and Identity Politics

BARBARA EPSTEIN

February 26, 1992

I hesitate to use the term "political correctness" without quotation marks because I have never heard it used on the left except in a joking way; as far as I know, it is not used to refer to a politics that anyone actually endorses. Also, I hesitate to adopt a term that carries the right-wing agenda of the neoconservatives. But the term does get at what seems to me to be a troubling atmosphere having to do with the intersection of identity, politics and moralism.

The neoconservatives describe "politically correct" students and faculty denouncing and intimidating liberals, and clearly there are instances of this—but what I am more aware of is a process of self-intimidation in the name of sensitivity to racism, sexism and homophobia, which tends to close down discussion and make communication more difficult.

In an article on PC in *New York* magazine, John Taylor claims that the guiding principle of PC is: "Watch what you say." People are being denounced, he wrote, for speaking of Indians rather than Native Americans or blacks rather than African-Americans, or for using the word "girl" rather than "woman"—even when the person in question is a teen-ager. One can object that we *should* watch what we say: that this is what is required to criticize and, ideally, transform a culture that is deeply imbued with racism, sexism and homophobia. Still, there is a difference between maintaining a critical awareness of the assumptions behind our language and creating a subculture in which everyone fears being charged with bias or is on the lookout for opportunities to accuse others of it. . . .

The tendency to use ideology as a bludgeon is an ever-present danger for a social movement. The an ambitious program of economic self-organization on the part of small landholders, shopkeepers, urban reformers and industrial workers—most of the same people who still inhabit the "Middle America" of the 21st-century pundit's mind. The main tributary of the 19th-century Populist insurgency was the Southern Farmers Alliance, which began as an effort to combat debt peonage of the tenant farmer, and evolved into a wide-ranging crusade to set the nation's economic accounts on a strict course reflecting the interests of the producers of wealth. Populists sought to nationalize utilities and railroads, bust trusts of land and resources, and transform the nation's currency, both by eliminating the gold standard and by instituting a "Subtreasury Land and Loan System" weighting exchange to crop production.

Even though the Populist movement flamed out in the spectacular catastrophe of fusion with the Democrats in 1896, it has cast a singularly long shadow on American reform politics. Much of the Populist agenda became diluted and later enacted into law via the labors of the Progressive movement, but its most lasting, if unexpected, legacy has been in the vocabulary of cultural confrontation, which has shrewdly bypassed—and indeed, baldly inverted—the Populist economic vision of democratic class conflict. This has been a long, bumpy, complicated transformation, in which the rhetoric of Populist producerist participation has been supplanted (on the left and right alike) by a resentful demand for greater consumer representation.

The People of the original Populist worldview were defined, loosely, by their capacities as creators and cultivators of plenty—their role in what was widely known among the reformers of the 19th century as the "cooperative commonwealth." The People of our own post-ideological political age, on the other hand, are defined principally by their sense of profound symbolic exclusion. On the right, they are cynically championed by the practitioners of the 1960s backlash—the astonishingly

Terry LaBan

A politics organized solely around defending identities makes it more difficult to create the coalitions needed to build a movement for progressive change.

"correct lineism" of the Marxist tradition involved a humorless, single-minded focus on results. By contrast, today's "political correctness" comes out of a movement, or a political atmosphere, that is dominated by identity politics. It is more oriented toward moral than strategic thinking; it often seems more concerned with what language is used than with what changes are made in the social structure. The danger is not so much regimentation as preachiness, a search for moral self-justification, the assigning of moral status in terms of exclusion and subordination, and the use of moral judgments as clubs against ourselves and others.

Perhaps today's "political correctness" bears some relation to the peculiar situation in which we find ourselves in the '80s and '90s. We have considerable cultural influence, at least in some areas (notably the university and intellectual circles) but virtually no political clout. This state of affairs can lead to frustration, cynicism about the possibility of political effectiveness, and a temptation to focus on berating each other rather than finding grounds for unity.

In a world of shifting identities, emphasizing one's difference from others can give organizations, and people, a sense of security. But it can also stymie efforts to find common ground for action. I am not arguing that we should soften our opposition to racist, sexist and homophobic language, but that a politics that is organized around defending identities based on race, gender or sexuality forces people's experience into categories that are too narrow and also makes it difficult for us to speak to one another across the boundaries of the identities—let alone create the coalitions needed to build a movement for progressive change.

Sell the Kids for Food

SCOTT McLEMEE

May 2, 1994

Kurt Cobain had not been dead long at all before his suicide was transformed into a media fetish. His body was discovered on a Friday. By the next Monday, his face was on the cover of *Newsweek*. Give it a few months and every Kurt Cobain demo tape, every stray guitar squeak, will be available as part of a CD boxed set.

But in the meantime, the suicide has served as the latest symbolic commodity on the market, distributed by the Twentysomething Anguish Division of Culture Industry Inc. A few hours after Cobain's body was discovered, the *Washington Post* had located some interview subjects who knew the Generation X script well enough to say what they were supposed to: "He killed himself for the same reason I'd kill myself. We lack something. We have no core."

Get a clue, kids. Suicide is not a tattoo. Putting a 12-gauge to one's head and pulling the trigger is not a statement of protest. And the manner in which Cobain chose to end his life is not incidental: He meant to get the job done. He obeyed a compulsion—emerging from unknown sources within a deeply wounded personality—to die.

long-legged demonization of the welfare state as cultural revolution by other means that has fueled successive rightist insurgencies from George Wallace to Richard Nixon to Ronald Reagan to Newt Gingrich.

On the left, they are championed—no less cynically, but far less effectively—by critics and academicians of the popular culture renaissance known as cultural studies. Like the backlashers, leftist cultural populists firmly believe culture determines all political life—and that our politicized popular culture represents, in a time of collapsed left electoral ambitions, the most beguiling forum for political transformation. (These beliefs, like other articles of leftist faith, claim little allegiance among aspirants to political power but positively transfix leftist critics and writers who are, astonishingly enough, influential mainly in academic circles.)

The cross-ideological consensus of cultural populism has been abetted by the sweeping nature of populist terminology. Once "producerism" ceased being a viable category of economic self-description for many Americans—indeed, once the United States became the mother of all consumer republics—the Populist tradition was pretty much up for grabs. Anyone who stepped forward to produce a jeremiad against some nefarious conspiracy or another could become, by sheer force of imputed exclusion, a voice of The People. Thus the welter of confused interpretations that has sprouted since large-P Populism passed from the historical stage. The populist label has been affixed to any and all movements with a whiff of mass-democratic delusion about them—from Coughlinism and McCarthyism to the New Left and the curious phenomenon of H. Ross Perot.

Yet over the past generation or so, the promiscuous identification of the Populist movement with what political scientists of the Cold War called "plebiscatory democracy" has ceded ground to the rampant conflation of populism with the culture wars. This odd development is itself eloquent testimony to the utter, through-the-looking-glass character of latter-day political reckoning with the notion of social class in America. The rhetoric of class and the masses has given way to the amorphous, self-conscious quandaries of taste and attitude: One is no longer an oppressor or a robber baron in the world of the culture lord; one is an "elitist"—that all-purpose villain who dares to question the ultimate liberating power of mass culture or the pieties of audience reception theory (or, if the self-styled populist in question is a right-winger, the conniving elitist is a liberal journalist, a PC professor or an ACLU attorney). Likewise, one is only "radical" nowadays in the land of perception and attitudes: By pursuing a politics of "representation" in the mass media, by endorsing corporate campaigns of "diversity" hiring and sensitivity, by treating universities as principal sites of political conflict, the left has adapted itself quite comfortably to the prevailing terms of political engagement.

Now the really curious thing about the culturalization of populism is that it owes its birthright to neoconservatism. Indeed, the neoconservative appropriation of class in our time, via the famed "New Class" hypothesis, makes up one of the most influential and interesting right-wing conspiracies going, far more momentous than anything perpetrated by Kenneth Starr or Richard Mellon Scaife.

The New Class cabal begins, fittingly enough, with a reconstructed Trotskyist, *The National Interest* founder and Reagan strategist named Irving Kristol. Following the lead of other defectors to the right, such as managerial theorist James Burnham (and appropriating Yugoslavian leftist Milovan Djilas' critique of the Communist *nomenklatura*), Kristol laid out a class-based explanation of liberalism's ongoing appeal in an age when (by neocon reckoning) liberal government was producing policy disaster after policy disaster. Kristol was not merely appealing to crude historical materialism here—he was, like most of his ideological opposite numbers in today's left academy, a student of the more nuanced, but supremely powerful, political instrument of cultural hegemony. Culture—the media, the university, the

In brief, Kurt Cobain's final exit had no connection whatsoever with the grungewear you bought last month at The Gap. . . .

But that is not the story we want to hear. And so the media has reconstituted the private motives of Cobain's suicide within a spectacular public narrative—tailored to fit the demands of the consuming public.

In this version of the story, Cobain's life was the punk-rock equivalent of the Horatio Alger myth. As *Newsweek* explained, Nirvana "hated the slick, MTV-driven rock establishment so much they took it over." Sure they did. Sort of like the Remington Micro-Screen Shaver guy in reverse; they hated it so much, they bought the company.

A working-class kid, a sickly boy with divorced parents, a high school dropout whose father pressured him into taking a test to join the Navy (he smoked a joint and thought better of it)—Kurt Cobain sat down one day with a couple friends and launched a hostile takeover of a major culture industry.

And just wait for the made-for-TV movie—by now doubtlessly into production. See the young Kurt sell his Journey and Pat Benatar albums (the audience smirks knowingly) to buy a ticket to a Black Flag show. Watch Kurt's band record its first album for $600. And listen to him, 10 million Nirvana records later, singing to a stadium of fans:

He's the one / who likes all our pretty songs / and he likes to sing along / and he likes to shoot his gun / but he don't know what it means / don't know what it means. . . .

During the week following Cobain's death, I listened to his songs and carefully watched the press and television coverage of the suicide. By degrees I came to feel bitter. The immersion left me sick of instant psychosocial diagnoses—like *Newsweek*'s conclusion that "grunge is what happens when children of divorce get their hands on guitars." And I was disgusted by the cultural machinery of lifestyle capitalism, which wasted not a second in appropriating the death for its own ends.

Mostly, though, I was angry—immoderately angry—at Cobain himself. At 30, I am a little too old to carry on like the kids interviewed in the *Post*. And I recognize that only his friends and family can properly claim to grieve a personal loss. Yet artistic talent is, in some complex way, a kind of public resource. It should not be destroyed. That Cobain did destroy it seems unforgivable.

To some extent, Cobain did seem to have a sense of the political responsibility inherent in his public role. "I have a request for our fans," he wrote in the liner notes to *Incesticide*. "If any of you in any way hate homosexuals, people of a different color, or women, please do this one favor for us—leave us the fuck alone!"

Had his personal demons been banished, he might have played a greater role in fighting the public evils tormenting others. That is, had he refused the Hemingway solution, that last fatal gesture of macho.

Textual Reckoning

THOMAS FRANK

May 27, 1996

Almost from its inception, the playful practice of poststructuralism has been dogged by a curious sense of its own absurdity. The high theorists of the genre often veer toward—and sometimes beyond—high silliness. There's something about the field's combination of nearly incomprehensible jargon, its grand claims of subversiveness and its practitioners' air of self-importance and professorial correctness that makes it a natural, even

arts and education bureaucracies—formed the procrustean bed where the New Class proliferated.

It lacked all sorts of analytical persuasiveness, but Kristol's notion was well-timed: It burrowed headlong into long-festering resentments among the lower-middle- and working-class white ethnic voters who would come to be designated as Reagan Democrats. It's not hard, on one level, to see why the idea caught on, and continues to exert considerable appeal in such circles: It touches on a class animus that liberalism easily inspired, as it continued to hemorrhage its traditional constituencies among lower-middle- and working-class Americans.

And its American appeal was precisely in its swift consignment of class identity to forces of cultural determinism. By Kristol's account, the members of the New Class were pre-eminently a cultural elite, a breed who strenuously set themselves apart from the everyday trials of working life. They regarded Great Society social engineering as a sort of self-administered full-employment plan, garlanding their evermore arrogant sense of bureaucratic entitlement with a rhetoric of enlightened social uplift. (Kristol's neocon colleague Daniel Patrick Moynihan would characterize the typical member of the New Class as the sort of government consultant who spent most of his time on the train between Washington and New York—a man, in other words, much like Moynihan himself.)

New Class apparatchiks were also political elitists of the first order, disdaining the effort to put their beliefs to the test of democratic procedure, opting instead for top-down transfusions of political authority from the courts—the most elite of American political institutions. The New Class was, in other words, shifty, overeducated and power-mad: They knew what was best for you, and they knew how to compel your obedience. In cultural matters, they oozed fastidious detachment from ordinary Americans and their preoccupations: The New Class typically inhabited suburbs or rapidly gentrifying urban enclaves. From such perches, they would peer down on the remote, lower-class folkways of Middle America with a certain appalled alienation—or, at best, bemused condescension. The exotic mores of the lower-middle class—parochial ethnic pride, rigid family discipline, religious belief—furnished curios of antiquarian or ironic cultural interest, against which members of the New Class could burnish their own sense of sophistication or hard-earned worldly detachment.

What has proven remarkable about the New Class thesis is not its descriptive power. It conspicuously omits, for example, the overlords of the state and corporation, who have no need to compose themselves into scheming bureaucratic elites, since their grip on the machinery of both economic and cultural power is uncontested and openly celebrated. And as Christopher Lasch observed, the New Class critique, by focusing obsessively on the alleged liberal and relativist assaults on political virtue and cultural self-discipline, overlooks how consumer capitalism wreaks infinitely more destructive damage on the self and the *gemeinschaft* alike.

No, the New Class thesis has been successful in a much greater, and prototypically American, project: It has transposed all notions of class conflict onto the battlefield of culture. As a result, right-wing professors, journalists and think-tank intellectuals—themselves, of course, all but card-carrying members of the New Class—have long been able to pose as champions of The People, simply by demonizing their opposite numbers in the welfare state, the liberal media and the left professoriate.

Today's populists of the right indulge this self-dramatizing reflex in richly diverse idioms and arenas. Some, of a libertarian bent—P. J. O'Rourke, Russ Smith, Fred Barnes—fancy themselves as celebrants of individual expression and even a certain Dionysian hedonism, defending the sundry pleasures of cars, tobacco, predatory sex and warfare from the frumpy elites who would regulate or outlaw them. Other obsessively self-documenting prisoners of the "PC" culture—such as Robert Bork, Gertrude Himmelfarb and William Bennett—

Peter Hannan

The high theorists of poststructuralism often veer toward—and sometimes beyond—high silliness.

obligatory, target of parody and farce. A discipline that makes much of puns and cleverness, it issues a standing challenge to the prank-inclined: I dare you to outwit me. . . .

This is why most of the professors and graduate students I know reacted with giddiness when they heard about physicist Alan Sokal's admission in *Lingua Franca* that his article on postmodern science that appeared in the Spring/Summer 1996 issue of *Social Text*, the respected journal of cultural studies and theory, was in fact a hoax. Sokal's essay bears all the earmarks of a classic prank: Plausible enough on the surface to get by *Social Text*'s panel of respected academic editors, it is spotted as a hoax immediately by those who are more skeptical of the magazine's mission.

Titled "Transgressing the Boundaries: Toward a Transformative Hermeneutics of Quantum Gravity," it conforms to the genre's conventions with a hilariously studied slavishness. Sokal carefully includes the usual pious references to the "subversive" power of interdisciplinarity; he takes pains to flatter and agree with the editors of *Social Text* and goes out of his way to assail their usual targets; he summons the usual barrage of references and quotations, many of them predictably impenetrable; and he closes with confused calls for an "emancipatory mathematics" and "a liberatory postmodern science."

"I confess, I don't understand half of the jargon I used," Sokal says. "But that's part of the point, that one can get an article accepted and look like an expert even if you don't understand what you're talking about." A long-standing leftist (Sokal taught in Nicaragua under the Sandinista government, a fact he takes pains to foreground whenever discussing his deed) and disturbed by what he calls "sloppy thinking" in the academic left's critique of science, Sokal resolved to intervene in a forcible and humiliating manner. "I took the silliest things written about physics and mathematics by the most prominent people," he recalls, then "invented an argument relating it all." . . .

The most revealing reactions to the prank are those of *Social Text*'s publishers. In spite of its usual tendency to celebrate the upending of authority, the twitting of order and anti-hierarchical gestures, the journal has retreated quickly into talk of professional ethics and betrayal of academic good faith. Even Stanley Fish, executive director of Duke University Press (*Social Text*'s publisher) and a scholar who has deftly transmuted textual indeterminacy into professional renown, has gotten involved in the question, issuing a statement supporting *Social Text* and chiding Sokal for using his "professional credentials" to deceive.

And one can't help but conclude that, in one sense, maybe Fish has got it right: For all the big issues that appear to be involved, this is ultimately a battle over competing definitions of professionalism, nothing more. The poststructuralist jargon Sokal deployed so devastatingly is the sacred talk of a professional group, a private banter whose function is precisely to keep outsiders like Sokal out. But call for a complete culture-wide rehabilitation of America's moral sense, a sort of Maoist assault on every last remnant of '60s sensibility, even though countercultural rebellion is now the heart and soul of our commercial consumer culture, from the sloganeering of Apple Computers to the investor anodynes of thestreet.com.

All of which points up the woozy unreality of the class-to-culture alchemy. The great elastic demonology of cultural populism works in all settings, trained against any available straw man—say, the record industry or "the culture of welfare"—while the forever unmobilized (and no less symbolic) constituency of The People languishes somewhere far offstage as the designated benefactors of the Kulturkampf's spoils: the forgotten middle class, the silent majority, the sober churchgoers who work hard and play by the rules.

Yet the truly astonishing thing is how the left has taken the bait. After ceding the main premises of the New Class critique—that culture determines all, that symbolic exclusion trumps class inequality, that controlling the media and the university produces the most meaningful form of political power—the left now devotes most of its discursive energies in the matters of class to asking how deeply the New Class critique batters its own self-image. There is no longer much question, it seems, of mobilizing actual working people into the ranks of the nonexistent left; instead there is the endless, anxious self-examination over the staggeringly hypothetical question of who gets to speak *on behalf* of such unmobilized constituencies and why.

The spoils of cultural populism predictably have been far more meager on the left than on the right: Instead of electing progressive political leaders, it has accomplished little more than launching a new path to tenure and letting a thousand journal articles bloom. Examples can be multiplied at numbing length, from the high tide of '80s cultural studies scholarship, when ephemeral productions from *Pee-wee's Playhouse* to *Dynasty* were accorded serious treatment as subversive documents of cultural dissent, down through the efforts of writers such as Andrew Ross and Ellen Willis to theorize a politics of left dissent that celebrated mass culture while thrillingly parting company with the discredited shibboleths of merely economic-minded left majoritarianism—or, in other words, any viable political strategizing.

But left cultural populism gained its greatest cachet when the frenzy of President Clinton's impeachment kicked into high gear. Here was a moment when a Democratic president (who by a certain exercise of political fantasy was held to be a liberal hero, singled out, so the fable went, by Ken Starr's inquisition for his laughably inert political convictions) was held to public view as the victim (as his no-less opportunistic wife famously put it) of a "vast right-wing conspiracy." What was more, the American public approved of his job performance and disavowed Congress' great cultural *anschluss* (many Clintonites with a straight face labeled the impeachment vote in Congress an attempted coup, even though it was a televised legal proceeding; and it's hard, in any event, to see what rightist coup objective would be achieved in installing Al Gore to the Oval Office).

Right down to the smallest flourishes of personal attitude and comportment, this was a culture war all but ordered up from central casting: Reps. Henry Hyde, Bill McCollum, Bob Barr and company were all tightly wound religious moralists with bad hair, and many of them were Southerners to boot. Ken Starr liked to pray when he jogged—and his button-down surrogates who conducted the president through his grand-jury testimony were grim Comstocks of the old school, typically repressed yet secretly titillated by all the salacious details of the president's dalliances.

Here was a cultural populist godsend, in other words, affording Clinton enthusiasts on the left the opportunity to celebrate the president's cultural transgressions—*and* invoke the will of The People! No sooner had the Starr Report

it's a jargon with a curious twist, a professional language that celebrates anti-professionalism, that fetishizes the subversive power of transgression and the virtue of the democratic multitude. Over the years it has always moved quickly enough—obsoleting itself as soon as it is taken up by a wider audience—to stay ahead of the crushing consequences of this contradiction, allowing cultural studies academics to present themselves, with only limited difficulty, as a professional vanguard of the popular will. But it is the exposing of this contradiction that gives Sokal's deed such resonance.

Cynical and Proud

CHRIS LEHMANN

May 12, 1997

Over and over again, hapless news readers and viewers hear that the fabric of American democracy has been coarsened by the reflexive "gotcha" coverage that governs political reporting—the procedure of catching candidates, leaders and other public figures in small, ostensible hypocrisies.

In fact, all press protestations to the contrary, the American public is almost twice as cynical as the media. According to a 1995 survey, some 77 percent of the public rated the honesty and ethics of Washington officials as low. Only 40 percent of national journalists held this admittedly cynical view.

Given this curious juxtaposition, perhaps it's time to make a fresh, and more open-minded, appraisal of the virtues of public cynicism. Sure, a certain kind of petulant, knee-jerk cynicism among citizens can translate into a lowest-common-denominator, "what's-in-it-for-me?" view of politics. But wouldn't it be infinitely more disturbing if the public hadn't responded with cynicism to the swelling nexus of finance scandals issuing from the White House? After all, cynicism, strictly speaking, is nothing more than the view that self-interest governs most human affairs—and the Clinton campaign finance scandals certainly bear abundant testimony to that proposition.

Moreover, cynicism has an upside: an honorable philosophical pedigree and a demonstrated usefulness in the struggle to reclaim democracy. After all, Diogenes, the original cynic, wasn't a glib forerunner of Beavis and Butthead, looking for quick debunking opportunities. He sought out an honest man, and ultimately found more palatable company among the dogs (the term cynic, indeed, stems from the Greek word for "dog"). And in latter-day authoritarian regimes, we've had plenty of avowed cynics rally impressively to the daunting, draining work of civic reform and reclamation. Nelson Mandela, Lech Walesa and Vaclav Havel, to

Kit Boyce

Perhaps the media should take the cynicism of the public more seriously.

surfaced than liberal writers set about christening the president—suddenly no longer the world's most powerful leader—as an oppressed, Romantic anti-hero in the blessed image of cultural liberation. Toni Morrison famously dilated in the pages of *The New Yorker* on how Clinton—Southern and poor, raised by a strong mother in a single-parent family—was actually the nation's first black president. Screenwriter Joe Eszterhas constructed a fictionalized account of both Clinton's sexual history and the tangled Lewinsky affair (featuring, among other things, a talking presidential, uh, staff) all by way of declaring Clinton both an archetype of Boomer maleness and a "rock-'n'-roll" leader of the free world.

Then rock critic and cultural historian Greil Marcus, in what seems an all-but-inevitable dialectical synthesis, pronounced the symbolic convergence of Clinton and Elvis, White Negro and rock 'n' roller par excellence. And tellingly, the one thing that each of these pop icons truly shared in common—their regional class backgrounds—is breathlessly minted, by Marcus' peculiarly disheveled method of critical free association, into the eternally weightless currency of cultural liberation. Here is but one of Marcus' typical effusions on this score:

> The unknowableness, or unseeableness, of Elvis Presley and Bill Clinton is part of their common status as outsiders in an America rewritten in the 1950s by means of a newly magical, newly dominant and altogether unitary media, which from 1945 rushed in to fill the huge gap in the nation's public life, its sense of purpose and definition, left by the death of Franklin Roosevelt. It was an era when images of the good, of what it meant to be American and to be taken seriously as such, were framed by a very few sources: *Life* magazine, daily newspapers, three television networks and advertisements for cars, refrigerators and Scotch. As white male southerners without family money (hillbillies, no 'counts, white trash—the source, of course, of much of the identification made

between Bill Clinton and Elvis Presley, and of Clinton's own heartfelt or cynical identification of himself with Elvis), Presley and Clinton always had to prove themselves—and they never could, not without abandoning themselves in some essential way, some way that one or the other or both could perhaps desire but never master.

In Marcus' America, a political leader who dismantled the foundations of the American welfare state (and who not incidentally, concealed evidence, suborned testimony, lied under oath and resorted to wag-the-dog bombing raids throughout the lowest sort of self-inflicted political crisis) is cognate with the man who crooned "Love Me Tender." Somehow, a man who delivers 550 speeches a year, before all manner of global media, is invisible—just as, by the same neo-Faulknerian logic, a Memphis truck driver who was trying his best to sound like Bing Crosby is a delectably orientalized other of the "no 'count" American South. Just squint, and through the kudzu you can behold both men treading fraternally through the travails of their "unseeableness" in the culture, struggling heroically to efface their standing as "outsiders" in a world of cold, indifferent photo magazines and refrigerator ads. It was also Marcus' response, as he records it, to Clinton's sax-blowing performance of "Heartbreak Hotel" on *The Arsenio Hall Show* in 1992, that a new cultural-cum-social contract was being forged: "I know that political speech cannot make the body politic speak," Marcus grandiosely proclaims. "Only cultural speech can do that."

Well, no, actually. Whatever Marcus may mean by "cultural speech" (try, if you can, to imagine what *acultural* speech may sound like) it has fatally abetted the flight of public discourse from anything resembling the body politic. This sort of pseudo-populist culture-speak manages at every turn to substitute the taste preferences of the interpreting self for the lineaments of any useful public distinctions of morality, legal accountability and—not least by a long shot—class, which emerges here as but a fungible tic of personal history,

name just three prominent examples, have all been practicing cynics, brandishing in spades the very traits that seem to worry the American pundit class: an open distrust of their government, a refusal to believe that official spokespeople were telling the truth or serving anything other than their own interests, and even, in some cases, a disarming ability to question their own reform-minded motives. These are all qualities that democracies would do well to cultivate.

Yet none of this ever seems to occur to the tribunes of American political debate, who resolutely cling to the conviction that the minds of most Americans are made of sealing wax, and that a more or less perfect correspondence obtains between the attitudes encoded in national press coverage and the outlook of the public.

A frank acknowledgment of the true scope of public cynicism would force journalists to give up the flattering notion of their own world-historical influence. "I think if we become more cynical about our institutions here, we also risk people around the world becoming more cynical about the true power and values of the American society," *Time* managing editor Walter Isaacson told the *Los Angeles Times* last year. The power of the American ideal, he explained, "comes basically from the authority and credibility we have as journalists."

Such magisterial pronouncements (redolent of Isaacson's predecessor Henry Luce) are further undermined by recent poll data suggesting that—horrors!—the American people are cynical consumers of news as well. A majority of respondents in another April poll, conducted by the Pew Center for the People and the Press, said they found news coverage to be "often inaccurate," up more than 20 percent from the results of a 1985 Pew Center poll. Fifty-four percent replied that the media get in the way of solving social problems, citing sensationalism and bias as the chief obstacles to more productive news coverage. Moreover, just as they are voting with their feet in our debauched elections, more and more Americans are choosing not to tune in to Peter Jennings & Co. Only 41 percent watch network news regularly, compared to 60 percent in 1993. Could it be that Americans, impressionable saps that they are, think that news organizations owned by massive corporations cheapen their coverage and distort the truth? . . .

Perhaps if the media took the cynicism of the public more seriously—imagining it as something other than their own creation—they could find their way to a "civic" journalism more in tune with the people they claim to represent.

Operation Infinite Jest

CHRIS LEHMANN

January 21, 2002

The current, reigning vision of America's war on terror as a pitched battle of towering, intractable civilizational premises seems certain to guarantee that the culture warriors on the left and right alike will continue exploiting the conflict for their pet domestic agendas. It seems all the more likely to proceed further down this course, indeed, now that the military phase of the Afghan war has yielded such unexpected, immediate results. In this setting, the egghead-baiting of the right and the fundamentalist-baiting of the left are two sides of the same well-worn coin: The selective vetting of an extreme minority body of opinion is made, via the curious alchemy of culture determinism, to stand in for an entire sensibility imagined to be gaining covert command of the culture at large.

And on it goes. No sooner had John Walker Lindh, the 20-year-old Taliban warrior from Marin County, California, stumbled out of a Mazzar-e-Sharif prison compound than a fresh round of pun-

another cultural identity card invoked and discarded en route to mass approval.

To see the full breadth of this sort of wish-fulfillment fantasizing, substitute in Marcus' wistful reverie the threadbare family background and pinched young adulthood of Richard Nixon—founded on a pitiful grocer's patrimony and a Whittier College law degree—over against Bill Clinton's sunny, successive tours through Georgetown, Oxford and Yale, and see whether it elicits the same measure of glib professed sympathy for the arduous rounds of self-reinvention and self-abandonment.

These high culturalist word-pictures are, in other words, but the reassuring photographic negative of the pundits' Red and Blue Two Americas. As in that vision, the telling considerations of our public life are expressed in imagined clashes of taste preference and sensibility. Both visions accede, moreover, to the pseudo-populism that places "out-of-touch" elites—the stalwarts of the bureaucratic welfare state, on the one hand, those latter-day Puritans who would scowlingly censor the quivering torsos of the King and the president, on the other. Politics here serve principally as a sounding board for the inchoate cravings expressed in mass taste and mass belief.

Psychodramas of the self and culture—that splendidly gossamer, endlessly debatable, agreeably inconclusive quantity of American life—steadily supplant all the incorrigible barriers of class that have only hardened and deepened in our culture-blinkered age. So as we continue to the dither over the wills-o'-the-wisp that shape-shift with every news cycle into this or that mortal threat to our cultural well-being, the leaders of our actual political life now consign one formerly universal social good after another—public schools, health care, job security, gas and electric utilities, Social Security—to the less than tender mercies of market privatization.

Each time we are presented with the beguiling cultural lullaby that Two Americas clash over our heads—square and hipster, religious and secular, the savvy libertarian entrepreneur and the grimly earnest entitlement addict, Ken Starr and Bill Clinton—we do well to remember that there is, in fact, a Third America.

This is the country in which real wages have failed, even throughout the Great '90s Boom, to keep pace with basic gains in productivity. This is the country that has racked up world-historic levels of consumer debt—to the tune of revolving, seasonally adjusted $664 billion in 2000—and witnessed, in 2000, the largest percentage of its citizens in their twenties declaring bankruptcy in history (indeed, this is the first time since the Great Depression that the country has had a negative savings rate).

This America imprisons a third of its young black men, chiefly via the prosecution of a self-defeating, horribly punitive cultural war on drugs. This is the country that has thrown over most meaningful federal forms of income support and housing assistance as relics of meddlesome, know-it-all liberal elitism. This America sees fit, across major-party lines, to issue continued tax cuts (and retroactive ones at that) to its most privileged citizens, while scrupulously eradicating all notions of equality of condition from our national life. (Even official poverty-assistance is now slated to be largely "faith-based," which apart from provoking obvious constitutional controversies, subtly confers upon the faithful giving class the discretionary power to define the deserving poor.)

This America has hemorrhaged membership in labor unions—thanks to laws that render most forms of labor organizing all but illegal—even as it has accumulated a fearsome, unprecedented trade deficit and entered into a number of regional trading alliances that keep American workers in competition with the lowest-wage (and the greatest resource-despoiling) economies in the world. This America gleefully fashions its fiscal policy, its employment goals, its trade protocols, all in the interests of the investor class (which controls fully 39 percent of the nation's wealth) to the chronic detriment of the living standards and spending power of the

dit-flak from culture alarmists commenced. It turns out that, as a troubled teen, Walker had posed on an Internet listserv as a street-tough rap music connoisseur. He'd converted to Islam after reading *The Autobiography of Malcolm X*, was named for John Lennon, and enjoyed the full doting attentions of divorced parents who encouraged their son to sample the teachings of other religious traditions. Presto, English professor Shelby Steele announced on the *Wall Street Journal*'s op-ed page: "A certain cultural liberalism cleared the way for [Walker's] strange odyssey of belief."

Walker was prepared for his seduction by Islam, Steele opines, by a "post-'60s cultural liberalism (more than political liberalism) that gave every step toward treason a feel of authenticity and authority. . . . This liberalism thrives as a subversive, winking, countercultural hipness. We saw it in the stream of 'hip'

Terry LaBan

Culture warriors on both sides have exploited the war on terror for their pet domestic agendas.

academics and intellectuals who—no sooner than the planes had struck—began to slash at their own country as if to keep it from gaining any victim's authority of its own." . . .

Steele opportunistically overstuffs an already prominent adolescent psyche with his own didactic script of culture warfare. It seems quite plain, however, that if John Walker had not existed, conservative culture warriors would have had to invent him—as indeed they have, in spite of knowing next to nothing about his actual existence. One awaits with a weary heart the arrival of the first leftish op-ed depicting Walker as the wholesale product of a divorced couple wrestling with the intolerable contradictions of a Catholic morality.

There should be some exit point from such giddy invocations of the iron determinism of culture, especially since they spring from a little-noted paradox: Our generation of high-culture warfare invests the products of American culture with this sort of world-historical import at the very time when its chosen content is so resolutely trivial.

growing ranks of its working poor.

And, of course, this America effectively forbids serious public discussion of all such conditions amid the grand mythologies of our deep cultural divisions. So it shall remain, indeed, until the left can begin to forswear the shadow play of cultural populism, to stake out a respectable position of conscientious objection to the culture wars, and to set about launching a new economic populism for this new Gilded Age.

The Secret of Their Success

BILL BOISVERT

December 13, 1998

Nothing succeeds like failure.

Christopher Reeve is proof of it, having transcended near total paralysis to regain the limelight as a busy director, best-selling author, sought-after speaker, and advocate for the disabled. Only a few years ago, Reeve's career languished. He was forced to make do with bit parts in Merchant Ivory productions, his starring roles in *Superman* blockbusters only a fading memory. There is a divide between Success in the '70s and Success in the '90s, an inexplicable cultural barrier that separates the Mark Hamills from the Harrison Fords, and Reeve spent many years on the wrong side of that wall. Until, one day, his horse jumped over it.

Mike Werner

True success, according to the experts, is a truly arduous undertaking.

And so he became a poster child for Success '98, a traveling series of day-long seminar extravaganzas of hope and encouragement. Reeve shared the stage recently at a Success '98 gathering in Chicago with Maya Angelou, Colin Powell, Elizabeth Dole and Chicago Bears great Walter Payton, all of whom rounded out the program with plentiful tales of racism overcome, stage fright faced down, and rejection dealt with constructively.

Success '98 is the brainchild of Peter Lowe, an ex-computer salesman and son of Anglican missionaries who calls himself "The Success Authority." Run by his non-profit organization, Peter Lowe International, Success '98 is billed as the most popular business seminar series in the country, a claim that's easy to believe looking at the 13,000 mostly middle-aged professionals and managers packed into Chicago's United Center arena. Lowe himself is an uncharismatic man with bright orange hair, bulging eyes and a nasal, whinnying voice. Aside from some press-packet hyperbole (he was apparently named "The Most Admired Man of the Decade" by something called the American Biographical Institute), he hasn't developed the sort of fire-walking cult of personality that other success vendors nurture. Instead, he seems to be a front man for an entire consortium of motivational gurus who, in between the celebrity speeches, give their own stage presentations and hawk their individual lines of books, tapes, thought-for-the-day planners, exercise programs and sales props.

The central theme of the Success '98 seminars is that success, far from being a random misstep in the steeplechase of life, is a coherent strategy, a diagrammable interplay of goal-setting, attitude adjustment, networking and prayer. But the sheer eclecticism of the speaker list—actor, poet, athlete, soldier, political animal—undermines this notion; such widely divergent life paths have nothing in common except their intersection at a seminar podium. The Boston Success '98 offers an even more incongruous mix, featuring ice-cream moguls Ben and Jerry side-by-side with trend-spotter Faith Popcorn and cold warrior Henry Kissinger (whose success strategies—"How To Strengthen Your Diplomacy," "Methods of Expanding Your Circle of Influence"—all sound like euphemisms for low-intensity warfare). It is the job of Lowe and his fellow motivational experts to tease out the thread that weaves these disparate lives together. But while there is a consensus on what it means to be a success authority—you (1) used to be a salesman and (2) have a personal relationship with Jesus Christ—the question of what it means to be a success is trickier.

What is known for sure is that it involves listening to inspirational audiotapes during the daily commute. Lowe himself has developed a sideline of Success Talk tapes ($4.95 per monthly installment) that pair interviews with role models like former British Prime Minister John Major with Lowe's own positive-thinking homilies ("How to Succeed When You're Frantic, Frazzled and Stressed Out!"). The other gurus also recommend tape-listening, a methodology known in the success industry as "Lifelong Learning," which requires a hefty commitment of money as well as time. Tom Hopkins, "the No. 1 sales trainer in the world," suggests that we "turn cars into classrooms" with his $350 line of products. Legendary salesman and motivator Zig Ziglar urges us to attend his "Automobile University" for a whole range of course offerings, including "Career and Family," with a 30-minute sex education segment, and a six-tape album titled "Christian Motivation" (tuition $1,595).

That these motivational "libraries" are mere compendia of feel-good bromides is precisely the point, Ziglar acknowledges, as he offers us a biochemical rationale for their effectiveness. It turns out that scientists who analyzed blood samples taken from audience members at Ziglar's lectures found that levels of the neurotransmitters norepinephrine, dopamine and serotonin ("the feel-good-about-yourself neurotransmitter") had risen by up to 300 percent. This excess, moreover, is stored in "minute blisters" in the nerve cell. Thus the high you get from "saturating your mind" with Ziglar's pep-talks persists in the form of stored neurotransmitters, providing you with a reservoir of "mental and emotional energy" you can draw on to ward off stress.

You're going to need that reservoir, because true success, according to the experts, is a truly arduous undertaking, requiring unlimited achievement in every facet of existence—career, money, health, family relationships, spiritual growth. Since "everything is connected," no dimension of success can be slighted; yet the difficulty of juggling them all forms the basis of our need for success expertise. That the quest for success might involve trade-offs between irreconcilable demands is a possibility that is both denied and harped upon by the speakers. Ziglar begins his talk with a cautionary tale about a man who jeopardizes his marriage by putting in too many hours at the office, and then ends it with a warning that we might be missing out on promotions that we could get if we would "just hold steady, work a little harder." This insistence that we balance family togetherness with workaholism is typical of the seminars' project of exacerbating the contradictions inherent in the psychology of success, the better to keep us in the market for solutions to our agonizing time-management dilemmas. Complacency and despair being the twin obstacles to the purchase of motivational materials, Success '98 tries to keep us poised in a dynamic tension between hope and dissatisfaction, self-affirmation and self-loathing. Yes, we can lead contented lives, but only if they are suffused with unfulfilled ambitions that compel us to take risks, embrace "change" and "dream crazy dreams."

All of this brings to mind the distinction made by sociologist David Riesman between the inner-directed personality, whose integrity and autonomy comes from strongly held internal values, and the other-directed personality, whose self-esteem depends on approval and acceptance from those around him. A celebration of pure, contentless self-actualizing, the mania for goal-setting gets at the crux of success ideology. It expresses the yearning for a more inner-directed consciousness, a yearning that reflects the deep links between the success industry and the fields of sales and marketing, those bellwethers of our evermore other-directed economy. In ages past, people could directly perceive success in the burgeoning fruits of their labor, which took the palpable form of acres cleared, bushels harvested, horseshoes forged or trackage laid. Nowadays, in an economy centered around the diffuse provisioning of intangible services, the emblematic figure is the salesman, who measures success solely in terms of "customer satisfaction," sallying forth each day to try to soften the stony mask of consumer indifference.

Ironically, the success movement promotes inner-directedness by the most patently other-directed means: through celebrity hero worship and the rush hour consumption of prerecorded platitudes. Zig Ziglar follows the logic to its endpoint by urging us to give ourselves daily pep-talks designed to transform negative feelings into positive thinking. In this "life-changing procedure," Zig instructs us to stand in front of a mirror and recite out loud, "with passion and enthusiasm," a long and tedious auto-encomium, one small fragment of which reads, "I am a supportive, giving and forgiving, clean, kind, unselfish, affectionate, loving, family-oriented human being, and I am a sincere and open-minded good listener who is trustworthy." In this exercise, it is as if our internal monologues themselves could no longer register unless externalized to mimic the longed-for testimonial from a satisfied customer or grateful boss.

In this almost parodic sketch of divided consciousness, we see the real message of the success industry, which knows full well that there's no profit to be had from gaining the whole world if we thereby lose our own souls. The profit comes from selling those souls right back to us.

Embracing Utopia

NOW IS THE MOMENT FOR NEW VISIONS

Illustration by Steve Anderson

Twenty-three

DAVID GRAEBER

FROM ROUGHLY 1980 TO 1999, THE LEFT WAS IN SOMETHING OF A ROUT. WHOLE SOCIAL MOVEMENTS DISAPPEARED; ALMOST EVERY GOVERNMENT that considered itself to be based on leftist principles either abandoned them or collapsed entirely; increasingly virulent strains of capitalism seemed everywhere triumphant. For obvious reasons, a lot of us did some soul-searching. How could a bunch of venomous cretins like Margaret Thatcher and Ronald Reagan ever have beaten us?

Gradually, a consensus began to take shape. The left's great mistake was its naive utopianism. Fixed on daydreams of a radically different, impossibly ideal society, we ignored human realities and human nature. As a result, revolutionary movements were either doomed to political ineffectiveness, carping at the margins of the capitalist order; or, if extraordinary circumstances did catapult them into power, to the creation of horrific killing fields as they tried to twist societies in shapes they simply would not go. More moderate types, such as European social democrats, at least had managed to create somewhat more humane, livable societies by abandoning all this wild-eyed nonsense about destroying capitalism or smashing the state, and concentrating on attainable ends like providing universal health care and collective bargaining. If we are ever to free ourselves from our current downward spiral, the argument went, we needed to stop demanding the impossible.

The only problem with this assessment was that it was almost entirely, systematically wrong. One need only examine the results. Abandoning utopian dreams did not lead to the birth of a new, vital, pragmatic left. Instead, the collapse of revolutionary movements was almost invariably accompanied not by a renaissance of liberalism and social democracy, but by the latter coming to seem like a pack of irrelevant has-beens. Everyone somehow managed to forget that the traditional division of labor within the left was that the radicals would set forth ideals, which the moderates could then go on to compromise.

In retrospect, the resultant disaster hardly should have come as a surprise. After all, what was all this anti-utopian wisdom but what right-wingers had been saying about us all along? It was really only a matter of time before, having soberly quaffed a potion offered by their mortal enemies, progressives would begin to wonder why they were starting to turn green and die. The surprising thing is that it took them so long. Or rather that so many of them indignantly cling to their new anti-utopianism, wondering, as they lie writhing and retching, if the problem is that perhaps they haven't drank quite enough.

One might take the measure of how much the right-wingers themselves ever really believed this critique by observing their own behavior. Because the moment the left dropped the visionary ball, right-wingers dashed in to snatch it up. The result was a strangely surreal, rather ridiculous historical moment. By the early '90s, the left had sunk largely into a politics of reaction, unable to raise their passions except to preserve things that were already there (social welfare policies, the ozone layer, rent control, trees)—yet "conservatives" suddenly had started posing as revolutionaries, thumping their Friedmans and Hayeks like so many little red books. The Internet swarmed with unprecedented beings: Republican cyberpunks, anarcho-capitalists, revolutionary Objectivists. For the first time in history, even science fiction was turning predominantly right-wing, and mainstream outlets like the *New York Times* were seriously trying to convince us that Che Guevara, were he alive today, would be a venture capitalist.

◎

That moment, mercifully, has already begun to pass. Republicans posing as revolutionaries were always a bit absurd; since the fall of Newt Gingrich, most have dropped

Prison Camp of the Mind

DAVID MOBERG

December 13, 1978

GEORGETOWN, GUYANA—Jerry Parks, 45, a one-time grocery store manager, was drawn to this would-be utopia of the Rev. Jim Jones in the deep jungle of Guyana as a chance to "do something positive with my life." He had begun following Jones 23 years ago when he lived in Springfield, Ohio, because the controversial young preacher was "very sensitive to people's needs" and seemed to have "some sort of paranormal faculties."

Here was a man who must be good: He was so sincere, so kind, so devoted to humanitarian work, Parks, like many others, thought. Here was a man with purpose: He had a vision of the world reminiscent of the Christianity of the Bible that established churches had long forgotten. Here was a man who was powerful: He could heal the sick, read people's minds, promise "protection" for his "family," organize projects that would—as the verses of Matthew enjoined—feed the hungry and clothe the naked.

So Jerry Parks sold his $35,000 home and turned the money over to the People's Temple: With his mother, his wife, two adolescent daughters and his older son, a medic who was an established associate minister in the church, he followed Jones to the jungle kingdom of 3,824 acres established four years ago. He didn't find what he expected.

"We found it was a virtual prison camp. Once you got here you weren't allowed to leave. You weren't allowed to dissent. You couldn't talk about going back to the U.S. . . . The congregation got up at 6 A.M. and worked from 7 A.M. to 6 P.M. Then we came home and ate subsistence level food, took a shower and went to the pavilion at 7:30 to listen to the news. The last six weeks, it got to be every night they held those 'people's rallies.' He had people believing there was a conspiracy against us, a movement in the U.S. with CIA backing and the pretense. But in what we like to the call the Third World—that is, the countries where most people live—the changes inflicted during this period really have been revolutionary, and they have done unimaginable damage. Imposed "free market reforms" have impoverished millions, destroyed whole societies, plunged great swathes of the planet into despair and war. What has been done is truly one of the great crimes of human history, but if nothing else, I think it allows us to gain some kind of perspective on what it is that turns would-be revolutionaries into mass murderers. What made these crimes possible? Was it utopianism?

Well, it's hard to deny that there is a utopian element here. Neoliberals do have an ideal vision of a truly "free" market, one that has never really existed, and surely never could. The notion that a society could be regulated entirely by market forces is an impossible dream generated by imagining what the world would be like if everyone's behavior was utterly consistent with some abstract moral ideal (in this case, economic theories that assume all human action is based on calculating, systematic, but scrupulously law-abiding greed). This is classic utopianism. Of course, there is no reason to believe that any of its current apostles would any more welcome a genuinely free market society than a Stalinist would welcome the actual withering away of the state, but the vision clearly seems to inspire them and give them a sense of moral purpose. Still, it is pretty obvious that neoliberals do not kill just because they like to fantasize about free markets. They kill because, like Stalinists, they refuse to admit they are dealing with fantasies at all. They kill because they mistake their fantasies for scientific truths.

What made Stalinists capable of such terrible crimes was not that they dreamed mad dreams (Stalinists were notoriously short on imagination), but that they were convinced their version of Marxism gave them a scientific understanding of human history. History could only advance in one direction; they were merely its agents. It was this utter certainty that made it possible to cast aside all decency and

some defectors. His philosophy was rather than let them come in and destroy this, it was better to commit revolutionary suicide. But there was no revolution out there."

There was suicide, of course, as a shocked world now knows, with a latest count of 911 dead at Jonestown; five dead at the airstrip where the group of government officials, journalists and defectors were gunned down by Jones' security force; and four more in a combined murder-suicide in Georgetown, Guyana's capital. . . .

Not everyone remembers Jonestown the way Parks does, however. Parks had wanted to leave for a long time and made his move with his family when Congressman Leo Ryan visited. Mike Carter, 20, had not wanted to quit. . . . He left as the suicide began with a suitcase full of $5 million for the Soviet Embassy in Georgetown. As radio operator, he had been a member of the inner circle at Jonestown.

Mike Carter saw Jonestown as socialism in action—a society that successfully eliminated money, racism, sexism, ageism, elitism. He still describes it as a beautiful place where the only complaints came from "parasites" and "bourgeois city folk" unwilling to work or accept the need for "structure," a community that was on the verge of success if only the supplies for new housing and other new equipment had arrived before the fateful Ryan visit. "It was just like a community anywhere in the world," he said. "If you like living in the country, it was paradise." . . .

Jonestown is rightly discussed in such starkly contrasting terms as heaven and hell, good and evil, socialism and fascism. It was the promise of life-enhancing utopia that gave Jones the power to create a deathly disaster. Jones preyed on the best instincts of people to realize their worst fears. He turned the desire for collectivity into the service of tyranny. He turned the desire for a humane moral order into an amoral terrorism. In the name of love,

ITT Archives

It was the promise of utopia that gave Jim Jones the power to create a deathly disaster.

he was a sadist worthy of the Marquis' imagination. In the name of liberating Americans from impending fascism, he imprisoned those who sought freedom through him. ("There were some people who wanted to go back," Mike Carter explained, "but they had to be held so that thousands more who wanted to come could do so.") By preaching that the end justifies the means, he produced a result that was the antithesis of his expressed goals. Jones was the Monster Dialectician, the Cancer of Reason.

common sense. Millions of Russian peasants could thus be told: "Science has proven that this is the only way forward, so shut up and do what you're told. Even if for the moment it may mean untold disruption, suffering and death, somewhere down the road (we're not sure quite when) all this will lead to a paradise of freedom and prosperity."

Is this not exactly the same line that these Russian peasants—indeed just about every peasant in the world—are currently being handed by the IMF? Take away the show trials and muscular statues, and Stalinism and neoliberalism become almost indistinguishable: the same faith in a science of society; the same assumption that a trained elite, conversant in that science, should be in charge of all important policy matters; the same disdain for sentimentality and worship of ruthless efficiency; the same intentional encouragement of starvation; the same obsession with economic growth numbers as ends in themselves, without a thought to what they might mean to the quality of actual human lives. If nothing else, this makes it easier to understand why so many former Stalinists have found it so easy to simply switch hats overnight and declare themselves free market enthusiasts. Aside from the nature of the supposedly scientific doctrine, there really wasn't very much to change.

To understand what's really at stake here, it might help to consider how the political spectrum came to be divided between something called "left" and "right" to begin with. The terms themselves go back to seating arrangements in the French Estates-General of 1789, but the left's founding ideas trace back to Enlightenment philosophies of the previous generation. (The founding ideas of the right mainly rose in reaction to them.) Everyone agrees that this was a period of profound intellectual ferment, when ideas were hatched that really did change the world. But it is worth asking, what was really new about them?

It's not as if the Enlightenment invented the idea of revolution: History is full of peasant revolts, egalitarian doctrines, utopian prophets with visions of a just society, attempts—sometimes, even partly successful ones—to translate such visions into reality. But if one examines the record, one also finds that previous revolutionaries never did so quite self-consciously. Demands for a just society were presented as either (a) demands for the restoration of some past Golden Age or (b) direct revelation from God. What the Enlightenment introduced was the idea that it was possible—or even more, legitimate—to imagine a better society, and then try to bring it into being, not on the basis of any outside authority, but simply because it would be a better society. This was no little thing. It was a concept of human freedom—not just individual freedom, either, but collective freedom—unprecedented in human history.

Like most ideas of freedom, though, it has proved very difficult to maintain. Part of the problem is that from the very beginning, it came entangled with that other Enlightenment invention: progress, the faith that the growth of science and rationality, or class struggle, or other endless varieties of alternative Motors of History were inevitably going to lead us to a better world. The two have been so consistently entangled, in fact, that few have noticed they are completely contradictory. The first suggests that human beings are capable of making their own history. The second sees us as mere agents of "structural forces," which operate on their own accord—though ones which will, purportedly, hand us our freedom somewhere down the road. There are a thousand ways to try to integrate them, or at least reach a compromise (i.e., the inherent contradictions within capitalism will inevitably lead to periodic crises, and during *those* junctures, it might be possible to try to change the world . . .), and much radical theory has consisted in debating the relative merits of one or another such compromise. But there has been a certain tension as a result, to say the least.

A reasonable intellectual response to the collapse of Leninism would have been to scratch the determinism, which we can justly say has been proven wrong and dangerous, and

1984: Are We There Yet?

CHRISTOPHER LASCH

December 19, 1984

1984, written when George Orwell himself was dying of tuberculosis, derives its emotional power not from the political analysis Orwell borrowed from James Burnham, but from its dramatization of a world in which death has become unbearable because of the fear that future generations will take no interest in our affairs. This fear of a meaningless death reaches its climax in the brutal remark with which O'Brien destroys Winston Smith's last hope and the last shred of his resistance to the totalitarian state: "You must stop imagining that posterity will vindicate you, Winston. Posterity will never hear of you. You will be lifted clean out from the stream of history."

It is above all modern consumer culture that makes it hard for us to take an interest in the future, by conveying to us at every turn the implicit message that the future will bear no resemblance to the past and by urging us, moreover, to squander our natural resources and energy supplies without any reference to the needs of future generations. We live today in a curiously insubstantial world, a world of images and abstractions in which organized expertise has replaced practical experience and images of things have become more vivid than things themselves.

Orwell's reflections on this subject revolve around the concept of common sense, to which he gives a double meaning. Common sense is the experience we have in common, and it embodies the common people's empirical knowledge of things rather than abstractions invented by intellectuals. For Orwell . . . totalitarianism represents the final triumph of ideological abstractions over common sense. . . .

The image of totalitarianism hides more than it reveals. It encourages us to ask whether the welfare state shows signs of turning into a police state, when we might better ask whether political freedom any longer has much meaning if it serves only to make possible the "private enjoyment of life."

Philip Roth has aptly remarked on the contrast between Eastern Europe and the West, "In the West everything goes and nothing matters; there, nothing goes and everything matters." If this puts the contrast too sharply, it still alerts us to the danger that individual autonomy, as Orwell called it somewhat misleadingly—that is, the capacity of moral judgment and self-regulation, the capacity for self-sacrifice, the willingness to accept the consequences of one's actions—can be weakened as effectively by the empty freedom of consumerism as by dictatorship and regimentation.

What Kind of Change?

MICHAEL HARRINGTON

February 24, 1988

There is no question now as to whether there will be radical change in the immediate future. It is already underway. The only issue is how it will be carried out. Will it come from on high, at the social and economic cost of the mass of people in every society and through a repression of freedom? Or can socialists, faced with a reality they never imagined, work out effective programs of structural change that move in the direction of a truly democratic socialization of the world?

There is now "too much" food in the world—and people starving to death; "too much" steel capacity and masses desperately in need of housing and transit. And there will be, within the next year or two, a crisis of the world economy that will not automatically engender a progressive response, but which will make such a political response

to get back to work on some more compelling visions. To figure out what sort of world we would really like to live in but, this time, work toward it in the full awareness that there are no inevitable laws of history—not progress, not the dialectic, not anything—which are guaranteed to bring us there. (Or, for that matter, that will necessarily stop us.) To accept that history is, really, nothing more or less than what we make of it. But the first reaction, at least, was often precisely the opposite: Witness all those Marxist economists one used to see at scholarly conferences in the early '90s, who seemed to have switched almost seamlessly from talking about a capitalism that would inevitably self-destruct because of the weight of its internal contradictions, to one that will inevitably roll over anything that tries to stand in its way.

The one thing they seemed utterly unwilling to consider is that the future might just be up to us. I suppose in a certain way it's understandable. At the very least, making everything seem inevitable is (as it was for the Stalinists) a way of denying any sort of historical responsibility. Since after all, if capitalism's recent victories were *not* inevitable, then we've obviously been doing a pretty rotten job of fighting it. We are talking a fuck-up on an unprecedented, world-historic scale. It's easy to see how one might wish to deny responsibility. But this is not much of a basis on which to build a movement, is it? What sort of slogan are they suggesting? "Join us. We're doomed!"

Another element of the collapse of Leninism was a gigantic intellectual assault on the very idea of collective political action—one that came not just from the right, but from within the left itself; particularly from within those intellectual and cultural circles that must play a crucial role in helping shape any revolutionary vision. This is the one great theme that runs through the endless strains of what's usually called "postmodernism," which really consists of a thousand different arguments against the idea that people should try to bring such collective visions into being. In fact, one of the fascinating things about this period was the degree to which neoliberal arguments were anticipated by academics who clearly felt they were engaging in cutting-edge radicalism.

Since the '80s, it has become common to be presented with a series of arguments that might be summarized like this:

1. We now live in a postmodern age. The world has changed; no one is responsible, it simply happened as a result of inexorable processes; we can't do anything about it, so we must simply adapt ourselves to new conditions.

2. One result of our new postmodern condition is that schemes to change the world or human society through collective political action are no longer viable. Everything is broken up and fragmented; anyway, such schemes will inevitably prove either impossible or produce totalitarian nightmares.

3. While this might seem to leave little room for human agency in history, one need not despair completely. Legitimate political action can take place, provided it is on a personal level: through the fashioning of subversive identities, forms of creative consumption and the like.

Compare these to the popular media arguments promulgated in the '90s about a phenomenon called "globalization":

1. We now live in the age of the global market. The world has changed; no one is responsible, it simply happened as the result of inexorable processes; neither can we do anything about it, but must simply adapt ourselves to new conditions.

2. One result is that schemes aiming to change society through collective political action are no longer viable. Dreams of revolution have been proven impossible or, worse, bound to produce totalitarian nightmares.

3. If this might seem to leave little room for democracy, one need not despair: market behavior, particularly individual consumption decisions, are democracy.

David Vita

"Those who join the movement for the immediate rewards of power," Michael Harrington said, "are advised to apply elsewhere."

possible. At that point, some of those who now assume that the determinants of Reagan's America (and Thatcher's Britain, Kohl's Germany, Chirac's France) are eternal will look around for a socialist movement with positive answers. These cannot be predicted now, but it is clear that they will be distinctively internationalist, anti-racist, feminist and green as well as oriented to the working class both old and new. . . .

Those who lose heart at the very eve of a new generation of change should remember the profound truth Antonio Gramsci articulated from a jail cell in a decade that saw the triumph of fascism. . . . Socialism, Gramsci said, was not a matter of a political victory on this or that day, or even this or that decade. It was not an economic program, a recipe. It was a "moral and intellectual reformation," a fight to transform the culture and will of those who, from time immemorial, had been made subordinate, the epochal work of the creation of a new civilization.

We live today in the most radical of times even though the temporary ascendancy of Reagan and his similars often conceals that fact. Humanity is fighting at this very moment over the content of that new civilization—of a new planet, if you will—and that struggle will go beyond the lifetime of every one of us. . . . Those who join the movement for the immediate rewards of power are advised to apply elsewhere. Those who are willing to wager their lives on the possibility of freedom and justice and solidarity should pay their dues.

The New Language of Protest

DAVID GRAEBER

September 3, 2001

GENOA, ITALY—Compare two abandoned streets in Genoa during the weekend of the G8 summit, immediately after confrontations between protesters and police. The first, a mile-long stretch along Via Tolemaide overlooking a train yard where Ya Basta! had faced off against riot cops on July 20, was scattered with oddly whimsical debris: slabs of rubber padding, bits of mock-Roman foam armor, balloons and abandoned plexiglas shields with inscriptions like "Yuri Gagarin Memorial Space Brigade."

The other, along Corso Marconi (one of the city's main thoroughfares) the next day, was the sort of scene one might see in the aftermath of a riot almost anywhere: shattered glass from storefront

There is, of course, one enormous difference between the two arguments. The central claim of those who celebrated postmodernism is that we have entered a world in which all totalizing systems—science, humanity, nation, truth and so forth—have been shattered; where there are no longer any grand mechanisms for stitching together a world now broken into incommensurable fragments. One can no longer even imagine that there could be a single standard of value by which to measure things. The neoliberals, on the other hand, are singing the praises of a global market which is, in fact, the single greatest and most monolithic system of measurement ever created, a totalizing system that subordinates everything—every object, every piece of land, every human capacity or relationship—on the planet to a single standard of value.

By now it has become increasingly obvious that what those who celebrated postmodernism were describing was largely the effect of this universal market system—which, like any totalizing system of value, tends to throw all others into doubt and disarray. By ignoring this, abandoning all faith in the ability of revolutionary movements to transform society, and blindly throwing themselves on the bandwagon of whatever structural forces seemed to be transforming the world, academic radicals suddenly find themselves in an impossible quandary. For years, they had been writing essays that sounded like position papers for some vast social movement that did not exist: denouncing one another as racists or sexists or imperialists for errors of theory; acting, in short, as if what they were doing made some kind of difference. Over the past few years, the situation has become, if anything, more embarrassing. Suddenly, new social movements have been cropping up all over the world to oppose neoliberalism, and most academic radicals—insofar as they are even aware such movements exist—have almost nothing to say to them.

All this is rather too bad because the *new* New Left could probably use a little help in this area. Granted, my own experience with groups like the Direct Action Network has made it pretty clear that in most ways the activists are way ahead of the intellectuals at this point. Young activists are showing a refreshing willingness to experiment, and an even more refreshing refusal to be ashamed of their ideals, or resist following them through to their logical conclusions. Still, there is a bit of a hitch: Activists are by nature practical people, and this generation in particular has been so (understandably) chary of repeating past mistakes that there has been a certain reluctance to talk about any ideals that cannot immediately be put into practice. Hence, while there has been a brilliant outpouring of ideas about direct democracy, consensus decision-making, decentralized forms of organization and the like, there's also a certain hesitancy about letting one's visions flower into the sort of wild utopian speculation that might really grab the public's imagination. I suspect this is one reason that the movement has had a little trouble presenting its message even to the older, "progressive" community (which for the most part has been unable to grasp that the new New Left has any unifying ideals at all). It is the normal role of intellectuals to do this kind of work; and existing radical thinkers have never been less disposed to do their part.

Of course, there was never a point where everyone on the left—even all leftists intellectuals—entirely abandoned the idea of envisioning an unprecedented social order, and then trying to bring it about on the grounds that it would be right. Feminism, most obviously, always has been based on doing exactly that; the gay and lesbian movement even more so. Is it a coincidence these are also the social movements which, even during our time of troubles, showed the least inclination to fade away? And while socialist dreams have been put on hold in a lot of places, how do we know that the only reason past experiments didn't work out was because they never seriously challenged the patriarchal family? Perhaps it's just impossible to build an egalitarian

ITT Archives

Maybe the left hasn't been utopian enough.

windows, charred automobile parts, and, everywhere, spent tear-gas canisters and jagged rocks. It was the first kind of confrontation, not the second, that was anathema to the Italian police. The *carabinieri* set out to create a riot, and that was exactly what they managed to produce.

A word of background: Ya Basta! is an Italian social movement most famous for their *tutti bianchi*, or "white overalls," a kind of nonviolent army who gear up in elaborate forms of padding, ranging from foam armor to inner tubes to rubber-ducky flotation devices, helmets and their signature chemical-proof white jumpsuits to create what Italian activists like to call a "new language" of direct action. Where once the only choice seemed to be between the Gandhian approach or outright insurrection—either Martin Luther King Jr. or Watts, with nothing in between—Ya Basta! has been trying to invent a completely new territory. The *tutti bianci* completely eschew any action that would cause harm to people or even property (usually), but at the same time do everything possible to avoid arrest or injury.

Ya Basta!—which began as a Zapatista solidarity group but has since evolved into a political network linking dozens of squats and social centers in major Italian cities—combines innovative tactics and an increasingly broad and sophisticated set of demands. To the usual calls for direct democracy, the *leitmotif* of the "anti-globalization" movement everywhere, they've made three major additions: A principle of global citizenship, the elimination of all controls over freedom of movement in the world (Ya Basta! especially has targeted immigration detention facilities); a universally guaranteed "basic income" to replace programs like welfare and unemployment (originally derived from the French MAUSS group); and free access to new technologies—in effect, extreme limits to the enforcement of intellectual property rights. . . .

What is called the anti-globalization movement (increasingly, people within it are just calling it the "globalization movement") is trying to change the direction of history—ultimately, the very structure of society—without resort to weapons. What makes this feasible is globalization itself: the increasing speed with which it is possible to move people, possessions and ideas around.

What politicians and the corporate press call "globalization," of course, is really the creation and maintenance of institutions (the WTO, G8 summits, the IMF) meant to limit and control that process so as to guarantee it produces nothing that would discomfit a tiny governing elite: Tariffs can be lowered, but immigration restrictions have to be increased; large corporations are free to take profits wherever and however they like, but any ideas about forms of economic organization that would not look like large profit-seeking corporations must be strictly censored, etc. The threat of real global democracy is probably their greatest fear, and the unprecedented growth of the movement—Seattle was considered huge at 50,000 protesters; Genoa, a year and a half

social order on the basis of a domestic order that ensures people will experience inequality from the moment they are born. Maybe otherwise, it would have worked just fine. Maybe not—but do we know? It seems to me that before giving up on the future of humanity, we should at least be *fairly* sure.

The last thing we need to be doing is penance for supposed past sins of utopianism. This is the moment for new, grandiose visions, experiments, inspirations and wild fantasies. (Myself, I would vote for a feminist-led revival of anarcho-syndicalism, but maybe that's just me. For now, I'd happily settle for a world in which suggesting this would not seem so ridiculous.) We need multiple visions; ways of imagining how completely different utopian experiments could all, somehow, coexist. In fact, we need to think of alternatives to the market not just in terms of what would be more just or equitable, but in terms of how to leave people most free to conduct collective experiments in more fulfilling ways of living.

We need to start asking questions like how many hours would people really need to work if we got rid of stupid, unnecessary jobs like lawyers, bureaucrats and telemarketers, and distributed the necessary ones more equally? How much apparently necessary work could be entirely eliminated if all our greatest technological minds were free to set themselves to eliminating them, rather than creating Star Wars satellites or day-trading software? (This, of course, is what they would immediately start doing if responsibility for performing unpleasant jobs were distributed equally, so they had to do them too. House-cleaning and coal-mining robots would be invented overnight.) How could we ensure these technologies were also ecologically sustainable? What is the optimal size for a truly livable community, and how could we begin reorganizing cities and neighborhoods to allow everyone to live in one? And these are the relatively simple questions.

Critiques are fun and have their place, but most people already know the existing social order is stupid and unfair. What most lack is some reason to believe there's a viable alternative—or increasingly, among people whose only source of information is the corporate media, any idea of what an alternative might look like. Whose fault is that?

The problem with the left is not that it has been too utopian. The problem is that it has not been utopian enough.

later, drew perhaps 200,000—must seem utterly terrifying.

This is why the battle of images is so strategic. Ya Basta! understands that "protection" for activists can never consist primarily of foam-rubber padding. When the state really wishes to take off the gloves, it can. Violence is something states do very well. If their hands are tied, it is because centuries of political struggle have produced a situation in which politicians and police have to be at least minimally responsive to a public that has come to believe that living in a civilized society means living in one in which young idealists cannot, in fact, be murdered in their beds. It is precisely this kind of padding that the rulers of our world are now frantically trying to strip away.

Will Americans decide to further fortify their sphere, or risk stepping out of it?

Steve Kagan

Love Thy Neighbor

SLAVOJ ZIZEK

October 29, 2001

So what about the phrase that reverberates everywhere, "Nothing will be the same after September 11"? Significantly, this phrase is never further elaborated—it's just an empty gesture of saying something "deep" without really knowing what we want to say. So our reaction to this phrase should be: Really? Or is it rather that the only thing effectively changed was that America was forced to realize the kind of world it is part of?

Such changes in perception are never without consequences, since the way we perceive our situation determines the way we act in it. Recall the processes of collapse of a political regime—say, the collapse of the communist regimes in Eastern Europe. At a certain moment, people all of a sudden became aware that the game was over, that the communists had lost. The break was purely symbolic, nothing changed "in reality"—and, nonetheless, from that moment on, the final collapse of the regime was just a question of days.

What if something of the same order did occur on September 11? We don't yet know what consequences in economy, ideology, politics and war this event will have, but one thing is sure: The United States, which, until now, perceived itself as an island exempted from this kind of violence, witnessing these kind of things only from the safe distance of a TV screen, is now directly involved.

So the question is: Will Americans decide to further fortify their sphere, or risk stepping out of it? America has two choices. It can persist in or even amplify its deeply immoral attitude of "Why should this happen to us? Things like this don't happen here," leading to even more aggression toward the outside world—just like a paranoiac acting out. Or America can finally risk stepping through the fantasmatic screen separating it from the Outside . . . and thus make the long-overdue move from "A thing like this should not happen *here*" to "A thing like this should not happen *anywhere*!"

Therein resides the true lesson of the attacks: The only way to ensure that it will not happen here again is to prevent it from going on *anywhere* else. America should learn to humbly accept its own vulnerability as part of this world, enacting the punishment of those responsible as a sad duty, not as an exhilarating retaliation. Even though America's peace was brought by the catastrophes going on elsewhere, the predominant point of view remains that of an innocent gaze confronting unspeakable evil that struck from the Outside. One needs to gather the courage to recognize that the seed of evil is within us too.

In his campaign for the presidency, George W. Bush named Jesus Christ as the most important person in his life. Now he has a unique chance to prove that he meant it seriously. For him, as for all Americans today, "Love thy neighbor" means "Love the Muslims." Or it means nothing at all.

Contributors

CRAIG AARON is managing editor of *In These Times* and editor of *Appeal to Reason: 25 Years In These Times.* His writing also has appeared in *The Progressive, The Memphis Flyer* and *Internet Underground.* He lives in Chicago.

PAT AUFDERHEIDE, professor and director of the Center for Social Media in the School of Communication at American University in Washington, was culture editor of *In These Times* from 1978 to 1982. Now a senior editor of the magazine, her most recent book is *The Daily Planet: A Critic on the Capitalist Culture Beat.*

DEAN BAKER is the co-director of the Center for Economic and Policy Research in Washington and the author of the "Economic Reporting Review," an online weekly analysis of economic news coverage. Baker is also co-author of *Social Security: The Phony Crisis.*

DENNIS BERNSTEIN is an investigative reporter and radio host who, along with **VINCE BIELSKI**, first broke the story of the Contra-cocaine connection. Bernstein is the co-author, most recently, of *Henry Hyde's Moral Universe.* Bielski has been a senior editor at *SF Weekly* and *The Industry Standard.*

JOEL BLEIFUSS is the editor and publisher of *In These Times,* where he has worked as a writer, columnist and editor since 1986. Bleifuss has had more stories on Project Censored's annual list of the "10 Most Censored Stories" than any other journalist.

SIDNEY BLUMENTHAL, who served as *In These Times'* Boston correspondent in the late '70s, has been a staff writer for the *Washington Post, The New Republic* and *The New Yorker.* Blumenthal has published five books. He was also a senior adviser in the White House to President Bill Clinton.

BILL BOISVERT is a contributing editor of *In These Times* and a freelance writer in New York. His work has appeared in the *Chicago Reader, The Baffler* and other publications.

ROY BOURGEOIS is a Vietnam veteran and recipient of the purple heart. After military service, he became a Catholic priest with the Maryknoll Missionary Order and worked in Latin America for six years. He is founder of the School of the Americas Watch.

DAVID BROWER was the most influential environmentalist of the second half of the 20th century. The first executive director of the Sierra Club, he transformed that organization from a hiking club into the most powerful conservation organization in the nation. He founded Friends of the Earth, now in 65 countries, the Earth Island Institute and the League of Conservation Voters. He died in November 2000 at the age of 88.

WILFRED BURCHETT was a war correspondent for more than four decades. He was the first correspondent to go into Hiroshima after the dropping of the atomic bomb in 1945 and covered the Korean and Vietnam wars, often as a correspondent for New York's *Guardian.* Burchett died in 1983.

TERRY CARR is an editorial writer for the *Anchorage Daily News.*

ANA CARRIGAN has been an independent filmmaker whose work includes *Roses in December* and *Miskito Come Home,* and is the author of *Salvador Witness: The Life and Calling of Jean Donovan* and *The Palace of Justice: A Colombian Tragedy.*

NOAM CHOMSKY is a political activist, writer and professor of linguistics at the Massachusetts Institute of Technology, where he has taught since 1955. His many books include *9-11, A New Generation Draws the Line, Rogue States, Profit Over People, The New Military Humanism, The Fateful Triangle* and *Manufacturing Consent.*

MARC COOPER has traveled the world covering politics and culture for myriad press outlets. A contributing editor of *The Nation*, his latest book is *Pinochet and Me: An Anti-Memoir.*

NEIL DEMAUSE, a regular contributor to *In These Times*, is the author of *Field of Schemes.* He lives in Brooklyn, where he writes for *Extra!* and *The Village Voice* and edits the 'zine *here.*

ARIEL DORFMAN is a distinguished professor of literature and Latin American studies at Duke University and the author of *Blake's Therapy, Death and the Maiden,* and *Heading South, Looking North: A Bilingual Journey.*

SUSAN J. DOUGLAS is a professor of communication studies at the University of Michigan and an *In These Times* columnist. She is the author of *Where the Girls Are: Growing Up Female with the Mass Media* and *Listening In: Radio and the American Imagination.*

JOSHUA DRESSLER, a former *In These Times* columnist, is the Edwin M. Cooperman Designated Professor of Law at the Michael E. Moritz College of Law, Ohio State University. He is the editor-in-chief of the four-volume *Encyclopedia of Crime and Justice.*

MARTIN DUBERMAN is a distinguished professor of history at the City University of New York's Lehman College and the CUNY Graduate School, where he was the founder and first director of the Center for Lesbian and Gay Studies. He is the author of more than a dozen books, including *Paul Robeson, Cures, Left Out, Stonewall* and *Black Mountain.*

LOUIS DUBOSE, who has covered Texas politics for nearly two decades, is the former editor of *The Texas Observer* and co-author with Molly Ivins of *Shrub: The Short but Happy Political Life of George W. Bush.*

BARBARA EHRENREICH is a journalist and author, who writes regularly for *The Progressive, Harper's, Time* and *In These Times*, where a version of this article originally appeared. Her recent books include *Nickel and Dimed: On (Not) Getting by in America* and *Blood Rites: Origins and History of the Passions of War.*

BARBARA EPSTEIN teaches in the History of Consciousness Department of the University of California, Santa Cruz and is the author of *The Politics of Domesticity* and *Political Protest and Cultural Revolution.*

DAVID EVANS spent 20 years as a U.S. Marine Corps artillery officer and military readiness and budget expert at the Pentagon. He later covered the military for the *Chicago Tribune* and now writes about safety and security issues in the airline industry for *Air Safety Week.*

THOMAS FRANK is editor of *The Baffler* and author of *One Market Under God* and *The Conquest of Cool.*

ANNETTE FUENTES is a New York-based journalist and adjunct professor of journalism at Columbia University who writes frequently on health care and social policy issues. A contributing editor of *In These Times*, she is co-author with Barbara Ehrenreich of *Women in the Global Factory.*

DAVID FUTRELLE is a former culture editor of *In These Times* whose writing on culture, technology and finance has appeared in the *New York Times, Newsday* and *Salon.* He is currently a staff writer at *Money* magazine.

EDUARDO GALEANO, one of Latin America's most distinguished writers, is the author of the *Memory of Fire* trilogy, *Open Veins of Latin America, Soccer in Sun and Shadow* and *Upside Down.* The article reprinted here originally appeared in a longer form in *Le Monde Diplomatique* in 1991. Translated by Kevin O'Donnell. Reprinted by permission of Susan Bergholz Literary Services, New York.

JOHN GARDNER, a former labor organizer, is a member of the Milwaukee School Board.

JUAN GONZALEZ is a columnist for New York's *Daily News* and *In These Times.* The winner of a 1998 George Polk journalism award, he is the author of *Roll Down Your Window: Stories of a Forgotten America* and *Harvest of Empire: A History of Latinos in America,* where a version of this essay originally appeared.

ARIEL GORE is the editor of the 'zine *Hip Mama* and the author of *The Hip Mama Survival Guide, The Mother Trip* and *Breeder: Real-Life Stories From the New Generation of Mothers.*

DAVID GRAEBER is a professor of anthropology at Yale University and author of *Toward an Anthropological Theory of Value: The False Coin of Our Own Dreams.* A contributing editor of *In These Times,* he is currently working with the Direct Action Network, Ya Basta! and other activist groups.

FRED HALLIDAY teaches international relations at the London School of Economics. His recent books include *Two Hours that Shook the World, Islam and the Myth of Confrontation, Revolution and World Politics: The Rise and Fall of the Sixth Great Power* and *The World at 2000.* An expanded version of this essay will appear in *The New International Agenda.*

MICHAEL HARRINGTON's 1962 book, *The Other America,* is credited with sparking the federal anti-poverty program. His other books include *Twilight of Capitalism, The Politics at God's Funeral, The Next Left* and *Socialism: Past and Future.* He first joined the Catholic Worker movement in 1951, headed the U.S. Socialist Party from 1968 to 1972, and later chaired the Democratic Socialist Organizing Committee and its successor, the Democratic Socialists of America. He died in 1989.

DAVID HELVARG, a former *In These Times* war correspondent, is a commentator for *Marketplace Radio* and author of *The War Against the Greens* and *Blue Frontier: Saving America's Living Seas.*

DOUG HENWOOD is the editor and publisher of the *Left Business Observer* and the author of *Wall Street: How It Works and For Whom* and *A New Economy?*

MARK HERTSGAARD is a journalist and author whose work has appeared in *The New Yorker, Harper's, The Nation,* the *New York Times, Salon* and *Mother Jones.* His books include *On Bended Knee, A Day in the Life* and *Earth Odyssey.* His new book, *The Eagle's Shadow: Why America Fascinates and Infuriates the World,* will be published in fall 2002.

CHRISTOPHER HITCHENS is a columnist for *Vanity Fair* and *The Nation* whose recent books include *Letters to a Young Contrarian, The Trial of Henry Kissinger* and *No One Left To Lie To.*

PAUL HOCKENOS has written for *In These Times* from Eastern Europe since 1989 and is the author of *Free to Hate: The Rise of the Right in Post-Communist Eastern Europe.* From 1997 to 1999, Hockenos worked for the OSCE Mission to Bosnia Herzegovina. He is presently writing a book about the role exile and diaspora groups played in the Balkan conflicts.

DOUG IRELAND has been writing about power, politics and the media since 1977. A former columnist for *The Village Voice, The New York Observer* and the Paris daily *Libération,* among others, his articles have appeared everywhere from *The Nation* to *Vanity Fair* to *POZ.* He's a contributing editor of *In These Times.*

MATTHEW JARDINE is the author *East Timor: Genocide in Paradise* and co-author of *East Timor's Unfinished Struggle: Inside the Timorese Resistance.* He is currently writing a book on the making of "Ground Zero" in East Timor in 1999.

DIANA JOHNSTONE was *In These Times* European correspondent and senior editor from 1979 to 1990. She is the author of *Deadly Connections* and *The Politics of Euromissiles.* From 1990 to 1996, she served as a press officer for the Greens in the European Parliament.

ALISA JOYCE covered China for ABC News in the late '80s and '90s. She currently works as Western bureau chief of National Public Radio and lives in San Diego with her husband and four kids.

JOHN B. JUDIS was West Coast editor, foreign editor and then senior editor of *In These Times* from 1976 to 1992. He is a senior editor of *The New Republic* and author of *The Paradox of American Democracy: Elites, Special Interests and the Betrayal of the Public Trust* and *William F. Buckley Jr.: Patron Saint of the Conservatives.* He is working on a book, with co-author Ruy Teixeira, on the emerging Democratic majority.

PAULA KAMEN, a Chicago journalist and playwright, is the author of *Her Way: Young Women Remake the Sexual Revolution.* Her play, *Jane: Abortion and the Underground,* has been performed by student groups across the country.

RICHARD KAYE is assistant professor in the Department of English at Hunter College, City University of New York. Kaye is the author of *The Flirt's Tragedy: Desire Without End in Victorian and Edwardian Fiction.*

MICHAEL T. KLARE is a professor of peace and world security studies at Hampshire College in Amherst, Massachusetts, and an expert on international military issues. He is the author of *Rogue States and Nuclear Outlaws* and *Resource Wars.*

NAOMI KLEIN, a syndicated columnist whose work appears regularly in the *Globe and Mail* and the *Guardian.* Also an *In These Times* contributing editor, she is the author of *No Logo: Taking Aim at the Brand Bullies.*

DAN LA BOTZ is a visiting professor at Miami University in Oxford, Ohio, and the author of *Made in Indonesia, Rank-and-File Rebellion, Mask of Democracy* and *Democracy in Mexico.*

CHRISTOPHER LASCH was a historian at the University of Rochester, whose works include *The New Radicalism in America, The Agony of the American Left, Haven in a Heartless World, The Culture of Narcissism, The Minimal Self* and *The True and Only Heaven.* He died in 1994.

DANIEL LAZARE is the author, most recently, of *America's Undeclared War: What's Killing Our Cities and How We Can Stop It* and *The Velvet Coup: The Constitution, the Supreme Court and the Decline of American Democracy.*

CHRIS LEHMANN, a former culture and managing editor of *In These Times,* is a senior editor for the *Washington Post Book World.* A former editor of *Newsday*'s Sunday "Currents" section, his work also has appeared in *The Baffler, Feed, The Atlantic Monthly, Harper's, Salon* and *Suck.*

BETH MASCHINOT is director of program development and evaluation at the Mental Health Association in Illinois and a former assistant editor of *In These Times.*

NELSON LICHTENSTEIN, who teaches history at the University of California, Santa Barbara, is the author of *Walter Reuther: The Most Dangerous Man in Detroit* and *State of the Union: A Century of American Labor.* He is a founding member of Scholars, Artists, and Writers for Social Justice.

ROBERT W. McCHESNEY is a professor of communications at the University of Illinois at Urbana-Champaign and co-editor of *Monthly Review.* He is the author, most recently, of *Rich Media, Poor Democracy: Communication Politics in Dubious Times.*

BILL McKIBBEN is an environmentalist and former staff writer for *The New Yorker* whose work has appeared in *Outside, Rolling Stone, Harper's* and many other publications. He is the author of *The End of Nature* and seven other books.

SCOTT McLEMEE writes about the humanities for *The Chronicle of Higher Education.* He has published numerous reviews and essays in *In These Times* as well as in *The Nation, Lingua Franca,* the *New York Times* and many other publications.

BRUCE MIRKEN, a longtime freelance writer, recently moved to Washington to become assistant director of communications at the Marijuana Policy Project. He strongly believes that freelance writers deserve to be paid for the re-use of their work, despite *In These Times*' refusal to do so in the production of this book.

DAVID MOBERG, a senior editor of *In These Times*, has been on the staff of the magazine since it began publishing. Before joining *In These Times*, he completed his work for a Ph.D. in anthropology at the University of Chicago and worked for *Newsweek*. Recently he has received fellowships from the John D. and Catherine T. MacArthur Foundation and the Nation Institute for research on the new global economy.

MICHAEL MOORE is a filmmaker whose work includes *Roger and Me* and *The Big One* as well as the television shows *TV Nation* and *The Awful Truth*. His latest book is *Stupid White Men: . . . and Other Sorry Excuses for the State of the Nation*.

CARLOS MORTON has authored two collections of plays, *The Many Deaths of Danny Rosales* and *Johnny Tenorio*. He has lived on the border between Mexico and the United States since 1981, and is currently a professor of theater at the University of California, Riverside.

SALIM MUWAKKIL is a senior editor of *In These Times*, where he has worked since 1983, and a weekly op-ed columnist for the *Chicago Tribune*. He is currently a Crime and Communities Media Fellow of the Open Society Institute, examining the impact of ex-inmates and gang leaders in leadership positions in the black community.

ALLAN NAIRN is an award-winning investigative reporter whose work has appeared in *The New Yorker*, the *Washington Post*, the *New York Times*, *The New Republic*, *Harper's*, *The Nation* and many other publications.

JIM NAURECKAS got his start covering the Iran-Contra scandal for *In These Times* as a staff writer in the '80s. He is now the editor of *Extra!*, published by the media watch group FAIR.

ZACK NAUTH was a journalist who wrote for the *New Orleans Times-Picayune*, But he is most proud of being a union organizer for Service Employees International Union Local 100 in Louisiana and Local 880 in Illinois.

JOHN NICHOLS is a fellow with The Nation Institute who writes "The Beat" column and covers national politics for *The Nation*. He is also an associate editor for the *Capital Times* in Madison, Wisconsin, and a regular contributor to *In These Times* and *The Progressive*. He is the author, most recently, of *Jews for Buchanan: Did You Hear the One About the Theft of the American Presidency?*

JAMES NORTH has reported for *In These Times* since 1977 from Europe, Africa, Latin America, the Middle East and Asia. He is the author of *Freedom Rising*, a book about his years in South Africa, and is currently completing *Structures of Sin*, a first-hand look at global inequality.

NELL IRVIN PAINTER is the Edwards Professor of American History at Princeton University and author of *Sojourner Truth: A Life, A Symbol* and *Southern History Across the Color Line*. She is currently completing *The History of White People*.

ROBERT PARRY, as an investigative reporter for Associated Press from 1980 to 1987, helped uncover Oliver North's Contra aid network, Ronald Reagan's secret approval of the operation, and the CIA's covert "assassination manual." He has also been a reporter for *Newsweek* and a correspondent for the PBS series *Frontline*. He is the author of *Fooling America*, *Trick or Treason* and *Lost History*.

RICK PERLSTEIN is the author of *Before the Storm: Barry Goldwater and the Undoing of the American Consensus.* In 2000, *The Village Voice* named him one of its "Writers on the Verge." He lives in New York.

JOHN PILGER is a documentary filmmaker, journalist and author who has twice won Britain's highest award for journalism, journalist of the year. His documentaries have won Academy Awards in the United States and the United Kingdom. A regular contributor to the *Guardian* and *New Statesman,* he is the author of *Hidden Agendas, A Secret Country* and *Distant Voices.* Reprinted by permission of South End Press

FRANCES FOX PIVEN currently teaches at the Graduate Center of the City University of New York. She is the co-author, with Richard Cloward, of *Regulating the Poor, Poor Peoples' Movements, The Breaking of the American Social Compact* and, most recently, *Why Americans Still Don't Vote.*

JEFFREY L. REYNOLDS is the vice president of the Long Island Association for AIDS Care and writes often on public health issues and social justice.

MATT ROTH is a writer who lives in New York.

ARUNDHATI ROY was trained as an architect. She is the author of the novel *The God of Small Things,* for which she received the Booker Prize, *The Cost of Living* and *Power Politics,* from which this article is excerpted. Roy lives in New Delhi, India. Reprinted by permission of South End Press.

EDWARD SAID is University Professor of English and Comparative Literature at Columbia University. He is the author of more than 20 books, the most recent of which is *Power, Politics and Culture.*

BERNIE SANDERS represents Vermont as an at-large member of the House of Representatives, where he has served since 1991. Before being elected to Congress, Sanders was a four-term mayor of Burlington. He is the author (with Huck Gutman) of a political autobiography, *Outsider in the House.*

JIM SHULTZ, executive director of The Democracy Center, lives in Cochabamba, Bolivia, and is the author of *The Democracy Owners' Manual.* His work for *In These Times* earned him first place on Project Censored's 2001 list of the year's most underreported stories.

TERRY SOUTHERN wrote the screenplays for *Dr. Strangelove* and *Easy Rider* as well as the novels *Candy, Red-Dirt Marijuana and Other Tastes* and *Blue Movie.* He died in 1995. Reprinted by permission of the Terry Southern Estate.

ILAN STAVANS is Lewis-Sebring Professor in Latin American and Latino Culture at Amherst College. His books include *On Borrowed Words, Art and Anger, The Hispanic Condition* and *Octavio Paz: A Meditation.*

BARRY STAVRO is an assistant business editor at the *Los Angeles Times,* where he has worked in various posts for 15 years. He previously served as the Chicago bureau chief for *Forbes* magazine and also worked for the *St. Petersburg Times.*

SANDRA STEINGRABER is on the faculty of Cornell University. She is the author of *Living Downstream* and, most recently, *Having Faith: An Ecologist's Journey to Motherhood.*

JEFFREY ST. CLAIR is a contributing editor of *In These Times* and co-editor with Alexander Cockburn of the investigative newsletter *Counterpunch.* He is also the co-author of *White Out : The CIA, Drugs and the Press, A Pocket Guide to Environmental Bad Guys* and *Al Gore: A User's Manual.*

JASON VEST is a reporter based in Washington, where he covers defense, intelligence and foreign policy matters. A former associate editor for *U.S. News and World Report,* Vest has been a Washington correspondent for *The Village Voice* and *The Boston Phoenix.*

ALICE WALKER's numerous books include *Meridian, The Color Purple* (a winner of the Pulitzer Prize) and *By the Light of My Father's Smile.*

HARVEY WASSERMAN is a longtime safe energy activist and commentator. His most recent book is *The Last Energy War: The Battle Over Utility Deregulation.*

JAMES WEINSTEIN is founding editor and publisher of *In These Times.* He also founded the journal *Socialist Review* and the Modern Times bookstore in San Francisco. Weinstein is the author of several books, including *The Corporate Ideal in the Liberal State, 1900–1918* and *The Decline of Socialism in America, 1912–1925.* His latest book, *Whatever Happened to Socialism?*, is in the works.

FRED WEIR is a Moscow correspondent for *In These Times* and regular contributor to the *Christian Science Monitor*, the London *Independent*, *Canadian Press* and the *South China Morning Post.* He is the co-author of *Revolution from Above: The Demise of the Soviet System.*

PAUL WELLSTONE is a Democratic senator from Minnesota. Before being elected to the Senate in 1990, he taught at Carleton College for 21 years.

LAWRENCE WESCHLER has been a staff writer for *The New Yorker* since 1981 and is the author of *A Miracle, A Universe: Settling Accounts with Torturers*, *Calamities of Exile* and eight other books. He is also the director of the New York Institute for the Humanities at New York University.

ELLEN WILLIS directs the cultural reporting and criticism program at New York University and is a Freda Kirchwey fellow of the Nation Institute. Her latest book is *Don't Think, Smile! Notes on a Decade of Denial.*

WILLIAM UPSKI WIMSATT co-founded the Active Element Foundation in Harlem, which funds youth organizing nationwide and publishes *The Future 500.* Wimsatt is the author of *No More Prisons*, *Bomb the Suburbs*, and *The Passion Brokers.*

ALAN WOLFE is the director of the Boisi Center for Religion and American Public Life at Boston College. He is the author of more than 10 books, including *Marginalized in the Middle* and *One Nation, After All.*

G. PASCAL ZACHARY is a contributing editor of *In These Times* and formerly a senior writer at the *Wall Street Journal.* He is the author of *Endless Frontier: Vannevar Bush, Engineer of the American Century* and, most recently, *The Global Me: New Cosmopolitans and the Competitive Edge.* He lives in Berkeley, California.

SLAVOJ ZIZEK, a philosopher and psychoanalyst, is a senior researcher at the Institute for the Advanced Study in the Humanities in Essen, Germany. He is the author of, among other books, *On Belief* and *The Opera's Second Death.*

HEATHER ZWICKER is an associate professor of English at the University of Alberta. Her teaching and research interests include postcolonialism, feminism and queer theory.

Index